Jewish Literature
between the
Bible and the Mishnah

"The re-edition of George Nickelsburg's introduction updates and expands an extremely valuable tool for the study of Jewish literature of the Second Temple period. Nickelsburg carefully sets a wide range of literature within the complex political and social context of the history of Israel in this period. Nickelsburg deftly introduces the primary sources and the problems of their interpretation. He does so in magisterial dialogue with an impressive array of recent scholarship, which will provide a solid foundation for any students engaging in the study of this phase of Jewish life and letters."

—Harold Attridge

Jewish Literature

between the

Bible and the Mishnah

A Historical and Literary Introduction

Second Edition

George W. E. Nickelsburg

Fortress Press
Minneapolis

JEWISH LITERATURE BETWEEN THE BIBLE AND THE MISHNAH
A Historical and Literary Introduction
Second Edition

Cover image: Extant fragment of columns 2–4 of 4QEn^g, containing the Aramaic of 1 Enoch 91:10—94:1. Photo reproduced by permission of the Israel Antiquities Authority.
Author photo: Marilyn Nickelsburg
Cover design: James Korsmo
Book design and typesetting: The HK Scriptorium

Library of Congress Cataloging-in-Publication Data

Nickelsburg, George W. E., 1934–
    Jewish literature between the Bible and the Mishnah : a literary and historical introduction / George W. E. Nickelsburg.— 2nd ed.
        p.   cm.
    Includes bibliographical references and index.
    ISBN 0-8006-3768-2 (hardcover : alk. paper) — ISBN 0-8006-3779-8 (pbk. : alk. paper)
    1. Bible. O.T. Apocrypha—Introductions. 2. Apocryphal books (Old Testament)—Introductions. 3. Dead Sea scrolls. I. Title.

    BS1700.N48   2005
    296.1—dc22

                                        2005019096

2   3   4   5   6   7   8   9   10

For Miles and Spencer
Sam and Max

Contents

Preface

When I wrote the first edition of this book twenty-four years ago, serious scholarly engagement with the history and literature of Second Temple Judaism was a luxury limited almost exclusively to persons working on the Dead Sea Scrolls. In the past two and a half decades the situation has changed dramatically, as is attested by the thousands of articles and monographs that have appeared not only on the Scrolls but on the "Apocrypha" and "Pseudepigrapha," as well as on Philo and Josephus and numerous topics about the history and sociology of the period. Scholars and publishers have initiated new periodicals and monograph series, commentaries are beginning to appear, universities have established chairs in Judaic studies, and courses are finding their way into curricula that were almost the exclusive domain of the canonical Scriptures. With this geometric increase in the scholarship and now the complete publication of the Dead Sea Scrolls, a new edition of this book is not only desirable but necessary.

My revisions are threefold. First, I have broadened my treatment of the literature. With the addition of *The Story of Darius's Bodyguards* from 1 Esdras, *The Prayer of Manasseh*, and *Psalm 151*, my coverage of the Apocrypha is complete. To my discussion of the Dead Sea Scrolls I have added nine texts: *The War Scroll*; *A Halakic Letter (4QMMT)*; *The Rule of the Congregation (1QSa)*; *Songs of the Sabbath Sacrifice (Angelic Liturgy)*; *The Temple Scroll*; *The Aramaic Levi Document*; *The Psalms Scroll*; *Instruction for a Student (Sapiential Work A)*; and *The New Jerusalem*. Together with the other Dead Sea texts that I previously discussed, they are now gathered in a chapter of their own, where I present them as a representative sampling of the range of sectarian and nonsectarian texts found in the Qumran caves. To round out my treatment of Second Temple texts, I have also provided introductions to *Philo of Alexandria* and *Flavius Josephus* and sketched some of the issues relating to the *Greek Jewish Scriptures* (the so-called Septuagint).

In my second type of revision, I have consulted hundreds of articles and monographs and updated my discussion of texts previously treated. I have documented scholarship that both agrees and disagrees with opinions that I still consider valid, and I have revised my interpretations where it seemed warranted. The results of this can be found both in the notes and in the bibliographies, to which I have added hundreds of new entries.

Third, I have made one revision in the structure of the book, dropping my chapter "The Exposition of Israel's Scriptures," and moving most of its texts into a final chapter "Texts of Disputed Provenance." Here I have included works whose date and place of origin are debated and whose Jewish or Christian origin is a lively topic of discussion.

The last change in the book is a digital download that contains the full, searchable text of the book, a library of nearly one hundred images that help bring the texts and the locations to life, along with a Study Guide that includes chapter summaries, study questions, and links to important web sites. A link at the head of each chapter takes you to the corresponding study materials. Asterisks throughout the text of the book are linked to related images.

As in the first edition, I have structured the book chronologically, following a sequence that runs from the beginning of the Hellenistic period to the Jewish War (ca. 325 B.C.E.–100 C.E.). The prologue provides background for the whole book and a context for chapter 1, which treats early texts of the dispersion. In chapters 2–5 and 7–8, the history of the Jews in Palestine is the organizing principle for discussing texts that appear to have been written between roughly 325 B.C.E. and 100 C.E. In chapter 6 I treat texts of Egyptian origin composed between 150 B.C.E. and 70 C.E. The last chapter, as I have noted, includes texts that I did not feel comfortable including in the other chapters. While there is some risk in organizing texts in such a historical sequence (rather than, e.g., by genres), my conviction that texts are historical artifacts and not timeless entities leads me to run the risk, indicating where the judgments are more or less certain and where the issues are fuzzy.

Seven of the chapters begin with a capsule history that provides context for the texts to be discussed. These short introductions touch only on matters necessary for a basic understanding of the literature. Bibliographies at the ends of the chapters provide resources for a more detailed study of the historical data.

I am pleased to acknowledge and thank friends and colleagues for their help and encouragement. Over two and a half decades I have learned much from my graduate students and from my colleagues in the Society of Biblical Literature Pseudepigrapha Group and the Society's group on Wisdom and Apocalypticism in Early Judaism and Early Christianity, as well as from the members of the Taskforce on Apocalypticism of the Wissenschaftliche Gesellschaft für Theologie, who adopted me as an honorary member of their group. As always I have profited from discussions with Birger Pearson and Norman Petersen, my perennial roommates at the SBL Annual Meetings. As an emeritus professor I have made prolific use of the extensive collection of The University of Iowa Main Library, and I have been especially well served by the prompt and courteous help of the staff of the Library's Interlibrary Loan office. Without these resources, I could not have completed this revision.

With the massive proliferation and specialization of the literature, I am indebted to those colleagues and friends who have read various parts of the manuscript and made suggestions and offered corrections. They include Mordechai Aviam, Roland Deines, Esther Eshel, Hanan Eshel, Erich Gruen, Daniel Harrington, Charlotte Hempel, Adam

Kamesar, Steve Mason, Sarianna Metso, Carol Newsom, Birger Pearson, Andrei Orlov, Lawrence Schiffman, Gregory Sterling, Michael Stone, Eugene Ulrich, Sidnie White Crawford, James VanderKam, and Benjamin Wright. Though responsibility for the contents is my own, they have in many ways made this a better book.

At Fortress Press, Harold Rast, John Hollar, K. C. Hanson, and Michael West encouraged me to revise the book. James Korsmo worked closely and patiently with me in the editing of the book. Gary Lee attended to the copy-editing with great care. At the HK Scriptorium Maurya Horgan, Paul Kobelski, and Jeska Horgan-Kobelski went out of their way to expedite the design and typesetting of the volume. To facilitate the revision, Robert Kraft at the University of Pennsylvania supervised the scanning of the text of the first edition.

My special thanks go to Marilyn, who after twenty-five years waited and watched for the second time as the scroll unrolled to its end. I dedicated the first edition of the book to our young children, Jeanne and Michael. This time around Jeanne edited the scanned copy, and now I am delighted to dedicate the book to our four grandsons, whose interest I hope will someday be aroused by its contents.

G. W. E. N.
Iowa City, Iowa
June 2005

Abbreviations

AB	Anchor Bible
ABD	*Anchor Bible Dictionary.* 6 vols. Edited by David Noel Freedman. Garden City, N.Y.: Doubleday, 1992
AbrN	*Abr-Nahrain*
Add Esth	Additions to Esther
AGAJU	Arbeiten zur Geschichte des antiken Judentums und des Urchristentums
AJSL	*American Journal of Semitic Languages and Literature*
ALD	Aramaic Levi Document
ALGHJ	Arbeiten zur Literatur und Geschichte des hellenistischen Judentums
AnBib	Analecta biblica
ANF	*Ante-Nicene Fathers*
ANRW	*Aufstieg und Niedergang der römischen Welt*
ANTZ	Arbeiten zur neutestamentlichen Theologie und Zeitgeschichte
AOT	*Apocryphal Old Testament.* Edited by H. F. D. Sparks. Oxford: Clarendon, 1984
Ap. Con.	*Apostolic Constitutions*
Apoc. Abr.	Apocalypse of Abraham
APOT	*The Apocrypha and Pseudepigrapha of the Old Testament.* Edited by R. H. Charles. 2 vols. Oxford: Clarendon, 1913
Aram.	Aramaic
(A)ASOR	(Annual of the) American Schools of Oriental Research
ATDan	Acta theologica danica
AUSS	*Andrews University Seminary Studies*
BA	*Biblical Archaeologist*
Bar	Baruch (in the Apocrypha)
2, 3 Bar	Syriac, Greek Apocalypse of Baruch
Barn.	*Epistle of Barnabas*
BASOR	*Bulletin of the American Schools of Oriental Research*

BBB	Bonner biblische Beiträge
B.C.E.	Before the Common Era (= B.C.)
BEATAJ	Beiträge zur Erforschung des Alten Testaments und des antiken Judentum
Bel	Bel and the Serpent (Bel and the Dragon)
BETL	Bibliotheca ephemeridum theologicarum lovaniensium
Bib	*Biblica*
BibOr	Biblica et orientalia
Bijdr	*Bijdragen: Tijdschrift voor filosofie en theologie*
BIS	Biblical Interpretation Series
BJRL	*Bulletin of the John Rylands University Library of Manchester*
BJS	Brown Judaic Studies
BO	Biblioteca Orientalis
BZ	*Biblische Zeitschrift*
BZAW	Beihefte zur Zeitschrift für die alttestamentliche Wissenschaft
BZNW	Beihefte zur Zeitschrift für die neutestamentliche Wissenschaft
ca.	circa, about
CBC	Cambridge Bible Commentary
CBQ	*Catholic Biblical Quarterly*
CBQMS	Catholic Biblical Quarterly Monograph Series
CD	Cairo Genizah copy of the Damascus Document
C.E.	Common Era (= A.D.)
CEJL	Commentaries on Early Jewish Literature
cf.	compare with
chap(s).	chapter(s)
1, 2 Chr	1, 2 Chronicles
Col	Colossians
col(s).	column(s)
comm.	commentary
ConBNT	Coniectanea biblica: New Testament
1, 2 Cor	1, 2 Corinthians
CQS	Companion to the Qumran Scrolls
CRINT	Compendia rerum iudaicarum ad Novum Testamentum
CScA	Contributi all Scienza dell' Antichità
CSCO	Corpus scriptorum christianorum orientalium
CTM	*Concordia Theological Monthly*
CurBS	*Currents in Research: Biblical Studies*
Dan	Daniel
Deut	Deuteronomy
diss.	dissertation
DJD	Discoveries in the Judaean Desert. Oxford: Clarendon, 1955–
DSD	*Dead Sea Discoveries*

DSSHAGT	*The Dead Sea Scrolls: Hebrew, Aramaic, and Greek Texts with English Translations.* Edited by James H. Charlesworth. Tübingen: Mohr Siebeck; Louisville: Westminster John Knox, 1994–
DSSR	*The Dead Sea Scrolls Reader,* edited by Donald W. Parry and Emanuel Tov. 6 vols. Leiden: Brill, 2004–5
EBib	Études bibliques
Eccl	Ecclesiastes (Qoheleth)
ed(s).	editor(s), edited by, edition
EDSS	*Encyclopedia of the Dead Sea Scrolls.* Edited by Lawrence H. Schiffman and James C. VanderKam. 2 vols. Oxford and New York: Oxford Univ. Press, 2000
EncJud	*Encyclopaedia Judaica.* Edited by Cecil Roth and Geoffrey Wigoder. 16 vols. Jerusalem: Keter; New York: Macmillan, 1971–72
Eng.	English
Ep Jer	Epistle of Jeremiah
Eph	Ephesians
1 Esd	1 Esdras
esp.	especially
EstBib	*Estudios bíblicos*
Esth	Esther
et al.	*et alii,* and others
Exod	Exodus
Ezek	Ezekiel
fasc.	fascicle
FB	Forschung zur Bibel
fig(s).	figure(s)
frg(s).	fragment(s)
FRLANT	Forschungen zur Religion und Literatur des Alten und Neuen Testaments
FS	Festschrift
Gal	Galatians
GAP	Guides to Apocrypha and Pseudepigrapha
GCS	Die griechischen christlichen Schriftsteller der ersten drei Jahrhunderte
Gen	Genesis
Gk.	Greek
GNP	*George W. E. Nickelsburg in Perspective: An Ongoing Dialogue in Learning,* edited by Jacob Neusner and Alan J. Avery-Peck. 2 vols. JSJSup 80. Leiden: Brill, 2003 (repr. of Nickelsburg's articles with commentary)
Hab	Habakkuk
HAR	Hebrew Annual Review

HDR	Harvard Dissertations in Religion
Heb	Hebrews
Heb.	Hebrew
Hen	*Henoch*
HeyJ	*Heythrop Journal*
HNT	Handbuch zum Neuen Testament
Homer	
Od.	*Odyssey*
HR	*History of Religions*
HSM	Harvard Semitic Monographs
HSS	Harvard Semitic Studies
HTR	*Harvard Theological Review*
HTS	Harvard Theological Studies
HUCA	*Hebrew Union College Annual*
HUCM	Hebrew Union College Monographs
IDB	*The Interpreter's Dictionary of the Bible.* Edited by George A. Buttrick. 4 vols. Nashville: Abingdon, 1962
IDBSup	*Interpreter's Dictionary of the Bible: Supplementary Volume.* Edited by Keith Crim. Nashville: Abingdon, 1976
IEJ	*Israel Exploration Journal*
IOSCS	International Organization of Septuagint and Cognate Studies
Isa	Isaiah
JAL	Jewish Apocryphal Literature
JAOS	*Journal of the American Oriental Society*
Jas	James
JBL	*Journal of Biblical Literature*
JBR	*Journal of Bible and Religion*
Jdt	Judith
Jer	Jeremiah
JJS	*Journal of Jewish Studies*
JNES	*Journal of Near Eastern Studies*
Jos. Asen.	Joseph and Aseneth
Josephus	
Ag. Ap.	*Against Apion*
Ant.	*Jewish Antiquities*
J.W.	*Jewish War*
Josh	Joshua
JQR	*Jewish Quarterly Review*
JRS	*Journal of Roman Studies*
JSHRZ	Jüdische Schriften aus hellenistisch-römischer Zeit
JSJ	*Journal for the Study of Judaism in the Persian, Hellenistic, and Roman Periods*

JSJSup	Journal for the Study of Judaism Supplements
JSNT	*Journal for the Study of the New Testament*
JSNTSup	Supplements to the Journal for the Study of the New Testament
JSOT	*Journal for the Study of the Old Testament*
JSOTSup	Journal for the Study of the Old Testament Supplements
JSP	*Journal for the Study of the Pseudepigrapha*
JSPSup	Journal for the Study of the Pseudepigrapha Supplements
JSS	*Journal of Semitic Studies*
JTS	*Journal of Theological Studies*
Jub.	Jubilees
Judg	Judges
1, 2 Kgs	1, 2 Kings
l(l).	line(s)
L.A.B.	Liber antiquitatum biblicarum (Pseudo-Philo)
LCL	Loeb Classical Library
Let. Aris.	Letter of Aristeas
lit.	literally
LT	*Literature and Theology*
LXX	Septuagint (common abbreviation for the Greek OT)
m.	Mishnah
1, 2, 3, 4 Macc	1, 2, 3, 4 Maccabees
Mal	Malachi
Mas	Masada
Matt	Matthew
Mic	Micah
Mnem	*Mnemosyne*
ms(s).	manuscript(s)
n(n).	note(s)
Neot	*Neotestamentica*
NIB	*New Interpreter's Bible.* Edited by Leander E. Keck. 13 vols. Nashville: Abingdon, 1994–2004
NovT	*Novum Testamentum*
NovTSup	Supplements to Novum Testamentum
NRSV	New Revised Standard Version
n.s.	new series
NT	New Testament
NTS	*New Testament Studies*
Num	Numbers
NumenSup	Supplements to Numen
OBO	Orbis biblicus et orientalis
ÖBS	Österreichische biblische Studien
OBT	Overtures to Biblical Theology

OLZ	*Orientalistische Literaturzeitung*
OT	Old Testament
OTL	Old Testament Library
OTP	*Old Testament Pseudepigrapha.* Edited by James H. Charlesworth. 2 vols. Garden City, N.Y.: Doubleday, 1983–85
OtSt	Oudtestamentische Studien
PAAJR	*Proceedings of the American Academy of Jewish Research*
Par. Jer.	Paraleipomena of Jeremiah
Phil	Philippians
Philo	Philo of Alexandria
Cher.	*On the Cherubim*
Conf.	*On the Confusion of Tongues*
Dreams	*On Dreams*
Drunkenness	*On Drunkenness*
Flight	*On Flight and Finding*
Jos.	*On the Life of Joseph*
Mig.	*On the Migration of Abraham*
Names	*On the Change of Names*
Plant.	*On Planting*
Spec. Laws	*On the Special Laws*
pl(s).	plate(s)
Plato	Plato
Rep.	*Respublica*
Pliny	Pliny the Elder
Nat. Hist.	*Naturalis Historia*
Pr Azar	Prayer of Azariah
Pr Man	Prayer of Manasseh
Prol.	Prologue
Prov	Proverbs
Ps(s)	Psalm(s)
Ps.-Clem. Hom.	*Pseudo-Clementine Homilies*
Pss. Sol.	Psalms of Solomon
PVTG	Pseudepigrapha Veteris Testamenti Graece
Q	Qumran, preceded by the number of the cave of discovery and followed by short title or ms. number. Scrolls identified by number (e.g., 4Q417) follow the standard in DJD 39 and in most recent editions and translations of the Qumran corpus. Other abbreviations are as follows:
1QapGen	Genesis Apocryphon
1QH(ab)	Hodayot or Thanksgiving Hymns
1QM	Milḥamah or War Scroll
1QpHab	Pesher on Habakkuk

1QS	Serek Hayaḥad or Rule of the Community
1QSa	Rule of the Congregation
4QEn^g	Enoch manuscript (4Q212)
4QLevi	Aramaic Levi Document
4QMMT	Halakhic Letter
4QpapTob^aar	Tobit manuscript (4Q196)
4QpIsa^c	Pesher on Isaiah (4Q163)
4QpNah	Pesher on Nahum (4Q169)
4QpPs^a	Pesher on Psalms (4Q171)
4QPrNab	Prayer of Nabonidus (4Q242)
11QPs^a	Psalms Scroll (11Q5)
11QTemple	Temple Scroll (11Q19)
RAC	*Reallexikon für Antike und Christentum*. Edited by Theodor Klauser. Vols. 1–. Stuttgart: Hiersemann, 1950–. Supplementary vol. 1, 2001
RB	*Revue biblique*
RechBib	Recherches bibliques
REJ	*Revue des études juives*
RelSRev	*Religious Studies Review*
repr.	reprint, reprinted
Rev	Revelation
rev.	revised
RevQ	*Revue de Qumran*
RevScRel	*Revue des sciences religieuses*
Rom	Romans
RSV	Revised Standard Version
RTL	*Revue théologique de Louvain*
1, 2 Sam	1, 2 Samuel
SAOC	Studies in Ancient Oriental Civilizations
SBLDS	Society of Biblical Literature Dissertation Series
SBLEJL	SBL Early Judaism and Its Literature
SBLMS	SBL Monograph Series
SBLRBS	SBL Resources for Biblical Study
SBLSBL	SBL Studies in Biblical Literature
SBLSBS	SBL Sources for Biblical Study
SBLSCS	SBL Septuagint and Cognate Studies
SBLSP	*SBL Seminar Papers*
SBLSS	SBL Symposium Series
SBLTT	SBL Texts and Translations
SBLTTPS	SBL Texts and Translations Pseudepigrapha Series
SBT	Studies in Biblical Theology
SC	Sources chrétiennes
ScRel/StRel	*Sciences Religieuses/Studies in Religion*

ScrHier	*Scripta hierosolymitana*
SecCent	*Second Century*
Sem	*Semitica*
sg.	singular
SHR	Studies in the History of Religions (supplement to *Numen*)
Sib. Or.	Sibylline Oracles
Sir	Wisdom of Joshua Ben Sira (Sirach or Ecclesiasticus)
SJLA	Studies in Judaism in Late Antiquity
SNTSMS	Society of New Testament Studies Monographs
SPB	Studia post-biblica
SR	*Studies in Religion*
SSN	Studia semitica neerlandica
STDJ	Studies on the Texts of the Desert of Judah
SUNT	Studien zur Umwelt des Neuen Testaments
Sup	Supplement
Sus	Susanna
SVTG	Septuaginta: Vetus Testamentum Graecum, Auctoritate Academiae Litterarum Gottingensis. Göttingen: Vandenhoeck & Ruprecht, 1939–
SVTP	Studia in Veteris Testamenti Pseudepigraphica
T. Abr.	Testament of Abraham
T. Job	Testament of Job
T. Mos.	Testament of Moses
T. 12 Patr.	Testaments of the Twelve Patriarchs
T. Ash.	Testament of Asher
T. Benj.	Testament of Benjamin
T. Dan	Testament of Dan
T. Iss.	Testament of Issachar
T. Jos.	Testament of Joseph
T. Jud.	Testament of Judah
T. Levi	Testament of Levi
T. Naph.	Testament of Naphtali
T. Reub.	Testament of Reuben
T. Sim.	Testament of Simeon
T. Zeb.	Testament of Zebulun
TANZ	Texte und Arbeiten zum neutestamentlichen Zeitalter
Tertullian	
De cult. fem.	*De cultu feminarum (Appeal of Women)*
Pat.	*De patientia (Patience)*
TextsS	Texts and Studies
Tg. Neof.	*Targum Neofiti*
Tg. Ps.-J.	*Targum Pseudo-Jonathan*

Tob	Tobit
TSAJ	Texte und Studien zum antiken Judentum
TThSt	Trierer theologische Studien
TZ	*Theologische Zeitschrift*
v(v)	verse(s)
VC	*Vigiliae christianae*
VCSup	Supplements to *Vigiliae christianae*
vol(s).	volume(s)
VT	*Vetus Testamentum*
VTSup	Supplements to *Vetus Testamentum*
Wis	Wisdom of Solomon
WMANT	Wissenschaftliche Monographien zum Alten und Neuen Testament
WUNT	Wissenschaftliche Untersuchungen zum Neuen Testament
YCS	*Yale Classical Studies*
ZAW	*Zeitschrift für die alttestamentliche Wissenschaft*
Zech	Zechariah
ZNW	*Zeitschrift für die neutestamentliche Wissenschaft und die Kunde der älteren Kirche*
ZWT	*Zeitschrift für wissenschaftliche Theologie*

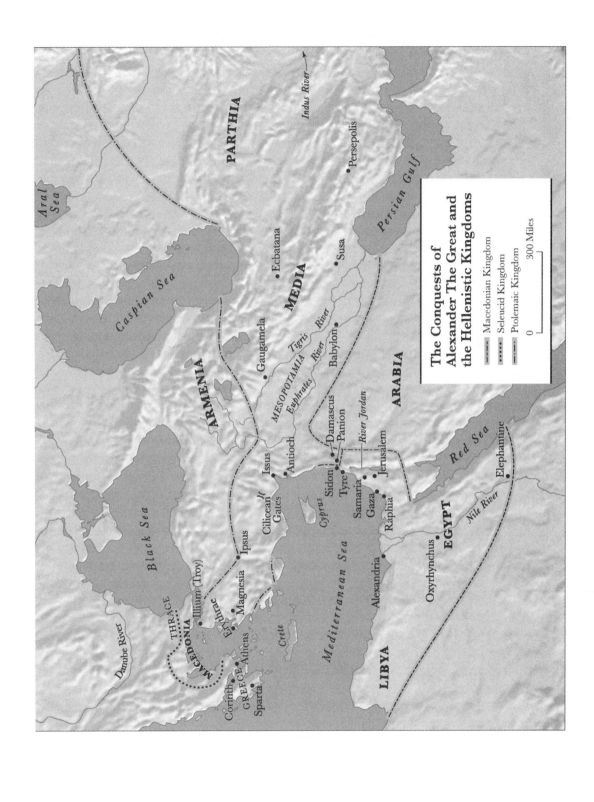

The Conquests of
Alexander The Great and
the Hellenistic Kingdoms

Macedonian Kingdom
Seleucid Kingdom
Ptolemaic Kingdom

0   300 Miles

Palestine in the Hellenistic and Hasmonean Period

□ Fortress   ● City or Town

—·—·— Kingdom of Alexander Janneus

•••••• Free City

0   30 Miles

Sidon

Damascus

Mt. Lebanon

Anti-Lebanon Mts.

Mt. Hermon

Tyre

Dan

Panion

PHONECIA

Ptolemais

Sea of Galilee

Hippos

Gamala

GALILEE

Gadara

Mt. Carmel

GILEAD

Strato's Tower

Scythopolis

Pella

Gerasa

Mediterranean Sea

Samaria

Shechem

SAMARIA

River Jordan

Alexandrium

AMMON

Joppa

Wadi ed-Daliyeh

Modein

Dok

Tyros

Philadelphia

Jamnia

Jericho

Azotus

Jerusalem

Qumran

Ascalon

Hyrcania

Bethzur

Machaerus

Gaza

JUDEA

Raphia

Masada

Dead Sea

I D U M E A

N A B A T A E A

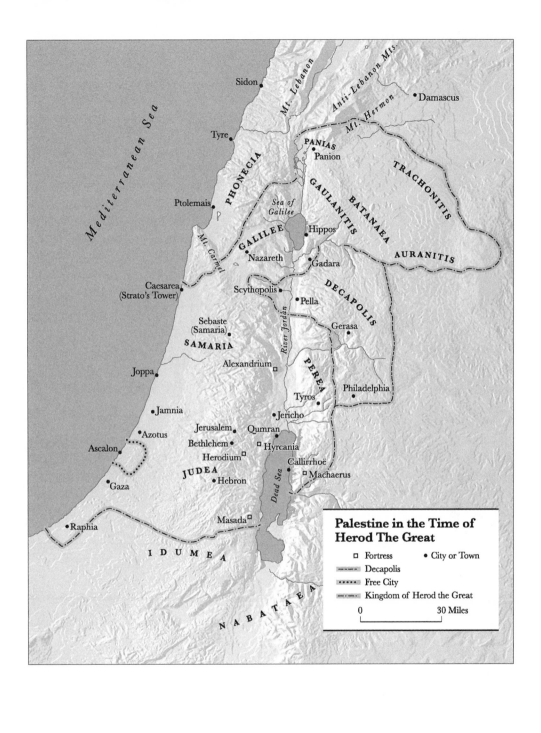

Mediterranean Sea

Sidon
Damascus
Mt. Lebanon
Anti-Lebanon Mts.
Tyre
Mt. Hermon
PANIAS
Panion
PHONECIA
TRACHONITIS
GAULANITIS
BATANAEA
Ptolemais
Sea of Galilee
AURANITIS
GALILEE
Hippos
Nazareth
Gadara
Mt. Carmel
Caesarea (Strato's Tower)
Scythopolis
DECAPOLIS
Pella
Sebaste (Samaria)
Gerasa
River Jordan
SAMARIA
Joppa
Alexandrium
PEREA
Tyros
Philadelphia
Jamnia
Jericho
Azotus
Jerusalem
Qumran
Ascalon
Bethlehem
Hyrcania
Herodium
Callirrhoë
Machaerus
JUDEA
Hebron
Gaza
Dead Sea
Raphia
Masada
IDUMEA
NABATAEA

Palestine in the Time of Herod The Great

□ Fortress   • City or Town
----- Decapolis
····· Free City
-·-·- Kingdom of Herod the Great

0   30 Miles

Mediterranean Sea

Sidon

Tyre

Mt. Lebanon

Anti-Lebanon Mts.

Mt. Hermon

Damascus

PHONECIA

PANIAS

Panion

TRACHONITIS

Ptolemais

Gischala

GAULANITIS

BATANAEA

Raphana

Sea of
Galilee

GALILEE

Hippos

Tiberias

Dion

AURANITIS

Kanatha

Nazareth

Gadara

Abila

DECAPOLIS

Mt. Carmel

Caesarea

Scythopolis

Pella

Gerasa

Sebaste
(Samaria)

Shechem

River Jordan

SAMARIA

Joppa

Alexandrium

PEREA

Philadelphia

Jamnia

Jericho

Tyros

Azotus

Jerusalem

Qumran

Ascalon

Bethlehem

Herodium

Gaza

JUDEA

Hebron

Machaerus

Dead Sea

Raphia

Masada

I D U M E A

N A B A T A E A

**Palestine in the Time
of the Early Procurators**

□ Fortress   ● City or Town

▪▪▪▪ Tetrarchy of Philip

▪—▪— Tetrarchy of Herod Antipas

—▪— Administration of Pontius Pilate

—▪▪— Decapolis

▪▪▪▪ Area under special control

0   30 Miles

Introduction

The five centuries that spawned the literature that is the subject of this book were times of crisis, transition, and creativity for the Judeo-Christian tradition. At the beginning of the third century (300 B.C.E.) most of the literature that would later become the Scriptures of the Jewish people had already been written. By the mid-second century C.E. both rabbinic Judaism and early Christianity had emerged. Both religions claimed to be the heirs of God's promises to Israel and embraced the earlier writings as Scripture. At this point, however, these religions had been shaped by the events and developments that had transpired during these five centuries. Thus the study of early rabbinic Judaism and early Christianity must reckon with this period and with the literature that grew out of it and that testifies to it.

Fundamental and far-reaching changes shook the Jewish people during these centuries. The Persian Empire fell. Alexander's victories brought Greek language and culture to the East. The persecution of the Jews by the Macedonian king, Antiochus IV Epiphanes, tested the mettle of Jewish faith and threatened to exterminate the religion. After a brief period of independence Palestine bowed to the sovereignty of Rome. New turmoil brought revolt. Palestine was devastated, Jerusalem was sacked, and the temple was leveled.

These events and others like them made their inevitable impact on the shape of Jewish life, religion, and thought. Persecution, oppression, and political domination were met with capitulation in some cases, but they also spawned varieties of resistance and the theoretical undergirdings for it: militant zeal and passive resistance; apocalyptic revelations about help from the heavenly sphere and hopes for a human helper, a messiah; speculations about God's justice in an unjust world. The Jewish community divided into parties and groups and sects. In and through this process individuals and members of various religious communities wrestled with the events that touched and troubled their lives, and they sought to make sense of them by interpreting their religious heritage and by creating new traditions that spoke with relevance and force to their circumstances. The literature of this period provides us with the evidence and some of the actual substance of this religious, cultural, and intellectual process. Moreover, this literature reveals, in various stages of development, literary forms of biblical interpretation three to four centuries before they

1

emerge in the writings of the rabbis. Thus from almost any viewpoint the literature of this period is crucial to an understanding of the emergence of early rabbinic Judaism.

The situation is basically the same for the study of early Christianity. The seedbed of the church was first-century Judaism. As Jews, Jesus of Nazareth and his disciples breathed the air of this religious and cultural environment and spoke its idiom. They received their Bible from the Jewish community, as it was interpreted by that community. Indeed, the very early church was a messianic movement within the bosom of Judaism, and fundamental aspects of its early history are intelligible only when viewed against the rejection of its messianic views and expectations by the majority of contemporary Jews. Thus in a variety of ways the literature of this period provides an indispensable key for the understanding of the rise of Christianity.

Unfortunately, Christian study of Judaism has often been imperialistic. Its purpose has been to enhance the study of Christianity, and often to do so by contrast. Thus Judaism is mocked up as the dark "background" against which is played the glorious drama of Christian origins. A more appropriate model is that of "roots." To the extent that I deal with the issue or imply it, I wish to show how both early rabbinic Judaism and early Christianity sprang from the same seedbed.

The problem of Christians coming to terms with their Jewish roots is particularly acute. Centuries of overt stereotype and polemic and the continued unconscious use of prejudicial concepts and terminology obscure the facts and issues. Consider the following configuration:

B(efore) C(hrist)				A(nno) D(omini)
Old Testament	| Intertestamental	|| New Testament
Israelite	| (Late) Jewish	|| Christian

The very chronological terminology that we regularly employ presupposes a Christian confession, dividing time "before Christ" and according to the "year of our Lord." Similarly, the application of the term "intertestamental" to the Jewish literature of this period presumes the Christian belief that in Jesus there is a "new covenant" (i.e., testament), which has replaced the "old covenant." Another distinction separates early Hebrew or Israelite religion and theology qualitatively from its Jewish development, and the latter from its Christian successor. On the one hand this distinction sees Judaism as a legalistic or wildly apocalyptic perversion of inspired Israelite religion. On the other hand it fails to admit the profound debt that early Christian faith and theology owed to Judaism. In its more arrogant and blind form it has defined the Judaism of this period as "Late Judaism," as if this religion had come to an end with the emergence of Christianity.

In order to avoid these pitfalls and to sensitize the reader I shall employ more neutral terminology. My chronological determiner will be the common existence of Judaism and Christianity; hence the Common Era (C.E.) and Before the Common Era (B.C.E.). While in keeping with Christian self-understanding I shall speak of the "New Testament," I shall also refer to the "(Hebrew) Bible" or "Scriptures," imposing no category of oldness on the covenant that Jews still consider viable. Similarly, recognizing the present existence of Judaism I shall speak of the period under consideration as "Early (postbiblical) Judaism."

APPROACH AND METHOD

As I have already suggested in the preface, I believe that literature is rooted in history and is affected by it. Theological conceptions arise not in a vacuum but in response to historical circumstances and events, and they reflect their social matrices and cultural contexts. While it is not always possible to determine these, particularly when we are dealing with ancient documents, our relative ability to understand milieu affects our understanding of literature. Thus I have arranged the book historically, I have provided most of the chapters with historical introductions, and I have raised historical considerations when and where they are relevant. At the same time, I have indicated where there are historical problems, uncertainties, and ambiguities.

Within this historical framework I treat the subject matter as literature. I am interested not simply or primarily in ideas or motifs or in contents in some amorphous sense, but in literature that has form and direction: in narrative that has plot with beginning, middle, and end (or situation, complication, and resolution); in other types of literature that use particular forms and rhetorical devices with consistency and purpose. The critic's task is to find these forms and directions and to interpret the text with reference to them. Not infrequently it is a difficult and ambiguous task. Nonetheless, I invite the reader to search with me for the logic that caused things to be written in the manner and the order in which they were written.

Above all I wish to emphasize that this volume is not a substitute for the ancient texts themselves. When I retell a story in brief form, my purpose is not to save the reader the trouble of interacting with the original. Here, as throughout, I offer a possible road map, a grid, an ordering of relationships and emphases as I see them. To some extent I intend this as a prolegomenon for a study of the exegetical *details*, and this is the way in which I have used the book in the classroom. At the same time, I hope that my interpretations will challenge the reader to find equally or more viable ways to read the texts. The history of interpretation and criticism is precisely such an ongoing process.

I have attempted to strike a balance between a study of the parts and a study of the whole. In general the overarching question is: wherein lies the integrity, the wholeness, the gist of a particular text? At the same time, some writings more than others are patently composites of earlier, shorter writings. Occasionally I discuss these parts separately. In some cases I have attempted to separate levels of tradition, but for the most part this has been a task secondary and consequent to an interpretation of the whole.

PROBLEMS AND PERSPECTIVE

The study and interpretation of ancient literature is fraught with difficulties. We must deal first with the time gap. As people of the twenty-first century, we are reading the literary products of an age and culture separated from us by two millennia and thousands of miles. Even if we are able to read the texts in their original languages, we face the barrier of strange thought patterns and modes of expression. At times even persons who are familiar with the canonical biblical literature find themselves in a strange world.

The problems of interpretation are compounded by our individual prejudices and tastes. I have already mentioned false and derogatory Christian presuppositions, which must be neutralized if the literature is to be read fairly and in its own right. Taste presents another kind of problem. Distaste for mythic thought can erect a barrier to understanding it. A preference for clear, logical, conceptualized exposition may hinder the interpretation and appreciation of narrative. Empathy must precede criticism. The critic must first enter the artist's world and view it from within before criticizing the manner in which that world has been expounded or delineated.

Our experience and appreciation of modern forms of literature may also create difficulties for our study and evaluation of these ancient writings. As one adapts to more complicated and "sophisticated" art forms, older forms may seem not only simple but simplistic. The person who has experienced William Walton's boisterous oratorio interpretation of Belshazzar's feast may find it difficult to appreciate George Frederick Handel's exposition of the same story. But that is hardly fair to Handel, who wrote in his own time and place and wrote well. Similarly, we should judge the artistry of the narrative literature of early Judaism in terms of its own environment and not in the context of the modern short story or novel.

One important factor that holds together the largest part of this corpus of literature is its common setting in hard times: persecution, oppression, other kinds of disaster, the loneliness and pressures of a minority living out its convictions in an alien environment. Within this context we can read and appreciate these writings as a sometimes powerful expression of the depths and the heights of our humanity and of human religiousness and religious experience. In them we may see ourselves as we have been or are or might be: the desperate puzzlement of Enoch's decimated humanity; the anguish and then the ecstasy of a Tobit; the courage of a Susanna or a Judith; the defiant tenacity of the Maccabean martyrs; the desolate abandonment of an Aseneth; and the persistent questioning of an Ezra.

Through it all is told the story of a people from whom sprang Jesus of Nazareth and Hillel, Akiba and Paul. Those who live in these two traditions, long ago tragically sprung apart, may find here some commonality. For others the story is recited as part of the human saga, as a source of interest, wonderment, and perhaps enlightenment.

CORPUS

The noncanonical literature of early Judaism, which bulks considerably larger than the New Testament, and indeed larger than the Hebrew Bible, is traditionally divided into five categories. The term "Apocrypha" (from the Greek for "hidden books") was employed by Saint Jerome to refer to those books or parts of books not found in the Hebrew Bible but included in its Greek translation, the so-called Septuagint (see below, pp. 192–93). Jerome included these texts in the Vulgate, his Latin translation of the Bible, together with another popular work, the apocalypse 2 Esdras (4 Ezra). In 1546 the Council of Trent declared all these writings except 1 and 2 Esdras and the Prayer of Manasseh to be part of the canonical Scriptures.

"Pseudepigrapha" (from the Greek for "pseudonymous writings") is a term applied to other noncanonical Jewish literature, though not all of it is written under a false name.

The Dead Sea Scrolls, or Qumran Scrolls, were found in the 1940s in caves near the ruins of Khirbet Qumran, by the northwest shore of the Dead Sea. They include all the books of the Hebrew Bible except Esther and possibly Nehemiah, several of the Apocrypha and Pseudepigrapha, numerous sectarian writings composed by a group who lived at Qumran or by related groups, and a spate of other literature of unknown origin.

Two other categories of Jewish writings are tied to known authors. In the mid-first century C.E., Philo of Alexandria composed a large number of exegetical and philosophical writings and a few treatises in defense of Judaism. In the last part of the first century Flavius Josephus wrote *The History of the Jewish War* of 66–72 C.E. In the last decade of the century he composed his *Jewish Antiquities*, an extensive rewriting of the Bible and related traditions, tracing the history of the Jews from Adam to the Herods, as well as a treatise in defense of the Jews.

Although I occasionally use the terms "Apocrypha," "Pseudepigrapha," and "Qumran Scrolls," the terms are problematic. If we treat these works in their own context, the canon-related term "Apocrypha" is after the fact and therefore irrelevant for historical study. "Pseudepigrapha" focuses on an aspect of a widely varied group of texts that is not their central defining characteristic. It also ignores the fact that some of the Apocrypha (e.g., Tobit and the Wisdom of Solomon) and some canonical writings are also pseudonymous. The Scrolls, as I have noted, are a mixed collection. A more proper literary categorization of these writings divides them into genres: apocalypses, narrative fiction, testaments, history, commentaries, philosophy, and the like, and it requires that we include the writings of Philo and Josephus.

BIBLIOGRAPHY

Bibliographies for the individual texts appear at the end of each chapter and divide into several sections. In the first of these sections I cite several readily available translations of the various works. The books of the Apocrypha are available in all editions of the Bible formally approved by the Roman Catholic and Eastern Orthodox churches, in many other editions of the English Bible, and under separate cover. The Pseudepigrapha are cited according to the two volumes edited by James H. Charlesworth, *The Old Testament*

Pseudepigrapha (Garden City, N.Y.: Doubleday, 1983–85), and the handy but less encompassing volume edited by H. F. D. Sparks, *The Apocryphal Old Testament* (Oxford: Clarendon, 1984). The Qumran Scrolls are cited according to the translations by Florentino García Martínez, *The Dead Sea Scrolls Translated: The Qumran Texts in English* (2d ed.; Grand Rapids: Eerdmans, 1996); Geza Vermes, *The Dead Sea Scrolls in English* (4th ed.; Harmondsworth: Penguin, 1995); idem, *The Complete Dead Sea Scrolls in English* (Allen Lane: Penguin, 1997); Michael Wise, Martin Abegg, and Edward Cook, eds., *The Dead Sea Scrolls: A New Translation* (2d ed.; San Francisco: HarperSanFrancisco, 2005); the text and translation editions of Florentino García Martínez and Eibert J. C. Tigchelaar, eds., *The Dead Sea Scrolls: A Study Edition* (2 vols.; Grand Rapids: Eerdmans; Leiden: Brill, 1997–98); and Donald W. Parry and Emanuel Tov, eds., *The Dead Sea Scrolls Reader* (6 vols.; Leiden: Brill, 2004–5). In the second section of each bibliography I list editions of the works in their original languages or ancient versions, and, in a few cases, in additional English translations. In the third section I list secondary literature, and, where relevant, I subdivide it into literature surveys, commentaries, and other literature, citing the authors in alphabetical order. In the notes of the respective chapters, literature listed in the bibliographies is cited by short title.

In my notes I have cited the secondary literature prolifically, but by no means exhaustively. For additional bibliography one should consult Lorenza DiTommaso, *A Bibliography of Pseudepigrapha Research 1850–1999* (JSPSup 39; Sheffield: Sheffield Academic Press, 2001), an exhaustive resource, albeit somewhat difficult to use; and Andreas Lehnardt, *Bibliographie zu den jüdischen Schriften aus hellenistisch-römischer Zeit* (JSHRZ 6/2; Gütersloh: Gütersloher Verlagshaus, 1999), which covers the Apocrypha as well as the Pseudepigrapha. Bibliographical resources for the Qumran Scrolls, Philo, and Josephus are cited at the end of the appropriate chapters. One can find bibliographical updates on the American Theological Library Association database, available in most research libraries, but one should note that it is by no means exhaustive in the entries it provides.

A few comprehensive works are worth noting. John J. Collins has written two useful introductory volumes, *Between Athens and Jerusalem: Jewish Identity in the Hellenistic Diaspora* (New York: Crossroad, 1983) and *The Apocalyptic Imagination: An Introduction to the Jewish Matrix of Christianity* (New York: Crossroad, 1984). Broad coverage of the literary corpora treated here is provided in Michael E. Stone, ed., *Jewish Writings of the Second Temple Period* (CRINT 2/2; Philadelphia: Fortress Press, 1984), as well as in volume 3/1–2 of the revision of Emil Schürer, *The History of the Jewish People in the Age of Jesus Christ (175 B.C.–A.D. 135)*, edited by Geza Vermes, et al. (Edinburgh: T. & T. Clark, 1986–87). On the history of the period and its institutions, in addition to volumes 1–2 of the revised Schürer, one may consult Lester Grabbe, *Judaism from Cyrus to Hadrian* (2 vols.; Minneapolis: Fortress Press, 1992); and Frederick J. Murphy, *The Religious World of Jesus: An Introduction to Second Temple Judaism* (Nashville: Abingdon, 1991). A detailed history of post-1945 research on early Judaism has been compiled in Robert A. Kraft and George W. E. Nickelsburg, eds., *Early Judaism and Its Modern Inter-*

preters (Philadelphia: Fortress Press; Atlanta: Scholars Press, 1986). Finally, as a companion to this volume, I have written *Ancient Judaism and Christian Origins: Diversity, Continuity, and Transformation* (Minneapolis: Fortress Press, 2003), which treats the diversity of Jewish religious expression of the Second Temple period topically, comparing and contrasting it with the diversity of first-century Christianity.

Prologue

Exile—Return—Dispersion

When the battering rams of Nebuchadnezzar's army breached the walls of Jerusalem in 587 B.C.E., they effectively opened a new era in the history of Israel and the religion of its people. Three facts dominated Jewish history in the sixth and fifth centuries: the fall of Jerusalem and the ensuing exile in Babylon; the return from the exile and the restoration of the Jewish community; and the continued dispersion of a large number of Jews. These facts would continue to exert a powerful influence on the lives, thought, and religion of this people for centuries to come. Subsequent Jewish history was postexilic not only chronologically but also in its essence. Thus certain perspectives on the facts and events of sixth- and fifth-century Jewish history, as these perspectives are expressed in the biblical literature of this period, provide us with an interpretive key for understanding the history and literature of later, postbiblical Judaism. In the biblical literature we see the emergence of certain theological conceptions whose paths we can then trace through the literature of postbiblical Judaism.

DESTRUCTION AND EXILE

Tragedy was already a well-established fact of life for the Hebrew people. In 722 B.C.E. Samaria, the capital of the northern kingdom of Israel, fell to the army of Shalmaneser V, king of Assyria; and under the reign of his successor, Sargon II, many Israelite citizens were deported to Assyria and Media never to return. In their place the Assyrians resettled foreigners, who intermingled with the surviving Israelite population. In Jewish accounts their descendants would reappear later as the Samaritans.

Subsequent Assyrian invasions reduced the southern kingdom of Judah to a vassal state, though Jerusalem, its capital, and the Davidic monarchy remained intact. The collapse of the Assyrian Empire before the rising power of Babylon (612–609) provided Judah with a new overlord. Rebellion was in the air in Jerusalem, but to no avail. In 597 the city surrendered. The royal family and many of the Judean aristocracy were deported to Babylon. Zedekiah was appointed king in place of his nephew Jehoiachin, the reigning monarch.

The events of the next ten years are recounted in some detail in the biographical sections of Jeremiah. Again rebellion flared up. The prophet foresaw disaster and sought to stave it off by counseling surrender. When his advice was rejected, Jerusalem fell in 587 to Nebuchadnezzar's army. The city was burned, its walls leveled, and the temple plundered and destroyed. Zedekiah was blinded and deported. The leading citizens were either executed or exiled to Babylon. Gedaliah, a Judean noble, was appointed governor. Shortly thereafter he was assassinated by compatriots, and his friends fled to Egypt, taking Jeremiah with them. A third deportation to Babylon took place in 582.

We can scarcely overestimate the trauma inflicted by the fall of Judah and Jerusalem. The enormity of the human tragedy will be evident to anyone familiar with the disasters of war. There was also a religious dimension. The people of Judah understood themselves to be the chosen people of YHWH, who was unique and all-powerful among the gods of the nations. Jerusalem was the site of his temple, the place where he caused his name to dwell (Deut 12:11; 2 Kgs 21:4), the cultic center of his religion, where sacrifice was offered and where "the tribes go up . . . to give thanks to the name of YHWH" (Ps 122:4). Little wonder that Jeremiah had to contend with the theory that the Jerusalem temple was under divine protection from violation (Jer 7:2-15; 26:2-24). Thus the shock waves resulting from the fall of Jerusalem and the destruction of the temple are deeply etched into all the contemporary Israelite sources. Moreover, these events became a prototype for similar disasters in the future inflicted by Antiochus Epiphanes (168 B.C.E.) and Titus (70 C.E.).[1]

Our knowledge about the particulars of life in the exile is scant.

> Transported to southern Mesopotamia not far from Babylon itself, [the Judean exiles] . . . were . . . apparently placed in settlements of their own (cf. Ezek 3:15; Ezra 2:59; 8:17). . . . . They were not free; but they were not prisoners either. They were allowed to build houses, to engage in agriculture (Jer 29:5-6), and, apparently, to earn their living in any way they could. They were able to assemble and to continue some sort of community life (cf. Ezek 8:1; 14:1; 33:20-21).[2]

To what degree the assemblies mentioned by Ezekiel represent one of the roots of the institution later known as the synagogue is uncertain.[3] In any event the exiles had to come to terms with the practice of their religion at great physical distance from Jerusalem and in spite of the annihilation of its cultic center. This religious aspect of life in the exile is attested in the prolific theological productivity of the period. It was a time for serious reflection upon the tragedy of 587 and its causes, for consolidation of the Israelite religion through the preservation of its traditions, and for nourishing the hope of restoration.

The Deuteronomistic History (Deuteronomy through 2 Kings) received its final form during the exile or shortly thereafter. The fall of Jerusalem was seen to be the result of the sins of King Manasseh (687–642)—an interpretation consonant with the original Deuteronomist's emphasis on sin and punishment. The reversal of this divine punishment of sin would be found in a return to obedience.

The author of the so-called Priestly work was particularly interested in Torah, especially cultic law. He anticipated a return to the homeland and a resumption of the cult.

Closely related to the circles of this author was the prophet and priest Ezekiel. Brought to Babylon in the first wave of exiles, he issued his indictment against the sins of Judah and announced that YHWH would abandon his sanctuary. Exile was punishment. Nonetheless, the future would bring restoration (chaps. 34–39). God would renew the covenant broken by the people's disobedience. He would put sinew, flesh, and skin on the dry bones of those who lay "dead" in the graves of their captivity. He would gather the lost and the scattered of both Israel and Judah, uniting them again as one people under the care of his shepherd, the Davidic prince. Then YHWH would return in glory and dwell in a new temple (chaps. 40–48).

Return and renewal are the heart of the message of the so-called Second (Deutero-) Isaiah, an unknown exilic prophet or group of prophets whose elegant poetry has been preserved in some of the later chapters of Isaiah (chaps. 40–55).[4] Deutero-Isaiah's oracles, composed during the latter part of the exile, breathe hope and optimism.[5] Babylon will soon topple before the army of the Persian king Cyrus. A return to the homeland is imminent. Israel has more than paid for its sins (40:2). YHWH, the universal king who moves people and history toward his own purposes, is prepared to do a new thing. He himself will lead a new exodus out of Babylon, across the wilderness, and into the land, where he will again reside in Jerusalem (40:3-11; 43:15-21). Speaking in eloquent metaphor the prophet calls on "Mother Zion"—at once barren, widowed, and divorced by God for her unfaithfulness—to make ready for the return of her dispersed children and the renewed compassion of her estranged husband (50:1; 52:1-2; 54:1-17).

Integral to Second Isaiah's message are the songs about the Servant of YHWH.[6] This anonymous figure is depicted in largely prophetic terms. YHWH presents him as one on whom he has put his Spirit (42:1-4). The Servant describes his prophetic call (49:1-6). He has received divine inspiration, that he may be the spokesman of YHWH (50:4-9). His destiny is to suffer and die (50:7-9; 52:13—53:12). The precise identification of the Servant vacillates in Second Isaiah. He is both explicitly identified with Israel (e.g., 44:1) and described as having a mission to restore Israel (49:6). The last two songs present a remarkable view of suffering, interpreted within the framework of a pattern of humiliation and exaltation, misunderstanding and vindication. Suffering cannot be construed simply as divine punishment for sin. The kings and the nations, who have thus understood the Servant's suffering, view his exaltation in astonishment. They confess that their original interpretation was wrong and that indeed he had suffered in their behalf (52:13—53:12). Later, this daring interpretation of suffering will have a profound influence on theologies formulated in response to persecution.

The offices of prophet and king undergo a transformation in the theology of Second Isaiah. Israel, the Servant purified by exile, has as a whole the responsibility to be a light to the nations (49:6). The Davidic dynasty is of little significance. Cyrus is YHWH's "anointed one" (45:1).[7] David is referred to only as "a leader and commander for the peoples," and the Davidic covenant is extended to all Israel (55:3-4).

We have noted how Second Isaiah's metaphors flow into one another. Of a similar order is the prophet's easy, sometimes almost imperceptible fluctuation between present and past history and between history and myth. The prophet celebrates a historical fact—the triumph of Cyrus, king of the Persian Empire. Yet as he anticipates the return to Zion, he mixes present events with past history. The trek through the wilderness will be a new exodus. Similarly, the description of the first exodus is itself not told as straight history. The dividing of the Red Sea was at the same time the conquering of the ancient dragon, the chaos monster (51:9-11), and the passage is an appeal to the Divine Warrior to strike out against chaos as he had in the past: "Awake, awake, put on strength, O arm of YHWH; awake as in the days of old." The triumph of Cyrus against Babylon, Israel's historical enemy, is at the same time the triumph of the Divine Warrior against his primordial foe. Similarly, a new exodus involves a new act of creation when the wilderness will be made "like Eden" (51:3).

There is a finality about the new act of God that Second Isaiah awaits. The prophet anticipates a new age, qualitatively different from the present one. The shape of nature itself will change, as the Creator re-forms the topography of the land, the structures of its water systems, and the growth patterns of its vegetation (40:3-4; 41:18-20; 42:15-16; 43:19-20).

In his use of myth, his portrayal of an imminent future as qualitatively different from the historical past, and his assertion of a coming universal kingship of God over all nature and history, Second Isaiah brings us to the verge of the eschatology that will characterize the apocalypses that we shall discuss later. For Second Isaiah the kingdom of God was at hand.

RETURN AND RESTORATION

In 538 B.C.E. Cyrus issued an edict in which he directed the Jerusalem temple to be rebuilt and its sacred vessels, which had been taken by Nebuchadnezzar, to be returned. Leading a first group of Jewish returnees was a certain Sheshbazzar, about whose activities we know very little.[8] In 520 he was succeeded as governor of Judah by Zerubbabel, the grandson of Jehoiachin.[9] Under Zerubbabel's supervision and after considerable delay, the rebuilding of the temple went forward. His colleague was the high priest Joshua, a descendant of Zadok, the Solomonic high priest whose descendants had dominated the Jerusalem priesthood for centuries. Among Joshua's and Zerubbabel's allies were the prophets Haggai and Zechariah. Haggai predicted that the completion of the temple would mark the dawn of a new era, and he hailed Zerubbabel, the descendant of David, as YHWH's "servant," whom he had "chosen" and would "make like a signet ring" (2:23). Zechariah dubbed Zerubbabel and Joshua the "sons of oil," that is, the anointed (and thus divinely legitimated) leaders of the community. The Jerusalem temple was completed in 515, but in spite of the glowing expectations of Haggai (2:7-9) it was a far cry from the splendid edifice built by Solomon. Thus the hope for a more glorious sanctuary would persist in the postbiblical literature. With completion of the temple, Zerubbabel disappears from the historical sources. With him went the presence of a Davidic heir as ruler of Judah. The hopes of Jeremiah and Ezekiel for a restoration of the dynasty would continue to be applied to the future, to an unknown figure whom God would enthrone as God's "anointed" king. Meanwhile, civil authority would reside increasingly in the high priest.

A very different side of the events of 538–515 is reflected in the anonymous oracles in Zechariah 9–14 (Deutero-Zechariah) and in the last chapters of Isaiah (chaps. 56–66). These latter are the product of an anonymous "pupil" of Second Isaiah, usually called Third (Trito-) Isaiah. The change in mood from Isaiah 55 to 56 is immediately evident. High optimism has given way to disillusionment. The return did not initiate a glorious new age. The temple still lay in ruins, and the Jerusalem community was split into factions and locked in acrimonious controversy.[10] Third Isaiah's transformation of the traditions of Second Isaiah reflects the change in situation and the dire straits in which Third Isaiah sees himself and those of his persuasion. (1) Second Isaiah described the whole of a purified Israel as YHWH's Servant, his "chosen one," in opposition to Babylon and the nations. Third Isaiah, reflecting the split in the community, speaks of "the servants" and "the chosen ones" of YHWH, contrasting them with the wicked of the Israelite community. (2) Whereas Second Isaiah spoke of the doom of Babylon, Third Isaiah envisions an imminent judgment that will separate the righteous and wicked of Israel. This message is carried in a new oracular form that combines words of doom for the wicked of the community with words of promise for the righteous.[11] (3) Although Second Isaiah used mythic language to describe God's new act, he identified that new act with a chain of historical events: the victories of Cyrus, the fall of Babylon, the return. For Third Isaiah, judgment and end time lie in the future, and they are depicted almost entirely in mythic, ahistorical terms: the direct intervention of God's self (59:15-20; 64:1-3; 66:15-16) and the creation of new heavens and a new earth (65:17-25; 66:22).

In Third Isaiah we have the primary ingredients for the third- and second-century apocalyptic theology of 1 Enoch and Daniel: an oppressed minority who deem themselves the righteous; the expectation of an imminent judgment to alleviate the present situation; the dawn of a new age qualitatively different from the present one; the use of mythic, ahistorical language to depict these future events.[12]

Third Isaiah's expectation of judgment and the creation of new heavens and a new earth were not realized, and the expectations of Haggai and Zechariah were not fulfilled. The Davidic dynasty was not restored. The temple was completed, but, as we learn from the prophet Malachi, cultic practice disintegrated. The priests grew weary of their duties. They accepted sick and injured sacrificial animals, which the Torah forbade to be offered (Mal 1:6-14). As teachers of the Torah they caused the laity to sin, and they showed partiality in their legal decisions (2:1-9). The people were not bringing to the temple the tithes and offerings prescribed in the Torah (3:8-9). The prophet also rebuked the Jewish men for their intermarriage with non-Jewish women and for their practice of divorce and remarriage (2:10-16).

This situation provided the context for the appearance of Ezra, "the scribe of the Torah of the God of heaven." There is a great deal of scholarly debate about the figure of Ezra, what his status was, when he came to Jerusalem, how long he stayed, and what he did.[13] According to the account in Ezra 7–10, upon his arrival in Jerusalem, he reacted with great shock to the widespread intermarriage and called for immediate divorce of foreign women, using the authority of his royal commission to enforce his orders. According to Nehemiah 8 he gathered the people in a public square and read to them from "the book of the Torah of Moses," most likely a penultimate form of the Pentateuch.

In 445, either after or before Ezra (depending on one's chronology), Nehemiah, the cupbearer to Artaxerxes I, came to Jerusalem to take up his post as governor of Judah. His principal task was to rebuild the walls of Jerusalem and thus provide the little community with protection from harassment by neighboring peoples. After a twelve-year tenure as governor, Nehemiah returned to the Persian court, only to reappear once more in Jerusalem. During his second stay he enacted a number of reform measures: enforcement of the payment of tithes, prohibition of violations of the Sabbath rest, and once more the dissolving of mixed marriages.[14]

Ezra and Nehemiah found the Jewish people in a state of religious chaos. They must have understood the mixed marriages of Jews and foreigners to be not only a violation of the holiness of God's people but also a threat to their existence as an identifiable people and hence to the continued existence of the Jewish faith. It was this faith that they sought to preserve through their reform measures. Theirs was a task of consolidation around the Torah of Moses. In this sense Ezra's public reading of the Torah was highly symbolic. Although the Pentateuch did not yet have formal authority as Scripture, the work of Ezra and Nehemiah was an important step toward its establishment as the revealed record of God's gracious deeds in behalf of his people and the normative instruction and law for the conduct of their lives.

With the close of Nehemiah's memoirs we enter a period of Palestinian Jewish history about which we know very little. Its one historical witness is the author of 1–2 Chronicles, who, probably in the mid-third century, recast the Deuteronomic History with a focus on the importance of the temple and cult and on the covenant with David.[15] Whether this latter emphasis implied the restoration of the Davidic dynasty is uncertain.[16] Within decades of the writings of 1–2 Chronicles, in 333 B.C.E., the rise of Alexander the Great would set in motion a series of events and circumstances whose impact on Jewish life, culture, and religion would rival the influence of the events we have just summarized.

DISPERSION

The deportation of Israelites in 722 and the exile to Babylon in 597 and 587 marked the beginnings of a widespread dispersion of the Hebrew people beyond the borders of their homeland. The precise extent of this dispersion during the sixth and fifth centuries is unknown. One party of Jews fled to Egypt taking Jeremiah with them (Jer 42–43), and still other Jews were located there at this time (44:1). We also know of a Jewish military colony at Elephantine at the first cataract of the Nile during the fifth century.[17] Jeremiah speaks of Jews in Moab, Ammon, and Edom (40:11). The exilic and postexilic prophets refer to a dispersion in all directions (Isa 49:12; 60:4-9; 66:19-20; Zech 8:7-8). It seems likely that part of this dispersion was caused by migration rather than by flight from Assyrian or Babylonian enemies, although the time, reason, and circumstances for such migrations are unknown.

Prophets from Isaiah to Zechariah expressed their hope for a return of the dispersed people of God. This hope was never realized. The Israelite deportees were evidently assimilated among their neighbors. A significant number of Jews remained in Babylon, and large numbers continued to live in Egypt. Many Jewish exiles chose to remain in dispersion long after the restraints of exile had been removed.

Life in the Dispersion created problems and opportunities that are the subject of a number of postbiblical writings: How does one practice one's religion in a non-Jewish environment that is often hostile or at least filled with enticements to apostasy? What are the possibilities that non-Jews will turn to the one, true, and living God?

For some Jews of the postbiblical period the Dispersion continued to be a theological problem, and a massive return from the Dispersion, often portrayed in the language of Second and Third Isaiah, became a staple in description of the end time.

SUMMARY

The events of the sixth and fifth centuries B.C.E. had a profound and lasting effect on the shape of postbiblical Judaism. (1) The Dispersion transformed the geographical configurations of the Jewish people and opened up the possibility for the propagation of the Jewish faith to non-Jews. It also moved this religion into a cosmopolitan setting in which complex interactions took place between religion and culture. (2) The codification of legal traditions (the Pentateuch) during the exile was carried out in part under the belief that the tragedy of 587 was the result of Israel's disobedience to their God and his will as expressed in this Torah. The work of Ezra and Nehemiah was a crucial step in the canonization of the Torah and its developing centrality in the postbiblical period. (3) The events of the sixth century spawned a literature that, along with the Torah, would deeply influence the shape of postbiblical Jewish religion and theology. These writings (Second and Third Isaiah above all) were quoted, paraphrased, and alluded to, and their theological modes of expression, especially the emerging eschatology of Second and Third Isaiah, found new relevance and use in the dark hours of Jewish history that followed. (4) The destruction of Jerusalem and the exile meant the disruption of life and the breaking up of institutions whose original form was never fully restored. Much of postbiblical Jewish theology and literature was influenced and sometimes governed by a hope for such a restoration: a return of the dispersed; the appearance of a Davidic heir to throw off the shackles of foreign domination and restore Israel's sovereignty; and the gathering of one people around a new and glorified temple.

BIBLIOGRAPHY

Peter R. **Ackroyd**, *Exile and Restoration* (OTL; Philadelphia: Westminster, 1968), general historical and literary introduction. Rainer **Albertz**, *Israel in Exile: The History and Literature of the Sixth Century B.C.E.* (trans. John Bowden; SBLSBL 3; Atlanta: Society of Biblical Literature, 2003). Jon L. **Berquist**, *Judaism in Persia's Shadow: A Social and Historical Approach* (Minneapolis: Fortress Press, 1995). Lester L. **Grabbe**, *Judaism from Cyrus to Hadrian* (2 vols.; Minneapolis: Fortress Press, 1991). Volume 1 focuses on the history of the period with a critical assessment of the scholarship. Erich S. **Gruen**, *Diaspora: Jews amidst Greeks and Romans* (Cambridge: Harvard Univ. Press, 2002), history of Jewish life in the Diaspora and an analysis of the literature it generated. Ralph W. **Klein**, *Israel in Exile: A Theological Interpretation* (OBT; Philadelphia: Fortress Press, 1979). Menachem **Stern**, "The Jewish Diaspora," in S. Safrai and M. Stern, eds., *Jewish People in the First Century* (CRINT 1/1; Assen: Van Gorcum, 1974) 117–83, the extent and nature of the Dispersion in the first century.

The Book of Tobit. Fragments of a mid-first-century B.C.E. Qumran Aramaic papyrus (4QpapTob[a] ar) preserving parts of Tob1:17—2:3. Photograph is courtesy of the Israel Antiquities Authority.

1

Tales of the Dispersion

The Eastern Dispersion (Babylon and Assyria) is the setting for the stories and other texts that we shall consider in this chapter. Because these writings show minimal effect from the revolution begun by Alexander's conquest, it is convenient to discuss them before turning to the Hellenistic period.

Daniel 1–6

The book of Daniel owes its present form to a Palestinian author who wrote between 167 and 164 B.C.E.[1] For the first half of the book this author used a collection of older stories that had probably already been edited into the form and order in which we know them.[2]

The setting of these stories is the royal court in Babylon during the exile. The dramatis personae include certain youths of the Judean aristocracy exiled in Babylon and the reigning monarch and his entourage of sages, magicians, and political officials. The climax of each story is a demonstration of the unique power and sovereignty of the God of Israel, most often acclaimed by the monarch himself. This demonstration results either from a contest of skills that pits the Judean youths against the monarch's sages or a power struggle between the Judeans and the monarch's political administrators.[3]

The principal hero in these stories is Daniel, whose deeds are central to chapters 1–2 and 4–6.[4] His ability to predict the future through the interpretation of dreams, his persecution by enemies, and his exaltation to a high position in the court are all reminiscent of the biblical figure of Joseph.[5]

The present order of the stories presumes the Jewish editor's interpretation of the four kingdoms in Daniel 2:36-45: Babylon (represented by Nebuchadnezzar and Belshazzar), Media (represented by Darius), Persia (represented by Cyrus, whose accession marks the end of Daniel's activity, according to 1:21), and Macedonia (yet to come, from the viewpoint of the stories).[6]

Daniel 1

Quite possibly composed by the editor as an introduction to the collection,[7] this chapter provides the setting, introduces the heroes (1:1-7), and recounts two incidents that foreshadow the principal motifs and the structure of the stories in chapters 2-6: (1) Daniel refuses the king's food on religious grounds and requests a vegetarian diet. At the end of the trial period the superior physical appearance of Daniel and his friends vindicates their piety and implies the miraculous power of their God. A similar vindication of the youths' obedience to their God is the subject of chapters 3 and 6. (2) As to their schooling in the wisdom of Babylon,

> God *gave them* learning and skill in all letters and wisdom; and Daniel had understanding in all visions and dreams. . . . The king . . . found them ten times better than all the magicians and enchanters that were in all his kingdom. (1:17, 20)

The demonstration of Daniel's divinely given wisdom is central to the action in chapters 2, 4, and 5.

Daniel 2

This story of Nebuchadnezzar's dream about a colossus made of four metals and its destruction has many parallels in ancient Near Eastern literature, and literary analysis suggests that the story went through several stages before it reached its present form.[8] As the story now stands, the four metals of the colossus represent four successive *kingdoms*: Babylonia, Media, Persia, and Macedonia. In the traditions the story drew on, the order of the metals depicted gradual decline (gold, silver, bronze, and iron), but in Daniel, the iron does not function as a final and base metal; it is the material of weapons and symbolizes the war and violence of the present time (v 40; cf. Dan 7:7). Moreover, the mixture of clay and iron represents the division of the empire under Alexander's successors, the Seleucids and the Ptolemies (vv 41-42). Finally, in what appears to be a secondary interpretation (v 43), the temporary mixture of clay and iron symbolizes the marriage of the Seleucid king Antiochus II and Berenice, daughter of Ptolemy II (252 B.C.E.), and the subsequent disruption of the peace brought about by that marriage when Antiochus died in 246.

The colossus is itself suggestive of an idol, and it is composed of the materials from which idols are made (cf. 5:23). Thus it appears to represent the idolatrous kingdoms of the world, which will all be destroyed by the transcendent power of the God of heaven.[9] The power and sovereignty of this God are evident in the contest that pits God's servant Daniel against the Babylonian sages. Nebuchadnezzar demands that "the magicians, the enchanters, the sorcerers, and the Chaldeans" reveal the content of his dream, as well as its interpretation. "Impossible!" they cry.

> There is no one on earth who can reveal what the king demands. . . . No one can reveal it to the king except the gods, whose dwelling is not with mortals. (2:10-11)

In the kind of unreasoning fury permitted only a monarch, the king orders the annihilation of all the sages in Babylon, including Daniel and his companions. The Jewish youths pray for deliverance, and the mystery of the dream is revealed to Daniel. His prayer of thanksgiving is an acclamation of his God, whose sovereignty extends over nature and the kings of the earth and who gives wisdom and revelation to the wise (2:20-23). The "exile from Judah" (2:25) is brought before the king. In Daniel's interpretation of the dream he makes the following points: only God can reveal mysteries, and I, Daniel, am God's spokesman (2:27-30); Nebuchadnezzar, the "king of kings," rules only by divine consent (2:37); over against the kingdoms of Nebuchadnezzar and his successors, which will be destroyed like the colossus in the dream, God will establish a kingdom that will never be destroyed (2:37-44). Nebuchadnezzar responds by paying Daniel homage and acclaiming,

> Truly, your God is God of gods and Lord of kings, and a revealer of mysteries. (2:47)

The dream will come true. The triumph of the God of heaven will become fact. Different from the other tales in chapters 1–6, this story, with its reference to successive kingdoms and recent events, contains an eschatological element that ties this half of Daniel to the second half and its eschatological visions, notably chapter 7 and its vision of the four kingdoms.[10]

Daniel 4

The king in the original version of this story was probably Nabonidus, the father of Belshazzar.[11] The narrative line demonstrates the absolute sovereignty of Daniel's God. This note is struck in the opening verses of the chapter, which are a royal edict, addressed to "all peoples, nations, and languages that live throughout the earth," acclaiming "the Most High God":

> How great are his signs,
>   how mighty his wonders!
> His kingdom is an everlasting kingdom,
>   and his sovereignty is from generation to generation. (4:1-3)

The story that follows recounts the events that led to this edict. The king had refused to accept the sovereignty of the Most High and to admit that he (the king) ruled only by divine permission. In a dream that Daniel interpreted when "the magicians, the enchanters, the Chaldeans, and the diviners" again failed, the king was told that he would be punished "*until you have learned* that the Most High has sovereignty over the kingdom of mortals and gives it to whom he will" (4:25). The events occurred as foretold, and the king learned his lesson. Reestablished in his kingdom, he now issues the universal edict acclaiming this God (4:37). The first-person singular form of the narrative gives the whole the force of a confession of faith.

Daniel 5

The tale of Belshazzar's feast is explicitly linked to the previous story. The king did not learn the lesson taught his father (5:18-21) but arrogantly exalted himself against the Lord of heaven (5:22).[12] The dramatic element in the Danielic stories reaches its high point in this tale. A royal banquet of massive proportions—blasphemous, idolatrous, and rowdy! Then suddenly the ghastly apparition: the disembodied hand etching its cryptic message into the plaster of the palace wall. The arrogant king turns white, his knees knocking in sheer terror.[13] The narrator's pace slackens as he uses a lengthy contrast between the Babylonian sages and Daniel to build up the suspense, which is relaxed only when Daniel interprets the writing, uttering the word of doom. The king fulfills his promise to reward Daniel, and then the story moves swiftly to its conclusion. That very night the God "who deposes kings" (2:21) brings Belshazzar's kingdom to an end (5:26). The king is slain, and his kingdom is given to Darius (5:30-31). Here alone among the stories in chapters 2–6 does the king not acclaim the God of the Jews. The acclamation, however, is implicit in the king's investiture and acclamation of Daniel (5:29), which come as a consequence of the revelation that Daniel received from the God whose sovereignty was affronted.

Daniel 6

The king here is "Darius the Mede."[14] We are now in the world of palace intrigues. Daniel's rivals are not Babylonian sages but colleagues among the "presidents and satraps" of Darius's kingdom who hatch a conspiracy against Daniel. The story has parallels and precursors in the biblical story of Joseph (Gen 37, 39–45), the material about Mordecai in the book of Esther, and the non-Jewish story of Ahiqar.[15] The protagonist in these stories is a wise man[16] whose actions arouse the wrath of his enemies or rivals, who then plot his death. He is condemned, but rescued, sometimes at the brink of death, exalted to the highest rank in the royal court, invested and acclaimed, and vindicated of the charges against him. Daniel 6 follows this basic plot line, but with several significant variants. Daniel's wisdom is not stressed here. He is a *righteous* man who obeys his God, knowing that this behavior will lead inevitably to his condemnation but trusting in God to deliver him (6:23). His miraculous rescue by divine intervention vindicates his initial act of obedience (6:16, 20-23, 27) and leads to a royal acclamation of his God.

These variations notwithstanding, the basic structure that we have observed in the other Danielic stories recurs in this story and is especially evident in the king's speeches. As Daniel is thrown into the pit of lions Darius says, "*May your God,* whom you faithfully serve, *deliver you*" (6:16). He returns the next morning and asks, "O Daniel, servant of the living God, *has your God,* whom you faithfully serve, *been able to deliver you?*" (6:20). When the king discovers that this is the case, he issues an edict "to all peoples, nations, and languages that live throughout the earth." All in his realm should worship the God of Daniel,

> for he is the living God,
>   enduring forever;
> his kingdom shall never be destroyed,
>   and his dominion shall be to the end.
> He *delivers and rescues,*
>   he works signs and wonders
>   in heaven and on earth,
> he who *has saved Daniel*
>   from the power of the lions. (6:25-27)

Thus Daniel's condemnation was a challenge to the power of the God whom he obeyed, and his rescue is an open demonstration of his God's power, which the king acclaims in an edict demanding universal obedience and worship of that God.

Daniel 3

This is the one story in the collection in which Daniel plays no role. The heroes are his companions, Shadrach, Meshach, and Abednego. Like chapter 6, this is a story of persecution and deliverance, of trusting obedience (3:16-17) and vindication (3:28). As in chapter 6 the king's edicts and speech carry the theme and structure common to the other stories. Nebuchadnezzar issues an edict demanding under penalty of death that "*all the peoples, nations, and languages*" fall down and worship a colossal image (3:6-7). The king verbalizes his challenge of the God of Shadrach, Meshach, and Abednego and construes their imminent death as an ordeal.

> If you do not worship, you shall immediately be thrown into a furnace of blazing fire; and *who is the god that will deliver you out of my hands?* (3:15)

Their subsequent deliverance proves that their God is sovereign.

Nebuchadnezzar now confesses his faith in this God and reverses his previous challenge to that faith. He does so first in an acclamation:

> Blessed be the God of Shadrach, Meshach, and Abednego, *who . . . delivered* his servants who trusted in him . . . rather than serve and worship any god except their own God. (3:28)

He then issues an edict that negates his first edict:

> *Any people, nation, or language* that utters blasphemy against the God of Shadrach,

Meshach, and Abednego shall he torn limb from limb; . . . for there is *no other god who is able to deliver* in this way. (3:29)

Summary

The stories in Daniel 1–6 are the end product of a long and complex process of transmission, from oral composition to literary redaction to their incorporation into the present book of Daniel.[17] In their present form, all six chapters embody a common theme: the testing, the demonstration, and the acclamation of the power and sovereignty of the God of the Jews. The placing of this acclamation on the lips of the monarchs stresses the universality of this sovereignty: *The God of the Jews is God also in the land of captivity and is lord over the captors and their gods.* The assembling of such a collection of stories with a common setting in the Babylonian Dispersion suggests that the collection was made in the Dispersion.[18] In their various stages of development, the stories may have had a number of functions. The use of the same cast of characters and the uniform structure of the stories may indicate that the stories served to provide, through the narration of past history, an example for Jewish sages in foreign courts and in the service of foreign monarchs.[19] When these courtiers remain faithful, their God protects them from danger and causes their activities to prosper (chaps. 1, 3, 6). Furthermore, their God enlightens them so that they can be divine spokesmen in their foreign environment (chaps. 2, 4, 5). The youths' witness to their God is a constant theme in all the stories. A striking result of this witness is the veritable conversion of the monarchs and their unabashed confession of faith in the uniqueness and universal sovereignty of the God of the Jews. Perhaps the authors of these stories nourished such a hope for their own times and through their own activities. In addition to this, however, the stories may well have circulated among Jews in the Dispersion in order to affirm "the possibility of participating fully in the life of a foreign nation."[20] While a Jew must abide by the Torah, this need not mean total separation from the Gentiles. In addition, the emphasis on Daniel as a wise interpreter of dreams fits well with the second half of the book, where he is the recipient of dreams, and it comports well with the thesis that the redactors of the book of Daniel came from the ranks of "the wise" (*maśkîlîm*) mentioned in 12:3.[21]

ADDITIONS TO THE BOOK OF DANIEL

The stories about Daniel and his friends were part of a living body of tradition. Although they may have been of diverse origin, they crystallized as a collection in what we call Daniel 1–6. Between 167 and 164 B.C.E. this collection was supplemented by a cycle of visions ascribed to Daniel (chaps. 7–12), and together they were issued as a single book (see below p. 83). The older forms of the tradition were, however, not completely lost. The Qumran Prayer of Nabonidus was a reworked form of the tradition behind Daniel 4 (see n. 11).

Less than a century after its compilation, Daniel 1–12 was itself expanded. The ancient Greek translations of the book—one known as the Old Greek and the other ascribed to a Jewish proselyte of the second century C.E. named Theodotion—included three lengthy additions that served to enrich and enhance the cycle of stories about Daniel and the three young men.[22] Two of these additions are stories similar to those in chapters 1–6. While the complex history of the traditions in these supplementary stories may have arisen apart from the figure of Daniel, in their present form the stories center on the heroics of Daniel and constitute an integral part of the Greek version of the book that bears his name. The third addition is of a different sort. Here two liturgical pieces (a prayer of confession and a hymn of thanksgiving) that originated independently of the book of Daniel have been integrated into the story about the three young men.

Susanna

This is a story of persecution and vindication in the tradition of Daniel 3 and 6. Susanna is cast in the role of the righteous one, conspired against by the elders, condemned to death because of her obedience to God, rescued by Daniel—the divinely sent savior figure—and vindicated of the charges against her. As in some of the other stories, the acclamation at the end is directed to the God who saves (v 60).[23]

Susanna's piety and innocence are evident in a variety of ways in the story. Her name in Hebrew means "lily."[24] She is introduced as a God-fearing woman (vv 1-4). When she is propositioned by the elders, she makes a conscious and explicit choice to obey God (vv 22-23; cf. Dan 3:17), whom she trusts (v 35) and to whom she prays for deliverance (vv 42-43). Throughout, her innocence and piety are contrasted with the wickedness and lechery of the elders (contrast vv 1-3|5; vv 20-21|22-23; v 31|32; v 56|57). The story appears to have been influenced by the story of Joseph and Potiphar's wife, with the male and female roles here reversed.[25]

The similarities to the old court tales in Genesis 37, 39–45, Ahiqar, Esther, and Daniel 3–6 notwithstanding, the story of Susanna has its own contours. The theme of persecution and vindication is here democratized; the central character is a woman rather than a man, and an ordinary, God-fearing person rather than a sage. Her enemies are not a king or his courtiers but Jewish compatriots. The cross-examination that leads to Susanna's exculpation serves as a dramatic device that builds tension. At the same time, its counterpoising of the young Daniel and the wicked, hypocritical elders from Israel suggests that the story has a number of points to make: God's vindication of the righteous and punishment of the wicked; the need for careful and just legal process; a critical stance toward the status quo; a Jewish, anti-Samaritan polemic; and possibly a countercultural tension between young and old and a similar counterpositioning of a virtuous woman and two hypocritical male religious leaders. A modern feminist reader may see in the story the vulnerability of the protagonist in a male world composed of lecherous would-be violators, an inept husband, and Daniel, her deliverer. All of these complex possibilities exemplify the problems involved in developing a simple, single-tiered interpretation of a text.[26]

The common dating of the Old Greek translation of Daniel to 100 B.C.E. indicates this as the terminus ad quem for the composition of Susanna; however, the fact that it was not included in the original book of Daniel does not necessarily indicate a mid- or late-second-century date of composition. It could have been written at any time in the Hellenistic or late Persian period.[27]

The place of writing is uncertain. The confrontation between Jew and foreigner, essential to Daniel 1–6, is lacking here. This is a story about life in the Jewish community. The setting in Babylon functions only to allow for the presence of Daniel, the famed sage of Babylon. The story could have been written anywhere for the purpose of encouraging obedience to God in the midst of the temptations and pressures that arise in the Jewish community. The original language of the story's composition could have been either Hebrew or Greek.[28]

The placement of the story of Susanna differs in the two Greek versions, but each one explicitly ties the story to the figure of Daniel. In the Old Greek it stands at the end of the book of Daniel either before or after the tale of Bel and the Serpent. The story concludes by praising the single-minded, pious, and wise youths of Israel—epitomized by Daniel. This conclusion diverts the story's focus from the virtuous conduct of the protagonist to the upright behavior of her deliverer, who is the main character of the book to which the story is attached. In the Theodotionic tradition, the story is placed at the beginning of the book of Daniel and explains how this incident contributed to Daniel's rise to prominence (v 64). The Theodotionic version, however, presents a more elaborate form of the story and is marked by an increased focus on Susanna.[29]

Bel and the Serpent[30]

The theme typical of Daniel 1–6 is here elaborated in a pair of episodes that are inextricably interwoven into a single plot (the conversion of Cyrus) that is resolved only at the end of the second episode.[31]

A. Bel:	Living God	vs.	idol
	Daniel	vs.	priests
	Daniel	vs.	king

Ordeal:
Cyrus acclaims Bel
Daniel is vindicated
Priests are killed
Bel is destroyed
King is not converted

   B. Serpent: Living God   vs.   serpent
                    Daniel   vs.   king

                       Ordeal vindicates Daniel
                       King is converted

      Daniel and king   vs.   Babylonians

                       Daniel is sentenced to death
                       Daniel is rescued
                       King acclaims Daniel's God
                       Babylonians are killed

The emphasis of the story is found in its explicit and repeated polemic against idolatry. The term "living God" is frequent in Jewish polemics against idolatry, and the present story is a demonstration of the impotence of the Babylonian gods in the face of the superior wisdom of Daniel, the servant of the living God.[32] Cyrus's acclamation is a fitting climax to the story and a natural inference from the action:

> You are great, O Lord, the God of Daniel,
> and there is no other besides you. (v 41)

A number of remarkable parallels to Isaiah 45–46 suggest that our story may have been colored by these chapters of Second Isaiah. There YHWH addresses Cyrus (45:1), who does not know the God of Israel but will come to know that God (45:3). He is YHWH; besides him there is no other God (e.g., 45:5, 6; cf. Bel 41). He is creator (Isa 45:18; cf. Bel 5). Isaiah 46 begins its polemic against idols with the words "Bel has fallen" (so LXX).

Bel and the Serpent is a delightful, entertaining tale with its own touches of humor: the priests and their families confidently moving about in the recesses of the temple, blissfully unaware of the telltale footprints they are leaving behind; and the serpent bursting asunder from his diet of pitch, fat, and hair cakes. Such humor is typical of Jewish writings that polemicize against idols by mocking them.[33]

The precise relationship of Bel and the Serpent to the stories in Daniel 1–6 is ambiguous and, perhaps, complex. Certain elements in the story appear to be typologically later. The plot is more complex than its Danielic counterparts. It lacks the court setting and is placed more generally in idolatrous Babylon. Daniel's enemies are not rival sages or princes but pagan priests and "Babylonians." The king's conversion is explicit: "The king has become a Jew" (Bel 28). The story knows the tradition that Daniel served under Cyrus (Dan 10:1; cf. 6:28), and at least in its present context it provides a conversion story about the last of Daniel's overlords. Some of the narrative elements in the episode of the lions' den seem secondary to the version in Daniel 6.[34] Some other considerations suggest that Daniel 6 could be dependent on a form of Bel and the Serpent, or that the two versions developed independently of one another.[35] The original language of composition is uncertain.[36]

The Prayer of Azariah and the Song of the Three Young Men

This addition to Daniel, inserted between 3:23 and 24, consists of a prayer of confession attributed to Azariah (Abednego) and a hymn of thanksgiving placed on the lips of the three young men. These two poetic pieces are joined to each other and to vv 23 and 24 by some brief narrative prose.[37]

Azariah's prayer is a confession of the nation's sins based on traditional Israelite covenant theology. Its closest parallels are Baruch 1:15—3:8 (see below, pp. 94–95) and Daniel 9:4-19 (see below, pp. 79–80), although these prayers make more frequent and explicit reference to Deuteronomy 28–32.[38] Verses 3-10 praise God, acknowledging that God's judgments are righteous.[39] Through their sins the people have broken the covenant and thus deserve to be delivered to their enemies. The author appeals to God's covenantal mercy and to the promise made to the patriarchs (vv 11-13). As God had warned, this promise to create a great nation (Gen 15:5) has been nullified because the nation broke the covenant (Deut 28:62; Pr Azar 13–14).[40] Moreover, the people are without political leadership and prophetic voice, and they lack the sacrificial means to make things right with God (v 15). Following David's precedent, the author asks that their humbled and crushed spirits be accepted in lieu of sacrifice (vv 16-17; cf. Ps 51:16-17). Thereby he expresses and pleads the repentance that can restore the covenantal relationship (Pr Azar 6–10, 18; cf. Deut 30:1-3). The prayer for deliverance is made explicit (Pr Azar 19–20b) and is followed by a request that their enemies be subjugated (vv 20c-21; cf. Deut 28:7; 32:41-43) and be made to acknowledge God's universal sovereignty (Pr Azar 22)—a constant motif in Daniel 1–6, as we have seen in the first part of this chapter.

Azariah's prayer appears to have been a previously existent composition reused for its present purpose. Its insertion here conforms to a typical Jewish literary pattern: deliverance comes in response to prayer.[41] However, the contents of this prayer hardly fit the young men's present predicament. They are more appropriate to the general circumstances of the Babylonian exile or to the time of Antiochus Epiphanes' persecution of the Jews, that is, the supposed or the real setting of the book of Daniel (see below, chap. 3). Reference to the cessation of the cult and lack of leadership (v 15) and to the unjust and wicked king (v 9) may indicate that the prayer was actually composed during the persecution.[42]

The prose insertion following the prayer forms a transition to the second half of the addition. Verses 23-25 emphasize the ferocity of the fire, thus heightening the miracle, although v 25 may be an answer to the prayer in vv 20c-21.[43] Verses 26-27 describe the miraculous deliverance for the curious reader and provide cause for the three young men to sing their hymn of praise.[44]

The hymn divides into four major sections. Verses 29-34 are a doxology to the God who is enthroned in the heavenly temple (vv 31-34). The rest of the hymn is a threefold appeal for the whole creation to join in the praise of God. Verses 35-51 are addressed to heaven, its inhabitants and its elements. Verses 52-60 extend the appeal to the earth, its components and its inhabitants, following in general the order of creation in Genesis 1. Having mentioned the last-created beings, "the sons of men," the author now addresses Israel in particular (vv 61-65). Finally, as a climax, v 66 refers to the three young men and the reason for singing the hymn. The brevity of this reference in the context of such a long hymn suggests once again that the author of the addition has employed an extant liturgical work, inserting this verse to make the hymn relevant to its new context.

The hymn cannot be dated with any certainty. Its theme is perennial. The influence of the canonical Psalter is evident in several ways. The content of the hymn appears to para-phrase Psalm 148.[45] Its structure, with an identical refrain after each line, recalls Psalm 136, and the wording of vv 67-68 reflects Psalm 136:1-3. The liturgical character of this hymn has not been lost; it is still to be found in Christian hymnals and liturgies, often under its Latin name, *Benedicite opera omnia*.

These two poetic compositions were most likely composed in Hebrew and inserted into Daniel by the Greek translator, who composed the narrative transitions.[46]

The long addition has the effect of breaking up the continuity of the story in Daniel 3. However, the sharp contrast between the tone and genres of the two poems underscores the change in the action from disaster to salvation. The poems convert the story from mere narrative to quasi-liturgical drama, eliciting the involvement of an audience attuned to such liturgical tradition.[47]

The Story of Darius's Bodyguards (1 Esdras 3–4)

First Esdras is extant only in the Greek Bible and the versions dependent on it. Its con-tents parallel 2 Chronicles 35–36, the book of Ezra, and Nehemiah 7:73—8:13. The order of some of the material from Ezra has been rearranged, and there are some addi-tions from other sources. The most significant of these is the present story.[48]

In its context in 1 Esdras, the story relates the incident responsible for the completion of the Second Temple. King Darius has summoned all his rulers and feted them with a great banquet (3:1-3). Afterward, when he has retired, his three bodyguards devise a con-test. Each of them will propose one thing that he considers "the strongest." The king will then bestow great honors on the one whose proposal seems the wisest (3:4-7). The next day the king summons his rulers to his council chamber and commands the three body-guards to defend their proposals (3:13-17a).

The speeches parallel one another in form and rhetoric.[49] The authors' ingenuity lies not simply in the cleverness and humor of their assertions and in their ability to support the respective propositions, but, more important, in the manner in which each speaker oversteps the previous arguments.[50]

For the first bodyguard, wine is the strongest (3:17b-24). Its power is evident in its capacity to transform and lead astray the minds of all who drink it and to erase all social distinctions. According to the second bodyguard, the king is the strongest (4:1-12). As the king's rulers here present can attest, men are strong, for they rule over land and seas and all that is in them. The king, however, is stronger, because he is lord over all these rulers. The point is illustrated by a series of examples, all formulated in a stereotyped way. The third bodyguard—now identified as Zerubbabel—discourses first on women and then on truth (4:13-32, 33-40). He agrees that the king is great, men are many, and wine is strong. But it is women who rule and lord it over all of these. They give birth to the king, rulers (cf. 4:2), and those who plant the vineyards that produce the wine. In that sense women are superior to all that the previous speeches have acclaimed as strongest. Furthermore, women receive the same attention, obedience, and benefits that kings receive. If wine leads men's minds astray, women cause men to *lose* their minds (4:26). Surely, the king is mighty and feared by all, but even he is not exempt from the power of women. With a touch of ironic humor, Zerubbabel depicts Darius as a captive to the whims and antics of his concubine Apame (4:29-31).

The king and his nobles look at one another, probably less in agreement with his wisdom than in astonishment at his outspokenness. Before they can respond, however, Zerubbabel outdoes himself by launching into a second speech (4:33-41) on the unsurpassed power of truth. It is a brilliant stroke. While the speech is interesting and important in its own right and refutes all the previous speeches, its immediate function is to disarm any objections to Zerubbabel's irreverent observations about the king's conduct. If these observations are true, one cannot object to them. This is, in effect, admitted at the end, when everyone acclaims truth.

In this speech Zerubbabel follows the technique employed in the previous speeches, arguing and asserting the superiority of the object of his praise over those previously discussed. Here, however, it is not simply a matter of superiority. Rather, the absoluteness of truth relativizes all that has been previously mentioned. "Truth" here is a polyvalent term. It has connotations not only of truth but also of rightness, steadfastness, and uprightness.[51] As a quality of God, it excludes its opposite, unrighteousness, which characterizes everything that has been previously praised: wine, the king, women, all humans and their deeds (4:36b-37). Moreover, truth exacts righteous judgment from all who are unjust and wicked and shows no partiality (a further defense of Zerubbabel's asserting the truth about the king). Thus to truth belong all the qualities that would seem to belong to wine, the king, and women: strength, kingship, authority, and greatness, and they belong to truth forever. Therefore, "Blessed is the God of truth" (4:40).

The people acclaim truth as great and strongest of all (4:41), and the king offers Zerubbabel the great honors that the bodyguards had anticipated (4:42). When he requests, instead, that the temple be rebuilt and its vessels returned to Jerusalem, Darius agrees (4:43-57). Zerubbabel's prayer makes clear that it was God who gave him the wisdom that was victorious in this contest (4:58-60; cf. 3:5-6).

Although the story makes good sense in its present form and context, a number of literary problems suggest that it has been altered and revised in the course of its transmission. A difficulty is immediately evident in the opening verses.[52] According to 3:3, King Darius awoke before the guards devised their contest, although the subsequent action suggests that the king was still asleep (see especially v 13). Moreover, it is unclear, under these circumstances, how the guards could be certain that the king would reward the winner of the contest. The version of the story in Josephus (*Ant.* 11.34-36 [§3.2]) solves the problem by having Darius propose the contest and promise the rewards. Furthermore, a number of literary considerations suggest that the speech about truth is an intrusion into a story describing three guards giving three speeches, and that the original story placed the speech about the king before the one about wine.[53] A natural (and naive) beginning is that the king is the strongest. The second bodyguard refutes this by showing how wine neutralizes the power of the king. The third shows how both of these are subject to the power of women. How the story might have ended and dealt with the affront to the king's dignity is uncertain.

In its present form and context, the tale of the bodyguards is a Jewish story that explains how the builder of the Second Temple came to accomplish this feat. In doing so, it employs a tradition known in the stories of Daniel 1–6. The Jewish youth pits his divinely given wisdom (4:58-60) against that of his Gentile colleagues in the Mesopotamian court, and he wins both the contest and the king's favor.[54] The story climaxes with an acclamation of God and a doxology of God's truth. Other features in the story—the various observations about wine and women and kings—have many parallels in Jewish wisdom literature, and the Jewish audience of 1 Esdras would have read them in such a context.[55] Especially close to the Bible are statements about a man forsaking his parents for his wife (4:20-21; cf. Gen 2:24) and claims about the power and eternity of truth (1 Esd 4:38; cf. Pss 117:2; 146:6).[56]

Nonetheless, the story is most likely of non-Jewish origin.[57] Even the formulation about the eternity of truth—though it may have been drawn from the Bible—has close parallels in Egyptian wisdom sayings.[58] When the story is read apart from its present context, there is little in it that is unambiguously Jewish. The identification of the third bodyguard as Zerubbabel is a secondary intrusion.[59] The parallels to the Danielic stories, which provide a broad literary analogy to the tale, are based on non-Jewish models.[60] Taken as a whole, the story has numerous parallels in the folklore of many nations.[61] In short, the Jewish author of 1 Esdras has revised a Gentile story and reused it as a catalyst for a crucial event in Israelite history.

The story was probably composed in Aramaic in a time and place that are uncertain.[62] The circumstances and manner in which the story was incorporated into 1 Esdras and the literary origins of 1 Esdras itself are matters that continue to be discussed.[63]

Tobit

God is with us, even in the midst of trouble and suffering! This is the theme that the author of Tobit[64] artfully develops in this complex and often ambiguous story about disorder, deliverance, and hope among the Israelite exiles in Assyria. Running through the narrative are elements of dark and lighthearted humor, serious theological reflection, cross-cultural borrowing, and a creative appropriation of Israel's sacred traditions.

The opening genealogy introduces Tobit as a genuine Israelite (1:1-2). As the narrative commences, Tobit describes his many acts of cultic devotion and deeds of kindness (1:3-18). His righteous deeds, however, are precisely the source of his trouble. He is persecuted for burying the bodies of fugitive Jews whom the king has executed (1:16-20).[65] Later, after his restoration to favor, he buries a dead Israelite and, being ritually unclean, sleeps in an open courtyard. As a reward for his piety, he is blinded by the droppings from some sparrows who were roosting on the wall.[66] Tobit's life falls apart and disintegrates into domestic squabbles (2:1-14).

Innocent suffering is not the lot of Tobit alone. Far from his home but at exactly the same time (3:7), a distant relative of Tobit, the young woman Sarah, finds herself in a similar predicament. She has been married seven times, and each of her husbands has been killed on the wedding night by a demon who is in love with Sarah. Like her ancestor of the same name, she is childless and the object of domestic reproach (cf. Gen 16:1-6). The author presents the introductions to these two stories one immediately after the other (Tob 2:1—3:6; 3:7-15), relating the events in close literary symmetry.

Tobit's piety (2:1-7)	Sarah's innocence (presumed, e.g., 3:14)
His blindness (2:9-10)	The demon (3:8a)
He is reproached (2:14b)	She is reproached (3:7, 8b-9)
His prayer (3:1-6)	Her prayer (3:10-15)

In a moment of despondency two righteous people, the victims of senseless suffering and the objects of reproach, pray for death as a release.

The author now introduces the third plot, which will resolve the problems raised by the first two. God responds to the prayers by sending the angel Raphael (the name means "God has healed"), who uses Tobiah (Tobit's son) as his agent to drive off the demon and to heal Tobit's blindness (3:16ff.). But that is to get ahead of our story.

Presuming that God will answer his prayer by taking his life, Tobit summons Tobiah for some "deathbed" instructions:

Live uprightly . . . and do not walk in the ways of wrongdoing. For if you do what is true, your ways will prosper through your deeds. Give alms from your possessions. . . . Do not turn your face away from any poor person, and the face of God will not be turned away from you. If you have many possessions, make your gift from them in proportion; if few, do not be afraid to give according to the little you have. So you will be laying up a good treasure for yourself against the day of necessity. For almsgiving delivers from death. . . . Do not hold over till the next day the wages of anyone who works for you, but pay the person at once; and if you serve God you will receive payment. (4:5-10, 14; cf. 14:8-11)

Given Tobit's situation, the irony of his words is readily evident. Tobit commands his son to act as he himself has acted, and he promises him that God rewards such piety. Yet Tobit's experience belies his fatherly instruction. God has not repaid him in kind, and his deeds of charity have not delivered him from the premature death he now awaits.

A humorous interlude follows. Tobit is seeking someone to accompany Tobiah on a journey to recover some money he had deposited in another city. Raphael appears in human guise. When Tobit inquires about his identity, Raphael presents bogus credentials (cf. 5:12 and 12:15), and poor, blind Tobit, falling for the line, hook and sinker, joyfully welcomes the angel as the son of a long-lost relative.[67] Then he sends Tobiah off to seek his fortune with these words: "Go with this man; God who dwells in heaven will prosper your way, and may his angel attend you" (5:16). He reassures Hannah, his heartbroken wife, that "a good angel will go with him" (5:21). The reader can chuckle with the author, aware of the real truth of the words that Tobit has unwittingly uttered.

The heart of the book unfolds the resolution of the plots. As they approach the Tigris River, a large fish leaps from the water and attacks Tobiah. Raphael instructs Tobiah to wrestle the beast to the ground and cut out its heart and liver. These will provide the necessary magical equipment to drive off the demon and heal Tobit (6:1-8). Raphael informs Tobiah of the girl's predicament, but his reassurances move the anxious youth to deep love for the troubled Sarah (6:9-17). The tension builds in chapter 7 as Sarah's parents expect the inevitable tragedy of another dead son-in-law. (In 7:9-10, for "Eat, drink, and be merry, for it is your right to take my child," perhaps one should read "Eat, drink, and be merry, for tomorrow you will be dead"; cf. v 11, "*for the present* be merry.")[68] But Raphael's magic works; the demon is rendered inoperative and exiled to Egypt. Tobit's money is returned. His suffering is alleviated. His son has married the right kind of wife, and they present him with sons and grandsons. He lives to a ripe old age. Thus the truth of Tobit's instruction to his son becomes evident, and he repeats the moral of the story in his testament (14:8-11). In similar fashion Raphael comments,

> For almsgiving delivers from death,
>   and it will purge away every sin.
> Those who perform deeds of charity and of righteousness will
>   have fullness of life;
>   but those who commit sin are the enemies of their own lives.
>   (12:9-10)

The action of the story has proven the truth of these assertions. God has rewarded God's pious servants.

For Tobit the way from piety to reward was long and tortuous and led through the valley of deep suffering. It is with this suffering and its resolution that our author is especially concerned. The story depicts a complex chain of events and the interweaving of multiple plots. Tobiah's marriage to Sarah solves the problem of her widowhood, and conversely her widowhood makes her available to be the kind of wife that Tobit admonished Tobiah to seek (4:12-15). Moreover, the possibility of Tobiah's finding Sarah was provided by the money Tobit had deposited in Rages, by the circumstances that made it impossible for him to collect it (1:14-15), and by Tobit's suffering and his consequent death wish, which led him to remember the money and send Tobiah off in search of it. Thus each problem contains the germ of a solution for the other. The combination of these plots for the common alleviation of everyone's suffering is not simply evidence of the author's literary genius. In effect, it creates a portrait of a God who carefully orchestrates, or at least successfully negotiates, the dark events of human life and history, working them toward gracious ends. Indeed, this God had "destined" Sarah for Tobiah "before eternity" (6:17). And so it happened. Our author presents a hypothetical case that serves as a window into the workings of divine sovereignty that operates in spite of suffering and the presence of demonic evil.[69] Although the case is hypothetical, the use of a narrative genre, set in a particular time and place with lifelike characters, asserts the reality of the divine operation in history.

If through the structure of the plots our author suggests *how* God works through suffering, the author also addresses the *why* of suffering. Tobit himself provides us with a clue to the author's view:

> For you have scourged me,
>   but you have had mercy on me. (11:15)

"Mercy" and "to have mercy" are the author's most frequent terms for God's saving activity. This mercy means release from "scourging." But why should Tobit the righteous man be scourged? The lengthy descriptions of Tobit's piety do not imply that he is sinless. His own prayer includes a confession of sin (3:3). His harsh judgment of his wife (2:11-14) and his lapses into unfaith (3:6; 10:1-3), and perhaps some self-righteousness on his part, are further indications that his piety notwithstanding, our author's righteous man is not perfect.[70]

Although this analysis may suggest that Tobit is a treatise on the suffering righteous person not totally dissimilar from the book of Job,[71] there is one substantive difference. Whereas the book of Job confines its treatment to an individual, the fate of the nation is of great concern in the book of Tobit, which focuses on it exclusively in the last two chapters.[72] In his earlier prayer Tobit lamented Israel's sin and God's punishment of the nation through plunder, captivity, death, and dispersion (3:4-5). He voiced this sentiment in the midst of a complaint about his own suffering. Now, in the light of his newfound health, he utters a hymn of praise to the God who will also save Israel. The exile and dispersion are God's punishment for Israel's sins, but the punishment is not final. Thus Tobit applies the formula "scourge/have mercy" several times to Israel's present situation and future destiny (13:2, 5, 9; cf. 13:14; 14:5). In parallel literature this formula occurs most frequently in connection with the nation.[73] This suggests that the problem of exile and dispersion and the hope for a regathering of the people are of foremost concern to the author and that its application to Tobit's own suffering is secondary. The return from dispersion will have as its focus proper pan-Israelite worship in a Jerusalem rebuilt according to the promises of Isaiah 54 and 60 (Tob 13:9-18; 14:5). In his testamentary forecast (14:4-7) Tobit envisages the Babylonian exile, the return, the rebuilding of the Jerusalem temple, and then in the end time the rebuilding of a glorious Jerusalem and the conversion of the Gentiles.

A key for our understanding of the author's *situation* and *purpose* can be found in the manner in which the book develops Tobit's character and unfolds the events related to his life. Deeply stamped into the early chapters is the senseless suffering of Tobit and Sarah and their families. Their prayers are spoken out of a sense of despair, and they are paradoxical in nature. While God may be addressed and even blessed (3:11), the best one can hope for is death, which brings release from a life that is effectively devoid of the gracious presence of God. Tobit addresses God as righteous judge and begs forgiveness in the form of quick dismissal from the continual reproach of others. God responds to his and Sarah's prayers in a totally unexpected way. God's angel is sent, through whom God "is with" Tobit and Sarah,[74] healing their ills and moving the course of events toward a beneficent conclusion. When this conclusion has become apparent Tobit bursts into a hymn of unmitigated praise to the God who "scourges" but "has mercy." The figure of Tobit is paradigmatic in his movement from despair (or rather a vacillation between despair and faith) to doxology. The author is addressing the Tobits of his own time, assuring them of God's gracious presence and activity and calling them to doxology, repentance, and the pious life. In the midst of senseless suffering one may still, like Tobit, assert the justice of God. For the reader, Tobit's assurances of an angelic presence are humorous, but they are also statements of the author's belief in the real presence of God in his own time.

The book of Tobit is profoundly doxological in content and tone. In addition to the three hymns of praise, there are numerous references (usually exhortations) to the praise of God.[75] When Raphael has revealed himself, he commissions Tobit to write a book that has an implicit doxological function:

> Bless God forevermore.... Bless him every day, praise him.... And now give thanks to God, for I am ascending to him who sent me. Write in a book everything that has happened.... So they confessed the great and wonderful works of God and acknowledged that the angel of the Lord had appeared to them. (12:17-22)

The readers are to utter praise because God is with them now and because their future is in God's hand. The dispersion of God's people, their absence from "the good land" (14:4), and their inability to gather as a single worshiping community in Jerusalem are problems of the first magnitude for our author. Nonetheless, the readers are exhorted to praise the God who will gather the scattered and bring the nations to worship at the temple in Jerusalem.

Our author also calls the readers to the pious and upright life as is evident from the several sections of formal teaching (4:3-21; 12:6-10; 14:9-11). The gathering of the Dispersion presupposes repentance (13:6) and the living of such a life. This piety and righteousness involves prayer, fasting, almsgiving (12:8), and deeds of kindness to others according to one's ability and station in life (4:7-11), as well as devotion to one's family and the maintenance of one's Israelite identity through endogamous marriage (4:12-13).[76]

The book's emphasis on marriage and family appears in a number of scenes that depict interactions between spouses and that reflect current attitudes about parents and children. Within this domestic sphere the men dominate, although the portrayal of Hannah mitigates somewhat this patriarchal familial structure. When the author focuses on religious matters and interactions with the divine sphere, men are clearly privileged and superior to women.[77]

The complexity of the story of Tobit is evident in its many parallels with biblical and non-Jewish literature.[78] The broad plot line, from start to finish, is similar to that of Job (see n. 71). The material about Tobit in the Assyrian court recalls the tales in Daniel 1–6 and the story of Ahiqar (see n. 15), and there are several allusions to characters and events in Ahiqar (Tob 1:21-22; 2:10; 14:10). The subplot about Tobiah and Sarah is reminiscent of the story of Isaac's quest for a wife (Gen 24) as interpreted in other Jewish texts.[79] Aspects of Tobiah's interaction with Raphael parallel the events involving Telemachus and the goddess Athena in Homer's *Odyssey,* and other details in the story are strikingly similar to other material in the *Odyssey.*[80] In all of these respects the book of Tobit evidences characteristics typical of the folktales and fiction of many cultures.[81] The folktale core of the story, however, has been embellished through the incorporation of motifs, forms, and formulas typical of biblical Deuteronomic theology and biblical and postbiblical Jewish sapiential and apocalyptic literature.[82]

From this emerges a multifaceted "didactic novel" that can be understood and appreciated on several levels.[83] Its central figure is lifelike, vacillating between faith and doubt, from despondency and perhaps self-pity to hope and optimism, and whose piety does not put him above domestic quarrels and perhaps a touch of self-righteousness. The book also provides a window into Jewish attitudes about suffering and theodicy that both parallel and differ from contemporary apocalyptic expressions of the same issues. To what extent, we might ask, did the readers of this text believe that their woes and their alleviation were functions of an invisible but very real spirit world?[84] This serious theological reflection notwithstanding, the book can be appreciated for its many moments of irony and humor.[85] For this author, the ways of God are sometimes funny, and humor protects religion from being dull or fanatical.

The place of the book's writing is disputed.[86] However, several factors point to the Dispersion: Tobit's persecution and reproach by foreigners (1:16-20); the long exhortation to marry within the nation and the incorporation of this theme into the narrative; and the continuous concern with a return from the problems and threats of the Dispersion.

Within such a context the message and purpose of the book may be delineated more specifically. The author repeatedly affirms the universal sovereignty of Israel's God and God's presence and activity among the dispersed in spite of distress. The people are exhorted to maintain their identity in the land of their dispersion. The source of such identity is in the family, in a respect for one's parents, and in the preservation of the purity of the line. Repentance and piety will lead to the gathering of the Dispersion, when the disorder and instability that characterize life away from home will be over-come.[87] Meanwhile Israel is to acknowledge God among the nations (13:6), that they might be converted and join in that universal praise of God that constitutes the heart of Tobit's vision for the future. Thus Tobit is remarkably similar to the stories in Daniel 1–6.

The date of Tobit is uncertain. The last historical event mentioned is the rebuilding of the Jerusalem temple (515 B.C.E.).[88] We may posit a date before the persecution of the Jews by Antiochus Epiphanes (168 B.C.E.) since the historical summary in chapter 14 makes no reference to it—a glaring omission in a book so concerned with sin, punishment, and Israel's suffering.[89] Many scholars suggest that the reference to "the prophets" (14:5) does not allow a date before about 200 B.C.E., when the prophetic corpus was presumably canonized. However, the author need not be referring to the whole collection of prophetic writings as we know them, and he does not speak of "the Law and the Prophets" together, thus implying canonicity for the latter. Like the other Apocrypha, the book of Tobit is preserved in manuscripts of the Greek Bible and its daughter translations. Its origin as a Semitic text has generally been recognized, however, and the Dead Sea Scrolls have preserved fragments of one Hebrew and four Aramaic manuscripts of the book.[90]

The Epistle of Jeremiah

Satirical polemics against idols and idolatry are a developing mode of expression in exilic and postexilic literature.[91] Taking a cue from one such text in Jeremiah 10:2-15 and from the prophet's letter in Jeremiah 29, this author has composed a tractate alleged to be the copy of another letter that Jeremiah wrote to the exiles in Babylon.[92] Beyond this claim in the superscription (v 1), however, there are no indicators in the text that it is either Jeremianic or a letter.

In the introduction (vv 2-7) the author tells the readers that they will see gods of silver, gold, and wood carried in procession and worshiped and feared by the Gentiles. Such fear should not possess the Jews. In their hearts they should determine to worship the Lord, whose angel is with them to witness their thoughts and requite them.[93]

Following this introduction are ten sections of unequal length (vv 8-16, 17-23, 24-29, 30-40a, 40b-44, 45-52, 53-56, 57-65, 66-69, 70-73) in which the author heaps up arguments and evidences that demonstrate that idols are not what the Gentiles suppose or claim them to be. The uniqueness of the Epistle of Jeremiah lies not in the types of arguments presented, many of which have parallels elsewhere, but in the persistence with which the author pursues a point by means of repetition and rhetorical devices that make this point in a variety of ways.

The author's message is explicit in a refrainlike formula that punctuates and concludes each of the ten sections. The wording varies slightly from place to place, but the point is always the same.[94] Typical is v 23:

Thence you will know that they are not gods.
Therefore do not fear them.

Four distinct elements occur in this refrain: (1) The initial word, "thence,"[95] indicates that the content of the refrain is an inference based on the paragraph it is bringing to a conclusion. (2) Each occurrence of the refrain contains a word denoting knowledge; the readers are to learn something from what they have read. (3) What they learn is that the alleged gods of the Gentiles are in fact not gods.[96] (4) Consequently ("therefore") the readers need not fear these false gods (vv 16, 23, 29, 65, 69). Thus the theme in vv 4-5 is repeated.[97]

The claim that idols are not gods is negative in form and antithetical in function. The author rejects the religious claims of the Gentiles, refutes their beliefs, implies that their religious practices are inappropriate, and, in general, argues that reality contradicts appearance. This is done by means of a number of specific arguments and rhetorical and grammatical devices that are explicitly or implicitly antithetical.

The most persistent idiom in this work is the use of the negative. The claim that idols "are not gods" is a conclusion drawn from a multitude of observations about the things that idols do not and, more strongly, "cannot" (vv 8, 19, 34, 35) do.[98] Idols do not and cannot do all the things that gods do. They cannot set up or depose kings, bestow wealth, enforce the keeping of oaths, rescue from death, deliver the weak from the strong, give sight to the blind, deliver a person in distress, show mercy to the widow and treat the orphan kindly (vv 34-38), send rain (v 53), administer justice and act beneficently (v 64), curse or bless kings, show heavenly portents, shine like the sun and give light like the moon (vv 66-67). In a parallel argument that remains implicit, the author recounts without comment practices in the idol cult or by its priests that are considered inappropriate. Thus from a Jewish point of view, the touching of sacrifices by women in a state of ritual impurity, the service of women at cultic meals, and cultic prostitution (vv 29, 30, 43) speak for themselves. Equally devastating are the hypocrisy and cynicism of the priests who steal gold and silver and robes from the idols and sell for profit the sacrifices offered to them (vv 10, 28, 33).

Carrying the argument one step further, the author points out that these false gods cannot even do the things that humans do: speak, see, and breathe (vv 8, 19, 25). Put in the strongest way possible, they cannot even help themselves (vv 12-14, 18, 24, 27, 55). This last point is also implied by describing how the idols are the object of a number of human actions: they are decked out with crowns and robes (vv 9-12), carried in procession (v 26), and hidden in time of war or calamity (v 48). But, most fundamentally, they are fabricated by human beings (vv 8, 45-51). They are nothing more than what they have been made by the human beings who revere them as gods. The fabrication process itself is a parable of their falseness: gold and silver on the outside but wood underneath; they are not what they appear or are claimed to be (vv 50, 44).

The ironic use of simile provides the author with yet another means of mocking the false gods. They are likened to all manner of things that are useless and altogether inappropriate as images of the Deity: a broken dish (v 17), an imprisoned criminal (v 18), a scarecrow that guards nothing, a thornbush on which birds light, a discarded corpse (vv 70-71). Thus lifeless, disintegrating (vv 12, 20, 72), and useless, they are not to be feared. They will perish in disgrace, and the reader will do well to dissociate himself or herself from them and hence avoid this disgrace (vv 72-73).

Although our author's purpose is argumentative, the progression of the book shows little development in the argument. Similar arguments, techniques, and implications recur from section to section. The author's technique is to overpower the reader by repetition and reinforcement.

The date of the work cannot be determined with any certainty. A clear reference to the Epistle of Jeremiah in 2 Maccabees 2:2 indicates a date before 100 B.C.E.[99] Reference to an exilic period of up to seven generations (Ep Jer 3) may indicate a date no later than 317 B.C.E.[100] The author's evident familiarity with aspects of Babylonian religion may indicate composition in Mesopotamia, although an author so informed could have written the book anyplace where idolatry presented a threat.[101] Although the epistle is extant only in Greek, it may well have been translated from Hebrew.[102] This suggests that the intended audience was Jewish, as seems to be indicated by vv 29-30, 43, which assume that the audience shares the Jewish presuppositions of the author's critique of Babylonian religion. In the Greek Bible and some oriental versions dependent on it, the book is placed either between Lamentations and Ezekiel, as a separate book, or more often as a last chapter in the book of Baruch (see below, p. 97).

BIBLIOGRAPHY

Daniel

Translation: The Bible and the Apocrypha.

Text: Joseph **Ziegler**, ed., *Susanna, Daniel, Bel et Draco* (SVTG 16/2; Göttingen: Vandenhoeck & Ruprecht, 1954), critical edition of the Greek texts, including the Additions.

Commentaries: John J. **Collins**, *Daniel: A Commentary on the Book of Daniel* (Hermeneia; Minneapolis: Fortress Press, 1993). Carey A. **Moore**, *Daniel, Esther, and Jeremiah: The Additions* (AB 44; Garden City, N.Y.: Doubleday, 1977) 23–149.

Literature: On the stories in Dan 1–6 see Elias J. **Bickerman**, *Four Strange Books of the Bible* (New York: Schocken, 1967) 61–100; Pamela J. **Milne**, *Vladimir Propp and the Study of Structure in Hebrew Narrative* (Sheffield: Almond, 1988) 179–292; George W. E. **Nickelsburg**, *Resurrection, Immortality, and Eternal Life in Intertestamental Judaism* (HTS 26; Cambridge: Harvard Univ. Press, 1972) 49–58; Lawrence M. **Wills**, *The Jew in the Court of the Foreign King: Ancient Jewish Court Legends* (HSM 26; Minneapolis: Fortress Press, 1990). Amy-Jill **Levine**, "'Hemmed in on Every Side': Jews and Women in the Book of Susanna," in Fernando F. Segovia and Mary Ann Tolbert, eds., *Reading from This Place* (Minneapolis: Fortress Press, 1995) 175–90, an excellent feminist reading of Susanna. Tim **McLay**, *The OG and Th Versions of Daniel* (SBLSCS 43; Atlanta: Scholars Press, 1997), analysis of the relationship of the two translations. Ellen **Spolsky**, ed., *The Judgment of Susanna* (SBLEJL 11; Atlanta: Scholars Press, 1996), a multidisciplinary discussion of the story of Susanna and its interpretation in the West.

The Story of Darius's Guardsmen

Translation: The Apocrypha.

Text: Robert **Hanhart**, ed., *Esdrae liber I* (SVTG 8/1; Göttingen: Vandenhoeck & Ruprecht, 1974), critical edition of the Greek text.

Literature: James L. **Crenshaw**, "The Contest of Darius' Guards," in Burke O. Long, ed., *Images of Man and God: Old Testament Stories in Literary Focus* (Sheffield: Almond, 1980) 74–88, 119–20. A. **Hilhorst**, "The Speech on Truth in 1 Esdras 4:34–41," in F. García Martínez, A. Hilhorst, and C. J. Labuschagne, eds., *The Scriptures and the Scrolls*, FS A. S. van der Woude (VTSup 49; Leiden: Brill, 1992) 134–51. George W. E. **Nickelsburg**, "The Bible Rewritten and Expanded," in Michael E. Stone, ed., *Jewish Writings of the Second Temple Period* (CRINT 2/2; Assen: Van Gorcum; Philadelphia: Fortress Press, 1984) 131–35, additional details and documentation for the present account. Robert H. **Pfeiffer**, *History of New Testament Times with an Introduction to the Apocrypha* (New York: Harper, 1949) 250–57. K.-F. **Pohlmann**, *Studien zum dritten Esra* (FRLANT 104; Göttingen: Vandenhoeck & Ruprecht, 1970). Charles C. **Torrey**, "The Story of the Three Youths," *AJSL* 23 (1907) 177–201, repr. in idem, *Ezra Studies* (New York: KTAV, 1970) 37–61. Zipora **Talshir** (with David Talshir), *1 Esdras: From Origin to Translation* (SBLSCS 47; Atlanta: Society of Biblical Literature, 1999) 58–109, composition and original language of the story. Zipora **Talshir** (with David Talshir), *1 Esdras: A Text Critical Commentary* (SBLSCS 50; Atlanta: Society of Biblical Literature, 2001) 125–243, detailed commentary with a focus on text-critical and philological issues.

Tobit

Translation: The Apocrypha.

Texts and Other Translations: Robert **Hanhart**, ed., *Tobit* (SVTG 8/5; Göttingen: Vandenhoeck & Ruprecht, 1983), critical edition of the Greek text. Joseph A. **Fitzmyer**, DJD 19 (1995) 1–79, edition and translation of the Qumran Aramaic and Hebrew texts. Stewart **Weeks**, Simon **Gathercole**, and Loren **Stuckenbruck**, eds., *The Book of Tobit: Texts from the Principal Ancient and Medieval Traditions: With Synopsis, Concordances, and Annotated Texts in Aramaic, Hebrew, Greek, Latin, and Syriac* (Fontes et Subsidia 3; Berlin/New York: de Gruyter, 2004). Frank **Zimmermann**, *The Book of Tobit* (JAL; New York: Harper, 1958), introduction, the Greek texts, annotated English translation.

Commentaries: Carey A. **Moore**, *Tobit* (AB 40A; New York: Doubleday, 1996), introduction, translation, and the best commentary in English. Joseph A. **Fitzmyer**, *Tobit* (CEJL; Berlin and New York: de Gruyter, 2003), introduction, translation, and commentary that focuses especially on text-critical and philological matters.

Literature Survey: Richard A **Spencer**, "The Book of Tobit in Recent Research," *CurBS* 7 (1999) 147–80.

Literature: Amy-Jill **Levine**, "Diaspora as Metaphor: Bodies and Boundaries in the Book of

Tobit," in J. Andrew Overman and Robert S. MacLennan, eds., *Diaspora Jews and Judaism: Essays in Honor of, and in Dialogue with, A. Thomas Kraabel* (South Florida Studies in the History of Judaism 41; Atlanta: Scholars Press, 1992) 107–17, the text's social location. George W. E. **Nickelsburg**, "Stories of Biblical and Early Post-Biblical Times: Tobit," in Michael E. Stone, ed., *Jewish Writings of the Second Temple Period* (CRINT 2/2; Assen: Van Gorcum; Philadelphia: Fortress Press, 1984), 40–46; George W. E. **Nickelsburg**, "Tobit," in James L. Mays, ed., *The HarperCollins Bible Commentary* (San Francisco: HarperSanFrancisco, 2000) 719–31, additional details and documentation on this exposition. Benedikt **Otzen**, *Tobit and Judith* (GAP; Sheffield: Sheffield Academic Press, 2002) 2–66, introduction and history of scholarship. Norman R. **Petersen**, "Tobit," in Bernhard W. Anderson, ed., *The Books of the Bible* (New York: Scribner's, 1989) 2:35–442, a literary introduction. Lawrence M. **Wills**, *The Jewish Novel in the Ancient World* (Ithaca: Cornell Univ. Press, 1995) 68–92, excellent discussion, especially in light of contemporary literary parallels.

The Epistle of Jeremiah

Translation: The Apocrypha.

Text: Joseph **Ziegler**, ed., *Ieremias, Baruch, Threni, Epistula Ieremiae* (SVTG 15; Göttingen: Vandenhoeck & Ruprecht, 1957) 494–504, critical edition of the Greek text.

Commentary: Carey A. **Moore**, *Daniel, Esther, and Jeremiah: The Additions* (AB 44; Garden City, N.Y.: Doubleday, 1977) 316–58.

Literature: Weigand **Naumann**, *Untersuchungen über den apokryphen Jeremiasbrief* (BZAW 25; Giessen: Töpelmann, 1913) 1–53.

The Wisdom of Ben Sira. Fragments of four columns of a second–first-century B.C.E. Hebrew manuscript found at Masada preserving parts of Sir 39:27—43:30. Photograph is courtesy of the Israel Museum and the Shrine of the Book.

2

Palestine in the Wake of Alexander the Great

THE OVERLORDS OF PALESTINE

For about two centuries, the Persian Empire founded by Cyrus the Great held sway over the lands around the eastern Mediterranean. Only the Greeks, and the Scythians to the north of them, successfully withstood attempts at Persian domination. Nonetheless, the vast empire that stretched from the borders of India in the east to Egypt and Thrace in the west was difficult to hold together. The reign of Artaxerxes I (during the time of Ezra and Nehemiah) saw the beginning of unrest and rebellion.

The mortal threat arose in the little backwoods kingdom of Macedonia. Its king, Philip II (359–336 B.C.E.), maneuvering with equal expertise on the battlefield and in the political arena, succeeded in making himself master of almost all of Greece, which was now spent from the agonies of the numerous internal wars. Philip's conquest of Thrace set the stage for a massive confrontation with Persia. When he was assassinated at the age of forty-six, the task fell to his twenty-year-old son, Alexander III ("the Great").

Once he had consolidated his power, the young general moved with incredible speed and efficiency. In four years the fragile Persian Empire crumbled before the relentless drive of Alexander's military machine. In 334 he crossed the Hellespont and defeated the Persian army at the River Granicus near the site of ancient Troy. There was no other sizable Persian force in the whole of Asia Minor. In a year Alexander swept across the peninsula and stood facing the armies of Darius II at the Cilician Gates near Issus (333). The Persian army was routed, and the king fled for his life, leaving his family and possessions behind. Alexander marched south along the coast, accepting the surrender of one Phoenician seaport after the other. Only the island of Tyre resisted, its inhabitants feeling secure in their position a quarter of a mile off the coast. Alexander's army constructed a causeway from the mainland to the island.* After seven months of hard labor and bitter siege, the city fell and its walls were leveled. Alexander continued south into Palestine. Gaza capitulated after a two-month siege, and for its resistance, it too was razed (332). Egypt welcomed Alexander as successor to the pharaohs and acclaimed him son of the god Amon. He then started north again toward Syria (330). A revolt in Samaria was swiftly punished, the city was destroyed, and a Macedonian garrison was installed.[1*]

With Asia Minor, Syria-Palestine, and Egypt now firmly in his control, Alexander turned eastward toward the heartland of the empire. He engaged the army of Darius at Gaugamela just east of the Tigris River. Again the Persian army was badly defeated, and the king fled. Alexander turned to other conquests: Babylon, Susa, Persepolis (the Persian capital), and Ecbatana. From Ecbatana he pursued the fugitive Darius, but the king was murdered by his own subordinates (330).

Alexander was now sole ruler of the Persian Empire. His ambitions carried him on through the eastern reaches of his empire to the Indus River. He would have gone farther, but his troops rebelled at the prospect and he was forced to return west (326). He spent his last year in Babylon consolidating his gains and administering his empire. The end came swiftly. He died in 323 at the age of thirty-three.

The young Alexander left no eligible heir to his empire. Immediately after his death his generals appointed Perdiccas, one of their number, to be regent over the whole empire. He in turn appointed his colleagues to be satraps over the various provinces. The orderly arrangement was short-lived, however. In 321 Perdiccas was assassinated by his own commanders, and chaos broke out as the generals and satraps maneuvered for control. These wars of the Diadochi ("successors") lasted forty years.

The province of Coele-Syria (southern Syria and Palestine) was a frequent bone of contention because it was located along the principal trade routes by land and sea and served as a major military highway between Egypt and the countries to the north and east. In a period of twenty-one years (323–302) it changed hands seven times and was frequently the site of military campaigns. Ptolemy, the satrap of Egypt, invaded Coele-Syria in 320. He drove out its rightful governor, Laomedon, and annexed it to Egypt. Meanwhile Antigonus, who was satrap of parts of Asia Minor, began to annex other parts of the empire as he sought to make himself sole successor to Alexander. Ptolemy, Seleucus (whom Antigonus had expelled from Babylon), and other satraps formed an alliance against Antigonus, demanding that he accept Ptolemy's sovereignty over Coele-Syria. Antigonus responded in 315 by invading the country and bringing it under his control. Ptolemy countered in 312, defeating Antigonus's son Demetrius while his father was engaged elsewhere. Antigonus returned, Ptolemy fled, and control over Coele-Syria reverted to Antigonus. In 302 the Macedonian generals once more made common cause against Antigonus. Ptolemy swept through Palestine. At Sidon he heard a rumor that Antigonus had defeated his allies, and he retreated swiftly to Egypt. The rumor was false. The decisive battle took place at Ipsus in central Asia Minor. Antigonus was slain in battle, his army was defeated, and his territory was divided.

The precise details of this settlement are disputed by historians. They were also disputed by the principals, Ptolemy and Seleucus, both of whom claimed the right to rule Coele-Syria. For the present time, however, Ptolemy's armies were in the province, and he and his successors continued to rule there until the beginning of the second century. Thus the result of Ipsus was the following division of the empire: Lysimachus in Thrace and western Asia Minor; Ptolemy in Egypt and Coele-Syria; Seleucus in northern Syria and Babylon. In 281 Seleucus defeated Lysimachus and annexed Asia Minor to his kingdom. Seleucus and Ptolemy were now the sole successors of Alexander, and their heirs would rule two rival kingdoms.

Ptolemaic Palestine remained peaceful for almost a hundred years. In 219 the old feud between the two dynasties flared up again as the Seleucid king Antiochus III ("the Great") sought control over Palestine. A series of battles ensued, and Ptolemy IV defeated him at Raphia in 217. When Ptolemy died in 204 and was succeeded by his five-year-old son, Antiochus once more set out to take Coele-Syria. The final battle was fought in 198 at the Panion (the shrine of the god Pan) near the sources of the Jordan River. Antiochus was victorious, and Palestine passed into the hands of the Seleucid house, where it would remain until the successful conclusion of the Jewish wars of independence later in the century.

EARLY HELLENIZATION IN PALESTINE

Alexander was a Macedonian steeped in Greek culture and schooled under Aristotle. His military conquest and political domination helped to expand Hellenic culture in the East. Alexandria was the first of some thirty cities that he established. The settlement of soldiers, some of whom married foreign wives, served to spread Greek institutions, religion, and language.

Alexander's successors also furthered the Greek way of life. Some thirty cities were founded in Palestine by order of the Macedonian kings. They were located in three areas, which excepted the territory of Judah: the Mediterranean coast; Samaria and Galilee; and Transjordan, where they formed the nucleus of what would later be the Decapolis (or league of "ten cities"). These cities adopted the political structure of the Greek *polis* ("city") and had an official enrollment of Greek "citizens." Some of their inhabitants assumed Greek names. Greek educational institutions were established, and temples, theaters, and other fine buildings were constructed.

It is a matter of debate to what extent and in what ways Palestinian Judaism was hellenized before the momentous events of 175 B.C.E., of which we shall speak in the next chapter. In any event, Judah did not remain isolated from its environment, and we shall note evidences of Hellenistic influence in the writings we discuss in the present chapter.

LITERATURE ATTRIBUTED TO ENOCH

Enoch walked with God; and he was not, for God took him (Gen 5:24).

The two halves of this cryptic passage suggest *in nuce* the two principal elements of a sizable amount of Jewish revelatory literature that is attached to the name of this ancient patriarch: (1) Enoch was righteous in an unrighteous age. (2) Therefore God saw fit to remove Enoch from this earth in order to transmit to him esoteric revelation about the nature of the universe and about the end time; Enoch wrote down this revelation so that it could be transmitted to the righteous who would live in the last days. The portrayal of Enoch in this literature reflects an interesting blend of motifs that are at home in Jewish theology and elements that appear to have been drawn from Babylonian flood traditions.[2]

A considerable number and variety of these pseudo-Enochic traditions, dating from various times in the three centuries B.C.E., have been collected in a writing that has come to be known as 1 Enoch. Most, if not all, of these traditions were composed in Aramaic. The collection was translated into Greek and from Greek into Ge'ez, the language of ancient Ethiopia, in which version alone the entire collection is preserved as part of the Ethiopic Bible. Fragments of eleven Aramaic manuscripts of various sections of 1 Enoch have been identified among the Dead Sea Scrolls.[3] We shall discuss the individual sections in their likely historical settings.[4]

The Book of the Luminaries (1 Enoch 72–82)

These chapters constitute a major treatise on cosmic and astronomical phenomena. Originally a more extensive form of this text existed as an independent Enochic work. Four fragmentary manuscripts of the Aramaic version of this longer work have been found among the Dead Sea Scrolls—in all cases separate from those manuscripts containing other parts of 1 Enoch.[5] Since 1 Enoch 1–36 (e.g., chaps. 2–4 and 33–36) employs material from these chapters, it is evident that the Book of the Luminaries is one of the oldest sections of the collection, dating back at least well into the third century B.C.E.

The Book of the Luminaries is presented as revelation. The archangel Uriel (meaning "God is my light") guided Enoch through the cosmos and explained the laws by which these phenomena operate. Enoch now writes an account of this journey and transmits the information to his son, Methuselah. With monotonous repetition and with calculations and predictions ad infinitum, the treatise demonstrates the uniformity and order of God's creation as it is evidenced in the movements of the luminaries and the blowing of the winds. The universe is very much alive, with thousands of angels in charge of its many facets and functions.

Enoch's heaven is a great hemispherical vault stretched over the flat disk of the earth and set upon its outer edge (like an oversized cup inverted on a saucer). At the juncture of the firmament and the earth are twelve gates through which the sun and the moon rise and set during their respective annual and monthly cycles. Alongside these gates are numerous windows through which the stars emerge and exit.

Crucial to this treatise is a solar calendar of 364 days, twelve months of thirty days, with four days intercalated in the third, sixth, ninth, and twelfth months. The first, very long part of the book, which has been preserved only in the fragments of Qumran Aramaic manuscripts a and b (4Q208 and 209), consisted of a tabulation that synchronized the movements of the sun and the moon over the course of a 364-day solar year. This was presumably prefaced by a brief narrative that set the scene and introduced the speaker.[6]

The Ethiopic version begins with this superscription:

The Book about the Motion of the Heavenly Luminaries, all as they are in their kinds, their jurisdiction, their time, their name, their origins, and their months, which Uriel, the holy angel who was with me (and) who is their leader, showed me. The entire book about them, as it is, he showed me and how every year of the world will be forever, until a new creation lasting forever is made. (72:1)[7]

Thus, like much of the rest of 1 Enoch, as we shall see, this section is presented as angelic revelation, and the cosmological shape of its subject matter notwithstanding, it has an eschatological perspective. The present shape of the cosmos will continue until the everlasting new creation (cf. 91:16-17, below, p. 111).

Chapter 72:2-37 presents "the first law of the luminaries"—the movement of the sun. It rises from an eastern gate and sets through the corresponding western gate (presumably returning behind the north or south side of the firmament), and it moves north and south along the six eastern and six western gates, as its zenith approaches and recedes from perpendicular—a function of what we now understand to be the earth's ecliptic. The calculation of this movement north and south does not coincide with empirical reality, but seems to have been based on an a priori scheme that demonstrates mathematical uniformity in the heavens. The next two laws of the luminaries relate to the phases of the moon (chap. 73) and the moon's movement along the aforementioned twelve gates (74:1-9). In these cases Enoch's calculations are close enough to empirical reality to have been based on actual observation.[8]

Chapter 74:10-17, with its comparison of the solar and lunar years, may be a remnant of the synchronistic calendar,[9] and 75:1-3 continues with reference to the four intercalary days and the angels that are in charge of them. The twelve gates in the four quarters of the heaven, and the winds that blow in and out of them for blessing and curse, are the subject of 75:4—76:14, and a description of the four quarters of the earth and their mountains and rivers follows (chap. 77). The text then returns to the subject of the sun and the moon (chap. 78). The summary in chapter 79 may indicate that some discussion of the stars has dropped from the text (79:1; but cf. 82:9-20). After what appears to be a final summarizing statement (80:1) comes a short poem that differs from the preceding material in two respects (80:2-8). It posits a violation in the order of nature not previously envisioned, and it associates this with "the days of the sinners" (80:2). Only in 75:2 have we seen such a polemic.

Chapters 81:1—82:3 are a misplaced block of narrative about Enoch's return to earth, which has more in common with chapters 12–36 than the Book of the Luminaries (see below, p. 114). Then another polemic contrasts right and wrong calendrical practice (82:4-8). The book concludes with a description of the stars, their leaders, and the four seasons (82:9-20). The description of the third and fourth seasons has been lost in the Ethiopic version, but one Aramaic manuscript preserves some fragments of it (4Q211 1 1–3).[10]

The precise provenance of the Book of the Luminaries is uncertain, but its contents suggest an association with "traditional, intellectual groups," namely scribes and priests.[11]

The 364-day solar that is the centerpiece for the Book of the Luminaries is also advocated in the Book of Jubilees (see below, chapter 3), which invests it with special religious status and strongly polemicizes against the "Gentile" lunar calendar. Such a polemical element is largely lacking in the Book of the Luminaries, although 75:2; 80:2-8; and 82:4-6 indicate that this material was employed for such a purpose at some point in the document's literary history, and the book's revelatory form may indicate that some such dispute lies in the background. Nonetheless, it is striking that Book of the Luminaries—both in the Ethiopic 1 Enoch and in the Qumran Aramaic fragments—contains detailed descriptions of the daily movements of the moon and of the relationships between the movements and locations of the sun and the moon. Other Qumranic calendrical texts also refer to lunar phases and movements.[12] There is, to date, no explanation for the presence at Qumran of multiple copies of both the antilunar Book of Jubilees and the Enochic and non-Enochic solar/lunar texts. The Enochic treatise provided the theoretical undergirding for Jubilees' dispute with the Jewish religious establishment (see below, pp. 69, 74), but it is unclear exactly how the Enochic authors themselves and the Qumran community may, at any given time, have fit into such a dispute.[13]

The Book of the Watchers (1 Enoch 1–36)

These chapters are a collection of revelatory traditions that have accreted over a period of time. We shall treat the component sections in the order of their appearance in 1 Enoch. Our earliest Aramaic manuscript evidence indicates that at least chapters 1–11 were already a literary unit in the first half of the second century B.C.E.[14] As we shall see, chapters 1–5 are the introduction to a larger number of chapters, probably 6–36. Evidence in 1 Enoch 85–90 indicates that 1 Enoch 1–36 was known before the death of Judas Maccabeus in 160 B.C.E.[15] Hence we are justified in treating these chapters as a product of the period before 175 B.C.E.

A. Introduction	chaps.	1–5
B. The rebellion of the angels		6–11
C. Enoch's heavenly commissioning		12–16
D. Enoch's journey to the west		17–19
E. Additional journey traditions		20–36
1. List of accompanying angels		20
2. Journey back from the west		21–27
3. Journey to the east		28–33
4. Journeys to the four corners of the earth		34–36

1 Enoch 1–5

Presently these chapters are the introduction to the whole of 1 Enoch, announcing the coming of the great judgment as a revelation that Enoch had received and transmitted for the benefit of the righteous chosen who would be living in the last days, that is, the real author's own time. The emphasis on the judgment and other points of similarity with chapters 20–36 suggest that chapters 1–5 were *composed* as an introduction to chapters 6–36.[16]

The opening verses (1:1-2) paraphrase Deuteronomy 33:1 (the Blessing of Moses) and Numbers 24:3-4 (one of Balaam's oracles). Thus the author sets himself in the line of the prophets and cites heavenly visions and auditions as the authority for the revelations that follow. The passages that frame the section (1:4-9 + 5:4-9) are a lengthy oracle in late prophetic style announcing the theme of the book: an imminent judgment in which God will vindicate the righteous and punish the wicked.[17] The first half of the oracle (1:4-9) recalls such biblical theophanic texts as Deuteronomy 33, Micah 1, and Zechariah 14:5. The latter half (1 Enoch 5:4-9) draws on the imagery and language of Isaiah 65 with its contrast between the long life and blessing awaiting the righteous and the curses that will befall the wicked. The prose passage in the middle of the oracle (1 Enoch 2:1—5:3), written in a style typical of wisdom literature,[18] contrasts nature's obedience with human rebellion. Sinful humans are culpable because they do not obey the moral order that God has created in the cosmos.

1 Enoch 6–11

This story about the rebellion of the angels ("the watchers") and their judgment is the nucleus and fountainhead of the traditions in chapters 1–36 and is presumed throughout. With the possible exception of chapters 72–82, it is the earliest tradition in 1 Enoch. Unlike the other sections of 1 Enoch, chapters 6–11 contain no references to Enoch himself or any indications that they were composed in his name.

A. The Proposal (Gen 6:1-2a)		6:1-8	
B. The Deed (Gen 6:2b, 4b)		7:1abc	
[Teaching			7:1de]
C. The Results (Gen 6:4cd, 4a)		7:2-5	
1. Birth of the giants	7:2		
2. Ensuing desolation	7:3-5		
D. The Plea		7:6—8:4	
1. Of the earth (Gen 4:10)	7:6		
[2. What Asael taught			8:1]
[3. Its results			8:1-2]
[4. What the other angels taught			8:3]
5. Of humanity	8:4		

E. The Holy Ones' Response (Gen 6:5)   9:1-8
   1. They hear   9:1-3
   2. They intercede   9:4-11
     [a. Asael   9:6]
     [b. Shemihazah and mysteries   9:8c]
F. God's Response (Gen 6:13)   10–11
   1. Sariel sent to Noah   10:1-3
   [2. Raphael sent to Asael   10:4-8]
   [3. Gabriel sent against giants   10:9-10]
   4. Michael sent
     a. Against Shemihazah   10:11-14
     b. Against the giants   10:15
     c. To cleanse the earth   10:16, 20
   5. Description of the end time (Gen 9) 10:17-19, 21—11:2

Literary analysis suggests that the passages bracketed in the outline are secondary additions to a story about the rebellion and punishment of the angelic chieftain, Shemihazah, his subordinates, and their progeny, the giants.[19] The original story was an elaboration of Genesis 6:1-4. It divides into three parts, each with significant departures from the biblical text:[20]

I. *The origins of a devastated world* (A–C): The intercourse between the sons of God and the daughters of men (Gen 6:1-2, 4) is here explicitly an act of conscious and deliberate angelic rebellion against God. The giants are described in detail as a race of powerful and bellicose half-breeds who devour the fruits of the earth, slaughter humankind and the animal kingdom, and then turn on one another. Thus the human race and "all flesh" are not the perpetrators of great evil, which God will punish (Gen 6:5-7, 11-13), but the victims of that evil, which has been committed by the giants.

II. *The turning point: a plea for help* (D–E): Here the archangels, and not God (Gen 6:5), view the state of the earth. The author places on their lips a long, eloquent, and impassioned plea in behalf of humanity.

III. *The divine resolution of the situation* (F): The divine Judge issues orders to the archangels. Sariel instructs Noah about the ark. Michael is commissioned to bind the rebel watchers until their final punishment on the day of judgment and to destroy the giants. The passage then flows into a divine commission to obliterate all evil and to cleanse the earth. It concludes with a description of a renewed earth, in which elements from Genesis 9 have been modified, intensified, and augmented with mythic material that is appropriate to a description of the end time: fabulous fertility and life span, the permanent absence of all evil of every sort, the conversion of the Gentiles—in short the final and full actualization of God's sovereignty on earth.

In addition to being biblical interpretation, this story is myth. Conditions in the author's world are the result of events in the unseen, heavenly realm. Moreover, the end time will be characterized by a quality that is beyond human ken and experience.

The author's thought is also typological. The events of the last days (the author's own time) mirror the events of primordial times. At the time of the flood, God judged a wicked earth and its inhabitants and started things anew. Once again the world has gone askew, but judgment is imminent and a new age will begin. Within the framework of this typological scheme, the variations from the biblical text may be read as reflections of the author's purposes and of the events and circumstances of the author's own time, when the enemy is a breed of mighty warriors whose bloody deeds threaten the very existence of creation. Since the archangels are intercessors between humanity and God, their prayer relays the prayer of the author's constituency and reflects a crisis in the faith of the people, who ponder the contradiction between God's complete foreknowledge and God's inactivity in the midst of the present disaster. The author's answer is placed in the mouth of God, who has given orders to the archangels. The judgment is at hand!

Our author is making a statement about the nature of contemporary evil and about its obliteration. This evil is more than the wicked deeds of violent people. Behind the mighty of the earth stand demonic powers. Given the supernatural origins of this evil, only God and God's heavenly agents can annihilate it. And they will do so. Therefore the audience can find comfort and take heart. Thus, in its viewpoint and function, this story foreshadows the apocalyptic literature of the second century to which we shall turn in the next chapter.

Because the story of Shemihazah is set in primordial times, attempts to determine the concrete historical setting of its composition will always fall short of absolute certainty.[21] Given this qualification, a possible setting appears to be the Diadochian wars. Alexander's conquests had begun a period of war and bloodshed. The large number of the Diadochi, the repeated campaigns in Palestine, and the multiplicity of wars and assassinations provide a suitable context for the descriptions of the battles of the giants—their devastation of the earth and humanity and their destruction of one another. Within this context, the myth of supernatural procreation may be read as a parody of the claims of divine procreation attached to certain of the Diadochi.[22] The author would be saying, yes, the parentage of the "giants" is supernatural, but their fathers are demons and rebels against heaven.

At some point the Shemihazah story was expanded either by ad hoc elaboration or through the addition of other traditions about rebel angels.[23] Now the rebellion involves the revelation of two kinds of heavenly secrets. Shemihazah and his subordinates reveal the magical arts and various kinds of astrological and cosmic prognostication (7:1de; 8:3). In addition, Shemihazah's lieutenant Asael is identified with an angelic rebel chieftain who reveals the arts of metallurgy and mining;[24] the result is the creation of weapons and seductive cosmetics. The material about Asael reflects the influence of Greek myths about Prometheus or perhaps other Near Eastern myths about similar figures.[25] In subsequent developing tradition, the figure of Asael comes to be identified with Azazel in Leviticus 16.[26]

The mythic character of this polemic against prohibited revelations is consonant with that of the Shemihazah story. Primordial rebellion is the cause of present evils: occult knowledge, bloodshed, and sexual misconduct. The precise object of the polemic against magic and prognostication is uncertain. While one might cite Gentile practices, magic was practiced also by Jews, and the Qumran Scrolls include both a horoscope and a brontological document (prognostication on the basis of thunderclaps).[27] The Scrolls document a Jewish community that collected texts with cosmic prognostications as well as other texts that polemicized against such prognostication.

1 Enoch 12–16[28]

This section of 1 Enoch reinforces the message of chapters 6–11. It does not retell the story of the watchers' revolt, but it does refer to it. Like chapters 6–11, it anticipates the coming judgment of the watchers. This announcement comes from the mouth of Enoch, "the scribe of righteousness," who is the central figure in these chapters.

Enoch is the recipient and transmitter of revelation about the nature and implications of the angelic revolt. He first receives this revelation from an angel. When he informs the watchers of their coming judgment, they ask Enoch to intercede for them. In response to this prayer, he sees a vision of heaven that reinforces the first revelation. As he relates this to the watchers (chaps. 14–16), he describes in great detail his ascent to heaven and his vision of the divine throne room. This description has a specific function within the narrative. Because the watchers have come from heaven, they know what it is like. By telling them of his experience of heaven, Enoch leaves no doubt in their minds that the message he brings comes straight from the divine throne room. This fictional (Enochic) setting in the story quite likely reveals the real setting for this piece of literature. The *author* presents an interpretation of chapters 6–11 and offers it to *his* audience as a piece of divine revelation. The descriptions of his ascent and of the throne room are his documentation.

These chapters mention only briefly the angelic revelation of secrets. They focus instead on the watchers' sinful intercourse with women. The act involved the unnatural mixture of heavenly and earthly, spirit and flesh (12:4; 15:3-7), and violated the divine order of creation. As such it was bound to fail and result in disaster. The union of angels and women could produce only half-breeds and bastards, and the deed could not be easily undone. When the giants died, their spirits were set loose in the world as evil spirits (15:8-12). The author interprets chapters 6–11 as a description of the incarnation of evil into the world, but he does so with his own nuance. The giants were an ancient race whose evil spirits—the progeny and incarnation of the watchers' rebellious spirits—now infest a troubled world.

The narrative of Enoch's call to preach to the rebel angels imitates the form of biblical prophetic commissionings. The author is especially beholden to Ezekiel 1–2 and to the account of that prophet's tour of the eschatological temple in Ezekiel 40–48. Making use of these materials, the author depicts Enoch's ascent to heaven and his progress through the courts of the heavenly temple right up to its holy of holies, where the Deity is enthroned. This use of the prophetic commissioning form suggests that the author saw himself in the line of the prophets. At the same time these chapters mark an important transitional point at which the tradition about Ezekiel's throne vision is moving in the direction of later Jewish mysticism. The description of the heavenly temple is shot through with paradox. The temple is constructed of hailstones, ice, and snow but is surrounded by fire. When Enoch enters it, he is as hot as fire and as cold as ice. The throne room at the heart of the ice temple is a raging inferno. The transcendence of the Deity, which is presumed and depicted throughout, foreshadows the viewpoint of later mysticism.

The oracles against the watchers depict them as priests of the heavenly temple who have forsaken their stations and defiled their purity (15:3-4; cf. 12:4). The language is reminiscent of polemics against the Jerusalem priesthood.[29] Taken in conjunction with elements in chapters 12–13 that parallel the story of Ezra,[30] they may indicate that the author looked upon the Jerusalem priesthood as in some sense defiled. The events in these chapters are set in upper Galilee near Mount Hermon. The multiple references to this area, and their accuracy, suggest that this tradition emanated from this geographical region, which had a long history as sacred territory for Israelites, Christians, and pagans.[31] *

1 Enoch 17–19

Angelic guides lead Enoch on a cosmic tour. With the exception of 18:1-5 (a *topically* arranged section about the seer's visit to the winds and about their functions), the direction of his journey is toward the west and culminates beyond the mountain throne of God in the northwest with a vision of the watchers' places of punishment. In its pattern the present section presumes chapters 12–16; like them it relates a journey to the throne of God, climaxing in a vision in which Enoch hears a word of judgment against the rebellious watchers. Here, however, the narrative has been shaped after the model of the Greek *nekyia*, a literary form that recounted a journey to the place of the dead and a vision of their punishments.[32] The author has employed and nuanced that form as a means of reinforcing the message of the book as a whole, namely, the judgment and punishment of the watchers. Temporally oriented predictions about that judgment are here given a locative referent: Enoch sees *the places* where the announced judgment will occur. As in chapters 14–16, the rapid listing of the places in the cosmos through which Enoch passes provides the reader with a kind of documentation that Enoch has made the trip all the way out there. The places listed indicate that the author was familiar with popular Near Eastern and Greek mythic geography.[33]

The author's subscript in 19:3 concludes a work whose central theme is the coming judgment (chaps. 6–19 or 1–19). The primary focus throughout is on the angelic, supernatural level—on the rebel angels, the giants, and the demons, who are the cause of the present evil, and on the divine figures and functionaries who will execute judgment on them.

1 Enoch 20–36

These chapters gather a second set of traditions about Enoch's cosmic journeys. Chapter 20 introduces the cast of angels who serve as Enoch's guides. Thereafter a stereotyped vision form is employed: arrival, vision, question, angelic interpretation, blessing ("I came to . . . I saw . . . I asked the angel . . . he said. . . . Then I blessed the Lord").

In chapters 21–27 Enoch retraces his journey from the far northwest eastward to Jerusalem, the center of the earth. The point of departure and direction of the journey indicates that this journey narrative presumes the existence of chapters 17–19. Doublets of the traditions in those chapters are here interpolated with eschatological elements and are interwoven with descriptions of places of special eschatological significance. Chapter 21 describes the places of punishment that have already been described in 18:10—19:2.[34] In chapter 22 Enoch arrives at the place of the dead, whose spirits are compartmentalized according to type until the day of judgment. Here the righteous receive a foretaste of their coming bliss while the wicked are already suffering.

In chapters 24–25 the seer is once again at the mountain throne of God. The description of 18:6-9 has been augmented by reference to God's final visitation of the earth, mention of the tree of life, and a description of the blessings that the righteous will experience in the new Jerusalem. Enoch's vision of the Holy City in chapters 26–27 has a similar emphasis. Chapters 25–27 take up eschatological predictions in Isaiah 65–66 and set them in the revelatory form that is typical of these chapters of 1 Enoch. Chapters 28:1—32:2 modify this vision form. Paralleling 17:1-5 they rapidly recount landmarks that document the seer's journey along the eastern spice routes, which culminates in his arrival at paradise (again the vision form in 32:3-6) and beyond it at the ends of the earth (33:1). In 33:2-4 Enoch refers to the astronomical treatise (chaps. 72–82). Chapters 34–36 summarize his vision of the winds (chap. 76). The book closes with an expanded form of the blessing that concludes most of the visions in chapters 21–33.

The Apocalyptic Worldview of 1 Enoch

Chapters 1–36 of 1 Enoch are our earliest extant example of a Jewish text that is governed by a full-blown apocalyptic worldview, in which a set of complementary dualisms or polarities is relieved by means of a revealed message received by an ancient sage.[35] A *spatial* dualism contrasts the inhabited world, the site of violence and injustice, with the heavenly realm, where God's will is done and judgment is being prepared, and with the outer reaches of earth's disk, the location of the places of reward and punishment. A *temporal* dualism juxtaposes the present time of evil with the primordial time of angelic rebellion and the future time of adjudication. An *ontological* dualism sets humanity over against the rebel watchers and demons on the one hand, and God and God's good angels on the other hand. The seer has traveled to heaven and the outer reaches of the cosmos and has seen into both the past and the future. His revelation, or apocalypse, to a world bereft of justice is that God's will, which is being done in heaven, will be fulfilled on earth when the imminent future judgment eradicates the present evil that was spawned in the past. This good news, contained in the writings of the ancient sage and seer, constitutes the eschatological community of the chosen, who abide by Enoch's law and trust in his promise of imminent deliverance. This same message will reappear in other parts of

1 Enoch and in a modified form in writings like the book of Daniel (for both, see below, pp. 77–86) and the New Testament book of Revelation.

Enochic apocalypticism blends a variety of traditions, themes, and literary forms from the Bible and noncanonical Jewish literature, as well as from non-Jewish sources. Drawing on Israelite precursors, it provides an eschatological interpretation of Genesis 6:1-4, rewrites history from Genesis to the Maccabees (1 Enoch 85–90), employs the themes and forms of prophecy, and takes up themes and forms found in biblical and nonbiblical wisdom texts.[36] The blend is dominated especially by the dualistic worldview described above, the book's claim to a new revelation (presented as very old), and the emphasis on eschatology. The Enochic use of pagan mythological motifs and its preachments against Gentile oppression are clear marks of this text's setting in the Hellenistic world and of its complex interaction with the events and culture of that world. The next book of concern to us offers a contemporary blend of some of the same elements from Israelite tradition, albeit with a very different emphasis and set of concerns.[37] It also presents another important witness to the interaction of Palestinian Judaism and Hellenistic culture.

The Wisdom of Ben Sira (Sirach or Ecclesiasticus)

Joshua Ben ("the son of") Eleazar Ben Sira[38] was a professional sage and scribe who studied and taught in Jerusalem during the first quarter of the second century B.C.E. He collected the fruits of his labors in a volume that he published in his own name (50:27), a fact that makes it almost unique in our literature. "The Wisdom of Jesus the Son of Sirach," the title of the book found in most English editions, employs the Greek form of his names and is derived from manuscripts of a Greek translation of the work that Ben Sira's grandson made from its Hebrew original.[39]

The book's genre and contents appear, at first, to be quite similar to the biblical book of Proverbs, although it is roughly twice as long as its canonical counterpart.[40] For much of his fifty-one chapters, Ben Sira employs the traditional form of the proverb to expound his views on right and wrong conduct and their consequences. Closer comparison of the two books, however, indicates some significant differences in genre, authorial concerns, and theological perspective. In addition to the proverbial form, Ben Sira includes some autobiographical narrative, two petitionary prayers, some prophetic forms, a long hymn in praise of the fathers, and some poems about "Lady Wisdom." He focuses on persons and events in Israelite history, emphasizes the critical importance of temple and cult (religious ritual), and indicates interest in the prophets and eschatology. For him wisdom is, to no small degree, embodied in the Mosaic Torah, although he also appreciates and sometimes speaks in the idiom of Hellenistic intellectual tradition.

Author

Ben Sira offers us a few glimpses of himself in his professional activities.[41] In 38:24—39:11 he contrasts the labor of the farmer and the tradesman with that of the scribe.

Each had "set his heart" on his particular task (38:26-28, 30; 39:5). For his part, the scribe (38:24) devoted himself full-time to a study of "the *law* of the Most High . . . the *wisdom* of all the ancients . . . and *prophecies*." Thus he was a scholar of what would later emerge as Israel's Scriptures and what in part was already recognized as such (Torah and Prophets). Moreover, his study included not only Israelite wisdom traditions but also the wisdom lore of other parts of the ancient Near East (cf. 39:4 and 39:1, "*all* the ancients").[42] Especially noteworthy is his sense of being a recipient of, participant in, and transmitter of traditional wisdom (24:25-33).[43] As a sage he served as counselor to rulers (39:4; cf. 38:33). His experience was not limited to his homeland; he traveled abroad, where he "tested the good and evil among humans" (39:4; cf. 34:9-12 [Gk. 31:9-13]). In addition to being a scholar, the scribe was also a teacher (39:8; cf. 24:33; 51:23).[44] To judge from Ben Sira's warning about association with the unscrupulous rich and powerful, his instructions on etiquette at banquets, and his frequent advice on riches, lending, and almsgiving, his students must have included in good part the youth of the Jerusalem aristocracy.[45] Whether, in addition to or in connection with his roles as scribe, scholar, and sage, Ben Sira was a member of the Jerusalem priesthood is disputed. He makes many positive references to the priesthood and the temple cult, and he identifies Jerusalem as the place where divine Wisdom dwells and "serves" (24:10-11). His strong support of the temple, cult, and priesthood may point in that direction (see below, pp. 59–60), although these statements may reflect rather his status as a "retainer" of the priestly and governing class.[46]

Literary Aspects

Prefixed to the Wisdom of Joshua Ben Sira is the translator's prologue. The structure of the body of the book is a matter of scholarly debate, and there is some evidence that the book was subject to a process of ongoing composition and editing rather than being a onetime composition.[47] There is general agreement, however, that, in its present form, the Greek text divides into two major sections. The first begins with a poem about Wisdom (chaps. 1–2), and an analogous poem in chapter 24 divides the book in two. The work climaxes with a doxology to the Creator (42:15—43:33) and a recitation of Israel's history in the form of an extensive song of praise to the heroes of the past (chaps. 44–50).[48] It concludes in the first-person singular with an author's subscript and a blessing on the reader (50:27-29),[49] a psalm of thanksgiving for deliverance from death (51:1-12), and a poem about the seeking of Wisdom (51:13-22)[50] that topically relates back to chapter 1 and links with 51:23-30, the author's final exhortation that the reader join with him in the pursuit of Wisdom.[51]

The selective analysis of chapters 1–23 that follows provides entree to the literary forms and techniques employed by Ben Sira and offers a basis on which the reader may analyze the literary aspects of chapters 24–51. Chapters 1–2 are the first of a number of sections on the personified figure of Wisdom (4:11-19; 6:18-37; 14:20—15:10; 24:1-29; 51:13-22). Chapters 2:1—4:10 are addressed to the sage's pupil(s) under the familiar title "child" or "children" (2:1; 3:1, 17; 4:1).[52] Continuing the theme of "the fear of God" in 1:11-30,[53] chapter 2 exhorts the reader to the patient pursuit of Wisdom and the testing that it brings with it. In 3:1-16 Ben Sira discusses, from a variety of perspectives, the honoring of one's parents. The verses below are typical of this reflection and of the distich (a proverb of two parallel lines), which constitutes the basic building block of this work (as it does of the book of Proverbs).

> He who honors his father atones for sins,
>> and like one who lays up treasure is he who glorifies his mother.
>>> (3:3-4)
> He who honors his father will be gladdened by his own children,
>> and in the day of his prayer he will be heard. (3:5)
> Honor your father in deed and word,
>> that a blessing from him may come upon you. (3:8)
> For the blessing of a father strengthens the houses of his children,
>> but the curse of a mother uproots their foundations. (3:9)

Here, as often, the idea of action and consequence is expressed, whether in the two halves of a line (vv 3-4, 9), in the succession of lines (v 8), or in both (v 5). Typical of Ben Sira is the combination of related proverbs with an identical formula ("He who honors/glorifies his father," vv 3, 5, 6) and the linking of proverbs by word association or catchword ("blessing," vv 8-9). The result is a more polished literary product than is found in many analogous collections in Proverbs (cf., e.g., Prov 12:13-23 on speech). In Sirach 3:17-31 Ben Sira develops the theme of humility and pride, which may have been placed here because the reference to almsgiving in 3:30 links with 4:1-10 and its exhortations to help the poor and needy. To be a father to the orphans is to be like a son of the Most High (4:10), a thought that links with another section on Wisdom (4:11-19), who "exalts her sons" (4:11).

The proper and improper use of speech is the topic of 4:23—6:1. An apparently unrelated section on wealth (5:1-8) has been attached, possibly because of the introductory formula "Do not *say*" in 5:3-6. A discussion of friendship (6:5-17) follows the section on speech, perhaps due to word association—the reference to "voice" and "tongue" in 6:5. Common introductory formulas are again evident (6:8-10, 14-16), indicating a conscious literary style. Another poem on Wisdom follows (6:19-31), with some related injunctions attached to it (6:32-37).

The negative imperative is a formal device that holds together 7:1-16, although topical subsections on public office (vv 4-7), escaping God's judgment (vv 8-9), and speech (vv 11-14) are in evidence. The use of the negative imperative in 7:18-20 may have been the linking device at the beginning of a major section that discusses: human relations and associations (7:18—9:18); friends and family (7:18-28); the priesthood (7:29-31, linked to the previous subsection by the common idea of gift in v 28 and vv 29-31); the poor and troubled (7:32-36); the rich and powerful (8:1-2); boors (8:3-4); the aged (8:6-9); sinners and the insolent (8:10-11); those stronger than oneself (8:12-14, perhaps originally connected with 8:1-2); other undesirables (8:15-19); women (9:1-9); and others desirable and undesirable (9:10-16). A section on magistrates and rulers (10:1—11:9), interpolated with a subsection on honor and riches (10:19—11:1), leads to a long discussion of poverty and wealth, rich and poor (11:10—14:19), which again indicates subcollections and subtopics. Another poem on Wisdom follows (14:20—15:10).

In 15:11—18:14 Ben Sira switches from his practical, deed-oriented discussion to theological speculation. His topic, however, is related. He discusses responsibility for one's deeds, the certainty of divine knowledge and retribution, creation, covenant and Torah, and the possibility of repenting of one's sinful deeds.

Returning to the realm of the practical and specific, Ben Sira discusses caution in speech and other matters (18:19—19:17, introduced by several other sayings on speech [18:15-18]). Four sayings beginning with "Question!" constitute a subunit (19:13-17). A brief section on wisdom and folly is connected by word association (19:30) with another lengthy discussion of proper and improper speech (chap. 20). Sin and the sinner are the topic of 21:1-10. Given the essential identity of sin and folly in the wisdom tradition, we have a natural transition to 21:11—22:18, where "fool" is the primary catchword in a wide variety of observations. Ben Sira uses a similar device in 41:17—42:8, a catalog of things of which one should be ashamed or not ashamed. Likewise, in 40:18-26 he combines diverse ideas by a common formula (x and y are good, but z is better).

The catchword "heart" connects 22:18 with 22:19, which begins a section on speech (22:19—23:15) that includes a prayer (22:27—23:6) with a brief mention of that subject (22:27). At the conclusion of the first major section of the book, a discussion of sexual sins (23:16-27) with its reference to an adulterous woman offers a transition to the praise of her foil or counterpart, Lady Wisdom (chap. 24), who is celebrated also at the end of part two (51:13-22).[54]

Our analysis of chapters 1–23 has laid out the major literary forms and devices employed by Ben Sira: short two-line proverbs, some of them with similar formulas, assembled in topical collections; the use of word association and common topics and formulas to link these collections to others; and the interweaving of sections on concrete topics and examples with poems about Wisdom, prayers and hymns, and extended theological discussion.

Wisdom in Ben Sira

Ben Sira includes under the category of wisdom instruction a spectrum of interests and concerns ranging from practical to speculative, from secular to religious and theological.[55]

Practical Advice

The sage writes about such down-to-earth matters as table etiquette (31:12—32:13 [Gk. 34:12—35:17]), caution in one's dealings with others (18:15—19:17), and wise and unwise associations (12:8—13:20). In treating these topics Ben Sira speaks as a man of experience, accumulating examples as he looks at the topic from a variety of viewpoints, and many of his observations and admonitions still ring true today. Wisdom about life is not simple, and proper action requires the discernment that comes from experience. As a man of experience, Ben Sira knows that a mistake or faux pas in these matters can have the gravest consequences. These consequences are generally seen to be natural and inevitable and are seldom defined as divine retribution, as they are when he is speaking of breaches of God's law.

Wisdom and Torah

It is in Ben Sira's identification of Wisdom and Torah that we find the heart and dynamic of his thought.[56] The practical sides of his advice notwithstanding, he is concerned for the most part with one's conduct vis-à-vis the Torah and with the consequences of that conduct. Although the book of Proverbs identifies the fear of God as the beginning of wisdom, and the author of Psalm 119 extols at great length the joy of the Torah, the Wisdom of Joshua Ben Sira is the earliest datable work in our literature that discusses the relationship of Wisdom and Torah in detail and in theory.[57]

In chapter 24 Ben Sira lays out his speculation about Wisdom and Torah.[58] This long passage is a counterpart to Proverbs 8 and also bears striking resemblance to Hellenistic texts about the goddess Isis.[59] The main part of the chapter is a hymn of four strophes, in which Wisdom praises herself (vv 3-7, 8-12, 13-15, 16-22).[60] Here Wisdom is personified and depicted as a female, the first of God's creatures (24:3; cf. 1:4; Prov 8:22), who is at home in the heavenly council (Sir 24:2). Proceeding from God's mouth (24:3), she participated in the creative process (cf. Prov 8:30)—whether as God's creative word (Gen 1:3), as God's breath construed as the life-giving mist that covered the barren primordial earth (Sir 24:3; cf. Gen 2:4-6), or as God's endowment on created beings (Sir 24:6; cf. 1:9). After Wisdom had pierced the heights of the ether and plumbed the depths of the abyss (24:4-6), God commanded this denizen of the angelic council (24:2) to pitch her tent and find her resting place in Israel, where she would minister to God in the Jerusalem temple (24:8-11). Thus the universal endowment of humankind became the Creator's unique gift to the chosen people. Employing the language of simile, Wisdom now describes how she took root and grew in Israel like a pleasant tree (24:12-18), and she concludes by inviting her hearers to partake of her life-giving fruit, which satisfies any hunger and quenches all thirst (24:19-22).[61]

Ben Sira then interprets Wisdom's hymn:

> All this is the book of the covenant of the Most High God,
>> the law that Moses commanded us
>> as an inheritance for the congregations of Jacob. (24:23)

Employing a new simile, the sage likens Torah to the Jordan River and to the life-giving streams that surrounded paradise (Gen 2:10-14). As such it gushes forth Wisdom into a boundless ocean and a fathomless and inexhaustible abyss (Sir 24:25-29).

There is a further stage in the mediation of Wisdom. The sage, in this case Ben Sira, is a channel that conveys the life-giving waters of Torah's Wisdom into another sea—his collective teaching, to be found in his book (24:30-34). In another simile, like Wisdom he is an enlightener of Israel (24:32; cf. v 27). Through prayerful, inspired study of Torah, wisdom, and prophecy (39:1-8), the sage or scribe becomes a secondary but evidently necessary channel of God's Wisdom. The place of prophecy has been taken by the scribe's study[62] and interpretation of the ancient writings, especially the Torah. This produces a deposit of teaching that Ben Sira considers to be authoritative, to judge from his claim that he speaks like a prophet (24:33) and perhaps from his use of prophetic forms.[63]

Ben Sira presents a kind of drama of salvation—salvation not in the sense of deliverance from something but as the bestowal of well-being, blessing, and life. His theological starting point is the biblical (esp. the Deuteronomic) view of covenant and Torah.[64] Through the covenant, God bestowed on Israel its status as the chosen people. In the same covenant, God set the divine commandments before them. The alternative possibilities to obey and disobey these commandments would lead like two roads to blessing and life or to curse and death.[65] One could not short-circuit the process that led from the grace of covenantal election to the fullness of covenantal blessing and life. Responsible obedience to the commandments of Torah was an integral and necessary part of the covenant. In this sense Torah was a gift that brought the possibility of life.

The focus of Ben Sira's covenantal theology is governed first by the fact that he is a teacher of ethics. For this reason, though he takes for granted Israel's covenantal status as God's chosen people (24:12; 46:1), he rarely speaks of the covenant except in the context of Torah.[66] From this same perspective his recitation of Israel's history—a rarity in Israelite wisdom literature—focuses on the right deeds, piety, and obedience of individual Israelites of renown. The catalog provides, in part, a multiplicity of examples of the life and attitudes Ben Sira seeks to inculcate throughout the book.[67]

Ben Sira's covenantal theology is also marked by a kind of mythicizing that superimposes an ahistorical and heavenly dimension onto the historical phenomenon of Torah. The chronological starting point for his drama of salvation is not Mount Sinai or even the exodus. In the beginning was Wisdom. This personified entity is functionally an agent or power. She first brought life to the world. At a particular point in history, she was sent to earth and embodied in Torah, where she offers the dynamic for obedience and hence the possibility for life. Thus Ben Sira's myth of Wisdom is the story of how God's freely given, innervating, vivifying goodness has been made present in Torah. It is the story of grace told from the perspective of eternity.

In chapter 24 and in his other poems about Wisdom (chaps. 1–2; 4:11-19; 6:18-31; 14:20—15:10; 51:13-30), Ben Sira describes several aspects of the Wisdom that resides in Torah.[68] Through Torah, Wisdom enlightens and instructs, revealing the will of God that leads to life if it is obeyed. Wisdom is also a means toward obedience. She is preacher and proclaimer (24:19-22; 51:23-30 through the mouth of the teacher) and helper (4:11). However, Ben Sira is under no illusion that the way of obedience is easy. It requires steadfastness, perseverance, and endurance (2:1-18).[69] Wisdom has her own tortuous discipline, her fetter, yoke, and collar (4:17; 6:18-31; 51:26). Nonetheless, those who pursue her she will feed and exalt and bless with gladness and goodness and the life and blessing that God offers through the covenant (4:18; 6:28-31; 15:1-6).[70] The theme of blessing through discipline we have already met in the story of Tobit.[71]

The myth of Wisdom reappears in the book of Baruch with explicit reference to the Deuteronomic covenant.[72] Early Christianity also employs the Wisdom myth, substituting Jesus of Nazareth for Torah as the unique historical embodiment of Wisdom.[73]

Ethical and Religious Teaching

As a teacher of Torah, Ben Sira is concerned more with ethical matters than ritual matters. A great deal of his advice relates to household relationships.[74] In 3:1-16 and 7:27-28 he expounds the commandment to honor one's parents.[75] Elsewhere he writes about relationships to one's wife, children, and slaves.[76] Ben Sira's attitude toward sexual matters is based on the biblical viewpoint. Incest and adultery are wrong (23:16–18). Other sexual relationships without benefit of marriage are not condemned per se, but they are to be avoided from a pragmatic point of view (9:1-9, where his advice applies also to adultery). Ben Sira's attitude toward women is thoroughly male-oriented, outright disparaging in places, and offensive to modern sensitivities.[77] To no small degree it reflected the values and, perhaps, the anxieties of a patriarchal society that saw "females' function as part of a cultural symbol system embodied in the concepts of honor and shame."[78]

Other interpersonal relationships are of special concern to Ben Sira.[79] Friendship stands high on his agenda,[80] and he celebrates the goodness of friendship, the need for caution in choosing one's friends, and the importance of faithfulness to those who are chosen.[81] For Ben Sira forgiveness is an important quality, and one passage that provides a context for the Lord's Prayer speaks of the reciprocity of forgiveness (28:1-7; cf. Matt 6:12).[82] Repeatedly Ben Sira turns to the topic of wealth, discussing its ethical implications.[83] He contrasts generosity and stinginess (Sir 14:3-8); enjoins almsgiving and other acts of kindness to the poor and needy (4:1-6; 7:32-36; 29:9-13); recommends lending, with all its problems (29:1-7, 14-20); and warns against fraud and ill-gotten riches (5:8; 21:8). Wealth in itself is not wrong, but Ben Sira is not optimistic about the possibility of the rich remaining honest and God-pleasing in their dealings with others (26:29—27:2; 31:1-11). Although Ben Sira is a protagonist of the poor and humble, his treatment of the topic is nuanced by "his ambiguous status vis-à-vis his rich superiors."[84]

Although Ben Sira concentrates on ethical issues, he is also concerned about the Jerusalem temple cult; he holds the priesthood in high regard. Among the strands of the Pentateuch, it is the Priestly redaction to which he is most closely related.[85] In his catalog of heroes he devotes twice as much space to Aaron as he does to Moses (45:6-22; cf. vv 1-5), and he concludes his hymn to these men of renown with a lengthy section in praise of the high priest Simon.[86] In a passage that expands on the biblical commandment to love God (Deut 6:5), he commands his readers to honor the priests and to give them their due (Sir 7:29-31). The cult is God's means of repairing violations of the covenant (45:16), and Ben Sira encourages participation in the cult (35:4-11 [Gk. 32:6-13]). Nonetheless, in true prophetic style he warns against contradictions between cult and life, specifically the offering of sacrifices from ill-gotten riches and possessions. Alternatively, obedience and deeds of charity function like cultic acts and provide "atonement" (34:18—35:3, 12-20 [Gk. 31:21—32:5, 14-26]; 3:3, 30). Ben Sira includes three prayers in his wisdom collection (23:1-6; 36:1-17 [Gk. 33:1-13 + 36:16-22]; 51:1-12).

Ben Sira: Between Wisdom and Torah

As we have seen, Ben Sira deals with ethical and ritual matters that are treated in the Torah. Indeed, words for "law," "commandments," and "covenant" occur more than fifty times in his book.[87] Yet, with the exception of 3:1-16, where he ruminates on the commandment to obey one's parents, one is hard-pressed to find any extended reference to a biblical law or commandment. Ben Sira is not a halakic interpreter of the Torah, one who spells out how one should observe the Torah in this or that situation. In 3:1-16 there is scarcely a reference to *what* specifically constitutes honoring one's parents; the substance of the passage is the commandment and the consequences of obedience and disobedience, spelled out in typical proverbial form.[88] Thus he has taken one paradigm for instruction in the right life—Mosaic covenantal Torah—and he has folded it into another paradigm—the wisdom tradition of moral admonition.[89] A similar melding occurs in the Qumran 4QInstruction and perhaps in the later strata of 1 Enoch.[90]

Retribution and Theodicy

Divine retribution in the form of blessing and curse was essential to the covenant, as we have seen. The idea is built into the very structure of many of Ben Sira's proverbs that describe the consequences of one's conduct. Where such conduct involves obedience or disobedience of Torah, the consequences are understood as divine retribution.

> Lay up your treasure according to the commandments of the Most High,
> and it will profit you more than gold.
> Store up almsgiving in your treasury,
> and it will rescue you from all affliction. (29:11-12)

Ben Sira did not, of course, expect perfection, and he speaks of the means of atonement and of forgiveness (2:11; 28:2). Nonetheless, one is not to presume on God's mercy, as if God would continue to forgive a multitude of sins heaped one on the other (5:4-7).[91] On a number of occasions Ben Sira speaks about retribution in polemical fashion.[92] He argues against the idea that God does not see sin or is not concerned with punishing it (15:19-20; 16:17-23; 17:20; 23:18-20). His programmatic treatment of the subject is in 15:11—18:14. The passage appears to be arguing on a theoretical and intellectual level against certain fixed points of view: the kind of determinism that excludes free will (15:11-20) and the theory that there can be no retribution in the universe (16:17).[93] While this possibility cannot be excluded,[94] it should be noted that Ben Sira's argument moves in a practical direction. He discusses creation (16:26—17:6), God's covenant with Israel (17:7-17), and God's charge that they obey the divine commandments and heed God's warning of retribution (17:14-23). He then moves into an exhortation to repent (17:24-29) and concludes with a passage in praise of God's uniqueness, especially God's patience and compassion (17:30—18:14). Ben Sira appears to be less interested in arguing for free will and retribution than in preaching and in exhorting his audience to act responsibly within the covenant. The same practical direction in his argument is evident in 5:7 and 23:21.

A doctrine of creation is central to Ben Sira's understanding of covenantal responsibility and retribution. God created humans with the free will that places in their hands the choice to obey or disobey (15:14-17).[95] Thus Deuteronomy 30:15-19 is put in the context of creation. Humanity's created endowments are the presupposition for covenant obedience also in Sirach 17:1-13. Ben Sira spells out his understanding of creation in his so-called doctrine of opposites: "every element in creation obeys God and carries out the purpose for which it was designed, either for good or for bad; sometimes the same element has the capacity to function either way" (17:7; 33:14, 15b; 39:33-34; 42:24).[96] In this way Ben Sira can maintain the goodness of creation (Gen 1:31) while allowing the presence of both good and bad. The Creator uses the creation to bless and curse the obedient and the disobedient. God's knowledge of human actions, which is the presupposition for divine judgment, is an aspect of God's creative power (Sir 42:18-21). God knows that which God has created. But in the final analysis, theology gives way to doxology. God's creative deeds are described in order that God might be praised (39:16-35; 42:15—43:33). As to the problem of evil in the world, Ben Sira, sounding somewhat like a Stoic, and positing a doctrine of opposite pairs, asserts that everything has its place in God's creation (33:7-15).[97]

Eschatology: God's Acts in the Future

It is generally thought that a wisdom book like Ben Sira's has no place for eschatology, such as one finds, for example, in 1 Enoch (see above, pp. 46–53). For this author divine retribution takes place here and now in this life. Different from 1 Enoch, death is followed by a gloomy existence in Sheol, from which there is no resurrection to a new life (40:1—41:13).[98] Thus the expectation of divine judgment in the future is not a major motif for Ben Sira. Nonetheless, a couple of passages may indicate some interest in the topic. In 48:24-25 Ben Sira says of Isaiah:

> By the spirit of might, he saw what would come after,
>   and he comforted the mourners in Zion;
> he revealed what would occur at the end of the age,
>   the hidden things before they come to pass.

As we have seen, the latter chapters of Isaiah were an important resource for the eschatology of 1 Enoch. Another passage speaks of Elijah as the one who is ready to return to calm God's wrath and to restore the tribes of Israel (Sir 48:10).[99] Whether Ben Sira espoused a hope in a future Davidic king is a disputed question. The relevant passages are 45:25; 47:11, 22, which refer to God's covenant with David. Two of these texts are particularly striking. In 45:25 the Davidic covenant is mentioned out of historical order and in tandem with the priestly covenant with Phinehas. This calls to mind Qumranic expectations about the coming of two "anointed ones"—a priest and a king (see below, pp. 150–51). Also striking is 47:22, where Ben Sira employs the negative four times to assert that God will never abolish the covenant with David.[100] A final passage with an eschatological tone is the prayer in 36:1-17, which appeals to God to vindicate Israel and destroys its enemies, although scholars debate whether this text is part of Ben Sira's original composition or a later interpolation.[101] Even if the prayer is considered a later interpolation, the other passages discussed above indicate that Ben Sira does not exclude future decisive acts of salvation from his purview. Such an outlook is present in other wisdom texts such as Tobit (see above, pp. 33, 35), Baruch (see below, p. 46), and 4QInstruction (see below, pp. 170–72). In this respect these texts differ from earlier wisdom texts like Proverbs and Ecclesiastes.

Date, Setting, and Purpose

The Wisdom of Ben Sira was written between 196 and 175 B.C.E. The high date is set by the death of the high priest Simon II, the last of Ben Sira's men of renown (50:1-21), who is described as a figure of the past.[102] The low date is the beginning of the Hellenistic reform under Antiochus IV (see chapter 3 below). Had Ben Sira written after that time, his deep concern for Torah would scarcely have permitted him to bypass sure and certain references to those events.

Given the date and place of the book's composition, it is to be expected that Ben Sira would be writing at least partly in response to the increasing inroads of Hellenism among the Jews. That this response was, to no small degree, negative and defensive has been argued in detail by a number of prominent historians.[103] However, the evidence is not all that clear. While it is possible that some of Ben Sira's statements are polemics against hellenizing tendencies, they are general enough to have had other intended applications.[104] Indeed, this book is striking for its lack of specific, pointed, and explicit polemics against Hellenism.[105] On the other hand, Ben Sira's thought is sometimes couched in language that was at home in Hellenistic philosophy[106] and shows a thorough knowledge and creative use of Hellenistic rhetoric and literary genres.[107] Clearly Ben Sira opposed "the dismantling of Judaism" in favor of Greek thought;[108] however, the extent to which he was able to express his Judaism in the language and forms of non-Judaic traditions is a complex and interesting example of religious cross-culturalism with many parallels in the Hebrew Bible's adaptation of elements in its Near Eastern environment.[109]

Although it is an exaggeration to portray Ben Sira simply as a polemicist against the alien elements in his environment, his book does indicate points of religious, cultural, and social tension and attempts to deal with them. His praise of Simon and the cult over which he presides offers a powerful brief for the temple establishment during a time of increasing struggle over the priesthood, and especially the high priesthood.[110] In addition, Ben Sira appears to polemicize against the kind of apocalyptic wisdom found in the Enochic corpus.[111]At the same time, his mythicizing of Wisdom—depicting it as a heavenly figure (chap. 24)—can be seen as an attempt to bring order to a unstable world[112] by means of an intellectual construct that has a precise parallel in 1 Enoch (cf. esp. 81:1—82:3). Other of his concerns, for example, his attitudes toward women, may be functions of an intensified "coinage of honor and shame" that was the result of "stress generated by the profound cultural, political, and ultimately religious flux of Ben Sira's day."[113] In any case, it is clear that Sirach and 1 Enoch need to be read side by side, each to enlighten the other and both to help us understand a critical time in Israel's history—one that will move rapidly to its tumultuous climax in the events to be described in our next chapter.

Language of Composition and History of Usage

Ben Sira wrote in Hebrew. His grandson translated the book into Greek in Egypt near the end of the second century B.C.E.[114] Fragments of three manuscripts of the Hebrew original have been found at Qumran and in the ruins of the Herodian fortress at Masada.[115] Large parts of the remainder of the Hebrew text have been recovered from six fragmentary medieval manuscripts.[116] The work was widely circulated and held in high regard by the Jews, and it was still referred to after the decision not to include it in the Hebrew Bible.[117] In the early Latin church the book was known as Ecclesiasticus, "belonging to the church," that is, the deuterocanonical book par excellence.[118]

BIBLIOGRAPHY

Hellenism

John J. **Collins** and Gregory R. **Sterling**, eds., *Hellenism in the Land of Israel* (Christianity and Judaism in Antiquity 13; Notre Dame: Univ. of Notre Dame Press, 2001), collection of papers.

Erich S. **Gruen**, *Heritage and Hellenism: The Reinvention of Jewish Tradition* (Berkeley: Univ. of California Press, 1998). T. Francis **Glasson**, *Greek Influence in Jewish Eschatology* (London: SPCK, 1961). Martin **Hengel**, *Judaism and Hellenism* (trans. John Bowden; 2 vols.; Philadelphia: Fortress Press, 1974), indispensable treatment of the encounter of Judaism and Hellenism in Palestine. W. W. **Tarn** and G. T. **Griffith**, *Hellenistic Civilization* (3d ed.; London: Arnold, 1952), wide-ranging account of the period from 323 to 31 B.C.E. Victor A. **Tcherikover**, *Hellenistic Civilization and the Jews* (Philadelphia: Jewish Publication Society of America, 1959) 1–151, political, economic, and social history of Palestine from Alexander to Antiochus IV.

1 Enoch

Translation: George W. E. **Nickelsburg** and James C. **VanderKam**, *1 Enoch: A New Translation* (Minneapolis: Fortress Press, 2004).

Texts and Other Translations: Michael A. **Knibb**, *The Ethiopic Book of Enoch: A New Edition in the Light of the Aramaic Dead Sea Fragments* (2 vols.; Oxford: Clarendon, 1978), vol. 1 contains a reproduction of one Ethiopic ms., with a full critical apparatus; vol. 2, translation of that ms. with detailed textual notes referring to the Greek texts and the Aramaic fragments. Michael A. **Knibb**, "1 Enoch," *AOT*, 169–319, same translation as the previous. Matthew **Black**, *Apocalypsis Henochi Graece* (PVTG 3; Leiden: Brill, 1970), text of the extant Greek manuscripts. J. T. **Milik**, *The Books of Enoch: Aramaic Fragments of Qumran Cave 4* (Oxford: Clarendon, 1976), the text of the Qumran fragments with prolific reconstruction and detailed notes on textual and other matters, historical introduction, a wealth of material. Florentino **García Martínez** and Eibert J. C. **Tigchelaar**, DJD 36:95–171, fragments of Qumran mss. a and b of the Book of the Luminaries; R. H. **Charles**, *APOT* 2:163–281; Ephraim **Isaac**, *OTP* 1:5–89, translation of one Ethiopic ms.

Commentaries: R. H. **Charles**, *The Book of Enoch* (Oxford: Clarendon, 1912), introduction, translation, and useful, though often outdated, commentary. Matthew **Black**, *The Book of Enoch or 1 Enoch: A New English Edition* (SVTP 7; Leiden: Brill, 1985), introduction, translation, and commentary. George W. E. **Nickelsburg**, *1 Enoch 1: A Commentary on the Book of 1 Enoch, Chapters 1–36; 81–108* (Hermeneia; Minneapolis: Fortress Press, 2001), introduction, translation, detailed textual apparatus, and commentary.

Literature: Matthias **Albani**, *Astronomie und Schöpfungsglaube* (WMANT 68; Neukirchen-Vluyn: Neukirchener Verlag, 1994). Randal A. **Argall**, *1 Enoch and Sirach: A Comparative Literary and Conceptual Analysis of the Themes of Revelation, Creation, and Judgment* (SBLEJL 8; Atlanta: Scholars Press, 1995). Kelley Coblenz **Bautch**, *A Study of the Geography of 1 Enoch 17–19: "No One Has Seen What I Have Seen"* (JSJSup 81; Leiden: Brill, 2003). Andreas **Bedenbender**, *Der Gott der Welt tritt auf den Sina* (ANTZ 8; Berlin: Institut Kirche und Judentum, 2000), 1 Enoch and the rise of Jewish apocalypticism. Lars **Hartman**, *Asking for a Meaning: A Study of 1 Enoch 1–5* (ConBNT 12; Lund: Gleerup, 1979). Eckhard **Rau**, "Kosmologie, Eschatologie und die Lehrautorität Henochs" (diss., Hamburg, 1974), discussion of chaps. 1–5 and 72–82. Michael E. **Stone**, "The Book of Enoch and Judaism in the Third Century B.C.E.," *CBQ* 40 (1978) 479–92. Eibert J. C. **Tigchelaar**, *Prophets of Old and the Day of the End: Zechariah, the Book of Watchers, and Apocalyptic* (OtSt 35; Leiden: Brill, 1996). James C. **VanderKam**, *Enoch: A Man for All Generations* (Columbia: Univ. of South Carolina Press, 1995), the figure of Enoch in Jewish and early Christian literature. James C. **VanderKam**, *Enoch and the Growth of an Apocalyptic Tradition* (CBQMS 16; Washington, D.C.: Catholic Biblical Association, 1984), broad-ranging discussion of the Enochic materials in their biblical and ancient Near Eastern contexts. James C. **Van-derKam**, *Calendars in the Dead Sea Scrolls: Measuring Time* (London and New York: Routledge, 1998).

The Wisdom of Ben Sira

Translation: The Apocrypha.

Texts and Other Translations: Joseph **Ziegler**, *Sapientia Iesu Filii Sirach* (SVTG 12/2; Göttingen: Vandenhoeck & Ruprecht, 1965), critical edition of the Greek text. Francesco **Vattioni**, *Ecclesiastico* (Naples: Instituto Orientale di Napoli, 1968), Greek, Latin, Syriac, and most of the Hebrew texts. *Historical Dictionary of the Hebrew Language: The Book of Ben Sira: Text, Concordance and an Analysis of the Vocabulary* (Jerusalem: Academy for the Hebrew Language and the Shrine of the Book, 1973). Pancratius C. **Beentjes**, *The Book of Ben Sira in Hebrew: A Text Edition of All Extant Hebrew Manuscripts and a Synopsis of All Parallel Hebrew Ben Sira Texts* (VTSup 68; Leiden: Brill, 1997); see, however, the review of Alexander A. **Di Lella**, *CBQ* 60 (1998) 107–8.

Commentary: Patrick W. **Skehan** and Alexander A. **Di Lella**, *The Wisdom of Ben Sira* (AB 39; Garden City, N.Y.: Doubleday, 1987), fresh translation with critical apparatus and commentary.

Literature Surveys: Daniel J. **Harrington**, "Sirach Research since 1965: Progress and Directions," in John C. Reeves and John Kampen, eds., *Pursuing the Text: Studies in Honor of Ben Zion Wacholder on the Occasion of His Seventieth Birthday* (JSOTSup 184; Sheffield: Sheffield Academic Press, 1994) 164–75. Alexander A. **Di Lella**, "The Wisdom of Ben Sira: Resources and Recent Research," *CurBS* 4 (1996) 161–81, annotated bibliography with some comments on editions of texts and versions. Pancratius C. **Beentjes**, ed., *The Book of Ben Sira in Modern Research* (BZAW 255; Berlin: de Gruyter, 1997); see especially Friederich V. **Reiterer**, "Review of Recent Research on the Book of Ben Sira (1980–96)," in Beentjes, *Ben Sira in Modern Research*, 23–60.

Literature: Richard J. **Coggins**, *Sirach* (GAP; Sheffield: Sheffield Academic Press, 1998), introduction to the book and its issues and problems. John J. **Collins**, *Jewish Wisdom in the Hellenistic Age* (Louisville: Westminster/John Knox, 1997) 22–111, extensive introduction to the book and its issues and problems. Alexander A. **Di Lella**, *The Hebrew Text of Sirach: A Text-Critical and Historical Study* (The Hague: Mouton, 1966). Renate **Egger-Wenzel** and Ingrid **Krammer**, eds., *Der Einzelne und seine Gemeinschaft bei Ben Sira* (BZAW 270; Berlin: de Gruyter, 1998). Burton L. **Mack**, *Wisdom and the Hebrew Epic* (Chicago: Univ. of Chicago Press, 1985), a careful and perceptive study of chaps. 44–50 in relationship to Israelite and Greek literature and as a key to understanding the context and function of the book. Jack T. **Sanders**, *Ben Sira and Demotic Wisdom* (SBLMS 28; Chico, Calif.: Scholars Press, 1983). Helge **Stadelmann**, *Ben Sira als Schriftgelehrter* (WUNT 26; Tübingen: Mohr, 1980). Benjamin G. **Wright**, *No Small Difference: Sirach's Relation to Its Hebrew Parent Text* (SBLSCS 26; Atlanta: Scholars Press, 1989).

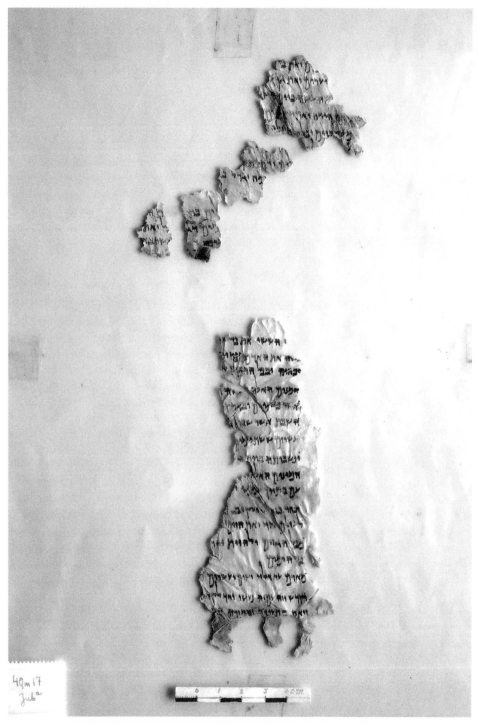

The Book of Jubilees. Fragments of two columns of a mid-first-century B.C.E. Qumran Hebrew manuscript (4Q Jubᵃ) preserving parts of Jub. 2:7-24. Photograph is courtesy of the Israel Antiquities Authority.

3

Reform—Repression—Revolt

THE EVENTS

Antiochus III extended many benefits to the Jews after his victory over the Ptolemies in 198 B.C.E. Included were the right to live "according to their ancestral laws," subvention of the Jerusalem temple cult, tax exemptions, and the return of slaves and property. Although the high priest was not mentioned in Antiochus's decree, he would serve as civil head of state.

The afterglow of Antiochus's victory was short-lived. The military might of Rome loomed on the horizon. In 190 the army of Scipio Africanus dealt Antiochus a crushing blow at the battle of Magnesia in Asia Minor, and the Seleucid emperor was forced to pay heavy indemnities. Three years later he was killed and was succeeded by his son, Seleucus IV. The financial burdens imposed by Rome weighed upon him. This was probably the cause of the unsuccessful attempt of his agent Heliodorus to confiscate money deposited in the treasury of the Jerusalem temple (2 Macc 3; Dan 11:20). Seleucus was succeeded in 175 by his brother, Antiochus IV ("Epiphanes"), who had been a hostage in Rome since 189. Events in Palestine took a turn for the worse.*

Those Jews who thought it was to their advantage to take up the Greek way of life found their champion in a priest named Jason (a Greek substitute for the Hebrew name Joshua), the brother of Onias III, the reigning high priest. Jason obtained an audience with Antiochus and offered him a large sum of money for the privilege of establishing a community of Antiochenes in Jerusalem.* Antiochus accepted Jason's proposal and appointed him high priest in place of his brother. Jason returned home to draw up a list of citizens and to establish the typical Greek educational institutions, the *gymnasion* and the *ephebeion*, which were to increase the roll of citizens. The athletic games of the *gymnasion* were a big attraction in which even some of the priests participated. Some Jews, evidently ashamed of their circumcision (considered a barbarism by the Greeks), resorted to surgical means to remove the sign of the covenant.

Three years later Jason was beaten at his own game when his envoy to Antiochus, Menelaus, offered the king a sizable amount of revenue and obtained the office of high priest. Jason fled across the Jordan River to the land of Ammon. Menelaus was unable to meet the heavy payments he had promised Antiochus. When the king was away from his capital, Menelaus bribed Antiochus's minister Andronicus with gold vessels taken from the temple. When this action was decried by Onias (the former high priest), Menelaus convinced Andronicus to entice Onias out of his place of asylum and murder him. Antiochus learned of the affair and had Andronicus executed, but Menelaus escaped any blame and continued his imperious ways. About this time sources begin to indicate considerable Jewish opposition to Menelaus's policies and practices. A bloody clash took place between these Jews and the soldiers of Lysimachus, Menelaus's brother, who had plundered the temple vessels. Lysimachus himself was killed. The Jews accused Menelaus before the king, but the high priest was acquitted when he successfully bribed one of Antiochus's counselors.

In 170/169 Antiochus mounted a military expedition against Egypt and overran most of the country. When the rumor came back to Asia that Antiochus was dead, Jason rallied his supporters, crossed the Jordan, and attacked Jerusalem. Pious Jews in the city seized the opportunity to take up arms against both Menelaus and Jason.[1] Antiochus returned rapidly from Egypt, stormed the city, slaughtered much of the population, sold some into slavery, and plundered the temple. He confirmed Menelaus as high priest and left a certain Philip the Phrygian to keep order in the city. Two years later (early in 167), evidently in response to more unrest among the pious Jews, Antiochus dispatched his lieutenant Apollonius, who fell upon the city on a Sabbath and repeated the terrible massacre of two years previous. Apollonius fortified the "Akra," the citadel near the temple, and manned it with a garrison of troops, who would continue to trouble the Jerusalemites for twenty-six years.

Antiochus had had his fill of uprisings, and so he struck at the heart of the matter. Religion according to the Torah had been responsible for the rebellions, and so religion in that form was proscribed by royal edict. Circumcision and the celebration of festivals, including the Sabbath, were forbidden. All copies of the Torah were to be burned. A polytheistic cult was instituted in the Jerusalem temple, and Jews were forced to eat swine's flesh, which was unclean according to the Torah. Opposition to the edict was punishable by death. On the fifteenth day of Chislev (December) 167, the "desolating sacrilege," an idolatrous structure, was erected upon the sacrificial altar in Jerusalem. Thus the temple in Jerusalem was defiled, and throughout Judea the king's officers enforced violation of the Torah. Sides had to be chosen. Many forsook the covenant in order to save their lives, but many pious Jews took their stand and chose to die rather than transgress the laws of their ancestors. Others fled to the wilderness and hid in caves; and many died, refusing to defend themselves on the Sabbath.

The Hasmonean family now appeared on the scene: a priest named Mattathias and his sons John, Simon, Judas, Eleazar, and Jonathan. They quickly brought direction and much-needed leadership to the dispersed bands of the pious, striking out against both apostatizing Jews and government troops. When the old patriarch died, the leadership passed on to his son, Judas. Nicknamed Maccabeus (perhaps meaning "hammer"), this brilliant general possessed all the advantages of a warrior employing guerrilla tactics in his home territory to defend a cause for which he was willing to die. He took on Antiochus's finest commanders and picked troops, and in a series of lightning strokes his little army put to flight the hordes of the foreign invader. In three years, punctuated by battles, negotiations, and accords,[2] the Temple Mount was retaken and, in December 164, the sanctuary was purified, its lights rekindled, and the orthodox cult reestablished.

A Response in Apocalyptic Literature

Out of the turbulence and violence of the years 169–164, a series of writings appeared that exhorted pious, Torah-abiding Jews to endure in the face of persecution, confident of swift divine judgment against their enemies. Each of these writings claimed to be a revelation written by an ancient prophet or sage: Moses, Daniel, Enoch.

The Book of Jubilees

The longest of these writings, the Book of Jubilees, is an extensive elaboration of Genesis 1–Exodus 12, presented as a secret revelation that the angels of God's presence transmitted to Moses on Mount Sinai.[3] With a few exceptions it follows the order of the Bible itself; however, the author treats the *wording* of the biblical text in a variety of ways.[4] Often he reproduces the text verbatim. Occasionally he deletes what he does not find useful. Most typically, however, he recasts the narrative or elaborates on it to fit his interests and purposes. Many of his alterations serve to smooth out perceived difficulties or problems in the biblical text.

The author is especially interested in halakah (from the Hebrew verb "to walk"), a "way" of life spelled out in teachings, ordinances, and practices derived from the interpretation of biblical laws. He employs a number of techniques to incorporate this legal material into the biblical narratives.

Running throughout the book is a chronological framework that presupposes and advocates the use of a solar calendar.[5] Events in biblical history and the establishment of religious festivals are dated according to this calendar, and the date of the end time is reckoned by it.[6] The calendar, moreover, has the force of law because it is rooted in the created structure of the universe. This structure is the subject of the Book of the Luminaries in 1 Enoch (see above, pp. 44–46), to which Jubilees 4:17 makes reference.

Typical expansions of the biblical narratives depict the patriarchs observing the Torah. Noah offered a proper sacrifice (7:3-5), and Levi discharged the office of priest (32:4-9). Major holy days were observed by the patriarchs: Firstfruits by Noah, Abraham, Isaac, Jacob, and Ishmael (6:18; 15:1-2; 22:1-5); Tabernacles by Abraham (16:20-31); and the Day of Atonement by Jacob (34:12-20). Special prescriptions are given for Passover, the Jubilee Year, and the Sabbath (chaps. 49–50).[7] In all of these the author's calendrical interests are evident.

On occasion the author exhorts his readers through admonitions that he places in the mouth of a patriarch. On his deathbed Abraham delivers three exhortations to his sons and grandsons, warning them against fornication, intermarriage with the Canaanites, idolatry, the consuming of blood, and other cultic abominations (chaps. 20–22).

Especially important among the author's additions are a number of brief halakic commentaries that often begin with the expression, "For this reason it is written (or 'ordained') in the heavenly tablets that. . . ." In these commentaries the author utilizes an element in the biblical narrative as the basis for his exposition of a point of law. God's clothing of Adam and Eve shows that nakedness is prohibited (3:31). Various events relating to the flood and its abatement demonstrate that feasts are to be observed according to the solar calendar (6:17-22). The vengeance of Simeon and Levi on Shechem and their refusal to allow him to marry Dinah show that marriage to a foreign spouse is categorically prohibited (30:7-23). The stories about Reuben and Bilhah and Judah and Tamar illustrate the forbidden sin of incest (33:10-20; 41:23-27).

For this author, Torah is eternal and immutable, recorded on the heavenly tablets.[8] His alleged source of authority is angelic revelation; an angel of the Presence dictated these halakot to Moses.[9] In the case of the solar calendar, details of the celestial structures on which it is based were revealed to Enoch by the angel Uriel (4:17; cf. 1 Enoch 72:1). Alongside these claims to direct revelation, the author also provides an exegetical base for some of the laws contained in the book; specific laws derive from some item or detail in the biblical text that he is transmitting (and interpreting through revision!).[10]

The nonhalakic revisions of the biblical text vary in their content and function. Some implicitly exhort the reader to proper behavior. Others "predict" or explain the origin of situations in the author's own time. Still others make a theological point. Some of these revisions were composed by the author. Others derived from oral or written tradition.[11]

We have already noted formal exhortations placed in the mouths of the ancients. In other cases, moral admonitions are implied by narrative additions and commentaries on them. Especially noteworthy in this respect are the stories about Abraham, who is depicted as a model of a variety of virtues. He is a paragon of wisdom and insight. As such, he sees through the folly of idolatry, teaches the Chaldeans the science of agriculture, learns of the futility of astrological forecasting, and studies "the books of his fathers" (11:5—12:27). Moreover, his zeal leads him to burn the local idolatrous temple (12:12).[12]

The stories of the sacrifice of Isaac and the purchase of the Cave of Machpelah are expanded to depict Abraham as a paragon of faithfulness and patient endurance under trial. The biblical story of the sacrifice states simply that "God tested Abraham" (Gen 22:1). His celebrated *faith* is mentioned not in Genesis 22 but in Genesis 15:6 with reference to his belief in God's promise of a son. Taking the biblical motif of testing as his point of departure, the author transforms the biblical story (which is repeated almost verbatim) into a full-blown courtroom scene.[13] The story is prefaced by a confrontation between the angel(s) of the Presence and the satanic accuser, "the prince of *mastēmā*," which is reminiscent of Job 1–2 (Jub. 17:15-16), and concludes with the defeat of the accuser (18:9-12). The incident, moreover, was but one example (though probably the example par excellence) of Abraham's lifetime of faithfulness to God and patient endurance (17:17-18). This notion appears to have drawn on a tradition about the ten trials of Abraham, of which he names the bargaining over the Cave of Machpelah as the tenth (19:1-9).[14] In short, characteristics that the Bible attributes to Abraham in one situation are applied to his behavior in a number of circumstances.[15]

Yet another set of important revisions of the biblical text relates to the role of women in the patriarchal history.[16] According to these texts, non-Israelite women who marry Israelite men lead to their downfall, while patriarchal marriages to women of their own kin are instrumental in furthering God's purposes in Israel. Thus, applying standards of priestly purity to the whole of Israel, "a kingdom of priests," the author declares mixed marriages in his own time as, in principle, contrary to God's will and the cause of defilement in the nation.

Other of Jubilees' additions to the biblical narrative also allude to events in the author's own time. Chapters 35–38 are a lengthy expansion on the list of Edomite kings in Genesis 36:31-39 (Jub. 38:15-24). The passage reflects contemporary Jewish-Idumean hostility and explains its origin, stressing Jewish superiority. The point is made in a lengthy narrative describing relationships between Jacob and Esau that culminate in a war in which Jacob kills Esau. The author alludes to other contemporary events by means of predictions that are included in some of his commentaries (e.g., 6:34).

Frequently the biblical text is expanded to make a theological point. The author interpolates a substantial set of traditions from 1 Enoch 6–16 (see above, pp. 47–51) into the story of the flood and its aftermath in order to explain the causes of the flood (Jub. 5 and 7) and, more important, the origin of the demonic world that is presupposed throughout the book.[17] These evil spirits have come forth from the giants who were born to the rebel angels and the daughters of men. Far from being exterminated by the flood, these spirits seduce the children of Noah into committing the same sins that led to the extermination of the giants (7:20-33). References to the judgment in 1 Enoch 10 are drawn into the narrative at Jubilees 5:10-16 and are expanded. Other eschatological additions occur from place to place.

The longest of the eschatological additions in Jubilees is 23:16-32. In form it is a historical apocalypse, that is, an account of events that lie in the future of the alleged narrator, who is a reliable revealer (an angel of the Presence who speaks to Moses; cf. 23:32). It shares a common outline with several other texts to which we shall turn later in this chapter. It begins with a prediction of events that are described in increasing detail and lead up to the present crisis. The crisis is resolved in a judgment that involves direct divine or angelic intervention and that ushers in a new age in which the earth or the whole cosmos is restored permanently to the state that the Creator had intended.

In context, Jubilees 23:16-32 is a commentary on Genesis 25:7, "These are the days of the years of Abraham's life, a hundred and seventy-five years" (cf. Jub. 23:8).[18] Abraham's life was much shorter than those of the patriarchs before the flood, but after him human life would become increasingly shorter, due to sin. When repentance takes place, human life will be restored to its former longevity. Verses 11-15 describe in stereotyped terms the terrible woes that will come in post-Abrahamic times. From v 16 on we are in the midst of a description of the times of Antiochus. The apocalypse may be schematized as follows:

1. Sin   vv 16-21
2. Punishment   vv 22-25
3. Turning point   v 26
4. Salvation   vv 27-31

Part 1 describes a deep schism between Jews who "forsake the covenant" (v 16; cf. v 19) and their compatriots who take up arms to bring them back to "the path of righteousness" (vv 16, 19, 20). Although much blood is shed, the apostates continue in their sinful ways and even "defile the holy of holies with their uncleanness and the corruption of their pollution" (v 21). The description fits admirably the events in Jerusalem before Antiochus's decree of 167: the apostasy of the hellenizers; the strife in Jerusalem at the time of Jason's attempted coup; and the continued presence of Menelaus, the corrupt and bloody high priest.

According to part 2, God punishes this generation (v 22), sending against them the merciless "sinners of the Gentiles" (vv 22-23). These verses are in accord with the bloody reprisals of Antiochus and Apollonius in 169 and 167.[19] Almost all the other sources from this time make specific reference to the person of Antiochus and to various details of his decree. The lack of any such specificity in the present passage argues for a date no later than early 167. Verse 25 continues the theme of premature old age that runs throughout the passage.

The crucial event in the action occurs in v 26 (part 3). If apostasy is responsible for God's punishment, the return of God's favor requires repentance—a return to "the path of righteousness." This is precipitated by a study of the laws.

As the author moves to the events of salvation (part 4), his language breaks the bounds of human experience, and history gives way to myth. Life will return to its primordial longevity (v 27; cf. v 9). It will be characterized by peace, blessing, healing, and the absence of Satan and evil. The passage reflects Third Isaiah's descriptions of life on the renewed earth and in the new Jerusalem (Isa 65:17-25). It supersedes that prophet's vision with a promise that death itself will be conquered. The bones of the righteous will rest in the earth, but their spirits will experience the joy of heaven (Jub. 23:31—probably an interpretation of Isa 66:14).[20]

Parts 1 and 2 of the passage are marked by a tension. On the one hand, there is a clear distinction between the apostates and the pious Jews who attempt to bring them back to the way of righteousness. On the other hand, the suffering of Israel as a whole is due to its sins. There is a deep sense of corporate guilt, which recurs in other documents dealing with this period of time. In any event, it is not clear who the children are that will return to the path of righteousness (v 26). Does the author expect that some of the apostates will repent when the power of the oppressor has reached its full fury, or does the passage refer to the righteous who share the guilt of Israel but will turn the tide by their increased righteousness?[21]

The explicit reference to Moses in v 32 and the command to write down these words are striking because they are reminiscent of Deuteronomy 31:19 and the broader context of Deuteronomy 28–32, where the pattern of sin–punishment–(repentance)–salvation is spelled out. This same pattern, with unmistakable verbal echoes of Deuteronomy 28ff., occurs in Jubilees 1 and in the Testament of Moses, which as a whole is a rewriting of the last chapters of Deuteronomy (see next section below).

The date of composition of Jubilees can be discussed in two stages.[22] Several factors indicate about 175 and 100–75 B.C.E. as the outer limits. The terminus post quem is provided by passages reflecting matters that were at issue in the Hellenistic reform. Prohibitions of nudity and uncircumcision à la Gentiles (3:31; 15:34) are cases in point.[23] Explicit citation of Jubilees in the Qumran Damascus Document (CD 16:3-4) indicates a lower limit of about 100–75 B.C.E. Paleographical evidence from Qumran manuscripts of Jubilees suggests a date closer to 100 B.C.E. Within this time span, two dates are possible.

A high date would be 168 B.C.E., contemporaneous with the composition of the apocalypse in chapter 23. Several elements in the book support this date. The author's many prohibitions of contact with and imitations of the Gentiles suit a document stemming from this period. Among the practices interdicted are nudity and uncircumcision (3:31; 15:33-34); observance of "the feasts of the Gentiles," that is, the lunar calendar (6:35); intermarriage (20:4; 22:20; 25:1; 27:10; 30:1-15); idolatry (20:7-9; 22:16-18); and consuming blood (6:12-14; 7:30; 21:6).[24] In the context of such a date, the Book of Jubilees would be that corpus of laws referred to in 23:26. Israel's study of these laws and obedient return to them will catalyze the return of fortune and the inception of the end time described in vv 27-31.

A second possible date of composition would be between 161 and 152–140 B.C.E.[25] Supposed references to the Maccabean wars (34:2-4; 37–38) would provide the terminus post quem. The terminus ad quem would be the rise of the Hasmonean high priesthood and the establishment of the Qumran community (see below, pp. 129–31), both of which stand in tension with the book's high appraisal of the priesthood and the Jerusalem cult. Three difficulties attach to this dating. First, we cannot be certain that 34:2-4 and chapters 37–38 refer to the Maccabean wars.[26] Second, if one accepts the dating, one must minimize the import of the many anti-Gentile polemics, reading them as post-factum reflections of the enormity of the deeds that brought on the disaster of the 160s or as otherwise undocumented evidence of the kind of hellenization and Jew–Gentile contact decried in the book. Third, if the book was written later and the earlier apocalypse in chapter 23 incorporated into it, we might expect the latter to be updated with some reference to the person of Antiochus IV, his pollution of the temple, and his edict.[27]

These considerations suggest to me that Jubilees was written in the early 160s rather than later, and that its purpose was to emphasize the uniqueness of Israel vis-à-vis the Gentiles and to exhort the nation to return to the obedience to the true Torah that would effect a change in Israel's fortunes. If one opts for a later date, one must give full weight to the book's anti-Gentile stance (see above, p. 73), which relates it more closely to the events of the 160s than to the anti-Hasmonean issues that arose in the 150s (see below, pp. 109, 121, 124, 130). Such a dating might emphasize the calendrical material in Jubilees and seek to relate it to debates that may have been a major issue in the 150s. In either case, with its appeal to heavenly tablets, its claim to angelic mediation, and its purported Mosaic authorship, it is set forth as a revealed, authoritative statement of the issues with which it deals and it is presented as, in some real sense, on a par with the pentateuchal material that it paraphrases.[28]

The exact provenance of Jubilees is uncertain. Similarities to texts from the community at Qumran (see below, pp. 119–22) are especially close.[29] The Damascus Document cites it as authoritative (CD 16:3-4). Twelve fragmentary Hebrew manuscripts of Jubilees have been found at Qumran. The book reflects priestly concerns,[30] and other religious ideas, theology, and laws in Jubilees closely parallel and are often identical with those in writings unique to Qumran. Either of the dates suggested above precludes its actual composition at Qumran, and there are some differences between Jubilees and the Qumran texts. The Book of Jubilees issued from an unnamed reformist group related to those responsible for the composition of 1 Enoch 72–82, 85–90, and 93:1-10 + 91:11-17. The specific historical relationships between these groups and the Qumran sect are now obscure, but the latter was heir to their literature.

Jubilees was composed in Hebrew, then translated into Greek and from Greek into Ethiopic, in which language alone it is extant in its entirety.[31] The book is still printed in editions of the Ethiopic Bible.

Like the Wisdom of Ben Sira, Jubilees reflects the increasing significance of Scripture and the importance of its interpretation. The centrality of halakah (lacking in Ben Sira) is symptomatic of the growing concern to expound the Torah—the revelation of God's will for the covenantal people—in a way that spoke relevantly to their needs and situations. However, the stress on halakah should not obscure the expositor's other tasks: to instruct, encourage, and admonish.[32] These twin features of the biblical interpretation in Jubilees would continue to characterize Judaism in the centuries to come. Their later counterparts are the so-called halakic and haggadic exegesis of the rabbis. In this exegesis, as in the Qumran commentaries (see below, pp. 128–32), the mixture of scriptural quotation and paraphrase used in Jubilees has been replaced by the format of quotation and commentary—evidence of the growing authority of Scripture.

The Testament of Moses

The Testament of Moses (commonly known as the *Assumption of Moses*)[33] is, in its present form, a product of the first decades of the Common Era (see below, pp. 247–48). However, literary analysis of the text suggests that the references to the Hasmonean princes and to Herod and his sons (chaps. 6–7) are secondary to the original form of the work, which was composed in the time of Antiochus Epiphanes.[34]

The Testament of Moses retells the events described in Deuteronomy 31–34, with the following elements in common:[35]

1. Announcement of Moses' death	Deut 31:1, 14	T. Mos. 1:15
2. Commissioning of Joshua	Deut 31:7, 14, 23	T. Mos. 1:7-11
3. Commands to preserve the book	Deut 31:19, 25-26	T. Mos. 1:16-18
4. Extensive revelation of Israel's history	Deut 32 (also 28–30)	T. Mos. 2–9
5. Blessing of Moses	Deut 33	Cf. T. Mos. 10
(6. Moses' death and burial	Deut 34	In the lost conclusion of T. Moses)

By beginning his revision of Deuteronomy where he does (and presumably ending it with an account of Moses's death and burial corresponding to the end of Deuteronomy),[36] the author structures his book as a testament—a writing containing the alleged last words of a famous figure of the past (see below, pp. 302–22). Integral to the author's conception of his work is his rewriting of Deuteronomy 31:24-26 in Testament of Moses 1:16-18. Moses is transmitting to Joshua secret prophecies that are to be stored in earthenware vessels until it is time to reveal them in the days before "the consummation of the end of days." In 12:4 he again refers to the "end of the age." Our author's belief that he is living in the last times has led him to rewrite the prophecies of Deuteronomy, employing a double cycle of the Deuteronomic historical scheme (T. Mos. 2–4 and 5–10):

	Testament of Moses		Deuteronomy	
1. Sin	2	5:1—6:1	28:15	32:15-18
2. Punishment	3:1-4	8	28:16-68	32:19-27
3. Turning point	3:5—4:4	9	30:2	32:28-34
4. Salvation	4:5-9	10	30:3-10	32:35-43

However, he has fleshed out that scheme with clearly identifiable events in the nation's history. In the second cycle of the scheme (chaps. 5–9), he describes the events of his own time in great and explicit detail. His reasoning is as follows: I am living in the end times; therefore what Moses the prophet wrote refers to the present. He then rewrites Deuteronomy as if Moses himself were describing the specific events.

In the first cycle, the author establishes the validity of the Deuteronomic scheme by reciting earlier history. Judah sinned (2:7-9). God punished them at the hand of Nebuchadnezzar (3:1-3). The people recalled the words of Moses in his song (3:10-14). An unnamed intercessor pleaded their case (4:1-4). The Lord had compassion and returned them to their land. The scheme did not come to complete fulfillment, however, and life in restored Judah still left much to be desired (4:8).

The cycle has repeated itself in the events contemporary to the author. The hellenizers and their opponents are divided with respect to the truth (5:2). Special mention is made of the deeds of the priests who defile the sanctuary (5:3). Chapters 6 and 7 are late additions, at least in their present form.[37] The persecution of Antiochus, described in unmistakable detail in chapter 8, is God's punishment ("visitation," 8:1) of the sins of the nation. The very end of 8:5 appears to contain a reference to the notorious "desolating sacrilege" erected above the altar. Chapter 9 then functions as the turning point in the scheme. The mysterious Taxo gathers his sons about him and echoes the sentiment that both 1 and 2 Maccabees later attribute to the pious Jews during the persecution, "Let us die rather than transgress the commands of the Lord of Lords, the God of our fathers" (9:6). They die with an appeal that God avenge their blood (9:7). Taxo's words echo Deuteronomy 32:43. The repetition of the theme in Testament of Moses 10:2 indicates that God will hear their prayer. Their innocent deaths and their cry for vengeance will trigger the wrath of God and move the drama into its final act, described in chapter 10.

Here history gives way to myth. Unlike the corresponding part of the first cycle of the scheme, salvation now is final and surpasses human experience, and the end time reverts to ancient times. Drawing on the language of Deuteronomy 33, the author describes God's final epiphany in terms of the ancient appearance on Sinai (10:3). God's victory will be complete, and the divine reign will be evident throughout all of God's creation (10:1). Satan, the power of evil and the opponent of God, will be annihilated; and in answer to the expectation of Taxo (9:7), the Gentiles—the persecutors of God's people— will be punished (10:7; cf. 10:2),[38] and their idols will be obliterated. And then the incredible—Israel will be exalted to the stars (10:9). The boundary between the mortal and the immortal will be transcended. Heaven will become the dwelling place of God's people while earth will be converted into the place of punishment for their enemies. The Testament ended, most likely, with an account of Moses' death and burial, perhaps involving a dispute between Michael the archangel and Satan.[39]

Our author writes some time after the beginning of Antiochus's persecution. The last datable event is the construction of the desolating sacrilege (December 167). Judas Maccabeus is not yet on the horizon, or at least he is not mentioned. Instead, this author expects deliverance in the form of direct divine intervention. The event precipitating the judgment is the innocent deaths of the pious. The author may have witnessed such, or he may be writing to encourage such deaths—perhaps both. In any event, he trusts in the faithfulness of God's ancient word through Moses. God will speedily answer the cry of the righteous.

We do not know to what group our author belonged. Although there are similarities in form and content with Jubilees 23 (see above, pp. 71–72), there are significant differences. There is no mention of the righteous taking up arms against their Jewish compatriots (cf. Jub. 23:20), nor is there any militant ideology.[40] A consuming interest in temple matters, which are scarcely mentioned in Jubilees 23, runs through the Testament of Moses and raises some interesting though probably unanswerable questions. Was the author a priest? What then do we make of his statement about the substandard nature of postexilic sacrifices (4:8)? Is this simply a reflection of the common view that Zerubbabel's temple was far inferior to the Solomonic edifice? Or are these sour grapes from a member of some group of disenfranchised priests?[41]

The Testament of Moses was composed either in Hebrew or in Aramaic[42] and then translated into Greek. It is extant in only one incomplete, corrupt, and partly illegible manuscript of a Latin translation of the Greek version.

Daniel 7–12

The second half of the book of Daniel contains a series of visions that Daniel allegedly saw during the reigns of Belshazzar, Darius, and Cyrus. In reality, the visions date from the time of Antiochus's persecution of the Jews, and they reflect various events in that persecution. Through the use of mythic symbolism, they depict the persecution as rebellion against heaven and announce an act of divine judgment that will quash the rebellion and usher in an era of salvation.[43]

Daniel 7

A. The Vision			vv 1-14
1. The first three beasts appear		vv 1-6	
2. The fourth beast		vv 7-11	
a. The beast appears	v 7		
b. The eleventh horn	v 8		
c. The heavenly court	vv 9-10		
d. The judgment of the beast	v 11		
3. The other beasts neutralized		v 12	
4. Exaltation of one like a son of man		vv 13-14	
B. The Interpretation			vv 15-27
1. Of the four beasts		vv 15-18	
2. Of the fourth beast, the eleventh horn, and the judgment		vv 19-26	
3. Of the exaltation		v 27	

The action in the vision takes place on two levels. The beasts appear, act, and are destroyed on earth (1, 2a, b, d, 3). The court is in heaven, and it is there that the one like a son of man is exalted (2c, 4).

Daniel 7 continues the tradition in Daniel 2 (see above, pp. 18–19), with the beasts representing four kingdoms, the last of these being the Macedonian. The imagery of the beasts arising from the sea is reminiscent of ancient Near Eastern myths that depict the ancient chaos monster of the sea and his combat with and ultimate defeat by the high god.[44] Here all four beasts are powerful and fearful predators, emphasizing the military might that reaches its climax in Macedon. The iron teeth of the fourth beast suggest the army's weaponry and correspond to the iron feet of the statue in chapter 2. The ten horns plus one represent Macedonian kings, the last of these being Antiochus IV.

The vision focuses on the fourth beast, and especially the eleventh horn, on their confrontation with heaven, and on their judgment and destruction. After a description of the warlike deeds of this ferocious beast and the boastful words of the little horn, the action moves to the heavenly court (vv 9-10), where God, described as an old man, is seated on his throne in the midst of his angelic entourage. The judgment passed in heaven has immediate consequences on the earthly level. The fourth beast is destroyed. The Macedonian kingdom (and hence its king, Antiochus) is annihilated (v 11). Reference to the other three beasts is perfunctory (v 12).

The scene moves back to heaven for the final act of the drama:

> And behold with the clouds of heaven there came one like a son of man,
>> and he came to the Ancient of Days,
>> and he was presented before him. (v 13)

The Semitic expression "son of man" means simply a human being. A humanlike figure is brought before the divine throne. However, the author does not say that the figure *is* a man. In 8:15 a similar expression describes the angel Gabriel (cf. 10:18; 9:21), and in the present context of a heavenly scene, it almost certainly denotes an angel—quite likely Michael (cf. 12:1)—being presented before God. His humanlike appearance is mentioned perhaps in contrast to the beasts. Verse 14 indicates the reason for the presentation:

> And to him was given dominion and glory and kingdom,
>> that all peoples, nations, and languages should serve him;
> his dominion is an everlasting dominion, which shall not pass away;
>> and his kingdom one that shall not be destroyed.

The angel is invested with authority that has its repercussions on the earthly level: all human kingdoms will be subservient to this authority.

Daniel himself has been caught up into the vision and seeks an interpretation from a member of the heavenly court (vv 15-16).[45] The initial interpretation is brief (vv 17-18). The four beasts are four kingdoms,[46] and the investiture means that the holy ones of the Most High will receive the kingdom and possess it forever. The term "holy one" or "saint," as it is often translated, is a typical name for angels; as we shall see, however, there are broader implications.[47]

Daniel inquires further about the fourth beast and the eleventh horn, about whose actions we now hear more (vv 19-22). The interpreting angel responds (vv 23-27). The mouth of the little horn (Antiochus) has uttered blasphemy against the Most High (v 25). His persecution of the Jews involves the "wearing out" of the holy ones of the Most High (v 25), that is, war against their angelic patrons. Verse 25 goes on to allude to his proscription of the Torah and of the observance of religious festivals. The author expects that in three and a half years the persecution will end and Antiochus will be destroyed (vv 25-26).

The apocalypticist views reality on two separate but related levels. Events on earth have their counterparts in heaven and vice versa. When Antiochus persecutes the Jews, he is wearing out their heavenly angelic patrons. By the same token, the actions of the heavenly court have repercussions on earth. When judgment is passed in heaven, the earthly king and his kingdom fall. Furthermore, when dominion is given *in heaven* to the chief angelic patron of Israel, *the people* of the holy ones of the Most High are given dominion over all the kingdoms *under heaven* (v 27). Israel will be preeminent among the nations of the earth.[48] In and through God's people, God's everlasting and indestructible reign (kingdom) will be present and operative and will succeed the kingdoms of this world (cf. 2:44; 4:3, 34; 6:26). With this promise the author concludes his drama, which has moved from rebellion to judgment and from persecution to deliverance and exaltation. It will serve as the fountainhead of later Jewish and Christian traditions (see below, pp. 250–51, 275, 280).

Daniel 8

This chapter also divides into vision (vv 1-14) and interpretation (vv 15-26). The animal imagery symbolizes the military might of the kingdoms in question. The charging ram is the Medo-Persian kingdom, and the he-goat is the Macedonian kingdom. Alexander's lightning conquest of the Persian Empire is depicted by the goat's moving across the face of the earth without touching the ground (v 5; cf. Isa 41:3 of Cyrus).[49] Alexander dies; the great horn of the he-goat is broken (v 8). He is succeeded by four other kingdoms, represented by four little horns. As in chapter 7, the action focuses on the one little horn, which represents Antiochus (vv 9-12, 23-25). Antiochus's chief sin, according to this chapter, was his desolation of the temple, his abolition of the burnt offering in the temple (vv 12-13). This moratorium of the two daily sacrifices would continue for 1,150 days (2,300 mornings and evenings, v 14), a little more than three years. As in chapter 7, this prediction was made before the actual restoration of sacrifice in 165—just three years after its cessation. As in chapter 7, vv 11-12 and 24-25 depict Antiochus's actions as a challenge against heaven, an attack against the angelic host.[50] The imagery is reminiscent of Isaiah 14:12-14. There the arrogance of the king of Babylon is described in the imagery of the ancient Canaanite myth about Athtar, the god who attempts to sit on El's throne but must descend to earth. Although Antiochus magnifies himself, he will be cut down. By no human hand—that is, by God—he will be broken (cf. Dan 2:34).

Daniel 9

In v 2 "Daniel" ponders the meaning of Jeremiah's prophecy that Jerusalem would remain desolate for seventy years (Jer 25:11-12; 29:10). In reality, an author in Antiochan times is speaking about the king's desolation of the temple. Daniel's prayer for enlightenment is answered by the appearance of Gabriel, who interprets the seventy years (Dan 9:21-

27) to refer to seventy weeks of years, that is, 490 years. The precise meaning of this chronology is obscure.[51] The author divides it into three periods. The first of these ends in 538 with the appearance of an anointed one, either Zerubbabel or Joshua the high priest. The second period ends when an anointed one is cut off—evidently a reference to the removal or death of Onias III. The last week of years is the time of Antiochus's actions regarding Jerusalem. For a half week (three and a half years), the sacrifice would cease in Jerusalem. This chronology approximates that in chapters 7 and 8.

Verses 4-19 are a long prayer calling for the restoration of Jerusalem and the return of the Dispersion. The Deuteronomic pattern is presumed. The nation's present condition is a curse for their violation of the law of Moses (v 11). Their prayer reflects the repentance required for salvation and restoration. The prayer derives from a liturgical tradition that is also attested in Baruch 1:15—2:35.[52] In its present context it fits the typical literary pattern: prayer, epiphany.[53] Scholars continue to debate whether the prayer was part of the original form of chapter 9 or a later interpolation.[54]

Daniel 10–12

These chapters constitute the most detailed revelation in the second part of Daniel.

A. Introduction		10:1—11:2a
B. The Revelation		11:2b—12:3
1. Historical events	11:2b-39	
a. Persia	11:2b	
b. Alexander	11:3	
c. Breakup of the kingdom	11:4	
d. Wars between Syria and Egypt	11:5-9	
e. Antiochus III	11:10-19	
f. Seleucus IV	11:20	
g. Antiochus IV	11:21-39	
2. The Time of the End	11:40—12:3	
a. Events on earth	11:40-45	
b. Judgment, resurrection, everlasting life	12:1-3	
C. Conclusion		12:4-13

In its broadest outlines, this section employs the structure typical of biblical epiphanies and commissioning scenes:[55] (1) circumstantial introduction, 10:2-4; (2) appearance of the revealer, 10:5-7; (3) reaction, 10:7b-10; (4) response and reassurance, 10:11-12; (3') reaction, 10:15-17; (4') reassurance, 10:18-19; (5) message or commission, 11:2b—12:3; (6) conclusion, 12:4-13. In two significant aspects, however, these chapters differ from prophetic commissionings. First, the message given to the seer is not a brief oracle but a long prediction of events to come.[56] Second, the seer is not to proclaim this message but to write it down and seal the book until "the time of the end," when the events described will occur (12:4). At that time, the wise will read it and understand that it refers to their own time (12:9-10). The idea is paralleled in the Testament of Moses (see above, p. 75). The author is conscious of living at the time of the end, and he writes the book for his community. If one breaks the pseudepigraphic code, the command to seal the book until its publication at the end time is really a command for the author to proclaim his revelation to his contemporaries. In this sense the present text functions like a prophetic commissioning.

The primary content of the revelation is a recitation of selected events in the history of the Macedonian kingdom, particularly the dealings of the Ptolemies and the Seleucids with each other and with the Jews. This historical and earthly level has a corresponding heavenly and mythic level, on which there is a multitude of patron angels for the nations of the earth. War between the kings and the nations involves on the heavenly level a battle between their angelic princes. As Daniel is receiving the revelation during the reign of Cyrus, Michael the patron angel of Israel is battling with the "prince of Persia" (10:13). When the latter is defeated, Persia will fall (10:20). Then a battle will ensue with the prince of Greece (10:20). His fall will coincide with the death of Antiochus.[57]

Although the revelation is set in the time of Cyrus, the author moves quickly to the rise of the Macedonian Empire and beyond it, to the conflicts between the Ptolemies and the Seleucids, the kings of the south and the kings of the north.[58] He details the campaigns of Antiochus III at Raphia (11:11-12) and the Panion (v 15) and his defeat by the Romans at Magnesia (v 18). Although Antiochus III had done many good things for the Jews, for this author he was another example of royal arrogance (vv 16, 18). Antiochus's son Seleucus is mentioned in a single verse with reference to the incident of Heliodorus (v 20; cf. 2 Macc 3). The narrative then moves on to Antiochus IV, whose reign is portrayed as unmitigatedly evil.

Verses 30-35 describe Antiochus's relationship with the Jews. He makes common cause with the hellenizers, "who forsake the covenant" (v 30). Then he desecrates the temple, halts the sacrifice, and constructs the idolatrous "desolating sacrilege" (v 31). Verses 32-35 refer to his persecution of the Jewish people. Special mention is accorded "the wise," who "make many understand." These are the teachers who help the people stand fast in the persecution. Some of their number are put to death. The author of Daniel was doubtless one of these "wise," and his book was likely intended to help in the process of teaching and exhorting the people.[59]

In 11:36-39 the author employs biblical language to describe Antiochus's arrogant defiance of God as he storms heaven.[60] Verse 40 opens a new section. We have arrived at the "time of the end." Again the author draws heavily on biblical passages, believing that the prophets had foretold how things would be at the time of the end.[61]

In 11:40—12:3 the author moves from the historical back to the angelic and mythic realm. It is time for Michael to confront the heavenly prince of Greece. The patron angel of Israel takes his stand for the final battle.[62] Michael is both the warrior chieftain of the heavenly armies and God's appointed agent in the judgment. The final battle has the character of judgment. It will be a time of unprecedented trouble. Michael will strike down the demonic power behind Antiochus and his kingdom.

The judgment will also separate the righteous and wicked of Israel, that is, the hellenizers and the pious Jews. Only those whose names are written in the book of the living will be saved.

The judgment will extend also to the dead:

> Many of those who sleep in the land of dust will awake,
>   some to everlasting life, some to everlasting contempt. (12:2)

Here the author deals with the problem of the righteous who were unjustly put to death because they chose to obey the Torah. God will right the injustice of their deaths by raising them to a new life. Similarly, the apostates who have died will be raised in order to be punished.[63]

In chapter 11 the author mentioned the "wise" who made many to understand. Their special role during the persecution will entitle them to special glory at the end time:

> And those who are wise will shine like the brightness of the firmament,
>   and those who bring many to righteousness, like the stars forever and ever.
>   (12:3)

Although the author uses the language of simile, he may be implying an exaltation to heaven. As in Testament of Moses 10:9, the barrier between the heavenly and the earthly dissolves, and humanity is brought into the place of God. Our author draws on the language of Isaiah 52:13 and 53:11, identifying the righteous teachers of his time with the suffering servant of the Lord, whom God would exalt. The tradition on which he was drawing will recur in other writings that have their roots in this time.[64]

In his concluding section, the author speaks of the period of time until the end. As in chapters 7, 8, and 9, there will be three to three and a half years between the cessation of sacrifice and the end (12:7, 11). Verse 12 is a later recalculation of this time.

There are a number of similarities in the Testament of Moses, Daniel 10–12, and Jubilees 23:16ff. All three narratives have a similar outline, as noted above (recitation of historical events, judgment, new age). All three await the destruction of death. The Book of Jubilees and the Testament of Moses speak of the end of Satan. The same idea is implied in the mention of Michael, whose angelic opponent, the epitome of anti-God, is the equivalent of Satan.[65] Like Jubilees and the Testament of Moses, Daniel notes the distinction between the righteous Jews and the hellenizers, who forsake the covenant. However, the pattern of sin–punishment–repentance is missing from Daniel 11. Antiochus's action against the righteous is not construed as punishment for sin.

The visions in Daniel 7–12 were composed at some time between Antiochus's desecration of the temple (December 167) and Judas's recapture of the Temple Mount in 164. In 11:34 the author perhaps makes passing and not very complimentary reference to the battles of Judas. Judgment will come not by human hand but by direct divine intervention, and it will come quickly. Each of the visions posits a period of three to three and a half years.

The Composition of Daniel 1–12

Sometime during the persecution of Antiochus, the four visions in Daniel 7–12 were collected and combined with the collection of stories in chapters 1–6. The appropriateness of the stories is evident. Chapters 1, 3, and 6 describe faith and piety under pressure. The three youths and Daniel are examples of the persecuted righteous. Nebuchadnezzar in chapter 3 could readily be understood as a king like Antiochus. The willingness of the young men to go to their death with no expectation of deliverance (3:18) would have been especially appropriate during Antiochus's persecution. The two sections of Daniel are also connected through their portrait of Daniel. In the stories Daniel is depicted as a wise man who was able to predict the future through the interpretation of dreams. In chapters 7–12 Daniel is himself the recipient of visions about the future. Not only do these visions predict the future, they also bring the readers up to current events and thus assure them that they stand at the brink of the judgment, when God will destroy the oppressor and initiate the new age with all its blessings. The book is itself part of the exhortatory task of the wise.*

The Animal Vision (1 Enoch 85–90)

First Enoch 83–90 contains two "dream visions" about future events that Enoch saw when he was a young man. In the first of these he foresaw the flood (chaps. 83–84). The narrative in chapter 83 parallels stories about Noah in 1 Enoch 65 and 106–107,[66] and the prayer in chapter 84 is probably dependent on the angelic prayer in 1 Enoch 9 (see above, p. 48).

In his second dream vision (chaps. 85–90), Enoch saw the history of the world played out in allegorical form.[67] Human beings are depicted as animals,[68] the sinful angels are fallen stars, and the seven archangels are human beings.[69] The course of history is divided into three major eras.

1. From creation to the first judgment in the flood   85:3—89:8
2. From the renewal of creation after the flood to the great judgment   89:9—90:27
3. From the second renewal into an open future   90:28-38

The vision begins with a summary of Genesis 2–5 (1 Enoch 85:3-10). All the dramatis personae are depicted as cattle, either bulls or heifers. For his account of the events described in Genesis 6:1-4 (chaps. 86–88), the author has drawn heavily on 1 Enoch 6–11 (see above, pp. 47–50). The first star to fall is Asael (86:1-3; 88:1; cf. 10:4). Other stars descend from heaven, become bulls, and mate with the heifers (i.e., women), thus producing camels, elephants, and asses (i.e., the giants, 86:3-6).[70] The tendency to make Asael the chief of the rebel angels is clearly at work here, and Shemihazah is not at all distinguished from his companions.[71] The four archangels have the same functions here as Sariel, Gabriel, Michael, and Raphael in 1 Enoch 6–11. The three other angels who escort Enoch to heaven (or paradise) have their counterparts in Uriel, Remiel, and Raguel, who are part of Enoch's angelic entourage in his journey through the heavenly world in 1 Enoch 17–19, 20–36, and 81:5.[72]

Although the author is aware of the typology between primordial history and the end time employed in 1 Enoch 6–11, and although he himself implies it, he nevertheless maintains a clear distinction between the two periods. The fall of the angels, the birth of the giants, the binding of the angels, the destruction of the giants, and the flood are events of past history. Thus he provides a detailed account of the flood (89:1-9; cf. Gen 6:13—9:29), whereas in 1 Enoch 6–11 the flood is mainly a type of the coming judgment, which is described in detail. In addition, our author has moved humanity's cry for vindication (8:4), the angelic intercession (9:1-11), and the description of a renewed earth (10:7—11:2) from the narrative about Noachian times to his description of the last times (89:76; 90:3, 12-14, 20-38).

The period after the flood begins a second major historical era. Thus, in the first period of this era, Noah, a white bull, and his three sons, depicted as a white, a red, and a black bull (89:9), correspond to Adam and his three sons, who were depicted in the same way (85:3, 8). With the death of Noah the menagerie begins to diversify, signifying a developing differentiation between the patriarchs of Israel and the Gentiles. From the red and black bulls (Ham and Japheth) many species of animals and fowl arise, all of them unclean by Jewish standards and many of them predators or scavengers. From the line of Shem, a white bull, come Abraham and Isaac, also white bulls. Thereafter, cattle become an extinct species, and we enter a second period in this era of world history, marked by the creation of Israel. To Isaac are born a black wild boar—a derogatory representation of Esau, the patriarch of the hated Edomites—and a white sheep, Jacob, the patriarch of the twelve tribes of Israel (89:10-12).

The image of Israel as sheep is of course a common biblical metaphor,[73] but the author employs it consistently with two biblical nuances that are fundamental to his interpretation of Israelite history. First, the sheep are often blinded and go astray; that is, that nation is guilty of unbelief and apostasy (89:32-33, 41, 51-54, 74; 90:8).[74] The author's second nuance is that the sheep of Israel are frequently the helpless victims of the wild beasts that represent the Gentiles, often as divine punishment for their apostasy (89:13-21, 42, 55-57; 90:2-4, 11-13, 16).[75]

Israel's mounting apostasy leads to a third period in the nation's history, which begins with Manasseh's apostasy (89:59ff.).[76] The Lord of the sheep summons seventy angelic shepherds who will pasture the sheep until the end time. The conception is a conflation of several biblical ideas:[77] the guardian angels of the (seventy) nations;[78] the term "shepherd" used to describe the leaders of God's sheep;[79] the idea that these shepherds are derelict in their duty and will be called to task;[80] and the interpretation of Jeremiah's prediction of seventy years to refer to seventy periods of time.[81] For our author the shepherds are angelic patrons or overseers, each on duty for a particular period of time (89:64; 90:5). Over against these angels stands another angel, who records their misdeeds and pleads Israel's case before God (89:61-64, 68-71, 76-77; 90:14, 17, 20, 22). He is the equivalent of Michael in Daniel 12:1 and is quite likely to be identified with Michael (1 Enoch 90:22).

Like the Testament of Moses, Daniel 7–12, and Jubilees 23 (see above, pp. 71–83), this vision focuses in considerable detail on events during the Seleucid rule. This is a time of unmitigated violence. The sheep are picked clean to the bone (90:2-4). It is also a time of awakening. The younger generation (the pious Jews) open their eyes and appeal to the older ones (the hellenizers) to return from their wickedness, but to no avail (90:6-8; cf. Jub. 23:16-20). The violence continues up to Antiochus's and Apollonius's attacks against Jerusalem (1 Enoch 90:9-11). The text is difficult to decipher at this point. Verses 13-15 closely parallel vv 16-18. We have either the repetition of a formulaic narrative, or duplicate versions of the same block of text, or an updating of the original text of the visions.[82] In any event, in the present form of the vision the action centers on the ram with a great horn, namely, Judas Maccabeus. Verses 13-14 very likely reflect the tradition about a heavenly apparition at the battle of Beth-zur recounted in 2 Maccabees 11:6-12.[83]

The historical section of the vision concludes with a theophany (1 Enoch 90:18). God appears in order to judge (v 20).[84] A threefold judgment is executed against the rebel angels (v 24; cf. 10:7, 12), the disobedient shepherds (90:25), and the apostate Jews (vv 26-27; cf. 10:14). These last are thrown into the fire of the Valley of Hinnom in full sight of Jerusalem (cf. 27:1-3).[85]

With the judgment complete, the third and final era of human history begins. God removes the old Jerusalem and sets up a new one (90:28-29). All the Gentiles come to pay homage to the Jews (v 30; cf. Dan 7:14, 27). The dispersed people of God return, and, it would appear, the dead are raised (1 Enoch 90:33).[86] The sword given to the sheep is sealed up, for an era of peace has begun (90:34). However, the real sign of the new age is the birth of a white bull and the transformation of all the beasts and birds into white bulls or cattle (vv 37-38). The first white bull may be the Messiah,[87] although he has no active function here. More important is the imagery. The end time is a reversion to the primordial time of creation. Like Adam, this white bull is the first of many.[88] As with Noah (1 Enoch 106–107; see below, p. 115), his birth is the sign of a new era of salvation. The distinction between Jew and Gentile is obliterated (cf. 10:21). Therewith ends the strife between the sheep and the beasts and birds of prey. Israel's victimization at the hands of the Gentiles has ceased. Moreover, the omission of any reference to red and black bulls—as there were among the progeny of Adam and Noah—indicates the permanence of this new condition.

The outline of 1 Enoch 85–90 parallels the Testament of Moses, Daniel 10–12, and Jubilees 23 (see above, pp. 71–83), though with its own nuances. This historical survey from creation to end time is much more extensive.[89] A pattern of sin and punishment appears in the sections about Israel. The author's use of allegory is reminiscent of Daniel 7–8 but is far more detailed. In a way that is similar to Daniel 7–12, the author describes reality on two levels: the earthly realm of history and the heavenly sphere of angelic activity. It is from the latter that effective prayer for deliverance comes.

The precise date of the vision is disputed.[90] The existence of duplicate passages in vv 9-19 has long been noted, and there is general agreement that the final form of the vision derives from the time of the campaigns of Judas Maccabeus, that is, between 164 (Beth-zur) and 160 (Judas's death). Its initial composition may have been just a few years before its final editing, or it could date back to the first decade of the second century B.C.E.[91] In any case, given its references to the Maccabean wars, it is noteworthy that the vision makes no mention of Antiochus's decrees, his pollution of the temple, and Judas's restoration of the cult. This surprising omission may be due to the nature of the author's imagery[92] or to the author's tendency to concentrate on the clashes between Israel and the Gentiles as whole entities. Alternatively, it may be related to the author's stated opinion on the Second Temple. From the time of its rebuilding, all the bread on the altar was polluted and not pure (89:73). Taken at face value this statement mitigates the effect of Antiochus's deed. The Second Temple was polluted from its construction. This radical attitude is reminiscent of a similar statement in Testament of Moses 4:8.[93]

The precise provenance of the Animal Vision is uncertain, although we can identify key points in the author's theology and similarities with and differences from other texts.[94] The author wrote within an eschatological community that was constituted around a claim to revelation (90:6) obviously related to the chain of tradition preserved in earlier parts of the Enochic corpus. We have already noted the text's attitude toward the Second Temple. The author's celebration of the militant resistance of Judas Maccabeus differentiates the Vision from the Testament of Moses and Daniel and their espousal of passive resistance,[95] but provides a point of contact with the last chapters of 1 Enoch (see below, p. 112) and the attitude and actions that 1 Maccabees ascribes to the "Hasidim" (see below, p. 91). Especially striking are these two facts: the vision both celebrates the activity of Judas Maccabeus and was preserved by the Qumran community, a group with a strong brief against the brothers of Judas, the Hasmoneans (see below, pp. 130–31). Taken together, all these facts underscore the complex nature of the social, religious, and political situation in Israel during the fourth decade of the second century B.C.E.

SUMMARY

We have discussed in this chapter a series of writings from the period of Antiochus IV that purport to be revelations received in various ways[96] and transmitted by ancient prophets and sages. While the phenomenon of pseudonymity may suggest that in the Antiochan period prophecy in one's own name was not credible among many, the fact remains that behind these pseudonyms lies the authors' conviction that they had a revealed message to transmit. We know little enough about the sources and psychology of this self-consciousness. It is noteworthy, however, that it is often connected with an interpretation of Scripture. The author of Jubilees rewrites Genesis and Exodus. The Testament of Moses is a detailed contemporizing explication of the last chapters of Deuteronomy. In chapter 9 Daniel ponders over Jeremiah's seventy years until an angel reveals its "true" meaning. The author of Daniel 10–12 clothes his references to contemporary events in the language of biblical prophecy. Thus the belief that one lived in the last times was bound up at least in part with the conviction that these times were predicted and described in ancient prophecy.

In Jubilees 23, the Testament of Moses, Daniel (esp. chaps. 10–12), and 1 Enoch 85–90, the message of the imminent end is embodied in the form of historical apocalypses, which bring one in increasing detail up to the present moment. By describing events that lay behind him, the real author seeks credibility for his message about the imminent future. By ascribing the whole to a sage of the remote past, he builds into his apocalypse a determinism that views both the past and the future that he forecasts as irrevocable.[97] The extensive linear sweep of these historical surveys is complemented by a vertical cross section of the universe that sees a cosmic reality operative simultaneously in heaven and earth. The heavenly and earthly levels come together in the end time, when God or God's agents touch history with finality. Either (righteous) humanity is assumed to heaven, or the earth is transformed into the realm where God's intent and sovereignty are finally and fully realized.

In their conviction that God will soon act in superlative fashion to right the wrongs of an unjust world, these authors express an eschatology that is reminiscent of Third Isaiah. In their use of pseudonymity, their explicit claim to revelation (revelatory visions in Daniel and 1 Enoch), their dependence on Scripture (including Third Isaiah), their long deterministic historical surveys, the prominence of their two-storied view of reality, and their extension of God's future judgment and deliverance to include the dead, they have transcended the eschatology of Third Isaiah in qualitative and significant fashion.

Not all revelatory literature from this period took the form of historical apocalypses. In 1 Enoch 12–36 the message of an imminent judgment was carried in a commissioning scene based on Ezekiel 1–2 and in reports of a series of cosmic journeys.[98]

The texts that we have discussed are the literary remains of individuals and, doubtless in some cases, groups that resisted certain forms of the hellenization of Judaism and exhorted their fellow Jews to stand fast in, or to return to the faithful obedience to the Torah. This would restore the divine blessings that had been lost due to hellenizing apostasy or, more radically (1 Enoch 85–90), due to the sins that had led to the exile. The authority for these authors was revelation about the specifics of divine law (Jubilees and 1 Enoch 85–90 at least) and the imminent judgment that would vindicate righteous behavior and punish sin. Since each of these texts has its own nuances, emphases, and viewpoint, it is unlikely, or at least not demonstrable, that any two of them stem from the same group or individual. Nor can we trace any of them back to a known group such as the Hasidim.[99] Their common features and their differences attest the existence, in the early second century, of a multiheaded reform movement that opposed religious and social developments in Israel and sought to bring the nation back to what they considered to be right religious practice. Parallels to the early strata of 1 Enoch suggest that such a reforming tendency was not new (cf. 1 Enoch 2:1—5:9; 12–16). The preservation of these texts among the Dead Sea Scrolls and, as we shall see in chapter 5, parallels in the writings of the Qumran community attest the ongoing life of this reform movement, as it turned to a new situation after the death of Antiochus IV and the demise of Seleucid power in Israel.

BIBLIOGRAPHY

History

Schürer, *History*, 1:137–63. Elias J. **Bickerman**, *The God of the Maccabees* (SJLA 32; Leiden: Brill, 1979). Jonathan A. **Goldstein**, *1 Maccabees* (AB 41; Garden City, N.Y.: Doubleday, 1976) 104–73, detailed reconstruction of the civic and political policies of Antiochus IV. **Gruen**, *Heritage and Hellenism*, 1–40. **Hengel**, *Judaism*, 1:175–218, 255–314. **Tcherikover**, *Hellenistic Civilization*, 117–203, more detailed account with emphasis on social and economic factors. James C. **VanderKam**, *From Joshua to Caiaphas: High Priests after the Exile* (Minneapolis: Fortress Press, 2004) 137–226.

Jubilees

Translations: O. S. **Wintermute**, *OTP* 2:35–142. R. H. **Charles**, rev. Chaim **Rabin**, *AOT*, 1–139.

Commentary: R. H. **Charles**, *The Book of Jubilees* (Oxford: Clarendon, 1902), introduction, translation, brief commentary.

Text and Other Translations: James C. **VanderKam**, DJD 13:1–185, Qumran Hebrew fragments with translation and annotations. James C. **VanderKam**, *The Book of Jubilees* (2 vols.; CSCO 510–11; Leuven: Peeters, 1989), critical text of Ethiopic, Greek, Syriac, and Latin; fresh translation of the Ethiopic.

Literature: Matthias **Albani**, Jörg **Frey**, and Armin **Lange**, eds., *Studies in the Book of Jubilees* (TSAJ 65; Tübingen: Mohr Siebeck, 1997). Gene L. **Davenport**, *The Eschatology of the Book of Jubilees* (SPB 20; Leiden: Brill, 1971). John C. **Endres**, *Biblical Interpretation in the Book of Jubilees* (CBQMS 18; Washington, D.C.: Catholic Biblical Association, 1987). Betsy **Halpern-Amaru**, *The Empowerment of Women in the Book of Jubilees* (JSJSup 60; Leiden: Brill, 1999). M. **Testuz**, *Les idées religieuses du livre des Jubilés* (Geneva: Druz, 1960), introduction to the thought of the book. J. T. A. G. M. **van Ruiten**, *Primaeval History Interpreted* (JSJSup 66; Leiden: Brill, 2000). James C. **VanderKam**, *Textual and Historical Studies in the Book of Jubilees* (HSM 14; Missoula, Mont.: Scholars Press, 1977), comparison of all published Qumran Hebrew fragments with the Ethiopic mss., discussion of the biblical text employed in Jubilees, detailed investigation of the book's date and relationship to the Qumran community. James C. **VanderKam**, *The Book of Jubilees* (GAP; Sheffield: Sheffield Academic Press, 2001), introduction to major aspects of the book.

The Testament of Moses

Translation: John **Priest**, *OTP* 1:919–34.

Text, Translation, and Commentary: R. H. **Charles**, *The Assumption of Moses* (London: Black, 1897), Latin text, introduction, translation, brief commentary. R. H. **Charles**, rev. J. P. M. **Sweet**, *AOT*, 601–16. Johannes **Tromp**, *The Assumption of Moses: A Critical Edition with Commentary* (SVTP 10; Leiden: Brill, 1993), new edition of the Latin, with introduction, translation, and commentary.

Literature: Norbert Johannes **Hofmann**, *Die Assumptio Mosis: Studien zur Rezeption massgültiger Überlieferung* (JSJSup 67; Leiden: Brill, 2000), comprehensive study of the structure of the Testament, its rewriting of Deuteronomy 31–33, and its relationships to the literature of the second century B.C.E. to the first century C.E. George W. E. **Nickelsburg**, ed., *Studies on the Testament of Moses* (SBLSCS 4; Cambridge: Society of Biblical Literature, 1973), papers on the date, provenance, form, and function. On the figure of Taxo see: Charles C. **Torrey**, "'Taxo' in the Assumption of Moses," *JBL* 62 (1943) 1–7; H. H. **Rowley**, "The Figure of 'Taxo' in the Assumption of Moses," *JBL* 64 (1945) 141–43; Charles C. **Torrey**, "'Taxo' Once More," *JBL* 64 (1945) 395–97; Sigmund **Mowinckel**, "The Hebrew Equivalent of Taxo in Ass. Mos. ix," in *Congress Volume, Copenhagen 1953* (VTSup 1 Leiden: Brill, 1953) 88–96; Jacob **Licht**, "Taxo, or the Apocalyptic Doctrine of Vengeance," *JJS* 12 (1961) 95–103; **Nickelsburg**, *Resurrection*, 97–102; Johannes **Tromp**, "Taxo, the Messenger of the Lord," *JSJ* 21 (1990) 200–209.

Daniel

See bibliography for chapter 1.

1 Enoch 85–90

Texts and Translations: See bibliography for chapter 2.

Commentaries: George W. E. **Nickelsburg**, *1 Enoch 1: A Commentary on the Book of 1 Enoch Chapters 1–36, 81–108* (Hermeneia; Minneapolis: Fortress Press, 2001) 345–408, translation, critical apparatus, and commentary. Patrick A. **Tiller**, *A Commentary on the Animal Apocalypse of 1 Enoch* (SBLEJL 4; Atlanta: Scholars Press, 1993), transliterated Ethiopic text with Qumran Aramaic fragments, translation, introduction, and commentary.

The Epistle of Enoch. Fragments of three columns of a mid- to late-first-century B.C.E. Qumran Aramaic manuscript (4QEn^g) containing parts of 1 Enoch 91:10—94:1. Photograph is courtesy of the Israel Antiquities Authority.

4

The Hasmoneans and Their Opponents

FROM JUDAS TO ALEXANDRA

The victories of Judas and the restoration of the Jerusalem cult were followed by new problems for the Jewish people.[1] Perhaps troubled by these evidences of power, the neighboring peoples began to make war on the Jews who lived outside the borders of Judea. Judas and his brothers led a series of sorties against the Idumeans to the south, the Ammonites in Transjordan, and other Gentiles in Galilee and Gilead, and they brought the Jews from these latter two areas back to Judea, where they were resettled safe from Gentile oppression.

Antiochus IV died late in 164 and was succeeded by his young son Antiochus V Eupator and his regent Lysias. At the outset of his reign, the new king issued a proclamation that rescinded the decrees of Antiochus IV. The Jews now possessed religious freedom de jure.

In 162 Demetrius I Soter, the son of Seleucus IV (the brother and predecessor of Antiochus IV), seized the throne in Antioch. The army rallied to Demetrius and executed Antiochus V and Lysias. Demetrius then confirmed as high priest a certain Alcimus (Heb. *Yakim*), who replaced Menelaus, whom Lysias had deposed and executed. Alcimus was supported by members of the Jewish community who opposed Judas, and his credentials as a legitimate Aaronic high priest satisfied a group of scribes and the Hasidim, a group of pious Jews who may or may not have been identical with these scribes (1 Macc 7:12-18). After having received the support of the Hasidim, Alcimus turned on them and had sixty of them slaughtered in one day. As high priest, Alcimus found an ongoing opponent in Judas. When he appealed to the king, Demetrius sent his general Nicanor to dispatch Judas and install Alcimus in the temple. Nicanor, however, made peace with Judas. With continued pressure from Alcimus and under orders from Demetrius, Nicanor then proceeded against Judas. In the battle that followed, Nicanor was killed. His head and right hand, "which he had stretched out against the temple," were cut off and hung up as trophies in Jerusalem.

When Judas sought to consolidate his position through an alliance with Rome,

Demetrius sent his general Bacchides against Judas at the head of a huge army. Most of Judas's troops deserted him, but he rejected the counsel to retreat. In the bitter battle that ensued, the remnant of the Jewish army was crushed and Judas Maccabeus fell.

The followers of Judas chose his brother Jonathan as their leader, and for seventeen years he maneuvered successfully through a series of Syrian kings and pretenders, developing and consolidating military and political power.* In the year 160 Alcimus the high priest ordered the wall of the inner court of the temple demolished. His death shortly thereafter was viewed by some of the Jews as punishment for tearing down this "work of the prophets" (1 Macc 9:54-56). Alcimus appears not to have had an immediate successor; the sources indicate a four- or seven-year vacancy in the office, the so-called *intersacerdotium*.

Evidently Jonathan had become a force to be reckoned with. In the year 152 Demetrius had to defend his throne against Alexander Balas, a pretender who claimed to be the son of Antiochus IV. Both Demetrius and Alexander sought the help of Jonathan, who sided with Alexander when he appointed Jonathan as high priest. Two years later Alexander named Jonathan civil and military governor of the province of Judea.

In 145 Alexander was deposed by Demetrius II Nicator, the son of Demetrius I, whom Alexander had ousted. Although Jonathan had supported Alexander in this rivalry, he was able to win the favor of Demetrius II, who confirmed his former honors and listed him among "the first friends of the king."

Conflict over the throne of Syria flared up again when Trypho, a general of Alexander Balas, set up Alexander's young son Antiochus VI Epiphanes Dionysus as a rival of Demetrius. Eventually Jonathan went over to the side of Trypho, who defeated Demetrius. Evidently fearful of Jonathan's growing power, Trypho captured him by treachery and had him murdered. Simon buried his brother in the family tomb in their native city of Modein, where he erected a splendid monument of polished white marble, and he assumed the reins of leadership. The year was 143/142.

Events in Syria took yet another turn when Trypho took the throne after having the boy Antiochus killed. This time Simon sided with Demetrius II, who pardoned past offenses against the crown, legitimized fortifications, and granted tax exemption (142). "The yoke of the Gentiles was removed from Israel," according to the Hasmonean author of 1 Maccabees (13:41). This characterization of Demetrius's actions notwithstanding, the Jews still remained under the rule of the Seleucids. The following year, however, Simon succeeded in ending the Gentiles' twenty-seven-year occupation of the citadel in Jerusalem. The following year "the people" formally acclaimed him high priest, military commander, and ethnarch of the Jews, and it was decreed that he (and perhaps his family) should be high priest(s) in perpetuity—at least until God should send a prophet to declare otherwise (1 Macc 14:41). As matters evolved, the high priestly and princely dynasty of the Hasmoneans was being founded. For a few years the country was at peace.

When the Parthians captured Demetrius II in 139, his brother Antiochus VII Sidetes took up the struggle against Trypho, and the latter was killed in battle. At first Antiochus confirmed for Simon all the favors granted by past monarchs. Later he revoked these concessions, but he was not able to enforce his will. His army was defeated by Simon's.

Simon's reign would not end on this high point. In 135 he and his sons Mattathias and Judas were feted at a banquet in the fortress of Dok near Jericho. When all three were drunk they were assassinated by Ptolemy, the commander of the fortress and Simon's son-in-law. Thirty-two years after Mattathias's revolt, the last of his sons died a violent death.

Simon was succeeded by his surviving son, John (Heb. *Yehoḥanan*) Hyrcanus. He would be the first of seven Hasmonean princes or priests with a Hebrew and a Greek name. During the first year of his reign Antiochus VII once again invaded Judea. Besieged in Jerusalem, Hyrcanus sued for peace. The price was high: the demolition of fortifications, heavy tribute, and hostages.

Hyrcanus's setback was only temporary. When Antiochus VII was killed he was succeeded by Demetrius II, who returned from captivity. With the death of Demetrius and the rapidly waning power of the Seleucid Empire during the reigns of Antiochus VIII Grypus and Antiochus IX Cyzicenus, the time was ripe for new Jewish conquests. First Hyrcanus struck across the Jordan and took the city of Medeba, then he marched north. Some time earlier the Samaritans had broken religiously with Jerusalem and had built their own temple atop Mount Gerizim near Shechem. John captured the city, razed the temple, and subdued the people.* Then he moved south, where he conquered Idumea and forced the Idumeans to submit to circumcision and to accept the Torah. Later he again marched north and captured the important fortified city of Samaria.

It is in Josephus's account of Hyrcanus's reign that we first hear of the activities of the religious parties of the Pharisees and the Sadducees. Previously the Hasmoneans (or at least Hyrcanus) had been favorably disposed to the Pharisees. However, a falling out between Hyrcanus and the Pharisees led to the rise in power of the Sadducees, a group made up to some extent of priestly aristocrats who traced their descent back to the high priest Zadok.

The thirty-year reign of John Hyrcanus (134–104) witnessed the expansion of Judea's territorial limits and the growth of its political independence beyond anything that had been known since the Babylonian exile. The longest of the Hasmonean reigns was followed by the shortest. Hyrcanus's son Judas (Heb. *Yehudah*) Aristobulus ruled for only one year. Defying his father's will, he seized the secular power that had been delegated to his mother, and he sent his brothers and his mother into prison, where his mother died. He then became the first Hasmonean to assume the title "king." When Aristobulus died in 103, his widow, Salome (Heb. *Shelamzion*, meaning "peace of Zion") Alexandra, released the brothers and bestowed on the eldest, Alexander Janneus (Heb. *Yonathan*), the high priesthood and her hand in marriage.

Alexander's twenty-seven-year reign was marked by frequent wars and many conquests. Extending his control north into Galilee, east into Transjordan, and west along most of the Philistine coast, he governed an Israelite state larger than anything since Solomon.* Like his brother, he took the title "king." His reign, however, was badly marred by acts of incredible cruelty and a six- or seven-year civil war. On one occasion, when he was executing the high priestly office on the Feast of Tabernacles, the crowd pelted him with the citrons that they were carrying for ritual purposes. He responded by slaughtering large numbers of the people. Another time, after many Jews had deserted him in a battle against Demetrius III, it is said that he crucified eight hundred of his opponents in Jerusalem, while he feasted with his mistresses and forced the crucified to watch the slaughter of their own wives and children. It is usually alleged that antipathy between the Pharisees and the Hasmonean house was exacerbated during this period, but the evidence for this is slim.[2] After a three-year illness that resulted from overdrinking, Alexander died in 76 B.C.E.

Alexander's widow, Salome Alexandra, ascended the throne and appointed their son John Hyrcanus II high priest. Her reign was in general peaceful and prosperous, and saw the Pharisees exercising considerable political influence. When she died in 67 B.C.E., however, the scene was set for a confrontation between her sons Hyrcanus II and Aristobulus II that would eventually place Judea under the domination of the Roman Empire and bring an end to its short-lived independence.

Baruch

This is the first of several works attributed to Baruch, the secretary of Jeremiah.[3] The book divides into four sections that are probably of diverse origins: narrative introduction (1:1-14), prayer (1:15—3:8), Wisdom poem (3:9—4:4), and Zion poem (4:5—5:9). These sections are bound together by the common theme of exile and return, which is often expressed in biblical idiom.

The introduction describes the alleged purpose of the book and the circumstances of its origin. In the fifth year after the destruction of Jerusalem (i.e., in 582 B.C.E.), Baruch assembled the Jewish leaders in Babylon for a formal hearing of the book.[4] Then, after rituals of repentance (1:5), they contributed money to be sent to Jerusalem together with the temple vessels that Nebuchadnezzar had taken as booty (1:6-9). The high priest was to offer sacrifice, pray for Nebuchadnezzar and his son Belshazzar, and intercede for the exiles (1:10-13). Proper sacrifice could be offered only at the temple site, and the prayer that follows was to accompany the sacrifice and also be prayed "on the days of the feasts and at appointed seasons."

The prayer comprises a corporate confession of sins and a petition that God will withdraw God's wrath and return the exiles to their homeland.[5] Its logic follows the scheme of Deuteronomy 28–32, and the language of both Deuteronomy and Jeremiah has heavily influenced its wording.[6] Verbal parallels to Daniel 9:4-19 indicate a very close relationship also to that prayer.[7]

The inhabitants of Jerusalem are first to confess their own sins (1:15—2:5).[8] The people are to acknowledge God's righteousness, confess their rebellion against covenant and the prophetic word, and admit that they are now suffering the curses of the covenant that Moses predicted in Deuteronomy. The repetition of the confession (1:17-18, 21) and the admission that this sin has continued to the present (1:19-20)—both missing from Daniel 9[9]—underscore the sense of guilt that pervades the prayer. Also lacking in Daniel 9 is a counterpart to Baruch 2:3-5, which reflects Deuteronomy 28:53.

In a second, parallel confession the people in Jerusalem are to speak in the name of the exiles (2:6-10). Again the sense of guilt is expressed by a double confession (2:8, 10) and by the admission that the people have not turned away from their evil thoughts (2:8, missing from Dan 9:8).

The petitionary section of the prayer (2:11-18) begins with the formulaic "And now. . . ." Here, as throughout the prayer (and the introduction), God is addressed by the proper name YHWH (translated "LORD"), and the covenantal relationship is indicated by the title "God of Israel" (cf. 3:1, 4; and "our God," passim) and by reference to the exodus (cf. 1:20). The petition itself is preceded by yet another confession of sin (2:12). The exiles pray that God's wrath will turn from them (2:13), that God will deliver his people and grant them favor with their captors (2:14), and that God will look down and consider God's people (2:16-17). The language of Exodus 3:7-8, 20-21 is reflected throughout this passage, for the author, like Second Isaiah, construes return from exile as a second exodus (see above, pp. 10–11). Each of the three parts of the petition differs from its Danielic counterpart by referring to the situation in exile rather than to the desolation of the temple (cf. Dan 9:16-18).

In his penultimate word in 9:18, Daniel contrasts the people's lack of righteousness with God's mercy, to which he appeals as the grounds for God's action. Baruch 2:19 contrasts the fathers' lack of righteousness with God's mercy and employs this thought as a transition to yet another confession of sin (2:20-26). (At this point this prayer continues at length beyond Daniel 9.) The people fell under God's wrath because they did not obey the prophetic warning to submit to the king of Babylon (cf. Jer 27:11-12). The motif is reminiscent of Baruch's admonition in 1:11-12.[10] The pattern of sin and the fulfillment of predicted punishment (2:20-24) parallels 1:20—2:1.

In 2:27-35 the prayer returns to Deuteronomy for a word of hope.[11] Although God predicted punishment for sin, God promised that when the people repented in the land of their exile, God would return them to their land, increase their numbers, and make an everlasting covenant with them. In 3:1-8 the people do precisely what God had said they would do (cf. 2:31-33 and 3:7-8). The prayer breaks off without an explicit request for return, but the implications are clear.

Chapters 3:9—4:4 contain a Wisdom poem in the tradition of Sirach 24 (see above, pp. 57–58). Its poetic (as opposed to prose) form, its concentration on Torah as Wisdom, its dependence on the language of Job, and its use of "God" rather than "LORD" differ from the previous section. These differences notwithstanding, it has been made an integral part of Baruch.

The poem is connected to the previous section by 3:9-13.[12] Israel is "dead" in the land of their enemies (3:10-11; cf. 3:4)[13] because they have forsaken the fountain of wisdom (3:12; cf. Jer 2:13), that is, the Torah, the commandments of *life* (Bar 3:9).

The specific topic of the poem is the finding of Wisdom, and it is beholden to Job 28:12-28. The opening strophe admonishes the readers to learn where there is wisdom and strength and life (Bar 3:14). The next three strophes enumerate those who have *not* found Wisdom: the rulers of the Gentiles (3:15-19), others among the wise of the earth

(3:20-23), and the giants of old (3:24-28).[14] By contrast God alone found the way to Wisdom (3:29-37) and has given it to Israel alone among human beings (3:36). The last strophe (4:1-4) makes explicit the identification of Wisdom and Torah hinted at in the wording of 3:29-30 (cf. Deut 30:11-13). Like Sirach 24, this poem asserts that Wisdom is embodied in Torah and promises life to those who "hold her fast."[15] It threatens death to those who forsake her, which explains why Israel is now "dead" in the land of their captivity. The author appeals to the people to repent (Bar 4:2) and find life, which here implies return, and he ends with a blessing on the people (4:4; cf. Deut 33:29) who know God's will.

Although this poem paraphrases Job 28, its explicit nationalism is foreign to its archetype (cf. Bar 3:36-37 with Job 28:23-28), while it parallels Sirach 24 and fits well with the rest of Baruch. Explicit references to Israel (Bar 3:9, 24, 36; 4:2, 4) and "our God" (3:35) are complemented by the identification of Wisdom with Torah and the consequent distinction between Israel and the Gentiles.

The personification of Wisdom in Baruch 3:8—4:4 is less clear than it is in Sirach 24. This poem is *about* her rather than *by* her. She is the object of a search rather than the one who searches the universe. Only in Baruch 4:1 is she the subject of a verb of action.

Having appealed for that obedience that can change Israel's fortunes, the author begins his last major section (4:5—5:9), issuing the first of several exhortations to "take courage." God's punishment is not final (4:6; cf. 2 Macc 6:12). This section is again stamped with the language of Deuteronomy,[16] but the controlling metaphor is Second Isaiah's image of Mother Zion and her children.

Before the author turns to his hope of the future, he again rehearses the past. Israel's plight is due to her sin (Bar 4:6-20). This rebellion against God brought bereavement to their widowed mother, who describes to her neighbors how she had nurtured her children with joy but sent them into exile in sorrow (4:9-20). Now addressing her children in a pair of strophes that also begin with "take courage" (4:21-26, 27-29), she appeals to them to offer that prayer for deliverance that stands at the beginning of the book. The individual units of these strophes are generally marked by a contrast between past calamity and future salvation: the mother sent her sons out in sorrow, but God will return them in joy; captivity will turn to salvation; the enemy himself will be destroyed. Calamity will be turned to joy.

In view of this prospect the author addresses four strophes to Jerusalem herself, each beginning with an imperative to act out a stage of the unfolding drama of salvation. Like her sons she is to "take courage" (4:30-35) in view of the coming reversal that will inflict on the enemy the ills that Israel suffered (cf. 4:33 with 4:11).[17] Then Israel is to look to the east for the return of her sons (4:26-37).[18] She is to replace her mourning clothes (cf. 4:20) with glorious robes (5:1-4).[19] Then she is to ascend to the height to view the return of her children, led in procession by their God (5:5-9).[20]

With the prospect of return the author has solved the dilemma with which the book began. Prayer has been answered. Exile and dispersion have ended. Sorrow has turned to joy. It will be obvious by now that the various component parts of the book, whatever their origin, have been edited into an almost seamless unity, and it is possible that the work as a whole was composed not as a book in its own right, but as an appendix to the canonical book of Jeremiah.[21]

Baruch is a prime example of a book whose time of composition is difficult to date.[22] There are no unambiguous historical allusions. The theme of dispersion and return fits any period after 587 B.C.E. Attempts to date the book by comparing 1:15—3:8 with Daniel 9 and chapter 5 with Psalms of Solomon 11 fall short of certainty. The nature of the interrelationships is uncertain, as are the dates of the other documents in question.[23]

The style of the Greek in Baruch appears to provide a terminus ad quem in 116 B.C.E. There are indications that at least the first part of Baruch and the Hebrew of Jeremiah were translated by the same person and that the translation of the whole prophetic corpus was known to Ben Sira's grandson, who translated the Wisdom of Ben Sira before 116 B.C.E.[24]

There is some consensus that the book's fictional date (1:2) provides a clue to the date of composition.[25] If Nebuchadnezzar is a stand-in for Antiochus IV, the book is possibly to be dated to 164 B.C.E., five years after Antiochus's sack of Jerusalem and after Judas's purification of the temple. The high priest Jehoiakim would be none other than Alcimus. The book would be an appeal both to accept the authority of Antiochus V, the son of Antiochus IV (i.e., Belshazzar, son of Nebuchadnezzar; cf. 1:11-13 and the emphasis in 2:21-23), and to seek that obedience to the Torah that would facilitate the return of the Dispersion and God's own judgment of the Macedonian kingdom. Dating the book in this time would explain the fictional setting and would also fit well with the strong consciousness of sin, guilt, and punishment that pervades chapters 1–3.[26]

Judith

> For your power depends not upon numbers,
>   nor your might upon men of strength.
> For you are God of the lowly,
>   helper of the oppressed,
>   upholder of the weak,
>   protector of the forlorn,
>   savior of those without help. (Jdt 9:11)

With these words Judith summarizes the central assertion of the book named after her.[27] The plot of the story manifests the truth of this assertion and depicts the characters in diverse reactions to it.

Chapters 1–7 describe the developing crisis facing Israel. Nebuchadnezzar, the epitome of irresistible military might, breaches the impregnable defenses of his enemy to the east, "Arphaxad,"[28] and dispatches Holofernes, his general, against the nations that have refused him aid. Holofernes sweeps across Mesopotamia and down into Syria and

Palestine (2:21—3:10). The Israelites prepare to resist and seek divine help through prayer, fasting, and mourning (chap. 4). In a long recitation of Israelite history, Achior, "the leader of all the Ammonites" who are accompanying Holofernes, explains why they dare to resist (5:5-21). From their history one can see that their strength is not in their armies but in their God. When they are faithful to their God they are invincible. When they sin they go down in defeat. In the present situation, if there is no transgression in the nation they had best be left alone, lest the Assyrian army be put to shame before the whole world (5:21). Holofernes retorts in a mock oracle that acclaims Nebuchadnezzar as the only God, the lord of the whole earth, whose command to destroy his enemies will not be in vain (6:2-4). The fundamental tension in the story is now explicit. Who is God, YHWH or Nebuchadnezzar?[29] When Holofernes's army appears in full array at the city of Bethulia, the people's courage melts (chap. 7). They conclude that God has sold them into the hand of the foreigner, and the exhortations of Uzziah their ruler are futile. The people are "greatly depressed."

Judith's appearance serves as a turning point in the narrative. Her address to the rulers and her prayer are crucial in several ways (chaps. 8–9). They depict Judith as a person of great faith and as a wise and eloquent spokeswoman of that faith. Through them she presents a formal exposition of the view of God that the book as a whole dramatizes. Her censure of the people expresses the author's criticism of a lack of faith in this God. Judith's prayer wins the help of God.

Judith's wisdom has its practical side, and her faith becomes operative in deed. A clever and resourceful assassin, she allows no detail to escape her preparations (10:1-5). Once she is inside the Assyrian camp, deceit is her modus operandi (10:6—12:20). Her great beauty disarms the sentries and the rest of the army, leaving them wide-eyed with wonder and hence blind to her treacherous intent. Playing up to Holofernes's arrogant pretensions, Judith addresses him as if he were the king himself (11:8, 19). Her conversation is a string of lies, half-truths, and double entendres.[30] Dazzled by Judith's beauty, Holofernes "loses his head before it has been cut off."[31] His desire to possess Judith provides her with the opportunity she has been awaiting, and she parries his proposition with ambiguous answers (12:14, 18). Tossing caution to the winds, Holofernes drinks himself into a stupor. The time for ambiguities has ceased. Judith beheads the drunken general with his own sword and tumbles his body from the bed onto the floor. His humiliation "at the hand of a woman" is complete (13:1-10).

The various themes in the story now resolve themselves. Judith returns to the city, proclaiming that God is still with the people of Israel, showing mercy to them and destroying their enemies (13:11, 14). The Assyrian camp is the scene of chaos and terror. Bagoas, Holofernes's eunuch, laments their defeat and disgrace, describing the fallen Holofernes as if he were a toppled statue that had lost its head (14:18; cf. Dan 2:34-35). It is evident who alone is God. The God of Israel has fulfilled Achior's warning (Jdt 5:21; cf. 14:18b), has vindicated the faith of Uzziah (7:30; 13:14) and especially Judith (8:15-17; 9:11), and has shown the people's despair to have been groundless (7:24-28). Holofernes's challenge has been met (6:3). Nebuchadnezzar's pride has been turned to disgrace, and his attempt to be "lord of the whole earth" (2:5; 6:4) has been foiled by the hand of a woman (9:10; 13:15; 16:6). His army is routed, and we hear no more of him in the book (16:25). When Achior, the first exponent of the power of Israel's God, learns what has happened, he "believes firmly in God," undergoes the rite of circumcision, and "is added to the house of Israel" (14:6-10). Judith's song is a reprise of the central assertion in the book: the God of Israel is the champion of the weak and the oppressed, who destroys the power of the mighty and humbles the pride of the arrogant (16:1-17).

The book of Judith is a literary work of considerable artistic merit.[32] Chapters 1–7, which many consider to provide an imbalance of useless information overload,[33] actually constitute the first half of a carefully crafted literary diptych, in which the second part (chaps. 8–16) resolves events and issues presented in the first part, and in which each of the two parts contains a threefold, thematically unified chiastic structure within itself (A-B-C-C'-B'-A' | A-B-C-D-C'-B'-A').[34] Another aspect of the author's literary artistry is the sophisticated manner in which the author depicts Judith and Achior as counterparts to one another.[35] The use of multifaceted humor, including irony and absurdity, is also an important aspect of the author's literary artistry.[36] It is generally agreed that the Greek form of the book is a translation from a Hebrew original.[37]

Not surprisingly, the book of Judith has captured the interest of feminist scholars and other scholars concerned with feminist issues.[38] It is a rare example of a book in biblical and early postbiblical Jewish (and, for that matter, Christian) literature whose protagonist is a woman whose roles and actions often confound normal portrayals of gender relations.[39] As the narrative unfolds, Judith is consistently depicted as superior to the men with whom she is associated. It is she and not her husband Manasseh who is given a genealogy (8:1-2). She acts on her own initiative, while Uzziah and the elders are unable to deal with the situation. It is she and her handmaid, not the men of Bethulia, who rescue the city, and she lops off the head of the boastful and lustful Holofernes. She gives the orders for the counterattack of the Jews (14:1-5). As Bagoas must admit, "one Hebrew woman has brought disgrace on the house of Nebuchadnezzar" (14:18). At the end of the story Judith gains the plaudits of Uzziah, Achior, and Joakim the high priest. Although some passages state that God's power is operative through the weakest of human agents, that is, a woman (9:10; 14:18; 16:6-7), Judith is no weakling. Her courage, her trust in God, and her wisdom—all lacking in her male counterparts—save the day for Israel. Her use of deceit, and specifically of her sexuality, will seem offensive to modern sensitivities. For the author it is the opposite.[40] Judith wisely chooses the weapon in her arsenal that is appropriate to her enemy's weakness. She plays his game, knowing that he will lose. In so doing she makes fools out of a whole army of men and humiliates their general.

These facts notwithstanding, some feminist scholars argue that in this story Judith remains a woman in a male-dominated world, "who liberated neither herself nor her country-women from the status quo of the biblical gender ideology."[41] For the author to bring closure to the story, this dangerous female character must retire from the public arena and spend the rest of her life in her deceased husband's house and, after she dies, be laid to rest in her husband's burial cave (16:21-24). Only in this way can she "be tolerated, domesticated, and even treasured by Israelite society," which is by definition patriarchal.[42] Clearly the author was not a feminist in any modern sense of the word. Yet one may ask: why did this author, who lived in what was admittedly a patriarchal society, create a female protagonist, describe her as a savior who delivered Israel from mortal danger—as did Moses, other male heroes in the books of Judges and 1 Samuel, and Judas Maccabeus (see below)—and then sideline her at the end? The issues are complex and will continue to be debated.

The book of Judith is patently fiction, abounding in anachronisms and historical and geographical inaccuracies and absurdities.[43] Nebuchadnezzar is introduced as king of the Assyrians (1:1), who makes war on Israel *after* their return from the exile (5:18-19; 4:3). The story combines features of a number of biblical stories,[44] and Judith is the personification of several Israelite heroines: Miriam (Exod 15:20-21), Deborah and Jael (Judg 4–5),[45] the woman of Thebez (Judg 9:53-54), and the woman of Abel-beth-maacah (2 Sam 20:14-22). Her deed also recalls the story of David and Goliath (1 Sam 17:12-54),[46] and the book of Judith as a whole is a kind of reversal of the story of the rape of Dinah (Jdt 9:2-4, 8-10; cf. Gen 34).[47]

By conflating biblical characters and events, the author presents a condensation of Israelite history that has a parabolic quality.[48] It demonstrates how the God of Israel has acted—and continues to act—in history, and the confrontation between this God and Nebuchadnezzar/Holofernes is even reminiscent of the dualistic antagonism that characterizes some apocalyptic literature, though Judith is in no way an apocalyptic work.[49] Its parabolic character is also evident in the way in which it provides models for proper and improper human actions and reactions vis-à-vis this God. The God of Judith is the deliverer of God's people, yet remains sovereign and *not obligated* to act in their behalf (8:15-17). In moments of evident defeat this God tests the faith of God's people (8:25-27). The citizens of Bethulia and Judith exemplify, respectively, those who fail the test and she who passes it. Judith's activism is noteworthy. She does not passively await direct divine intervention. Her appeal to the activism of "my father Simeon" is reminiscent of 1 Maccabees 2:24-26, which cites Phinehas as a paradigm for Mattathias's activist zeal, and of the laudatory descriptions of Levi's participation in the slaughter at Shechem in Testament of Levi 2–6 and Jubilees 30.

Alongside its exposition of a view of God, the book of Judith as a religious text evinces considerable interest in matters relating to divine law, the Torah. Numerous narrative details depict Judith and the people faithfully adhering to the commandments of God as, doubtless, they were construed according to the halakah that was accepted in the author's own time and community. Fasting and morning rituals, dietary rules, ablutions, and morning and evening prayer are important constituents of this author's portrayal of his characters' piety.[50] Perhaps the most striking reference to religious practice is the conversion of Achior (14:10). Not only is this our earliest reference to a formal practice of accepting proselytes, but the convert belongs to one of the nations that the Torah forbade entrance into the people of Israel (Deut 23:3).[51]

Before considering the function(s) of the book, we must discuss its possible date. Because Judith is fiction, attempts to date it are tenuous, depending as they do upon the identification of events in the book with other events in real history. These events are usually sought in the late Persian period or in the wars of Judas Maccabeus.[52]

Several considerations indicate undeniable influence from the Persian period.[53] Holofernes and Bagoas have the same names as one of the generals of Artaxerxes III and his eunuch. Events in the story are paralleled in Artaxerxes' campaign against Phoenicia, Syria, and Egypt in 353 B.C.E.[54] and in the Satraps' Revolt during the reign of Artaxerxes II, which revolt spread across the western part of the Persian Empire. Many items in Judith reflect the sociohistorical situation during the Persian period.[55]

At the same time the story of Judith has striking similarities to the time of Judas Maccabeus.[56] Nebuchadnezzar may be understood as a figure for Antiochus IV.[57] The predominance of Holofernes tallies well with the presence of a number of Syrian generals in Palestine during the Maccabean uprising. The defeat of a vastly superior invading army parallels Judas's defeat of the Syrians. Especially noteworthy are the similarities between this story and Judas's defeat of Nicanor.[58] Although the setting of Judith is shortly after the return from the exile (4:3), the book speaks not of the rebuilding of the temple but of the consecration of the vessels, the altar, and the temple after their profanation. The similarity to Judas's consecration of the temple is noteworthy (1 Macc 4:36-51). Furthermore, Nicanor's subsequent threat against the temple, his defeat and decapitation, and the public display of his head in Jerusalem all find remarkable counterparts in the story of Judith (1 Macc 7:33-50).

If we accept a date in Hasmonean times, we can explain two of the patently unhistorical features of the book. The designation of Nebuchadnezzar (= Antiochus) as an Assyrian would correspond to the identification of the Assyria of biblical prophecy with Syria in some of the biblical interpretation of this period.[59] A deliberate allusion to events in the Maccabean wars would explain why the author has described a postexilic threat against the temple (5:12; 9:8) by a general of a preexilic king. Nicanor's defeat was significant enough to be commemorated in an annual celebration (1 Macc 7:48-49; 2 Macc 15:36).

Neither the connections with the Persian period nor the similarities to the Maccabean wars can be easily dismissed as coincidence. Perhaps we can best solve the problem of dating by suggesting that a tale that originated in the Persian period has been rewritten in Hasmonean times. The setting in Bethulia may indicate that the story was composed in Samaria near Dothan.[60] Alternatively, the prominence of a Samaritan location in a book whose action features the deliverance of the temple in Judean Jerusalem might indicate a time of composition after John Hyrcanus brought Samaria under his control.[61]

The function of the book of Judith can be related, first, to its Hasmonean dating. It is a strongly nationalistic text that celebrates God's victories over the Syrians. The name "Judith" itself may be a personification of Judea, while at the same time resonating with the name of the great Maccabean warrior who liberated the temple and then defeated and beheaded Nicanor, thus protecting the newly consecrated temple from destruction.

Judith's speech, at the heart of the book, suggests that the work has a didactic function.

In its literary context, this formal exposition of the ways of God and exhortation to act accordingly are addressed to the rulers of Bethulia. As the speech is read, however, the reader is addressed. At one point in her song Judith speaks like the mother of her people (16:5).[62] As such she also addresses the reader. The parabolic nature of the book reinforces Judith's message, placing events in the Maccabean time in the broader context of Israelite history. As God has recently acted, God will continue to act. Moreover, Judith's Torah piety sets an example to be followed.

The didactic character of the book suggests connections with the wisdom tradition. In the broad outlines of its plot and in certain particulars, Judith parallels some of the narrative wisdom literature that we discussed in chapter 1. Judith is "wise" (8:29; 11:8, 20-21). The story is reminiscent of Daniel 3. Speaking in the name of Nebuchadnezzar, Holofernes challenges the power of Israel's God to deliver God's people from the king's hand (Jdt 6:3; cf. Dan 3:15). As the spokeswoman of that God, Judith maintains that God has the power to save and will do so if God so chooses (Jdt 8:15-17; cf. Dan 3:17-18). Trusting in her God, she makes herself the test case. In the end Bagoas must acknowledge that Nebuchadnezzar has been defeated in the contest (Jdt 14:18; cf. Dan 3:28).

In several respects Judith is also reminiscent of Tobit. Each protagonist is depicted as a genuine Israelite (Tob 1:1; Jdt 8:1) whose piety is exemplary and beyond the call of duty. Like Tobit, the Israelites in Judith are brought from expressions of despair to the praise of the God who has delivered them. Both books end with a hymn and reference to the death of the protagonist, and both appropriate material from a wide variety of biblical narratives (see above).[63]

Long after it was excluded from the canon of the Hebrew Bible, the story of Judith continued as a living part of Jewish haggadic tradition.[64]

1 Maccabees

First Maccabees recounts the history of Israel from the Hellenistic reform to the death of Simon the Hasmonean. Different from the pseudonymous apocalypses that we have discussed in the last chapter and the fictional book of Judith, 1 Maccabees is straightforward historical narrative. Together with 2 Maccabees it constitutes our main source material for the history of Israel in the mid-second century B.C.E. Being a historian rather than a chronicler, this author *interprets* the events he recounts. His purpose is to defend the legitimacy of the Hasmonean high priestly dynasty by showing how the family of Mattathias delivered the Jews from the persecution, liberated Jerusalem and its temple, reimposed the rule of the Torah, and brought the nation to an era of peace and political independence.

Although 1 Maccabees is a work of history, careful rhetorical analysis indicates that its author has arranged his material with considerable literary artistry. The first two of three sections reveal a chiastic structure.[65]

Section 1

A 1:1-10 Alexander the Great dies; Antiochus IV is introduced

  B 1:11-15 Renegade Jews seek to join with the Gentiles around them

    C 1:16-64 The temple is desecrated by the Greeks

      D 2:1-70 Mattathias urges his sons to rebel

        E 3:1-26 Judas leads the Jewish revolt

      D' 3:27—4:35 Antiochus IV seeks to quell the Jewish revolt

    C' 4:36-61 The temple is liberated and rededicated by the Jews

  B' 5:1-68 Righteous Jews defeat the Gentiles around them

A' 6:1-17 Antiochus IV dies

Section 2

A 6:18—7:50 The Jews obtain freedom of religion

  B 8:1-32 The Jews make a treaty with Rome

    C 9:1—10:66 Jonathan rises to power

    C' 10:67—11:74 Jonathan maintains his powerful status

  B' 12:1-23 The Jews renew their treaty with Rome

A' 12:24—14:15 Simon liberates the citadel and obtains independence

Section 3 of the book (14:45—16:24) recounts events in the high priesthood of Simon and the transmittal of his high priesthood to his son John Hyrcanus I, albeit without the chiastic structure evident in the first two parts. Space does not permit a detailed exposition of this fine-tuned literary analysis. Instead we shall track the events as they move across the careers of Mattathias, Judas, Jonathan, and Simon, in a way that is consonant, however, with the above-described literary analysis.

Chapter 1 depicts the developing crisis in Israel. Alexander the Great, the champion of hellenization, appears on the scene. After his death and a string of successors, the villain of the piece, Antiochus Epiphanes, becomes lord of Syria Palestine (vv 1-10). A group of "lawless" Jews then set out to install Greek institutions in Jerusalem (vv 11-15). Following a raid on Egypt, Antiochus and subsequently Apollonius attack Jerusalem (vv 16-28 and 29-40) and then defile the temple, forbid the practice of the Jewish religion, and persecute those who disobey (vv 41-61). Because the Hasmoneans are to be the heroes of the piece, the author does not indicate that Antiochus's decrees are the result of pious Jewish opposition to the hellenizers.[66] He mentions Jewish resistance to the royal government only at the very end of chapter 1, when he is ready to introduce Mattathias and his sons as the ones who will turn away the "very great wrath" that has befallen Israel (vv 62-64).[67]

Chapter 2 is pivotal to the action of the book and the author's purpose. Mattathias is introduced as the father of John, Simon, Judas, Eleazar, and Jonathan (vv 2-5), whose heroics and accomplishments are the subject of chapters 3–16. In the present chapter, however, Mattathias is the main character, and his words and deeds predominate throughout. In vv 7-14 he is the spokesman of Israel's grief over its ill fortunes. In answer to the command to apostatize he rejects the officer's bribe and gives expression to the pious Jewish determination to adhere to the covenant (vv 15-22; cf. 1:63; contrast 1:15, 52). Mattathias's ideology is not pacifist, however; his zealous resistance is militant. He is likened to the priest Phinehas, whose zeal stayed God's wrath against Israel and won for him an eternal priestly covenant (vv 23-26; cf. Num 25:6-12). The author implies that Mattathias's deed has stayed God's wrath against Israel's apostasy, and his purpose is to recount the deed that was foundational for the high priestly credentials of the Hasmonean house.[68]

Only after Mattathias has issued his rallying cry to those who are zealous for the law and who support the covenant (1 Macc 2:27-28) do we hear of other Jews who flee to the wilderness (vv 29-38). The deaths of many of them in wilderness caves and their cries for heavenly vindication (vv 32-38) are reminiscent of the story of Taxo and his sons in Testament of Moses 9 (see above, p. 76). Thereafter Mattathias is depicted as the leader of a sizable resistance movement against the Syrian crown and its Jewish adherents (1 Macc 2:39-48).

In his testament at the end of the chapter (2:49-68) Mattathias duly transfers authority to his sons (vv 65-66). At the same time, he expresses his militant ideology, indicating that God exacts vengeance through human agents (vv 50, 66-68). In listing the heroes of faith, whose obedience brought them glory (vv 51-60), he both exhorts his sons to action and promises them deliverance and divine blessing, and he suggests that they will hold authority as rulers.[69] In the predictive style typical of testaments, Mattathias foretells the punishment of Antiochus and the failure of his oppressive measures (vv 61-63).

The chapter as a whole is remarkable for its many parallels, both to the story of Taxo and to the story of the seven brothers and their mother in 2 Maccabees 7 (see below, pp. 108–9 Each of the three stories relates in its own way what it considers to be the event that turns the course of history in this particular situation. First Maccabees 2 is unique and remarkable both for its militant ideology and for the special status that it grants to a historically identifiable person—the patriarch Mattathias.

The succession announced by Mattathias becomes fact when his son Judas "arises in his place [Gk. *anti*]" (3:1) as the leader of his brothers and of his father's followers (3:2). The author then devotes 40 percent of his history to an account of the exploits of Judas. This major part of the book is framed by a poem in praise of Judas as a warrior par excellence (3:3-9) and by this epilogue:

Now the rest of the acts of Judas, and his wars and the brave deeds that he did, and his greatness, have not been recorded, for they were very many. (9:22)[71]

These passages notwithstanding, our author does not simply sing the praises of a great hero. Judas's victories are possible only through divine help. He enters battle with prayer (3:46; 4:30-33; 5:33; 7:30-42) and celebrates victory by praising God (4:24, 33, 55). His exhortations to his army remind them of other times in the past when God supported

Israel against overwhelming odds (4:8-9, 30; 7:41). "It is not on the size of the army that victory in battle depends, but strength comes from heaven" (3:18-19). Some of the descriptions of Judas's wars make clear that he was following the ancient practices of holy warfare.[72] Our author believes that through Judas "the savior of Israel" (9:21) God "the savior of Israel" (4:30) delivered God's people.

When Judas dies in battle "the lawless" rise to power in Israel (9:23-27). Judas's friends approach Jonathan and ask him to fight in their behalf (9:28-31), and so he takes the leadership and arises "in the place of [Gk. *anti*] Judas his brother." The succession continues. Like his brother, Jonathan is a mighty warrior who also understands that his victory comes only through the help of heaven (9:43-46; 11:71; 12:15). Our author depicts Jonathan functioning as a ruler, like the judges of old (9:73),[73] and the sword ceases in Israel during this time. Although "lawless men" try to discredit him, he is vindicated in the eyes of the monarchs, Alexander and Demetrius (10:61; 11:21-27), and the land is quiet (11:38, 52). Of special importance for our author is Jonathan's appointment as high priest, and he notes the date on which he was invested with the robes of office (10:21). In contrast to Jonathan, Alcimus the priest is consistently depicted as a scoundrel who finally reaps the just rewards of his wicked deeds (7:9-25; 9:54-56).

When Jonathan is captured, Simon assembles "the people" and delivers a stirring speech that is both a summary of the glorious achievements of the Hasmonean house and an exhortation that the people accept his leadership (13:3-6). The people respond by acclaiming him their leader "in the place of" (Gk. *anti*) Judas and Jonathan (13:8-9). Thus the succession passes to Simon. Some three years later this popular acclamation is fully legitimized by "the great assembly of the priests and the people and the rulers of the nation and the elders of the country" (14:28). In keeping with his purpose the author preserves the full text of this decree, which rehearses the great deeds of the Hasmonean house and of Simon in particular (14:27-45). Thus he draws attention to the event toward which, in his opinion, the whole history of the period has been moving: the establishment of the Hasmonean house as the legitimate seat of the Jewish high priesthood and as the ruling dynasty in Israel. The author is quick to point out that the honors heaped on Simon were well deserved, and he lists the Hasmonean prince's accomplishments in considerable detail (13:33-53). Not least among these was the ushering in of a time of peace, which is described in a poetic passage that may well date from the reign of Simon (14:4-15). It is virtually a pastiche of biblical allusions, and it suggests that some of Simon's contemporaries believed that for all intents and purposes the messianic age had arrived. At the very least the poem attributes to Simon's era some of the glories of the Davidic and Solomonic age and the fulfillment of some of the hopes awaited in the golden age of the future. In context the poem, with its description of peace, stands in striking contrast to the description of Judas's warlike deeds in 3:3-9. Perhaps the author wished to frame the body of his work with two passages that would dramatize the progress made during these thirty years.

Although this history of the Hasmoneans reaches its climax with the reign of Simon, there remains a final act of succession. Simon appoints his two sons, John and Judas, to fight for their nation in the place of (*anti*) him and his brother (16:1-3). There follows the story of the treacherous assassination of Simon and his sons, Judas and Mattathias (16:11-17), and the mantle of leadership falls on John Hyrcanus. His deeds are only alluded to (16:23-24), partly because they have already been recorded, but also because the author has accomplished his purpose. He has recorded the history of the founding, the succession, and the establishment of the Hasmonean house, and he has documented its legitimacy by royal decree, popular acclaim, and the attestation of the God who has worked the divine purposes through the Hasmonean family and its early heroes. He has told the story of "the family of those men through whom deliverance was given to Israel" (5:62). Thereby he has proclaimed the gospel according to the Hasmoneans.

The reference to the chronicles of John Hyrcanus's high priesthood (16:23-24) suggests that 1 Maccabees was written after his death.[74] The favorable references to the Romans in chapter 8; 12:1-4; 14:24, 40; and 15:15-24 give no hint that Rome would later be the invader and overlord of Israel. Thus a date between 104 and 63 B.C.E. is probable. First Maccabees was very likely composed during the reign of Alexander Janneus, perhaps as propaganda against opponents of the Hasmoneans—including the Pharisees and the Essenes (see below, pp. 121, 124, 130). The book was composed in Hebrew and has been preserved in manuscripts of the Greek Bible and some of its daughter translations.[75]

2 Maccabees

Second Maccabees is a condensation of a five-volume history of Israel during the years 180–161 B.C.E., composed by one Jason of Cyrene. In his prologue the anonymous epitomizer describes Jason's work in a way that tallies well with the emphases and scope of 2 Maccabees (2:19-23).[76] For that reason, and because the epitomizer claims no originality in his work, we can view 2 Maccabees as a unified whole, without attempting to distinguish between Jason's work and the epitomizer's abridgment.

Second Maccabees supplements 1 Maccabees by providing our only detailed account of the situation just before and during the hellenizing of Jerusalem (chaps. 3–5). At the same time, different from 1 Maccabees, the history ends when Judas has defeated Nicanor and secured the city (chaps. 14–15||1 Macc 7). Four major elements color the author's exposition. First, he shapes his account according to a Deuteronomic scheme. Second, many and perhaps most of the events that he recounts are explicitly related to the Jerusalem temple and its fate. Third, of the members of the Hasmonean family, we hear almost exclusively of Judas Maccabeus. Fourth, the author delights in "playing strongly upon the emotions of the reader with vivid portrayals of atrocities and heroism and manifestations of divine power and with the copious use of sensational language and rhetoric, especially when presenting the feelings of the characters."[77] We can outline the book as follows:

As can be seen in C.1–5 of the outline, the author employs the same Deuteronomic scheme that governs the apocalyptic recitation of these events in Jubilees 23:16-31 and Testament of Moses 5, 8–10 (see above, pp. 72–73, 75). This scheme of sin and divine retribution is also the context of the author's frequent moralizing comments (3:1; 4:16-17, 26, 38, 42; 5:10, 19-20; 6:12-16; 15:32-33). Integral to his use of this scheme are the status and fate of the temple.

The peace and prosperity of Jerusalem and the Gentiles' high regard for the temple during the days of Onias III are attributed to the fact that the "laws were very well observed because of the piety of the high priest" (3:1-3). The angelic attack against Heliodorus demonstrates how God protects the temple as long as God's people are obedient (3:39; cf. 5:18). It is the first of a number of "manifestations" (Gk. *epiphaneia*) that illustrate divine intervention in the affairs of Israel. As told it draws the reader into an emotional involvement in the incident and the characters' various responses to it.

In his extensive account of hellenization in Jerusalem the author stresses that Israel or its leaders have forsaken the covenant and violated the laws (4:7, 11-15, 25, 34, 39, 50; 5:6). Herein lies the reason for the disaster that subsequently befalls the nation. Antiochus is the agent of God's judgment (5:17-18), and because the temple has been a principal site of the hellenizers' sin (4:14, 32, 42), judgment falls swiftly on the house of the Lord (5:15-20; 6:2-5). In 6:12-17 the author pauses to remind his readers that Israel is still God's people, subject to divine discipline but never to utter destruction. God will yet have mercy.[78]

The account of the martyrs' deaths in 6:18—7:42 is both the climax of the account of

Antiochus's cruelty (again told with typical emotional force) and the turning point in the historical drama. The paradox evident in Jubilees 23 and the Testament of Moses (see above, pp. 72, 76) is again present. The persecution is punishment for Israel's sins (7:18); nonetheless, these martyrs are put to death precisely because they refuse to capitulate to sin (6:27, 30; 7:2, 9, 11, 23, 37). This obedience to the Torah and these innocent deaths, together with the prayer of Judas and his companions (8:2-4), are instrumental in reversing Israel's dire circumstances. The brothers and their mother believe and confess that God will again have mercy on the people. As evidence they refer to what "Moses declared in his song" (7:6), quoting Deuteronomy 32:36, which describes God's salvation in the final part of the historical scheme. The last brother appeals to God that with these deaths God would show mercy and bring the divine wrath to an end (7:37-38). This is also the gist of the prayer in 8:2-4.

A comparison with Testament of Moses 9 and 1 Maccabees 2 indicates that we have here yet another version of the same story.[79] Each instance recounts the event that the respective author interprets as the catalyst that turns God's wrath from Israel and brings release from the persecution. Each is a story about parent and sons who are ready to die rather than transgress the Torah. The Testament of Moses, written in the heat of persecution, anticipates a cosmic denouement in which God will avenge the innocent blood of God's servants, notably Taxo and his sons. The Deuteronomic scheme of the Testament of Moses turns on this author's interpretation of Deuteronomy 32:43 (T. Mos. 9:7; 10:2). For the pro-Hasmonean author of 1 Maccabees, Mattathias's zealous deed stays God's wrath (cf. Num 25:8, 11). The Maccabean victories are an answer to the dying patriarch's appeal to execute judgment on the Syrians (1 Macc 2:66-68; cf. Deut 32:43). The version of the story in 2 Maccabees 7 takes cognizance of the fact that it was Judas Maccabeus who turned back the Syrian armies and brought deliverance to Israel. Although Taxo's prediction has not been fulfilled as stated, our author nevertheless espouses in part the ideology of the Testament of Moses. The innocent deaths of the martyrs and their appeal for vengeance before and after death (7:37; 8:3) contribute to turn God's wrath to mercy (8:5) and facilitate the Maccabean victories that are recounted through the rest of the book.

Thus the final act of the historical drama unfolds. True to the brothers' predictions (7:17, 19, 31, 35-37), Antiochus is struck down by divine judgment and is forced to confess the only God (chap. 9). The temple is regained, purified, and rededicated (10:1-8). Nicanor's final onslaught against it is foiled (chaps. 14–15), and the people sing praises to the God "who has kept his place undefiled" (15:34). The story has come full circle. Divine blessing has returned to Israel, and the sanctuary is once more secure.

Not only does our author depict God's judgment on the sins of Israel and the arrogance of Antiochus, but he also treats the theological problem of the unjust deaths of the martyrs. God will undo these violent and unjust deaths by raising the dead to life.[80] This theme of judgment is carried in the speeches of three of the brothers and their mother (7:9, 11, 14, 23). The brothers are tried and condemned for violating the king's command. Their civil disobedience is synonymous with their obedience to the divine law. At the resurrection their disobedience of the king's law will be vindicated in the divine court because they have obeyed the law of the "king of the world" (7:9). Theirs will be a bodily resurrection (7:10-11)—an appropriate remedy for their bodily tortures. God will heal what Antiochus has hurt; he will bring to life those whom Antiochus has killed.[81] What God created, God will re-create—in spite of the king's attempt to destroy it (7:22-23, 28-29; cf. 14:37-46).[82] The treatment of resurrection in this story has its roots in the theology of Second Isaiah. The theme of suffering and vindication draws on a traditional interpretation of Isaiah 52–53. Antiochus's arrogance and punishment, depicted in 2 Maccabees 9 in terms of Isaiah 14 (cf. above, pp. 79, 81), were also drawn from that tradition (see below, pp. 207–8). The mother represents Second Isaiah's Mother Zion, who awaits the return of her dispersed sons (2 Macc 7:17-29; cf. Isa 49:14-23; 54:1-8.; 60:4-9), and her language reflects the interpretation of Second Isaiah in Baruch 4:17-29 (see above, p. 96). The description of resurrection as new creation has its roots in Second Isaiah's theology of creation and redemption (Isa 43:1-2, 6-7; 44:1-2; 46:3-4). Thus the prophet's announcement of return from exile is here reinterpreted as deliverance and vindication in spite of death.

For a world of scholarship that (necessarily) creates tidy categories and distinctions in order to bring some order to the chaotic array of evidence that comes to us from the ancient world, 2 Maccabees is a refreshing example of a text that muddies the waters and breaks the stereotypes. Although the author clearly distinguishes between Jews and Gentiles and sees hellenization as a major sin committed by certain Jews, different from the author of 1 Maccabees, he allows for the existence of "good" Gentiles.[83] Despite his opposition to hellenization, he writes in the idiom of Greek literary genres,[84] even if—to compound the problem— there is no consensus as to the genre of his composition.[85] The Hellenistic literary character of his book notwithstanding, the author expounds a view of bodily resurrection that has often been associated with Semitic rather than Greek thought.[86] Although males play a major role in the action of the book and the author's society was doubtless "patriarchal," the dominant figure in the pivotal story in the book is a woman, who urges her sons to obey the Torah and whose own martyrdom is counterpoised to that of the scribe Eleazar, as well as the deaths of her sons (6:18—7:42).[87]

The purpose of the author of 1 Maccabees should be sought in three of the book's main features mentioned above. Mattathias the Hasmonean patriarch is never mentioned, and the story of the brothers and their mother is his version of 1 Maccabees 2 and its functional equivalent. When the exploits of Judas are mentioned, the central figures are never "Judas and his brothers," as in the early chapters of 1 Maccabees, but instead the more vague "Judas [or Maccabeus] and those with him." Jonathan is mentioned only once (8:22). Simon is referred to on two other occasions, both times in a bad light (10:20; 14:15-18). For 2 Maccabees, *the* Hasmonean hero is Judas (15:30).[88] The narrative ends before his death, and we never hear of the accomplishments of Jonathan and Simon. In view of the author's intense interest in temple and priesthood, and his emphasis on Judas as the deliverer of the temple, his silence about Jonathan and Simon may well indicate that he was opposed to the Hasmonean high priesthood.[89] This need not mean that his version of the story was intended to set straight what he considered to be the distortions of the account related in 1 Maccabees.[90] We should look more broadly:

> It is primarily temple propaganda—the defense of the temple and its surroundings by the patron deity. . . . By downplaying the heroism of the Maccabean family, by upgrading the role of the pious observers of the Law, and by placing God as the truly decisive actor in the divine drama, the author provides his readers with the proper religious perspective from which they can assess their present leaders.[91]

The Deuteronomic scheme provides the framework within which to see how this piety and God's reward of it are played out. The anti-Hasmonean tone of the work and its favorable view toward the Romans suggest that it was likely composed during the reign of Alexander Janneus.[92]

Second Maccabees and its source, the history of Jason, were composed in Greek. Two letters addressed to Jews in Egypt have been prefixed to 2 Maccabees. Their exhortation to celebrate the Feast of Dedication and the second letter's emphasis on God's accreditation of the Second Temple may be covert polemics against the Jewish temple that Onias IV built in Leontopolis in Egypt.[93]

The Epistle of Enoch (1 Enoch 92–105)[94]

Writing in the name of Enoch, this author has composed an epistle[95] that is ostensibly addressed to Enoch's children but is in fact directed to the author's own contemporaries—"the future generations that will practice righteousness and peace" (92:1; cf. 1:1-2; 37:2). On the basis of his revealed knowledge of the heavenly realm, he assures his readers that God's imminent judgment will bring vindication and eternal blessing to the righteous and swift punishment to their powerful oppressors. Thus, although the times are troubled, he can exhort the righteous to faith, steadfastness, and joy.

After the usual superscription that identifies the author and addressees (92:1), an initial comforting exhortation typical of these chapters (92:2), and a brief scenario of the coming salvation (92:3-5), the author has Enoch recite the Apocalypse of Weeks (93:1-10 + 91:11-17)[96] that is based on a threefold appeal to revelation (i.e., through a heavenly vision, the interpreting words of the angels, and the contents of the heavenly tablets, 93:2). The ancient sage summarizes world history from his time to the *eschaton*, employing a scheme of ten periods of uneven length called "weeks." The historical survey focuses on "the chosen of eternity" and "the plant of righteousness" (93:2). Initially this means Israel sprung from Abraham (93:5). Running through the apocalypse from its beginning is the countermotif of wickedness, often construed as violence, deceit, and apostasy (93:4, 8, 9; 91:11 [Aramaic]).[97] These are met by God's judgment in the flood and the exile, although an occasional righteous person is delivered (Noah and Elijah, 93:4, 8). History reaches its climax in the seventh week, which is the author's own time. God has pruned the plant of righteousness to a remnant of the chosen. These constitute the author's "group," which is endowed with revealed, sevenfold (i.e., complete) wisdom—that is, the contents of the author's message and perhaps much of the rest of the Enochic corpus. They will function as "witnesses of righteousness" and will be instrumental in uprooting the counterstructure of deceit (93:10 [Aramaic]). In the eighth week they will execute judgment against their oppressors. A second judgment will destroy all the grossly wicked, and the rest of humanity will turn to righteousness (91:14; cf. 10:21). With the *earth* thus purged of evil and the eschatological temple built (91:13), God will judge the rebel angels and renew the *heavens* and its luminaries (91:15-17).

Following the apocalypse is a prose section (only partly preserved) that meditates on the uniqueness of the revelation that Enoch has received (93:11-14). A comparison of 93:11 with Deuteronomy 5:26 indicates that an idea originally referring to Israel as a whole (they alone heard God's voice) is applied here to Enoch and the private recipients of his special knowledge.

A few verses of two-ways instruction (94:1-5; see above, pp. 139–40) provide a transition to the main section of the Epistle (94:6—104:8), which spells out (by condemnation) the way of wickedness that "sinners" pursue and encourages "the righteous" to be steadfast in the sure hope of vindication.

This central part of the Epistle divides into six discourses (94:6—96:3; 96:4—98:8; 98:9—99:10; 99:11—100:6; 100:7—102:3; 102:4—104:8).[98] The content of these discourses is embodied almost entirely in three literary forms that are well known from the biblical tradition, especially from the prophets.[99] All three feature the theme of the coming judgment. The woe (a distich in its simplest form) juxtaposes in its two major components the paradox that one experiences injustice in one's life and yet believes in divine judgment. The first part of the woe describes the sinners' misdeeds, and the second part announces the coming judgment that is the cause for the lament "Woe!" that introduces the form.

> Woe to you who repay your neighbor with evil;
> for you will be repaid according to your deeds. (95:5)

Collectively, the indictments in these woes provide a description of the author's world. The charges against the sinners are of two types. The first (attested esp. in 98:8—99:10) are religious strictly speaking. The sinners are guilty of idolatry (99:7) and of consuming blood (98:11), of blasphemy (94:9; 96:7) and cursing (95:4). Others among them disregard and pervert divine law as the righteous ("the wise") understand it (99:2; 98:9; 99:14), and as false teachers they "lead many astray" (98:15).[100] Most often, however, the misdeeds that the author attributes to the sinners are social in nature. The rich and powerful sinners abuse the righteous poor. They build sumptuous houses at the expense of others (94:6-7; 99:13), banquet in luxury while they make the righteous suffer (96:5-6), hoard wealth and food (97:8-9), parade about in fine clothes and jewelry (98:1-3), and perjure themselves (95:6). In the judgment the security they have sought in their riches will be suddenly undermined.[101]

The exhortations embody the same paradox as the woes. In their first line they call the righteous to courage, faith, and hope in their present troubled circumstances in view of the sinners' coming judgment described in the second line:

> Fear not the sinners, O righteous;
>> for the Lord will again deliver them into your hands,
>> so that you may execute judgment on them as you wish. (95:3)

The participation of the righteous in the judgment is reminiscent of the description of the eighth week in 91:12, and the phraseology reflects holy-war contexts in Numbers 21:34, Deuteronomy 3:2, and Joshua 8:1. A second kind of exhortation calls for courage in the face of present calamity (first part) on the basis of a promise of vindication and eternal life for the righteous (second part):

> Be of good courage, for you were formerly worn out through afflictions and
>> tribulations;
>> but now you will shine as the luminaries of heaven. (104:2)

The introductory words of these exhortations, as well as the frequent conclusions of the woes, "You will have no peace," are reminiscent of the language of Second Isaiah.

Descriptions of the judgment or events leading up to it are the third major form in these chapters. Generally introduced by the adverbial expressions "then" or "in those days," they call to mind parallel passages in the prophetic books.

The author's use of forms familiar from the prophets suggests that he is presenting his message as revelation. The impression is strengthened by his use of formulas that elsewhere introduce revelations and especially forecasts of the future: "Know!" "Be it known!" "I say to you." Stronger yet is the oath formula "I swear to you." References to happenings in the heavenly realm also presume Enoch's claim to revelation (97:6; 98:6-8).[102]

The main section of the Epistle reaches its climax in 102:4—104:8, which takes the form of a disputation about the existence or nonexistence of retribution, that is, the judgment that has been the Epistle's main subject. In each of the four parts of this disputation the author addresses a particular group, quotes certain words about or by them, and then refutes these words with an appeal to revelation. The first part is an expanded exhortation addressed to the righteous dead (102:4—103:4). In spite of the claims of the sinners, the sad lot of the righteous in life, their grievous death, and their lamentable existence in Sheol do not belie divine justice. Enoch reveals a mystery he has read on the "heavenly tablets." The spirits of the righteous will come to life, and they will receive all the good things that they missed in life and that (according to the next part) the sinners had enjoyed in theirs. The second part is an expanded woe addressed to the dead sinners (103:5-8). It asserts the converse of the first part. The sinners, prosperous and happy in life and honored in their death, face an intensified and eternal form of the miseries that the righteous had experienced in their lives.

In the third and fourth parts of the dispute (103:9—104:6; 104:7-8) the author refutes words the living righteous and sinners speak about themselves. The righteous complain that they are experiencing the covenantal curses described in Deuteronomy 28 (103:9-15).[103] Again citing his knowledge of the heavenly realm, the author assures them that their frustrated cries for vindication have been heard in heaven, that their oppressors will be judged, and that they themselves have a blessed heavenly existence awaiting them (104:1-6). To the wicked who claim that their sins are not seen he announces that the angels record their deeds, and this testimony will seal their doom on the day of judgment (104:7-8).

The Epistle closes with explicit reference to the transmission of Enoch's teaching. In the end time his books will be given to the righteous (cf. 93:10) and will be a source of wisdom, faith, and joy (104:11-13), and they will serve as a testimony to the children of earth (105:1-2). With this reference to the future generation, the paths of righteousness, and the peace that belongs to the righteous, the author returns to the themes of his superscription (92:1).

The author of the Epistle has created a symbolic universe that depicts the structure of reality in terms of a set of polar opposites. The first of these contrasts good and evil and their human embodiment in, respectively, the chosen, pious, and righteous, and the sinners, godless, and wicked. The second contrasts what is, or seems to be (present injustice) with what ought to be (justice) or really is (God's seeing eye and hearing ear) or what will come to be (final judgment). In the final judgment, the tables will be turned. The righteous and the wicked will get their just deserts, which means for each the reversal of their present situation.

In the kind of situation it presumes, the message it conveys, and the purpose for which it was written, the Epistle resembles other apocalyptic writings. The author exhorts his readers to steadfastness on the basis of a revealed message about an imminent judgment that will remove oppression and adjudicate injustice. This work shares with the apocalypses we have treated the claim that it is an ancient writing intended for latter-day readers. It differs from them in form, however. Although it contains a brief, sketchy apocalypse, as a whole it is not an ordered account of events to come, but an extended exhortation based on such knowledge of the future.

Certain aspects of the Epistle of Enoch are reminiscent of the Qumran literature. In its movement toward the formation of the chosen community of the end time constituted by revelation, the Apocalypse of Weeks is similar to column 1 of the *Damascus Document* (see below, p. 123).[104] Reference to false teachers and halakic disputes also have parallels in the Scrolls. However, the author of the Epistle does not specify the exact nature of these disputes. It is best to suggest that this writing, or parts of it, may have emanated from a sectarian group that was somehow related to the Qumran community or its ancestors. The broader context of the Enochic literature, with its emphasis on the solar calendar and possible allusions to irregularities in the Jerusalem priesthood (see above, pp. 51, 86), may indicate yet a closer relationship.

Contrasting these chapters with Ben Sira's admonitions about the problematic nature of wealth, scholars have tended to date the Epistle to the late Hasmonean period and to detect in it polemical references to the excesses of Alexander Janneus or perhaps John Hyrcanus.[105] The suggestion should be adopted with caution. Although the tension between rich and poor appears to be much sharper here than in the Wisdom of Ben Sira,[106] the two writings have very different settings. Ben Sira addresses the rich, admonishing them to use their wealth responsibly. That a group of the poor living in Ben Sira's time could have perceived the actions of the wealthy as "Enoch" does and might have cursed the rich among themselves as he does is certainly possible. Hence the date of these chapters remains in question. One piece of external evidence may indicate an earlier date for these chapters. Writing around 169 B.C.E.,[107] the author of Jubilees recounts the written works of Enoch (Jub. 4:17-19). Prominent in this list is reference to Enoch's testimony and testifying. This language is most closely paralleled in 1 Enoch 81:5—82:2; 91:3; 104:11-13; 105:1. If the last two passages were part of the original epistle, and the first two, part of the redactional framework that connected the Epistle to the first chapters of 1 Enoch (see below), then the Epistle may have been written early in the second century B.C.E.[108]

POSSIBLE STAGES IN THE LITERARY DEVELOPMENT OF 1 ENOCH

The growth of the components of 1 Enoch into a corpus of texts constitutes a literary puzzle. Our earliest evidence comes from Qumran.[109] Among the eleven manuscripts of the Aramaic text, the Book of Luminaries (chaps. 72–82) is always written on its own, separate scroll. The Book of Parables (chaps. 37–71) appears not to have been known at Qumran. One manuscript (4QEn^g) contains a bit of chapter 91 and parts of chapters 92–94. Yet another scroll (4QEn^c) seems to have contained chapters 1–36, 85–90, at least the end of the Epistle, and chapters 106–107.

Qumran manuscript c provides no evidence what literary shape or the rationale of this collection may have been. However, the Ethiopic text of 1 Enoch may provide some indications and remnants of such a rationale. Chapters 81:1—82:3 contain a block of narrative that describes Enoch's return from his cosmic journeys and his testamentary instruction to his sons. This narrative has elements in common with the accounts of his journeys in chapters 1–36 and with the Epistle, but little in common with its present context in the Book of Luminaries.[110] In addition, this testamentary narrative finds its natural complement and sequel in chapter 91, which immediately precedes the Epistle in 1 Enoch and in the Aramaic 4QEn^g. From this, we may hypothesize that chapters 1–36, the Dream Visions (chaps. 85–90), and the Epistle were shaped into a literary unity as a testamentary collection of Enochic writings. Since chapters 81–82 are found neither in this Qumran manuscript nor in the Qumran manuscripts of the Book of Luminaries, it is uncertain at what point the collection might have taken on such a testamentary shape. However, the juxtaposition of chapter 91 and the Epistle in 4QEn^g is suggestive, since its initial words, "And now my son Methuselah," presuppose some sort of prior narrative context.

The following elements in these chapters suggest the outline of such a collection: Enoch ascends to heaven and visits the cosmos, learning the secrets of both. These journeys culminate in his meeting with Uriel (chap. 33) and his viewing of the heavenly tablets (81:1; cf. 80:1 and the reference to Uriel). After he has blessed God (81:3; cf. the similar blessings in chaps. 22–36) the angels return him to earth with the command that he instruct and testify to his sons. He writes his books and delivers them to Methuselah (82:1-3). Chapter 91 provides the testamentary setting for Enoch's final instructions to his children, which climaxes in the Epistle. The hypothetical testamentary collection that we are suggesting may have been modeled on Deuteronomy 31–33. The first part of the opening oracle (1 Enoch 1:1-9) echoes the introduction to Moses's final blessing in Deuteronomy 33:1-2. Chapters 81:5—82:2 + 91 parallel parts of Deuteronomy 31. The prose and poetic predictions in 91:5-10 and the Apocalypse of Weeks have counterparts in Deuteronomy 31:16-18 + 32:1ff.[111]

However one construes the details of this development, the account of Noah's birth (chaps. 106–107) was added to chapter 105. As in chapters 6–11, the flood is a type of the coming judgment and the collection ends with the promise of this salvation.[112] At some later time chapters 72–80 were inserted by attraction to 33:2-4, and then chapters 37–71 were inserted between these two. Chapter 108 was appended to form the book as we know it.

BIBLIOGRAPHY

History

Schürer, *History*, 1:164–232. Jonathan A. **Goldstein**, *1 Maccabees* (AB 41; Garden City, N.Y.: Doubleday, 1976) 168–73, chronology of the Hasmonean period through Alexander Janneus. **Gruen**, *Heritage and Hellenism*, 12–40, hellenization in the Hasmonean period. **VanderKam**, *From Joshua to Caiaphas*, 240–393, history of the Hasmonean high priests. Ehud **Netzer**, *The Palaces of the Hasmoneans and Herod the Great* (Jerusalem: Israel Exploration Society, 2001).

Baruch

Translation: The Apocrypha.
Text: Joseph **Ziegler**, ed., *Ieremias, Baruch, Threni, Epistula Ieremiae* (SVTG 15; Göttingen: Vandenhoeck & Ruprecht, 1957) 450–67, critical edition of the Greek text. Emanuel **Tov**, *The Book of Baruch: Also Called 1 Baruch* (SBLTT 8; Missoula, Mont.: Scholars Press, 1975), Greek text and translation; for 1:1—3:8, a retroversion into Hebrew with linguistic parallels from the Bible.
Commentaries: J. J. **Kneucker**, *Das Buch Baruch* (Leipzig: Brock, 1879), translation, introduction, and commentary. Carey A. **Moore**, *Daniel, Esther, and Jeremiah: The Additions* (AB 44; Garden City, N.Y.: Doubleday, 1977) 55–316, translation, introduction, and commentary.

Literature: David G. Burke, *The Poetry of Baruch: A Reconstruction and Analysis of the Original Hebrew Text of Baruch 3:9—5:9* (SBLSCS 10; Chico, Calif.: Scholars Press, 1982). André Kabaselle **Mukenge**, *L'unité littéraire du livre de Baruch* (EBib 38; Paris: Gabalda, 1998). Odil Hannes **Steck**, *Das apokryphe Baruchbuch: Studien zu Rezeption und Konzentration "kanonischer" Überlieferung* (FRLANT 160; Göttingen: Vandenhoeck & Ruprecht, 1993). Emanuel **Tov**, *The Septuagint Translation of Jeremiah and Baruch* (HSM 8; Missoula, Mont.: Scholars Press, 1976).

Judith

Translation: The Apocrypha.

Texts and Other Translations: Robert **Hanhart**, ed., *Iudith* (SVTG 8/4; Göttingen: Vandenhoeck & Ruprecht, 1978), critical edition of the Greek text. Morton S. **Enslin** and Solomon **Zeitlin**, *The Book of Judith* (JAL; Leiden: Brill, 1972), introduction, Greek text, and annotated translation. Erich **Zenger**, *Historische und legendarische Erzählungen* (JSHRZ 1/6; Gütersloh: Mohn, 1981), introduction and translation.

Commentaries: Y. M. **Grintz**, *Sefer Yehudith* (Jerusalem: Bialik Institute, 1957 [Hebrew with English summary]), introduction, commentary, and retroversion into Hebrew. Carey A. **Moore**, *Judith* (AB 40; Garden City, N.Y.: Doubleday, 1985), fresh translation, introduction, and commentary.

Literature Surveys: Toni **Craven**, "The Book of Judith in the Context of Twentieth Century Studies of the Apocryphal/Deuterocanonical Books," *CurBS* 12 (2003) 187–229. See also Benedikt **Otzen**, *Tobit and Judith*, 68–142 (GAP; Sheffield: Sheffield Academic Press, 2002).

Literature: Luis **Alonso-Schöckel**, "Narrative Structures in the Book of Judith," in *Protocol of the Colloquy of the Center for Hermeneutical Studies in Hellenistic and Modern Culture* 11 (Berkeley: Graduate Theological Union, 1975) 1–20. Toni **Craven**, *Artistry and Faith in the Book of Judith* (SBLDS 70; Chico, Calif.; Scholars Press, 1983), literary, rhetorical analysis. A.-M. **Dubarle**, *Judith* (AnBib 24; 2 vols.; Rome: Biblical Institute Press, 1966), studies the Greek and Latin texts in relation to the Hebrew, traces the story through the midrashim and early Christian writers, presents texts and translations of the hypothetical Hebrew and the midrashim. Y. M. **Grintz**, "Judith, Book of," *EncJud* 10:451–61, summary of Grintz's arguments in his commentary (above), editorial addenda on Judith in the arts. Ernst **Haag**, *Studien zum Buch Judith* (TThSt 16; Trier: Paulinus, 1963). Ulrike **Mittmann-Richert**, *Einführung zu den historischen und legendarischen Erzählungen* (JSHRZ 6/1,1; Gütersloh: Gütersloher Verlagshaus, 2000) 82–96, introduction. **Otzen**, *Tobit and Judith*, 68–142, comprehensive introduction incorporating a survey of the literature. Margarita **Stocker**, *Judith, Sexual Warrior: Women and Power in Western Culture* (New Haven: Yale Univ. Press, 1998). James C. **VanderKam**, ed., *"No One Spoke Ill of Her": Essays on Judith* (SBLEJL 2; Atlanta: Scholars Press, 1992). Lawrence M. **Wills**, *The Jewish Novel in the Ancient World* (Ithaca: Cornell Univ. Press, 1995) 132–57, excellent discussion of literary issues. Paul **Winter**, "Judith, Book of," *IDB* 2:1023–26.

1 and 2 Maccabees

Translation: The Apocrypha.

Text: Werner **Kappler**, *Maccabaeorum liber*, fasc. 1 (2d ed.; SVTG 9/1; Göttingen: Vandenhoeck & Ruprecht, 1967), critical edition of the Greek text. Werner **Kappler** and Robert **Hanhart**, eds., *Maccabaeorum liber,* fasc. 2 (2d ed.; SVTG 9/2; 1976), critical edition of the Greek text.

Commentaries: F.-M. **Abel,** *Les livres des Maccabées* (EBib; Paris: Gabalda, 1949); F.-M. **Abel** and J. **Starcky,** *Les livres des Maccabées* (EBib; Paris: Cerf, 1961); Jonathan A. **Goldstein,** *1 Maccabees* (AB 41; Garden City, N.Y.: Doubleday, 1976); Jonathan A. **Goldstein,** *2 Maccabees* (AB 41a; Garden City, N.Y.: Doubleday, 1983).

Literature: Robert **Doran,** *Temple Propaganda: The Purpose and Character of 2 Maccabees* (CBQMS 12; Washington, D.C.: Catholic Biblical Association, 1981). David S. **Williams,** *The Structure of 1 Maccabees* (CBQMS 31; Washington, D.C.: Catholic Biblical Association, 1999).

1 Enoch 91–108

For relevant bibliography also pertaining to the whole of 1 Enoch see the bibliography for chapter 2.

Translation: **Nickelsburg** and **VanderKam,** *1 Enoch: A New Translation,* 137–70.

Text: Campbell **Bonner,** *The Last Chapters of Enoch in Greek* (London: Christophers, 1937), introduction and annotated text of the Greek papyrus of 1 Enoch 97:6—107:3. Frederic G. **Kenyon,** *The Chester Beatty Biblical Papyri: Descriptions and Texts of Twelve Manuscripts on Papyrus of the Greek Bible,* fasc. 8: *Enoch and Melito* (London: Walker, 1941), facsimile of the papyrus.

Commentary: **Nickelsburg,** *1 Enoch 1,* 409–560.

The **Damascus Document.** An almost complete column of an early- to mid-first-century B.C.E. Qumran Hebrew manuscript (4QD^a) containing the hitherto lost ending of the document. Photograph is courtesy of the Israel Antiquities Authority.

5

The People at Qumran and Their Predecessors

SCROLLS FROM THE DEAD SEA CAVES

Progress in the study of ancient history is sometimes due as much to accidental discovery as to painstaking scholarship. As the story is told, in the winter of 1946/1947 three Bedouin of the Taʿamireh tribe were wintering their flocks at the foot of the high limestone cliffs near the northwest shore of the Dead Sea. One of them, Jumʿa Muhammad Khalil, tossed a stone into a hole—one of the thousands that pockmark the cliffs. With an accuracy that defied aim, it shattered a ceramic jar that was embedded in the floor of the cave below. Two days later, Jumʿa's cousin, Muhammad "ed-Dhib" ("the wolf") returned looking for gold; instead he found ten large cylindrical jars and three scrolls in one of them. A few months later four more scrolls were recovered from the cave.[1] Ten other caves with scrolls were to be discovered and then archeologists would spend five seasons exploring the nearby ruins known as Khirbet Qumran.* When the dust and bat guano had settled in 1964, eleven caves had yielded nine scrolls, either complete or with large parts intact, and tens of thousands of large and small fragments from more than nine hundred Hebrew, Aramaic, and Greek manuscripts that had been inscribed between 250 B.C.E. and 68 C.E.[2]

Because they were in relatively good shape, the seven Cave 1 scrolls were published in short order. These included a complete and an incomplete text of Isaiah, a commentary on Habakkuk, a copy of a Rule of the Community, a scroll of Thanksgiving Hymns, a copy of the Rule of the War of the Sons of Light and the Sons of Darkness, and part of a long paraphrase of Genesis (the Genesis Apocryphon).* In subsequent years, an initial team of nine scholars, augmented by a few more, began to sort the fragments from the eleven caves in the vicinity of Qumran. Between 1955 and 1982 the team published parts of many texts in preliminary editions and produced definitive editions in seven volumes of the newly established series, Discoveries in the Judaean Desert, and in two other volumes. A three-volume edition of the Cave 11 Temple Scroll appeared in Hebrew in 1977 and in English in 1983.

Yet many of the forty thousand fragments from Cave 4 remained unpublished—for a variety of reasons: other academic responsibilities; lack of research funds; scholarly perfectionism; illness; but, especially, the sheer difficulty of identifying, assembling, and making sense of the masses of small fragments that constituted an unrealistic overload for the persons to whose care they had been committed.[3] Frustration mounted as a whole generation of scholars stood near the promised land waiting for access to the unpublished material. Rumors circulated and charges were hurled, alleging that scholars were protecting their pet theories or even that the Vatican was conspiring to quash documents that threatened the Christian faith. Popular authors and the media took up the cause, often without fully understanding it and without always fairly interpreting the facts. But even as the furor was mounting in the 1980s, new volumes of the Discoveries in the Judaean Desert were being completed.[4] It was the beginning of an incredible burst of scholarly energy and activity. Between 1990 and 2005 a team of around eighty scholars, which had been gradually expanded during the 1980s and 1990s, produced thirty-two folio volumes totaling more than ten thousand pages, which brought the Discoveries in the Judaean Desert just about to completion.[5]

The 664 identifiable Qumran manuscripts can be divided into three groups: every book of the traditional Hebrew Bible except Esther and Nehemiah (223 mss.); writings composed by the religious group that was resident at Qumran during the two centuries around the turn of the era (249 mss.); other Jewish religious texts from the Greco-Roman period, many of them hitherto unknown (192 mss.).[6] Many of the texts, biblical and otherwise, are attested in multiple copies: for example, 29 copies of Deuteronomy, 21 of Isaiah, and 34 of Psalms; at least 11 copies of the Rule of the Community; 11 copies of various parts of 1 Enoch, 14 copies of Jubilees, and 7 copies of an Aramaic text that purports to have been written by the patriarch Levi (see below, pp. 159–65).[7]

Scholars have employed many methods to assemble, date, and in other ways shed light on the scrolls. Parallels between the pottery found in some of the caves and in the ruins of Khirbet Qumran indicate that we should interpret the two bodies of evidence together. The dating of the pottery and coins provides a fixed chronological point for dating the scrolls. The typological development of the Hebrew, Aramaic, and Greek scripts (paleography) allows manuscripts to be dated within a generation or two, and accelerator mass spectrometry (an advanced form of carbon-14 dating) roughly confirms the paleographic dating.[8] The analysis of physical destruction patterns in the manuscripts has been greatly refined, so that one can more accurately place fragments physically and even estimate the length of a scroll and the scope of its contents.[9] DNA analysis and microscopic study of hair follicles in the leather also help in this respect. Digital imaging has produced new and more accurate readings of the texts. Developments in the analysis of archeological evidence provide new data about the material context of the community.[10]

Archeological excavations at Qumran have revealed two (some would say three) phases of Jewish occupation at the site between 100 (or 130) B.C.E. and 68 C.E., when the Roman army under Titus overran the site during the Jewish War (see below, pp. 264–65).[11] The manuscripts from Cave 4, which lies just a few hundred feet across a ravine from the ruins, appear to be the remnants of the literary collection belonging to the group that occupied Khirbet Qumran; the manuscripts from the other caves should be treated as part of the same corpus. Study of the pottery types, the architecture of the ruins, and the content of the texts shed light on the nature and identity of the Qumran group.

Since the first discoveries were announced, well over ten thousand books and articles have appeared in scores of languages, propounding almost every imaginable theory, hypothesis, and synthesis regarding the scrolls and the ruins. Nonetheless, a basic consensus exists among the large majority of those scholars who accept the validity of the archeological and paleographic evidence as it applies to the content of the scrolls. The scrolls and their material context reveal the thought, practice, and historical development of a Jewish religious group that understood itself to be exclusively the true Israel in voluntary exile. Disillusioned by the conduct of the temple cult in Jerusalem as the Hasmonean high priests presided over it in the latter part of second century B.C.E., these people retreated to the wilderness to seek and to do God's will. Informed and inspired by their leader, "the Teacher of Righteousness," they concluded that they were living at the end of the evil age, whose events had been predicted in the writings of the biblical prophets, and they claimed to possess a uniquely revealed interpretation of the Mosaic Torah, which enabled them to live in a state of high ritual purity, mingling with the angels as they awaited the imminent end of the age.

Early in scrolls research, a consensus began to emerge about the *identity* of the Qumranites.[12] They were Essenes, a Jewish group whose beliefs and practices were described by the first-century Jewish authors Philo and Josephus, and whose location near the Dead Sea was attested by the Roman author Pliny the Elder. Although this theory still commands the assent of a majority of scholars, it has been challenged in recent years, notably by Jewish scholars who have found close parallels between some of the laws in the Qumran texts and legal interpretations espoused by the Sadducees (in opposition to the Pharisees). These data, however, are probably to be explained by a common origin of the Qumranites and the Sadducees in the Zadokite priesthood.[13]

Even if the Essene identity of the Qumranites is accepted, questions remain as to the origins and history of the group.[14] Previous notions that the Essenes derived from a group called the Hasidim are problematic since the term *Hasidim* is sometimes a generic term for pious Jews and little is known about a concrete group of that name. To judge from the multiple copies of 1 Enoch, Jubilees, and the Aramaic Levi Document found among the scrolls, the Qumranites had predecessors among the authors of these texts, but the precise connections are uncertain. The scrolls have demonstrated that the sociology of Jewish groups in the Greco-Roman period was considerably more complex than Josephus's triad of Pharisees, Sadducees, and Essenes. The Qumranites were part of a substantial reform movement in second-century Judaism. Equally uncertain and disputed are the details of the sect's history. The Qumranites were only one group of Essenes. Others lived in the countryside or in villages. The Qumran sect itself appears to have splintered.

The scrolls have also shown a number of other theories and stereotypes of Jewish religion and religious thought in this period to be false.[15] Biblical manuscripts from Qumran indicate that at many points the form of the biblical text was not yet fixed. Moreover, an authoritative corpus of religious writings had not yet emerged, and some groups held writings to be sacred that others did not accept as authoritative. Interpretations of Scripture varied. "Messianic" expectations were multiform; the Jews as a uniform group did not expect one Messiah; different people had different expectations, as we shall see below and throughout this book.

Finally, the scrolls have shed new light on Christian origins.[16] Their religious language and thought patterns, their rites and community organization provide a window into the kind of Judaism that formed the seedbed of earliest Christianity. Like the Qumran community, the early church was a subgroup in Judaism constituted by eschatological revelation—in this case, proclaimed by Jesus, the apostles, and the teachers of the church. It was one of a number of eschatological reformist groups. What was unique about Christianity was the linking of all this to the historical figure of Jesus of Nazareth, declared to be the Christ.

In the sections that follow we shall review a variety of texts from the literary corpus found in the Qumran caves. These include the nonbiblical scrolls from Cave 1, other texts that appear to have been authored by either the Qumran group or one of its predecessors, and a few texts that were popular at Qumran but do not indicate that the authors had sectarian concerns. We begin with several texts that offer some glimpses of their historical contexts (the Damascus Document and the biblical commentaries).

The Damascus Document (CD, 4QD, 5QD, 6QD)

This Hebrew text first came to the attention of modern scholars early in the twentieth century, after two incomplete medieval copies of it (designated A and B) had been discovered in the *genizah* or storeroom of a Cairo synagogue.[17] Although scholars generally recognized that this was a document from the Greco-Roman period, they disagreed on its provenance, seeing connections variously with the Hasidim, the Sadducees, and the Pharisees.[18] When the first Qumran scrolls came to light, references to the Teacher of Righteousness in both the Habakkuk Commentary and the Cairo document led to the conclusion that the text was Essene.[19] Eventually Caves 4, 5, and 6 yielded fragments from ten manuscripts of the work.[20] At first its references to the priests, "the sons of Zadok," had led to the designation "A Zadokite Work." Later, scholars adopted the title "Damascus Document" because of its emphasis on an exile in "(the land of) Damascus." The abbreviation "CD" denotes "Cairo Damascus." Column and line counts are based on the two Cairo manuscripts.

The writing divides into two main parts: an *admonition* to the hearer based on history, and *laws* for the life of the community.[21] The two Cairo manuscripts preserve most of the Admonition but a relatively small part of the Laws.[22] With a few exceptions, the text of the Qumran manuscripts coincides with the wording of the medieval manuscripts. In addition, they preserve part of the very beginning of the work, lost in Cairo manuscript A, as well as numerous additional columns of the Laws, which indicate that this part constituted perhaps as much as two-thirds of the work.[23] Thus, taken as a whole, the document is an exposition of the laws of the community with a long admonitory introduction.[24] Both parts are heavily dependent on the Scriptures. In the Admonition, *prophetic oracles* are frequently cited and interpreted as predictive descriptions of events relating to the life of the community. The second part presents the community's special interpretation of the *Torah*, sometimes with explicit appeal to *other biblical passages*.[25] In the literary form in which it is preserved in the Cairo texts and the Qumran fragments, the Damascus Document is a product of the Qumran community or a closely related sister group.[26] This form, however, is an edited composite that includes traditional material, some of which may well have derived from a parent group.[27] References to the death of the Teacher as a past event and paleographic analysis of the Qumran fragments suggest a date around 100 B.C.E. for the final form of the composition.[28]

The Admonition[29]

The introduction to the work, which is only partly preserved, sets the tone; according to the superscription, the sons of light are to keep their distance from the way of the wicked until the appointed time of God's judgment (4Q266 1 1:1-4). There follows the first of several appeals to "listen" as the author reveals information hidden from ordinary humans (4Q266 1 1:5-7). At the beginning of Cairo document A, in a second appeal to "listen," the author announces that he will recount God's dispute with the human race (CD 1:1-2). In fact, the author sketches the history of *Israel* from the Babylonian exile to the present time, focusing on God's creation of a remnant and their development into a community of the righteous (1:2—2:1). The imagery is reminiscent of the Apocalypse of Weeks in 1 Enoch 93:1-10 (see above, pp. 110–11), and the idea of an awakening has parallels in Jubilees 23 and 1 Enoch 90:6 (see above, pp. 71–72, 85).[30] The group finds a leader in the "Teacher of Righteousness," who will appear elsewhere in the Qumran literature. This teacher guides his followers on the right path and stands in opposition to "the Scoffer," a false leader and deceiver of Israel, and to those who "sought smooth things" (i.e., facile interpretations of God's law). The language of Isaiah 30:8-21 colors this section at a number of points (see below, pp. 131–32).

A third appeal that "those who enter the covenant" should "listen" to the author's revelation ("I will open your ears") introduces a theological section (2:2-13) with elements that parallel the two-ways teaching in the Qumran Rule of the Community (see below, p. 139). God's foreknowledge and predestination are asserted. God has chosen a remnant in the land and has shown them the truth, but has led the wicked astray (a second reference to the founding of a reform movement that is set over against its opponents). In spite of God's deterministic choice, each group will receive the reward or punishment of its actions.

A fourth appeal to "listen" to the author's revelation ("I will open your eyes") leads into the first major section of the Admonition (2:14—6:2). The author speaks of "the works of God" in history. Again we learn of two groups: (1) the wicked who were punished (the "watchers" of heaven, the children of Noah, the children of Jacob) and (2) the occasional righteous (Abraham, Isaac, and Jacob), who "were recorded as friends of God and party to the covenant forever." The author is particularly concerned with the latter-day manifestation of the righteous few, "the remnant" (a third reference to the founding and functions of a community, 3:12—4:12a). When the majority in Israel strays, this group remains faithful. To them has been revealed the proper interpretation of the Torah, including the correct calendar. Having left the land of Judah, they have dug a well to the waters of the Torah (Num 21:18) and will live forever, whereas the outsiders will "not live" (Deut 30:15). This remnant has been built as "a sure house in Israel" (cf. 1 Sam 2:35). Others may still join them, but the end of the age is near, and soon the wall of that house will be complete and outsiders will be excluded.

During this last time, Belial (Satan) breaks loose in Israel (4:12—5:19). A mark of the demonic chieftain's presence is the commonly accepted interpretation of the Torah, which has the appearance of "righteousness" (4:16-17). By not following the community's stricter interpretation, the Jerusalem priests have committed fornication and defiled the temple (5:6-11). Moreover, they blaspheme the laws of the covenant when they reject this stricter interpretation. The section concludes with the warning that anyone who goes near such persons will be punished, as God punished Israel in the past (5:15-19).

Now for the fourth time we are told of the founding of a community (5:20—6:11a). In a time of devastation and deceit, when Israel was led astray (5:20-21; cf. 1:1—2:1), God raised up sages, who left the land of Judah and lived in the land of Damascus, where they dug a well (6:3-7; cf. 3:16-17; 4:2-3). The "well" is the Torah. The "stave" with which it is dug appears to be an earlier leader in the history of the community who expounds the proper interpretation of the Torah and is succeeded by "one who will teach righteousness," whose appearance marks the end of days.

The next section of text spells out some specific obligations for the members of the community and the consequences of observing or not observing them (6:12—8:21a). First, the author quotes Malachi 1:10 in support of his prohibition from participating in the defiled temple cult (CD 6:12-14a; cf. 5:6). A series of twelve other prohibitions follow, which relate to halakic matters ("the interpretation of the law") that will be treated in the document's section on laws (6:14b—7:4a).[31] Those who "walk" according to these commandments (two-ways language) God will bless with a life (or a lineage) of "a thousand generations" (7:4b-9a), while those who disobey will suffer at the time of God's final judgment (7:4b-12a). Of special importance in this section is the reference to those who live in camps and marry and beget children (7:6-9). This passage and others in the Laws are striking because they envision life in communities quite different from the isolated and apparently celibate male community at Qumran.[32] An exegetical bridge leads to another reference to the sojourn in "Damascus" (7:12b-21a). Associated with this sojourn are two figures: "the interpreter of the Torah" and "the prince of the congregation," who in some sense correspond to the eschatological priestly and royal anointed ones ("messiahs"), of which we shall hear later (see below, pp. 150–51). At this point, Cairo manuscript A overlaps with column 1 of Cairo manuscript B, usually designated as CD 19. Scholars debate which of the two somewhat divergent texts may have been the original.[33]

Most of the remainder of the Admonition deals with apostates and disobedient members of the community (CD 19:33b—20:27a). Those who entered the covenant in the land of Damascus but then forsook the well of the Torah will be expelled from the community between the time of the death of the Teacher and the coming of "the anointed one of Aaron and Israel" (19:33b—20:1a). After reference to the temporary expulsion of the disobedient (20:1b–8a), the text continues with warnings against apostasy and the promise of blessings to the faithful (20:8b–34), who listen to the voice of the Teacher of Righteousness and adhere to his interpretation of the Torah (20:28, 32-33). Noteworthy in this section is the prediction of a forty-year period of wrath that begins with the death of the Teacher and appears to end with acts of mutual exhortation that bring on salvation (20:13-22). It is uncertain how this section relates to 20:28-34, where the theme of confession and obedience to the Teacher forms an *inclusio* that reprises the themes in the beginning of the main part of the Admonition (CD 1:7-11a).

The Laws

The second part of the Damascus Document, comprising perhaps two-thirds of the text, provides long lists that spell out the community's interpretation of the Torah. In Cairo manuscript A (with the columns reorganized to correspond to the Qumran fragments) this section includes columns 15–16 and 9–14. Five manuscripts from Qumran Cave 4 contain, variously, material from all of these columns. In addition, they include fragments of at least thirteen columns of legal material that is not in Cairo manuscript A.[34] The precise placement of some of this material is uncertain. Especially problematic is 4Q270 2 1–2, which contains a list of transgressions followed by an appeal to "listen" to revelation similar to those in the Admonition. Does this fragment belong in the Admonition, where it is formally at home, or in the Laws, where it is unique in Cairo manuscript A and the other preserved Qumran fragments?[35]

The section on Laws includes the topical treatment of the following issues: priestly duties and qualifications, purity rules, harvest laws, commercial dealings and marriage arrangements, oaths, judicial procedures, Sabbath rules, the purity of the temple and the temple city, treatment of blasphemers and Gentiles, dietary rules (4Q266 frgs. 5–9 2 and parallels in 4Q267–273 and CD 15–16, 9–12). The last section contains rules for the community (4Q266 9 3–10 2 and parallels in CD 13–14). In two Qumran manuscripts that preserve the end of their respective scrolls, the text concluded with a liturgy and rules for the expulsion of offenders (4Q266 11; 4Q270 7 2). The subscript identifies either this section or the whole document as "the elaboration of the laws to be followed during the entire period [of judgment . . .] during the periods of (God's) wrath . . .”; this may be a reprise of the document's opening words.[36]

Detailed consideration of the laws in the Damascus Document is not possible here. Since the publication of the Cave 4 fragments, the literature has been voluminous, and it will continue to grow.[37] Nonetheless, some generalizations are possible. The Damascus Laws are invaluable for reconstructing the history of Jewish law. Along with Jubilees and other texts in the Qumran corpus, they constitute the earliest extant examples of the halakic interpretation of the Torah.[38] Different from the laws in the rabbinic corpus, whose dating is uncertain, these texts provide early datable evidence for the content, forms, rationale, and social setting of such interpretation. Although the second part of the document is a collection of legal tradition that was generated over time,[39] its presence in one document used by one community provides some concrete and detailed sense of how one group lived out the covenant obligation to observe divine law. Both the ritual laws and the rules that governed community organization help us to envision community life in a way that is not possible, for example, with texts like 1 Enoch and Daniel or even Jubilees and Judith.

A comparative study of the laws helps to place the community that observed them in the context of groups like the Pharisees and Sadducees. In the latter case, we can see legal similarities that stand side by side with theological dissimilarities with regard, for example, to determinism and free will, as well as eschatology.[40] While some Qumran halakah parallels that of the Pharisees and their rabbinic successors, the differences are at least as striking.[41] With considerable justification, legal strictness is axiomatic in Christian descriptions of the Pharisees. In the view of the Qumranites, however, many instances of Pharisaic halakah were lax, and there is good reason to suppose that the expression “the seekers after smooth things,” attested in the Damascus Document and other Qumran texts, is a pejorative reference to what the Qumranites considered to be their facile, easy interpretations of the Torah.[42] Explicit references to Scripture in connection with some halakah also suggest a polemical context in some cases. Also striking is the claim— repeatedly asserted in the Admonition and reiterated in the Rule of the Community (see below, p. 140)—that the community's interpretation of the Torah is grounded in revelation.[43] The repeated counterpoising of the community and its opponents, who do not possess that interpretation, underscores the polemical character of the claim.

Of special interest is the Damascus Document's attitude toward the Jerusalem temple. On the one hand, one finds laws about temple purity that presuppose the sanctuary's crucial place in Jewish religion. On the other hand, a couple of passages declare the cult to be defiled due to halakic improprieties.[44] The critiques are paralleled in texts such as 1 Enoch and the Psalms of Solomon (see above, pp. 51, 86, and below, pp. 239–40), and they also find parallels in the New Testament, although there the issue does not seem to be halakah. Finally, occasional parallels to the Gospels belie the simple stereotype that— at least in the perception of some early Christians—in comparison to the Pharisees, Jesus was soft on the Torah.[45]

— Hardliness

Summary

The Damascus Document is a complex document with an extended literary history that reflects the developing history of community or communities that would emerge in one form in the community that gathered at Qumran.[46] Early on, we learn, certain people left the land of Judah and took up residence in ("the land of") Damascus, where they generated their authoritative interpretations of the Torah. Whether "Damascus" denotes the Syrian city and its environs or is a code word for another place is a point of debate.[47] In any case, this exodus is a vivid and essential part of the historical memory of the group responsible for the final compilation of the document, which also incorporates some of the laws that governed the early community or communities.

In its final form, as a Qumranic text, the document provides a window into a community with a polarized worldview that sees a sharp distinction between the in-group and the outsiders. The community understands itself to be the true people of God, bound together by a new covenant and having the correct, revealed understanding of the Torah, explicated in the document but hidden from the outsiders. As such they separate themselves from the rest of the Jewish people and boycott the Jerusalem temple, which they claim has been profaned by the priestly establishment. The end of the age is at hand, and the full fury of Satan is loose in the land, as witnessed by the wickedness of their opponents. However, God's messianic figure(s) will appear, and God will come as judge, to punish the wicked and bless those who have been faithful to the Torah.

PESHARIM

> And God told Habakkuk to write down that which would happen to the final generation, but He did not make known to him when time would come to an end. . . . God made known (to the Teacher of Righteousness) all the mysteries of the words of His servants the Prophets. (Comm. on Hab 2:1-2; Vermes)

Here in a nutshell is the principle of interpretation that governs a corpus of Qumran texts whose function is to expound the interpretation (Heb. *pēsher*) of the Bible.[48] The prophets (Moses and David included) wrote about the events that would take place at the end time. The group at Qumran believed that they were living during that crucial period. Thus the prophetic texts contained cryptic references ("mysteries") to contemporary events.[49] God had given the Teacher of Righteousness special insight to interpret these mysteries.

The Teacher was not the first to understand Scripture in this way. We have already seen various forms of such interpretation in a number of second-century texts. The author of the Testament of Moses rewrites Moses' prophecy so that it makes explicit ref-

who doens't

erence to contemporary events. Jubilees 23, Daniel 10–12, and 1 Enoch 85–90 employ phrases from the prophets and allusions to these books to describe contemporary events and to flesh out descriptions of the imminent end. The author of Daniel 9 reinterprets Jeremiah's seventy years as seventy weeks of years that reach their culmination in the author's own time.

Continuous Commentaries

Among the Qumran documents, *pesher* exegesis occurs for the most part in a set of Hebrew texts that comment verse by verse on substantial blocks of text—parts of Isaiah (four commentaries), Hosea, Micah, Nahum, Habakkuk, Zephaniah, and the Psalter (three commentaries).[50] Typically a passage is quoted and then followed by the interpretation, which is formally introduced with the words "Its interpretation concerns" (*pishrô ʿal*) or "the interpretation of the passage is" (*pēsher hā-dābār*). The Hebrew *pēsher* ("interpretation") is the same word employed in the stories about Joseph and Daniel, where the seer offers a divinely revealed interpretation of a mysterious dream or message. Here it denotes the unraveling of the mysteries hidden in Scripture.

In keeping with this viewpoint, the content of the interpretations is generally limited to the identification of events and persons mentioned in the Bible with contemporary events and persons and to some explication as to how the biblical text is being fulfilled in detail in the present time. Most of the commentaries appear to have been written during the second half of the first century B.C.E. and are extant in only one copy each—perhaps in some cases the autograph (original copy).[51] They are evidently a compilation of the sect's interpretive traditions, reaching back to the Teacher himself and covering events from a century of the sect's history—from the Teacher's conflict with the Wicked Priest to the Roman occupation of Palestine.

The commentaries are the earliest examples of a literary genre that became popular in rabbinic circles in the second century C.E. and later. Certain similarities are evident: the technique of commenting on lengthy blocks of Scripture; the format of quotation and interpretation (although the rabbis did not use the same formal introduction to the interpretation); and the quotation of parallel passages from Scripture. The differences, however, are just as significant and help us to understand the peculiar nature of the Qumran commentaries. The rabbinic commentaries concentrate on the Torah and the Writings. The exposition is of two types: halakic (how the laws are to be applied in specific circumstances) and haggadic (largely homiletical comments). The commentaries compile the opinions of many rabbis, who are mentioned by name. In the Qumran commentaries the interpretations are anonymous and reflect community interpretation. They deal mainly with the prophetic writings, but even in the Psalms Commentary the interpretations are limited to the type discussed above. We should not be far off the mark in describing the commentaries as an eschatological key or index to the Scriptures.

The Habakkuk Commentary (1QpHab)

This is the best preserved of the Qumran commentaries. Its thirteen columns contain comments on the whole of Habakkuk 1–2.* For the most part these comments relate to two series of events: (1) circumstances relating to the Teacher of Righteousness and his conflict with the "the Liar" (lit. "the man of the lie") and "the Wicked Priest"; and (2) the appearance of the Roman army in Palestine (see below, pp. 231–32).

The Habakkuk Commentary 2:10—6:17 deals almost entirely with the Romans, who appear under the name "Kittim."[52] The section describes how the irresistible Roman military machine grinds out its victories with merciless ferocity. The descriptions have the marks of fresh memory, and the document was probably written only a decade after the fact.[53]

The second set of historical allusions concerns the history of the community and provides tantalizing but vague information about the Teacher of Righteousness and his opponents, the Liar and the Wicked Priest. The Teacher was an inspired interpreter of the prophetic Scriptures (1QpHab 2:6-10; 7:4-8; comm. on 1:5 and 2:1-2). In this role he met with two divergent reactions. A community of the faithful gathered around him:

> "But the righteous shall live by his faith" (Hab 2:4). Its interpretation concerns all who observe the Torah in the House of Judah, whom God will deliver from the House of Judgment because of their toils and their faith in the Teacher of Righteousness." (1QpHab 7:17—8:3)

The faithful are the faithful doers of the Torah, presumably as it was expounded by the Teacher, and this piety is described in terms of "faith in" or "faithfulness to" the Teacher. Their way of life causes toil or suffering for the group, as it does for the master. Elsewhere in the commentary the group is known as "the chosen," a term with exclusivistic and sectarian connotations (1QpHab 5:4; 9:12; 10:13).[54] The community of the pious, however, has its counterpart: the unfaithful, who reject the covenant and the Torah and do not heed the revelation received by the Teacher (1QpHab 2:1-4; comm. on 1:5).

Rejection of the Teacher is epitomized in the (Wicked) Priest[55] and "the Liar." The priest is the main subject of the commentary on 2:5-17 (1QpHab 8:3—11:17). The list of charges against him is considerable. He is a rebel against God and he amasses great wealth (1QpHab 8:3-12; comm. on 2:5-6) and uses this to complete his building projects (1QpHab 9:11—10:5; comm. on 2:9-11). He persecutes the Teacher and his community (1QpHab 11:2-8; comm. on 2:15). His indulgence in abominable and unclean things defiles the temple (1QpHab 12:6-9; cf. 8:13; comm. on 2:17). Noteworthy in these passages is the repeated stress on the punishment or judgment (variously described) meted out to the Wicked Priest.

Scholarly opinion is divided on the interpretation of these passages as it relates to the identity of the Wicked Priest.[56] The two most frequently mentioned candidates for the dishonor are the first Hasmonean high priests, Jonathan and Simon. It has also been argued that the sobriquet is here applied to more than one of the Hasmonean priests.[57]

Several passages in the commentary refer to an opponent of the Teacher of Righteousness as the "Man of Lies" and the "Dripper of Lies" (i.e., "False Oracle"; cf. Mic 2:11; 1Q pHab 2:1-2; 5:9-12; 10:5-13; comm. on 1:5, 13; 2:12-13), who leads many astray.[58] While some have argued that these are a different set of names for the Wicked Priest, it seems more likely that they refer to another opponent of the sect, who was construed as a false teacher.[59]

A Commentary on Psalms (4QpPs^a [4Q171])

Parts of four columns of this commentary have been preserved. They contain comments primarily on Psalm 37 and, immediately after it, on Psalm 45. The commentary on Psalm 37 makes evident reference to the Teacher of Righteousness and his opponent, the Wicked Priest (4Q171 3:15-16; 4:8-9; comm. on vv 23, 32). Both passages are broken by lacunae in the manuscript. The latter passage appears to refer to the Wicked Priest's attempt on the Teacher's life. If we may judge from the biblical passage being interpreted, the attempt was unsuccessful, for God "will not abandon" his righteous one. The Wicked Priest, however, is given over into the hands of violent Gentiles. The Man of Lies is mentioned at least once in a passage closely parallel to the description of the False Oracle in the Habakkuk Commentary. "Its (interpretation) concerns the Liar, who has led many astray by his lying words so that they chose frivolous things and heeded not the interpreter of knowledge" (4Q171 1:26-27; comm. on v 7). The interpreter of knowledge is presumably the Teacher, and the passage combines elements from 1Q pHab 2:1-3 and 10:9-13. The Man of Lies stands in opposition to the Teacher and gathers his own following, who disregard the words of the Teacher. The expression "lead many astray" is a technical term for the activity of false teachers, which we shall meet again in the Commentary on Nahum. The term par excellence for the Teacher's community is "the chosen" (4Q171 2:5; 3:5; 4:12; comm. on vv 9, 20, 34), and a sense of community is evident in the repeated use of the term "congregation" ("congregation of his chosen," "congregation of the poor," etc.). The community is defined as "those who observe the Torah" (4Q171 2:14-15, 22-23; comm. on vv 12-13, 16), "those who turn back to the Torah, who do not refuse to turn from their evil" (4Q171 2:2-3; comm. on vv 8-9). Running through the commentary is the prediction of punishment for the wicked and also reward for the righteous, often triggered by the psalmic refrain that the righteous "will possess the land." The commentary on vv 21-22 (4Q171 3:10-11) promises that they will possess the high mountain of Israel, that is, Mount Zion and the sanctuary, a promise of considerable significance to a group who had separated themselves from the temple because they considered it to be defiled. The commentary anticipates the time when all this will be changed.

The Nahum Commentary (4QpNah [4Q169])

The events described in column 1 took place during the reign of Alexander Janneus, when on two occasions Alexander slaughtered large numbers of his enemies (see above, pp. 93–94).* While it is generally assumed that these enemies of Alexander were Pharisees, the assumption finds little support in Josephus, who does not mention the Pharisees in connection with this incident.[60] The present text, however, indicates that the Pharisees were among these enemies.

The "Lion of Wrath" is Alexander, who wreaks vengeance on his enemies by "hanging them alive" (i.e., crucifying them). The commentary applies to these enemies the title "the Seekers after Smooth Things" (*dôrshê hā-ḥălāqôt*). The Hebrew *dārash* is a technical term for the kind of "seeking" that goes on in biblical interpretation, and hence the phrase can be translated "the Facile Interpreters." It is not surprising that the Essenes should so describe the Pharisees. Essene interpretation of the Torah was often stricter than that of the Pharisees (see above, p. 126). Very likely we have a wordplay between the Hebrew *hălākôt* ("legal prescriptions") and *hălāqôt*. That is, Pharisaic legal interpretations (*hălākôt*) are really facile bypasses (*hălāqôt*) of the strict intent of the Torah. Thus the use of the term stresses what we have already seen in the commentaries, namely, that the Qumran group considered themselves to be the genuine observers of the Torah. The Facile Interpreters are mentioned five times in the extant fragments of the Nahum Commentary. "They conduct themselves [Heb. *hālak*, perhaps a wordplay] in lies and falsehood" (4Q pNah 2:2; comm. on 3:1ab). They "lead many astray by their false teaching, their lying tongue, and their deceitful lips" (4Q pNah 2:8; comm. on 3:4; cf. 4Q pNah 3:3, 6-8; comm. on 3:6-7a, 7b).[61] We have already seen this same terminology in the Damascus Document, the Habakkuk Commentary, and the Psalms Commentary (see above, pp. 123, 130).[62] The indictments of this group, which are at odds with the Qumran community, could hardly be stronger, and their punishment is repeatedly mentioned. They received their just deserts from Alexander, whose title seems to imply that he was the instrument of God's wrath; and their influence will come to an end.[63]

This commentary is noteworthy for its use of both historical and symbolic references. The author mentions both Demetrius and Antiochus by name (1Q pNah 1:2-3), but also employs many symbolic designations. In addition to the "Seekers after Smooth Things," he refers to "the simple ones of Ephraim" (the legally naive), "Manasseh" (perhaps the Sadducees), "Judah" (the Qumran community), and "the Kittim" (the Romans).[64]

A Commentary on Isaiah (4QpIsa^c [4Q163])

Fragments of five commentaries on Isaiah have been recovered.[65] The third commentary contains comments on Isaiah 30–31. It mentions the "congregation of those who seek smooth things, which is in Jerusalem." It is almost certain that the expression "the Facile

Interpreters" (see the previous section) is derived ultimately from this portion of Scripture, specifically Isaiah 30:10:

> who say to the seers, "See not"; and to the prophets, "Prophesy to us what is right; speak to us *smooth things*, prophesy illusions, leave the way, turn aside from the path."[66]

That this portion of Scripture would have been especially meaningful to the Qumran community is understandable in light of the passage that follows shortly thereafter:

> And though the Lord give you the bread of adversity and the water of affliction, yet your *Teacher* will not hide himself anymore, but your eyes shall see your Teacher. And your ears shall hear a word behind you, saying, "This is the way, walk in it." (Isa 30:20-21)

Florilegium (1Q174), Melchizedek (11Q13), Testimonia (4Q175): Three Thematic Exegetical Texts

A *pesher*-like exegesis of Scripture occurs not only in continuous commentaries, but also in texts whose unity is in their theme.[67] The so-called Florilegium (4Q174), to judge from what is left of its fragments—especially its third column—is unified around the theme of place or house: the Jerusalem temple, past, present, and future; the eschatological community; and the house of the Davidic messiah, who is mentioned in tandem with his eschatological twin, "the Interpreter of the Law" (*dōrēsh ha-tôrāh*), the awaited priestly messiah.[68] Presumed throughout is the notion that ancient Scripture has yet to be fulfilled. This point is repeatedly made by explicating one passage though the citation of another.

Another thematically unified text of two fragmented columns anticipates eschatological salvation through the agency of Melchizedek. This priestly and royal figure mentioned in Genesis 14:18-20 and Psalm 110 is here a heavenly figure similar to, if not identical with the angel Michael and the prince of Light (see below, p. 139).[69]

A text of a different sort, but based on similar exegetical principles, is the so-called Testimonia (4Q175).[70] Its single column quotes without comment three passages (Deut 18:18-19; Num 24:15-17; Deut 33:8-11) that are evidently intended to be scriptural references to three eschatological figures awaited by the community: the prophet like Moses, the royal messiah, and the priestly messiah. Then it adds a quotation from a nonbiblical book of Joshua, which appears to refer to an enemy of the community, "the accursed man" and his two sons.[71]

The Thanksgiving Hymns (1QH[ab], 4QH)

Among the seven scrolls found in Qumran Cave 1 was a collection of thanksgiving hymns that originally ran to at least twenty-eight columns (1QH[a]).[72*] In the columns that are still intact, we can count at least twenty-five separate compositions, each of which begins (where the beginning is preserved) with an expression of thanksgiving or praise: "I give thanks to you, O Lord [or 'God']" (Heb. *ʾôdĕkāh ʾădônāy/ʾēlî*); "Blessed are you, O Lord" (Heb. *bārûk ʾattāh ʾădônāy*). The Hebrew of the primary thanksgiving formula led to the common designation of the collection as *Hodayot*. Some fragments of a second Hymn Scroll (1QH[b]) were also identified, and Cave 4 yielded fragments of six other scrolls.[73] The number of copies of the collection and "the impeccable material crafting" of 1QH[a] attest the high esteem in which the Qumranites held these compositions.[74] Parallels to the language and concepts in other Qumran texts indicate that they belong to a core group of texts that were authored in this community.[75] Paleographic analysis of 4QH[b] indicates a date shortly after 100 B.C.E., suggesting that the hymns were composed in the last quarter of the second century B.C.E., in the early days of the community's history.[76] These hymns, which are of various lengths, belong to two major types.

Hymns of the Teacher

Included in this group are at least seven hymns: 10(2):1-19; 10(2):31-39; 12(4):5—13(5):4; 13(5):5-19; 13(5):20—15(7):5; 15(7):6-25; and 16(8):4-40.[77] The speaker and principal figure in this group is a teacher or revealer of saving knowledge who is persecuted by his enemies but delivered by God. The author of at least some of these compositions may well have been the Teacher of Righteousness himself.[78]

1QH[a] 10(2):1-19

The first-person singular dominates the hymn: "I have been . . . to . . ."; "You have made me . . . to. . . ." By the use of these forms the speaker describes his contrasting relationships to the righteous and the wicked:

> to the righteous chosen you have made me a banner,
>> and a discerning interpreter of wonderful mysteries.
>> (10[2]:13, Vermes adapted)

The author's followers are "the righteous chosen," the true people of God. He has been an eschatological rallying point for them (cf. Isa 11:12; 49:22; 62:10), and he is the interpreter of the marvelous mysteries about the end time that God is now revealing in the end time:

> I have been a snare to those who rebel,
>> but healing to those of them who repent. (10[2]:8-9; Vermes adapted)

He is a touchstone. To the repentant he brings divine healing (i.e., salvation), but in the wicked he creates an adverse effect and is a cause for sin (cf. 10[2]:8).

The speaker's opponents are not just the wicked in general but a group of opposing teachers: "deceivers," "interpreters of error," and the familiar "interpreters of smooth things." The opposition, instigated by Belial, leads to persecution (10[2]:17). The speaker sees himself at the center of a battle between heaven and hell. The revelation he mediates brings salvation to the community of the chosen, his followers. It triggers satanic reaction through his opponents, who counter his teaching and seek to annihilate its source—and do so to their own damnation. The purpose of the hymn is to thank God for deliverance.

1QHᵃ 10(2):31-37

The speaker's teaching activity may be inferred from the description of his opponents: "the congregation of those who interpret smooth things," "interpreters of falsehood." His special function is described as "your service" (10[2]:33, 36). Because he has served the Lord, his opponents have plotted to kill him (10[2]:32-34). Unlike the previous hymn, the speaker is here in every case the *object* of a verb. His enemies seek to destroy him. God has "delivered," "redeemed," and "helped" him. This is the occasion for thanksgiving.

1QHᵃ 12(4):5—13(5):4

The speaker gives thanks to the Lord for enlightenment, for divinely given insight into the true nature of the covenant (12[4]:5-6a). It is with respect to this understanding of Torah that his enemies take issue with him. In two sections he mentions their erring interpretations and then expresses the threat of divine judgment (12[4]:6b-12a | 12b-13a; 13b-18a | 18b-21a). The lying interpreters and false seers attempt to lead astray the community of the righteous by opposing the speaker's interpretation, which God has engraved in his heart (i.e., revealed to him). They hope to make the group sin with respect to the observance of their sectarian holy days (cf. 1QpHab 11:2-8; comm. on 2:15). Persecution here seems to take the form of banishment, and the speaker uses language from Isaiah 53:3 to describe his rejection by his opponents (1QHᵃ 12[4]:8). Moreover, at the time of judgment he will take part in their destruction (12[4]:21-22; cf. below, pp. 206–8, on Wis 5). His thought moves on to his relationship to his followers (1QHᵃ 12[4]:23-29a). The enlightenment he has received he has mediated to them. He is God's instrument for revelation. But that treasure is contained in a clay vessel (12[4]:29b-33a). In a passage typical of the hymns, he contrasts the power, righteousness, and holiness of God with his own humanity. The thought of it leads him to shudder as he meditates upon his sin. Do the onslaughts of the enemy mean that God has forsaken him because of that sin? Surely not. With God there is forgiveness and mercy, and therefore he can take courage, confident that God's judgment will be the final word (12[4]:33—13[5]:4). The hymn as a whole provides a remarkable insight into the public and private sides of the speaker as he deals with fighting without and fear within.

1QH^a 13(5):20—15(7):5

If in the hymn we have just discussed the speaker had voiced his earlier doubts about being "abandoned," both there and in 13[5]:5, he gives thanks precisely because God has not abandoned him. When he has given thanks for God's presence (13[5]:20-22), he moves into a long description of his predicament (13[5]:22b—14[6]:3). Even members of his group have forsaken him, heeding the words of his opponents.

The passage is filled with biblical clichés, and hence it is impossible to discover the actual events of his persecution. The heaping up of descriptive phrases functions to portray his situation in the darkest possible colors. All this contrasts with the affirmation of God's deliverance that follows (14[6]:4-19). In the midst of the tumult he has the vision of God's final triumph and God's vindication of those who belong to the community. Again he repeats the cycle of thought (14[6]:22-34). He is like a sailor tossed on the chaotic waves and brought to the very gates of Death itself. But again there is deliverance. Within his community, the true city of God, he finds refuge as in a fortress. He depicts it as if it were the heavenly Jerusalem itself—impregnable to the invasion of the enemy. He anticipates the imminent time of judgment, when its gates will open and its members will sally forth in the final battle. Meanwhile, the turmoil goes on (15[7]:1-5).

1QH^a 15(7):6-24

This hymn contains many of the motifs we have already seen. God is to be thanked for giving the speaker strength to face the troubles connected with his office (15[7]:6-8a). Here he applies the metaphor of the fortress to himself to describe the security that God affords him, or others through him (15[7]:8b-9). As true teacher he will be God's criterion in the judgment (15[7]:10-12). People will be saved or damned according to how they have responded to his teaching. Again he reflects on his own humanity and on the grace of God (15[7]:13-19). He likens his relationship to the community as that of father—or nurse—to child (15[7]:19b-22a). He concludes with reference to the judgment and the time when he will be exalted in glory. The passage is reminiscent of Daniel 12:3 and its reference to the glorification of the persecuted righteous teachers.

Summary

These hymns constitute a consistent body of literature. The speaker is the recipient of divine truths that he passes on to his community, which is construed as the true people of God gathered around the correct understanding of the Torah. In his activities the teacher is challenged and persecuted by opponents who are also teachers. At times they are successful in eroding his support. Nevertheless, he is confident of God's support and saving activity, and he looks forward to the resolution of the situation in the coming judgment, when he will be exalted and his enemies will be condemned for their opposition to him.

Hymns of the Community

A second group of hymns speak of the sectarian's place in the community.[79] Lacking are references to the teacher and his relationship to the community and his persecution at the hands of his enemies.

1QH^a 11(3):19-23

In the introductory section the author praises the Lord, who has rescued him from the pit of Sheol (11[3]:19-20a). He then explicates the nature of his redemption (11[3]:20b-23b). He has been created anew from the "dust" of his humanity, cleansed from sin, and brought into fellowship with the angels. He has been delivered from the wiles of Belial, the snares of hell, and the furious judgment of the Almighty (11[3]:26-36). The imagery is strongly eschatological in tone. Contemporary Jewish writings apply the notion of "inheritance" or "lot" to eschatological salvation, and it is in descriptions of this salvation that the righteous are depicted in the presence of the angels (cf. 1 Enoch 39:8 and esp. Wis 5:5, below, pp. 207). Thus the blessings of the *eschaton* are already a reality for this author. Upon his entrance into the community, he passed from the sphere of death into the realm of life, and he describes this graphically as ascent from Sheol to the "eternal height" (i.e., heaven). The community, as the true people of God, is the arena of salvation. The final section (1QH^a 11[3]:28b-35) describes either the speaker's plight before his entrance into the community or, more likely, his status in the world, which is still the realm of wickedness. In such a case the passage introduces a tension between the "now" and the "not yet." The full consummation of salvation belongs to the future.

1QH^a 19(11):3-14

The author gives thanks because God has made him, a mere human being ("dust," "creature of clay"), the recipient of divine revelation and enabled him to sing his Creator's praise (19[11]:3-5a). The emphasis on the receipt of revelation is repeated in 19(11):9-10. God has cleansed humanity from sin, and therefore certain consequences follow (19[11]:10b-14). He is now holy to the Lord, and he stands in the company of the sons of God's truth, the community of the eschatological chosen ones. Moreover, God has taken a human being, who is in a state of alienation ("the perverse spirit") and prone to death ("dust," "mortal worm"), and given him access to the divine mysteries and to the immortal company of the holy ones, the angels. As in the previous hymn, entrance into the community is an eschatological event, and it is depicted in language traditionally used of the *eschaton*: resurrection from the dead.[80]

Summary

From the point of view of these hymns, the community is the arena of salvation. Outside is the realm of death. To enter the community is "to pass from death to life." It is construed as an event of eschatological salvation. Entrance involves access to divine mysteries and knowledge. Presumably these involve insights into God's purposes and activities in the present time, as well as the proper interpretation of the Torah. That such knowledge is crucial for salvation is a natural (sectarian) inference from the Jewish understanding of Torah. Within the compass of the covenant, God gives certain laws and commandments. The obedient receive the blessings ("life"), the disobedient are cursed ("death"). It follows that one can "live" only if one has a correct perception of the requirements of the covenant. The Qumran group narrows the scope of Torah to mean "Torah as we perceive it," that is, as it has been divinely revealed through the Teacher. Thus the shape of the covenant is recast in narrow sectarian and eschatological terms. True Israel is equated with the sect, the Torah with the sect's interpretation of it, and blessing and curse with eternal life and eternal destruction. For this community, election is the presupposition for membership in the covenantal community. Hence they call themselves "the chosen." However, such election is not their birthright as natural-born Jews. It is due to an eternal decree of God that divides through the midst of Israel itself. The hymns state their sectarianism in another way. Not only is Israel outside their community damned, but the situation is even more radical. Humanity qua humanity, "dust," "ashes," "clay," and "flesh," is alienated from God and doomed to destruction. Only by an act of divine salvation—variously construed as re-creation, revelation, justification, and renewal—are such human beings enabled to stand in God's presence (see, in addition to the hymns discussed, 1QH 5:18-28 [13:10-20]; 7:24-25 [15:21-22]; 23 [18:9-29]; 1QS 11:2-22). The hymns continually emphasize that this salvation belongs to the members of the community and celebrate the process by which one obtains this salvation. It is quite likely that the hymns were used in the initiation ceremonies, thus providing an opportunity for the initiate to give thanks for his newfound salvation, and for daily periods of prayer.[81]

The Rule of the Community (1QS, 4QS, 5QS)

Of the seven scrolls discovered in Cave 1, it was this Hebrew document that first shed light on the community that lived at Qumran.[82*] Detailed parallels between parts of the Rule and the descriptions of Essene belief and practice in the writings of Josephus and Philo led rather quickly to a wide consensus that the community described in the Rule was a group of Essenes, and archeological evidence indicated that the building complex that lay in ruins at Khirbet Qumran had been the center of their activities. The subsequent recovery of fragments of eleven copies of the Rule from Caves 4 and 5, in close proximity to the ruins, confirmed the connection.

The text entitles itself the "Book of the Rule of the Community" (Heb. *sēper serek ha-yaḥad*, 1QS 1:1; 4Q papSᵃ 1:1). As such it lays out the rules and regulations that governed the lifestyle and religious practices of the community, together with their theological rationale. Paleographic analysis dates 1QS between 100 and 75 B.C.E. and the other manuscripts between 125–100 B.C.E. and 1–50 C.E.[83] This range of dates roots the document in the time of the community's foundation in the mid- or late second century B.C.E. and indicates that it was a viable text during the entire history of the community.

The issue is not so simple, however. As scholars have long recognized, 1QS is a composite text, rather than one written as a single piece, and hypotheses to explain its literary history have been floated since the 1950s.[84] The publication of the Cave 4 fragments in 1998 has complicated matters even more because the fragments indicate that these manuscripts contained different assemblages of the components in 1QS, as well as shorter and longer forms of the same passages and sometimes different wording.[85] Since these data have not yet produced a consensus regarding the literary genesis of the document, I shall discuss 1QS from start to finish as a text in its own right that represents one stage in the document's development.

Introduction (1:1-15)

The opening lines of the Rule serve as an introduction to the *whole* document, which sets forth the goals and ideals of the community: wholehearted obedience to the commandments of God (not least the observance of the right calendar) as expounded by Moses and all the prophets and avoidance of what is evil; love for all the members of the community (the sons of light), and hatred toward all the outsiders (the sons of darkness). When the initiates freely volunteer to enter the community, they are to bring with them "all their understanding, their strength, and their possessions."[86] The polarity of good and evil, insiders and outsider, anticipates the dualism of the two-spirits section that will follow in 3:13—4:26. The repeated use of the adjective "all" (sixteen times) underscores the radicality of the commitment assumed by members of the community.

Initiation into the Community and Its Implications (1:16—3:12)

The reference to the initiates and their entrance into the community in 1:1-15 prepares one for the liturgy of initiation that follows (1:16—2:18). To enter the community and assume the obligations of "the rule of the community" is to enter into a covenant with God (1:16-18). The presumption is that those outside the community stand outside the covenant.[87] That is, the community *is* Israel. The liturgy is saturated with biblical idiom and has much in common particularly with the biblical covenant forms (esp. Deut 28–31). This suggests that initiation took place on the occasion of an annual covenant-renewal ceremony (see also 1QS 2:19).[88] The liturgy begins with a doxology by the priests and Levites, which the initiates echo with a double "Amen" ("Indeed") (1:18b-20). The priests and Levites then recite, respectively, God's mighty acts and, in contrast to these, the wicked deeds of Israel (1:18-23); grace has been met by rebellion. The initiates confess their participation in these sinful acts (1:24-26) but assert their

as a living temple

faith in God's everlasting mercy (2:1a). Reminiscent of the ancient covenant ceremony described in Joshua 24, the choruses of the priests and the Levites respond, one after the other, with the pronouncement of blessings and curses (1QS 2:1b-9). The blessing, which is an expansion of the Aaronic benediction (2:2b-4; cf. Num 6:24-26), invokes God's mercy on the new members of the covenantal community.[89] The curses, which are aimed at the outsiders, embody a reversal of the Aaronic benediction (1QS 2:8-9).[90] Then priests and Levites pronounce a curse on anyone whose commitment is not sincere or wholehearted (2:11-17). The initiates respond to each of the choruses with the words "Amen, Amen" (2:10, 18). Thus they are at one with the sentiments of the community.

This liturgy is followed by a rubric for convocation at the annual ceremony (2:19-25a). One's ranking in the community is of the essence. The next section picks up the theme of 2:11-14a: outward ceremony and ritual ablution are ineffective without inward conversion (2:25b—3:12). Parallel themes occur in the two halves of the passage, in negative and then positive forms (2:25a—3:6a; 3:6b-12).

Instruction about the Two Spirits and the Two Ways (3:13—4:26)

This section spells out systematically the religious worldview that undergirds the lifestyle and rituals of the community.[91] The covenantal form that structured the liturgy of initiation and was led by the priests and Levites is here used to shape a didactic passage that is to be explicated by the teacher of the community, the *maśkil*.[92]

The passage begins with a prologue about the acts of God in creation (rather than in Israel's history, as is typical of the covenantal form) (3:15b—4:1). God has created everything, including two angels identified as the Prince of Lights and the Angel of Darkness. These two cosmic beings exercise supervision over the human beings who have been assigned to their respective lots: the sons of light and the sons of darkness, and the angels function as guides along the ways of light and the ways of darkness. It is a highly deterministic and dualistic system.

With the scheme set, the author describes the ways of the righteous (4:2-6a) and the ways of the wicked (4:9-11). Although traditional two-ways theology focuses on *the deeds* of the righteous, in this particular text there is no mention of concrete deeds; the lists are catalogs of virtues and vices—good psychological and intellectual dispositions (4:2-6a) and evil dispositions that are sometimes spelled out through the use of physical metaphors (4:9-11a). This anticipates the anthropological character and activity of the two cosmic spirits.

Next, the passage describes the rewards and punishments that result from them.[93] In traditional covenantal theology and two-ways passages, rewards and punishments are temporal and this-worldly. In the present case, the rewards of righteous conduct are partly temporal and partly eternal (4:6b-8), and the visitation of those who walk along the path of darkness is only eternal and postmortem (4:11b-14).

The section on the two spirits and the two ways concludes by depicting the war

NEED FOR ESCHATOLOGY FOR TOTAL CLEANSING

between the two spirits and God's resolution of it.[94] First the author traces the battle from creation to the *eschaton* (4:15-18a, 18b-23a). The terminology in 4:18-21 implies that the water ablutions that were part of the Qumran ritual life were only partially and temporarily effective. Only at the *eschaton* will God cleanse humanity completely of its wicked and perverse deeds. Only then all evil will be annihilated and "man" (*ʾādām*) will revert to his original glory. The passage is reminiscent of motifs in the description of the *eschaton* in 1 Enoch 10:16-22. Although the author has asserted that human beings belong to either the sons of light or the sons of darkness, he recognizes that the former can and do sin. Thus he concludes that the great battle between the two cosmic forces is also waged within the human heart, and people act according to their particular proportions of light and darkness, which generate the good and evil inner dispositions mentioned previously. The technique of describing this ongoing battle and celebrating God's eschatological victory parallels the doxologies in some of the Hymns, which give thanks for God's salvation but mourn human weakness and propensity to sin (cf. 1QH 11[3]:19-36; 19[11]:3-14; 20[12]:4-36; 21[18]:1-16).

Separateness

Rules for Communal Life (5:1—7:27)

With the liturgy for initiation and the community's theological presuppositions explicated, the document turns to its announced subject matter, the rules that govern the organization and operation of the community. The introduction to this main section (5:1-7a) echoes phrases and ideas first sounded in the introduction to the document (1:1-15): "This is *the rule* for the men of *the community*, who *freely volunteer to convert from all evil* and to *keep themselves steadfast in all he commanded*. They should *keep apart* from the congregation of the men of injustice in order to constitute a community in Torah and *possessions*. . . . No one should walk in the *stubbornness of his heart* to go astray." They are "to lay a foundation of truth for Israel, for the community of the eternal covenant." It also establishes the authority of the Zadokite priests and the majority of the laypeople of the community.

As in column 1, this introduction is followed by a section that deals (in its own way) with admission to the community (5:7b—6:1bα), first with the oath of admission (5:7b-20a) and then with the examination of the candidate and its annual sequels (5:20b—6:1bα). Explicit in this section is a sectarianism of the strictest sort. To join the community is to "enter into the covenant of God" (5:8). Although the initiate is an Israelite by birth, he stands outside the covenantal relationship. To enter the covenant is "to be converted to the Mosaic Torah," which one is to obey "with all one's heart and soul, (abiding by) everything of it that is revealed to the sons of Zadok" (5:8-9). In short, a covenantal relationship with the God of Israel can exist only within this community and as one abides by its unique, revealed understanding of the Torah.

The implication is simple. Those who enter the community must break all relationships with outsiders, who are "perverse men who walk in the way of wickedness" (5:10-

11) and who are doomed to damnation. Entrance into the community is taken up again at 5:20. One is examined, and within the community itself there is a strict ranking of the members according to their "understanding" and their "perfection" of conduct, as evidenced in their annual examination (5:20b-24). Community means mutual concern, which reflects itself in reproof that is spoken out of "faithfulness, humility, and loving kindness." Grudges may not be harbored, nor is anyone to publicly denounce another unless the process has first been carried out privately before witnesses (5:24b—6:1bα).

The document now turns to the rules that govern the sessions of the community. The first of two sections appears to refer to a plurality of settlements that exist apart from Qumran (6:1bβ-8aα).[95] Provisions are made for smaller groups of ten persons (6:2-8aα). In each of these there is to be a priest who presides over the common meal, and the study of the Torah is to go on perpetually. A formal heading ("And this is the rule for the session of 'the Many'") introduces the parliamentary procedure for the conduct of the assembly (6:8aβ-13). Seating and the order of speaking are determined by one's rank. No one may interrupt another. Only the "Inspector" (Heb. *měbaqqēr*), who presides over the session, can speak without the consent of the majority (6:8-13).

Continuing with regulations that pertain to "the Many," the text resumes in more detail the process that leads to membership in the community (6:13b-23). At some points, however, the text is not altogether clear.[96] The initiate must be a natural-born Israelite. The probationary period divides into stages and is at least two years. The initiate is instructed in the community's halakot and is examined and voted on at various points. Full membership and full table fellowship in the pure meals of the community are granted at the end of the process.

A formal heading ("And these are the regulations by which they shall judge ...") leads to the community's penal code (6:24—7:27), which comprises a heterogeneous collection of rules, doubtless generated as a result of the community's experience.[97] Most of the offenses that are listed reflect communal tensions and may be described as "violations of community"—actions carried out without respect for, or in defiance of, other members of the community or of the community as a whole. The list culminates in rules dealing with apostasy.

A Program or Charter for the
Founding of a Community (8:1—9:25a)

It is generally believed that this section of 1QS constitutes, in part or almost as a whole, a program for the foundation of the Qumran community or its immediate predecessor.[98] It divides into two major sections. The first (8:1-16a + 9:3-11) prescribes the founding of the community, and the second (9:12-27) lays out regulations for its wise leader (maskil; cf. 1:1; 3:13). In the midst of this text have been interpolated two later sets of rules for the discipline of backsliding members of the community (8:16b-19 and 8:20—9:2).[99] The community is to be formed of twelve laymen (representing the twelve tribes of Israel) and three priests. They will be a remnant dedicated to the righteous conduct that will effect expiation in the land (8:3-10). Evidently, they serve in lieu of the Jerusalem temple, whose cult is considered to be ineffective. For two years (8:10-12) they will live in the land, nevertheless keeping themselves, their possessions, and their understanding of the Torah separate from "the men of perversity." During this time they open God's "way" in the desert through the study or exposition (*midrash*) of the Torah (8:13-16). One passage in column 9 (3–11), which is missing from 4QS[e], may be a later expansion of material in 8:4-14.[100] Most notably it identifies the terminus of the community's activity with the coming of "the prophet . . . and the anointed ones of Aaron and Israel" (9:11). The section as a whole concludes with two sets of regulations for the maskil (9:12-21a, 21b-26a).

The Prayer of the Maskil (9:26b—11:22)

The version of the Rule of the Community preserved in 1QS concludes with an extensive prayer ascribed to the maskil. Its first major part is a calendric section that refers to the community's times of prayer (8:26b—10:8). The remainder (and longest part) of the prayer expresses the maskil's intention to carry out his appointed functions as leader of the community (10:9—11:2a). This exalted status notwithstanding, the author concludes with a series of observations about his own humanity, drawing on the idiom typical of the hymns of the teacher in the Hymn Scroll (see above, pp. 134–35).

Summary

The Rule of the Community as it is recorded in 1QS is a coherent document that presents the rules and regulations that governed the Qumran community along with some of their theological rationale. It recalls the origin of the group, describes its self-understanding as the true and exclusive Israel, records the ritual and procedures by which one became a member, and spells out the rules that governed membership and meetings, as well as expulsion from the group. Parallels in Philo and especially Josephus indicate that the community is best understood as a group of Essenes, although differences in these accounts warn against a one-to-one equivalence.[101] Other parallels in the Damascus Document, both in its narratives of community origins and in its legal code, must also be fit into the picture.[102] The picture is complicated, however by the Cave 4 fragments of the Rule.[103] For example, 4QS[d], which was copied later than 1QS, omits columns 1–4. Is it an abbreviated form of the document, which included only the rules that governed the community,[104] or is it a later copy of an earlier form, to which 1QS added the ritual of initiation and an introduction to the whole document that drew motifs from the original introduction in column 5?[105] Column 5 of this same Cave 4 manuscript omits two references to the authority of the "sons of Zadok," the priests (5:2,

9), and ascribes that authority to "the Many." Does this shorter text attest diminution of priestly authority, or does 1QS indicate that early on the sons of Zadok took over authority that originally belonged to "the Many"? We could cite many other examples of long and short texts in one or another manuscript, which are variously interpreted by students of the texts. While the dating of the manuscripts must be taken seriously, it is also possible that later manuscripts are copies of early forms of the text, and that the document continued to circulate in several forms. This is the case with some biblical texts found at Qumran. The discussion will continue, and perhaps its outcome will shed some light on the development of the Qumran community.

The War Scroll (1QM, 4QM)

The War Scroll is a Hebrew document that records the rules for the conduct of the eschatological war that its author expected to be waged between Israel and the nations that were antagonistic to it. Drawing on language from its first two lines, its first editor named it "The War of the Sons of Light with the Sons of Darkness."[106] The manuscript, one of the seven scrolls found in Cave 1, contains eighteen continuous columns of text (with a break in one of them) and the remnant of a nineteenth column. Of the estimated twenty-one or twenty-two lines per column, each column except the last contains sixteen to eighteen lines, with the remainder lost due to the deterioration of the bottom of the scroll.[107] In short, it preserves extensive runs of text and, doubtless, most of the scroll. Fragments of six Cave 4 manuscripts attest the document's popularity at Qumran and seem to indicate that it was copied in various long and short textual forms.[108] Although literary analysis indicates that 1QM is a composite of earlier texts and/or traditions, our discussion will follow the present order of 1QM. The text of the War Scroll divides into four major parts.[109]

1. Introduction   1:1-17+
2. Organization and tactics   1:end—9:17+
3. Military liturgies   9:end—14:18+
4. The war against the Kittim   14:end—19:13+

From the outset, in the introductory paragraph (1:1-7), the author identifies the war of the end time as a clash between cosmic powers whose activity is embodied in human agents.[110] The "sons of light" will launch their attack against the "sons of darkness," who are, in effect, "the army of Belial," the archdemon. This army is identified with the troops of the nations that surround Israel and with the "Kittim," who are in league with "the violators of the covenant." The war will result in salvation for "the people of God" and the final destruction of "the lot of Belial" and the dominion of the Kittim (1:1-7). The remainder of the introduction reiterates these themes, focusing on the opposition of the sons of light and the sons of darkness and the destruction of the Kittim (1:8-17+).

The war divides into seven periods, three in which the sons of light will prevail, three in which the army of Belial will force the sons of light into retreat, and then the final victory by the God of Israel (1:13b-15).[111] A more detailed account of the war appears in columns 15–19.

The lost bottom lines of column 1 began a new section that laid out the rules for the conduct of the war. Thus, as column 2 begins, we have moved from the scroll's overarching mythology to a focus on the real world of human beings and their activity in time. On the Israelite side, it is a world that is dominated by the high priest, the heads of tribes, and other subordinates. The feasts and the sacrificial system are central.[112] The war will span forty years, which include thirty-five years of battle—five six-year periods (each followed by a sabbatical year of release) and then a final five-year period (2:6-9a). Of the thirty-five years, six will be spent preparing for the war and twenty-nine executing it in segments of nine, ten, and ten years (2:9b-15).

The largest part of section 2 spells out a series of "rules" (Heb. *serek*, as in *serek ha-yaḥad*, "The Rule of the Community"). The first three of these rules specify the wording to be inscribed on the instruments of war (2:16—5:2). The wording on the war trumpets, in most cases, proclaims God's power to defeat the enemy and deliver God's people (2:16—3:11). The subsequent two subsections prescribe the slogans to be placed on the battle standards, as well as the size of the standards, which diminish in relation to the size of the unit (3:13—4:17+). The beginning of column 5 mentions "the Prince of the whole congregation," evidently a reference, but the only extant reference, to the royal messiah.[113] The last and longest subsection provides instructions for battle formations (5:3—9:16+). One paragraph lists the qualifications for the personnel: the appropriate ages for the various functions (7:1-4a), as well as classes of persons who are disqualified because of physical defects or because they could bring impurity into the camp (7:4b-7). The latter is important because "the holy angels" are marching with the armies. This same motif appears in the descriptions of the battle towers (9:10-16), which are to carry on them the names, respectively, of the four archangels (Michael, Gabriel, Sariel, and Raphael).[114]

Section 3 of the War Scroll contains several liturgical compositions to be used in connection with the battles of the war. To judge from its introductory rubric, the first hymn is to be employed as the army approaches the battle (see the quotations of Deut 20:2-5 and Num 10:9 at 1QM 10:1-8a). Its introductory paragraph stresses the uniqueness of the God of Israel and the uniqueness of God's people. They have been chosen from all the nations and are bound in a covenantal relationship with their God. Like "the holy angels," they are "holy" and are the recipients of revelation, both of the law and of God's activity as creator of the cosmos (1QM 10:8b-16). Citing examples from Israel's history (David and Goliath, the later Philistines, Pharaoh at the Red Sea), the heart of the prayer affirms that it is God and God's might that bring Israel victory in battle against the overwhelming odds (11:1-18+) that are identified as "the troops of Belial" (11:8). This victory is accomplished through the activity of Belial's counterpart, "the multitude of holy ones in heaven and the hosts of angels in your holy dwelling" (12:1-5). This unit closes with a paragraph that addresses God in its first sentence. The remainder of the paragraph calls upon the army to strike against the enemy, and exhorts Zion and Jerusalem to rejoice in the victory to come (12:7-17+).

The second composition in section 3 begins, like the first, with instructions to the priests and Levites and elders to bless "God of Israel and all the deeds of his truth" and to curse "Belial and all the spirits of his lot" (12:end—13:2a). The next lines contain the words of the blessing and curse (13:2b-6). The blessing/curse formula is reminiscent of the liturgy in 1QS 1:21—2:18. The remainder of the column continues the address to God in the form of a blessing and an extensive exposition of Israel's status (13:7-18+). The nation, which is bound by a covenant to God, belongs to the lot of light under the care of "the Prince of Light" (Michael) and his angels and stands in opposition to "all the sons of darkness," who are under the tutelage of Belial and "the angels of destruction." The section parallels the theology of 1QS 3:13-26.

The rubric that precedes the final composition in this section sets it in the aftermath of battle, as the armies "wash their clothes and cleanse themselves of the blood of guilty corpses" (13:end—14:4a). The substance of the hymn is a pair of blessings on the God of Israel who has kept covenant in the past during the dominion of Belial and now through the destruction of his armies (14:4b-15).

The fourth and final extant part of the War Scroll (14:end—19:14+) describes the battle against the Kittim first mentioned in column 1. The connection between these two sections is indicated by the frequent occurrence of "the Kittim" in the two columns (1:2, 4, 6, 9, 12; 15:2; 16:3, 6, 8, 9; 17:12, 14-15; 18:2, 4; 19:9, 13) and by the reference to "the third lot" in 17:16 (cf. 1:13-14). Precisely how the seven "lots" play out in this narrative is uncertain due to the substantial deterioration of the end of the scroll. The narrative may have run something like this:[115]

a. Introduction	14:end—16:1
b. First attack (lot 1)	16:3-9
c. Counterattack by Belial (lot 2)	16:11—17:9
d. Second attack (lot 3)	17:10-16
e. Counterattack–attack–counterattack (lots 4–6)	[17:17+]
f. God's final intervention (lot 7)	17:end—18:6a
g. Blessings and hymn of rejoicing	18:6b—19:8
h. Aftermath of the battle	19:9-13+

Part a is indicated by the rubric that continues down to 16:1. In 16:3 the action begins with the sounding of the trumpets (16:3-8a), and then the text briefly describes the attack (16:8b-9). After a blank line in the manuscript, the counterattack by the army of Belial is noted (16:11). As in earlier columns, the priests play a prominent role, encouraging the army of Israel (16:13—17:9). The second attack (and third lot, 17:16) begins with the blast of the priestly trumpets and ends with the route of the enemy. The narration of the decisive intervention of God seems to have begun at the end of column 17 and is under way at the beginning of column 18. Lines 5-6 describe the conclusion of the battle as "the sun travels toward its setting on that day." The blessing in 18:6-8 recalls earlier liturgical material, as does an additional section in 18:10-15+. Column 19 is preserved in only a fragment. Lines 1-8 duplicate the hymn of exultation in 12:7-18, and line 9 returns to a narrative mode that is set on the morning after the battle.

Central to the War Scroll is a traditional theme in Israelite biblical and postbiblical literature: the antagonism between Israel the covenant people and their enemies among the nations, here epitomized in the Kittim. This antagonism is in focus especially in texts composed during periods of foreign domination and oppression (see, e.g., the texts discussed here in chaps. 3, 6, and 8). The antagonism is the more acute here because it is construed as a realization of the cosmic battle between God and God's angels and Belial and his hordes. Israelite troops mingle with God's angels, and the armies of the nations are the host of the principle of evil, the archenemy of God. By the same token, when Michael's dominion is exalted in heaven, Israel will rule over all humanity (17:6-8). This is the author's message and promise: the God of Israel is in control of the events of history and will vindicate the covenant people and exterminate evil.[116]

Discussion of the date and setting of the War Scroll is complicated by the composite nature of the document. If we focus first on the form of the text as it exists in 1QM, several facts are clear. Aspects of its language and content are thoroughly at home at Qumran: the terminology of the "sons of light" and the "sons of darkness"; the central role of the priests; the presumption of a 364-day calendar;[117] the close association between the sectarians and the angels (cf., e.g., 1QH[a] 11[3]:21-23; 19[11]:11-13). In such a context, the paleographical dating of 1QM to the decades before or after the turn of the era suggests that the text's final redaction was carried out with a view toward what its author perceived to be the threat of Roman military might.[118] As in the Qumran Habakkuk Commentary, the Kittim would have been understood to be the Romans (see above, p. 129), although the expression may originally have referred to the Seleucids.[119]

Although scholars generally agree that the War Scroll is a composite of earlier texts and/or traditions, no reconstruction of the scroll's literary history has found a consensus.[120] According to one view, columns 1 and 15–19 represent a late redaction of texts (preserved in the heart of the document) that reflect knowledge of Maccabean war practices and that date to the mid-second century B.C.E.[121] Another explanation posits that columns 2–14 fill in an earlier text about the war that comprised columns 1 and 15–19. This explanation notes that the dualism of the War Scroll is located typologically between the dualistic worldviews of the book of Daniel and the Qumran Rule of the Community.[122] In Daniel 10–12 the wars between nations are enactments of battles among heavenly angelic princes, who are the patrons of the respective nations, and the fundamental antagonism between Israel and the Seleucid kingdom involves a conflict between Michael, the patron of Israel, and the spirit power behind the throne of Antiochus Epiphanes (see above, pp. 81–82). Different from Daniel, the Rule of the Community depicts the spirit of darkness as a cosmic principle of moral evil, albeit one whom God has created (1QS 3:1—4:26). Moreover, it identifies the children of light and the children of darkness—the clients of the two spirits—with the members of the Qumran

[handwritten margin notes: "Israel vs BELLI AL⟩ cosmic moral evil generally"]

community and those who stand outside the covenant of the community. That is, on the human level the dualistic distinction is not between Israel and the nations, but between righteous and sinful Israelites. Further, the battle between the two spirits is waged in the human heart, and not on the battlefield of military war.

The War Scroll agrees with Daniel and differs from the Rule of the Community in associating its dualism with the antagonism between Israel and the nations. It differs from Daniel and agrees with 1QS 3:13—4:26 in identifying the antagonistic spirit as Belial, the principle of cosmic moral evil. Thus the typological location of the scroll's dualism may reflect its chronological origins—between Daniel and the sectarian dualism on the Rule of the Community. Of course, it is not impossible that both groups of material reflect early tradition.

Alongside these observations about the nonsectarian character of the War Scroll's dualism is another, related factor—the broad use of the terms "(God of) Israel," "nation," and "covenant" to relate to Israel as a whole over against the Gentiles. How did an author/editor who was at home in the sectarian use of "sons of light" and "sons of darkness," "Israel," and "covenant" come to use (or retain) these terms in a nonsectarian manner throughout the text of the Scroll?[123] What made a person who lived in a world that distinguished between his group, the true Israel, and those who stood outside the covenant erase these distinctions and draw the line between ethnic Israel as a whole and the nations? And how did this text with its Israel/Gentiles polarity function in a community for whom the divisions between the saved and the damned fell within ethnic Israel itself? The Rule of the Congregation (see below, pp. 150–51) seems to provide an analogy to the War Scroll in this respect, albeit not an explanation for the change of viewpoint.[124]

With all these ambiguities, the War Scroll continues to challenge scholars to ask new questions about the text itself, the persons that created and edited it, and the community that preserved it in multiple copies. What were the roots of its traditions? How did it evolve to the literary form attested in 1QM? By what intellectual or theological processes did the pacifist ideology of the apocalyptic book of Daniel—to which 1QM owes so much—fuse with biblical holy war ideologies to create the realistic, activist, militant ideology of the War Scroll?[125] How might these processes have compared to those that led to the militant holy war language of the apocalyptic Animal Vision and Epistle of Enoch (see above, pp. 85, 111–112)?[126] Do any of these texts tell us anything about possible eschatological dimensions in the Maccabean wars? How do we relate the militancy of the War Scroll to claims that the Essenes were a pacifist group?[127]

A Halakic Letter (4QMMT)

The text of this untitled, anonymous Hebrew document has been painstakingly reconstructed from the fragments of six manuscripts recovered from Cave 4.[128] Its central concern is the proper observance of certain precepts of the Torah that pertain to the conduct of the Jerusalem temple cult. The frequent use of "we" and "you" has suggested that the document is a kind of public letter or treatise sent from one party to another regarding important matters of mutual concern.[129] The text divides into three main parts, identified by the editors as A, B, and C. Section A outlines the details of a 364-day calendar. Section B treats a number of disputed points of law. Section C is a hortatory conclusion that appeals to the addressees to accept the senders' interpretations of the Torah "for your own good and the good of Israel."* The siglum MMT abbreviates the Hebrew *miqṣat maʿăśê ha-tôrāh* ("some precepts of the Torah," C 27), which, in the editors' view, aptly summarizes the contents of the document.[130]

Part A listed in terse form the days of the year on which the Sabbaths, the feasts, and the epagomenal (extra) thirty-first day at the end of each quarter fell, and it concluded with: "the year is complete—three hundred and s[ixty-four] days." Approximately one half of this tabulation has been preserved in the remnants of six columns of one manuscript (4Q394). Since this part seems to have little in common with the rest of the text and since it is not attested in any of the other five manuscripts, it is uncertain whether it was part of the original form of the document.[131] The 364-day calendar, however, is attested in other Qumran texts.[132]

Part B, which has been reconstructed from the fragments of five manuscripts to a length of eighty-two lines, recorded the legal opinions of the author and his group on issues related to the Jerusalem temple, its purity, and the proper conduct of its sacrificial system. The extant parts touch on at least seventeen issues.[133] The topics and subtopics are introduced by "And concerning x, . . ." and in the preserved text, the cited opinion and practice are introduced seven times by "we consider that . . ." (Heb. *ḥāshab*, B 29, 36, 37, 42) or "we say . . ." (Heb. *ʾāmar*, B 55, [65], 73). Four times the author cites the authority of Scripture ("it is written," B 66, [70], 76, 77), but in some cases the accepted practice is simply stated categorically.[134] The double occurrence of "you [pl.] know" (B 68, 80) indicates that the document is directed to an outside group that is differentiated from the "we" of the author's group.

Part C has been reconstructed from three manuscripts to a length of thirty-two lines. Between the last extant line of part B and the first preserved line of part C an estimated twenty lines have been lost, and it is impossible to know where one section ended and the other began.[135] The end of the document, however, has been preserved in fragments of two manuscripts (4Q398 and 399). Different from part B, this part is hortatory rather than descriptive. The author, speaking again for "us," addresses a "you," which in all but two cases (C 7, 8) appears in the singular. The cast of characters is further enhanced in the statement that "we have separated ourselves from the multitude of the people" and from the things they do (C 7-8). The gist of this section is as follows: We have separated ourselves from the sinful majority in Israel. In the book (of Moses) it is written that God's curse will fall on those who disobey the Torah. This has happened, and now that the "end of days" has come, or is imminent, it is time to repent and return to God, so that the blessings of the covenant may come upon Israel (C 13–16; cf. Deut 30:1-3). To this end, we have written you, laying out the true understanding of the Torah, so that you may study the Scriptures (Moses, the Prophets, and David). Therein you will discover how God blessed the kings of Israel who were "seekers of the Torah."[136] If you follow their example and recognize that our understanding of the Torah is correct, this will result in "good [i.e., blessing] for you and your people . . . for you and for Israel."[137]

Thus parts B and C are closely related to one another. Part B spells out the right understanding of the Torah, and part C encourages the addressee(s) to adhere to these practices and thus receive God's blessing. The rhetoric in part C indicates that the author seeks to co-opt rather than confront the addressee(s).

We may draw some general historical conclusions from this fascinating text. The presence at Qumran of six manuscripts whose dates range from the mid-first century B.C.E. to the mid-first century C.E. speaks for the document's long-term importance for this group.[138] Its references to disputes over the interpretation and practice of the Torah, especially as it relates to purity and temple cult, echo concerns in other Qumran texts.[139] However, its irenic tone, its lack of a sharp insider/outsider polarity, to say nothing of terms like "sons of light" and "sons of darkness," "the Liar," the "Wicked Priest," and the "Seekers after Smooth Things," suggest that it derives from an early period of Qumranite history (before divisions hardened) or from an antecedent group.[140] The appeal for "you" to act in a way that will bring blessing also to Israel, "your people," and the citing of the example of the Torah-abiding kings of Israel, suggest that it was addressed to a current leader of Israel, presumably one of the Hasmoneans—albeit before such a leader came into direct confrontation with the Qumranites.[141] At this point opinions differ. For example, might the author have been the "Teacher of Righteousness," and might this very document have triggered a reaction that led to the confrontation mentioned in the Qumran commentary on Psalm 37:32-33 (4Q171 4:7-9)?[142] While this is possible, we are in the realm of speculation.

Another question pertains to the nature of the legal opinions in part C and the light they may shed on the origin of the Qumran group. In three or four cases, the cited opinions correspond to opinions that the Mishnah attributes to the Sadducees in their opposition to the Pharisees.[143] This appears to support the notion that the Qumranites derived from circles of the Zadokite priesthood, which also developed into the second-century Sadducees. Details on how this happened, however, are uncertain, and some scholars are more hesitant than others to press the parallels.[144] However one resolves these issues, MMT provides a precious piece of primary historical evidence about Qumran origins, even if we cannot with certainty identify its precise date and determine the precise identity of the spokesman of the "us" and the leader of Israel to whom he speaks.

We may derive two other historical data from this text. It is one of our earliest attestations of the threefold structure of the Scriptures, with the third part identified as "David" (C 10). Like the Book of Jubilees, it demonstrates how the specific interpretation of the Torah can be tied together in one document to the contemporizing interpretation of the Deuteronomic interpretation of history (see above, p. 72).

Rule of the Congregation (1QSa)

This two-column Hebrew text was inscribed on the same scroll that contained the Cave 1 copy of the Rule of the Community.[145] In this location it is, in effect, an eschatologically focused appendix to the Rule of the Community. Its first line identifies it as "the rule for all the congregation of Israel in the end of days" (1:1), and to a large extent it lays out the laws and regulations that govern assemblies of people. The first section (1:1-5) describes a solemn assembly of men, women, and children who gather for a formal hearing of the Torah, so that they can commit themselves to the covenant that has been observed by "the sons of Zadok, the priests," the others in the community, and especially the members of the counsel of the community, "who have kept the covenant in the midst of wickedness and atoned for the land." The section expands on aspects of 1QS 8:1-10. The text is noteworthy because it broadens the sectarian horizon of salvation in 1QS to include Israelites, who have not been members of the community (see above, pp. 138–42).

The second section of the document (1QSa 1:6-25a) sets forth the regulations for the composition of the armies that will do battle in the eschatological war (cf. 1QM, above, pp. 143–47) and for those who otherwise serve the community.[146] Duties are distributed according to age, mental competence, and the "perfection" of one's behavior; and certain persons (the mentally incompetent) are excluded from service. This is the only section of the document that does not deal with ad hoc assemblies, though an army is, of course, an assemblage of persons.

The third section (1QSa 1:25b—2:10) deals with formal legal assemblies, whether for judgment, or for the convocation of the council, or to make a decision about war. As in the previous section, the principal concern is with one's qualifications. The issue here is ritual impurity (2:3-4), moral deformity reflected in a physical imperfection (2:4b-7a),[147] or disability due to old age (2:7b). Such persons are excluded from the assembly because "the holy angels" sit in their midst (cf. 1QM 7:3-7). If such a person has anything to say to the group, it must be communicated outside the assembly hall (1QSa 2:9b-10).

The next section (2:11-17a) prescribes the protocol for a gathering of the community council in the presence of the "anointed one of Israel," that is, the messianic king of the end time. Here, as befits the presence of the king, the issue is rank (cf. 1QS 6:8b-23). First the high priest enters, then the rest of the priests and the laypeople enter and are seated according to their "dignity" (lit. "glory"). Next, the anointed one enters, and then all the members of congregation enter and sit before him according to their dignity.

The final section of the Rule (1QSa 2:17b-22) provides the rubrics for the communal meal (cf. 1QS 6:2b-6), as it is to be celebrated in the presence of the high priest and the anointed one of Israel. Again, rank is crucial. First the priest stretches his hand and blesses the bread and the wine. Then the anointed one of Israel stretches his hand for blessing. Finally, all the members of the community pronounce the blessing in the order of their dignity (or the two leaders bless the whole congregation in the order of their dignity).[148] The meaning of the last line of the section is uncertain. Unless one supposes that the anointed one was expected to meet regularly with every small group, it seems to imply that whenever ten or more men gather to eat their common meal, they do so as if the high priest and the anointed one of Israel were present. That is, the meal anticipates the coming of the messianic king. Such an interpretation might provide a parallel to some early Christian communal meals, but the parallels need to be treated with care.[149]

The Rule of the Congregation is directed to Israelites living in "the end of days," that is, the last period of history before the end.[150] Perhaps its sections are to be understood chronologically. It begins with an assembly in which the Israelites commit themselves to the Torah as it has been understood and observed by "the sons of Zadok" and their group (section 1). The regulations that follow in sections 2 and 3 deal with subsequent events: the eschatological war and various assemblies. The last two sections deal with the final, messianic segment of the "end of days." If we accept this interpretation, which construes this whole period as one period, then it is understandable, for example, that small groups living during this time would eat their meals in an atmosphere in which the cloud of future messianic fulfillment hovered over their present practice.[151]

The dating of this document is problematic. Its only more or less intact copy was inscribed in the early first century B.C.E.[152] Nonetheless, although it served as an eschatologically focused appendix to the Rule of the Community to which it was juxtaposed, its openness to salvation for "all the congregation of Israel" may point to an earlier date when some of the rules in 1QS were already in place, but before the Qumran community has developed the sectarian mentality that is evidenced in 1QS.[153] In this respect, it would agree typologically with the viewpoint in the War Scroll, the Halakic Letter, and an early stratum of the Damascus Document (see above, pp. 146–47, 149).[154]

The pairing of the high priest and the messianic king in the Rule of the Congregation is a feature typical of some Qumran eschatology.[155] Thus 1QS 9:11 cites as a terminus the coming of the eschatological prophet and the anointed ones of Aaron and Israel. 4QTestimonia presumes the same triad in the same order (see above, p. 132). One manuscript of the Damascus Document also awaits the coming of "the anointed one(s) of Aaron and Israel" (CD A 12:23—13:1; 14:19; B 19:10-11; 20:1). The pairing has its roots in the ideology expressed in Zechariah 3–4, where Joshua the anointed high priest and Zerubbabel the Davidic heir are described as the "sons of oil," who stand in God's presence (4:14). The pairing notwithstanding, some Qumran texts focus on the military activity of the Davidic king,[156] while a pre-Qumranic text like the Aramaic Levi Document features the future high priest and even associates with him biblical language about the Davidic king (see below, pp. 161–62). This messianic variation at Qumran suggests that we must be cautious not to assume that the New Testament title "Christ" must always refer to Jesus as the Davidic king.[157]

Songs of the Sabbath Sacrifice (The Angelic Liturgy)

Shîrôt ʿôlat ha-shabbat is a collection of thirteen songs in Hebrew associated with the Sabbath praise that the angelic choirs utter in the heavenly sanctuary. It is preserved in nine fragmentary copies found at Qumran and one discovered at the fortress of Masada thirty-three miles to the south.[158] The fragmentary state of the manuscripts notwithstanding, overlaps between them and the formulaic character of the text allow some sense of the document as a whole. The songs, seven of which have substantial parts preserved, were dated for each of the thirteen Sabbaths of the first quarter of the year. The superscriptions are stereotyped: "For the *maśkîl*"; "song of the sacrifice of the nth Sabbath on the nth (day) of the nth month"; an invocation for a group of angels to praise God.[159]

The songs divide into three groups. Songs 1–5 describe the establishment of the angelic priesthood, their duties, and the praise that these priests utter. The first song is dated to the first Sabbath of the first month, which corresponds to the week that the Temple Scroll designates as a commemoration of the ordination of priests (11Q19 15:3; see below, p. 155). Appropriately, the song describes how the most holy ones (lit. "the holy ones of the holy ones") have been appointed as priests in the heavenly sanctuary. The nouns "holy ones," "the holy of holies" (i.e., the sanctuary), and "holiness" and the verb "sanctify" (lit. "make holy") permeate the preserved section of the song (4Q400 1 1–20). Those who stand in the presence of the holy God must themselves be holy and keep God's presence pure from any uncleanness. (The term "holy" is never used of God in this section, but God's holy priests are called *ʾĕlōhîm*, the most frequent name for God throughout the composition.) The other specific functions ascribed to the angels are to propitiate God's goodwill and thus effect forgiveness for those who repent of their transgressions (line 16)—a typical priestly function—and (it would appear) to execute God's "jealous vengeance"—a function that the Bible and later literature also ascribe to priests.[160] The second song, to judge from its few fragments, focused on the angels' responsibility to praise God. Appropriately, God is here depicted several times as "king," and words like "majesty" and "glory" recur. The song also refers to the priestly status of the human beings who utter this song, contrasting their earthly knowledge with that of the "divine beings" (4Q400 2:6-9). The third song is lost, and the fourth has only a few words preserved. The fragments of the fifth song indicate that God's knowledge, discernment, and providential plan were its subject, and the middle of the song depicted the angels as divine warriors (4Q402 4; cf. the War Scroll, above, pp. 144–45).

The middle group of songs (6–8) focuses on the angelic praise of God. Thick with formulaic repetition, Song 6 lists the psalms that the seven chief princes utter seven times in praise of God, and it follows this with reference to the sevenfold blessings that they speak over the various groups in the heavenly chorus (Mas 1k col. 2). The first half of Song 7 (4Q403 1 1:30-40) addresses these groups in the heavenly host, calling on them variously to "magnify," "laud," "exalt," "exult," "confess," and "praise." In the song's second part, the structures in the heavenly sanctuary are called upon to praise God, anticipating things to come in the later songs (4Q403 1 1:30-46; 1 2:1-16). Song 8 takes up again the call for the chief princes, the deputy princes, and various sevenfold groups to praise God in sevenfold ways (4Q403 1 2:18-37).

In the final section of the composition (Songs 9–13), the praise of the angels is set within a vivid, graphic recitation of the architectural features of the sanctuary, as the mind and the emotions move progressively toward the heart of the heavenly palace.[161] Here a tumult of praise arises from those who bless the divine chariot throne, the portals of the temple glorify the divine king, and the angelic priests offer sacrifice.

The aforementioned subject matter is not unique to this text among Jewish writings of the Greco-Roman period. It is rooted in the vision of the chariot in Ezekiel 1–2,[162] which is also elaborated in 1 Enoch 14–16 in the description of Enoch's ascent to the heavenly palace and his progress to the door of its throne room, where the heavenly priests and the myriads of angels surround God's throne and utter God's praise.[163] The Parables of Enoch focus on the angelic praise of God (1 Enoch 39; 61:6-13; see below, p. 250). However, the Songs of the Sabbath Sacrifice are to these heavenly visions what the text about the New Jerusalem (see below, pp. 177-79) is to the Zion hymns in Tobit 13 and 11QPs[a] 22. They offer a detailed, close-up exposition of what is elsewhere treated thematically and in general. They lift one up emotionally and imaginatively into the midst of the heavenly choirs. Whether the songs are an expansion on the apocalyptic visions or the visions (esp. in the Parables of Enoch) presuppose knowledge of something like these songs is a point that would be worth discussing. However one resolves that, the thirteen songs constitute a remarkable religious phenomenon in their own right. To what end were they composed, and how were they in fact used?

In general, their content is not technically liturgical; that is, the songs do not address themselves to the Deity.[164] Instead they *describe* the angelic worship and appeal to the angels to engage in that worship. Thus we may see them "as the means for a communion with angels in the act of praise, in short as a form of communal mysticism."[165] They created an experience by which the community on earth was brought emotionally and imaginatively into the presence of the angels and, indeed, before the very throne of the Deity.[166]

Two elements in the Songs fit well with the situation at Qumran. First, the angels are repeatedly described as priests.[167] Second, and conversely, God's priests and the worship of God take place in the heavenly sanctuary. Through the medium of these songs, priests in the community at Qumran could attune themselves with their counterparts, the heavenly priests (cf. 1QH[a] 11[3]:20-23; 19[11]:10-14). Moreover, they were assured that although the Jerusalem cult was polluted and ineffective, the praise due the heavenly king was in fact taking place in heaven, that forgiveness was effected through the instrumentality of the heavenly priests, and that God's kingship, which was yet to be realized on earth, was already established in heaven.[168]

This text was clearly a popular item at Qumran, as the nine manuscripts attest. Moreover, the initial address to the maskil parallels similar superscriptions in texts probably authored at Qumran,[169] and all the manuscripts date from the time of the community (75 B.C.E.–50 C.E.).[170] Since they lack the terminology typical of the Qumran sectarian texts, however, it is uncertain whether they were composed there. They could have originated prior to the formation of the Qumran community in "circles" that were disaffected with the Jerusalem temple and priesthood and that also gave rise to some of the Enochic literature and the priestly Aramaic Levi Document.[171]

Whatever their origin, the Songs of the Sabbath Sacrifice attest an important variant in the tradition that led from the throne vision in Ezekiel 1–2 through the account of Enoch's ascent in 1 Enoch 14–16, to the Parables of Enoch and the book of Revelation, and on to the later texts of Jewish *merkabah* mysticism.[172] The peculiar nuances of the text demonstrate, as we have so often seen, the complexity in Jewish religion in the period between the Bible and the texts of the rabbinic period.

The Temple Scroll

The Temple Scroll (11Q19) was the last Qumran scroll to come into the hands of scholars.[173] It is also the largest of the intact Qumran scrolls, being more than 8 meters (26 feet) long and consisting of sixty-seven columns.[174] Unfortunately, this prize scroll sustained severe damage before it was purchased.[175] Columns 2–5 are preserved only in a single 13–17–line fragment each. Columns 6–40 consist of generally increasingly larger fragments, most which contain the bottom margin and part of the full width of the columns. Columns 41–67 preserve the bottom two-thirds to three-quarters of the scroll (15 to 21 lines of the original 22 to 26). Thus we have small portions of the first 7 percent of the scroll, larger parts of the next 53 percent, and from two-thirds to three-quarters of the final 40 percent of the scroll. From these remains we can extract a good deal of information about its original contents, although the large gaps in the manuscript create some major unsolved issues.[176]

The scroll, written in Hebrew, was a collection of laws and prescriptions primarily about the Jerusalem temple and the Holy City, drawn mainly from the Pentateuch, systematically reorganized in five major clusters, and presented as definitive revealed Torah, notably through the substitution of the pronoun "I" for the Divine Name. Thus biblical laws about YHWH are here laws explicitly spoken *by* YHWH. The title of the scroll, not found in the scroll itself, reflects the predominant place that it gives to the construction of the sanctuary, the sacrifices that are offered in it, and the maintenance of its purity. The contents, which draw on four or five (written) sources, can be outlined as follows, although there are overlapping transitions between several of them:[177]

Narrative setting and introduction	cols.	1–2
1a. Construction of the sanctuary and altar		3–13
2. Calendar of annual festivals, their sacrifices		13–29
1b. Construction of courtyards and their buildings		30–45
3. Purity laws for the temple and Jerusalem		45–51
4. Rewriting of Deuteronomy 12–23		52–66+
Conclusion?		67:1–5

To judge from its first major section (1a), the fictive setting for the contents of the scroll was either the account of the ratification of the covenant on Mount Sinai (Exod 24–31;

11QTemple 51:7) in which God gives Moses the two tables of the Torah (Exod 24:12) and the prescriptions for the tabernacle and its service (chaps. 25–31), or the account of the renewal of the covenant on Mount Sinai in Exodus 34 and the construction of the tabernacle in Exodus 35–40. Elements from both contexts appear in this part of the scroll.[178] The fragment of column 2, which preserves a bit of the introduction, appears to have focused on God's covenantal relationship with Israel and—appropriate to its context in the Scroll—on the prohibition of the worship of other gods.[179] Its language derives from Exodus 34:10-16 and Deuteronomy 7 and exemplifies the author's conflation of related biblical texts.[180]

The fragment of column 3 indicates that the author has begun to lay out the prescriptions for the construction of the sanctuary. These begin at the heart of the temple, with the temple building, its furnishings, and the sacrificial altar (cols. 3—13:9). The narrative will pick up again at column 30 and continue outward through the three temple courts (cols. 30–45). The details of the prescriptions are drawn from the descriptions of the tabernacle in Exodus 35 and 26, Solomon's temple in 1 Kings 6 and 2 Chronicles 3–4, and the vision of the postexilic temple in Ezekiel 40–48.[181] This conflation of material from diverse biblical sources is, again, typical of the author's technique in the scroll as a whole.

At 13:10, after having reached the sacrificial altar, the author breaks his narrative about the temple itself and makes a transition to its cult. After prescriptions about the daily burnt offerings (*tamid*) and the supplementary Sabbath offerings (13:10—14:top),[182] the author begins an extensive exposition (14:top—29:10) of the laws that govern the sacrifices and rituals that are prescribed for each of the annual festivals. The section is usually described as a "calendar."[183] Given the respective apportionment of space and the section's context, however, we should perhaps consider the calendar as providing the skeleton or structure for an extensive exposition of sacrificial laws.

The annual festivals are as follows.[184] (1) *The New Year*, on the New Moon of the first month (Nisan) (14:9—15:3a). (2) *An annual commemoration of the ordination of the priests*, the first seven days of that month (15:3b—17:5). (3) *Passover*, on the 14th of the month (17:6-16). (4) *Four successive festivals of firstfruits* at fifty-day intervals, beginning on the 26th of the first month: (a) Barley (18:1-10a); (b) Wheat (18:10b—19:10); (c) Wine (19:11—21:11); (d) Oil (21:12—23:2a). (5) *The Wood Festival*, on the 23rd to 29th of the sixth month (23:2b—25:2a). (6) *The Day of Memorial*, begun with the blast of the trumpets, the first day of the seventh month (25:2b-10a).[185] (7) *The Day of Atonement*, the 10th of the month (25:10b—27:10a). (8) *The Feast of Booths*, the 15th to the 21st of the month, followed by the solemn assembly on the following day, the eighth day of the feast (27:10b—29:1). A summary at the end of the section (29:2-6) leads to God's promise that God will dwell with the covenant people until God creates the new, eschatological temple (29:7-10).

The author's principal biblical sources are Numbers 28–29 and Leviticus 23, although he draws on other passages to fill in perceived gaps in the regulations and to resolve problems caused by texts that seem to be at odds with one another. Among the listed festivals several have no biblical basis: the annual ordination of the priests, the four feasts of firstfruits (rather than one), and the Wood Offering.[186] Moreover, the author follows the 364-day calendar found in 1 Enoch 72–82 (see above, pp. 44–46), the Book of Jubilees (see above, pp. 69–74), and several other texts found at Qumran, including the Halakic Letter (see above, pp. 147–49).[187]

With his exposition of the festivals and their rituals complete, the author returns to his narrative about the construction of the temple, starting with the inner court and working to the outer one (cols. 30–45).[188] The three courts are square. The inner court measures 280 cubits (480 feet) on each side. Within it are five structures in addition to the sacrificial altar: a stair-house that provided access to the roof of the temple building and its upper chamber (30:3—31:9); a "house of the laver," where the priests washed after performing the sacrifices (31:10—33:7); a house of utensils, where the sacrificial vessels and fire pans were stored (33:8—34:top); an open-air slaughterhouse (34:top—35:9); and a stoa of columns used to tether the sacrificial animals (35:10-15a). The wall of the court was lined by a columned stoa, and one gate on each side provided access to the sacred precinct for each of the four divisions of the tribe of Levi.[189] The middle court (38:12—40:top) was 480 cubits (750 feet) square, providing 100 cubits (156 feet) on all sides of the inner wall. The court was reserved for ritually pure Israelite males twenty years of age or older,[190] and its four walls were pierced by three gates each, one for each of the twelve tribes of Israel. The description of the outer court and the perimeter of the temple runs from column 40:top to 46:12. The court provides the opportunity for ritually pure Israelite women, children, and proselytes to participate in the public festivals of the temple.[191] Its dimensions are gargantuan—2,500 feet (a half mile) on each side,[192] enclosing an area roughly four times the size of the *temenos* that Herod would construct for his temple. The wall, like that of the middle court, has twelve gates.

Toward the end of his description of this court, the author turns to the subject that has been the presupposition for the temple's architecture, the preservation of the sanctuary's purity (45:7—46:12). First come a series of rules that exclude from the temple, and in most cases from the Holy City, men who have had genital discharges, blind persons, those who have had contact with a corpse, and diseased persons (45:7a—46:1). This is followed by a few final architectural details. The outer wall will have devices to ward off birds from defiling the temple courts, and a trench 150 feet wide will prevent anyone from accidentally wandering from the city into the temple and thus defiling it (46:2-12b).[193] In short, the temple's architecture provides a series of barriers that keep at various removes persons whose respective states of impurity would threaten the purity of the sanctuary.[194]

The topic of impurity now moves outside the temple precincts to the surrounding area—Jerusalem, other cities, and the whole of Israel (46:13—51:10).[195] The laws in this section are sprinkled with geographical and spatial references (the/my city, their/your cities, your land, the house) and prescribe which actions that foster impurity are permitted in what places and which defiling acts are forbidden to all of Israel, God's holy people, who are separate from the nations (48:1-12). This legislation, taken together with the account of the temple architecture, defines zones of decreasing purity spreading out from the temple building where God dwells, into the inner court, where the Levitically pure priests function, through the middle and outer temple courts, to the city, to its immediate environs, and from there into the towns and cities of the land of Israel.

The last major section of the scroll is a rewritten form of Deuteronomy 12–23 (cols. 51:11—67:top).[196] It begins with a command that quotes Deuteronomy 16:18-20 about the appointment of judges and their responsibility to act justly (11QTemple 51:11-18). This abrupt opening is perhaps bound to the previous section by the biblical qualification "in all your towns" (51:11; cf. Deut 16:18). Following the cue of its biblical source (Deut 16:21-22 and 17:1), the text of this section switches to a treatment of cultic matters, first idolatry (11QTemple 51:19—52:3) and then prescriptions about animals to be sacrificed and animals to be eaten, again with a distinction being made between clean and unclean and between "all your towns" and the temple and its environs (52:4—53:8). At this point we are at the beginning of a running paraphrase of most of Deuteronomy 12–23, except chapters 14–16 (most of which the author treats elsewhere in the scroll).[197] The exposition, which closely follows the order of the biblical text, adds relevant material from other sources (as elsewhere in the scroll) and continues to the end of the document (66:17 and originally to the top of col. 67).

The major expansion in this section of the scroll is in columns 56–59. The author quotes Deuteronomy 17:14-20 (11QTemple 56:12—57:top seven lines), which anticipates the election of a king and summarizes his qualifications and responsibilities, including the obligation to write out a copy of "this law" (i.e., Deuteronomy) and to consult it and learn from it. At this point, the author has inserted an estimated seventy-three lines, which in effect define "this law" (56:21).[198] This so-called Law of the King (57:1—59:21) expands on Deuteronomy 17:14-17, laying out prescriptions and rules that are to govern the king's activities and responsibilities as military chief, head of state, and guardian of justice (11QTemple 57:1—59:top) as well as the curses and blessings that will result from his wrong or right conduct (59:top-21+). The function of the section as a whole appears to be to place certain limits on the king and to guard against excessive autocracy. There are restrictions on the waging of war. The king is to administer justice and interpret the law in consultation with a council of priests and Levites. The king must marry an Israelite woman from his own clan and family, and he can neither divorce her nor marry a second wife while the first is alive.[199] The seriousness of the king's responsibility is underscored by the curses and blessings, which comprise roughly one-third of the section and paraphrase parts of Deuteronomy 28 and 30 (and some related biblical passages), tying them to the behavior of the king rather than the people.

The text of 51:11—66:21+ constitutes roughly one-quarter of the Temple Scroll. The text of this section does not clearly indicate the rationale for its inclusion in a document that is devoted to the temple and its cult and issues of purity and impurity that relate to these. It is possible that the author wishes to lay out regulations concerning life in the land of Israel, thus continuing the pattern that had begun in the description of the temple, its courts, the city and its outlying districts, and the rest of the land.[200] The concerns here are different, however, and the overall content of the section is governed by the content of Deuteronomy. An emphasis on place and purity appears only in columns 51–53. Thereafter the issue of the cult and a contrast with the Holy City and the temple are lacking.

The genre and function of the Temple Scroll should be sought in its relationship to Israel's Scriptures, especially the Pentateuch. It is a book of Torah rewritten in the first-person singular and thus presented as God's own revelation of the divine will. As such it is intended either to replace the laws that it presents or, more likely, to present the definitive interpretation of those laws accomplished through harmonization and supplementation.[201] The scroll offers a utopian view. When its prescriptions are followed—as they relate to the rebuilding of the temple, the conduct of its sacrificial system, the maintenance of purity in the Holy City, the just rule of the king, and the observance of other aspects of God's will—then the dispersion of Israel will return and God will dwell in glory among God's people.[202]

The date and provenance of the Temple Scroll are disputed.[203] The quotation of the book of Chronicles provides a terminus post quem around 350 B.C.E.,[204] and the law about the importation of animal hides into Jerusalem suggests a date closer to 175 B.C.E.[205] The paleographic dating of 11Q19 indicates a terminus a quo around the turn of the era.[206] The "Law of the King" has suggested to some that the text should be dated during the reign of John Hyrcanus or Alexander Janneus (134–67 B.C.E.), whose activities the author would have considered repugnant.[207] However, a fragmentary copy of perhaps an early edition of the document (4Q524), written in a script dated to 150–125 B.C.E., suggests an earlier date.[208]

The text's precise connection with the Qumran community is uncertain. The presence of three copies of the document in Caves 4 and 11, and the recopying of columns 1–5 in 11Q19 by a scribe in the early first century C.E., indicate an ongoing interest in the text at Qumran.[209] The scroll's priestly concerns are compatible with Qumranic theology and the makeup of the community. A number of legal interpretations in the text have parallels in the Halakic Letter and suggest some substantive connection.[210] A few points of law correspond to Josephus's accounts of the Essenes.[211] The scroll shares a 364-day calendar with 4QMMT and other Qumran texts (see above, p. 156). Lacking in the scroll, however, is any of the language typical of the Qumran sectarian scrolls,[212] nor does one find other sorts of polemical in-group/out-group polarity or, indeed, any language referring to an organized group of any sort. These data—the early dating of 4Q524, the lack of a sectarian ideology, and the parallels to 4QMMT—suggest that the text was composed before the foundation of the Qumran community, but in a social context ancestral to the community.[213] Consonant with that conclusion are some similarities between the Temple Scroll and the Book of Jubilees, which antedates the Qumran community but was of considerable interest to the group.[214] Both authors "operate with the same 364-day cultic calendar, never conflict with one another regarding festivals, and agree almost completely about sacrifices and procedures for their holidays."[215] Both authors write in Hebrew and claim to present authentic, specially revealed Torah given on Mount Sinai (Jubilees as it was delivered by angels recited from the tablets, the Temple Scroll as it came directly from the mouth of God), and the of the two texts cover successive parts of the Pentateuch (Genesis–Exodus, L Deuteronomy).[216] Both authors present their Torah in the hope that obedience to it will reverse Israel's present situation. In this respect the two texts also parallel the Halakic Letter.

With this we must leave the matter. The Temple Scroll is one of several texts found at Qumran that were not authored there but that reflect the religious situation in Israel around or before the mid-second century and that testify to the religious antecedents of the Qumran community. It is one of several texts that reflect dissatisfaction with the Jerusalem temple establishment, in this case not through overt polemic but by means of a utopian vision for a new temple.[217] That vision would have offered the Qumranites hope for a change in one aspect of the status quo that was profoundly disturbing to them and that was at least partly constitutive of their organization as a religious community.

The Aramaic Levi Document (1Q21, 4Q213–214b)

The Aramaic Levi Document is a narrative text in which the patriarch of the Israelite priesthood, speaking in the first-person singular, recounts the events of his life, instructs his sons about cultic and ethical issues, and transmits information about future events. The document, which was a source for the Greek Testament of Levi (see below, pp. 306–8), has been preserved only in fragments. These include the surviving text from six pages of a tenth-century Aramaic codex discovered in the Cairo Genizah,[218] several interpolations in an eleventh-century Greek manuscript of the Testament of Levi found in the monastery on Mount Athos,[219] and the remnants of seven first-century B.C.E. Aramaic manuscripts from Qumran.[220] Taken together, this manuscript evidence provides us with several pieces of running text that offer glimpses of an important Jewish text from the third century or early second century B.C.E.

Thanks to some overlaps in the Greek and Aramaic texts, there is consensus as to the original order of all but the first three major fragments.[221] In the order that we shall follow here,[222] the first fragment (which contains only four full lines and five half lines),[223] is the remnant of an account of the rape of Dinah, and the revenge that Levi and Simeon exacted on Shechem (1:1-3; Cambridge Genizah ms. col. a; cf. Gen 34; Jub. 30). The next fragment (ALD 2:1-5; Cambridge ms. col. b, on the reverse side of the first and separated from it by sixty lines)[224] mentions Shechem twice, as well as Levi's brothers Reuben and Judah, but it is uncertain whether it preserves the end of the Dinah story or an account of the wars of the sons of Jacob, which are not recounted in the Bible but are attested elsewhere in the later literature.[225]

The next episode attested by the fragments (2:4—3:18; Mt. Athos interpolation at T. Levi 2:3 and 4QLevi[b] 1–2) is an account of Levi's prayer, preceded by a brief description of Levi performing a ritual ablution of his clothes and his body.* Although ablution is not a normal ritual before prayer,[226] the action could reflect that Levi is entering some sort of sacred space in order to pray (cf. ALD 7:1). Alternatively, it may be the conclusion of either the Shechem episode or the aforementioned wars of the sons of Jacob.[227] In this case, Levi is purifying himself of the blood he had shed in one or the other of these events. Perhaps this brief narrative links the two events; Levi must purify himself from blood before entering God's presence.

Levi's prayer has two aspects. First, read in its narrative context, its function is to petition God to equip Levi to be a fit and worthy priest. That Levi makes this request and that he has previously performed ritual ablutions appropriate to the priesthood indicate that a previous part of the text now lost stated that God had appointed Levi to be a priest, presumably because of his zeal in avenging the rape of Dinah (cf. Jub. 30:18-19).[228] Second, with respect to its genre and function, the prayer is an "apotropaic" prayer, that is, one that intends to "turn away" or ward off evil spirits.[229] After a narrative introduction (ALD 3:1-2), the prayer begins with the typical assertion of God's omniscience,[230] which is here related to the human thoughts with which Levi is particularly concerned (3:3). The reference to the presence of Levi's children is puzzling and would fit better in a testamentary context (3:4a). The prayer presumes a two-spirits theology similar to that in the Qumran Rule of the Community (see above, pp. 139–40).[231] Levi asks God to drive off the spirit of iniquity that leads to evil thoughts and fornication and to give him "the holy spirit" that enables him to do what is pleasing to God (3:5-8). In 3:9 Levi identifies the (an) evil spirit as a "satan."[232] Both in 3:4b-5 and 3:9 the evil spirit appears to be associated with a two-ways theology, as the two spirits are in 1QS 3–4.[233] In ALD 3:6 the activity of the good spirit is explicated in the language of Isaiah 11:2, which is part of a Davidic oracle that comes to be applied to the Davidic messiah in Pss. Sol. 17:37 (42) (see below, p. 242)—one indication that this text has combined the functions of the royal and priestly messiahs.[234] Levi's role as priest is emphasized in ALD 3:10, 13, 16-17. He is to have access to God, to serve God, to be pure, and to be the teacher of the wisdom that pertains to the priestly office. The apotropaic function of the prayer, introduced in 3:5 and reiterated in 3:9, recurs in 3:11, where God's peace and power are said to be Levi's wall and shelter from evil. Reference to the obliteration of evil from the earth (3:12) perhaps hints at the Noachic source of Levi's priesthood (see below).[235] The pericope concludes with the terse statement that Levi continued his prayer in silence (3:18c).

The next unit in the text, which follows immediately after the prayer (4QLevi[b] frg. 2), describes how, on his way to meet his father, Levi is granted a dream vision or visions (4:1-13). The sequence of prayer and vision is typical in our literature (cf. Dan 9; 1 Enoch 13:4-10). The text is extremely fragmentary, but it appears that in the vision(s) Levi is taken up into heaven, where he is installed a high priest and where seven angels speak to him about his new office.[236] The section ends as Levi notes that he revealed its contents to no one (cf. the narrative in Mark 16:8; cf. the contrasting commands in Dan 12:9 and Rev 22:10).

The details of the action in the section that follows immediately in the Genizah text

(Bodleian col. a:8) are less than clear, though they may be clarified by the Greek Testament of Levi.[237] Levi goes to Isaac, who blesses him (ALD 5:1). Then suddenly he is with Jacob, presumably at Bethel, who learns that he has been appointed priest and invests him with the priestly robes and consecrates him (lit. "he filled my hands") as "a priest of the God of eternity." Levi offers sacrifices and blesses Jacob and his own brothers. The entourage then moves on to Hebron to visit Isaac.

When he learns of Levi's priesthood, Isaac proceeds, in the first person singular, to instruct Levi in "the law of the priesthood" (5:8).[238] This instruction, which is the longest of the preserved sections of the document,[239] divides into four interlocking sections plus a conclusion.[240] The first section treats the subject of sexual and familial purity (6:1, 3-5), a topic that was introduced already in Levi's prayer (3:5, 13). Levi is to be holy as the sanctuary is holy because he has access to God and to all God's holy ones (i.e., the angels). The second section provides prescriptions for the wood that is to be burned under the sacrifices (7:1-7). As is typical in the instruction, the section begins with a transition from the previous one: Levi is to *purify* himself by washing three times: before entering the sanctuary, before approaching the altar, and before offering the sacrifice (cf. 2:4-5). Along with this prescription for purity is a commandment regarding the perfection of sacrificial material. Levi is to split the wood to be certain it is free of worms.[241] Moreover, the wood for the sacrifice is limited to twelve species of trees.[242] The specifications for the wood lead naturally in the next section to a set of prescriptions regarding the offering of the sacrifice to be placed on the wood (8:1-6). After the transitional verse (8:1) comes once again the commandment to wash (8:2), then the specification of the order in which the sacrificial animal is to be sacrificed (8:3-4). Proper order is of the essence, as are the proper amounts of salt, fine flour, oil, wine, and frankincense that are to accompany the sacrifice (8:5-7).[243] This transition leads to the final prescriptive section, concerning the proper amounts for the wood, salt, fine flour, oil, wine, and frankincense (9:1-16), and then the specifications for the various measures (9:17-18).[244] Isaac frames the conclusion to his instructions (10:1-14) with references to the perpetual priesthood that has been allotted to Levi and his descendants (10:1-2, 12-14). Related to this is the assertion that the priestly commandments follow a line of transmission: to Levi's sons from Levi, to Levi from Isaac, to Isaac from Abraham, who had read them in the book of Noah (10:2, 3, 10). The center of the section reprises the topics in the previous sections: the offering of sacrifice, the salt and fine flour, the wine and frankincense, the need to make proper ablutions (10:4-7). This last topic pertains specifically to the removal of blood, and this, in turn, brings Isaac to his reference to "the book of Noah concerning the blood" (10:10).

Isaac's reference to Levi's descendants (10:12-14) leads naturally to a biographical section (11:1—12:9), in which Levi—now once again the speaker in the first person—recounts his marriage and the births of his sons, his grandsons, and his great-grandsons, setting these events within the chronology of his life as calculated by a 364-day solar calendar.[245] Two other details are noteworthy in this genealogical material. First, in the explanation of Kohath's name (11:6), the author has "applied Israelite messianic language to the Priestly Levitical messiah."[246] Thus, in this text there is no room for a Davidic messiah. Second, the list of descendants ends with the generation of Amram, whose name is tied not to his son Aaron, the priestly patriarch, but to his other son Moses, the one who will "raise up the people from the land of Egypt" (12:4).[247] The biographical section ends with Levi's reference to his 137th year, the year of his death, which obviously has not yet occurred (12:9).

The next preserved section of the document, which follows immediately (Cambridge col. c:82), offers a flashback to Levi's 118th year, when he began to instruct his sons and their sons (thus fulfilling the command of Isaac; 13:1). Different from Isaac's instructions, which are legal prescriptions for priestly ritual, Levi's instructions take the form of a poem about wisdom that does not contain a word about anything that is peculiar to the priesthood.[248] The poem, to the extent that it has been preserved, can be divided into four parts of uneven length (13:2-3, 4-10b, 10c-14, 15-16). The first section sets the theme of deed and consequence. Righteousness and truth on the one hand and evil on the other hand bring their inevitable results. Different from much wisdom instruction, the idea of twofold actions and results is embodied not in the image of the two ways, but in the metaphor of sowing and harvesting (cf. Gal 6:7-9). The beginning of the next section is marked by the phrase "and now, my sons" (ALD 13:4). Its subject is the teaching and learning of reading and writing and the wisdom that derives from these, and the results that follow. The model for Levi's sons in this respect is his brother Joseph, the noted sage and counselor of the Egyptian pharaoh (cf. 13:4, 6), and his rise to great honor is the promised outcome for those who follow his example. "Wisdom" and "honor" are the catchwords that provide a link to the next section (13:10c; cf. 13:9b, 10a). Here the central concept is wisdom as treasure. Even if a city is despoiled, invading kings and their armies cannot find and plunder the treasury of wisdom. The final partly preserved section of the poem, which again begins with the phrase "and now, my sons," returns to the central motif in the second section (13:15; cf. 13:4, 6), and seems, as in that section, to promise "great honor" to his sons (13:16h; cf. 13:4, 5, 6, 9, 10).

Among the Qumran fragments that cannot be certainly located in the document is a brief piece of broken text (4QLevi[a] frg. 4) that predicts that Levi's descendants will abandon the paths of truth that Levi sought in his prayer (3:4).[249] Perhaps it indicates that the author found fault with some priestly practices in his own time.

Due to the fragmentary nature of the manuscripts, we cannot determine the precise literary genre of the document.[250] If we look at its parts, we can discern a number of literary forms: narrative, a prayer, a dream vision or two, priestly halakah, wisdom instruction. Such a mosaic has counterparts in other texts such as 1 Enoch and the book of Tobit.[251] When we look for a macrostructure, to the extent that we can discern such in a fragmentary text, one aspect becomes obvious. The preserved parts are unified by the fact that they constitute a first-person narrative almost all of whose episodes focus on Levi's priesthood. His zeal against Shechem leads to his appointment as priest. He prays for the wisdom and divine protection that will equip him to be a priest. This leads to a vision in which he ascends to heaven and is installed as priest. Jacob recognizes his priesthood and invests him with the priestly robes. Isaac, in turn, transmits to him the law of the priesthood first written down by Noah and instructs Levi to transmit this to his sons, who will be priests after him. Levi recounts events in his life, including the births of his priestly descendants. He then fulfills Isaac's commandment by instructing his sons. The text obviously takes its point of departure from Scripture, but at least in the case of the preserved fragments, little of its wording and few of its events are drawn from Scripture.

It is tempting to characterize this text as a testament because it is a major source for the Levitic testament that was included among the Greek Testaments of the Twelve Patriarchs, and because the narrative is cast in the first-person singular, as testaments are, of necessity.[252] Nonetheless, we must exercise caution for two reasons. First, the fragments do not preserve the beginning and the end of the document and hence lack the explicit testamentary setting. Second, as other documents such as the Genesis Apocryphon attest, first-person narrative about the events of one's life need not indicate the form of a testament (see below, pp. 172–77).

Nonetheless, the narrative setting of the wisdom poem is reminiscent of testamentary settings. Levi summons his sons and addresses them in an idiom that is typical of such settings—both his introductory words and the sapiential form of his discourse (13:1-2; cf., e.g., 1 Enoch 91).[253] Moreover, this instruction is preceded immediately by a reference to the year of Levi's death, and although this instruction is placed twenty years earlier, it is dated to the time of the death of Joseph, whom Levi has cited as a model of the true sage (ALD 13:6). Perhaps the author took a cue from an early form of the Enochic corpus, in which a first-person narrative was followed by testamentary wisdom instruction. Tobit, a text contemporary with the Levi Document, may provide another analogy, with its occasional use of first-person narrative and its two testamentary sections and their wisdom instruction (see above, pp. 30–34). Perhaps it is best to think of fully articulated testaments as a genre that emerged gradually from earlier texts that had testamentary elements in their narratives (beginning with chap. 49 in Genesis and chaps. 31–33 in Deuteronomy).

The function of the text appears to have been didactic—to offer a portrait of the ideal priest, to anchor the priesthood in ancient tradition (the life of Levi and by implication in the patriarchal tradition back to Noah), to present some minimum albeit basic instruction relating to the cult, and evidently to make "predictions" about the author's own time.[254]

Among the attributes that the Levi Document ascribes to the priesthood, the most obvious is its sapiential character.[255] In order to equip him to be priest, Levi prays for a spirit of wisdom and understanding. He is the recipient of a dream vision. His instruction to his sons emphasizes the teaching of reading and writing and the pursuit of wisdom (properly scribal functions) rather than the observance of right halakah. Joseph the sage is his ideal. In various respects these emphases are reminiscent of the Wisdom of Ben Sira and the apocalyptic and mantic wisdom of Daniel and Enoch. Similarly, the metrological detail in Isaac's instructions adds an intellective, "scientific" dimension to the practice of the priesthood and the cult.[256] One must know weights and measures as well as the order of cultic procedure. In short, although one may be inclined to think of the (high) priest in ritual terms as one who performs the cult, or theological/religious terms as the mediator between humans and the Deity, or politically as a civil ruler,[257] or even militarily as the executor of divine judgment,[258] in the preserved fragments of the Aramaic Levi Document he is also a sage and teacher.

Several other aspects of the Levi Document's view of the priesthood and the cult deserve mention in summary. Despite the broad currency of Aaron's role as the first high priest and the priestly patriarch in the Bible and postbiblical literature,[259] the priesthood here is broadly Levitic and not narrowly Aaronic. Moreover, Levi's priestly tradition is traced back to Noah.[260] The document presumes the observance of a 364-day solar calendar. Finally, this document affirms the importance of the priesthood in its attribution of royal messianic elements to the future Levitical messiah. We do not know how any of these tenets of belief and practice may have worked out in the real world of the author's "circle," but it is noteworthy that neither is presented in a polemical fashion.[261] Indeed, for all of their insistence on right procedure and moral and ritual purity, none of the major preserved fragments indulges in polemic or reveals a sectarian, "us-against-them" mentality. Only in the case of 4QLevi^a frg. 4 is there the possibility of a polemic against the priesthood, but we cannot ascertain the nature of the complaint. It need not have been a broadside against the Jerusalem priesthood.

Although the Aramaic Levi Document came to light only among the discarded texts of the Cairo Genizah and the lost and forgotten manuscripts in the Qumran Caves, the document was influential in contemporary Jewish circles and in some Christian circles. Its narrative was incorporated into the biblical haggadah of the Book of Jubilees,[262] and its ignoring of Aaron is perhaps the more noteworthy in Jubilees' complete failure to mention the brother of its alleged author. It also came to be the first in a triad of texts attested at Qumran that included the Testament of Kohath (one copy) and the Visions of Amram (seven copies) and that may have been intended to "legitimate the continuity of the priestly line and its teaching."[263] Its popularity at Qumran is noteworthy, given the important role of the Aaronic priesthood in some of the scrolls.[264] In Christian circles the Aramaic Levi Document provided the major source for the Testament of Levi, arguably the central text among the Testaments of the Twelve Patriarchs, a corpus that seems to have been composed in the second century C.E.[265] Additionally, the Testament of Isaac, a Christian text of uncertain date and provenance, highlights Isaac's status as priest and emphasizes some of the same elements found in Isaac's instructions in the Aramaic Levi Document (T. Isaac 4).[266]

Three data provide benchmarks for dating the Levi Document.[267] The oldest Qumran manuscripts date from the second half of the first century B.C.E., thus indicating that time as a terminus ante quem for the composition of the document.[268] Since the text is cited in the Damascus Document, which is dated to the late second century, the date can be moved back a half century.[269] This date can be moved back at least another half century since the Book of Jubilees, which draws from its narratives, is to be dated to the first half of the second century B.C.E. (see above, pp. 73–74). This suggests a date of composition in the third century or, at the latest, in the early second century B.C.E.[270] By all accounts, the text was composed in Aramaic.[271]

Although the provenance of the Levi Document is unknown, it appears to have been composed in priestly "circles" that were perhaps related to those that generated the Temple Scroll and that were in some sense ancestral to the reformist circles that created Jubilees and that were antecedent to the Qumran community.[272] Although arguments from silence are tenuous, to judge from the preserved fragments and their lack of polemics, the developing socioreligious tensions evident in Jubilees and the Qumran sectarian literature were not (a major) part of its immediate social world. Thus it constitutes one tessera in the complex social and religious mosaic that has begun to become evident through the discovery and publication of the Dead Sea Scrolls.

An Unusual Psalms Scroll (11QPs^a)

The Psalms Scroll from Qumran Cave 11 presents some surprises for the person accustomed to the content and order of the canonical Psalter. It is one of the largest and best-preserved Qumran scrolls, with the upper two-thirds of twenty-four running columns of text (4.25 meters of scroll), along with parts of four other columns and five fragments of more than three others.[273] The scroll contains Psalms 101–104, 105, 109, 118–119, and 121–150 in Hebrew, though not in the order of the Hebrew canon (and English translations).[274] Moreover, interspersed in the last ten columns are nine compositions not found in the Hebrew canon.[275] These include: two psalms that have been combined in Psalm 151, the last psalm in the Greek translation of the Psalter; a version of the poem in Sirach 51 (see below, p. 355 n. 50); three psalms previously known from manuscripts of the Syriac translation of the Bible; three other psalms hitherto unknown; and a prose composition that describes David's poetic output. The Psalms Scroll probably contained, originally, most of Psalms 101–150 plus the aforementioned additions.[276] While its fuller contents and its ordering of the canonical psalms could reflect the assembling of an ad hoc liturgical collection, more likely it represents an alternative form of the Psalter stemming from a period before the collection achieved its final canonical form.[277] The two psalms that we will treat below (cols. 18 and 22) indicate that the 11Q Psalter probably emanated from a group of pious Jews who were in some sense the predecessors of the Qumran group.[278] That the collection was still being copied at Qumran in the first half of the first century C.E. speaks for its relevance and utility in that community (see below).[279]

A Davidic Psalter

As we have seen in the Halakic Letter (4QMMT C 10), the third part of the emerging Hebrew canon, which included the Psalms, could be referred to in shorthand as "David."

Several elements in columns 26 to 28 of the Psalms Scroll indicate that this scroll as a whole (whatever its original fuller content) presented itself as a Davidic Psalter.[280] The end of column 26 (now lost) and the beginning of column 27 contained 1 Samuel 23:1-7, "the last words of David" (1 Sam 23:1). This is followed immediately by a prose composition mentioned above, which informs us that David wrote 3,600 psalms, as well as 364 songs to accompany the daily *tamid* sacrifice, fifty-two more for the Sabbath offering, thirty for various special occasions, and four for persons "stricken" by evil spirits—a total of 4,050.

Two elements in this composition tie it to the special interests of the Qumran community. First, it assumes the 364-day solar calendar in use at Qumran. Second, the last line of the composition states: "All these he spoke through prophecy which was given to him from the presence of the Most High." This identification of David as a prophet is consonant with the fact that the Qumran commentaries exegete not only the books of the biblical prophetic corpus but also some of the Psalms (see above, p. 130).

Psalm 151

The final Davidic element in the scroll is, as we might call it, David's autobiographical signature to the corpus, written in the first-person singular (28:3-14). It includes the Hebrew archetype of the Greek Psalm 151 and a fragment of a narrative about David's encounter with Goliath, evidently also known by the author/editor of Psalm 151.[281]

The superscription of the Hebrew psalm describes it as "A Hallelujah of David the Son of Jesse." The body of the psalm comprises seven units, each a pair of parallel distichs. Its basis is the narrative of David's anointing in 1 Samuel 16. According to v 1, Jesse made David "shepherd of his flock and ruler over his kids" because he was the smallest and youngest of his sons. Verses 2-4 describe David's activity as a shepherd and YHWH's response to it. The environment is the mountain and hills, the trees and Jesse's flock. David makes a lyre and sings praises to God. When the mountains and hills are mute and no one can properly recount God's deeds (vv 3ab, 4ab), David's unique gift becomes apparent. He even charms the trees and the flock (v 3cd)—a motif that may recall the gift of Orpheus, the legendary singer of Greek antiquity.[282] YHWH sees and hears David and chooses him to be his anointed (vv 4cd-5ab). Thus the tall stature and attractive characteristics of Jesse's other sons notwithstanding (vv 5c-6b), YHWH makes little David (v 1ab) great (v 5b) and appoints the shepherd of the flock and ruler of the kids (v 1cd) the leader of YHWH's people and the ruler over the sons of YHWH's covenant (v 7cd). It is a remarkable poem, beautifully and symmetrically composed, that expounds what the author perceives to be the heart of the Davidic story: YHWH takes the insignificant boy, finds in him true devotion, and raises him to greatness—from a caretaker of animals to the shepherd of YHWH's flock, Israel. In context the poem identifies the quality that made David great as the poetic gift, born of devotion to YHWH, that is displayed in the collection of psalms that it brings to a conclusion.

The last two preserved lines of the column begin a short autobiographical narrative about David's encounter with Goliath, based on 1 Samuel 17. The Greek Psalm 151 is a shortened form of the Hebrew psalm, which omits vv 2c-3 and concludes by replacing the *inclusio* in v 7 with a reference to the Goliath encounter that corresponds to the narrative at the bottom of column 28.[283]

Psalms of the Pious

Column 18 of the Psalms Scroll contains one of three compositions in the scroll that were previously known from two Syriac Bible manuscripts and some manuscripts of a Syriac "Book of Discipline."[284] The Syriac texts make it possible to reconstruct the beginning and end of the psalm, which have been lost at the bottoms of columns 17 and 18. The psalm is a call for the community of the righteous and pious to praise God and to make YHWH's deeds known to others.[285] Three groups are mentioned. The author's group is known as "the upright," "the faithful," "the good ones," "the perfect," "the righteous," and "the pious." Their opposite number are "the wicked" and "the arrogant" (l. 15). In between is a group described as "the simple *or* untaught *or* naive" and "those lacking judgment" (ll. 3, 4b–5a). The author's group is called upon to "glorify God," to "recount" God's deeds of salvation, and to "instruct" the simple.

The communal setting of the psalm is clear in the opening strophe. God's praise is to be sung in "the congregation of the many" and "the multitude of the upright" and "the faithful." The next strophe continues the motif: "form an assembly" (Heb. *yaḥad*) together with the "good ones" and the "perfect" in order to make known God's salvation (ll. 1–2). In parallel with this is the admonition to make God's might and greatness known to "all the simple." The third strophe explicates the grounds for this (ll. 3b–6a). "Wisdom is given" (by God) to make known YHWH's glory and many deeds to the simple and people lacking in judgment. Thus the distinction is clear: the author's group, with their divinely given insight, are distinct from all others, but they are to gather in those who are teachable and instruct them (Heb. *haśkil*, lit. "make wise"). The next strophe identifies "the Most High" and "the God of Jacob" as the object of worship and then makes the remarkable point that such worship is the equivalent of temple sacrifice (ll. 6b–11).[286] In the fifth strophe (ll. 12–15) we learn something new about these religious assemblies. They are an occasion on which "the righteous" and "the congregation of the pious" (*qahal ha-ḥăsîdîm*) gather for communal meals, during which the group meditates on the Torah of the Most High. All this stands in opposition to the activity of "the wicked" and "the haughty." The last strophe describes God's response to the worship of "the good ones" by increasing mercy (*ḥesed*) and delivering them in time of need from the clutches of "foreigners" and "the wicked." The final pair of strophes add a future perspective, when God will redeem "Jacob" and "Israel" and abide forever in (the temple in) Jerusalem.

This psalm can be compared and contrasted with the sectarian texts from Qumran.[287]

The author construes piety and worship of God as a group activity. He even uses the common Qumranic term *yaḥad*. Moreover, as at Qumran, communal gatherings are the occasion for the study of the Torah. The enlightened worshiping and meditating community, however, stands in opposition not to persons described as liars and false teachers, but to those who pose a physical threat to the group. By contrast, the unenlightened and simple are to be the object of the group's proclamation of God's greatness and goodness.

The date of this psalm is uncertain, but the form of its Hebrew is consonant with a date in the late Persian or early Hellenistic period (400–250 B.C.E.),[288] and its language is consonant with contemporary wisdom literature.[289] The psalm emanated from a group of Jews who understood themselves to be "the righteous" and "the pious," in opposition to those who were not. The term "congregation of the pious" can be understood generically and need not refer to a formal organized group with the name *ḥăsîdîm*."[290] As we shall see, the term recurs with this meaning in the Psalms of Solomon (see below, p. 247). The presence of this psalm in a Qumran Psalter suggests that the Qumran community had a predecessor or predecessors in a group or groups who gathered for worship and study of the Torah. Such groups may also have been ancestral to the later institution—the synagogues, which emerged as worshiping communities and then found homes in special buildings set aside for worship and other communal activities.[291] The references to a worshiping and meditating *yaḥad* would have made the psalm compatible in a Qumran setting, and its statements about instructing the simple and unlearned could be construed with reference to persons who were recruited into the community.

A second composition in the Psalms Scroll that emanated from the circles of "the pious" is the so-called Apostrophe to Zion (col. 22:1-15). In a way it is a companion piece to the previous one. The future glory of Zion, briefly alluded to in the last distich of the former, is its subject matter, and Zion is addressed six times (ll. 1, 2, 8, 10 [bis], 14). Moreover, "salvation," which the previous psalm attributed to God, is here explicitly directed to Zion (ll. 3, 8, 15); and glory, which the previous psalm attributed to God, here belongs to Zion (ll. 3, 4, 5, 15). The psalm's three strophes are made up of distichs, except for its first and last units, which are tristichs. In form it is an acrostic, that is, the first words in successive lines or units begin with successive letters of the Hebrew alphabet.

The first strophe (ll. 1–6a) looks to the future peace, salvation, and glory of Zion. Its future inhabitants will be generations of *ḥasidim* (l. 3b), and Zion will remember the pious acts (*ḥesed*) of the prophets and will glory in the deeds of her pious (*ḥasidim*). The second strophe indicates why Zion's glory is a future hope. Presently she is marked by violence, falsehood, and injustice (ll. 6b–7a), which must be removed. The word pair "violence" and "falsehood" are noteworthy, since in the Apocalypse of Weeks they occur together as shorthand for what is wrong (see above, pp. 110–11). Different from the previous psalm, where the enemies are those of the pious and righteous, here they are Zion's enemies (ll. 10–11). The third strophe returns to the theme of the first. The author utters a blessing on Zion (l. 12; cf. l. 2), and Zion's future glory, promised by the prophets, is again in focus.

This psalm is one of a group that look for the deliverance of Zion (cf. Sir 36:1-17, esp.

vv 14-17; Tob 13:9-18; Bar 4:30—5:9; Pss. Sol. 11). The emphasis on the vision of the prophets (11QPsᵃ 22:14) is mirrored in Sirach 36:15-16 and is implied in the heavy use of language from Third Isaiah in the other compositions. For the Qumranites who read this scroll, the promise of future glory for Zion would have spoken to their complaints about the Hasmoneans' abuse of power ("violence") and observance of wrong halakah ("falsehood").

Instruction for a Student
(4QInstruction [4Q415–418])

The text known variously as "Sapiential Work A," "4QInstruction," and "*Mûsar lĕ-Mēvîn*" (the editors' proposed Hebrew title translated above) exemplifies how a single Qumran document can present a scholar with problems and puzzles, significant new information, and major challenges to the imagination and intellect. Its seven or eight manuscripts attest its popularity and importance at Qumran, but their fragmentary condition often makes it difficult or impossible to make interpretive decisions.[292] The content of the scroll is sometimes consonant with aspects of the sectarian scrolls, while at other times it presumes a social setting totally different from the isolated environment of Qumran.[293] The text's mixture of wisdom instruction and eschatology and its lack of an equation of wisdom and the Mosaic Torah call into question traditional categories and stereotypes applied to Jewish literature of this period. At the same time they challenge the scholar to deal with literary and theological data that are as varied as the social complexities of Judaism in the Greco-Roman period.

The Instruction for a Student was a large sapiential text, estimated to have been between twenty-three and thirty or more columns long.[294] The seven or eight manuscripts that preserve parts of the text comprise well over four hundred fragments. Of these fragments a half dozen cover the larger part of a column, another half dozen contain substantial pieces of text, and a few more preserve enough text to read parts of a succession of lines. Several dozen overlaps among manuscripts help to fill in some of the gaps.[295] As a result, the relatively small portion of the composition that has been preserved provides a series of smaller or larger glimpses of the contents of the work, but it has led to no consensus as to the sequence of the parts,[296] no picture of the whole, and no certainty as to whether the manuscripts attest different "editions" of the work.[297] Nonetheless, we can make some thematic observations and draw some tentative conclusions as to how the components may have related to one another. To judge from its large fragments, the Instruction was a compilation of units of practical wisdom, loosely strung together,[298] and related to a theological framework with cosmological and eschatological components. The text's admonitions are expressed mainly in the second-person singular and are sometimes addressed to a *mēvîn*, literally "one who understands [or 'is learned'],", a student, or expert in the making.[299]

The author's interest in practical advice is best exemplified in 4Q416 2 2–4, where parts of three successive columns provide the largest preserved piece of more or less running text.[300] Here, as elsewhere in the document, the author addresses his reader in the second-person masculine singular. The longest part of the section deals with the use of money and possessions or, conversely, how to cope with poverty.[301] One should pay back one's creditors and not lend money foolishly (2:4-6). Monetary transactions also require some sophistication in human relations (2:10-16).[302] Grasping for money and overextending oneself financially can be dangerous (2:17—3:8a). Do not sell yourself into the service of others (2:17-18a). Do not live beyond your means (2:18b-21a). Do not borrow from money that has been entrusted to you (3:3b-8a). If one is poor, one should accept that status, recognizing that it is God who apportions poverty and wealth (3:8-12). This insight will come as one studies "the mystery to be" (3:8b-15a; see below).

With no apparent reason for the transition, the author moves on to exhort the student to "honor your father in your poverty and your mother in your low estate."[303] It is they who brought you into the world, whom God set in authority over you, and who taught you "the mystery to be." To honor them is to gain long life. The section as a whole (3:15b-19a) is an expansion and reinterpretation of the biblical commandment about parents (cf. Sir 3:1-16, on which see above, p. 55). The discussion about one's parents leads naturally to a consideration of one's relationship to one's wife and children (3:19b—4:13+), again within the context of one's poverty: "You have taken a wife in your poverty; take her offspring [in your low estate]." Alluding to Genesis 2:20-25, the text goes on to assert the unity and companionship of husband and wife, but also the husband's authority over his wife.[304]

A substantial fragment of column 1 of 4Q416 preserves part of what appears to be a prologue to the document, which provides a theological rationale for the advice that the instructor is giving to his student.[305] The passage deals with both cosmology and eschatology. The first preserved lines emphasize the orderliness of the cosmos, in which the heavenly bodies carry out the tasks that God has allotted to them (1 1:1-10). The following section focuses on the final judgment, with an emphasis on the punishment of the wicked (ll. 10–14).[306] The point of the text appears to be that everything and everyone have their allotted tasks and that God's judgment will be based on their obedience or disobedience.[307] Lines 14b-15 appear to be the beginning of an admonition to the righteous to understand this and act accordingly. The topic of eschatology recurs in 417 1 (2) 1:7-16. Especially noteworthy is the reference to a pair of heavenly books written in God's presence, the one containing the punishments that will befall the wicked, and the other a Book of Memorial in which are written the names of those "who keep his word" (ll. 14–16; cf. Mal 3:16-18).

The cosmological and eschatological assertions in the Instruction are the object of revelation, to which the author repeatedly appeals in his references to the "mystery that is to be" (*Heb. raz nihyeh*). The expression occurs more than twenty times in the preserved fragments of the document, frequently as the object of verbs like "gaze upon," "reveal," and "study" (*darash*).[308] The meaning of the expression is itself open to multiple translations: "the mystery that is to be," "the mystery that is to come," "the mystery of existence."[309] The imperfect tense of the verb "to be" suggests that the content of the mystery includes eschatological speculation; however, it can also be associated with God's acts in the past, including creation itself.[310] Thus we may construe it as "the plan by which [God] designed the world and its foundations."[311] It is this cosmic structure of things, both temporal and spatial, that puts human activity in perspective. Thus, in the middle of his exhortations as to how one is to conduct oneself in one's concrete circumstances, the author can appeal to the *raz nihyeh* as a means to gain a perspective on God's purposes and will (4Q416 2 3:14-15, 17-18).[312] Precisely where and how one finds the *raz nihyeh* is not said; however, the verb *dāraš* (lit. "search") is used in other contexts to refer to the careful study of the Torah.[313] This suggests at least some consultation of a book or books.[314]

The aspects of the Instruction on which we have touched invite comparison with contemporary writings that have been classified as sapiential and those that have been called apocalyptic. The obvious parallel is the Wisdom of Ben Sira, and notably its emphasis on practical wisdom regarding marriage, home, and family, as well as interpersonal relationships and the use of money (see above, p. 59).[315] The differences between the two works, however, are just as striking. Ben Sira expounds his wisdom to the rich young men of Jerusalem. The author of the Instruction assumes the possibility, if not always the fact, of poverty.[316] Ben Sira employs the form of the proverb; the preserved parts of the Instruction use almost exclusively the form of second-person singular imperative. For Ben Sira, wisdom is equated with the Mosaic Torah (see above, pp. 57–59). The term *Torah* never occurs in the preserved parts of the Instruction, and one rarely finds other terminology elsewhere associated with the Torah.[317] Like Ben Sira, the author of the Instruction employs the language of intellection and learning, calling on the reader to observe, learn, and consider how things are or should be. A striking difference between the two, however, is the object of one's consideration. According to Ben Sira, one is to pursue wisdom. In the preserved fragments of the Instruction, the word "wisdom" occurs perhaps twice in the sense of God's wisdom;[318] instead it is the *raz nihyeh* that is to be the object of one's search and study. Moreover, while Ben Sira seems to have some interest in the things to come (see above, pp. 61–62), the Instruction espouses an eschatology that includes a major final judgment that results in the punishment of the wicked and eternal life for the righteous (4Q416 1 1:10-16; 4Q417 1 1:7-18; 2 [1] 1:10-12).[319]

The differences between the Instruction and the Wisdom of Ben Sira are, in some important respects, points of similarity between the Instruction and the apocalyptic texts of the Enochic corpus.[320] Both texts embody aspects of the sapiential tradition, and both downplay the importance of the Mosaic Torah and the notion of covenant. For both texts, revelation comprises cosmological, eschatological, and ethical knowledge. Both imagine a heavenly realm where the punishments of the wicked and the names of the righteous are written down in God's presence,[321] and both envision an end time when iniquity will be destroyed and the righteous will be rewarded. Both 1 Enoch and 4Q416 begin by placing the obedience of the heavenly bodies in the context of human behavior that will be punished in the coming judgment.[322] The two works parallel one another in their use of a number of other ideas and motifs.[323] While all of this does not prove that one text was literarily dependent on the other, it suggests that the Instruction represents a stage in the Israelite sapiential tradition that was foundational both for 1 Enoch and the Wisdom of Ben Sira.[324]

Although seven or eight manuscripts of the Instruction have been identified among the Qumran finds, a number of elements either present in or absent from the fragments complicate any attempt to relate the setting of this text's origin to the Qumran context. Lacking in the fragments is the in-group/out-group language of the Qumran sectarian scrolls and, indeed, any indication of a religious community setting.[325] To the contrary, the document employs the second-person *singular*, and the implied communal setting is one's home and family. Thus the person addressed is expected to marry, to raise a family, and to engage in business transactions rather than to live in an isolated wilderness setting. At the same time, there are numerous parallels between the language of the Instruction and the *non*sectarian language of the Instruction on the Two Spirits in 1QS 3–4.[326] All of these factors together may indicate that the Instruction was composed prior to the founding of the community and apart from its sectarian antecedents, albeit among persons who were steeped in the vocabulary and worldview that would emerge in early apocalyptic texts and the sectarian texts of Qumran.[327] Its purpose was to stimulate intellectual and religious reflection among young men to prepare them for an intelligent and righteous life according to God's purpose and with a view toward God's promised reward.[328]

It is uncertain what function the text may have served at Qumran. Its numerous copies, all dating from the mid- to (mainly) late first century B.C.E., indicate the work was popular there.[329] Perhaps some of the manuscripts were imported from Essene communities where family life was the norm. The Qumranites may have considered the work profitable because of its repeated exhortations to study and mediate and its many references to a life lived in poverty. Possibly other aspects of its vocabulary, which it had in common with the Rule of the Community, resonated with members of the Qumran community. Finally, since we possess only a small part of the text, we do not know how the parts now lost may have fit into the religious environment of Qumran. Thus, as we noted at the beginning, the document is valuable for the light it sheds on the complexity of first-century Judaism, for the literary variety that it attests at Qumran, and for the frustrating, unanswered questions that it raises for historians who need to be reminded that our knowledge is partial and our conclusions tentative.

The Genesis Apocryphon (1QapGen)

Of the seven scrolls discovered in Qumran Cave 1, this compilation of narratives about the patriarchs was in the worst state of deterioration. It has also benefited the most from technological advances in the decipherment of ancient manuscripts. Although when it was first unrolled in 1955 the scroll contained substantial remnants of twenty-two columns, it was possible to decipher the largest part of the writing of only five columns (2, 19–22, with 155 of 170 lines). Of the remaining columns, parts of only 34 lines were legible.[330] Now, through the use of advanced infrared technology and digital imaging equipment, it is possible to read sometimes large parts of an additional 164 lines.[331]

The extant columns of this Aramaic scroll (beginning with col. 2) trace the history of the patriarchs from Lamech (Noah's father) to Abraham. The narratives are, for the most part, supplements to the Genesis accounts written almost entirely in the first-person singular. In the last columns of the scroll (20:33—22:34), the author reproduces some of the actual wording of the Bible, but more often he expansively paraphrases it. Some of the supplements to the Genesis account parallel contemporary written sources such as 1 Enoch and Jubilees.

The first reasonably well-preserved column of the Apocryphon (col. 2, with 26 of 37 lines) begins with a narrative about the birth of Noah already in progress.[332] Since a parallel version of the narrative has been preserved in full in 1 Enoch 106–107, we can reconstruct the story line in the Apocryphon and identify some of the points of difference between the two versions.[333] To judge from 1 Enoch 106, the story in the Apocryphon began perhaps in the middle of present column 1.[334] Moreover, since the myth of the watchers and the women is presupposed at several points in column 2, it is likely that such an account preceded the Noah story in the scroll. We cannot determine, however, how much space this story may have occupied.

The story in the Apocryphon seems to have progressed as follows. Lamech marries Bitenosh, who gives birth to Noah (col. 1||1 Enoch 106:1), whose glorious appearance is then described (col. 1||106:2-3). Lamech concludes from the child's appearance that his wife was impregnated by one of the watchers (2:1||106:5-6) and is struck with fear at the prospect (2:2-3||106:4a). He confronts Bitenosh, demanding that she speak the truth under oath, but she insists that the child is Lamech's (2:3-18||–). Lamech then runs to Methuselah, asking that he, in turn, request Enoch to query the holy ones about the truth of the matter (2:19-21a||106:4-7). Methuselah goes to Enoch and tells him about the miraculous birth (2:21b-26+[27-37]||106:8-12). Enoch responds at great length, describing the sin of the watchers, the judgment that will come through the flood, and Noah's role in that judgment (cols. 3–4||106:13-17, signaled by 3:3||106:13b). He assures Methuselah that the child is Lamech's (5:3-8) and tells Methuselah to return with that news (5:9-±11||106:18). He then continues his speech with a description of the *eschaton*, which will be marked by increasing sin and a second judgment (5:±11-23||106:18—107:2). Methuselah returns to Lamech, conveying Enoch's information (5:24-25||107:3). The section concludes with a brief description of Lamech's positive response to the news (5:26-27).

A comparison of the two versions of the story indicates the following. The beginnings of the two stories may have been roughly the same length. Lamech's suspicion that Noah's conception was of angelic origin (2:1-2; cf. 1 Enoch 106:6) leads to a long, emotional scene that is totally absent from 1 Enoch. Lamech adjures his wife to reveal the truth of the matter, and she responds by reminding Lamech of the pleasure of their love-making (1QapGen 2:3-18). Lamech's speech to Methuselah is briefly summarized in the Apocryphon, but Methuselah's description of the wunderkind in his conversation with Enoch is expanded, thus focusing on the importance of the extraordinary child.[335] Enoch's oracle about the flood and the second judgment in the *eschaton* is more than six times as long as its counterpart in 1 Enoch 106–107 (1QapGen 3:10—5:27).

Several tendencies are evident in the Apocryphon's interpretation of Genesis.[336] First, from start to finish, the narrator is Lamech, who speaks in the first-person singular and quotes others doing the same thing. Second, the author draws heavily on traditions, motifs, and language that are at home in 1 Enoch: the story as a whole, of course (1 Enoch 106–107); the myth of the watchers and the women (1 Enoch 6–11); Methuselah as the transmitter of Enochic revelation (1 Enoch 72–82; 83–84; 85–90); Enoch's association with the angels (1 Enoch 12:1-3); terminology found in 1 Enoch, but not in chapters 106–107. Third, like 1 Enoch 106–107, the Apocryphon draws a parallel between ancient time and the end time, with the flood serving as the prototype of the final judgment, and like 1 Enoch 106–107, he most probably sees the glory of the newborn Noah as a sign of his function as primordial savior and a type of the salvation to come.[337] Fourth, Enoch's role as revealer, which is the presupposition for the whole Enochic corpus and is emphasized in 1 Enoch 106–107, is enhanced in the Apocryphon's substantial expansion of his oracle. Fifth, notwithstanding his emphasis on theological topics, the author of the Apocryphon has a keen interest in the psychological dynamics and interchange between his characters. This dimension of human characterization is largely missing from 1 Enoch as a whole. As to the relationship between the two stories, it is likely that the Genesis Apocryphon represents a rewriting of the story in 1 Enoch 106–107.[338]

The second major part of the preserved scroll begins with the superscription: "[A Copy of] the Book of the Words of Noah" (5:29).[339] Its extensive text ran from column 5 to the end of column 17 or the beginning of column 18. Although much of the text is illegible, enough of it can be deciphered to indicate some of the ways in which it interpreted Genesis and reiterated some of the tendencies in the Lamech story. The expression "I, Noah," occurs four times in the preserved text (6:6, 23; 11:1, 11; cf. 15:21), and the narrator consistently speaks in the first-person singular. Noah's life up to the time that he prepares for the flood is summarized in a few lines (5:30—6:11a). Elaborating on the biblical account (Gen 6:9), Noah portrays himself as righteous from his mother's womb (1QapGen 6:1-2), employing the image of the paths of truth and falsehood typical of 1 Enoch 92–105 (1QapGen 6:2-3; see below, pp. 175–76). Diverging from the biblical account, and employing motifs also found in 1 Enoch, Noah refers to a vision in which he learned of the activities of the watchers and the women, and a second vision in which a watcher and holy one appeared to him (6:11a-15). The broken text that follows recounted the violence of the giants, thus tying the flood story to Genesis 6:1-4 as it is interpreted in 1 Enoch 6–11. Columns 7–8 described the flood, and columns 9–12, the events that followed his disembarkation. The remnants of columns 13–15 narrate some parts of an extensive dream vision that featured a variety of trees, one of which (a cedar) symbolized Noah the righteous plant (cf. 1 Enoch 10:3),[340] as well as a fragment of its interpretation, presumably by an angel (1QapGen 14:9—15:20). The narrative in columns 16 and 17 described Noah's division of the land among his sons and their distribution of their portions to their sons (cf. Gen 10 and its expansion in Jub. 8:10—9:13).

The third and final extant portion of the scroll recounted the story of Abram/Abraham. It began probably in column 18, but since it is badly deteriorated, the transition between the Noah story and the Abram story is unknown.[341] Columns 19–22 retell the events in Genesis 12:8—15:4. The fragmented beginning of column 19 (ll. 7–10a) appears to parallel the slightly expanded version of Genesis 12:1-7 in Jubilees 13:8-10. The suture marks on the margin after column 22 indicate that one or more sheets of manuscript once followed this column, but were removed before the scroll was rolled up.[342]

The story of Abram's sojourn in Egypt (Gen 12:10-20) has been expanded in columns 19:10—20:32 to nine times its original size.[343] In this transformation, the tightly written Genesis account has been interpolated with additional narrative details, motifs, and whole genres completely absent from Genesis. As the story begins, Abram has a dream, which he interprets for Sarai (19:14-19). Then, in the account of Sarai's abduction, the comment in Genesis 12:15—that the princes have praised Sarai's beauty—is elaborated into a lengthy poetic passage that dwells in delicious detail on the features of her physical beauty.[344] After Sarai's abduction, Abram's prayer for vindication catalyzes Pharaoh's affliction (20:12-16). Then the account of Pharaoh's affliction and healing is narrated as a contest in which Abram accomplishes what the Egyptian magicians and healers cannot do.

The Apocryphon's retelling of the Genesis story is shaped by a number of elements that parallel the previous two parts of the scroll and the sources, traditions, and tendencies that influenced especially the story of Noah's birth.[345] First, as the text of the Abram story emerges at the top of column 19, it is Abram, the major character, who is narrating the story. The first-person narrative continues well into column 21, to the beginning of the section corresponding to Genesis 14.[346] Second, like the Apocryphon's narrative of Noah's birth, this story is interested in the characters' emotions (1QapGen 19:18, 21, 23; 20:10, 12, 16). Third, the long, explicit description of Sarai's beauty, notably lacking in Genesis, fits well with the erotic tone of Bitenosh's double reference to her sexual pleasure. Fourth, Abram is the recipient and interpreter of revelation.[347] Different from Genesis, Abram's apprehension about Sarai's abduction is the result of "a dream in the night." This narrative element recalls Noah's two dreams, and Abram's interpretation of the dream parallels Enoch's function as revealer in the story of Noah's birth. Fifth, the attribution of Pharaoh's affliction to a demon parallels 1 Enoch 15:11—16:1 and especially Jubilees 10:1-13, where evil spirits are the cause of sickness. Sixth, in depicting Abram as an exorcist who cures Pharaoh and as an interpreter of dreams, the author recasts the patriarch in the mold of the sage and seer Daniel (Prayer of Nabonidus; Dan 2; 7–12).[348]

Several additions to the Genesis story tie the Apocryphon to the Enochic tradition.

At 19:25 the author appears to describe Abram reading to the Egyptian princes from "the [book] of the words of Enoch."[349] This respect for the Enochic corpus parallels its usage in both the story of the birth of Noah and the further allusions to the story of the watchers and the women in the account of Noah's preparation for the flood. Especially noteworthy here is the way in which the author has reshaped the Genesis 12 story to conform to the story of the watchers and the women. The parallels are the following:[350]

1 Enoch 6–11	1QapGen 20
Sons of heaven see beauty of women	Pharaoh sees Sarai's beauty
They desire them	He loves her
They take them as their wives	He takes her as his wife
They have intercourse with them	
The dead, the earth, the holy ones pray	Abram prays
God sends angels for judgment	God sends a spirit
	Pharaoh does not have intercourse with Sarai

In Genesis 12:15 Pharaoh simply hears the princes' report about Sarai's beauty. Here he witnesses it for himself (1QapGen 19:?—20:8). His love for her (20:8) parallels the desire ascribed to the watchers (6:2). The reference to Pharaoh's taking her as his wife (Gen 12:19) is drawn into the Apocryphon's narrative much earlier (1QapGen 20:9), at a point that corresponds to 1 Enoch 6:2; 7:1. Of necessity, the reference to intercourse is deferred until later in the narrative. Abram prays for divine vindication (20:12-15) in the idiom of the prayer for vindication in 1 Enoch 9. It is specifically in response to this prayer that God exacts justice in behalf of Abram and does so through the agency of a spirit (1QapGen 20:16-20; cf. 1 Enoch 10). The stories differ in this respect. Here God's judgment prevents intercourse between Pharaoh and Sarai, whereas in 1 Enoch 6–11 the judgment comes after the divine–human mating has produced the giants, whose devastating activity triggers the prayer. In both stories the plot depicts an erotic triangle, in which a husband agonizes over a possible sexual relationship between his wife and a larger-than-life figure—in one case an angelic watcher, in the other the pharaoh of Egypt. In both cases the apprehension is unfounded. The author's precise point is uncertain; perhaps it reflects concern about the vulnerability Israelite women in a world populated by "strangers" (Gentiles?).[351]

Columns 20:33—21:7 retell the story of Abram and Lot (Gen 13:1-13) in compressed form. God's promise and command to Abram (Gen 13:14-18) are reproduced almost in their entirety, with additions containing geographical information (1QapGen 21:10-12, 15-19). Genesis 14 is paraphrased in somewhat compressed form (1QapGen 21:23—22:26). The scroll breaks off midway through an expanded version of Genesis 15:1-4 (1QapGen 22:27-34).

With respect to its genre and its motifs and emphases, the Genesis Apocryphon is a remarkably complex document. Its three preserved components draw on the mythic, revelatory, and eschatological dimensions of the Enochic corpus and thus offer serious theological reflection about the world and Israel's place in its history. These authorial concerns, however, are not embodied in an apocalypse. Instead the author retells and supplements biblical stories, bringing them together in sequential narrative that recasts a sizable part of Genesis. In this respect he parallels the Book of Jubilees, which he may have used as a source.[352] But, different from Jubilees, his wording is a much freer paraphrase of Genesis, and he evinces little interest in halakic matters and moral exhortation. Instead, he treats his characters with sensitivity to the emotions and reactions that reflect their humanity. The use of the first-person singular in each of the three preserved parts of the scroll strengthens the reliability of the narrative by increasing its vividness.[353]

The author seems to have presented a set of patriarchal memoirs—copies of the books of the words of Lamech, Noah, and Abraham. The story of the watchers and the women that preceded the Lamech story may well have been presented as a copy of the "book of the words of Enoch" (cf. 19:25). The pervasive influence of the Enochic corpus in the three preserved components of the scroll may indicate that the narrative began not at Genesis 1–3 but with Genesis 6, which was the biblical basis for the story of the watchers and the women that was so central to the Enochic corpus.[354] In any case, like Jubilees, the Apocryphon attests the ongoing significance of the Enoch tradition.

The Genesis Apocryphon indicates none of the sectarian concerns that typify the texts that appear to have been composed at Qumran or in its orbit. Nonetheless, the text's emphasis on eschatology and its use of the Enochic tradition would have made it a good fit at Qumran. Conversely, its focus on the sexuality of its protagonists is surprising in the evident celibate environment of Qumran and would have been more at home in an Essene community in which marriage was the norm.[355]

The document appears to have been composed in Aramaic some time around the turn of the era.[356] The complex elements that constitute the warp and weft of the document and the fragmentary state of its preservation warn the interpreter against any simple definition of the author's purpose.

The New Jerusalem (1Q, 2Q, 4Q, 5Q, 11Q)

The New Jerusalem is a detailed and imaginative attempt to concretize one aspect of Israelite expectations about the future. The prophet Ezekiel, when in exile in Babylonia, was taken "in the spirit" to the land of Israel, where his guiding angel gave him a tour of the city and temple of the future, measuring it all with a yardstick (Ezek 40–48). At roughly the same time, Second Isaiah, whose theology centered on a return to Zion, offered a brief description of the future, when the city's walls and gates would be constructed of precious stones (Isa 54:11-17). Isaiah 2:1-4 also anticipates the future glorification of Jerusalem and the nations flowing to it with their tribute. Zechariah 2:1-5 (Heb. 2:5-9) features the angel with the measuring rod, and the end of the book looks for the survivors of the nations to celebrate the Feast of Booths in the Holy City (14:16).

The Zion hymns in Tobit 13:9-18 and 11QPs[a] 22 pick up the theme of a glorious new Jerusalem (see above, pp. 33, 169), and the Animal Vision of 1 Enoch anticipates a new city large enough to accommodate all Israel and the converted of the nations as well (90:28-36; see above, p. 85). The Temple Scroll has its own utopian vision of the temple of the future and the Holy City in which it is situated (see above, pp. 156–57).

The New Jerusalem text, parts of which have been preserved in six fragmentary Aramaic texts from Caves 1, 2, 4, 5, and 11, draws on or parallels elements in these texts and provides a kind of architect's plan for the city of the future.[357] The form of the text parallels that of Ezekiel 40–48. A person, whose name is not preserved in the fragments, is guided through the city evidently by an angel, who measures its components. The visionary character of the text is indicated by the size of the city. It is fourteen by twenty miles, larger than almost any city in antiquity, and immensely larger than the city of Jerusalem known to its author.[358]

The scroll originally contained detailed descriptions of both the residential part of the city—its walls, gates, streets, and houses—and the temple and its courts.[359] Most of the latter has been lost, but the fragments preserve a few parts of a description of the temple complex and the enactment of its ritual. Access to the city was provided by twelve gates (three on each of its four sides) named for the twelve tribes of Israel (see 4Q554 1 1:12-21; 1 2:7-10). The city itself is divided into twelve segments divided by broad avenues, three east-west and three north-south. Each of the twelve segments is divided into twenty subsections, which are, in turn, divided into individual blocks with sixty two-storied houses each—a total of 4,480 blocks and 28,800 houses, with twenty-two dining couches each. This would have allowed for a population of 633,600 persons, although this number may refer not to the regular inhabitants but to the pilgrims who visited the city at festival times.[360] The streets are paved with "white stone . . . alabaster and onyx" (5Q15 1 1:6-7), its buildings are constructed of sapphire and rubies, and the windows are made of gold (4Q554 2 2:14-15).

The preserved details just summarized indicate that we are dealing with a utopian description of the Jerusalem of the future. Given the text's model in Ezekiel 40–48, the visionary account of the text and the presence of an interpreting angel do not require that we construe this as a description of the *heavenly* Jerusalem. Like the other texts cited above, with their precious stones and large size, the author anticipates the earthly Jerusalem of the end time.[361] Perhaps the examples of texts like 2 Baruch 4:1-6 and especially Revelation 21:10-21 indicate that the visionary saw a heavenly archetype of the future earthly Jerusalem. Another possible element in the eschatological picture is a fragment of an account of the eschatological war that parallels the opening column of the Qumran War Scroll (4Q554 2 3:14-21). If this fragment does belong to the New Jerusalem text,[362] a rationale for its association with that text may be found in Isaiah 2:1-4, where the elevation of Zion is connected with the end of warfare; in 1 Enoch 90, where the new Jerusalem is constructed after the final war and the final judgment; or in Zechariah 14:12-21, which juxtaposes the final war with the celebration of the Feast of Booths in Jerusalem.

Although the genre of the text is usually described as an apocalypse, it is unclear what formal features distinguish it from its prototype in Ezekiel 40–48.[363] The date and provenance of the New Jerusalem text are uncertain.[364] The Qumran manuscripts were copied between the second half of the first century B.C.E. and the mid-first century C.E.[365] The Aramaic in which it is written could date from the late third to the early second century B.C.E.[366] Since the fragments contain no language or ideas peculiar to the Qumran community, it could date from the first half of the second century B.C.E.[367] It is uncertain what the precise literary connection is between this text and the Temple Scroll, with which it has a number of similarities.[368] The six copies preserved in Qumran indicate that it was of considerable interest to the members of the community over a period of fifty to one hundred years. Like the Temple Scroll and the Zion hymn in 11QPsᵃ, it offered hope beyond the present pollution of the temple and its cult.

SUMMARY

In this chapter we have surveyed a representative sample of the texts found in the eleven caves in the environs of Qumran. Although they are the remnants of a literary collection that belonged to the members of the community at Qumran, we have no detailed information as to how they came to be at Qumran. There are two obvious general scenarios. Some were composed or copied at Qumran. Others were brought to Qumran by members of the community or by persons who visited the community and/or became members there. Although we cannot be certain in many instances which scrolls were actually copied at Qumran and which ones were imported, the collection sheds some light on the community that preserved them. Scrolls that were composed at Qumran reflect the religious worldview of the Qumran community. Scrolls that were brought to Qumran tell us something about the religious worldviews of the kind of people that the Dead Sea community attracted. What, in summary, do the scrolls from the Qumran caves, and especially those that we have discussed, tell us about the Qumran community?

We can begin with a note about the biblical scrolls, although we have not discussed them. The Qumran group held in high regard almost all the texts that were emerging into an authoritative canon of religious writings, to judge from the testimony of Ben Sira and his grandson. The five books of Moses constituted divine Torah. The Latter Prophets foretold events in the life of the community. The Psalms were also part of the prophetic corpus and played an important role in the community's liturgical practice.

The importance of the Torah, the Latter Prophets, and the Psalms is attested not only by the numerous copies of these texts preserved in the Qumran caves, but, as we have seen, by a whole range of other documents that interpreted them: legal collections (the Damascus Document and the Halakic Letter); haggadic expositions of biblical narrative (the Genesis Apocryphon); texts that combined these two elements (Jubilees); eschatological commentaries on the prophets. Moreover, the echoes of the texts of the Tanak (Hebrew Bible) resound in many other writings from the Qumran caves.

The issue of the biblical canon at Qumran is complicated, however, by the presence of other texts that claim to speak in the name of God. The relatively large number of manuscripts of the revelations given to the ancient prophet Enoch and of the Book of Jubilees, which claims to be the Torah as Moses received it on Mount Sinai, and the several manuscripts of the Temple Scroll, which presents Torah in the first-person voice of God, suggest that the Qumranites had a wider collection of authoritative religious texts than what would emerge in the Tanak.

The clear-cut distinction between authoritative Scripture and noncanonical texts is somewhat blurred, however, by the community's sense that it possessed inspired interpretation of the Torah and Prophets. As the Rule of the Community and the Damascus Document assert, right Torah is Torah as it has been revealed, variously, to the community, the sons of Aaron, the sons of Zadok, and "the Interpreter of the Torah." The Habakkuk Commentary attributes to the Teacher of Righteousness revealed knowledge of the meaning of the prophets, and such knowledge is presumed throughout the *pesharim*. Thus, while there is, in some instances, a formal distinction between Scripture and its traditional interpretation, the Qumran texts indicate that Scripture cannot be cleanly separated from its inspired interpretation. These texts reveal a process by which learned scholars "were seeking" (Heb. *dāraš*) the meaning of the sacred texts and the secrets that were hidden in them.

It is from the texts that arguably were composed at Qumran (or in very closely related predecessor or satellite communities) that we gain a reasonably certain picture of the religious worldview of the Qumranites. Among the texts that we have discussed, these include the Damascus Document, the *pesharim*, the *Hodayot*, and the Rule of the Community. From these texts emerges the picture of a community that understood itself to be exclusively the true Israel of the end time, observing divinely revealed Torah, constituted by divine revelation, and living in ritual purity in the presence of the angels. This self-image had a negative counterpart, namely, that the rest of humanity, including Israelites who had not entered their covenant, were bound for eternal damnation. Right versus wrong cultic praxis, including purity laws and the observance of a solar calendar, was a major factor in the equation.

From some other of the texts that we surveyed it is evident that this self-image and worldview did not appear fully formed at one time. The Halakic Letter and, perhaps, the Rule of the Congregation (and parts of the Damascus Document) attest a time when the antecedents to the community hoped to reform larger numbers in Israel, and a nucleus of the War Scroll seems also to have viewed Israel—more or less as a whole—as the children of light over against the Gentile children of darkness. Still other texts from the Qumran Caves, such as parts of 1 Enoch and Jubilees, derived from reforming, and to some extent sectarian, circles that existed prior to the formation of the Qumran community. These texts, as well as the Temple Scroll and the Aramaic Levi Document, focus on issues relating to cult and calendar. The Cave 11 Psalms Scroll is also oriented toward a 364-day solar calendar, and two of the "apocryphal" psalms in the collection, while they are not sectarian in the Qumran sense, evince a self-consciousness of one's being "the pious" and "the good" and "the righteous."

The eschatological consciousness that is apparent in a number of the sectarian texts was supported by texts that originated outside the community, notably the Enochic Animal Vision and Apocalypse of Weeks, but also the Enochic part of the Genesis Apocryphon, the Book of Jubilees, the New Jerusalem text, and the Instruction for a Student. Moreover, lest one forget it, the prophetic texts were understood as eschatological prophecy.

Much more work needs to be done before one can venture some sort of overall assessment of the multiple ways in which the Qumran collection anticipated, interacted with, reflected, and functioned within the Qumran milieu and beyond. Nonetheless, an imaginative reading of the Scrolls allows us to intuit some aspects of the religious and social life of this sectarian community. They lived in the wilderness isolated from the rest of the world, and in a highly regimented fashion they sought religious perfection and social harmony among themselves, as they read, copied, meditated on, and sought to penetrate the meaning of their traditions and the mysteries of their revelation, as they lived out divine Torah, as, through their liturgies and other rituals, they communed with their God and attuned themselves to the heavenly world (the Angelic Liturgy), and as they yearned for the full consummation of the salvation of which God had granted them a foretaste. The Qumran Scrolls are not simply a variegated compendium of theological ideas. In the concreteness of their detail, they offer us a snapshot of a moment in history when a group of human beings *lived and acted* their religion in the *present*, appropriating their *past*— reshaping and reformulating the traditions they had received from their predecessors— and aspiring for the *future* that they believed God had promised them.

BIBLIOGRAPHY

General

Translations: Michael A. **Knibb**, *The Qumran Community* (Cambridge Commentaries on Writings of the Jewish and Christian World 200 B.C. to A.D. 200; Cambridge: Cambridge Univ. Press, 1987), translations of major texts with commentary. Florentino **García Martínez**, *The Dead Sea Scrolls Translated: The Qumran Texts in English* (2d ed.; Leiden: Brill; Grand Rapids: Eerdmans, 1996), most of the nonbiblical texts. Geza **Vermes**, *The Dead Sea Scrolls in English* (4th ed.; London: Penguin, 1995), the major texts. Geza **Vermes**, *The Complete Dead Sea Scrolls in English* (London: Penguin, 1997), a more complete collection. Michael **Wise**, Martin **Abegg** Jr., and Edward **Cook**, eds., *The Dead Sea Scrolls: A New Translation* (2d ed.; San Francisco: HarperSanFrancisco, 2005), comprehensive collection of translations with brief introductions.

Texts and Concordance: Florentino **García Martínez** and Eibert J. C. **Tigchelaar**, eds., *The Dead Sea Scrolls Study Edition* (2 vols.; Grand Rapids: Eerdmans; Leiden: Brill, 1997), Hebrew and Aramaic texts with facing English translation. Daniel **Barthélemy**, et al., eds., Discoveries in the Judaean Desert (39 vols.; Oxford: Clarendon, 1951–), authoritative edition of all fragments from Caves 1–11. Donald W. **Parry** and Emanuel **Tov**, eds., *The Dead Sea Scrolls Reader* (6 vols.;

Leiden: Brill, 2004–5), all the Qumran compositions, organized by broad generic categories, with texts and facing translations taken primarily from Discoveries in the Judaean Desert. Martin G. **Abegg** with James E. **Bowley** and Edward M. **Cook,** *The Dead Sea Scrolls Concordance,* vol. 1: *The Non-Biblical Texts from Qumran* (2 parts in 2 vols.; Leiden: Brill, 2003).

Bibliographies: Joseph A. **Fitzmyer,** *The Dead Sea Scrolls: Major Publications and Tools for Study* (rev. ed.; Atlanta: Scholars Press, 1990) 97–98, bibliography of bibliographies. William Sanford **LaSor,** *Bibliography of the Dead Sea Scrolls: 1948–1957* = Fuller Library Bulletin 31 (1958) (Pasadena: The Library, Fuller Theological Seminary, 1958). B. **Jongeling,** *A Classified Bibliography of the Finds in the Desert of Judah: 1958–69* (STDJ 7; Leiden: Brill, 1971). Florentino **García Martínez** and Donald W. **Parry,** eds., *A Bibliography of the Finds in the Desert of Judah 1970–95* (STDJ 19; Leiden: Brill, 1996). Avital **Pinnick,** *The Orion Center Bibliography of the Dead Sea Scrolls (1995–2000)* (STDJ 41; Leiden: Brill, 2001). Subsequent updates of "The Orion Center Bibliography of the Dead Sea Scrolls" have appeared in *RevQ* 20 (2001–2) 323–55, 495–508, 599–623; 21 (2003) 137–61, 331–62; 21 (2004) 505–25. Online see http://orion.mscc.huji.ac.il/.

Survey Essays and Volumes: Alan J. **Avery-Peck,** Jacob **Neusner,** and Bruce **Chilton,** *The Judaism of Qumran: A Systematic Reading of the Dead Sea Scrolls* (2 vols.; Judaism in Late Antiquity 5/1–2; Leiden: Brill, 2001). Peter W. **Flint** and James C. **VanderKam,** eds., *The Dead Sea Scrolls after Fifty Years: A Comprehensive Assessment* (2 vols.; Leiden: Brill, 1998–99), articles on many specific topics. Robert A. **Kugler** and Eileen **Schuller,** eds., *The Dead Sea Scrolls at Fifty* (SBLEJL 15; Atlanta: Scholars Press, 1999), mainly a series of survey essays. Eileen **Schuller,** "Going on Fifty: Reflections on the Study of the Dead Sea Scrolls," *Canadian Society of Biblical Studies Bulletin and Abstracts 1995–96* (1996) 20–46. George W. E. **Nickelsburg,** *Ancient Judaism and Christian Origins: Diversity, Continuity, and Transformation* (Minneapolis: Fortress Press, 2003) 237 n. 141, 240 n. 179, some further bibliography.

Literature: For three excellent but very different introductions, see Lawrence H. **Schiffman,** *Reclaiming the Dead Sea Scrolls: Their True Meaning for Judaism and Christianity* (New York: Doubleday, 1994); Hartmut **Stegemann,** *The Library of Qumran* (Leiden: Brill; Grand Rapids: Eerdmans, 1998); James C. **VanderKam,** *The Dead Sea Scrolls Today* (Grand Rapids: Eerdmans, 1994). See also the collection of more popular articles edited by Hershel **Shanks,** *Understanding the Dead Sea Scrolls: A Reader from the Biblical Archaeology Review* (New York: Random House, 1992). On the archeology see Jodi **Magness,** *The Archaeology of Qumran and the Dead Sea Scrolls* (Grand Rapids: Eerdmans, 2002). For authoritative articles on almost every conceivable related topic see Lawrence H. **Schiffman** and James C. **VanderKam,** eds., *Encyclopedia of the Dead Sea Scrolls* (2 vols.; New York: Oxford Univ. Press, 2000). Two journals dedicated to the topic are *Dead Sea Discoveries* (Leiden: Brill, 1994–) and *Revue de Qumrân* (Paris: Gabalda, 1982–). An outstanding monograph series is Studies on the Texts of the Desert of Judah (Leiden: Brill, 1957–).

Damascus Document

Translations: García Martínez, *Scrolls,* 33–71. **Knibb,** *Qumran Community,* 13–76, translation with commentary. **Vermes,** *Scrolls,* 95–118. **Vermes,** *Complete Scrolls,* 125–45. **Wise, Abegg,** and **Cook,** *Scrolls* §1.

Texts: Joseph M. **Baumgarten**, ed., DJD 18 (1996), text and translation of all Cave 4 fragments. Joseph M. **Baumgarten** and Daniel R. **Schwartz**, "Damascus Document," in *DSSHAGT* 2 (1995) 4–79, introduction, texts, and translations of CD and Qumran fragments. Magen **Broshi**, ed., *The Damascus Document Reconsidered* (Jerusalem: Israel Exploration Society, Shrine of the Book, Israel Museum, 1992), plates and transcription of the Cairo texts, essay on the laws by Joseph M. Baumgarten, comprehensive bibliography. **García Martínez** and **Tigchelaar**, *Scrolls* 1:550–627, texts and translation of the Cairo mss. and the Cave 4 fragments. **Parry** and **Tov**, *DSSR* 1:78–179, text and translation of all Cave 4, 5, and 6 fragments.

Literature: Joseph M. **Baumgarten**, "Damascus Document," *EDSS* 1:166–70. Joseph M. **Baumgarten**, Esther G. **Chazon**, and Avital **Pinnick**, eds., *The Damascus Document: A Centennial of Discovery: Proceedings of the Third International Symposium of the Orion Center for the Study of the Dead Sea Scrolls and Associated Literature, 4–8 February, 1998* (STDJ 34; Leiden: Brill, 2000). Philip R. **Davies**, *The Damascus Covenant: An Interpretation of the "Damascus Document"* (JSOT-Sup 25; Sheffield: Sheffield Academic Press, 1983). Maxine L. **Grossman**, *Reading for History in the Damascus Document* (STDJ 45; Leiden: Brill, 2002). Charlotte **Hempel**, *The Laws of the Damascus Document: Sources, Tradition and Redaction* (STDJ 29; Leiden: Brill, 1998). Charlotte **Hempel**, *The Damascus Texts* (CQS 1; Sheffield: Sheffield Academic Press, 2000), compact and comprehensive introduction to the text with full attention to the history of scholarship. **Knibb**, *Qumran Community*, 13–76, commentary.

Pesharim

Translations and Texts:

Habakkuk Commentary: **García Martínez**, *Scrolls*, 197–202. **Knibb**, *Qumran Community*, 221–46. **Vermes**, *Scrolls*, 340–47. **Vermes**, *Complete Scrolls*, 478–85. **Wise**, **Abegg**, and **Cook**, *Scrolls*, §3. **García Martínez** and **Tigchelaar**, *Scrolls* 1:11–21, text and translation. Maurya P. **Horgan**, *Pesharim: Qumran Interpretations of Biblical Books* (CBQMS 8; Washington, D.C.: Catholic Biblical Association, 1979) 10–21. **Parry** and **Tov**, *DSSR* 2:78–93, text and translation.

Psalms Commentary[a]: **García Martínez**, *Scrolls*, 203–6. **Knibb**, *Qumran Community*, 247–55. **Vermes**, *Scrolls*, 348–52. **Vermes**, *Complete Scrolls*, 487–91. **Wise**, **Abegg**, and **Cook**, *Scrolls*, §23. **García Martínez** and **Tigchelaar**, *Scrolls*, 1:342–49, text and translation. **Horgan**, *Pesharim*, 192–200. **Parry** and **Tov**, *DSSR* 2:96–105, text and translation.

Nahum Commentary: **García Martínez**, *Scrolls*, 195–97. **Knibb**, *Qumran Community*, 209–19. **Vermes**, *Scrolls*, 336–39. **Vermes**, *Complete Scrolls*, 473–77. **Wise**, **Abegg**, and **Cook**, *Scrolls*, §22. **García Martínez** and **Tigchelaar**, *Scrolls*, 1:335–41, text and translation. **Horgan**, *Pesharim*, 158–66. **Parry** and **Tov**, *DSSR* 2:72–79, text and translation.

Isaiah Commentary[f]: **García Martínez**, *Scrolls*, 187–90. **Vermes**, *Scrolls*, 322. **Vermes**, *Complete Scrolls*, 468. **Wise**, **Abegg**, and **Cook**, *Scrolls*, §20. **García Martínez** and **Tigchelaar**, *Scrolls*, 1:318–27, text and translation. **Horgan**, *Pesharim*, 94–106. **Parry** and **Tov**, *DSSR* 2:30–47, text and translation.

Literature: **Horgan**, *Pesharim*, texts, translations, commentary, bibliography. Timothy H. **Lim**, *Pesharim* (CQS 3; London: Sheffield Academic Press, 2002), introduction, bibliography, attention to history of scholarship.

Other Exegetical Texts

Translations and Texts:
4Q174 (Florilegium): García Martínez, *Scrolls*, 136–37. Vermes, *Scrolls*, 353–54. Vermes, *Complete Scrolls*, 493–94. Wise, Abegg, and Cook, *Scrolls*, §24. García Martínez and Tigchelaar, *Scrolls*, 1:352–55, text and translation. Parry and Tov, *DSSR* 2:2–9, text and translation.

11Q13 (Melchizedek): García Martínez, *Scrolls*, 139–40. Vermes, *Scrolls*, 360–62. Vermes, *Complete Scrolls*, 500–502. Wise, Abegg, and Cook, *Scrolls*, §153. García Martínez and Tigchelaar, *Scrolls*, 2:1206–8, text and translation. Parry and Tov, *DSSR* 2:24–29, text and translation.

4Q175 (Testimonia): García Martínez, *Scrolls*, 137–38. Vermes, *Scrolls*, 355–56. Vermes, *Complete Scrolls*, 229–31. Wise, Abegg, and Cook, *Scrolls*, §25. García Martínez and Tigchelaar, *Scrolls*, 1:355–57, text and translation. Parry and Tov, *DSSR* 2:134–37, text and translation.

Literature: George J. Brooke, *Exegesis at Qumran: 4Q Florilegium in Its Jewish Context* (JSOT-Sup 29; Sheffield: Sheffield Academic Press, 1985). Annette Steudel, *Der Midrasch zur Eschatologie aus der Qumrangemeinde (4QMidrEschat^(ab))* (STDJ 13; Leiden: Brill, 1994), reconstruction of 1Q174 and 4Q177 fragments and commentary.

Thanksgiving Hymns

Translations and Text: García Martínez, *Scrolls*, 317–70. Vermes, *Scrolls*, 189–236. Vermes, *Complete Scrolls*, 243–300. Wise, Abegg, and Cook, *Scrolls*, §11. García Martínez and Tigchelaar, *Scrolls*, 1:146–205; 2:893–909, texts and translations. Eleazar L. Sukenik, ed., *The Dead Sea Scrolls of the Hebrew University* (Jerusalem: Magnes, 1955), editio princeps of 1QH^a. Eileen Schuller, DJD 29 (1999) 69–232, text, translation, and notes on Cave 4 fragments. Parry and Tov, *DSSR* 5:2–120, text and translation of 1QH^(ab) and Cave 4 fragments.

Bibliography: Eileen M. Schuller and Lorenzo DiTommaso, "A Bibliography of the Hodayot, 1948–1996," *DSD 4* (1997) 55–101.

Literature: Svend Holm-Nielsen, *Hodayot—Psalms from Qumran* (ATDan 2; Aarhus: Universitetsforlaget, 1960), commentary. Gert Jeremias, *Der Lehrer der Gerechtigkeit* (SUNT 2; Göttingen: Vandenhoeck & Ruprecht, 1963) 168–267, study of hymns of the teacher. Bonnie P. Kittel, *The Hymns of Qumran: Translation and Commentary* (SBLDS 50; Chico, Calif.: Scholars Press, 1981). Heinz-Wolfgang Kuhn, *Enderwartung und gegenwärtiges Heil* (SUNT 4; Göttingen: Vandenhoeck & Ruprecht, 1964), study of eschatology in the hymns of the community. Günter Morawe, *Aufbau und Abgrenzung der Loblieder von Qumran: Studien zur gattungsgeschichtlichen Einordnung der Hodayôth* (Theologische Arbeiten 16; Berlin: Evangelische Verlagsanstalt, 1961), the genre of the hymns. Émile Puech, "Hodayot," *EDSS* 1:365–69, good overview.

Rule of the Community

Translations: García Martínez, *Scrolls*, 3–32 (1QS, 4QS, 5QS). Knibb, *Qumran Community*, 77–144. Vermes, *Scrolls*, 69–94 (1QS and 4QS^(de)). Vermes, *Complete Scrolls*, 97–124 (1QS and 4QS^(de)). Wise, Abegg, and Cook, *Scrolls*, §6. Parry and Tov, *DSSR* 1:2–79, text and translation of 1QS and Cave 4 and 5 fragments.

Text: Philip A. **Alexander** and Geza **Vermes**, DJD 26 (1998), full publication of Cave 4 fragments. Frank Moore **Cross**, David Noel **Freedman**, and James **Sanders**, eds., *Scrolls from Qumrân Cave I: The Great Isaiah Scroll, the Order of the Community, the Pesher to Habukkuk, from photographs by John C. Trever* (Jerusalem: Albright Institute of Archaeological Research and the Shrine of the Book, 1972), splendid color photographs of the three original discovered scrolls, taken in 1948; for 1QS, see pp. 126–47. **García Martínez** and **Tigchelaar**, *Scrolls*, 1:68–99 (1QS), 511–45 (4QS), texts and translations. Elisha **Qimron** and James H. **Charlesworth**, *DSSHAGT* 1 (1994) 1–105, introduction, texts of 1QS and 4QS, and translations.

Commentaries: Charlotte **Hempel**, *Rules and Laws I* (Grand Rapids: Eerdmans, forthcoming). **Knibb**, *Qumran Community*, 77–144. A. R. C. **Leaney**, *The Rule of Qumran and Its Meaning* (Philadelphia: Westminster, 1966). P. **Wernberg-Møller**, *The Manual of Discipline: Translated and Annotated with an Introduction* (STDJ 1; Leiden: Brill, 1957).

Literature: Michael A. **Knibb**, "The Rule of the Community," *EDSS* 2:793–97. Sarianna **Metso**, *The Textual Development of the Qumran Community Rule* (STDJ 21; Leiden: Brill, 1997). Sarianna **Metso**, *The Serek Texts* (CQS 8; London: T. & T. Clark, 2006).

War Scroll

Translations and Texts: **García Martínez**, *Scrolls*, 95–123, 1QM and 4QM fragments. **Vermes**, *Scrolls*, 123–48, 1QM and some 4QM fragments. **Vermes**, *Complete Scrolls*, 161–86, 1QM and some 4QM fragments. **Wise**, **Abegg**, and **Cook**, *Scrolls*, §10, 1QM and 4Q fragments. Jean **Duhaime**, *DSSHAGT* 4 (1995) 80–203, introduction, text, and translation of 1QM and 4QM fragments. **García Martínez** and **Tigchelaar**, *Scrolls*, 1:112–45, 1QM; 2:970–91, 4QM fragments, texts, and translations. Eleazar L. **Sukenik**, ed., *The Dead Sea Scrolls of the Hebrew University* (Jerusalem: Magnes, 1955), editio princeps of the *War Scroll*. **Parry** and **Tov**, *DSSR* 1:208–47, text and translation of 1QM and Cave 4 fragments.

Commentaries: B. **Jongeling**, *Le rouleau de la guerre des manuscrits de Qumrân* (SSN 4; Assen: Van Gorcum, 1962). J. **van der Ploeg**, *Le Rouleau de la guerre traduit et annoté avec une introduction* (STDJ 2; Leiden: Brill, 1959). Yigael **Yadin**, *The Scroll of the War of the Sons of Light against the Sons of Darkness* (Oxford: Oxford Univ. Press, 1962), extensive introduction, Hebrew text and translation, commentary.

Literature: John J. **Collins**, *Apocalypticism in the Dead Sea Scrolls* (London and New York: Routledge, 1997) 93–107, good summary discussion. Philip R. **Davies**, *1QM, the War Scroll from Qumran: Its Structure and History* (BO 32; Rome: Biblical Institute Press, 1977). Philip R. **Davies**, "War of the Sons of Light against the Sons of Darkness," *EDSS* 2:965–68. Jean **Duhaime**, *DSSHAGT* 4 (1995) 80–95, extensive introduction with bibliography. Jean **Duhaime**, *The War Texts: 1QM and Related Manuscripts* (CQS 6; London/New York: T.&T. Clark, 2004). Peter **von der Osten Sacken**, *Gott und Belial: Traditionsgeschichtliche Untersuchungen zum Dualismus in den Texten aus Qumran* (SUNT 6; Göttingen: Vandenhoeck & Ruprecht, 1969) 28–115.

Halakic Letter

Translations and Text: **García Martínez**, *Scrolls*, 77–85. **Vermes**, *Complete Scrolls*, 220–28. **Wise**, **Abegg**, and **Cook**, *Scrolls*, §100. Elisha **Qimron** and John **Strugnell**, DJD 10 (1994), texts, composite text, translation, and commentary. García Martínez and Tigchelaar, *Scrolls*, 2:791–805, texts and translations of individual manuscripts. Parry and Tov, *DSSR* 1:326–35, text and translation.

Literature: John Kampen and Moshe J. Bernstein, eds., *Reading 4QMMT: New Perspectives on Qumran Law and History* (SBLSS 2; Atlanta: Scholars Press, 1996), collection of articles with extensive bibliography. Lawrence H. Schiffman, "Miqtsat Maʿasei ha-Torah," *EDSS* 1:558–60.

Rule of the Congregation

Translations and Text: García Martínez, *Scrolls*, 126–28. Vermes, *Scrolls*, 119–22. Vermes, *Complete Scrolls*, 157–60. Wise, Abegg, and Cook, *Scrolls*, §7. J. T. Milik, DJD 1 (1955) 108–18, text, French translation, and notes. James H. Charlesworth and Loren T. Stuckenbruck, *DSSHAGT* 1 (1994) 108–17, introduction, text, translation. Stephen J. Pfann, DJD 36 (2000) 515–74, Cave 4 cryptic fragments. García Martínez and Tigchelaar, *Scrolls*, 1:100–103, text and translation. Parry and Tov, *DSSR* 1:194–209, text and translation of 1QSa and Cave 4 cryptic fragments.

Literature: Knibb, *Qumran Community*, 145–55, translation and commentary. Lawrence H. Schiffman, "Rule of the Congregation," *EDSS* 2:797–99.

Songs of the Sabbath Sacrifice

Translations and Texts: García Martínez, *Scrolls*, 419–31, most of the fragments. Vermes, *Scrolls*, 254–63, some of the fragments. Vermes, *Complete Scrolls*, 321–30, the major fragments. Wise, Abegg, and Cook, *Scrolls*, §101. Carol Newsom, *Songs of the Sabbath Service: A Critical Edition* (HSS 27; Atlanta: Scholars Press, 1985), first edition of all the texts, with introduction and commentary. Carol Newsom, DJD 11 (1998) 173–401, official reedition of texts with translations and notes. Carol Newsom, et al., "The Angelic Liturgy: Songs of the Sabbath Sacrifice (4Q400–407, 11Q17, Mas 1k)," in *DSSHAGT* 4B (1999), detailed introduction, texts, translations, and a composite text of each of the songs. García Martínez and Tigchelaar, *Scrolls*, 2:804–37, 1212–19, text and translation. Parry and Tov, *DSSR* 5:356–425, text and translation of Cave 4 and Cave 11 fragments.

Literature: Crispin H. T. Fletcher-Lewis, *All the Glory of Adam: Liturgical Anthropology in the Dead Sea Scrolls* (STDJ 42; Leiden: Brill, 2002) 252–394. Newsom, *Songs*, commentary on the individual songs. Newsom, et al., "Angelic Liturgy," comprehensive introduction. Carol Newsom, "Songs of the Sabbath Sacrifice," *EDSS* 2:887–89, shorter introduction. Bilhah Nitzan, *Qumran Prayer and Religious Poetry* (STDJ 12; Leiden: Brill, 1994) 282–318, detailed discussion of setting and function.

Temple Scroll

Translations and Texts: García Martínez, *Scrolls*, 154–84. Vermes, *Dead Sea Scrolls*, 151–80. Vermes, *Complete Scrolls*, 190–219. Wise, Abegg, and Cook, *Scrolls*, §154. Yigael Yadin, *The Temple Scroll* (3 vols.; Jerusalem: Israel Exploration Society, 1983), splendid first edition in English of the major text (11Q19), with plates, transcription, notes, and extensive commentary. Florentino **García Martínez**, Eibert J. C. **Tigchelaar**, and Adam S. **van der Woude**, DJD 23 (1998) 357–414, text, translation, and notes on 11Q20 and 21. Émile **Puech**, DJD 25 (1998) 84–114, text, translation, and notes for 4Q524. Elisha **Qimron**, *The Temple Scroll: A Critical Edition with Extensive Reconstructions* (Beer Sheva: Ben-Gurion Univ. of the Negev Press; Jerusalem: Israel Exploration Society, 1996). **García Martínez** and **Tigchelaar**, *Scrolls*, 2:1228–1305, texts and translations of individual mss. based on Qimron's edition. **Parry** and **Tov**, *DSSR* 3:122–239, text and translation.

Literature: George J. **Brooke**, ed., *Temple Scrolls Studies* (JSPSup 7; Sheffield: Sheffield Academic Press, 1989). Sidnie White **Crawford**, *The Temple Scroll and Related Texts* (CQS 2; Sheffield: Sheffield Academic Press, 2000), excellent introduction with bibliography and attention to the history of scholarship. Florentino **García Martínez**, "Temple Scroll," *EDDS* 2:927–33, good summary treatment. Johann **Maier**, *The Temple Scroll: An Introduction, Translation and Commentary* (JSOTSup 34; Sheffield: JSOT Press, 1985). Donald D. **Swanson**, *The Temple Scroll and the Bible: The Methodology of 11QT* (STDJ 14; Leiden: Brill, 1995). Michael O. **Wise**, *A Critical Study of the Temple Scroll from Qumran Cave 11* (SAOC 49; Chicago: Oriental Institute of the Univ. of Chicago, 1990). Yigael **Yadin**, *The Temple Scroll: The Hidden Law of the Dead Sea Sect* (London: Weidenfeld and Nicolson, 1985), a popular treatment of Yadin's three-volume edition, without the text and translation.

Aramaic Levi Document

Translations and Texts: **García Martínez**, *Scrolls*, 266–69. **Vermes**, *Complete Scrolls*, 524–27. **Wise, Abegg,** and **Cook**, *Scrolls*, §38. **García Martínez** and **Tigchelaar**, *Scrolls*, 1:48–59, 446–55, text and translation of Genizah and Qumran fragments. Michael E. **Stone** and Jonas **Greenfield**, DJD 22 (1996) 1–72, text and translation of Qumran Cave 4 fragments, partly reconstructed on the basis of the Genizah fragment. Émile **Puech**, "Le Testament de Lévi en araméen de la Geniza du Caire," *RevQ* 20 (2002) 511–56, critical edition of the Genizah fragments with French translation. For reconstructions of the text and translations based on the Genizah and Qumran fragments and the Greek Testament of Levi, see Henryk **Drawnel**, *An Aramaic Wisdom Text from Qumran: A New Interpretation of the Levi Document* (JSJSup 86; Leiden: Brill, 2004); and Jonas C. **Greenfield**, Michael E. **Stone**, and Esther **Eshel**, *The Aramaic Levi Document: Edition, Translation, Commentary* (SVTP 19; Leiden: Brill, 2004). **Parry** and **Tov**, *DSSR* 3:378–403, text and translation.

Commentaries: **Drawnel**, *Aramaic Wisdom Text*, introduction, text, translation, commentary, Aramaic and Greek concordances. **Greenfield, Stone,** and **Eshel**, *Aramaic Levi Document*, introduction, text, translation, commentary, and Aramaic and Greek word indices.

Literature: Robert A. **Kugler**, *From Patriarch to Priest: The Levi-Priestly Tradition from Aramaic Levi to Testament of Levi* (SBLEJL 9; Atlanta: Scholars Press, 1996). Michael E. **Stone**, "Levi, Aramaic," *EDSS* 1:486–88.

Psalms Scroll

Translations and Text: James A. **Sanders**, DJD 4 (1965), text, translation, notes, plates. James A. **Sanders**, *The Dead Sea Psalms Scroll* (Ithaca: Cornell Univ. Press, 1967), translation with comments, foldout of whole scroll. Apocryphal psalms: **García Martínez**, *Scrolls*, 304–11. **Vermes**,

Scrolls, 237–43. **Vermes**, *Complete Scrolls*, 301–7. **Wise, Abegg**, and **Cook**, *Scrolls*, §150. **García Martínez** and **Tigchelaar**, *Scrolls*, 2:1171–79, text and translation. **Parry** and **Tov**, *DSSR* 5:190–203, text and translation.

Literature: Peter W. **Flint**, *The Dead Sea Psalms Scrolls and the Book of Psalms* (STJD 17; Leiden: Brill, 1997), discussion of all the Qumran Psalms scrolls.

Instruction for a Student

Translations and Text: **García Martínez**, *Scrolls*, 382–93. **Vermes**, *Complete Scrolls*, 402–12. **Wise, Abegg**, and **Cook**, *Scrolls*, §105. John **Strugnell** and Daniel J. **Harrington**, DJD 34 (1999), editio princeps, introduction, transcriptions of individual mss., translations, and copious notes. **García Martínez** and **Tigchelaar**, *Scrolls*, 2:844–89, texts and translations. **Parry** and **Tov**, *DSSR* 4:82–198, text and translation.

Literature: John J. **Collins**, *Jewish Wisdom in the Hellenistic Age* (Louisville: Westminster John Knox, 1997) 117–27, introduction to the work. Matthew J. **Goff**, *The Worldly and Heavenly Wisdom of 4QInstruction* (STDJ 50; Leiden: Brill, 2003), a comprehensive study of the "theology" of this text. Daniel J. **Harrington**, *Wisdom Texts from Qumran* (London and New York: Routledge, 1996) 40–59, translation of some major sections with brief commentary. Daniel J. **Harrington**, "Sapiential Work," *EDSS* 2:825–26, brief introduction. Eibert J. C. **Tigchelaar**, *To Increase Learning for the Understanding Ones: Reading and Reconstructing the Fragmentary Early Jewish Sapiential Work 4QInstruction* (STJD 44; Leiden: Brill, 2001), major study on the reconstruction of the text and some additional topics relating to the content.

Genesis Apocryphon

Translations and Text: **García Martínez**, *Scrolls*, 230–37. **Vermes**, *Scrolls*, 292–99. **Vermes**, *Complete Scrolls*, 448–59. **Wise, Abegg**, and **Cook**, *Scrolls*, §4. Nahman **Avigad** and Yigael **Yadin**, *A Genesis Apocryphon: A Scroll from the Wilderness of Judaea* (Jerusalem: Magnes and Heikal ha-Sefer, 1956), editio princeps, introduction, transcription, translation, and plates. Matthew **Morgenstern**, Elisha **Qimron**, and Daniel **Sivan** (with an appendix by Gregory **Bearman** and Sheila **Spiro**), "The Hitherto Unpublished Columns of the Genesis Apocryphon," *AbrN* 33 (1995) 30–54, transcription and translation of previously indecipherable text. **García Martínez** and **Tigchelaar**, *Scrolls*, 1:28–49, text and translation. **Parry** and **Tov**, *DSSR* 3:2–35, text and translation.

Commentary: Joseph A. **Fitzmyer**, *The Genesis Apocryphon of Qumran Cave 1 (1Q20): A Commentary* (3d ed.; BO 18B; Rome: Biblical Institute Press, 2004), text, translation, and commentary.

New Jerusalem

Translations and Texts: **García Martínez**, *Scrolls*, 129–35. **Vermes**, *Scrolls*, 224–27, 4Q554 and 5Q15. **Vermes**, *Complete Scrolls*, 568–70. **Wise, Abegg**, and **Cook**, *Scrolls*, §142. J. T. **Milik**,

DJD 1 (1955) 134–35, text and translation of 1Q32. J. T. **Milik**, DJD 3 (1962) 84–89, 184–93, texts and translations of 2Q24 and 5Q15. Florentino **García Martínez**, Eibert J. C. **Tigchelaar**, and Adam S. **van der Woude**, DJD 23 (1998) 305–55, text and translation of 11Q18. **García Martínez** and **Tigchelaar**, *Scrolls*, 1:110–13, 218–21; 2:1106–13, 1220–27, texts and translations. **Parry** and **Tov**, *DSSR* 6:38–75, text and translation of Cave 1, 2, 4, 5, 11 fragments.

Literature: Michael Chyutin, *The New Jerusalem Scroll from Qumran: A Comprehensive Reconstruction* (JSPSup 25; Sheffield: Sheffield Academic Press, 1997), an architect's assessment. Sidnie White **Crawford**, *The Temple Scroll and Related Texts* (CQS 2; Sheffield: Sheffield Academic Press, 2000) 66–76, summary introduction. Florentino **García Martínez**, "New Jerusalem," *EDSS* 2:606–10.

The Wisdom of Solomon. Codex Sinaiticus fol. 152b (fourth century C.E.) containing Wis 4:1—5:7 in Greek. Photograph is courtesy of the British Library.

6

Israel in Egypt

As early as the Babylonian exile, Egypt was the location of Jewish settlements. The written products of Egyptian Jewry comprise a large corpus of literary and nonliterary documents that run the gamut from everyday correspondence and business records to highly polished philosophical treatises. From the island of Elephantine we have the correspondence of a Jewish military colony in the fifth century B.C.E., as wells as Aramaic fragments of the story of Ahiqar, a court tale of Mesopotamian origin that migrated through Jewish and, later, Christian circles.[1] Sizable collections of papyri from Ptolemaic to Byzantine times have been uncovered in Oxyrhynchus and in other locations.[2] The Greek translation of the Pentateuch is itself a literary product of third-century Egyptian Judaism that reflects the interpretive traditions and cultural conditions in the land of its origin, and other parts of the Greek Bible may also stem from second- to first-century Egypt. The bulky works of Philo of Alexandria not only are a tribute to the fertile mind of this Jewish philosopher of the first century C.E. but also testify to how Jews participated in the intellectual climate of the great center of Hellenistic learning and ferment. Other religious works of possible Egyptian origin that we shall treat in subsequent chapters include the Testament of Abraham, the Testament of Job, and Joseph and Aseneth.

The primary focus of the present chapter will be six texts written between about 140 B.C.E. and 70 C.E. We treat them as a group because it is virtually certain that they were written in or for Egypt and because, with the exception of 2 Enoch, they share an explicit concern with life in the Dispersion. How ought one to relate or respond to one's Gentile neighbors and the culture that they represent? The answers vary. Aristeas recommends rapprochement. Book 3 of the Sibylline Oracles exhorts the Gentiles to worship the one true God. Wisdom of Solomon may be making a similar appeal to righteous conduct. At the same time, this book and 3 Maccabees are wary of the abuse of power by Gentile rulers and their rich friends, and these writers appear to be smarting from the experience. Opposition to pagan idolatry and sexual promiscuity is a common motif even in the writings that have a relatively positive view toward the Gentiles. On these issues there can be no compromise.

Their setting in the Dispersion notwithstanding, these authors reveal various concerns and connections with Palestinian Judaism. In different ways temple and cult are a topic of discussion, sometimes peripherally. Wisdom of Solomon knows apocalyptic traditions at home in Palestine, and 2 Enoch is a massive rewriting of what appears to have been a penultimate form of 1 Enoch.

Before turning to these texts, for the sake of completeness, I shall touch briefly on some issues that relate to the Greek translation of the Hebrew Scriptures. Toward the end of the chapter, I shall offer a brief introduction to the life and works of Philo of Alexandria and some comments on one of his biblical paraphrases.

Because we are dealing with a long time span and in view of the many complexities involved in reconstructing the history of Egyptian Judaism during this period, I shall make only brief historical observations as these relate to the individual books. The reader may consult the bibliography for detailed discussions.

The Greek Jewish Scriptures— The So-called Septuagint

A discussion of the Greek version of the Hebrew Scriptures is appropriate to this book because the collection constitutes the largest corpus of Jewish writings from the Greco-Roman period. Such a discussion, however, is complex in every way, and it is only possible to sketch some of the issues.[3]

The first issue is terminology. Although the term *Septuagint* (Lat. "seventy") is widely used to refer to the whole corpus of Greek Jewish Scriptures, it properly refers only to the Greek translation of the Pentateuch, which was carried out, according to legend, by seventy (or seventy-two) translators.[4] The historical kernel of this legend, first attested in the Letter to Aristeas (below, pp. 196–99), seems to be that the Hebrew Pentateuch was first translated into Greek in the third century B.C.E. to meet the needs of the Greek-speaking Jewish community in Alexandria.

This implies a related, historical issue. Although it is logical, and perhaps likely, that other parts of the Hebrew Scriptures were translated into Greek in Alexandria in the second and first centuries B.C.E., we have no certain information to confirm such a hypothesis.[5] Quite possibly, various parts of the Prophets and the Writings were translated at different times and in different places and appeared in multiple translations.[6] That is, the texts of the books of the Greek Bible, as they appear in different fourth-century C.E. codices, constitute mosaics of translations and/or revisions of translations of diverse origins, and even the text of a given biblical book in a particular codex may represent a collation. This process of translation, revision, and retranslation comes into clear historical light in the early centuries C.E., when new translations arose, partly with the intent of being more faithful to the letter of the Hebrew text, not least in cases where the Jewish translator took issue with Christian interpretations of the text.[7] The problem is more radical, however. Some variations in the early Greek translations reflect the fact that the text of the Hebrew and Aramaic Bible itself was not fixed in the pre-Christian era and in the first century C.E.[8] In short, as we think about the Greek texts that are bound between the covers of an edition of the "Septuagint," we need to distinguish among other things: "the Septuagint," a translation of the Pentateuch; other early translations, generally called collectively the "Old Greek"; some systematic revisions or "recensions" (text forms), sometimes called "Lucianic" and "proto-Lucianic"; and other, later translations that are attributed to "Aquila," "Symmachus," and "Theodotion."

Careful study of the texts of the Greek Jewish Scriptures has three important consequences for the student of antiquity. First, the "archeology" of the Greek text sometimes enables us to posit a form of the Hebrew or Aramaic that is arguably older than that preserved in the Hebrew Bible that was transmitted by the rabbis of the second and later centuries C.E. This is the purpose to which the study of the Greek Bible is usually put.[9]

Second, and more important for our purposes here, the Greek translations of the Hebrew and Aramaic Bible constitute a major event in Jewish history of the Greco-Roman period. It demonstrates the important role that these texts played in their religion and culture. In a manner that complements the other texts discussed in this volume, the Greek Bible reveals how Jews interpreted and reinterpreted their Scriptures to fit their new circumstances and how the use of the Greek language and its modes of expression of necessity transformed the meaning of the original Hebrew and Aramaic.[10] The careful study of the Greek Bible as a religious and cultural artifact in its own right—rather than simply as an aid to determining the shape of the ancient Hebrew and Aramaic documents—should be an important aspect of any comprehensive attempt to reconstruct Jewish history in the Greco-Roman period.

Finally, the Greek rather than the Hebrew and Aramaic Bible were the Scriptures of the church that created the New Testament,[11] and some of the interpretations that had been made by the Greek Jewish translators became important components in subsequent Christian arguments that the church, not the synagogue, was the true embodiment of the religion of Israel. Thus the Greek Jewish translation of the Bible, which began in Egypt, was an important moment of transition and adjustment in Jewish religious and cultural history, and it facilitated, supported, and enhanced the process by which Israel's religion in Christian garb became a major factor in the culture of the Mediterranean world.

The Sibylline Oracles, Book 3

"Sibyl" is a term that the ancients used to designate a woman who in a state of ecstasy uttered generally gloomy oracles about future events.[12] Our earliest sources speak of only one sibyl, who was believed to have lived in Erythrea in Ionia. Over the centuries, however, pagans, Jews, and Christians generated a massive oracular literature—most of it now lost—which was ascribed to some thirty or forty different sibyls. Our present collection of Sibylline Oracles comprises fourteen books and was compiled no earlier than 500 C.E. and perhaps as late as the mid-seventh century.[13]

The Sibyllines were composed in Greek hexameters and generally lack the parallelism typical of Semitic poetry. They are particularly noteworthy for their explicit references to political events in named places. These often function as signifiers of the end time. The oracles are also marked by a syncretistic use of pagan mythologies and conversely by powerful polemics against pagan idolatry and immorality. Frequent references to the uniqueness, eternity, and omnipotence of the God of the Jews dominate the compositions.

As an example of the Sibylline genre, we shall discuss book 3. Although in its final form the book must be dated no earlier than the late first century B.C.E., the major part of its contents appears to date to the mid-second century B.C.E. (see below). Lines 1-96 of book 3 are widely considered to be of an origin different from that of the rest of the book.[14] Lines 1-45 constitute a general introduction that proclaims the creative power and activity of God and indicts idolatry and immorality. The section is prefaced by an ecstatic prophetic formula that recurs several times in the book:

> But why does my heart shake again? And why is my spirit
> lashed by a whip, compelled from within to proclaim
> an oracle to all? (ll. 4-6)[15]

The introduction is followed by three oracles that describe events of the end time (ll. 46-62, 63-74, 75-96). The first and last of these oracles date from the time of Cleopatra (ca. 30 B.C.E.).[16] In the first oracle the author alludes to the second Roman triumvirate (l. 52) and announces that the kingdom of God will appear when Rome has conquered Egypt. The third oracle anticipates the dissolution of the universe during the reign of Cleopatra, the widow, who may be depicted as a personification of Isis, the universal queen (l. 77).[17] The second oracle is probably contemporary with book 5 and reflects the late-first-century C.E. legend of the return of Nero as a wonder-working, prophetic personification of Beliar (Satan).[18]

The succession of kingdoms and their fates is the subject matter of lines 97-349.[19] In the first major part of this section, the author uses the story of Babel (ll. 97-107; Gen 11) as preface to a summary of the Greek myths of the Titans (ll. 110-58), which provide a paradigm for the succession of the kingdoms listed in lines 158-61. A second list of kingdoms begins with "the house of Solomon" and continues through Greece and Rome to the "seventh reign," when a king of Greek origin will rule over Egypt (ll. 162-93). Then Israel will be great again, and the nations will be punished (ll. 194-210). There follows a survey of Israel's history from Abraham to the building of the Second Temple (ll. 211-94), including an impressive eulogy to the Jewish people (ll. 218-47), which acts as a foil to the anti-Gentile indictments that occur throughout the book. The section ends with a series of woes against the nations (ll. 295-349). Lines 316-18 allude to the struggle between Ptolemy VI Philometor and Ptolemy VIII Euergetes (169–145 B.C.E.) and thus identify the aforementioned "seventh reign" with that of either Philometor or Euergetes.

Lines 350-489 contain three oracles of diverse origin. Lines 350-80 date from the time of Cleopatra.[20] A strong anti-Macedonian bias is evident in lines 381-400. An oracle that originally referred to Alexander the Great (ll. 388-91) has been updated on the basis of Daniel 7 to refer to one of the kings of the Macedonian line (ll. 396-400).[21] The predominance of references to Asia in lines 401-58 suggests that this oracle is an adaptation of material originally attributed to the Erythrean sibyl.[22] An allusion to the Roman civil war (ll. 464-69) indicates a date after 88 B.C.E.[23]

After the typical prophetic formula (ll. 489-91) the woes that began in line 303 are continued (ll. 492-519). A lengthy indictment of the Greeks (ll. 520-72) leads to an even longer description of the end time (ll. 573-808). First the Jews are eulogized for their observance of law and cult, and this piety is here explicitly contrasted with the idolatry and immorality of the Gentiles (ll. 573-600). God's punishment will follow (ll. 601-15) during the time of the seventh king (l. 608), and then God will bring blessing and fertility to the human race (ll. 616-23). The wise reader is exhorted to repent and turn to the worship of the only God (ll. 624-31) lest he suffer God's wrath (ll. 632-51). God will send a king "from the sun" as executor of his judgment (ll. 652-55). The people of the mighty God will grow wealthy, and when the kings of the nations assault Jerusalem and its temple, God will turn the elements against them (ll. 657-701). Then the sons of the great God will dwell securely around his temple, and the nations will come confessing their sins and acknowledging him as God (ll. 702-31).[24] All this is a warning that Greece should repent (ll. 732-40; cf. ll. 520-72). The author again envisions the fecundity of the end time (ll. 741-60), and reference to God's wrath leads to a warning to shun immorality (ll. 761-66). When God ushers in the everlasting kingdom, all the nations will bring God tribute and the world will revert to paradisiacal peace (ll. 767-95). After a description of the signs of the end (ll. 796-808), the book closes with prophetic formulas and an ascription of the work to the sibyl of Erythrae (ll. 809-29).

Several factors suggest that the major part of the prophecies in book 3 was composed during the reign of Ptolemy VI Philometor around the mid-second century B.C.E.[25] As we have seen, the author connects the end time with the reign of the seventh king (ll. 193, 318, 608). Furthermore, he speaks of a savior king whom God will send "from the sun" (ll. 652-56). This terminology appears to refer to an Egyptian king, and the analogy of line 286 (God will send Cyrus) supports the idea that this author looks to the Ptolemaic line for a deliverer. The best setting for such a messianic expectation is the reign of Philometor, whose friendship for the Jews is recorded elsewhere.

Book 3 shows a remarkable openness to the Gentiles and may have been written to be read by them. It employs Greek literary forms and draws on motifs from Greek mythology. More important, its attacks on Gentile idolatry and immorality are balanced by exhortations that the Gentiles repent of these evils in order to escape divine judgment and obtain the blessings of the one true God. These demands notwithstanding, the author does not call for the wholesale surrender of the Hellenistic way of life, and, as we have seen, his messianic hope reflects an irenic attitude toward the ruling house of

Egypt. From this cross-cultural stance the author envisions the time when Jews and Gentiles may be joined in the worship of the one God, the universal Creator. It is uncertain to what extent the book was intended to convert to a Gentile audience or to affirm the self-esteem of a Jewish audience.[26]

Aristeas to Philocrates

In the whole of our literature this writing presents the most positive estimate of the Greeks and Greek culture and of the possibility for peaceful and productive coexistence between Jews and Greeks. The author has taken the name of Aristeas, who is alleged to be an influential courtier of Ptolemy II Philadelphus (283–247 B.C.E.). The book is a fictional account of the circumstances surrounding the Greek translation of the Torah, and it was purportedly written for the edification of Aristeas's brother Philocrates, whose interest in religious matters is duly noted in the prologue to the work (§§1–8).

The first major section of the book recounts the events surrounding Ptolemy's request for a translation of the Law (§§9–82). Narrative is interwoven with lengthy quotations of appropriate official documents. The request originates with Demetrius of Phalerum, who is alleged to have been in charge of the king's library in Alexandria (§§9–11).[27] When Ptolemy agrees to the project, Aristeas seizes this opportunity to convince the king that he should free all the Jewish slaves in his realm (§§12–20). The narrative in this section exemplifies the view of God to be propounded later. God answers prayer and rules the hearts of God's creatures and guides their actions. Aristeas documents the king's accession to his request by quoting the decree of emancipation (§§21–25), which may be a reworked version of a genuine decree of Ptolemy II calling for the registration of slaves in Egypt.[28] After the release of the slaves (§§26–27) Ptolemy requests from Demetrius an official memorandum regarding the translation, which is of course quoted (§§28–32). The Jewish Law is recommended as "thoroughly philosophical" (cf. 4 Macc 1:1; see below, p. 256) and "flawless," thanks to its divine origin, and the alleged opinion of the Greek historian Hecateus of Abdera is mustered in support of this viewpoint. Ptolemy orders gifts prepared for the Jerusalem temple (§§33–34). Aristeas reproduces in full Ptolemy's letter to Eleazar the high priest requesting the translation (§§35–40) and Eleazar's letter acceding to the request and listing the names of the seventy-two men who will be sent to Alexandria as translators (§§41–51). The section closes with a long and detailed description of the gifts sent to Jerusalem (§§51–82). Such descriptions were a well-known literary genre in the ancient world.[29] The description of the table of shewbread quotes the Greek translation of the biblical descriptions of this furnishing (Exod 25:23-30; 37:10-15).[30]

The second major section is set in Judea (§§83–171). Aristeas first describes the Jerusalem temple and its cult and the city (§§83–106). Twice he mentions his emotional responses to Eleazar's high priestly apparel and ministrations (§§96, 99; cf. Sir 50:1-21). His idealized description of the country is marked by utopian elements that characterize travelogues in classical and Hellenistic literature (Let. Aris. §§107–20).[31] After these extensive digressions Aristeas returns to his main topic, the translation (§§120–29). He praises the qualifications of the men chosen to be translators: their proficiency in both Jewish and Greek literature and their ability to carry on learned conversations about the Law. Aristeas then records Eleazar's lengthy speech on the Law (§§130–71). The first part stresses the justice of the code and of the omniscient God who gave it and enforces it (§§130–33). This one God, the Creator, is contrasted with the idols and idolatry of the Egyptians (§§134–38). In the heart of his speech Eleazar employs the allegorical method to explain and defend the rationality of the Jewish food laws in terms that would be understandable to his Greek audience and in large part compatible with their own views. Carnivorous animals are not to be eaten, because they "oppress the rest and procure their food with injustice" (§§144–49; Hadas). As we shall see, tyranny and justice are the ultimate vice and virtue in this author's theory of kingship. The parted hoof of kosher animals symbolizes the Jews' discrimination in their deeds and their being set apart from other people, especially those guilty of promiscuous sexual unions (§§150–52). The chewing of the cud of kosher animals is symbolic of the pious remembrance of God (§§153–60). Then Eleazar makes the weasel symbolic of the sinful practice of gossip and informing, employing a bit of folk physiology (weasels conceive through the ear and give birth through the mouth! §§165–67). The section as a whole foreshadows the massive use of allegory that will characterize the biblical exposition of Philo of Alexandria (see below, p. 219).

The longest and major section of the writing recounts Ptolemy's reception of the Jewish translators and the table talk during the banqueting that preceded the beginning of the translation work (§§172–300). The king is so anxious to meet the sages that he gives them immediate and unprecedented access to himself and pays homage to them and the divine Law (§§172–80). Thereupon they are feted at a daily banquet seven days in a row. Authors in antiquity often made such banquets the setting for wise and witty talk and for learned answers to the weighty questions posed by kings.[32] Here at each of the seven banquets the king addresses questions to ten or eleven of the seventy-two translators and compliments each on his prompt and sagacious response. The topic of conversation is the theory and practice of kingship. The seventy-two answers provide many variations on a few basic themes. Each answer climaxes with a reference to "God" or "divine" activity. God is the Creator, the "giver" of all good things, who inspires the human heart and rules, governs, and guides kings and kingdoms. God's help and guidance are readily accessible to those who pray for them, and the good and wise king imitates God's characteristics and virtues. Chief among these are justice, munificence, gentleness, mercy, and patience. Arrogance, cruelty, and tyranny are to be avoided. There is little that is peculiarly Jewish in these answers. Most of their contents and themes, including the references to God and the imitation of God, are paralleled in Hellenistic treatises on kingship.[33] It is all the more remarkable then that Ptolemy praises the sages for exceeding the philosophers in their wisdom and particularly in making God their starting point

(§235). Aristeas concludes his account of the banquets by commenting on the "incredible" instantaneous wisdom of these sages and affirming several times the veracity of the account (§§295–300).

Aristeas's account of the translation work itself is very brief (§§301–8). Translation results are compared and harmonized. Coincidentally, or possibly providentially, the work is completed in seventy-two days. Thereafter the translation is ratified by the Jewish community, whose rulers anathematize any revisions, additions, transpositions, or excisions (§§308–11). Then the entire translation is read to Ptolemy, who expresses his admiration for Moses' intellect. Demetrius recounts several incidents that stress the divine origin of the Law and explain why it cannot be copied or quoted by Gentile authors (§§312–16). After promising that the books will be cared for with great reverence, the king sends the translators home with great praise and lavish gifts (§§317–21). The book concludes with an epilogue addressed to Philocrates.

It is universally agreed that this work was written by a Jew rather than by an Egyptian courtier named Aristeas. Archaizing statements and historical anachronisms indicate that it was composed not during the reign of Ptolemy Philadelphus but at some later time.[34] Scholars do not agree on the actual date of composition, but linguistic and other considerations point to the last third of the second century B.C.E., specifically during the reign of Ptolemy VIII Euergetes, probably between 138 and 130.[35] Its milieu appears to have been Alexandria.

The author's message and general purpose are evident in his remarkable portrait of Gentiles and Jews and their interaction. Differences between Jews and Gentiles are reduced to a minimum. Among Gentile practices only idolatry and sexual immorality are singled out for serious criticism.[36] While the Law is binding on Jews, Eleazar emphasizes that the Law's intent is compatible with and implies the finest in Gentile ethics and wisdom. By the same token the author employs a variety of genres and motifs common to the Hellenistic literary world in general.[37] Particularly noteworthy is the manner in which things Jewish (temple, cult, land, Jewish wisdom, and of course the Law) are repeatedly the objects of Gentile admiration and amazement, expressed by Ptolemy and his courtiers, including Aristeas himself, whose alleged authorship of the book is surely tied to this function. Consonant with these reactions is the manner in which the one God, by definition the Creator and the God of Israel, effectively moves the heart of the king and catalyzes his action. Ptolemy's decree of emancipation comes in response to Aristeas's prayer. Moreover, the obvious should not be forgotten: it is at the suggestion of the Gentile courtier Demetrius and by request of his king that the Law is translated into a Greek version that is ratified as definitive in the Jewish community of Alexandria. The wisdom of the Jewish sages provides the theoretical undergirding for the view of God as universal sovereign and guide and mover of Gentile kings. In this portrait we see the assertion and probably the plea that Greeks can be right and good and beneficent and that the influence and acts of God make it possible for Jews, while maintaining their own identity, to coexist and interact with Gentiles to the mutual benefit of both.[38]

all for coexistence

Of the variegated contents of this book, it was the story of the translation attracted Jewish and Christian authors, who progressively embellished it into miraculous account.[39]

3 Maccabees

Persecution, oppression, and miraculous deliverance are the stuff of this piece of histori-cal fiction. Elaborate and often bombastic Greek is the language of its composition. In contrast to the irenic and inclusive approach of Aristeas, this work focuses on the Jews' status as God's special, protected people and shows considerable ambivalence toward a Gentile world that can be a serious threat to the chosen people. Ptolemaic Palestine and Egypt provide the settings for its two separate parts, which are held together loosely by a common theme and plot.

Chapters 1–2, the first part, are made up of two separate episodes. The original begin-ning of the book appears to have been lost,[40] and the story begins abruptly in the middle of a narrative that leads quickly to a brief but vivid account of the battle at Raphia in 217 B.C.E. between Ptolemy IV Philopator and Antiochus III ("the Great"). The accu-racy of some of the details in 1:1-7 indicates dependence on a reliable historical source.[41] Dositheus's loyalty to the crown and his later apostasy from Judaism (1:3) are motifs that foreshadow later developments in the book (2:31-33; 3:3).

Royal arrogance and divine judgment are the leitmotifs in the story of Ptolemy's visit to Jerusalem (1:8—2:24), and we shall meet them again in the second part of the book. When Ptolemy expresses his intention to enter the holy of holies, he provokes a mass demonstration, which the author relates at length as he describes the feelings of the characters and plays on the emotions of his readers (1:8-29). When Ptolemy is refused entrance to the holy of holies, curiosity gives way to arrogance (1:25-26). In his prayer for deliverance Simon the high priest repeatedly addresses God as (sole) King and Ruler and invokes God's judgment on Ptolemy's arrogance, citing similar incidents in the past as paradigms for intervention in the present (2:1-20). He confesses the nation's sins, which have caused subjugation to the Gentiles and led to the present disaster, and he beseeches God to vindicate the divine glory by protecting the place dedicated to God's name. The divine scourge rescues the temple from defilement but reinforces the king's arrogance (2:21-24; contrast 2 Macc 3:9-39 and the related story of Heliodorus, who learns his lesson).[42]

Intent upon revenge, Ptolemy returns to Egypt and orders a census of the Alexandrian Jews for the purpose of reducing them to the status of slaves (3 Macc 2:25-30). They may escape this burden and disgrace by being initiated in to the mysteries of Dionysus.[43] Some Jews accept the offer, thereby cutting themselves off from their compatriots. The scene highlights the king's arrogance and emphasizes the courage of the majority of Jews, who refuse to abandon their traditional religion for a cult incompatible with it.

For the second part of his book (chaps. 3–7) the author has reworked a legend originally set in the reign of Ptolemy VIII Euergetes (145–117 B.C.E.).[44] This new version of the legend identifies its main character with the villain of chapters 1–2, intertwines motifs from those chapters, and introduces yet others, so that the whole is shaped into a story about the persecution, vindication, and exaltation of the righteous (see above, p. 20; below, p. 208).[45] The thrust of the narrative is clear, but the conflation of sources and traditions leads to a good deal of confusion and contradiction.[46]

The legend behind these chapters is sketched by Josephus (*Ag. Ap.* 2.53–56). When Ptolemy VIII sought to exterminate the Jews of Alexandria by turning drunk elephants against them in the hippodrome, the animals turned on Ptolemy's friends, killing a large number of them. Upon seeing an apparition, and with the encouragement of his concubine, the king repented of his deed. The Jews, in turn, celebrated the event with an annual festival.

Ptolemy's intent to kill the Jews is tied in 3:1 to their refusal to apostatize (2:32-33) but is extended to include all the Jews of Egypt. Alongside this intent is a conspiracy by certain other people (3:2-7), an element typical of the story of the persecuted righteous. The Jews' loyalty to the king is contrasted with accusations of treason that grow out of their peculiar cultic and legal observances. The loyalty and innocence of the Jews is attested by certain "Greeks" and friends and neighbors, who, however, are unable to help them (3:8-10). Ptolemy's decree of extermination stresses their unique way of life, indicts them as traitors, and cites as evidence the incidents in 1:8—2:24 and 2:27-33.

The narrative that follows is characterized by motifs and literary devices already familiar to us from 3 Maccabees. The section as a whole reveals a number of contradictions. The people are brought from all over Egypt (4:1), yet they can fit into the confines of the hippodrome (4:11). Although they are marked for death, they are still subject to registration (4:14-21). As in the first part, the author narrates history in an emotional key (4:4-10; 5:25, 48-51). Three times Hermon the keeper of the elephants tries to carry out his orders (5:1-22, 23-35; 5:36—6:21). This repetition serves to build some suspense, to underscore the king's arrogance, and to stress God's sovereign power and response to prayer (5:12-13, 25, 27, 30, 35). These motifs come to a head in chapters 6–7. Eleazar's prayer—which parallels Simon's—cites previous examples of deliverance from Gentiles (in Jonah's case, from the depths of Sheol), contrasts Israel and their Gentile oppressors, and implores judgment and deliverance (6:2-15). The climax of the work is typical of the stories of the persecuted righteous. The enemy soldiers are killed (6:16-21). The Jews are vindicated of the accusations against them and are set free (6:24-29). In this scene and the decree that follows (7:1-9), the king publicly acclaims the God he had opposed. The Jews are granted authority to execute the apostates (7:10-15). Feasts of celebration are held, and the book ends on a note of jubilation and doxology. The elements typical of the stories of persecution and vindication dovetail nicely with another literary structure, which Aristotle calls *peripeteia*: "a change of events in the opposite direction." Events that menace the Jewish people have counterparts that effect their salvation from the menace.[47]

To a large extent, 3 Maccabees accentuates the differences between Jews and Gentiles and thus stands in marked contrast to Aristeas, a book with which it otherwise shares many literary and other features. Whereas Aristeas asserts that the best in Greek culture has much in common with Judaism and the intent of the Mosaic Law and that Jews and Gentiles can coexist peacefully, 3 Maccabees recounts how exclusivistic attitudes about the sanctity of the temple, the worship of the one God, and the observance of God's Law have been the object of Gentile derision and the cause of political and social oppression and persecution. In contrast to Pseudo-Aristeas's glowing portrait of Ptolemy II as a model ruler and a patron of the Jews, the present author depicts Ptolemy IV—the main character of this work—as the epitome, even the caricature, of the cruel, insolent, and unreasoning tyrant who instigates serious troubles for the Jews and is brought to their side only through direct, repeated intervention by God.[48] According to 3 Maccabees, Jerusalem suffers under Gentile subjugation and Egypt is a place of exile where the Jews live as strangers in a strange land (6:3, 10),[49] even if they sometimes find friends and neighbors who admire and help them.

Comparative interpretation of the two stories can also come to a very different conclusion by emphasizing such elements as the friendly help of the Jews' neighbors and the final, happy outcome of the story.[50] While these elements are certainly present, the focus appears to be quite different in the two texts. In Aristeas the Jews' slavery is quickly put out of the way, and the largest part of the text focuses on the salutary relationship between the monarch and the Jews and between beneficent Gentile kingship and Jewish Law. Third Maccabees arrives at such a salutary relationship only after devoting most of its narrative to the frictions between Jews and Gentiles. In short, Aristeas summarizes a dark act I and plays out a full, bright act II, while 3 Maccabees plays out a full act I and offers a summary of act II.

The precise setting and purpose of 3 Maccabees can be described in various ways.[51] Most likely, the references to apostasy indicate that the author perceives this as a real danger among his readers. At the same time, he celebrates the courage of those who stand fast and promises them deliverance and vindication. These are elements essential to the stories about persecution and vindication.[52]

Two different kinds of considerations suggest two different dates for 3 Maccabees. According to one viewpoint the Greek word for census (*laographia*) indicates a date between 20 and 15 B.C.E.[53] This interpretation finds the closest analogy to our narrative in the seventh year of Augustus's reign (24/23 B.C.E.), when a census was taken in Egypt for the purpose of imposing a poll tax that discriminated between the citizens of the Greek cities and the people of the land, who were effectively reduced to a degraded and enslaved status. With the *laographia* as a terminus post quem, a date during the reign of Gaius Caligula (38–41 C.E.; see below, p. 214) has also been suggested.[54] Another possible date for 3 Maccabees derives from literary considerations. According to this interpretation a comparison of parallels in 3 Maccabees and the Greek additions to Esther indicates the priority of 3 Maccabees,[55] which must then be dated before 77 B.C.E., the terminus ad quem for the translation of Esther (see below, p. 203). It is possible that these conflicting indications of different dates reflect different stages in the literary history of 3 Maccabees, which is patently a conflation of traditions or sources.

Third Maccabees is related to a number of other Jewish writings. The differences notwithstanding, its style and language, the content of Ptolemy's second decree, and its division into scenes in Jerusalem and Alexandria resemble similar features in Aristeas.[56] Its historical style is akin to that of 2 Maccabees, and the stories in 3 Maccabees 2 and 2 Maccabees 3 are obviously variants of the same tradition.[57] With respect to its genre 3 Maccabees is most closely paralleled in the tales of persecution and exaltation in Daniel 1–6 (see above, pp. 17–24) and Esther. Moreover, specific details in the plots of 3 Maccabees and the canonical book of Esther are essentially the same. Jews are cited for their peculiar laws and accused of disobeying royal law. Their death is decreed, but they are rescued and celebrate the occasion with a special feast. Even closer to 3 Maccabees is the Greek translation and expansion of Esther, in which the two royal decrees and the prayers of Mordecai and Esther reveal verbatim parallels with their counterparts in 3 Maccabees (see below, pp. 202–5). Finally, as a story of the persecuted and vindicated righteous, 3 Maccabees has important formal similarities with Wisdom 2, 4–5 as well as a number of verbal parallels (see below, pp. 207–8).[58]

Additions to the Book of Esther

The Greek translation of Esther includes six passages not found in the Hebrew, canonical version of the book. When Saint Jerome revised the Old Latin version of the Bible, he removed all but the last of them and appended them as a collection at the end of the canonical book. From this position they received the chapter and verse numbers found in modern editions. Here is the order of the Greek translation:

Sections from Hebrew	*The Additions*
	A. 11:2—12:6, introduction, Mordecai's dream, transition
1:1—3:13	
	B. 13:1-7, Artaxerxes' decree of extermination
3:14—4:17	
	C. 13:8—14:19, Mordecai's, Esther's prayers
5:1-2 (omitted)	D. 15:1-16, Esther before the king
5:3—8:12	
	E. 16:1-24, Artaxerxes' decree
8:13—10:3	
	F. 10:1—11:1, interpretation of dream, conclusion, colophon

The purpose of these additions was to supply information lacking in the Hebrew, to enhance the book's dramatic appeal, in part by bringing the characters' emotions to life, to add a note of authenticity by the inclusion of relevant "documents," and especially to bring an explicitly religious dimension to the original form of the book by making God (who is never mentioned in the Hebrew) its chief actor and by attending to issues of ritual law.[59] Alongside the additions certain passages in the Hebrew have been changed, usually for purposes of harmonization. Sections B and E appear to have been composed in Greek, while the others may translate additions already made to the Hebrew text.[60] The colophon, or "publisher's postscript," attributes the translation to "Lysimachus, the son of Ptolemy, one of the residents of Jerusalem," and indicates that it was brought to Egypt during the fourth year of the reign of Ptolemy and Cleopatra, that is, in 77 B.C.E. (11:1).[61]

Additions A and F

In framing the book by Mordecai's dream and its interpretation, the author places this character in the company of his visionary predecessors, Joseph and Daniel.[62] The dream presents a mystery to be pondered (11:12). After the fact, Mordecai can interpret its meaning (10:1). Preeminently, it depicts God's role as the savior of Israel. The battle of the dragons (Mordecai and Haman), the phenomena in heaven and earth, and the Gentiles' preparation for war against the Jews add a cosmic, otherworldly dimension to the tale, bringing it into the orbit of apocalyptic literature like Daniel, which combines narrative court tales with apocalyptic visions.[63] In the midst of this tumult Esther appears— a tiny spring has become a river, God's appointed deliverer sent in answer to the people's prayer (10:9). The "lots" from which the Feast of Purim takes its name (3:7; 9:24) are here the two portions into which God divides Israel and the nations (10:7-9), and they correspond to the dualistic use of this term in the Qumran texts.[64]

Chapter 12 expands on 2:21-23, which is altered at that place in the Greek translation to indicate that Mordecai's promotion was the cause of the conspiracy against the king (cf. Dan 6:3-4).[65]

Addition B

The inclusion of a "copy" of Artaxerxes' decree adds a note of authenticity to the narrative.[66] The charges against the Jews (13:3-5) elaborate on 3:8, stressing the Jews' peculiarity and alleged disobedience by adding the motifs of hostility and the strangeness of its laws and lifestyle. This hostility and other wording unique to 13:4-7 are paralleled in 3 Maccabees 3:7, 24-26.[67]

Addition C

The prayers of Mordecai and Esther add an important religious dimension that is not explicit in the Hebrew book. The deliverance of the Jews comes in response to prayer. Mordecai's prayer emphasizes God's power as creator and as savior of Israel. The traditional motif of God's omniscience is tied to an explanation of Mordecai's refusal to commit the idolatrous act of doing obeisance to Haman.[68] The prayer is roughly paralleled by the prayers of Simon and Eleazar in 3 Maccabees 2 and 6 (cf. Add Esth 13:9; 3 Macc 2:2). Mordecai's "remembrance" of "all the works of the Lord" (Add Esth 13:8) may indicate the priority of 3 Maccabees, where God's deeds are enumerated. In chapter 14 Esther's acts of self-abasement constitute a foil for her self-adornment in chapter 15. Her prayer is considerably longer than Mordecai's and deals in much more detail with her personal circumstances.[69] Verses 15-18 answer questions about the propriety and problems of Esther's Jewish-Gentile marriage and her life in the palace, as these relate to Jewish ritual law. It is a situation that she personally abhors, but she has managed to observe Jewish dietary laws. The prayer climaxes in a petition that God use her speech as an instrument of deliverance (14:13-14; cf. Jdt 9). The attack on the temple that Esther anticipates (Add Esth 14:9) is not mentioned earlier in the book. This seems to indicate the priority of 3 Maccabees, where the king attempts to enter the temple and then contemplates its destruction (chaps. 1–2; 5:42-43; cf. also Esth 14:8, 10; 2 Macc 4:16).

Addition D

This expansion and replacement of 5:1-2 adds a strong dramatic and emotive element to the story. The bland portrayal of Esther's audience with the king in the Hebrew text is here depicted with language at home in biblical epiphanies.[70] Before a resplendent and terrifying monarch, Esther is frozen with fear and faints.[71] Verses 2 and 8 interpret the king's response to Esther as an answer to her prayer, made all the more dramatic and miraculous by the king's sudden change of disposition.

Addition E

This decree again adds a note of authenticity. More important, it resolves tensions created in the first part of the story. God has judged the arrogant enemy who accused his people (16:2-6). Thereby God vindicates their innocence, which is acclaimed by the king (16:15-16), who also publicly acclaims the universal sovereignty of this God (16:21). These elements are all typical of the stories of the persecuted righteous (see above, pp. 19–20). Moreover, verbatim parallels indicate a close relationship between 16:3-6, 10-16 and 3 Macc 6:23-28, 7:2, 3:18, and 5:20.

In the Hebrew book of Esther the tale of the persecuted and exalted courtier (Mordecai) is the nucleus of a story about the persecution and rescue of the Jewish people.[72] The additions in the Greek version embellish and reinforce the genre, focusing on the fate of "the righteous nation." If our interpretation is correct, these additions were made on the analogy of 3 Maccabees. The occasion for the revision may have been to introduce the celebration of the Feast of Purim in the place of the festival that commemorated the Jews' deliverance from death in the hippodrome.[73]

The Wisdom of Solomon

The Wisdom of Solomon is an exhortation to pursue Wisdom and thereby to live the righteous life that issues in immortality. In order to accomplish his purpose the author combines the wisdom and apocalyptic traditions of Israel,[74] synthesizing them with an eclectic use of Greek philosophy and religious thought, and creatively and artistically shaping his material through the use of typical Hellenistic rhetorical devices and modes of expression.[75] In assuming the identity of King Solomon, he specifies wisdom as his chief topic, roots that wisdom in the religious tradition of Israel, and claims authority for his address to the kings and rulers of the earth (1:1; 6:1-11). The Wisdom of Solomon is divided into three closely related and interlocking parts: the "book of eschatology" (1:1—6:11), the "book of wisdom" (6:12—9:18), and the "book of history" (chaps. 10–19).[76]

God's judgment of the righteous and the ungodly is the subject of 1:1—6:11. This "book of eschatology" is framed by a pair of exhortations addressed to rulers, kings, and judges (1:1-15; 6:1-11). The initial exhortation introduces the major subjects of the work—wisdom, righteousness and sin, immortality and death—and indicates their interrelationship.[77] Wisdom is God's Spirit. This cosmic force, which fills the world and holds all things together (v 7), is also a divine gift that dwells within individuals (vv 2-5; cf. 7:27). She is God's self-manifestation to those who seek him in uprightness (v 1) and the means by which pious souls become friends of God and prophets (7:27). Wisdom also has a juridical function as witness against the ungodly (vv 6-11). Verses 12-15 contrast the consequences of sin and righteousness: death and immortality. Death is not the termination of biological life, nor is immortality something that is awaited beyond the grave. Death and immortality are states in which the ungodly and the righteous participate here and now and which continue unbroken in spite of biological death.[78]

As the primary vehicle of his thesis the author tells a two-part story (1:16—2:20; 4:16—5:13) that is narrated primarily in two matched speeches (2:1-20; 5:4-13). In the first of these "the ungodly" make a series of assertions; in the second they retract some of the assertions, while they recognize that others have come true. The basic claim of the ungodly is that death means extinction (2:1-5). Because there is only this life, one should enjoy it (2:6-11), even when this means the oppression and persecution of others (2:10-20). In vv 10-20, especially vv 12-20, the author takes up the typical elements of the story of the persecution and exaltation of the righteous one: the conspiracy and its cause, the condemnation, the construal of death as an ordeal (see above, pp. 20–22).[79] The hero of this story is an unnamed righteous man who preaches against the sins of the ungodly and legitimates his actions by claiming to be God's son or servant who is under special divine protection. In condemning him to death the ungodly propose to test his claims. When God does not rescue him from death they will have proven that the righteous one is not God's son and that there is no divine retribution. Because their argument is based on the premise that death is extinction, this rescue and retribution must occur in this life. The author has the ungodly narrate the story (as they expect it to happen) in order to have them set forth as forcefully as possible the false viewpoint he will later have them retract.

The author now offers his own refutation (2:21—3:9).[80] God created man in the divine image and destined him for incorruption. Therefore the righteous only *seem* to die. In reality they pass to the fullness of immortality; their souls are in the hands of God and rest in peace.[81] The ungodly, in their blindness and folly, fail to perceive the hidden purposes of God. What they offer as proof of their claim—the shameful "death" of the righteous one—is God's means of testing the righteous one and is the moment of his rescue. This rescue and the vindication and exaltation of the righteous one, as well as the punishment of the ungodly (3:7-11), will be narrated in the second part of the story.

Before he returns to the story of the *persecuted* righteous one, however, the author generalizes his discussion of right and wrong perspectives on judgment by declaring invalid certain classical examples of this-worldly reward and punishment (3:12—4:15). The undefiled barren woman "will have fruit" in the judgment. The righteous eunuch will have his place in the temple of the Lord. Conversely, the children of adulterous unions will suffer, and they will witness against their parents in the judgment. The author begins to return to his story. Premature death is no sign of divine punishment (4:7-9), as is evident from the case of Enoch, the righteous one par excellence (4:10-15).

Verses 16-17 provide a transition between the example of Enoch and the story of the persecuted righteous one, and a brief reference to the death of the ungodly in vv 18-19 leads to the second part of the story (4:20—5:13). As in the stories typical of the genre, it describes the exaltation and vindication of the persecuted righteous one and the punishment of the persecutors. In its form and nuances it provides a detailed reversal of the first part. When the ungodly come to the judgment, they meet the righteous one whom they persecuted and mocked. Exalted in the heavenly court, he confronts them as judge. In astonishment they finally see. He was rescued. With their premises shattered they quake in fear, anticipating the dreadful consequences of their false logic—the reality of the divine retribution they had previously denied. In repentance they utter a second speech that corresponds to the first. Assertions previously made with confidence must now be retracted. They who thought that the righteous one's life was madness were themselves the fools. In their view his dishonorable "death" disproved his claim to be God's son and under his protection. Now they must acknowledge that he stands among the angels, the sons of God par excellence. Moreover, they confess that they were guilty of sin, and thus they vindicate his indictment of them. In all these things they were wrong, but in one way they were right. They face the extinction they anticipated. This is so because they themselves summoned death (1:16), and now it claims them. Their nihilistic belief led to sinful actions, and these are punished by the annihilation they had posited in the first place. On the other hand, the righteous will live forever (5:15-16). Theirs is the gift of immortality in which they had believed. Thus God will protect those who trust in God to be their protector and will wreak vengeance on their foes, even the kings of the earth (5:15-23).

The "book of eschatology" ends with a second exhortation to the kings and judges (6:1-11). In view of God's judgment, mentioned in 1:6-12 and vividly portrayed in chapter 5, they should learn wisdom and avoid the iniquity of the ungodly.

Perhaps the most striking feature in these chapters is the repeated contrast between right and wrong perception.[82] Right knowledge, which is the medium of salvation, is the recognition that things are not as they appear to be. The righteous one, who typifies the righteous in general, has insight into God's secret world and hidden purposes. Because he trusts in God's deliverance—all appearances to the contrary—and lives in consonance with that trust, he is rewarded and vindicated. The ungodly are empiricists who view life and the world at face value. Because they act in accordance with this misperception of reality, they reap the consequences. In contrasting these two viewpoints the author is not engaging in an academic debate about life after death. His very *practical* purpose is evident in the exhortations that frame the book. He appeals to his readers to live righteously and pursue wisdom so that they may receive the crown of everlasting life. To accomplish his purpose he does not present rational arguments in favor of immortality. He *asserts* the validity of the paradoxical belief in God's hidden world and secret ways, and he appeals to his audience to espouse that belief. God's justice is a fact, all appearances to the contrary.[83]

These chapters have many close associations with apocalyptic and related literature.[84] The ultimate reality of the heavenly world is an important constituent of such texts as Daniel 7–12, 1 Enoch 37–71 and 92–105, and 2 Baruch 51. The emphasis on one's knowledge of God's hidden purposes (*mystēria*, Wis 2:22) is paralleled in Daniel 1–6 and in Qumranic biblical interpretation (see above, pp. 127–28). The structure and content of the argument in Wisdom 2:1—4:9 may be compared to 1 Enoch 102:6—103:15,[85] and the exaltation language in Wisdom 3:7-8 is reminiscent of Daniel 12:3 and 7:27 as well as 1 Enoch 104:2 and 2 Baruch 51:10.

Of special interest is the scene of exaltation and vindication in Wisdom 4:20—5:14. Here the author has reused an apocalyptic tradition that dates back at least to the persecution by Antiochus Epiphanes.[86] This tradition employed the structure of the last Servant poem of Second Isaiah (52:13—53:12), as the following comparison indicates:

implicit and explicit difference

Second Isaiah	*Wisdom of Solomon*
A. Exaltation of Servant (52:13)	Mention of exalted righteous man (5:1a)
B. Parenthetical comment on Servant's former state (52:14)	Righteous man's former state (5:1bc)
C. Reaction of nations and kings (52:15)	Reaction of persecutors (5:2)
D. Their confession (53:1-6)	Their confession (5:3-8)

Conflated with the scene of the Servant's exaltation was material from Isaiah 14, a lament over the king of Babylon, the anti-God figure who stormed heaven and was hurled down to Sheol. In this conflated tradition the prophetlike figure of the Servant (Isa 50:4-5) was interpreted to refer to the persecuted righteous teachers in the time of Antiochus (cf. Dan 12:3). The kings and nations, more or less neutral bystanders in Isaiah 52–53, were identified with the anti-God figure in Isaiah 14 and were interpreted to refer to the royal persecutor of the righteous. According to the tradition, after their death the persecuted righteous teachers would be exalted and would judge their persecutors. In the Wisdom of Solomon the Servant figure is identified with the wise protagonists in the stories of persecution and vindication. The scene of exaltation and vindication is preceded by a scene that contains most of the elements of the stories of persecution and exaltation (Wis 2:12-20). In order to match the lengthy speech in chapter 5 and to fulfill the author's purpose of assertion and refutation, this scene is narrated in the form of a speech. The description of the righteous one in chapter 2 has also been influenced by the language of Isaiah 52–53, as well as by Greco-Roman traditions about the hostile treatment of philosophers.[87] The heavy influence of Isaianic language is also evident in Wisdom 3:13—4:19, where the author's examples reflect Isaiah 54:1, 56:2-5, and 57:1-4, 20.[88]

In Wisdom 6:12—9:18 the author focuses on the figure of personified Wisdom, alternating references to Solomon's quest for Wisdom with descriptions of her characteristics and gifts.[89] Wisdom was introduced in 1:6-11. The last appeal in the exhortation in 6:1-11 was to learn wisdom (6:9). Verses 12-16 are related to the poems in the Wisdom of Ben Sira that describe the seeking and acquiring of Wisdom (see above, pp. 54–55). The sorites, or logical chain, in vv 17-20 may reflect 1 Kings 3:11-13. After a final exhortation to the kings (Wis 6:21; cf. 6:9), the author introduces the subject matter to follow (vv 22-25).

In chapters 7–9 the author assumes the identity of King Solomon and recounts his quest for Wisdom (1 Kgs 3:5-15), which leads to immortality and nearness to God.[90] Like all humans, Solomon was born mortal (Wis 7:1-6), in need of the immortality that Wisdom could grant (8:13). Therefore he prayed for her and received all good things (vv 7-14), including friendship with God (v 14; cf. v 27). Solomon will now describe her for the reader (vv 15-16). From her he learned the structure of the cosmos (vv 17-22). This catalog has points of contact with lists of secret things in apocalyptic literature, and it hints at the later development of a Solomonic literature that recounts his magical and demonological knowledge and his control of nature.[91]

Solomon now stresses those characteristics of Wisdom that enable her to permeate all creation (7:22b—8:1). He begins with a list of twenty-one attributes (vv 22b-23) and discusses her mobility and purity, which is related to her divine nature (vv 24-26). As in chapter 1 she is both the orderer of the cosmos (8:1) and God's gift to individuals. In all things she is God's life-giving, renewing agent.

Solomon describes his quest for Wisdom as the courting of a bride (8:2-18; cf. Sir 51:13-22, on which see below, p. 355 n. 50). A digression in Wisdom 8:3-8 again praises the characteristics and gifts of Wisdom, among them the four cardinal virtues celebrated by Platonic and Stoic philosophy (v 7; cf. 4 Macc 1:3-4). In Wisdom 8:10-16 Solomon anticipates the many benefits he will receive from his association with Wisdom, and he returns to the account of his search for her (vv 17-21). Verses 19-20 presume a view of the preexistence of the soul akin to that of Platonic philosophy.[92] Verse 21 stresses Wisdom's character as God's gift and leads to Solomon's prayer for that gift (chap. 9).

This carefully structured didactic prayer is governed by the belief that Wisdom is the agent of God's works and the divine gift without which no human can please God.[93] The doxology typically mentions God as Creator (9:1-3) but identifies God's word and Wisdom as the instruments of creation. Solomon then prays for Wisdom (v 4), without whom he cannot properly rule and fulfill God's command to build the temple (vv 5-8). He notes that Wisdom was God's companion at creation (cf. v 1) and that she is "with" God now and knows what is pleasing to God (v 9). He asks that God send her (cf. v 4) to be "with" *him* and teach him what is pleasing to God (vv 10-12). Verses 13-17 stress the plight of mortals apart from the gift of Wisdom and God's Spirit (cf. vv 5-6). Verse 18 provides a ground for Solomon's prayer: in the past Wisdom has taught what is pleasing to God. The verse also forms a transition to the third major part of this work, which begins with an account of Wisdom's works in history.

The "book of wisdom" is related to the "book of eschatology" in two important respects. First, Solomon's quest for Wisdom is paradigmatic of the search for Wisdom that the author recommends to his readers. Because Solomon was a king, his words have special relevance for the kings and rulers the author addresses. Second, the author's description of Wisdom clarifies why the quest for Wisdom is important and even necessary for salvation. Through his search for Wisdom, Solomon the mortal hopes to gain the immortality that is the gift of God. The indwelling presence of Wisdom, moreover, makes the eschatological gift of immortality a reality in the present life of the righteous.[94]

The figure of Wisdom in these chapters has characteristics in common with both Jewish wisdom speculation and Greek thought. Wisdom's presence at creation and her function as God's instrument are paralleled in Proverbs 8 and Sirach 24. Although Wisdom is not here identified with Torah, as she is in Sirach and Baruch, and Torah is only of marginal importance in this work (see below, p. 212), she is closely connected with righteousness and is the means to immortality (cf. Sir 24:19-24; Bar 4:1, where Wisdom grants life to the righteous). At the same time, the descriptions of Wisdom in these chapters employ language most likely drawn from the praises of Isis.[95] Other characteristics of Wisdom, notably her permeation of the cosmos and her ordering of all things, are beholden to Stoic conceptions.[96]

God's acts of judgment in history are the subject matter of chapters 10–19. The topic that chapters 2–5 treat with respect to individuals is here discussed with relationship to nations, mainly Israel and Egypt. Whereas chapters 2–5 are concerned with judgment after death, chapters 10–19 focus on history (esp. the exodus) and this world as the arena of God's activity. Within this arena God is operative through intrinsic, natural phenomena and causation rather than through extrinsic, transcendent intervention.[97] Wisdom, the pervading force in the universe, is God's agent, both the teacher and savior of the righteous and the executor of an essential part of the exposition in these chapters.

Chapter 10, which illustrates the last verse of Solomon's prayer (9:18), catalogs notable examples of Wisdom's activity in the lives of the prominent saints and sinners of old: Adam, Cain and Abel, Noah, Abraham, Lot and the people of the "Five Cities," Jacob, Joseph, Moses, Israel and the Egyptians. In each section Wisdom is the subject of verbs that denote salvation. The objects of Wisdom's activity are unnamed, like the hero and villains of chapters 2–5, because they are construed as types of the righteous or the ungodly. The list culminates in a relatively lengthy reference to the exodus, which is the subject matter of a large portion of the chapters that follow.

In 11:4-14 we have the first of seven comparisons that contrast God's dealings with Israel and the Egyptians.[98] The *synkrisis* was a common device in Greek literature. The first comparison shows how God slaked the thirst of the Israelites by giving them water from the rock, but punished the Egyptians by turning the water of the Nile into blood. These examples illustrate how God uses nature as a means of effecting divine judgment—a motif also found in the next verses and in the other comparisons.

God's mercy and forbearance are a central motif in 11:15—12:22. The subject of idolatry, which is of great importance in these chapters, is introduced in 11:15. Because the Egyptians worshiped animals, God appropriately punished them through plagues of frogs, flies, lice, and locusts (vv 15-16). Nonetheless, God showed mercy by not loosing on them the more ferocious beasts that were at the disposal of the Creator (vv 17-20). In 11:21—12:2 the author generalizes on God's mercy and God's use of discipline rather than outright punishment. In 12:3-11 he illustrates this with the case of the Canaanites. After stressing God's power and righteousness he applies the topic of God's chastisement to Israel, contrasting it with God's punishment of their enemies (cf. above, pp. 32–33, 107; below, pp. 244–46, 278).[99]

In 12:23-27 the author returns to the subject of animal worship, which leads up to the extensive critique of idolatry and paganism that stands in the center of this part of the Wisdom of Solomon.[100] Chapters 13–15 are structured in a concentric pattern (A-B-C-B'-A') that comes to focus in 14:21. This verse identifies the heart of the problem: falsely ascribing to idols the name that belongs to God.

I. 13:1-9:	The vanity of the philosophers, who divinized nature
II. 13:10—15:9:	The misery of those who worship idols, wrongly calling them gods
A. 13:10-19:	Idols of gold, silver, and especially wood; the role of the woodcutter
B. 14:1-10:	The invocation of God, reference to salvation, transition
C. 14:11-31:	The punishment of idols, the invention and consequences of idolatry, the punishment of idolaters
B'. 15:1-6:	Invocation of God, reference to salvation, transition
A'. 15:7-13:	Idols of clay, the role of the potter
III. 15:14-19:	The greatest folly is that of the Egyptians, who reckoned all the idols of the nations to be gods and who worship animals

This section, then, is a scorching polemic against idolatry in general and Egyptian paganism in particular. In many of its observations and arguments it parallels the prophetic corpus and such writings as Bel and the Serpent, the Epistle of Jeremiah, and the Apocalypse of Abraham (see above, pp. 24–26, 35–37, and below, p. 285). In combining a polemic against idolatry with an attack against sexual immorality, the author parallels book 3 of the Sibylline Oracles and Aristeas.

In chapters 16–19 the author takes up his series of comparisons between God's dealings with Israel and Egypt.[101] According to 16:1-4 God satisfied the hunger of the Israelites by providing them with quail, but God ruined the appetites of the Egyptians by turning a multitude of odious animals loose on them. God provided deliverance from the fiery serpents, but the Egyptians found no healing from the bites of locusts and flies (16:5-14). In v 12 God's "word" appears to be the functional equivalent of Wisdom (cf. 18:15 and 9:1b-2a). In the next comparison (16:15-29) fire, water, ice, and snow worked for both the benefit and the detriment of Israel and Egypt. The fifth comparison deals with darkness (17:1—18:4). The slaughter and protection of children are the subject of the sixth comparison (18:5-25). While the firstborn of Egypt were being slain, God protected God's people, whom the Egyptians had to acknowledge as his son (18:13; cf. 5:5). The final comparison contrasts Israel's passage through the Red Sea with the drowning of the Egyptians (19:1-8). Here again nature becomes the medium of God's deliverance (v 6). The final verses of chapter 9 conclude the subject of God's judgment and stress God's use of animate and inanimate creation (19:9-21). The book closes on a note of praise to God who has exalted, glorified, and helped God's people (19:22).

Cumulative evidence in the Wisdom of Solomon points to its composition in Egypt. In chapters 10–19 the author focuses on the exodus and God's judgment of Egypt, the enemy par excellence. He labels the Egyptians' idolatry as the height of pagan folly. Parallels between this work and the religious and philosophical thought of Philo of Alexandria are many and close.[102]

The date of the book's composition is debated. Linguistic evidence may point to the first decades of the Common Era.[103] The prominence of the story of the persecuted righteous one and the theme of Egypt's oppression of Israel may indicate that the book was written during the reign of Caligula (37–41 C.E.), when Jews in Alexandria suffered severely under Roman rule (see below, p. 214).[104]

The author may have intended his book for a mixed audience. On the one hand, the theme of chapters 2–5 and its extension in the discussion of God's contrasting judgments on Israel and Egypt (chaps. 10–19) would serve to comfort the Jews (thus esp. 19:22). On the other hand, the detailed attack on idolatry may well be directed to a Gentile audience. A similar indication is found in the exhortations to kings and rulers. The second of these exhortations implies that these readers are to avoid the excesses of the ungodly rich. Both the Israel/Egypt contrast in chapters 10–19 and the Dispersion setting of the work make it likely that these ungodly persecutors of the righteous are Gentiles rather than Jews.

The Wisdom of Solomon is of importance for the study of both early Judaism and early Christianity. It is an interesting example of a creative Judaism that synthesized Israelite and Hellenistic traditions,[105] and it represents a stage in the sapiential tradition that is accommodating itself to emerging importance of the Torah without surrendering the centrality of Wisdom to the Torah.[106] Aspects of the book also illuminate the New Testament. Its story of the persecuted righteous one was probably known by the author of the Gospel according to Matthew (cf. Wis 2:13, 18 and Matt 27:43). Paul's argument in Romans 1:18-27 bears important similarities to Wisdom 13–15. Likewise Paul's doctrine of the Holy Spirit as a witness as well as God's power for the godly life (e.g., Rom 8) parallels this author's understanding of Wisdom. These similarities do not prove Paul's direct dependence on Wisdom of Solomon, but they do suggest a common milieu in Hellenistic Judaism. Whatever one makes of these parallels, the book enjoyed great popularity in Christianity of the patristic era, and the story of the persecuted righteous one was interpreted to refer to Jesus.[107]

PHILO OF ALEXANDRIA

Philo Judaeus ("the Jew"), as he is often called, holds a special place for students of Judaism in the Greco-Roman period.[108] Along with the historian Flavius Josephus (see below, pp. 288–96), he is one of the two writers from that period whose names we know, about whose lives and activities we know a little, and whose writings have been preserved in considerable volume.[109] Because we are uniquely fortunate to know something about this author, and because his corpus is so large (see below), I shall diverge from my usual procedure here and focus on some details of his biography and context, on the broad contours of his literary ouevre, and only briefly on parts of one of his texts.

Biographical Data

Philo was born around 15 B.C.E. and died around 50 C.E. His birthplace was Alexandria, the cultural and educational center of the Hellenistic world. His family, one of the wealthiest in Alexandria, was a fascinating cultural mix. Philo's brother Alexander held a position of high authority in the Roman bureaucracy in Egypt and was rich enough to adorn the temple gates in Jerusalem with gold and silver plating and to provide the Jewish king Agrippa I (see below, pp. 236–37) with a loan of two hundred thousand drachmas.[110] Alexander's son Marcus married King Agrippa's daughter. His other son, and Philo's other nephew, Tiberius Julius Alexander, apostatized from Judaism and, like his father, held high positions in the Roman bureaucracy.[111] He was governor of Judea during Philo's last years and later was appointed prefect of Egypt. During the Roman siege of Jerusalem in 70 C.E. (see below, pp. 264–65), he moved to Judea and served as chief of staff under the general Titus.

Life and Activities as a Jew

An Observant Jew

Philo, for his part, remained faithful to the religion of his ancestors. He believed that the Jews were God's chosen people and perceived their peculiarity to be bound up in the ancestral traditions that were embodied in the Mosaic Law. In his view, the ritual prescriptions of the Torah, whether they related to circumcision, the observance of the Sabbath and the annual feasts, or the purity of the temple, were to be kept in their details (*Mig.* 89–94). We may presume that he frequented the Alexandrian synagogues and contributed to the instruction in the Torah that took place on the Sabbath.

A Writer and "Teacher"

We know Philo best as an author. His preserved writings comprise roughly 437,000 words in Greek,[112] and an additional substantial portion of his literary output has been lost.[113] In the largest part of his extant writing, Philo functions as an exegete of Scripture and specifically of the five books of Moses. These expositions constitute three different types of treatises. The first is a highly expansive paraphrase of the Pentateuch that recasts the biblical narrative and legal parts, intermingling the narrative with imaginative novelistic elaborations and supplementing the whole with extensive comments and explanations.[114] Philo's second set of writings, of which only a small part has been preserved, is a verse-by-verse commentary on the Pentateuch, cast in the form of questions and answers.[115] The third set of writings, which form the largest segment of his preserved literary corpus, includes a series of expositions on Genesis 2–41 that lay out the literal, and especially the allegorical, meaning of the biblical text.[116] For Philo these two levels of the text are complementary. The allegorical is, of course, the deeper meaning of the text and participates in the basic reality of the universe and of the relationship between God and humanity. Philo's fascination with the deeper meaning of the Torah makes all the more significant his assertion that one must, nevertheless, observe the literal details of the biblical laws, and he sharply criticizes those who use allegorical exegesis as the grounds for neglecting the explicit requirements of the Law (*Mig.* 89–94).

Philo appears to have written commentaries only on the Pentateuch. This reflects the centrality of the Torah in the Jewish religion in general, but also indicates Philo's high regard for Moses as the supreme revealer of God and God's will. As an interpreter of that divine will, Philo focuses on the ritual commandments of the Torah, but he also deals extensively with ethical issues. With respect to the latter, he cites the examples of the patriarchs whose lives are narrated in the Pentateuch rather than quoting the pointed and powerful oracles of the prophets. He does so even though he holds the prophets in high regard as inspired spokesmen of God and occasionally quotes from them.[117]

In addition to his paraphrases and commentaries, Philo composed a number of other works; some of them have been lost, others are preserved only in part. One group of writings takes up philosophical topics in dialogue with contemporary traditions.[118] They include a pair of treatises that argue that *Every Bad Man Is a Slave* (now lost) and *Every Good Man Is Free* (*Quod omnis probus liber sit*); two others *On the Eternity of the World* (*De aeternitate mundi*) and *On Providence* (*De providentia*); and a disputation with his nephew Tiberius Julius Alexander as to *Whether Dumb Animals Are Rational* (*De animalibus*). Of considerable historical value is *On the Contemplative Life* (*De vita contemplativa*), which provides detailed information about the Therapeutae, an ascetic group of men and women who settled near Alexandria and with whom Philo may have spent some time.[119] Other writings had an apologetic purpose. The *Hypothetica*, or *Apology for the Jews* (*Apologia pro Iudaeis*), was composed in response to Gentile criticisms of Judaism.[120] Two texts entitled *Against Flaccus* and *On the Embassy to Gaius* (*In Flaccum* and *Legatio ad Gaium*) appear to have been part of a larger set of five treatises that described the persecutions of the Jews and the retribution that was exacted against their enemies.[121] There is some debate about the extent to which these works were written for Gentile consumption, but some of them seem to presume such an audience.

A Public Servant of the Jewish Community

Although the bulk of Philo's literary oeuvre reflects considerable dedication to a scholarly and contemplative life, he states that he felt compelled to enter public life in the service of his people (*Spec. Laws* 3.1–6). This is reflected, in particular, in his treatise *On the Embassy to Gaius*. In 38 C.E. a bloody pogrom broke out in Alexandria.[122] The emperor Gaius Caligula had ordered that his statue be erected and homage paid to it. When the Jews refused to do so, members of the Alexandrian populace took to the streets against the Jews, and the Roman prefect Flaccus was drawn into the action. The emperor's image was set up in synagogues, while other of these buildings were burned. Jewish houses and shops were looted, and the people were violently assaulted. Flaccus was banished and eventually executed. But the situation remained tense. In 40 C.E. the Jews sent a delegation to Rome to plead their cause. That Philo was the leader of the delegation speaks for his activity in public affairs and for his stature in the Alexandrian Jewish community.

In sum, Philo viewed his world through the lens of the Jewish Scriptures and the Mosaic Torah in particular. He occupied himself with the task of interpreting those Scriptures as the benchmark and guide for the conduct of his fellow Alexandrian Jews. He was also active in public life and defended and interpreted Judaism in his Gentile environment.

Philo the Greek

His Education

Philo was, at the same time, a citizen of the Hellenistic world. As the son of a prominent Alexandrian family, he received a broad Greek education. This is evident first in his excellent command of the Greek language and his facile use of Greek literary forms and rhetoric. Additionally, he is acquainted with the persons and events of history and myth, the writings of the philosophers, the tragedians, and the poets. He can discourse on the arts, natural science, law, mathematics, and music, and he knows the workings of government. Among the authors that he cites, quotes, or alludes to are Aeschylus, Aristotle, Chrysippus, Democritus, Euripides, Hippocrates, Hesiod, Homer, Menander, Plato, Solon, Sophocles, Theophrastus, and Zeno.[123]

Philo's Exegesis: *On the Life of Joseph*

Philo's interpretation of the biblical texts reflects his Hellenistic training. As an example we may look briefly at his paraphrase of the pentateuchal story of Joseph the son of Jacob. He expands the version of the story in the Greek translation of the Torah to roughly three and a half times its size. We might characterize his form of the story as a moralistic novel. Its didactic nature is evident already in the title and introduction. Joseph is presented as a *politikos* (statesman). The text divides into four sections, three of them with alternating narrative and interpretation (§§2–5, 6–7; 8–10, 11–14; 15–21, 22–26; 27–44). However, the narrative itself is heavily interpretive. Although Philo follows closely the order of the biblical account, he transforms its tightly written prose into a flowing narrative that elaborates on events and their circumstances and that explicates the characters' emotions, motivations, and reactions to the events that are being narrated. He accomplishes this sometimes by placing long speeches in the characters' mouths. By means of these speeches, but in their narrative framework as well, Philo, in typical Hellenistic fashion, depicts his characters as the personifications of abstract moral virtues and vices—not least the four cardinal virtues of contemporary Greek philosophy: justice, courage, intelligence, and self-control. Thus the biblical story of Joseph, which explains how God engineers the events of history to God's own ends, becomes for Philo an occasion for good Greek ethical instruction. That is the first half of it. The second component in each of the first three sections of this text is an allegorical commentary on the narrative, which explicates the meaning that underlies the literal surface of the text. This kind of allegorical interpretation is also part and parcel of contemporary pagan Hellenistic exposition of texts. Thus throughout this treatise on Joseph, Philo, the Jewish exegete of a Jewish text, speaks the language of Greek philosophy, and he even quotes a tragedy of Euripides to illustrate his point (§78).

Philo the Philosopher

Thus, if the principal form of Philo's writing was exposition of the biblical text, its content was thoroughly informed by Greek philosophical speculation—more so than any other contemporary Jewish author whose works have been preserved. He drew eclectically from the traditions of the Platonists, the Stoics, and the Pythagoreans. The initial treatise of his paraphrase of the Pentateuch, *On the Creation of the World* (*De opificio mundi*), retells the Genesis story of creation "in terms of Plato's *Timaeus* as Philo understood it,"[124] and his lengthy expostulation on the number seven would have brought a gleam to a Pythagorean's eye. He is in constant critical dialog with Stoic cosmology, but draws deeply from their well as he expounds his ethics.[125] Philo's worldview is fundamentally Platonic. God is being itself, the unknowable, the one who exists. *Logos* is a multivalent term that denotes the complex ways in which God extends himself in order to form matter and to communicate and interact with the sensible, empirical world. *Logos* is the mind of the Creator in the act of creation, and it is the means by which God speaks through the mouth of Moses, in particular, and acts by means of angels and archangels. Aspects of this world have their counterparts in the world of forms, which is the lowest extension of the *Logos*.[126] The Jerusalem temple has its counterpart in the cosmic heavenly temple, and priestly purity reflects the image of God.[127] The Mosaic laws and the righteous *politikos* mediate true justice.

Philo's Mystical Religion

Philo's philosophy was not an end in itself; it was not speculating about the universe for the sake of speculation. Nor were his allegories simply a clever way to interpret old texts in a modern mode. Together they were a vehicle to explicate and facilitate what has been appropriately described as Philo's mystical religion, a type of religion that has analogies in the so-called mystery religions that populated Mediterranean antiquity.[128] The goal of Philo's religion is for earthbound humans to transcend their material existence and circumstances and to come to know the unknowable God. According to Philo's allegory, this path was already trodden by the patriarchs, notably by Abraham, Jacob, and Moses. Abraham's migration from Chaldea involved his rejection of the philosophy that saw the material world as the ultimate form of existence. His marriage to Sarah involved his union with Sophia, the divine effulgence of Wisdom that comes from God. Jacob, in taking the name Israel, is designated as the man who has seen God. Moses ascended the mountain and functioned as the divine Logos when he brought revelation to the people of Israel. Thus, in all of this, through the explication of allegory and the speculative systematization of philosophy, Philo propounds a form of the Jewish religion that begins with the ancient Scriptures and seeks to bring human beings into communion with the transcendent God. Such communion, moreover, enables one to live the righteous life that God demands of God's people.

Philo's Other Participation in Greek Culture

Philo's mysticism did not preclude his involvement in Alexandrian life. Moreover, he was a Greek not only when he sat at his desk. He did not simply think as a Greek and write as a Greek. In significant ways, he *lived* as a Greek. To judge from the illustrations in his writing, he was a knowledgeable spectator at athletic contests, attended the theater, and participated in banquets.[129]

Philo: A Citizen of Two Worlds

Philo lived in two worlds and imbibed the culture of both. He studied and interpreted his Jewish Bible and he observed its commandments, and through his writings he sought to teach his fellow Jews how to live the pious and God-fearing life and to aspire to communion with God. At the same time, he spoke Greek, not Hebrew or Aramaic; he was educated as a Greek; he participated in Greek culture; and he expounded his ancestral Scriptures in the language, rhetoric, and concepts of Greek philosophy and art. His loyalties clearly lay with Judaism, and he criticized the excesses of the dominant culture and defended Judaism against attacks of its cultured despisers and its persecutors. This fact notwithstanding, he believed that one could stand with one foot in each culture, that one could be, so to speak, a Jew and a Greek at the same time, and that the quest for truth could progress fruitfully through an appropriate synthesis of the two cultures.[130]

Characterizing Philo

As an exegete Philo is thoughtful, imaginative, clever—perhaps with a touch of humor—and sometimes brilliant. His comments are not an exercise in the ordinary and the obvious. In other ways, Philo is always looking for analogies or associations, to make his point clear or to show how things are really connected. He can use a simile or parable, or he can cite an example from athletics, art, commerce, or agriculture to illustrate a point. Thus the text is always a starting point that triggers an insight in his mind. The parade example of this is, of course, his allegorical exposition of Scripture. Even when he is not in his allegorical mode, however, he is making connections. He is imagining how or why this or that event happened, and what its consequences were in the lives of the people concerned. He has the rich imagination of a novelist or a playwright.

Philo's critical and synthetic mind is at its best when he reflects on the great Greek philosophical tradition, drawing on this, and rejecting that, and bringing it all together, not simply in its own terms, but as it relates to and illuminates his Jewish tradition.

Although Philo was a philosopher, he was very much in touch with the world, and he was particularly keen as an observer of human nature. His psychological insights were remarkably on target and even shed light on modern problems and situations. The Joseph story provides one example. Joseph's brothers pull him from the pit and sell him into slavery. When his brother Reuben, who has been absent, returns to find the pit empty, he "rent his garments and rushed up and down like a madman, beating his hands together and tearing his hands. 'Tell me, what has become of him. Is he dead or alive? If he is no more, show me his dead body, that I may weep over the corpse and thus make the calamity seem lighter. If I see him lying here I shall be comforted'" (*Jos.* §§16–17, translation Colson). His father expresses similar emotions at much greater length (§§22–27). Philo understood well the dynamics of grief and the necessity to bring closure after a death—long before modern psychology analyzed the phenomenon.[131]

In short, Philo of ancient Alexandria makes good reading in our own time: psychological insight into what makes humans tick, reflection on how things are, wisdom on how to deal with them, a respect for the tradition combined with an ability to express it in new ways. Of course, Philo had his blind spots, intellectually and psychologically. Perhaps the most notorious was his chauvinistic attitude toward the female sex,[132] but that should not obscure the admirable aspects of his intellect and his humanity.

Philo among Contemporary Jews: Continuity and Distinction

Philo was a preeminent representative the Hellenistic Judaism that blended its biblical heritage with contemporary Greek culture. In various respects his writings were similar to and differed from those of other Jewish writers who preceded him, followed him, or were roughly his contemporaries.

Attitude toward Scripture

For Philo the Jewish Scriptures were the word of God, and he was, at heart, an exegete of those Scriptures.[133] It was through the allegorical method that Philo and some of his contemporaries plumbed the individual words of the text for a deeper meaning. Such close attention to the minute details was not limited, however, to Greek allegorical exegesis. At the Qumran community, scholars hung on particular words as they probed the prophetic texts for clues about their own times (see above, pp. 127–32). The rabbis of a later period followed similar procedures and employed complex hermeneutical principles to milk the words of the divinely inspired text for every imaginable bit of meaning.[134]

Philo stood in a long tradition of writers who interpreted the sacred traditions by paraphrasing them. We have seen examples of this literary phenomenon in the Book of Jubilees and the Genesis Apocryphon. Other examples include the *Book of Biblical Antiquities* (see below, pp. 265–70) and Flavius Josephus's *Antiquities of the Jews* (see below, pp. 291–93). The uniqueness of Philo's paraphrase of the Pentateuch lies, at least in part, in the considerable length of Philo's expansions, in his novelistic recasting of the material, in his moralistic presentation of the patriarchs as personifications of virtue, and in his allegorical commentaries on the texts.

Commentaries were another vehicle for interpreting Scripture. The earliest preserved exemplars of the genre are the commentaries on the prophetic writings discovered in the caves of Qumran. The commentaries of Philo differ from the Qumran texts in significant ways. First, Philo limits himself to the books of the Pentateuch. Second, his commentaries are loaded with allegorical interpretations that are integrated into his worldview and his mystical religion, and that seek to encourage right conduct and the cultivation of a relationship to God. Third, eschatology, as such, is not a major facet of Philo's religious outlook. Commentaries on the Bible would continue to flourish among the Jewish rabbis of later centuries.[135]

The Use of Allegory

Allegory was a common hermeneutical method in the Greco-Roman period; interpreters of Homer used it to explain away difficulties in the texts. We find a similar usage in some preserved fragments of Aristobulus, an Alexandrian Jewish predecessor of Philo.[136] Aristeas employed the method to demonstrate how Jewish food laws really deal with moral vices and virtues and thus are relevant for both Jews and Gentiles (see above, pp. 196–97). Philo's allegorical usage parallels both of these approaches, but his principal use of allegory fits into his broader theological and philosophical purposes and focuses on the relationship between humanity and God.

Jewish Philosophy

Philo was not the first Jewish philosopher. In this role he was preceded by Aristobulus; however, his preserved fragments are so few and so small that we can not determine the breadth or quality of his philosophical program. The presence of Jewish philosophy in Alexandria is also attested in the Wisdom of Solomon, whose author, like Philo, blended Platonic and Stoic thought and equated *Logos* with divine Wisdom (see above, pp. 209–10). In Antioch the author of 4 Maccabees incorporated the story of the seven brothers and their mother (2 Macc 7) into a philosophical discourse that identifies the Torah as the true philosophy (see below, pp. 256–59). These texts demonstrate the developing tendency in the three centuries around the turn of the era to interpret Jewish religion in terms of Greek philosophy. While we must be cautious is drawing conclusions from limited evidence, it appears the Philo's was the most ambitious of the philosophical programs.

Expounding the Will of God

Judaism was a religion that was especially concerned about the imperative to live according to God's will as this is spelled out in the Mosaic Torah and the prophets. Jewish texts that we have discussed embody this concern in halakic exegesis (e.g., Jubilees) and wisdom forms (e.g., Wisdom of Ben Sira). One of the special qualities of Philo's ethical writing is his characterization of the patriarchs as embodiments of abstract virtues. We can apparently attribute this substantially to the Hellenistic sources of his thought; and some contemporary Jewish writings, such as 4 Maccabees and the Testament of Job, draw on the same sources (see below, pp. 256, 322).

To summarize, Philo of Alexandria was an important and significant figure in Hellenistic Jewry around the turn of the era, but he was not unique. On the basis of present evidence we may perhaps conclude that Philo was preeminent among such exegetes, teachers, and philosophers. What is certain is this: due to their sheer volume, the preserved works of Philo provide a unique window into the world of Hellenistic Judaism. Without his corpus, our knowledge of this religious and cultural phenomenon would be greatly impoverished, and thus we would be considerably hampered in our attempt to construct a balanced picture of the diversity of first-century Judaism as a whole.

Philo and Early Christianity

Philo of Alexandria is significant not only for our understanding of first-century Judaism, but also for the interpretation of the New Testament.[137] This is to be expected, since early Christianity arose as a sect within the matrix of Judaism and the books of the New Testament were written for communities that understood the religious language of the hellenized world and, in some cases, the vocabulary and worldview of Hellenistic Jewry.

The precise relationships between the New Testament and Philo, however, are complex and uncertain, and they continue to be debated—for two reasons.[138] First, Philo was one among many Hellenistic Jewish thinkers and writers. New Testament parallels to Philo may reflect currents in the broader stream of Hellenistic Judaism. Second, such parallels may also derive from other forms of Judaism, for example, apocalyptic Judaism. However we resolve the particular issues, the Philonic corpus helps us better to understand early Christianity as a religious phenomenon that has, in its own way, synthesized biblical religion and Hellenistic religion and culture.

One of the major developments in the Christian writings of the second century and thereafter is a tendency toward the philosophical defense and explication of the new religion. In this new development, parallels to Philo are closer than in the New Testament, and the actual influence of Philo can be demonstrated.

Explicit citation and prolific use of Philo appears first in the writings of Clement of

Alexandria, who taught and wrote between 175 and 220 C.E.[139] Evidently the library with which Clement worked contained most of Philo's writings, and he employed the thought of the Alexandrian Jew in his philosophically oriented biblical exegesis and his writings in defense of Christianity.

Closer to Philo, in a real sense, was Clement's successor, Origen, who wrote extensively in Alexandria in the first part of the third century and then moved to Caesarea in Palestine.[140] His affinity to Philo, whom he frequently quotes, lies in the form of his writing. His major genre, like Philo's, is biblical commentaries, which are shot through with Philonic themes, Platonic philosophy, and allegorical interpretation.

A few decades later, Eusebius, the Christian apologist and historian of Caesarea, employed and quoted from the works of Philo.[141] Modern editions of the works of Philo are, for the most part, ultimately based on manuscripts from this Philonic library in Caesarea, which Origen had transplanted from Alexandria.

Thus we come to a set of historical ironies. In the centuries after Philo's death, his works were discarded within Judaism, as that religion consolidated itself under the leadership of the rabbis.[142] However, these works of the Alexandrian Jew were cherished, used, and ultimately preserved by Christian theologians, precisely at a time when the church was differentiating itself from Judaism and polemicizing against its mother religion.[143]

2 Enoch

This apocalyptic work has been preserved in Slavonic in a long and a short recension. Scholars debate whether the long recension is an expansion of the short, or the short recension is a compression of the long one. The truth probably lies in between: there are expansions and compressions.[144] In the interest of not relying on possibly expansionistic elements, the discussion here follows the short recension, although occasional reference is made to possible original readings in the long recension.[145]

Second Enoch divides into three sections, which correspond to major blocks of material in 1 Enoch. Enoch's ascent to heaven, vision of God, and commissioning (chaps. 3–37) are the counterpart of 1 Enoch 12–36 (and perhaps 71). His return to earth and instruction of his children (chaps. 38–66) are analogous to 1 Enoch 81, 91–105. The narrative about Melchizedek's miraculous birth is the counterpart of 1 Enoch 106–107.

From a formal point of view 2 Enoch shares the characteristics of both an apocalypse and a testament. (On these literary forms see above, pp. 52–53, 87, and below, p. 302.) As an apocalypse the text has a narrative framework that provides the setting for an account of a heavenly ascent in which the central figure receives revelations about the cosmos (esp. heaven) and the hidden future, which he then transmits to his audience—both those in the narrative and those who will read his book. As a testament the work is set in the last year of Enoch's life (1:1). He is in his bed (1:3), and at the command of two angels, he summons his sons and household for instructions (1:8—2:4). His first-person account of his heavenly journey is the equivalent of the narrative sections in the typical testament. When he returns, he gathers his children for testamentary instruction (chaps. 38–66), after which he departs from their presence (chap. 67). Instead of a reference to his burial, the author recounts the construction of an altar at the place where he was taken to heaven (chap. 68).

Within these apocalyptic and testamentary macroforms, the author has shaped the contents of his work through the use of literary microforms that have counterparts in 1 Enoch and that draw on its contents (on which see above, pp. 50–52). The patriarch's ascent to heaven (2 Enoch 3–37) culminates at the divine throne with a divine commissioning that corresponds to 1 Enoch 12–16 and perhaps 71.[146] Enoch's journeys to places of cosmological and eschatological significance correspond to the journeys described in 1 Enoch 17–19 and 20–36 (and to the detailed accounts in chaps. 72–77) and reflect formal differences in 1 Enoch. Enoch's visions of the *celestial* phenomena in the first and fourth heavens (2 Enoch 3–6, 11–17), like their counterparts in 1 Enoch 17:1—18:6; 33–36; and 72–77, are narrated in a straightforward manner. He sees (or the angels show him) certain heavenly phenomena, which he recognizes, names, and describes. Alternatively, when the seer describes the visions of *eschatological* import in the second, third, and fifth heavens (2 Enoch 7–10, 18), he employs the form familiar from the visions in 1 Enoch 18:6—19:2 and especially 21–27 and 32: journey, vision, seer's comment or question, interpretation.[147] In his description of the rebel angels the seer distinguishes between two groups, as does 1 Enoch: the *egrēgoroi* ("watchers"), who sinned with the women (2 Enoch 18); and their "brethren" (18:7), called "apostates" (chap. 7), who may correspond to the angels as revealers.[148] Significant for this author's purpose are his descriptions of paradise and hell in the third heaven (chaps. 8–10). The complementary lists of sins and good deeds correspond to similar lists in Enoch's instruction later in the book and reflect the book's strong ethical emphasis.[149]

Enoch's ascent terminates in the divine throne room, which is located in the seventh heaven.[150] Although the scene parallels 1 Enoch 14:15—16:4 in its narrative introduction and its form as a commissioning scene, there are major differences that reflect a substantial magnification of Enoch's person and functions. After the collapsed seer has been rehabilitated, he is brought directly into the presence of God and transformed into a heavenly being, in effect an angel (2 Enoch 21:2—22:10; cf. 1 Enoch 14:14).[151] Having achieved this status, Enoch is able to enter God's presence and look at the face of God (see 2 Enoch 22:1-4 long recension, supported by his later report in 39:3-8 short recension),[152] something that is denied him in 1 Enoch 14:21.[153] In keeping with his elevated status and his traditional role as scribe,[154] Enoch is commissioned not to take a book of indictment back to the "watchers" (1 Enoch 13:10—14:1), but to write 360 books of cosmological and ethical teaching. After the seer has inscribed these books (2 Enoch 23) at an angel's dictation, God grants Enoch the privilege of hearing a lengthy account of the secrets of creation, which hitherto have been unknown even to the angels (chaps. 24–30).[155] In the short recension the account reflects Egyptian and Persian mythology,[156] while the author of the long recension has included material from Genesis 1–3, giving special attention to the creation of Adam (2 Enoch 30).[157] The climactic position of the creation narrative attests the theological prominence that this author has accorded to creation. Thus God comments on the narrative just completed by stressing God's own uniqueness as Creator and God's total sovereignty in the heavens (chap. 33), and God reveals that the flood will come because the human race refuses to acknowledge that uniqueness and sovereignty (chap. 34). As a remedy for this situation God commissions Enoch to bring to earth books that, as we shall see, stress creation as a rationale for ethics (chaps. 36–37). The description of Enoch's ascent has also emphasized God's creative power, which is evident in the cosmic phenomena and the places of eschatological signif- icance that God has "prepared" (9:1; 10:4).

Enoch's instruction is an epitome of the books he has written, and it is divided into three parts. The first of these is addressed to his children (chaps. 39–56), although it has no formal introduction in the present state of the text (but see 36:4).[158] Enoch asserts the divine origin and universality of his knowledge (39:1—40:1; cf. 1 Enoch 93:2)[159] and his role as the governor of God's world (2 Enoch 39:8; 43:1),[160] and he interweaves descrip- tion of the celestial and eschatological phenomena that he has seen with ethical exhorta- tions in the form of blessings and curses that correspond to the exhortations and woes of 1 Enoch 94–104.[161] In this section, proper conduct is construed largely in terms of one's deeds toward others. Such conduct is based on the double rationale of creation and eschatology.[162] One dare not hold other human beings in contempt; that is to hold God in contempt since God created humanity in the divine image (2 Enoch 44:1). Moreover, to do so invites God's wrath and great judgment (44:2). Elsewhere in this section the eschatological rationale is explicit (e.g., 49:2; 50:4—51:3), and it is implicit in descrip- tions of the places of judgment and reward and punishment (40:12—42:3) and in for- mulas of blessing and curse.

Enoch addresses his second body of instruction to Methuselah's brethren and to the elders of the people (chaps. 57–63). An initial description of creation provides the basis for instruction about responsibility toward animals and human beings (chaps. 58–60). This includes some brief instructions about proper animal sacrifice (59:1-4). The obliga- tion to clothe the naked and feed the hungry (63:1) was mentioned as a touchstone of judgment in Enoch's descriptions of paradise and hell (chaps. 9–10) and in the previous parenetic section (42:8).

Enoch's final instruction is addressed to "all his people" (chaps. 64–66). In it he com- bines creation and eschatology. The background of the author's thought is the teaching about two ages: the present age of sorrow and trouble and the glorious age to come (cf. 66:6 and 50:2 and see the discussion of 2 Baruch and 4 Ezra, below, pp. 270–77, 277–83). For the author of 2 Enoch, however, God created both the present time-bound and cir- cumscribed age of creatures and "the great age," the heavenly sphere, where every person goes at the time of death, whether to the place of reward or to the place of punishment. These two spheres—the heavenly and the earthly—continue to coexist until the time of the earthly and historical runs out, the great judgment takes place, and there exists only the one endless age.[163] This spatial dualism of heavenly and earthly is paralleled in such texts as the Wisdom of Solomon and the Testament of Job (see above, p. 205, and below, pp. 318–19), and it may have a counterpart in the eschatology of the Qumran Hymns (see above, pp. 136–37). After this eschatological instruction and a final brief admonition (2 Enoch 66), Enoch is taken to heaven (chap. 67).

The narrative that concludes 2 Enoch is concerned with the problem of continuity (chaps. 68–73).[164] The author presumes that Enoch was a priest (cf. 59 and 64:5), and the narrative traces the succession of the priesthood from Enoch to Methuselah, to his grandson Nir the younger brother of Noah, and to Melchizedek. The story of Melchizedek's birth and assumption to heaven until after the flood is remarkable in several respects. Its placement at the end of the apocalypse parallels the location of the story of Noah's birth in 1 Enoch 106–107. The miraculous circumstances attending Melchizedek's conception and birth, and some other narrative details, are reminiscent of the Noah story in 1 Enoch, although the suspicion of Nir more closely parallels the version of the Noah story in the Genesis Apocryphon (see above, pp. 173–74). Different from the Noah story, Melchizedek's conception occurs without benefit of a biological father. Also different from the Noah story, this narrative relates the problem of surviving the flood not to Noah and his sons, the patriarchs of a new humanity, but to Melchizedek the priest, who is whisked away to paradise. Moreover, it traces the priestly line back to Enoch and runs it through Nir rather than his elder brother Noah, who in the Bible and its interpretation in the Genesis Apocryphon (col. 10) is the first one to offer animal sacrifice. Taken together, this evidence suggests that 2 Enoch is presenting a tradition that rivals that of the Noachic priesthood.[165]

As we have seen, an important aspect of 2 Enoch is the author's appropriation of traditions found in 1 Enoch. The book begins with Enoch's ascent to heaven and tracks his journeys to places of cosmological and eschatological import. It features a commissioning scene in the divine throne room and depicts Enoch's return to earth, where he instructs his family in esoteric knowledge and ethical issues, and it concludes with the story of a miraculous conception and birth that is related to the family of Noah. This story's positing of a priesthood alternative to Noah's and the book's promotion of sacrificial procedure different from that practiced in the Jerusalem temple parallel some of 1 Enoch's concerns with the temple and its cult and priesthood.[166]

In appropriating Enochic tradition, the author also revises it in significant ways. The collection of developing tradition in 1 Enoch is here shaped into a coherent first-person narrative that then flows from Enoch's instruction into a second set of narratives that focus on continuity in the priesthood. Built into this narrative is also a change in cosmology. Enoch's journeys up to heaven and out to the ends of the cosmos in 1 Enoch are here integrated into a seven-heavens universe in which the places of punishment, for example, are up in the heavens rather than out on the edges of the earth's disk. The account of the patriarch's heavenly glorification in 2 Enoch may well presuppose the appendix in 1 Enoch 71, which transforms the story of Enoch's ascent to heaven and his journeys through the cosmos into an account of Enoch's installation as the heavenly son of man, the executor of the final judgment (on this text see below, p. 254). Here, how-ever, the author *centers* his narrative on Enoch's glorification and, through the use of the first-person singular and the expression "my children," keeps him in focus also in the section that recounts his instruction. In this way the book is not simply a collection of cosmological and eschatological lore, but is equally a story about the importance of Enoch as a figure. As such a central figure in God's economy, the glorified Enoch is also seen as the superior of Moses, as he is to some degree in 1 Enoch (see below, p. 358 n. 90),[167] and a kind of reincarnation of the primordial glorious Adam.[168] In these respects, to use an analogy, Enoch becomes for this author's cosmology and eschatology what the crucified and risen Christ is for the New Testament's various portrayals of the drama of salvation. Finally, 2 Enoch's transformation of earlier Enochic traditions is also a way station between 1 Enoch and the later mystical traditions now gathered in part in the so-called 3 Enoch.[169]

Parallels to Egyptian mythological motifs and traditions in Philo of Alexandria sug-gest that Egypt was the place of composition.[170] A date in the first century C.E. has often been suggested,[171] and the book's concern about animal sacrifice appears to presume the existence of the Second Temple.[172] The Slavonic text of 2 Enoch is a translation from Greek, which is most likely the language in which it was composed.[173]

While it is true that 2 Enoch is preserved only in Slavonic manuscripts written by Christian scribes and some have argued that it was composed by a Christian author, the internal evidence of the texts seems counterindicative of Christian authorship for two reasons.[174] First, it is most problematic to ascribe to Christian circles a text that rewrites the Enochic tradition so as to elevate the person of Enoch to the status of angel, unique interpreter come from God's presence, governor of the world, and central figure in God's economy, and that presents a Melchizedek narrative that gives no indication that Jesus was his latter-day counterpart. The author has written a theology that enhances the fig-ure of Enoch and has no place for the exalted Christ. Second, the book's location in a stream of tradition that runs from 1 Enoch to Jewish mystical circles points to Jewish authorship rather than to the Jewish appropriation of a Christian appropriation of Jew-ish Enoch material. Its propounding of halakah for animal sacrifices not in place in the Jerusalem temple may point to a provenance in sectarian Jewish circles of which we have no other certain evidence.

BIBLIOGRAPHY

History

Victor A. **Tcherikover** and Alexander **Fuks**, *Corpus Papyrorum Judaicarum* (3 vols.; Cam-bridge: Harvard Univ. Press, 1957) 1:1–93. Erich **Gruen**, *Diaspora: Jews amidst Greeks and Romans* (Cambridge: Harvard Univ. Press, 2002) 54–83. Peter **Fraser**, *Ptolemaic Alexandria* (3 vols.; Oxford: Clarendon, 1972), a history of life, culture, and learning. Menachem **Stern**,

"The Jewish Diaspora," in S. Safrai and M. Stern, eds., *The Jewish People in the First Century* (CRINT 1/1; Assen: Van Gorcum, 1974) 122–33.

The Greek Jewish Scriptures

Karen H. **Jobes** and Moisés **Silva**, *Invitation to the Septuagint* (Grand Rapids: Baker Academic, 2000), comprehensive introduction to the subject. Melvin K. H. **Peters**, "Septuagint," *ABD* 5:1093–1104. Emanuel Tov, "Jewish-Greek Scriptures," in Kraft and Nickelsburg, eds., *Early Judaism and Its Modern Interpreters*, 223–37. Eugene **Ulrich**, *The Dead Sea Scrolls and the Origins of the Bible* (Grand Rapids: Eerdmans, 1999) 165–289.

The Sibylline Oracles

Translations and Text: John J. **Collins**, *OTP* 1:362–472, translation of books 1–14.

Text and Other Translations: J. **Geffcken**, *Die Oracula Sibyllina* (GCS 8; Leipzig: Hinrichs, 1902), the Greek text of books 1–14, apparatus of textual variants, and history of religions parallels. H. C. O. **Lanchester**, *APOT* 2:368–406, translation and notes on books 3–5. Rieuwerd **Buitenwerf**, *Book III of the Sibylline Oracles and Its Social Setting: With an Introduction, Translation and Commentary* (SVTP 17; Leiden: Brill, 2003), translation of book 3.

Literature: **Buitenwerf**, *Book III of the Sibylline Oracles*. John J. **Collins**, *The Sibylline Oracles of Egyptian Judaism* (SBLDS 13; Missoula, Mont.: Scholars Press, 1974), origin, contents, purpose of books 3 and 5. John J. **Collins**, "The Development of the Sibylline Tradition," *ANRW* 2.20 (1987) 1:421–59. John J. **Collins**, "Sibylline Oracles," *ABD* 6:2–6. John J. **Collins**, "The Third Sibyl Revisited," in Esther **Chazon** and David **Satran**, eds., *Things Revealed: Studies in Honor of Michael E. Stone* (Leiden: Brill, 2004) 3–19. Erich **Gruen**, *Heritage and Hellenism* (Berkeley: Univ. of California Press, 1998) 268–91, discussion of book 3. Valentin **Nikiprowetzky**, *La Troisième Sibylle* (Études Juives 9; Paris: Mouton, 1970). Valentin **Nikiprowetzky**, "La Sibylle juive et la 'Troisième Livre' des 'Pseudo-Oracles Sibyllins' depuis Charles Alexandre," *ANRW* 2.20 (1987) 1:460–542.

Aristeas to Philocrates

Translation: R. J. H. **Shutt**, *OTP* 2:7–34.

Text and Other Translation: Moses **Hadas**, *Aristeas to Philocrates* (JAL; New York: Harper, 1951), excellent introduction, Greek text, and translation.

Literature: Jonathan A. **Goldstein**, "The Message of *Aristeas to Philocrates* in the Second Century B.C.E.: Obey the Torah, Venerate the Temple of Jerusalem, but Speak Greek, and Put Your Hopes in the Ptolemaic Dynasty," in Menachem **Mor**, ed., *Eretz Israel, Israel and the Jewish Diaspora: Mutual Relations* (Studies in Jewish Civilization 1; Lanham, Md.: Univ. Press of America, 1991) 1–23. Sidney **Jellicoe**, *The Septuagint in Modern Study* (Oxford: Clarendon, 1968) 29–55. Victor A. **Tcherikover**, "The Ideology of the Letter of Aristeas," *HTR* 51 (1958) 59–85.

3 Maccabees

Translation: The Apocrypha. Hugh Anderson, *OTP* 2:509–29, introduction, translation, notes.

Text and Other Translations: Robert **Hanhart**, *Maccabaeorum liber,* fasc. III (SVTG 9/3; Göttingen: Vandenhoeck & Ruprecht, 1960), critical edition of the Greek text. Moses **Hadas**, *The Third and Fourth Books of Maccabees* (JAL; New York: Harper, 1953), introduction, Greek text with facing annotated translation.

Literature: J. R. C. **Cousland**, "Reversal, Recidivism and Reward in 3 Maccabees: Structure and Purpose," *JSJ* 24 (2003) 39–51. John J. **Collins**, *Between Athens and Jerusalem: Jewish Identity in the Hellenistic Diaspora* (New York: Crossroad, 1983) 106–11. **Gruen**, *Heritage and Hellenism,* 222–36. Fausto **Parente**, "The Third Book of Maccabees as Ideological Document and Historical Source," *Hen* 10 (1988) 177, a comprehensive summary on the scholarship on 3 Maccabees. Victor **Tcherikover**, "The Third Book of Maccabees as a Historical Source," *ScrHier* 7 (1961) 1–26. Johannes **Tromp**, "The Formation of the Third Book of Maccabees," *Hen* 17 (1995) 311–28.

Additions to the Book of Esther

Translation: The Apocrypha.

Text: Robert **Hanhart**, *Esther* (SVTG 8/3; Göttingen: Vandenhoeck & Ruprecht, 1966), critical edition of the Greek text.

Commentaries: Sidnie White **Crawford**, "The Additions to Esther," in *NIB* 3:945–72, New American Bible and NRSV of the Additions with brief commentary. Carey A. **Moore**, *Daniel, Esther, and Jeremiah: The Additions* (AB 44; Garden City, N.Y.: Doubleday, 1977), annotated translation of the canonical Hebrew book, interwoven in order with a translation of the Additions and a commentary on them.

The Wisdom of Solomon

Translation: The Apocrypha.

Text and Other Translation: Joseph **Ziegler**, *Sapientia Salomonis* (SVTG 12/1; Göttingen: Vandenhoeck & Ruprecht, 1962), critical edition of the Greek text. Dieter **Georgi**, *Weisheit Salomos* (JSHRZ 3/4; Gütersloh: Mohn, 1980), introduction, translation, and notes.

Commentaries: C. **Larcher**, *Le Livre de la Sagesse ou la Sagesse de Salomon* (3 vols.; EBib n.s. 1, 3, 5; Paris: Gabalda, 1983–85), introduction and extensive commentary. David **Winston**, *Wisdom of Solomon* (AB 43; Garden City, N.Y.: Doubleday, 1979), translation and detailed commentary.

Literature: Nuria **Calduch-Benages** and Jacques **Vermeylen**, eds., *Treasures of Wisdom: Studies in Ben Sira and the Book of Wisdom,* FS M. Gilbert (BETL 143; Leuven: Leuven Univ. Press and Peeters, 1999) 241–396, collection of essays. Samuel **Cheon**, *The Exodus Story in the Wisdom of Solomon: A Study in Biblical Interpretation* (JSPSup 23; Sheffield: Sheffield Academic Press, 1997). John J. **Collins**, *Jewish Wisdom in the Hellenistic Age* (Louisville: Westminster John Knox,

1997) 178–95, introduction to major issues. Maurice **Gilbert**, *La critique des dieux dans le Livre de la Sagesse* (AnBib 53 Rome: Biblical Institute Press, 1973). Maurice **Gilbert**, "Wisdom Literature," in Michael E. **Stone**, ed., *Jewish Writings of the Second Temple Period* (CRINT 2/2: Assen: Van Gorcum; Philadelphia: Fortress Press, 1984) 301–13, introduction. Lester L. **Grabbe**, *Wisdom of Solomon* (GAP; Sheffield: Sheffield Academic Press, 1997), introduction to the major issues. Michael **Kolarcik**, *The Ambiguity of Death in the Book of Wisdom 1–6* (AnBib 127; Rome: Pontifical Institute Press, 1991). C. **Larcher**, *Études sur le Livre de la Sagesse* (EBib; Paris: Gabalda, 1969), encyclopedic study of the book's religious themes, its parallels in Jewish and pagan Hellenistic literature, and its influence on Christian theology. James M. **Reese**, *Hellenistic Influence on the Book of Wisdom and Its Consequences* (AnBib 41; Rome: Biblical Institute Press, 1970).

Philo of Alexandria

Translation and Texts: L. **Cohn** and P. **Wendland**, eds., *Philonis Alexandrini opera quae supersunt* (7 vols. in 8; repr. Berlin: Reimer, 1962), critical edition. F. H. **Colson** and G. H. **Whittaker**, *Philo with an English Translation* (12 vols.; LCL; Cambridge: Harvard Univ. Press, 1929–62), Greek text with English translation on facing pages.

Concordance: Peder **Borgen**, Kåre **Fuglseth**, and Roald **Skarsten**, *The Philo Index: A Complete Greek Word Index to the Writings of Philo of Alexandria* (Grand Rapids: Eerdmans; Leiden: Brill, 2000).

Bibliographies and Research Surveys: Peder **Borgen**, "Philo of Alexandria: A Critical and Synthetical Survey of Research since World War II," *ANRW* 2.21.1 (1984) 97–154. Howard L. **Goodhart** and Erwin R. **Goodenough**, "A General Bibliography of Philo," in **Goodenough**, *The Politics of Philo Judaeus: Practice and Theory* (New Haven: Yale Univ. Press, 1938) 125–318. Roberto **Radice** and David T. **Runia**, *Philo of Alexandria: An Annotated Bibliography 1937–1986* (VCSup 8; Leiden: Brill, 1988). David T. **Runia**, *Philo of Alexandria: An Annotated Bibliography 1987–1996 with Addenda for 1937–1986* (VCSup 57; Leiden: Brill, 2000). Updates appear each year in the *Studia Philonica Annual:* 12 (2000) 148–91; 13 (2001) 250–90; 14 (2002) 141–79.

Literature: Studia Philonica Annual, a major periodical devoted to scholarship on Philo. Peder **Borgen**, "Philo of Alexandria," in **Stone**, ed., *Jewish Writings*, 233–82. Peder **Borgen**, "Philo of Alexandria," *ABD* 5:333–42, introduction. Erwin R. **Goodenough**, *By Light, Light: The Mystic Gospel of Hellenistic Judaism* (New Haven: Yale Univ. Press, 1935). Erwin R. **Goodenough**, *An Introduction to Philo Judaeus* (2d ed.; New York: Barnes & Noble, 1962). Erwin R. **Goodenough**, *Politics of Philo Judaeus*. Jenny **Morris**, "The Jewish Philosopher Philo," in **Schürer**, *History*, 3/2:808–89, comprehensive introduction to Philo's life, setting, literary works, and philosophy and religious thought. David T. **Runia**, *Philo in Early Christian Literature: A Survey* (CRINT 3/3; Assen: Van Gorcum; Minneapolis: Fortress Press, 1993). Harry A. **Wolfson**, *Philo* (2 vols.; Cambridge: Harvard Univ. Press, 1962), Philo's philosophy.

2 Enoch

Translation: Francis I. **Andersen**, *OTP* 1:91–221, two recensions in parallel columns, including the Melchizedek narrative. A. **Pennington**, *AOT*, 321–62, translation of short recension.

Text and Other Translations: André **Vaillant**, *Le Livre des Secrets de l'Hénoch* (Paris: Institut d'études slaves, 1952), Slavonic text with facing French translation. W. R. **Morfill** and R. H. **Charles**, *The Book of the Secrets of Enoch* (Oxford: Clarendon, 1896), introduction, annotated translation of long recension.

Literature: Andrei A. **Orlov**, *The Enoch-Metatron Tradition* (TSAJ 107; Tübingen: Mohr Siebeck, 2005).

The Psalms of Solomon. Copenhagen manuscript 260 fol.181 verso (tenth–eleventh century C.E.) containing Ps. Sol. 17:21-32 in Greek translation. Photograph is courtesy of the Kongelige Bibliotek, Copenhagen, and Prof. Robert B. Wright.

7

The Romans and the House of Herod

THE HASMONEANS GIVE WAY TO ROME

The years 67–37 B.C.E. saw the Hasmonean house fall from power and Palestine submit to the yoke of Roman authority. When Queen Salome Alexandra died, she was succeeded by her elder son, John Hyrcanus II, who had already been serving as high priest. Almost immediately Hyrcanus's ambitious brother, Judas Aristobulus, raised the flag of revolt and wrested both civil and religious power from Hyrcanus, who quietly resigned from office.[1]

Other forces now came into play. The first of these was an Idumean named Antipater, who had served as governor of Idumea under Alexander Janneus and whose son, Herod, would later become king of Judea. Preferring to have Hyrcanus rather than Aristobulus as his king, Antipater used deceit and intrigue to convince Hyrcanus once more to seek the throne. Antipater and Hyrcanus found an ally in Aretas, the ruler of the Arabian kingdom of the Nabateans. Aristobulus was severely defeated in battle and when his army deserted him, he fled to Jerusalem, where he was besieged in the temple.

The resolution of the matter, however, lay in the hands of the Romans, who had long been a power to be reckoned within the eastern Mediterranean. At this very time (65 B.C.E.) the armies of Pompey were busy extending Roman rule over western Asia, and Pompey's commander, Aemilius Scaurus, was in Damascus. Both sides saw this as an opportunity to settle the dispute in their own favor. As bribe matched bribe, Scaurus decided in favor of Aristobulus. The temple siege was lifted.

But the family quarrel was not yet at an end. Early in 63 B.C.E. both Hyrcanus and Aristobulus appeared before Pompey in Damascus and again pleaded their causes, while a third party of Jews brought complaint against both brothers. Pompey deferred a decision and asked that all concerned keep the peace. In a series of rash and unwise actions, Aristobulus defied Pompey's request and incited his anger. He was arrested, and the situation quickly passed out of his control.

Partisan dissension and Roman military might finally decided the issue. Jerusalem was under threat of Roman siege. The followers of Aristobulus and Hyrcanus disputed whether to capitulate. Hyrcanus's party won out and opened the city gates; however, the partisans of Aristobulus locked themselves in the temple and prepared to resist. After a three-month siege in autumn 63, the wall was breached. Priests were slaughtered as they offered sacrifice, and according to Josephus some twelve thousand Jews perished. Pompey entered the holy of holies, but he took nothing and commanded that the cult be continued. The leaders of the resistance, however, were executed.

The Hasmonean dispute brought an end to Jewish independence. Much of the territory that had been won by Simon, John Hyrcanus I, and Alexander Janneus was removed from Jewish control and placed under the Roman governor of Syria. Jerusalem and the remainder of Judea were subject to Roman tribute. Hyrcanus was to govern them, but without the title "king."[2] Pompey returned to Rome in triumph, accompanied by Aristobulus (who was in chains), his daughters and sons, and a large number of other Jewish captives who were subsequently released in Rome.

Reappearing as if on a rotating stage, the principals of the Jewish civil war returned time and again to interact disastrously with the renowned figures of the last years of the Roman republic. It was a time of widespread nationalist feeling among the Jews.[3] In 57 B.C.E. Aristobulus's son Alexander, who had escaped on the way to Rome, gathered a sizable army and attempted to seize power in Palestine. He was defeated by Aulus Gabinius, the governor of Syria, and his lieutenant, Marc Antony. Hyrcanus, moreover, was stripped of his political authority, though he retained the office of high priest. The following year Aristobulus and his other son, Antigonus, escaped from Rome and made yet another abortive attempt to seize power. Alexander tried once again in 55 B.C.E. M. Licinius Crassus, who had joined Caesar and Pompey in Rome's "First Triumvirate," became governor of Syria in 54 and robbed the temple of its treasures. He was succeeded in 53 by C. Cassius Longinus (later one of the conspirators against Caesar), who dealt with still another insurrection by selling thirty thousand Jews into slavery.

The year 49 saw the beginning of the Roman civil wars, which took their toll on the whole Roman world. Pompey fled Rome ahead of Caesar, who released Aristobulus so that he could lead an army against Pompey in Syria. This time the ever-resilient Hasmonean met his end. He was poisoned by Pompey's supporters before he could leave Rome. His son Alexander was beheaded in Syria at Pompey's command. The following year (48 B.C.E.). Pompey himself was defeated, slain, and decapitated.

As Julius Caesar now set out to make himself master of the eastern world, he found a willing ally in Hyrcanus, whose loyalty was rewarded when, in 47, he was nominated as hereditary "ethnarch," thus receiving once again the political power he had lost. In point of fact the real power was given to the Idumean Antipater, who was nominated governor of Judea. He in turn nominated his sons Phasael and Herod as governors in Jerusalem and Galilee.

After the assassination of Caesar in 44 B.C.E. Brutus and Cassius fled east. For two years Cassius once more ruled Syria. Antipater and Herod sought his favor and helped raise the heavy taxes he demanded of Judea. Violence followed upon violence. In 43

Antipater was poisoned by a rival named Malichus, who in turn was murdered at the instigation of Herod and with the connivance of Cassius.

With the defeat of Cassius and Brutus at Philippi in 42, the balance of power swung again. Marc Antony was now master of Syria. Although they had previously supported Cassius, and in spite of formal complaints that an embassy of Jews brought against them, Phasael and Herod were able to secure Antony's favor. He nominated them as "tetrarchs" of the Jewish territory, while Hyrcanus remained nominal head of state with the title of "ethnarch."

During Antony's absence from Syria in 40 B.C.E., the Parthians swept across the East, took Syria, and marched into Jerusalem, plundering as they went. They were supported by Antigonus, the remaining son of Aristobulus, who sought the title of "king." Phasael and Hyrcanus were betrayed to the Parthians, but Herod escaped with his family. Phasael and Hyrcanus were turned over to Antigonus. Phasael committed suicide. Hyrcanus's ears were cut off, thus physically disqualifying him permanently from the high priesthood. The Parthians named Antigonus "king."

By diverse routes Herod eluded his enemies and arrived in Rome, where with the support of Antony and Octavian (Augustus) the Roman senate named him "king" of Judea. He returned to Syria the following year. While the Romans were engaged in defeating the Parthians, Herod moved on into Palestine. The army of Antigonus was defeated. In the spring of 37 Jerusalem was captured. At Herod's request and with Antony's permission, Antigonus, the last of the Hasmonean kings, was beheaded.

HEROD THE GREAT

The career of Herod the Great is a study in opposites and extremes. What was already evident in the record of his years as a general and governor is written in boldface type through the annals of his reign. High intelligence and an instinct for the appropriate action at the opportune moment combined and conflicted with incredible cruelty and ruthlessness and an irrepressible desire for revenge. In the political arena he maneuvered with shrewdness, skill, and resourcefulness; on the battlefield he fought with courage and distinction. He loved with passion and ruled with terror and cruelty. Not only among his people but also in his own family he was the object of opposition and conspiracy. Paranoia and conspiracy formed a vicious cycle that rapidly spiraled toward the end of his career. Although he had lived in splendor and style, he died unloved and unmourned.

During the first decade of his reign Herod consolidated his power. Already on the eve of his victory over Antigonus (spring 37 B.C.E.), he had married Mariamme, the granddaughter of Hyrcanus II. This alliance with the Hasmonean family was, however, of little political benefit to Herod, and it became the source of numerous and tragic problems. The many adherents of Antigonus were a threat to him, and he executed forty-five of the most prominent of them and confiscated property and wealth. Within his own family he had to deal with Alexandra, the mother of Mariamme. Both mother and daughter pressured Herod into appointing Mariamme's seventeen-year-old brother, Aristobulus, as high priest. When the young Hasmonean's popularity among the people became a threat to Herod, the king had him "accidentally" drowned after a banquet at Herod's palace in Jericho. In spite of Alexandra's pleas through Cleopatra, Herod was acquitted by Marc Antony.

Herod's next problem was Cleopatra. When she successfully demanded that Antony make her a present of sizable and rich parts of Herod's kingdom, Herod was forced to rent his own land from her. Then she attempted to seduce Herod, and the king sent her back to Egypt deftly and with great ceremony. In September 31 B.C.E. Augustus defeated Antony in the battle of Actium. In spite of his close relationship to Antony, Herod convinced Augustus that he would be a good ally, and he was confirmed as king. The following year, after Cleopatra's suicide, Augustus returned Herod's territory to him.

Other domestic tragedy marred Herod's reign during these years. A victim of his own suspicions and of the intrigue of his family, he executed his uncle, Joseph, who was also married to Herod's sister, Salome; the aged Hasmonean, Hyrcanus II; his own most beloved wife, Mariamme; and Salome's second husband, an Idumean named Costobar, who was making common cause with some distant relatives of the Hasmoneans.

The middle years of Herod's reign (25–13 B.C.E.) offered some respite from this domestic strife. It was a time for splendid building projects[4] and the importation of the trappings of high culture.[5] He secured the borders of his kingdom with fortresses and palaces—most of them on the sites of Hasmonean citadels*—and embellished cities through great public works. On the Mediterranean coast, Straton's Tower was converted into a magnificent harbor city named Caesarea in honor of Julius Caesar. Samaria was renamed Sebaste, after the Greek form of Augustus's name, and a temple was erected there in his honor.* Yet another temple to Augustus was built at the Panion, at the headwaters of the Jordan. The citadel in Jerusalem had already been rebuilt and named Antonia, in honor of Herod's patron Antony. In Hebron, at the reputed burial site of the patriarchs, Herod erected a magnificent memorial to Abraham, Isaac, and Jacob that, to this day, towers fifty-two feet into the air.* The greatest of his public works, however, was in Jerusalem, where he greatly extended and rebuilt Zerubbabel's temple, making it one of the architectural marvels of its time.* Work on it ceased only a few years before its destruction in 70 C.E.

The last nine years of Herod's reign were the worst. Domestic strife—Herod's constant demon—led to conspiracies, and conspiracies brought on a string of executions that whittled down the list of Herod's heirs. Early in his reign Herod had repudiated his Idumean wife Doris and her son Antipater. Herod's two sons by Mariamme—Alexander and Aristobulus—quarreled with Herod's sister Salome, who countered by making accusations against them. Herod brought back his son, Antipater, who fed the fires of suspicion. In 7 B.C.E., after alternating accusations and reconciliations, Alexander and Aristobulus were convicted of treason and executed. Meanwhile, Antipater was plotting to seize the throne. He was eventually found out and imprisoned. Antipas, Herod's youngest son, by his Samaritan wife Malthace, was named his heir. The seventy-year-old king was gravely ill, and a rumor of his impending death circulated. Two scribes named Judas and Matthias stirred up some of their followers to pull down a golden eagle that Herod had erected over one of the main gates of the temple. The instigators and executors of the deed were burned alive. Herod's illness became worse. In vain he sought a cure at the hot baths of Callirhoë, east of the Dead Sea. A few days before he died, Herod had his son Antipater executed. He rewrote his will, making his sons Archelaus and Philip coheirs with Antipas. His painful death came in the spring of 4 B.C.E.*

THE HOUSE OF HEROD

In the months following Herod's death, Jerusalem and to some extent the wider Jewish territory were the site of a number of uprisings. Archelaus put down one rebellion stemming from the incident of the golden eagle. Thereafter Archelaus, Antipas, and Philip left for Rome, each pressing his case against the other for the title of "king." During their absence Varus, the governor of Syria, quelled a rebellion in Jerusalem. Shortly thereafter Sabinus, the procurator of Judea, put down yet another uprising there and burned some of the buildings around the temple and plundered its treasury. Varus returned from Antioch, dealt with a rebellion in Galilee, and settled matters in Jerusalem. Two thousand rebels were crucified. In Rome Augustus confirmed Herod's will in all its essential points.

Philip, the son of Herod and Cleopatra of Jerusalem, was named tetrarch of Batanaea, Trachonitis, Auranitis, Gaulanitis, and Panias, north and east of the Sea of Galilee, where he reigned quietly from 4 B.C.E. to 34 C.E. He is remembered for his development of the area of Caesarea Philippi, around the shoulder of Mount Hermon, where he rebuilt the shrine at the Panion. He was married to Salome the daughter of Herodias.

Herod Antipas was appointed tetrarch of Galilee and Perea. He is the Herod most frequently mentioned in the Gospels, especially Luke. A connoisseur of fine architecture like his father, he built a splendid capital on the west shore of the Sea of Galilee, naming it Tiberias in honor of Augustus's successor, the emperor Tiberius.* Antipas is notorious for having taken as his wife Herodias, the wife of his half brother, Herod,[6] and for having executed John the Baptist when he reproved him for this deed. Antipas's alliance with Herodias proved to be his downfall. When his first wife heard that he planned to divorce her, she fled to her father, the Nabatean king Aretas IV, whose army dealt Antipas a severe defeat.* Subsequently, Tiberius's successor, Caligula, appointed Antipas's nephew, Agrippa, "king" over the tetrarchy of Philip. The ambitious Herodias prodded her husband to seek the same title. Charges were brought against Antipas. He was deposed and banished to Gaul in 39 C.E.

Archelaus had the worst reputation of the sons of Herod (cf. Matt 2:22), and his reign was the shortest. He ruled as ethnarch of Judea, Idumea, and Samaria from 4 B.C.E. to 6 C.E., when he was accused before Augustus, deposed, and banished to Gaul.

THE ROMAN GOVERNORS OF JUDEA

With the deposing of Archelaus, Judea, Samaria, and Idumea were placed under the direct rule of a Roman governor known first as a "prefect" and later as a "procurator." Holding both military and civil authority, these governors were beholden primarily to the emperor himself. In cases of emergency the legate of Syria could intervene.

At the beginning of this direct Roman rule over Judea, Quirinius, the Roman legate of Syria, conducted a census of the people (cf. Luke 2:2)[7] and quickly put down a rebellion of uncertain proportions led by a Galilean named Judas.

Six or seven Roman governors ruled Judea from 6 to 41 C.E. Of these the most famous, or infamous, was Pontius Pilate. From the very beginning of his rule he showed insensitivity and contempt for Jewish customs and desires, and on several occasions during his ten years as prefect he met protests with force of arms.* In this context his recorded capitulation to the crowd at the time of Jesus' trial seems odd and out of character, to say the least. A few years later, in 36 C.E., after an ill-advised attack on a group of Samaritans, Vedalias, the legate of Syria, ordered Pilate to Rome to answer for his conduct.

Other trouble erupted during the reign of the emperor Caligula (37–41 C.E.). In Egypt the Jewish community in Alexandria suffered bloody persecution, which was allowed if not abetted by the Roman governor (see above, p. 214). As for Judea, the emperor, taking claims of his own divine status seriously, ordered that his statue be erected in the Jerusalem temple. The Roman legate of Syria, Petronius, knowing that the Jews would violently oppose this action, hesitated and attempted to negotiate. Through the intercession of Agrippa, who was in Rome at this time, Caligula temporarily rescinded his order. In January 41 he was murdered before he could enforce a second such demand.

AGRIPPA I

Agrippa, the grandson of Herod the Great, was born in 10 B.C.E., just three years before the execution of his father, Aristobulus. In Rome he became an intimate of Tiberius's son and of Caligula. Although he was later imprisoned by Tiberius, Caligula released him after the old man's death and appointed him "king" of the tetrarchy of Philip, who had died in 34 C.E. When Herod's son Antipas sought the same title for himself and was removed from office, Agrippa was given his territories. After the murder of Caligula, Agrippa helped to secure the succession of Claudius as emperor, and for this service his territory was extended to include Judea and Samaria. Thus, from 41 to 44 C.E. Agrippa ruled as king over the realm that had once belonged to his grandfather. He was known as a pious and observant Jew. During the few years of his reign he strengthened and extended the fortifications of Jerusalem. According to the book of Acts he beheaded James the son of Zebedee and imprisoned the apostle Peter. After his sudden death his territories were placed under the direct supervision of Rome. Later, however, his son Agrippa II would receive back some of the family territories.

DOMINATION—OPPOSITION—EXPECTATION

Roman presence and domination were an overshadowing fact of life in Palestine during the century we have been discussing. Although Roman rule was exercised directly only in Judea and Samaria, and then only for thirty-five years, Jewish rulers held their power by permission of the Roman government, and positions and appointments were constantly subject to a succession of Roman governors, generals, and emperors.

To many, Roman rule doubtless appeared as just and as a relief from the infighting of the Hasmonean house in its waning years. Nonetheless, the advent of Roman power brought its own set of problems, burdens, oppression, and disastrous interaction with the population or segments of it. In the process of squelching Hasmonean power, Pompey desecrated the temple and slaughtered some of the population, and Cassius sold thousands into slavery. Gabinius practiced extortion. Crassus plundered the temple, and Antony extracted heavy taxes. Among the governors of Judea, Pilate was notorious for his cruelty. Only Caligula's murder prevented a terrible disaster. The cruel and ruthless lifestyle of Herod the Great could be oppressive to the extreme and doubtless alienated many.

There were periods during this century when oppression begat revolt and vice versa. The names of a few revolutionary leaders have been preserved. To what extent the uprisings they led were messianic in a strict sense, religious in a more general sense, or simply reactions without ideology is a question we cannot discuss here. But the times were certainly harsh and tense. Within this charged atmosphere, well attested by the writings of Josephus and Philo, were spawned the documents that we discuss in this chapter, with their messages of messianic hope and eschatological cataclysm and their exhortations to courage and resistance to death if necessary. To them must be added those writings from Qumran that date from this period, at least the Habakkuk Commentary and the War Scroll in its final form.

Finally, we must note, this was the context for the appearance of John the Baptist and Jesus of Nazareth. With the fire of a prophet and the certitude of an apocalyptist, John appealed for wholesale repentance in the face of an imminent judgment. The message of Jesus is more difficult to extract, for it is interwoven in the Gospels with the church's testimony to him. But it is evident that he spoke of the coming of God's kingdom and that he saw it breaking in through his own words and actions. Little that he said and little that the church said about him can be understood apart from the times we have sketched and those Jewish theologies that we have discussed in our previous chapters and that we take up here in the documents that were written and expanded in the years that encircle the turn of the era.

The Psalms of Solomon

The psalms in this collection were composed in the first century B.C.E. in circles that designated themselves as "the pious" and "the righteous." The titles of the psalms attribute them to King Solomon. This pseudonymous ascription may be late, and its rationale is not altogether clear. The last part of Psalm 2 is reminiscent of Wisdom 6, and the hope for an heir to the Davidic throne (Pss. Sol. 17) provides a superficial connection with Solomon, but there appears to be nothing uniquely Solomonic in any of the psalms.

The feature of the psalms that differentiates them from their canonical counterparts is their didactic character. The author not only petitions or praises God or gives thanks for deliverance from distress but also explicates how this distress serves as chastening for the righteous or the nation and punishment for Gentiles and for the sinners within the nation. Thus God's chief function according to the psalms is that of judge, justly dispensing reward and punishment for human deeds.

Psalms of the Nation

While the psalms have many points of similarity, they divide roughly into two categories, which deal respectively with the nation and its fate and with personal piety, usually in contrast with sinful behavior. Psalms in the first category either reflect upon events in the immediate past—the Roman conquest and related matters—or express Israel's eschatological hopes—the restoration of the Davidic monarchy and the return of the Dispersion.

Psalm 1

The speaker is Mother Jerusalem. When she first heard of the approach of the Roman army she was certain she would be spared. She had interpreted her prosperity as an indicator of her children's piety, a reasonable deduction from Deuteronomic presuppositions. In point of fact, however, God was preparing to punish the people for their secret sins, which exceeded the transgressions of their Roman conquerors. The people had polluted the sanctuary. This psalm may have been written as an introduction to the collection. Its last line provides a transition to the beginning of Psalm 2.

Psalm 2

The author plays a number of variations on the theme of sin and judgment, weaving them into a kind of narrative.[8]

A. Introduction: the Roman attack   vv 1-2
B. Reason: Israel's sin   v 3
C. Result: judgment   vv 4-10 (4-12)
D. Cause: Israel's sin   vv 11-14 (13-15)
E. Result: God's judgment   vv 15-21 (16-23)
F. Prayer for deliverance   vv 22-25 (24-29)
G. Answer: Pompey's judgment   vv 26-27 (30-31b)
H. Reason: his arrogance   vv 28-31 (31c-35)
I. Exhortation and summary   vv 32-36 (36-40)
J. Doxology   v 37 (41)

Pompey is able to breach the temple walls, and his army can trample on the altar because the Jews themselves have already defiled the sanctuary in their conduct of its cult (A-B). The mode of punishment corresponds to the nature of the sin. Verses 6-9 suggest that more Jews than just the family of Aristobulus were taken captive to Rome. Reference to sexual sins (vv 11-14 [13-15]) is repeated in 8:9-12 (10-13). Typical of these psalms is the stress on the impartial nature of God's judgment (vv 15-17 [16-19]). The author borrows imagery from Second Isaiah to describe the degradation of Jerusalem (vv 19-21 [20-22]; cf. Isa 52:1-2). Employing a theme reminiscent of Deuteronomy 32:19-33, he describes how the agent of God's judgment grows arrogant and is himself punished (G-H). Pompey's arrogance is similar to that attributed to Antiochus and his prototype, the king of Babylon (see above, pp. 79, 82), and the language here seems to be informed by the parallel passage in Ezekiel 28:1-10. The description of Pompey as a "dragon" is a reference to the mythological motif of the chaos monster. A similar combination of the dragon motif with the arrogant anti-God figure occurs later in Revelation 12:7-9, where it is applied to Satan. The author implies that Pompey's judgment is an answer to prayer.

Verses 30-35 (34-39) contain a number of motifs that are reminiscent of Wisdom 1–6 (see above, pp. 205–8): the persecution (v 35 [39]) and exaltation of the righteous (v 31 [35]); the arrogance and punishment of the oppressor (v 31 [35]); an address to the mighty, informing them of God's judgment (v 32 [36]; cf. v 30 [34]). Certain elements in vv 32-36 (36-40) stand in tension with the rest of the psalm. We have previously heard of God's punishment of the whole of Israel for their sins. Here a distinction is made between the righteous and the sinner within Israel, who will be judged "according to their deeds" (v 34 [38]). The psalm was composed some time after 48 B.C.E., the date of Pompey's death.

Psalm 7

This psalm is difficult to place in sequence with the others. Verses 2-3 and 5 imply that the conquest has not yet taken place. The psalm reflects none of the panic or anguish that one would expect in the face of imminent conquest (cf. 8:1-5 [1-6]). Perhaps it was composed when Rome first came on the horizon and before the parties of Aristobulus and Hyrcanus had invited disaster.

Psalm 8

Again the pattern of sin and punishment governs the structure of this psalm.

A.	Introduction: the coming of judgment	vv 1-7
B.	Israel's sins described	vv 8-13 (8-14)
C.	Pompey, the agent of divine judgment	vv 14-21 (15-24)
D.	Reprise: sin, judgment, doxology	vv 22-24 (25-29)
E.	Prayer: that judgment turn to mercy	vv 25-33 (30-39)
F.	Doxology	v 34 (40)

The author describes his terror at the approach of the Roman army. At first he thought that Jerusalem would be spared because of the righteousness of its inhabitants (v 6 [7a]; cf. 1:3-5), but this righteousness was an illusion. As in 1:8 and 2:3 the cardinal sin involved defilement of the sanctuary and the cult (8:11-13, 22 [12-14, 25-26]).

The events of 63 B.C.E. are clearly reflected in vv 15-23 (16-28). The party of Hyrcanus opens the gates of Jerusalem to the conqueror (vv 15-18 [16-20]). When he finally breaches the walls of the temple, great slaughter ensues (vv 19-20, 23b [21-23, 28]), and the family of Aristobulus (at least) is taken captive to Rome (v 21 [24]).

The prayer in vv 25-33 (30-39) corresponds to 2:21-25 (24-29) but with several significant differences. Here, as throughout this psalm, there is no reference to the arrogance of the conqueror. Foremost in the author's mind is an understanding of this conquest as God's righteous judgment. Second, the prayer is broader in scope. The author looks for a return of the Dispersion and a general turn of God's wrath to mercy. Because of the nature of the petition, the author still awaits its fulfillment. The psalm was composed between 63 and 48 B.C.E., the date of Pompey's death, which is not mentioned here, and thus is chronologically prior to Psalm 2.

Psalm 9

This psalm depicts the activities of God, who is both the righteous judge and the one who forgives those who repent. When Israel sinned, God judged them through the exile (vv 1-2 [1-4]). God can judge righteously because of a perfect knowledge of the sins and righteous deeds of all (v 3 [5-6]). The presupposition for God's judgment is the person's freedom to choose good or evil (v 4ab [7]), and "the doer of righteousness" and "doer of iniquity" bring upon themselves eternal life and destruction, respectively, because of God's righteous judgment (vv 4c-5 [8-10]). Nevertheless, there is forgiveness with God (vv 6-7 [11-15]). The doer of righteousness is not sinless, but when he repents and confesses his sin he is forgiven. The psalm concludes with an appeal for God's mercy on Israel, which is threatened by the Gentiles. The appeal is based on election and covenant (vv 8-10 [16-19]). This psalm shares characteristics of the two categories of compositions in the collection. The repetition of the name "Israel" and the repeated use of the first-person plural ("we, us") place it in the category of psalms of the nation; in its contrast between those who do righteousness and those who do iniquity, however, it shares an important motif with the second category of psalms, to be discussed below.

Psalm 11

The author's hope for a return of the Dispersion is expressed in a pastiche of phrases and imagery from Second Isaiah (cf., e.g., Isa 40:1-5; 41:19; 43:5-6; 49:6; 52:1-2; 60:1-7). A passage very closely connected with this psalm occurs in Baruch 4:36—5:9 (see above, p. 96). Like its biblical prototype and other texts that draw on it, this vision of the future lacks any reference to a future Davidic king.

Psalm 17

A. God is King	vv 1-3 (1-4)
B. The sons of David were to be the human agents of this kingship	v 4 (5)
C. Israel sinned	v 5a (6a)
D. Their punishment was the rise of the Hasmonean dynasty	vv 5b-6b (6b-8a)
E. God is punishing their arrogance	vv 7-20 (8b-22)
F. Prayer: restore the Davidic dynasty	v 21 (23)
G. Description of the Messiah and messianic times	vv 22-44 (24-50)
H. Final petition	v 45 (51ab)
I. God is King	v 46 (51c)

God's kingly power is the central concept and underlying theme that runs like a thread through this psalm. God is Israel's king forever (v 1). God's kingdom extends forever over the Gentiles as well (v 3 [4]). God chose David and his descendants to be the human agents exercising that reign (v 4 [5]). The Hasmoneans usurped the privilege of this monarchy (vv 5-6 [6-8a]).[9] Now they have been removed from power (vv 7-14 [8b-16]), but new and foreign powers are loose in the land. So, let now the Davidic heir arise, thrust out the enemy, and reign in Israel (vv 21-36 [23-41]); for God is Israel's king forever (v 46 [51c]).

The pattern of sin and punishment that is typical of Psalms 1, 2, and 8 appears here with its own peculiar emphases, although the identifications of the historical personages who play the various roles in this drama are less than certain. At the center of the action is the Hasmonean house. This dynasty arose as punishment for Israel's sin (vv 5-6 [6-8]), and it is they who are recompensed for their usurpation and perversion of the monarchy (vv 7-12 [8b-14]. But who is God's agent to punish the Hasmoneans? Traditionally, in keeping with Psalms 2 and 8, this person has been identified with Pompey, and the reference to the exile to the West (Rome, v 12 [14]) fits this identification. Verses 7-9 (8b-11) appear to contradict this identification, however. The Romans, rather than *extirpating* the Hasmonean house (vv 7a, 9b [8b, 11b]), turned civil power over to Hyrcanus II, albeit without the title of king. In fact, it was the Idumean Herod the Great who set out on a systematic program to annihilate the Hasmonean heirs.[10] For that reason it has been argued that vv 7-9a (8b-11a) with their future tenses anticipate Herod's plan of genocide.[11] The problem with this interpretation lies in the messianic scenario in vv 21-25 (23-27), which states three times that the Davidic king's mission is to remove the lawless Gentiles who have polluted and trampled the nations (plural) that trample down Jerusalem in destruction. Herod's Idumean ancestry notwithstanding, this appears to fit the Romans better than Herod.[12] However one resolves these problems, the text emphasizes how (a) the Hasmonean usurpation of the Davidic throne was punishment for Israel's sins; (b) their removal by the Romans and/or Herod was punishment for their arrogance; (c) the coming of the Davidic king would punish the arrogance of the conqueror and restore God's kingly presence in Israel and over the rest of the world.

The prayer for deliverance (vv 21-25 [23-27]) here takes a very specific form: that God send an heir to the Davidic throne, the anointed of the Lord (v 32 [36], Gk. *christos*, reflecting Heb. *mashiah*).[13] The major portion of this psalm is devoted to a description of this Messiah and the messianic era in Israel, and it presents us with the most detailed description of what at least some Jews of this period expected in such a figure.

The Messiah is a human being, a member of the family of David who is a latter-day fulfillment of God's ancient promise that the sons of David would rule over Israel *in perpetuum* (2 Sam 7:14; Ps 89:19-37). The continuity of that line had been broken with the exile. Thus, during the years of Persian and Hellenistic rule the biblical oracles about the Lord's anointed and promises of the restoration of the dynasty were applied to a king yet to come. Now the usurpation of the monarchy by the Hasmonean house and the domination of Israel by the Romans and/or Herod are sufficient to bring these hopes to full and rich expression in this psalm, and, as is usually the case, the messianic king is set in opposition to another figure of royal stature or status.[14] The author alludes to the biblical oracles, especially Psalm 2:9 and Isaiah 11:2-5 (Pss. Sol. 17:23-24, 37 [26-27, 42]).

Although the messianic king will be a human being, the author attributes to him semidivine characteristics that are typical of the older (esp. Isaianic) oracles. As God's vicar and agent on earth the king shares in, or embodies, divine qualities. He is the presence of wisdom, strength, and righteousness (vv 22, 27, 37, 39 [24, 29, 42, 44]) and is pure from sin (v 36 [41]). His word has power that is reminiscent of the mighty, creative, and effective power of God's word (vv 33-35a [37-39]; cf. Isa 11:4). He is the source of blessing (v 35b [40]). The Messiah cannot be seen apart from God. It is God who is Israel's king and the Messiah's king (v 34 [38]). However, the Messiah is the agent by whom and through whom God's reign and its consequences are actualized in this world. Thus God endows the Messiah with God's own divine characteristics, and the author may speak of the Messiah in divine superlatives.

The messianic king has a variety of functions. God's reign means the removal of foreign domination; he will drive the Gentiles out of the land, the promised inheritance of God's people (vv 22-24, 36, 45 [24-27, 41, 51]). He will gather the dispersed (vv 26, 44 [28, 50]) and restore the old tribal boundaries (v 28 [30]). This implies the expansion of the nation to its former borders during the united monarchy—an expectation not surprising for a superlative, latter-day manifestation of the Davidic dynasty. He will reign in Israel as ruler, judge, and shepherd of the flock of the Lord (cf. Ezek 34). However, because the Lord is king over all the world he will exalt Israel over all the Gentiles, who will flow to Jerusalem to bring their tribute (cf. Isa 60 and Dan 7:27).

The days of the Messiah will be ideal times. Israel will be cleansed of sin (vv 27, 32, 40 [29-30, 36, 45]), and God's kingly power will become evident in Israel and over all the world. The psalmist's prayer may be summarized pithily: "Your kingdom come; your will be done on earth as it is in heaven."

In its assertion of the final, total kingship of God, the eschatology of this psalm closely parallels many manifestations of apocalyptic eschatology, but with important distinctions. There is here no concept of two corresponding levels of reality—the heavenly and earthly, the mythical and the historical—and no transcendent revelation to mediate between the two. The author appeals for judgment against his enemies and the manifestation of God's kingly power in the form of a human agent, who will yet appear on the horizon of history. Finally, he awaits the messianic king "at the time that God sees" (v 21 [23]). That time is fixed, we may suppose, yet there is no indication that it will be in the imminent future, much less a claim that the author has revealed knowledge about that time. We miss here the white heat of apocalyptic expectation, stoked by revelation.

This psalm, with its references to Herod's extirpation of the Hasmonean house, can be dated between 37 and 30 B.C.E.[15]

Psalm 18

The author speaks mainly of Israel's present relationship to God and her future hope. The nation is described as God's firstborn, only begotten son (cf. Exod 4:22). In connection with this metaphor the present suffering is interpreted as God's parental chastisement or discipline (Ps. Sol. 18:4). The same interpretation occurs in 7:9 (8), 17:42 (47), and especially 3:4. The author stops short of calling the present calamity outright punishment for sin and presumes a relationship between God and the people that is different from that of judge and defendant. The bitter tragedy of 63 B.C.E. is somewhat muted. The emphasis is on the close relationship between God and God's people and on the hope for the blessed days of the messianic age. The psalm forms a fitting conclusion to the collection and may have been composed for that purpose.

Verses 10-12 (11-14) appear to belong to a different psalm, which has not been preserved in its entirety. Its theme is reminiscent of the hymn in column 10 of the Qumran Rule of the Community (see above, p. 142). Its emphasis on the Creator's power over the cosmos provides a fitting conclusion to the collection.

Psalms of the Righteous and the Pious

A second category of psalms depicts two types of people within Israel, their relationships to God, their deeds, and their fates at the hand of the divine Judge. The types are "the sinners" (also called "transgressors," "lawless," and "wicked") and "the righteous" (also called "the pious [of the Lord]," "those who fear the Lord," and "those who love the Lord"). True religion is expressed in the proper observance of Torah, that is, in righteous conduct. Nonetheless, the author's choice of names for the righteous also implies the internal roots of right religious conduct. The righteous are those who *fear* and *love* the Lord and who do so "in truth" (10:3 [4]; 14:1). They stand in opposition to the "people-pleasers" or hypocrites, who take their place in the company of the pious while their hearts are far from God (Ps. Sol. 4). Deeply influencing the portrait of the righteous in these psalms is a sense of the covenantal relationship, although the word "covenant" is rarely used (9:9-10 [17-18]). The righteous are the pious of *the Lord*, those who fear *the Lord*, those who love *the Lord*. They are the Lord's children: beloved, firstborn (13:9 [8]). Thus God deals with them in special ways, chastising and correcting rather than punishing, cleansing them and forgiving their sins. The righteous, for their part, express this relationship not only by striving to obey Torah but also through those acts of personal piety that explicitly enact the relationship, namely, prayer, praise, and thanksgiving.

Psalm 3

In two parallel sections the author contrasts the righteous and the sinners (vv 3-8 [3-10], 9-12 [11-15]). The righteous are not sinless or perfect. They are "righteous" because, being concerned about their sins and seeking atonement for them through fasting and acts of humiliation, they are "cleansed" by God (v 8 [10]). Thus they live in awareness of and open to God's grace (vv 3-5 [3-6]). The sinner, by contrast, shows no concern for God, but accumulates sin upon sin with no attempt to get right with God. Thus the sinner's "destruction" is eternal (vv 10b-11 [13-14]). Those who fear the Lord, however, will rise to eternal life in the presence of the eternal glory of the Lord (v 12 [16]).

Psalm 4

This powerful polemic against religious hypocrisy emphasizes that participation in the externals of the religious life is no barometer of true inward piety. Even among the congregation of the pious (v 1) who utter the Torah (v 8c [10]) there are those whose lust and greed lead to secret sins that intentionally contradict public profession. Again it is this willful and continuous sinning (vv 12, 24 [15, 28]) that characterizes "the sinner." God's judgment is sure to ensue.

Psalm 5

Written primarily in the first-person singular, this psalm focuses on God's providential care for "the poor," and "needy," and "humble" (vv 2, 11, 12 [2, 13, 14]), which is set in the context of God's generous care for the whole creation and becomes a paradigm for human generosity, a characteristic of the righteous.[16] The status of vv 16-19 (18-21) is uncertain. They may have been a separate psalm since vv 16 (18) and 19 (21) parallel the first and last verses of the next psalm (6:1, 5 [1, 9]); and 6:5d (9), with its reference to the Lord's mercy, parallels what would then be the last verse of the first part of Psalm 5 (v 15 [17]).

Psalm 6

All but two lines (v 3 [4-5]) mention God as the object of piety and devotion, the subject of a verb of deliverance, or both. Because the author fears and loves God and has experienced God's saving activity, he can stand fast in trouble (vv 2-3 [3-5]). This theme echoes elements in the first part of Psalm 5.

Psalm 10

God's judgment on the righteous is of a special sort. God judges not in order to punish but to chastise, to purge, to discipline them, so that they might be kept within the covenantal relationship (vv 1-2 [1-3]). The proper stance for the pious is to "endure" this discipline and to give thanks to God, who thus deals mercifully with them.[17]

Psalm 12

The first part of the psalm focuses on a description of the lawless and wicked man, who uses his lying tongue to wreck havoc (vv 1-3 [1-4]). The remainder of the psalm alternates between curses on the lawless ones and blessings on "the pious," "who fear" the Lord (vv 4, 5-6a, 6b, 6c [4b-5, 6-7a, 7b, 7c]). The result is the sinners' destruction and the pious inheriting God's promises (eternal life). These two alternative consequences of human behavior will be reiterated in succeeding psalms.

Psalm 13

The author contrasts God's dealings with the righteous and the sinners. In a recent calamity God punished the sinners but spared the righteous. Again the righteous is one who commits sins and who is indeed fearful that he will be punished for them.

Nevertheless, his misdeeds and sins committed in ignorance have not nullified his covenantal status as a child of God, dear and beloved. In keeping with this relationship God disciplines and corrects God's pious ones. Not only is God's judgment evident in this life, but life of the righteous and destruction of the sinners are eternal.

Psalm 14

A paraphrase of the canonical Psalm 1, this psalm contrasts the pious of the Lord, who endure God's chastening and follow the divine commandments, with the sinners, who spend their time sinning and ignoring God. As judge, God has full knowledge of these things, and in consequence of God's judgment, both the pious and the sinners will receive their just deserts: life and destruction, respectively.

Psalm 15

Here, as in Psalm 13, calamity enacts the judgment of God on the wicked, whereas the righteous escape. It is unclear whether vv 12b-13 (14-15) refer to a future day of judgment or to God's perennial judgmental activity, exemplified in the recent calamity. The idea that the righteous and the wicked have on them "a sign," which marks them for salvation or destruction, is reminiscent of passages like Genesis 4:15, Exodus 12:21-23, and Revelation 14:9-11.

Psalm 16

Again we hear of the foibles of the righteous. It is not clear whether the author actually committed a sexual transgression (so vv 7-8) for which God has forgiven him or avoided committing the deed. In either case he gives thanks to God who has chastised him and thus brought him to his senses so that he might escape the consequences of gross sin.

Date and Provenance

These psalms have often been often attributed to Pharisaic circles.[18] Many items in them are consonant with such an attribution: the assertion of human responsibility for actions (9:4 [7]); belief in a resurrection (although it is not specified as a resurrection of the body; 3:12 [16]); a deep concern for the righteous life and piety; and a conscious distinction between righteous and sinner. Lacking, however, are references to specific Pharisaic concerns like Sabbath laws and rules for table fellowship, although such arguments from silence are not necessarily persuasive. It has been suggested that the psalms emanate from an early stage of the Essene movement.[19] However, some literary parallels to the Qumran Scrolls are not proof of this, and the Psalms lack major features of the Qumran sectarian texts, for example, their dualism and their sharp distinction between the in-group and the outsiders (see above, pp. 127, 136–37). Moreover, we still know far too little about Essenism antecedent to and contemporary with Qumran (see above, p. 121). Indeed, since our knowledge of the social groupings of first-century Judaism is spotty and uncertain, it is best not to attribute these psalms to any specific, known group.[20]

What is noteworthy, however, is the use of the term "congregations of the pious" (*synagōgai/synedrion hosiōn*, 17:16 [18]; 4:1).[21] The expression, which is paralleled in other texts such as Psalm 149:1 and the Qumran apocryphal psalms (see above, pp. 167–68), indicates that these psalms were created and used in circles that considered themselves to be especially pious, righteous, and God-fearing and who gathered for purposes of worship, which probably included the recitation of some of these psalms.[22] The vivid references to Pompey's actions in Jerusalem suggest that these circles had their home, at least in part, in Jerusalem,[23] where they also found great displeasure with the present conduct of the temple cult.

The psalms were probably of diverse origin,[24] composed between at least 63 B.C.E. and 30 B.C.E.[25] Apart from the function of Psalms 1 and 18 as an introduction and a conclusion, the rationale for the present shape of the corpus is not altogether certain.[26] It is generally agreed that the Psalms, which are now extant in Greek and Syriac translations, were composed in Hebrew.[27]

The Testament of Moses—Revised

The expectation of an imminent judgment was an essential feature of Jewish apocalyptic eschatology. When this judgment did not happen as expected, apocalyptic literature and traditions might be revised and updated in a variety of ways. Daniel 12:12 revises the timetable announced in 12:11. Reinterpretations of the vision in Daniel 7 are found in Revelation 13, 1 Enoch 46–47 (see below, pp. 250–51), and 4 Ezra 11–13 (see below, p. 275). The Testament of Moses is an example of revision through interpolation.

As we have seen, the Testament of Moses was composed during the persecution by Antiochus Epiphanes (above, pp. 74–76). Chapter 5 refers to the events leading up to the persecution. Chapter 8 describes the persecution itself. According to chapter 9 the innocent deaths of Taxo and his sons will trigger God's vengeance and bring in the end time described in chapter 10. In fact the persecution did cease and the Gentile oppressor met his end, although not in the kind of cosmic catastrophe depicted in chapter 10.[28] The apocalypse was shelved, but it was not forgotten.

Almost two centuries later the work was dusted off and revised to make it relevant for new times. The editor's method was to insert between chapters 5 and 8 a sketch of events that would bring the reader to the present time. In chapter 6, v 1 refers to the Hasmonean high priests, whom the editor obviously despised. The rest of the chapter refers to events in the reigns of Herod the Great and his sons.[29] Since v 7 predicts that Herod's sons will rule for shorter periods of time than his thirty-four years (v 6), the latest date for the revision is 30 C.E., after which the reigns of both Antipas and Philip exceeded that of their father. The last identifiable events mentioned are in v 9: the burning of the buildings around the temple by Varus's commander, Sabinus, and Varus's crucifixion of the Jewish rebels in the months following Herod's death. The descriptions in chapter 7 are too stereotyped to be identifiable.

The net result of this interpolation is the transformation of the description of Antiochus's time into a kind of "eschatological tableau"[30] that recapitulated the earlier events that transpired during the terrible times of the 160s. The repetition of such events would usher in the end time.

There appears to be one final revision in 10:8. In the original version of the Testament this verse was most likely an allusion to Deuteronomy 33:29: Israel would tread on the necks of its enemies.[31] The reference to the wings of the eagle looks like an expansion that alludes to the incident of the golden eagle at the end of Herod's reign and perhaps to the eagle as symbol of the Roman Empire.[32]

In the months or years following Herod's death an apocalyptist with the same pacifist ideology expressed by the author of the Testament updated and reissued this work to encourage and exhort his comrades during the difficult years at the beginning of the Common Era.[33] For him, as for the writers of Revelation and 4 Ezra, the great enemy was no longer the Seleucid kingdom but the Roman Empire; the apocalyptic message, however, remained essentially the same.

The Parables of Enoch (1 Enoch 37–71)

These chapters of 1 Enoch were originally a separate Enochic writing that announced the coming of the great judgment, in which God would vindicate the "chosen and righteous" and punish their oppressors, "the kings and the mighty."[34] The book divides into three major sections called "parables" or "similitudes" (chaps. 38–44, 45–57, 58–69). As this term is employed in this book, it reflects the usage of biblical prophetic literature and denotes a revelatory discourse.[35] Since the expression occurs also in 1:2-3 and 93:1, 3 (Aramaic), it is less distinctive of chapters 37–71 than the universal scholarly designation the "Book of Parables" might indicate. The author's introduction entitles the work Enoch's "vision of wisdom" (37:1).[36]

Running through the Parables are four major types of material, which parallel other parts of 1 Enoch. The book as a whole depicts a journey or series of journeys. The seer ascends to the heavenly throne room (39:2—41:2). Then he visits the astronomical and other celestial phenomena (41:3-8; 43:1—44:1; 59:1-3; 60:11-22) and the places of punishment (esp. 52:1—56:4). The literary form that describes segments of these journeys is familiar from chapters 17–32: journey, vision, seer's question, interpretation by accompanying angel (see above, pp. 51–52). The second set of materials includes narratives about Noah and the flood (esp. 65:1—69:1). As in chapters 6–11 and 106–107, the flood is a type of the final judgment. The third group of materials consists of a series of heavenly tableaux, scenes in a developing drama that depict events leading up to the final judgment. Intermingled with these tableaux and often introduced by the words "in those days" (or "then") is a series of anticipatory allusions to the judgment. The closest Enochic parallels to the tableaux are the heavenly scenes in 1 Enoch 9–10 and 89:70-71, 76-77; 90:14, 17. Chapters 92–105 also presume such heavenly activity but do not present it in vision form. The anticipatory allusions have formal counterparts in chapters 92–105.[37]

Before turning to the drama itself, we must introduce the cast of characters. On the one side are God, God's heavenly entourage, the agents of divine judgment (primarily "the Chosen One," but also certain of God's angels), and God's people ("the chosen," "the righteous," and "the holy"). On the other side are the chief demon Azazel, his angels, and the kings and the mighty. God is usually called "the Lord of Spirits," a paraphrase of the biblical title "Lord of hosts" (cf. 39:12 and Isa 6:3)[38] or "the Head of Days," a title drawn from Daniel 7:9. The Chosen One combines the titles, attributes, and functions of the one like a son of man in Daniel 7, the Servant of YHWH in Second Isaiah, and the Davidic Messiah. "Son of man" is not a title. It is a Semitic way of saying "human being" and it is almost always qualified: "that son of man," "the son of man who has righteousness."[39] In the Parables the term is ambiguous. On the one hand it cannot be excluded that the author has in mind a human being glorified in heaven, with a face "like one of the holy angels" (46:1).[40] In chapter 71, which is probably an appendix, this figure is in fact identified with Enoch himself. On the other hand the usage of Daniel 8:15, 9:21, 10:5, and 12:6 indicates that an angel can be called "a/the man" or described as having "the appearance of a man." The Chosen One is the agent of God's judgment and as such is depicted with imagery that the early chapters of 1 Enoch ascribe to God. Related to his judgmental function is his role as the champion of God's people, and his titles "the Chosen One" and "the Righteous One" correspond to the titles "the chosen" and "the righteous ones." The salient features of God's people are their status as God's chosen ones, their righteousness, their suffering, and their faith in God's hidden world and God's vindication of their righteousness.[41] Named among God's angels are Michael, Raphael, Gabriel, and Phanuel, who correspond to the four archangels in chapters 9–11. Azazel and his hosts are the counterparts of Asael and of Shemihazah and his hosts in chapters 6–16. Here, as in chapters 12–16, Shemihazah is never mentioned. His function as archdemon is ascribed to the other angelic chieftain. Different from chapters 12–16, the angels' major sin here is the revelation of secrets rather than the spawning of bastard offspring. Although the Parables speak of "sinners," the references are usually very general. Where they are specific they seem to identify "the sinners" with "the kings and the mighty," the real villains of the piece (46:4; 62:2-3). The latter are notorious for denying the name of the Lord of Spirits and the heavenly world and for oppressing and persecuting the righteous. Their common destiny with the wicked angels suggests that they are agents of the latter.[42] In this respect and in their violent activity, they are counterparts of the giants begotten of the watchers in chapters 6–11 (see above, pp. 48–49).

The Unfolding Drama

The first parable is the shortest of the three. It introduces most of the dramatis personae, as well as the theme of judgment that is elaborated in the rest of the book. Together with the introduction to the book (chap. 37), it follows roughly the structure of the first chapters of 1 Enoch. Chapter 37 corresponds to 1:1-3. The repeated formula "I lifted up and said" (37:2, 5) parallels the repetition of "he (I) lifted up his (my) parable and said" in 1:2, 3 (and 93:1, 3). Also similar to 1:2 is the contrast between present and future in 37:2-3. Chapter 38 opens the first parable by introducing the subject of the coming judgment. Corresponding to the theophany predicted in 1:3-9 is the epiphany of "the Righteous One" (38:2).[43] The story of the descent of the angels (chaps. 6–7) is summarized in 39:1. Enoch is introduced in 39:2 (cf. 14:1).[44] Verse 3 mentions his ascent, which is described in chapter 14. After seeing the dwellings of the angels and the righteous, Enoch sees the one whose coming he has anticipated (38:2), here called "the Chosen One" (39:6-8). He is then caught up in the praises of the heavenly entourage (39:9-14). Enoch's vision of the divine throne room in chapter 40 corresponds to chapter 14, and the author here employs for the first time the format of vision (vv 2-7), question (v 8), and interpretation (v 9). Enoch views the judgment process and then moves on to the places of the celestial phenomena. There may be a literary displacement in chapters 41–44. In the present order, both 41:3-8 and 41:9 are separated from the sections to which they are naturally related. The original order may have been 41:1-2, 9; 42; 41:3-8; 43–44. The little Wisdom poem in chapter 42 suggests a parody on Sirach 24 and Baruch 3:9—4:4. Wisdom does not dwell in Israel; unrighteousness drove her back to heaven—a pithy and telling summary of the apocalyptic worldview (cf. 94:5).

The second parable, like the first, begins with a poetic introduction that anticipates the judgment and its consequences and refers to the Chosen One (chap. 45). Verse 3 is the first of several anticipatory references to the enthronement of the Chosen One. In spite of the heavenly setting of the Parables, the place of eternal life will be on earth, which will be purged of sinners (vv 4-6; cf. 10:16—11:2 and 91:14).

Chapters 46–47 present the first tableaux in the developing drama about the Chosen One and the judgment. In 46:1-3 the author draws on Daniel 7:9, 13, identifying his protagonist with the one like a son of man who is presented to the Ancient of Days in Daniel 7. The angelic answer to Enoch's inquiry employs or alludes to three of the four names of the protagonist (v 3). He is the son of man who has righteousness (son of man, the Righteous One) and whom God has chosen (the Chosen One). In 46:4-8 the angel anticipates the judgment scene in chapters 62–63, which has been constructed from an exegetical tradition that combined Isaiah 52–53 with Isaiah 13–14. Here the deeds and the fate of the kings and the mighty are depicted in language drawn from Isaiah 14.[45] Verse 7 suggests that these rulers are Gentiles, since they worship idols. Chapter 47 strikes a familiar Enochic theme. The blood of the righteous will be avenged. The interceding angels will relay the prayer of the righteous and thus trigger God's judgment.[46] Verse 2e alludes to Daniel 7:22 and introduces another tableau in v 3, which paraphrases Daniel 7:9-10.

Chapter 48 presents yet another tableau, the naming of "that son of man." Because it follows the enthronement of "the Head of Days," it may correspond to the presentation in Daniel 7:13 (cf. 1 Enoch 49:2d; the Chosen One now stands in the presence of the Lord of Spirits). The scene, however, expands on the call of the Servant in Isaiah 49,[47] thus drawing on this strand of the author's tradition. That son of man is both a helper of the righteous and a light to the Gentiles. The latter term is drawn from Isaiah 49:6 but is also consonant with the openness to the salvation of the Gentiles in 1 Enoch 10:21, 90:38, and 91:14. Language about the preexistence of that son of man and his name (vv 3, 6), read in the context of the many references to wisdom in chapters 48–49, may indicate that this figure is in some sense identified with or related to preexistent Wisdom.[48] This would fit with the usage of the Servant tradition in Wisdom 2, 4–5, where the righteous man is the bearer of preexistent Wisdom.[49] Linked to the tableau in 1 Enoch 48:1-7 is a section that describes the coming judgment of the kings and the mighty in language drawn from Exodus 15:7, 10 (the destruction of Pharaoh and his host).

The expression "kings of the earth"—found only here in the Parables—and the reference to "the Lord of Spirits and his Anointed" (48:8, 10) are drawn from Psalm 2:2 and indicate the third source of this author's description of the Chosen One—biblical language about the Davidic Messiah.[50] In 1 Enoch 49:1-2 the author returns to the theme of wisdom introduced in 48:1 and links it in v 3 to a paraphrase of the messianic oracle in Isaiah 11:2. Because of his wisdom the Chosen One can penetrate lies and judge rightly (1 Enoch 49:4, anticipating 62:3). Verse 4cd paraphrases Isaiah 42:1, the source of the Servant title "the Chosen One."

Chapters 50–51 anticipate future events connected with the judgment. Chapter 50 mentions a third group, in addition to the righteous and the sinners, who will be saved by repentance (cf. 100:6). Chapter 51 includes a resurrection among the events of the end time, and v 3 makes another anticipatory reference to the enthronement of the Chosen One. Verses 4-5 again designate earth as the locus of salvation and eternal life.

The journey and visions described in 52:1—56:4 are related to the myth of the angels and to the journey traditions in chapters 6–11 and 17–21. The vision of the mountains in chapter 52 contains several literary problems. Verse 1 refers back to Enoch's ascent (39:3). The double angelic interpretation in v 4 and in vv 5-9 may indicate that two traditions have been conflated, the first referring to a variety of things that Enoch saw and that will serve the Anointed One (vv 1a, 3-4), then a separate vision of the mountains (vv 1b-2), which is interpreted in vv 6-9. The mountains are reminiscent of the six mountains that flank the mountain of God in chapter 18. The interpretation of some of the metals as materials for warfare (v 8) suggests Asael's revelation of metallurgy in 8:1. Unlike 8:1, however, silver and gold are here (futile as) a means of buying deliverance (cf. 63:10). Verse 6 is of special significance. As in 38:2, the author has replaced the theophany of chapter 1 with an epiphany of the Chosen One, before whose presence the mountains and hills will melt (see also 53:6-7 and cf. 1:6). As in chapter 18, the mountains are located by a deep abyss that will serve as a place of eternal punishment. Chapter 53 describes the place of punishment for the kings and the mighty. The futility of bringing gifts and tribute parallels the motif in 52:7. A comparison of chapters 53 and 54 indicates that 54:2 has probably been displaced from chapter 53. In the respective valleys Enoch sees instruments of punishment being prepared (53:3; 54:3). He questions the angel (53:4; 54:4), who answers him (53:5; 54:5). As in 54:6, we expect in chapter 53 a reference to the actual punishment of the respective culprits. Thus 54:2 belongs after 53:5 and is out of place in chapter 54. As in chapter 18, there is a second abyss of punishment, this one for the hosts of Azazel (chap. 54). Verses 5-6 reflect 10:4-6. The description of the angels' place of punishment appears to have been interpolated by a tradition about the flood (54:7—55:2). Thus 55:3 picks up where 54:6 left off, with a reference to the angels' "taking hold of" the hosts of Azazel, and the passage concludes, as do chapters 52 and 53, with mention of the judgment by the Chosen One.[51] The whole section ends as the angels of punishment set out after certain "chosen and beloved ones," who are quite possibly to be identified with the kings and the mighty.

The reference to the Parthians and the Medes in 56:5 is the only explicit historical reference in the entire book. The author may well be referring to the invasion in 40 B.C.E., just before the beginning of the reign of Herod the Great.[52] This poetic passage describing the horror of the end time is followed by a vision of the return of the Dispersion or the coming of the Gentiles to worship in Jerusalem.

The third parable is the longest of the three. Like the other two it begins with a poetic section, which in this case anticipates the glorious theophanic light that will envelop the righteous after the judgment (chap. 58). The material in chapters 59–60 appears to have suffered a displacement. On the one hand 60:1-10 separates two blocks of astronomical lore (59:1-3 and 60:11-23). On the other hand 60:24 with its reference to the two monsters is separated from 60:7-10, which deals with the same subject. By placing 60:11-23 after chapter 59 we solve both problems and arrive at what may well have been the original order: 59; 60:11-23; 60:1-10, 24-25. The reference in 60:8 to "my great-grandfather who was taken up, the seventh from Adam" (i.e., Enoch), indicates that 60:1-10 + 24-25 is a tradition originally ascribed to Noah that is now placed in this Enochic book.[53]

In chapters 61–63 the drama of the judgment moves to its denouement. In 61:1-5 the angels prepare for the resurrection. Verses 6-13 are held together by the common theme of angelic praise. In v 8 the event occurs toward which the whole book has been pointing—the enthronement of the Chosen One. First he will judge the angels (v 9).

Chapters 62–63 describe the great judgment and its aftermath, which form the climax of this work. For this tableau the author has employed a traditional judgment scene, attested also in Wisdom 4–5 (see above, pp. 207–8), which expanded Isaiah 52:13—53:12 with material from Isaiah 13 and 14.[54] The Servant figure in Wisdom is the persecuted righteous man, now exalted, who judges his former persecutors, who are depicted in language drawn from Isaiah 14. These persecutors recognize him, react in terror, confess their sins, and anticipate their punishment, from which their riches cannot deliver them.

The present text begins with the exaltation of the Chosen One (a Servant title). Before him stand the kings and the mighty, the counterpart of the audience in Isaiah 52–53, whom the tradition transformed into the enemies of the righteous man. The recognition referred to in 1 Enoch 62:1 suggests that the kings and the mighty are to recognize in the Chosen One the chosen ones whom they have been persecuting.[55] Verse 2bc draws on the language of Isaiah 11:2, 4 and hence the messianic strand of the Chosen One tradition (cf. 1 Enoch 49:3). Verse 3de provides a further counterpart to 49:4, and v 7 to chapter 48. The kings and the mighty petition for mercy without success and are driven from the presence of the Lord and delivered to the angels of punishment (vv 9-12, anticipated in 53:3-5). The author then shifts the focus to the righteous and chosen and to their coming deliverance and fellowship with their helper and champion, that son of man (62:13-16). Verses 15-16 interpret Isaiah 52:1 and its reference to Mother Zion to refer to the community of the chosen. Chapter 63 is the counterpart of the confession in Isaiah 53:1-6 and Wisdom 5:6-8. The section ends with the banishment of the kings and the mighty, described in language reminiscent of the banishment from Eden (63:11; cf. 62:10, 12d and Gen 3:24). Chapter 64 with its reference to the angels has no clear connection with its context.[56]

Chapters 65–68 are a collection of Noachic traditions. The story in chapter 65 is closely related to chapters 83–84 and 106–107 and presumes a typology between the flood and the last judgment. God's oracle to Noah (67:1-3) is related to both 10:1-3 and 84:5. In chapter 66 and in 67:4 Noah appears to be a visionary guided by his grandfather Enoch, and 67:4 refers back to chapter 52, where Enoch had been guided by an angel. The parallel between the punishment of the angels and that of the kings and the mighty has been prepared for already in chapters 53–54. The description of that punishment in 67:5-13 has led many scholars to see here an allusion to the attempts of Herod the Great to find healing at the hot springs of Callirhoë.[57] The reference to "the Book of Parables" in the book itself (68:1) suggests that the Noachic traditions have been interpolated into an already extant work. The list of rebel angels in 69:2-3 is essentially the same as 6:7, while vv 4-12 present an alternative version. The precise meaning of 69:13-25 is uncertain. Reference to the oath that holds the earth together may be connected with the flood (see vv 17-19). If so, this passage may be related to the Noachic traditions in chapters 67–68 (cf. also the presence of Michael in 67:12-68 and 69:14-15).

After the materials in 64:1—69:25 the scene in 69:26-29 comes as something of a surprise. Clearly, it belongs with the judgment scene in chapters 62–63. It is an acclamation by the chosen and the righteous, who have witnessed the appearance of that son of man, his enthronement, and his judgment and banishment of the wicked. This connection may support our previous conjecture that the Noachic material, and perhaps most of 64:1—69:25, are an interpolation.

In its present form the Book of Parables has two conclusions. The first describes Enoch's final removal from earth (chap. 70).[58] The second conclusion (chap. 71) is an ascent vision that interprets chapters 14–16 and 46 in terms of one another. Enoch's ascent and commissioning as prophet of judgment (chaps. 14–16) are here interpreted as his presentation as "the son of man who was born for righteousness" (chap. 46; 71:14). In the present form of the book, this final tableau provides a climax and key to the work as a whole. The author of this chapter repeats the material in chapters 46–47 but identifies that son of man as Enoch, the righteous man par excellence, "the son of man born for righteousness." His ascent to heaven and his exalted status are a promise of the deliverance and vindication of the righteous in the coming judgment. This second conclusion is very likely a later appendix to the Book of Parables. The descriptions of Enoch's visions of the secrets of heaven (71:3-4) repeat in capsule form what has occurred previously in the book. This may indicate that chapter 71 once stood apart from the Book of Parables.[59]

The Parables are cast in the form of an apocalypse, with Enoch as the recipient of revelation mediated through heavenly visions interpreted by angels.[60] It is these revelations that are salvific, not the Mosaic covenant and Torah, which are never mentioned.[61] In this respect the Parables are similar to other parts of the Enochic corpus (see above, p. 358 n. 90).

Date and Provenance

The Parables of Enoch are notoriously difficult to date. Some scholars have argued for a late date because these chapters of 1 Enoch are not found in Qumran.[62] The arguments, however, are inconclusive. Although fragments of the earlier parts of 1 Enoch, which formed the basis for this work, were found at Qumran, they were not authored at Qumran and were not the sole property of that community. Not every Jewish apocalyptic work authored before 68 C.E. found its way into the Qumran collection, and thus the absence of the Parables in the Qumran collection proves nothing about the date of the work. Nonetheless, the passages usually cited as evidence for a relatively early date are suggestive but not conclusive.[63] The end of chapter 56 may refer to the invasion of Judea by the Parthians and the Medes in 40 B.C.E., or it may be a prediction of a future invasion written at some later time. Similarly, the punishment of the kings and the mighty in 67:8-13 may have as much to do with mythic geography in general as with Herod's treatment at Callirhoë.[64]

Several other considerations may indicate, however, that at least the traditions now collected in this book were known around the turn of the era. In the first place the judgment scene in chapters 62–63 is a reworked form of the tradition that occurs also in Wisdom 2, 4–5, the story of the persecuted righteous man, who is exalted as judge over his enemies. Wisdom 4:10-15 identifies Enoch as the prototype of this righteous one. This may indicate that the author of the Wisdom of Solomon knew that this tradition existed in an Enochic context and perhaps that the Chosen One was there identified with Enoch.

A second type of evidence comes from the New Testament.[65] In the Gospels the passages that pertain to the eschatological Son of Man presume that he will function as judge, or at least, in some cases, in a judicial role. Such a role contradicts Daniel 7, which these passages usually quote or allude to. In Daniel the one like a son of man appears *after* the judgment. The Parables offer us the exegetical basis for such a transformation: the conflation of Daniel 7 with the Isaianic tradition of the exalted righteous one and thus the identification of the one like a son of man with the Servant figure. Moreover, in Matthew 24:37-44||Luke 17:22-27 the typology between the days of Noah and the days of the Son of Man recalls the frequent Enochic typology of flood and final judgment and connects this judgment with the figure of the Son of Man, who is mentioned in 1 Enoch only in the Parables. Finally, the judgment scene in Matthew 25:31-46 may well reflect 1 Enoch 62–63.[66] For Matthew the touchstone of judgment is the manner in which people have treated the brethren of the Son of Man and hence the Son of Man himself. In 1 Enoch 62–63, as we have interpreted it, the solidarity between the Chosen One and the chosen ones enables the kings and the mighty to recognize in the Chosen One the chosen ones whom they have persecuted. That Matthew refers to the Son of Man as "the king" (25:34) is consonant with the title "the Anointed One" in the Parables.[67]

Some have argued that the Parables of Enoch are a Christian composition based on the Gospels.[68] Several factors tell against this hypothesis. There is nothing explicitly Christian in the Parables. To the contrary, in their present form the Parables identify the Chosen One with Enoch himself. It is unlikely and indemonstrable that Jews would have taken up such a Christian eschatological work and transformed it so as to identify the Chosen One (originally Jesus) with Enoch, as is presently the case. Finally, the traditions in the Parables give all indications of being earlier than those in the Gospels. They show us the exegetical steps by which the one like a son of man came to be judge. Moreover, the sheer repetition of the term "son of man" provides an intermediate step toward the usage of "the Son of Man" as a title and technical term in the Gospels. Conversely, the Parables employ the more Semitic and original meaning of the term in a nontitular sense ("human[like] being"). It is unlikely that this usage is a secondary resemiticizing of the Gospel's titular use of the term.

If this appraisal of the evidence is correct the Parables are a Jewish writing produced around the turn of the era.[69] Within that period the kings and the mighty would have had their counterparts among the many Roman generals, governors, triumvirs, and monarchs whose activities in Judea are well documented in the sources. The author might also have had in mind the late Hasmoneans and the Herods.[70]

The composition of the Parables cannot be attributed to any known Jewish group. We can only say that it originated among Jews whose experience, worldview, and eschatology were compatible with that sector of early Christianity that identified the one like a son of man with the risen and exalted Christ and that awaited his imminent coming as judge.[71]

The Parables of Enoch were most likely composed in Aramaic, and they may have been translated into the Ethiopic version in which they are now extant, with some access to the Aramaic as well as a Greek intermediary translation.[72]

4 Maccabees

Transformations of Jewish religious traditions are of many sorts. The author of 4 Maccabees transposes the stories of the martyrs in 2 Maccabees 6–7[73] into the key of Greek philosophy[74] and embodies them in a discourse that demonstrates—mainly on the basis of these stories—that reason is sovereign over the passions (1:13), which he divides into two categories, namely, pleasure and pain (1:20).[75]

In his introduction the author presents his thesis (1:1) and summarizes his argument (1:1-12). This thesis, a "thoroughly philosophical subject" (1:1, Hadas), was a standard doctrine of the Platonic and Stoic schools, and the author's enumeration of the four cardinal virtues (intelligence, self-control, justice, courage, 1:3-4), which stand in opposition to the passions, is similarly Platonic and Stoic.

In his definition of terms (1:13-30a) the author both agrees with his non-Jewish predecessors and sets himself apart from them. Reason is for him "the intellect choosing with correct judgment the life of wisdom," and he agrees with the Stoics that "wisdom is the knowledge of things human and divine" (1:15-16).[76] What defines his philosophy as Jewish is the assertion that "this wisdom is education in the law," that is, the Mosaic Torah (1:17).[77] His exposition will demonstrate how religious reason informed by the Law governed and subdued those passions that would have led the martyrs to violate the Law. The Law has five functions in the exposition of 4 Maccabees: "to teach the way of Jewish culture, to enable rational living, to encourage the faithful to persevere even in the face of persecution, to condemn/not condemn persons for their behavior, and to issue commands and prohibitions for right living."[78]

Before turning to the story of the martyrs the author illustrates his thesis with a number of examples, most of them from biblical history (1:30b—3:18). The citing of biblical figures as examples of abstract virtues (and vices) is typical of the didactic literature of this period. In the Testament of Joseph, as here, the young patriarch exemplifies self-control (sōphrosynē, 4 Macc 1:30—2:6; T. Jos. 3–9; see below, pp. 312–13).

The author places his discussion of the martyrs in the context of the events that led to their martyrdom (4 Macc 3:20—4:26; cf. 2 Macc 3:6-11). Although the heavy emphasis on divine judgment that runs through 2 Maccabees is here toned down, the persecution is still seen as punishment for hellenization (4:19-21), and the resistance of the innocent is contrasted with this sin (4:24-26). The deaths of the martyrs are described as three separate but closely linked episodes: Eleazar (chaps. 5–7), the seven brothers (8:1—14:10), their mother (14:11—17:6).

Chapters 5–7 retell the story in 2 Maccabees 6:18-31. Here the graybeard is not only an expert in the Law (cf. 2 Macc 6:18, "a scribe") but also a priest and a distinguished philosopher (4 Macc 5:4, 35). The discussion between Eleazar and Antiochus (who is not mentioned in 2 Macc 6) takes the form of a philosophical debate (4 Macc 5). The king derides Judaism as folly and nonsense, unworthy of a philosopher. Even if the Law is divine, sin committed out of necessity will be forgiven. Eleazar maintains that a Jew's prime necessity is to obey the Law in all its commandments. Far from being unreasonable, Judaism teaches self-control, courage, justice, and piety. Because God is Creator, divine law is fitting to the nature of God's people and appropriate to their souls.

Now reasoning gives way to straightforward refusal. Eleazar will not violate the Law, and in good Stoic-Cynic fashion he asserts that the tyrant cannot lord it over his reason. And so he faces death by torture. Unlike 2 Maccabees 6, Eleazar's tortures are here described in detail (4 Macc 6:1-11, 24-26), providing evidence for the old priest's claim that his philosophy furnishes him with the virtue of courage, which overcomes bodily pain (7:22-23; cf. 5:23). In the midst of his pain Eleazar continues to philosophize, declaring that his refusal to play the hypocrite is reasonable (6:12-22; cf. 2 Macc 6:21-23). His final words are an appeal that God accept his death as an expiation for the sins of the nation (4 Macc 6:26-29). Both this motif and the reference to eternal life in 7:19 are drawn from the story of the seven brothers and their mother in 2 Maccabees 7. By using them here and by other means, the author welds the two stories together. Employing a variety of images typical of Greek rhetoric (4 Macc 7:1-7) and reasserting his thesis—now demonstrated by Eleazar's actions—the author concludes this section by singing the praises of his hero.

Chapters 8–12 narrate the martyrdom of the seven brothers and thus correspond to 2 Maccabees 7. The introduction connects the story with the martyrdom of Eleazar (4 Macc 8:1-2; see also 9:5-6 and cf. 2 Macc 6:28, 31). In its outline the story approximates 2 Maccabees 7, connecting similar words and tortures with the respective brothers. The major omission is the material about the mother, which is gathered in the next section. The descriptions of the tortures are expanded, probably to emphasize the brothers' courage (see 4 Macc 8:16). The brothers' speeches are also lengthened and modified. Retained from 2 Maccabees 7 are the motifs of dying for the Law and the punishment of Antiochus. References to Israel's suffering for their sins are deleted, and the theme of resurrection—here immortality and eternal life—is mainly deferred until later. Additions in the narrative, the speeches, and the author's comments interpret the story as evidence of the book's thesis. This application is spelled out at length in the author's conclusion to the story in 13:1—14:10. Like chapter 7 it employs rhetorical imagery, sings the praises of the heroes (and of reason), and appeals to the audience to draw the proper conclusion from the story.

The mother of the seven brothers, whose speeches are integrated into the narrative of

2 Maccabees 7, is here treated in a separate section (4 Macc 14:11—17:6). She is the ultimate example of the author's thesis. In encouraging her sons to die for the Law she demonstrates how reason triumphed over the deepest of the pleasurable passions—a mother's love (15:4). Even her suicide to avoid defilement is applauded as a courageous religious act (15:23). The remainder of the work rounds off the discourse with a series of observations and applications (17:7—18:24): the thesis has been proven; the courageous deaths of the martyrs have expiated the sins of the people and purified the land; the audience is exhorted to emulate their example and to give praise to God.

Although the author's purpose was to demonstrate a philosophical thesis for the edification of his audience, he has significantly transformed and emended his tradition in other ways. Future resurrection of the body (2 Macc 7) is here replaced by immortality and an eternal life that begins at the moment of death (4 Macc 7:3; 9:22; 13:17; 14:5-6; 15:3; 16:13, 25; 17:12, 18-19).[79] God's creative power is cited as a reason for obedience (11:5; 13:13) rather than as a guarantee of resurrection, as it is in 2 Maccabees 7. Eternal life is God's reward for obedience to the Torah, not God's vindictive restoration of that which the martyrs have lost (i.e., their limbs, as in 2 Macc 7). In 2 Maccabees the placement of the stories of the martyrs enables them to serve as a turning point that changes God's wrath to mercy (see above, pp. 107–8). This function of the martyrs' deaths is explicit in 4 Maccabees, which employs categories of expiation and cleansing that find their closest analogies in non-Jewish Greek literature (1:11; 6:28-29; 9:24; 12:17-18; 17:19-22; 18:4-5).[80] The actions of the martyrs are likened to a battle in behalf of virtue or an athletic contest to be endured (9:8, 24; 17:11-16). This imagery and conception have parallels in traditions about Abraham, Joseph, and Job, and in Hebrews 10–12,[81] and it suggests that martyrdom is seen (here also) as the extreme example of the human striving for virtue.

Even if our author has been heavily influenced by Greek philosophical, religious, and rhetorical categories, he remains in his self-understanding a Jew. Judaism is the true philosophy. Right reason takes its stand on wisdom, which is the Torah. The martyrs were true children of Abraham (6:17, 22; 7:19; 9:21; 13:17; 15:28; 16:20; 17:6; 18:23) who took their place with other heroes of Israelite history as examples to be emulated by "the seed of Abraham, the children of Israel," who constitute the author's audience.

As to the time of 4 Maccabees' composition, Apollonius's title as "governor of Syria, Phoenicia, and Cilicia" (4:2) suggests the period between 20 and 54 C.E., when Syria and Cilicia were associated administratively in the Roman Empire.[82] The book was composed in Greek in the Diaspora, possibly in Syrian Antioch.[83] It bears the marks of a text that was intended for oral delivery.[84] Reference to "the season" (3:19) may indicate that the occasion for the work was a festival commemorating the deaths of the martyrs.[85] Its evident purpose was to show the compatibility of Judaism with some aspects of Hellenism, to indicate the boundaries beyond which a faithful Jew will not stray, and to exhort righteous behavior and, perhaps if necessary, perseverance in persecution.[86]

The accounts of the martyrs' deaths have strongly influenced both Jewish and Christian piety and tradition. In rabbinic tradition the death of a mother and her seven sons is dated to the time of Hadrian.[87] The church fathers made use of this book, and although it was not canonized by the Eastern churches, it has continued to influence their preaching and piety.[88]

BIBLIOGRAPHY

History

Schürer, *History*, 1:233–454. E. Mary **Smallwood**, *The Jews under Roman Rule* (SJLA 20; Leiden: Brill, 1976) 1–200. David C. **Rhoads**, *Israel in Revolution, 6–74 C.E.: A Political History Based on the Writings of Josephus* (Philadelphia: Fortress Press, 1976) 47–68. Nikos **Kokkinos**, *The Herodian Dynasty: Origins, Role in Society and Eclipse* (JSPSup 30; Sheffield: Sheffield Academic Press, 1998). Peter **Richardson**, *Herod: King of the Jews and Friend of the Romans* (Columbia: Univ. of South Carolina Press, 1996). Ehud **Netzer**, *The Palaces of the Hasmoneans and Herod the Great* (Jerusalem: Israel Exploration Society, 2001). Duane W. **Roller**, *The Building Program of Herod the Great* (Berkeley: Univ. of California Press, 1998). Abraham **Schalit**, *König Herodes: Der Mann und sein Werk* (Berlin: de Gruyter, 1969). Daniel R. **Schwartz**, *Agrippa I: The Last King of Judaea* (TSAJ 23; Tübingen: Mohr Siebeck, 1990). James **VanderKam**, *From Joshua to Caiaphas: High Priests after the Exile* (Minneapolis: Fortress Press, 2004) 337–436.

Psalms of Solomon

Translations: Robert B. **Wright**, *OTP* 2:639–70. Sebastian P. **Brock**, *AOT*, 649–82.

Texts and Other Translations: For the Greek text see an edition of the Septuagint. G. Buchanan **Gray**, *APOT* 2:625–52. Robert R. **Hann**, *The Manuscript History of the Psalms of Solomon* (SBLSCS 13; Chico, Calif.: Scholars Press, 1982), discussion of the Greek manuscripts. Joseph L. **Trafton**, *The Syriac Version of the Psalms of Solomon: A Critical Evaluation* (SBLSCS 11; Atlanta: Scholars Press, 1985), text, translation, and discussion of the Syriac version. Robert B. **Wright**, ed., *Psalms of Solomon: Greek and Syriac Manuscripts* (CD Version 4.1; Philadelphia: Temple Univ. Department of Religion, 2002), digital images of manuscripts.

Literature Survey: Joseph L. **Trafton**, "The Psalms of Solomon in Recent Research," *JSP* 12 (1994) 3–19.

Commentaries: Svend **Holm-Nielsen**, *Die Psalmen Salomos* (JSHRZ 4/2; Gütersloh: Mohn, 1977), introduction, translation, extensive notes. H. R. **Ryle** and M. R. **James**, *Psalmoi Solomōntos: Psalms of the Pharisees, Commonly Called the Psalms of Solomon* (Cambridge: Cambridge Univ. Press, 1891), introduction, Greek text, annotated translation. J. **Viteau**, *Les Psaumes de Salomon* (Paris: Letouzey & Ané, 1911), introduction, Greek text, facing annotated translation.

Literature: Kenneth **Atkinson**, *I Cried to the Lord: A Study of the Psalms of Solomon's Historical Background and Social Setting* (JSJSup 84; Leiden: Brill, 2004), detailed study of Psalms 2, 8, 17, more cursory treatment of the other psalms, discussion of their setting. Joachim **Schüpphaus**, *Die*

Psalmen Salomos: Ein Zeugnis Jerusalemer Theologie und Frömmigkeit in der Mitte des vorchristlichen Jahrhunderts (ALGHJ 7; Leiden: Brill, 1977).

Testament of Moses—Revised

See the bibliography for chapter 3. Adela Yarbro **Collins**, "Composition and Redaction of the Testament of Moses 10," *HTR* 69 (1976) 179–86.

1 Enoch 37–71

Text and Translations: See the bibliography for chapter 2.

Literature Survey: David W. **Suter**, "Weighed in the Balance: The Similitudes of Enoch in Recent Discussion," *RelSRev* 7 (1981) 217–21.

Commentary: Sabino **Chialà**, *Libro delle parabole di Enoc* (Studi Biblici 117; Brescia: Paideia, 1997).

The literature on the Parables of Enoch and the son of man is vast. A classic treatment of the latter is Erik **Sjöberg**, *Der Menschensohn im äthiopischen Henochbuch* (Acta Reg. Societatis Humaniorum Litterarum Lundensis 41; Lund: Gleerup, 1946). More recent discussions include John J. **Collins**, "The Heavenly Representative: The 'Son of Man' in the Similitudes of Enoch," in George W. E. **Nickelsburg** and John J. **Collins**, eds., *Ideal Figures in Ancient Judaism: Profiles and Paradigms* (SBLSCS 12; Chico, Calif.: Scholars Press, 1980) 111–33. George W. E. **Nick-elsburg**, "Son of Man," *ABD* 6:137–50. Johannes **Theisohn**, *Der auserwählte Richter* (SUNT 12; Göttingen: Vandenhoeck & Ruprecht, 1975). Leslie W. **Walck**, "The Son of Man in Matthew and the Similitudes of Enoch" (diss., Univ. of Notre Dame, 1999). For further bibliography see the articles by Frederick H. **Borsch**, Matthew **Black**, and James C. **VanderKam**, in James H. **Charlesworth**, ed., *The Messiah: Developments in Earliest Judaism and Christianity* (Minneapolis: Fortress Press, 1992) 130–221. On the date of the Parables see Jonas C. **Greenfield** and Michael E. **Stone**, "The Enochic Pentateuch and the Date of the Similitudes," *HTR* 71 (1977) 51–65; Michael **Knibb**, "The Date of the Parables of Enoch: A Critical Review," *NTS* 25 (1979) 344–57; Christopher L. **Mearns**, "Dating the Similitudes of Enoch," *NTS* 25 (1979) 360–69. On literary issues see David Winston **Suter**, *Tradition and Composition in the Parables of Enoch* (SBLDS 47; Missoula, Mont.: Scholars Press, 1979).

4 Maccabees

Translation: Many editions of the Apocrypha.

Texts and Other Translations: For the Greek text see an edition of the Septuagint. Hugh **Anderson**, *OTP* 2:531–64. R. B. **Townshend**, *APOT* 2:653–85.

Literature: Urs **Breitenstein**, *Beobachtungen zu Sprache, Stil und Gedankengut des Vierten Maccabaerbuches* (Basel: Schwabe, 1976). John J. **Collins**, *Between Athens and Jerusalem: Jewish Identity in the Hellenistic Diaspora* (New York: Crossroad, 1983) 187–91, good summary treatment. David A. **deSilva**, "The Noble Contest: Honor, Shame, and the Rhetorical Strategy of 4 Maccabees," *JSP* 13 (1995) 31–57. Moses **Hadas**, *The Third and Fourth Books of Maccabees* (JAL; New York: Harper, 1953), introduction with bibliography, Greek text with facing annotated translation—a good starting point. Hans-Jozsef **Klauck**, *4. Makkabäerbuch* (JSHRZ 3/6; Gütersloh: Mohn, 1989), German translation with substantial introduction. Paul L. **Redditt**, "The Concept of *Nomos* in Fourth Maccabees," *CBQ* 45 (1983) 249–70.

Fourth Ezra. The ninth-century Codex Ambianensis fol. 63 verso–64 recto containing 4 Ezra:7:63–86 in Latin translation. Photograph is courtesy of the Bibliothèque Municipale, Amiens.

8

Revolt—Destruction—Reconstruction

THE EVENTS

Events in Palestine in the second half of the first century C.E. threatened Jewish life and religion as they had not been threatened since the persecution by Antiochus IV some two centuries earlier. More exactly, these events paralleled the situation in the sixth century B.C.E. Chaos and revolt brought on the devastation of Judea and the destruction of Jerusalem and the temple. This in turn spawned a period of religious reflection and reconstruction.

After the death of Agrippa I in 44 C.E., his kingdom was constituted a province of the Roman Empire, governed by a procurator who was responsible to the legate of Syria. The land was relatively quiet during the rule of the first two of these procurators, but tensions with Rome were evident. The first procurator, Cuspius Fadus (44–±46), attempted to place the vestments of the high priest in Roman custody (as they had been before the time of Agrippa I), but Jewish protest prevented this. Fadus acted decisively when a prophet named Theudas led a large following to the Jordan River, where, he claimed, he would part the waters. Evidently suspecting political motives, Fadus sent his cavalry. Some of the crowd were killed and captured. Theudas was executed. Fadus was succeeded by Tiberius Julius Alexander (±46–48 C.E.), the nephew of the Jewish philosopher Philo of Alexandria (see above, pp. 212–13). He ordered the crucifixion of two sons of Judas of Gamala, who had led an uprising against the census of Quirinius in 6 C.E.[1]

During the procuratorship of Ventidius Cumanus (48–52 C.E.) events took a turn for the worse. One altercation in the Jerusalem temple, caused by a Roman soldier's obscene gesture, cost the lives of a host of Passover pilgrims. Some time later some Galilean Jews journeying to Jerusalem for a festival were murdered in a Samaritan village. When Cumanus accepted a bribe from the Samaritans and refused to take action, a band of Jewish brigands, led by a certain Eleazar, avenged the murders by burning several Samaritan towns and killing their inhabitants. Cumanus then attacked the Jews, killing some and capturing others. Quadratus, the legate of Syria, intervened, and both Jews and Samaritans were punished. Eventually, after a hearing in Rome, Claudius removed Cumanus from office because of his inept handling of the affair.

Cumanus's successor was a freedman named Felix (52–±60 C.E.). The appointment of a freedman as governor was unprecedented. That he was appointed and that his conduct

263

was tolerated is attributable to the influence that his brother, Pallas, exercised in the court of Claudius. During his rule conditions in Judea continued to deteriorate. He took strong action against the brigands and rebels who ravaged the countryside, crucifying many of them and punishing their sympathizers. One of their leaders, the aforementioned Eleazar, was captured and sent to Rome for trial. The *sicarii*, so named for the daggers (*sicae*) they carried, mingled with crowds in Jerusalem and assassinated their opponents, including the high priest Jonathan. Others sought freedom from Rome in less violent ways. Among these was an Egyptian Jew who gathered a large number of followers in the desert and prepared to march on Jerusalem, whose walls he expected to crumble before him.[2] Felix's soldiers attacked them, slaughtering and capturing many.

Felix was succeeded by Porcius Festus (±60–62 C.E.), a good man who was unable, however, to reverse the conditions that had been exacerbated by his predecessor. The *sicarii* continued their terrorist activities.

When Festus died in office Nero appointed Albinus as procurator. His rule (62–64 C.E.) was worse than that of Felix. He plundered public and private funds, accepted bribes, and allowed criminals, notably the *sicarii*, to be ransomed from prison. When he left office he emptied the prisons, thus filling the country with brigands.

According to Josephus, the next procurator, Gessius Florus (64–66 C.E.), made Albinus look like "the most righteous" of people. He plundered whole cities and cooperated with brigands, accepting a share of their booty. His robbery of the temple treasury led to an uprising in Jerusalem, which accelerated to the point of no return. The Roman troops were driven from Jerusalem, and the revolution began to spread to other cities. Cestius Gallus, the legate of Syria, marched on Judea with a sizable army, but he was unable to take Jerusalem. During the winter of 66/67 C.E. preparations were made for war.

Nero delegated the task of waging this war to his general Vespasian. The conflict began in Galilee. One city and fortress after another fell to the armies of Vespasian and his son Titus. By winter 67 the north of Palestine was again in Roman hands.

The war in Judea might have been short; in June 68 Vespasian was ready to besiege Jerusalem. The news of Nero's assassination, however, caused Vespasian temporarily to suspend his military operations. In January 69 Nero's successor Galba was assassinated. New uprisings in south Judea brought an end to Vespasian's inactivity. During the spring of 69 he reestablished the occupation of Judea. Meanwhile, Galba's successor, Otho, had committed suicide, and Vitellius had been acclaimed emperor by his troops. In July 69 Vespasian's army acclaimed their general as emperor. As Vespasian set out for Rome, where he would begin a ten-year reign, he entrusted the completion of the war to his son Titus. Only Jerusalem and the fortresses of the Herodium, Machaerus, and Masada remained to be conquered.

The siege of Jerusalem lasted some four months in 70 C.E. Within the city, the people were divided into factions. This had been the case for two and a half years since a certain John of the city of Gischala in Galilee had fled to Jerusalem, where he precipitated a civil war during the winter of 67/68. During the siege, factions fought not only the Romans but one another. In stages the Romans broke through the fortifications that ringed the city. On the 17th of Tammuz (June/July) the daily offering was suspended in the temple. On the 10th of Ab (July/August) the Romans broke into the temple. The sanctuary was set ablaze, and the Romans slaughtered everyone in sight. John of Gischala and his followers escaped across the central valley to the "Upper City," where they withstood further assault until the 8th of Elul (August/September), when the last bastions of the city fell. Titus ordered the entire city and the temple leveled, leaving only the three towers of Herod's citadel and a few levels of the walls here and there standing as a memorial of the dimension of the Jewish fortifications and hence of the Roman victory.* The following year Rome acclaimed the joint victory of Vespasian and Titus. A triumphal arch—built after Titus's death—still stands in the Forum in Rome, with a relief depicting the table of shewbread and the Menorah (seven-branched candelabrum) being carried in triumphal procession.*

Following the destruction of Jerusalem, Lucilius Bassus, the governor of Judea, subdued the fortresses of Herodium and Machaerus.* The prolonged siege of the fortress of Masada, which was held by the *sicarii*, lasted until spring of 73.*

The great war with Rome left Palestine in ruins and its people in shock. Leadership had failed. Large segments of the population had been killed. Cities had been demolished. Institutions were destroyed. Jerusalem and its temple were no more. In the decades that followed two other revolts against Rome would flare up and again prove disastrous for the Jewish people in the Diaspora and Palestine, but that is a story for another book.[3]

As had been the case in 587 B.C.E., the tragedy of 70 spawned reflection about the ways of God and soul-searching about the human situation. The agony of this process and the shock waves that set it in motion can still be felt in the writings that we shall discuss in this chapter.

If Judaism was to survive the events of the year 70, reflection had to be accompanied by reconstruction. Since the temple was not rebuilt, as it had been in the sixth century, the nature of reconstruction was radically different. The Torah, its study, definition, and observance, began to fill the vacuum created by the annihilation of the Jewish cultic center. Rabbis in the city of Yavneh (Jamnia on the Mediterranean) and elsewhere in the land of Israel, together with their students, began the process of crystallizing the interpretations of the Torah that were their heritage.[4] This crystallization of the tradition led to new definition and interpretation. Generations of rabbis would follow one another. The literary deposits of their activities are to be found in the bulky collections that we know as the Mishnah, the Tosefta, the Palestinian and Babylonian Talmuds, and the rabbinic commentaries.

The Book of Biblical Antiquities (Pseudo-Philo)

In this lengthy anonymous chronicle, which has been transmitted in the name of Philo of Alexandria, we encounter a type of literature that we have already seen in a variety of forms in the Book of Jubilees, the Animal Vision in 1 Enoch, the Testament of Moses, and the Genesis Apocryphon, namely, the recasting of biblical narrative—in this case, from Adam to the death of Saul.[5] The Antiquities' treatment of its biblical source material varies widely.[6] Extensive portions of Scripture are briefly summarized or completely bypassed. Other sections are paraphrased, with occasional verbatim quotations. Still others are interpolated with prayers, speeches, or narrative expansions. In a few cases whole new stories have been inserted or old ones have been radically revised.

Among the sections deleted are: Genesis 1–3; Genesis 12–50 (its contents are briefly summarized in L.A.B. 8); Exodus 3–13; all the legal material in Exodus except chapter 20; almost the entire book of Leviticus; all the legal material in Numbers; Deuteronomy 1–30; the descriptions of the conquest in Joshua (chaps. 3–21); and parts of 1 Samuel.

The book of Judges is a notable exception to the author's technique of excision and compression. The section corresponding to Judges constitutes one-third of the entire work (L.A.B. 25–49). Only Judges 1–3 have been deleted; however, they have been replaced by the lengthy story of Kenaz (L.A.B. 25–28). According to Judges 1:13 Kenaz was the father of Othniel; here he assumes Othniel's place as the first judge (Judg 3:7-14).[7] The stories of Deborah, Gideon, Abimelech, Jephthah, Samson, Micah, the Levite, and the war between Benjamin and Israel have been retained, though with many revisions.

Consonant with this concentration on the book of Judges is the Antiquities' orientation of Israelite history around persons who function as leaders—whether good or bad.[8] In the radically revised story of Abraham, the patriarch is present at the building of the tower of Babel (L.A.B. 6), and he and eleven others refuse to participate in the idolatrous enterprise. Even among these twelve, however, Abraham stands out as the only one who rejects the possibility of escape and confronts death in a fiery furnace (cf. Dan 3). The story of Moses' birth is prefaced by a lengthy episode involving his father, Amram (L.A.B. 9), who convinces the Israelite elders that God will protect the nation and leads a mass disobedience of the Pharaoh's decree. The other parts of the Pentateuch that are reproduced center mainly on the figure of Moses and his functions as mediator of the covenant, intercessor for his people, and spokesman of God and executor of God's judgment (chaps. 10–19). Thus he maintains his preeminent position in Israelite history (19:16). The author's treatment of the book of Joshua centers on the figure of Moses' successor (L.A.B. 20–24). As is indicated by the length of his story, Kenaz is a leader par excellence (cf. 49:1). The recasting of Judges makes specific moral judgments about Israel's leaders, often adding a motif of retribution that is lacking in the biblical text. Gideon, who dies unpunished for his idolatry (Judg 8:22-32), will be punished after death (L.A.B. 36:4).[9] Jephthah loses his daughter as punishment for his wicked vow (39:11), and she is said to be wiser than her father (40:4). Samson is blinded because his eyes went astray (43:5). Judges 17–20 is unified around the theme of Micah and his idolatry (L.A.B. 44–47). His punishment, not mentioned in Judges, is explicit here (47:12). Israel's initial defeat by Benjamin is punishment for those who do not oppose Micah's idolatry (chap. 47). The birth of Samuel is set in a vacuum of leadership in Israel, and he is designated as a ruler like Kenaz (49:1). The treatment of 1 Samuel focuses on the figures of Samuel, Saul, and David, which is consonant with the biblical book.

Fundamental to the Antiquities' historical narrative is the conviction that God chose Abraham as the patriarch of a people with whom God would be bound in an everlasting covenant.[10] Pseudo-Philo indicates Abraham's significance early on in the narrative, in its nonbiblical version of the Babel story, which establishes him as a man of faith and an example to his people (L.A.B. 6). This significance is underscored by repeated references to the incident and by interpolations into the flow of the biblical narrative that refer to or briefly summarize Abrahamic stories that have been moved from their original places in the biblical narrative.[11] This repetition calls the readers' attention to a point of primary significance.

Abraham's function as patriarch is essential to his election. The covenant with him carries the promise of land and, especially, of progeny, and though the Antiquities does not narrate the reestablishment of the covenant with Isaac and Jacob, later pericopes refer to the covenant or the promises made to the patriarchs.[12] This covenant is also reaffirmed or reestablished at Sinai (11:1-5); both covenants are one. In addition, the covenant is described as an *eternal* covenant, and the motif runs like a continuous thread through Pseudo-Philo's narrative.[13] This specification is noteworthy because the idea of an eternal covenant occurs in the Pentateuch only in Genesis 17, with reference to circumcision.

A corollary of Israel's election is the distinction between this people and the rest of the nations. This too is signaled in the first story about Abraham (L.A.B. 6–7). His election is tied to his act of faith at the time of the building of the tower.[14] What is a separate episode in Genesis 11:1-9 becomes the setting for a story whose protagonist is Abraham (Gen 12:1-3), the one who rejects Chaldean idolatry. As retold, the Babel story contrasts Abraham not only with the Semitic Chaldeans, but also with the children of Ham and Japheth, that is, the rest of humanity. The account of the giving of the Torah reemphasizes Israel's difference from the nations. Israel alone receives the Torah, and thereby they are glorified over the nations (L.A.B. 11:13). The Israel–Gentile contrast reappears frequently in subsequent references to the nation's covenantal election.

Pseudo-Philo's compositional technique has structured into the narrative the paradox that in spite of its unique election, Israel is perennially at the mercy of the nations from whom God as chosen and distinguished it. The Babel story foreshadows this situation; righteous Abraham and his companions are persecuted by their idolatrous contemporaries. The next major story depicts the covenant people as slaves in Egypt (L.A.B. 9). Pseudo-Philo then guarantees attention to this paradox by devoting the remainder of his work to the events described in Judges and 1 Samuel and by inserting specially composed speeches in which the characters articulate the paradox as a theological problem.[15]

Pseudo-Philo provides an explanation for this paradox. Israel's subjugation to the nations is an expression of God's wrath, which is directed against the people because they have violated their covenantal status and shown themselves to be no different from the nations.[16] Most frequently the sin involves capitulation to Gentile seductions to idolatry.[17] The author consistently emphasizes this fact when the biblical text mentions it, and frequently attributes the sin to the people in biblical stories that do not mention it. This focus on idolatry does not exclude other sins, however. Israel's failure to live up to its covenantal status and obligations is especially evident in a pair of contrasting stories. In the account of the giving of the Torah (L.A.B. 11), the commandments are enumerated as part of the Law that is the unique gift to Israel. At the time of Micah (L.A.B. 44), Israel is indicted for having broken the commandments, which are listed seriatim (vv 6-7).[18] As a result, God threatens to eliminate the whole human race, Israel included.

If the chosen people continually violate their covenantal status and obligations, will God eventually annul the covenant? In Pseudo-Philo's narrative, individual instances of Gentile subjugation often give rise to this question.[19] The possibility that God may permanently disenfranchise Israel can be suggested in the form of a question (Has God rejected us?) or in a refutation of the implied question (God has not rejected us). The frequency with which the issue surfaces in revisions of the biblical text suggests that it is an existential concern for the author and the book's audience.

Pseudo-Philo provides a consistent response to doubts about Israel's ongoing status: God's promises to Israel are rooted in an *eternal* covenant.[20] This assertion is sometimes embedded in an appeal to creation. God's created world itself will crumble before God annuls the covenant (9:3; 18:10). History is also an indicator. Israel's past history demonstrates, over and again, that God's merciful fidelity to the promises of the eternal covenant overrides human faithlessness.[21] Pseudo-Philo makes this assertion even after God threatens universal cataclysm at the time of Micah. The birth of Samuel, a leader like Kenaz, bodes well for the future and prepares for the rise of the Davidic dynasty. Statements by leaders like Kenaz and Deborah anticipate a future for Israel far beyond the sinful events narrated in the history (28:4-5; 32:13-17).

The historical pattern that pervades the narrative in the Antiquities suggests that its author lives in a time when the land of Israel suffers under Gentile domination. Through that same pattern, however, the author expresses the expectation that in fidelity to the covenant, God will once again send the appointed deliverer to rescue the people of Israel.[22] The day of Deborah stands as a promise (32:14). Figures from the past like Barak and Deborah, Kenaz, Samuel, and David offer hope for the future. Given both the importance of Kenaz, the ruler par excellence from the tribe of Judah, who fulfills the prophecy in Genesis 49:10 (L.A.B. 21:5), and the prominence of David, God's anointed (L.A.B. 59), one might suppose that this author expects that such a ruler will be a messianic scion from the tribe of Judah and the house of David. The fact that the Antiquities articulates no such hope has led commentators to doubt, or even deny, that the author cherished such a hope.[23] They correctly emphasize that hope in a Davidic messiah was not a staple in Jewish eschatological hope that must be assumed even where it is not expressed.[24] Nonetheless, the Antiquities' emphasis on human deliverers, its highlighting of Kenaz and David, and the fact that the Davidic king of the future is usually posited as a counterforce against oppressive rulers and kings might easily have lent itself to such an interpretation.[25] Perhaps the author was implying such a hope, or perhaps the author was being cautious and purposely vague. Pseudo-Philo should not be included among authors who nourished the hope of a Davidic messiah, nor should the text be used as proof that not every Jewish author in the Greco-Roman period awaited such a messiah.

What is clear about Pseudo-Philo's expectations about the future is the belief in the resurrection of the dead, a final judgment, and punishment for the wicked and eternal life for the righteous.[26] These expressed beliefs parallel similar statements in the contemporary apocalypses, 2 Baruch and 4 Ezra (see below, pp. 273, 279). The Antiquities is not an apocalypse, but a piece of "historical" narrative that does not claim to be a revelation. In these instances, however, it employs motifs at home in apocalyptic writings. Moreover, like the authors of these apocalypses, Pseudo-Philo believes that divine actions take place according to a preordained schedule (19:14-15; 56:2; 59:1; 61:3; 62:2, 9).

The Book of Biblical Antiquities has usually been dated shortly before or after the Jewish War.[27] A date before 100 C.E. is indicated by the type of biblical text that the author employs, a text type that fell out of use around the turn of the century under the influence of the rabbis.[28] A date close to the year 70 is suggested by the many close and substantial parallels with the wording and eschatological traditions in 2 Baruch and 4 Ezra (see below, pp. 270–85) and with traditions in the Antiquities of Josephus.[29] Moreover, the crisis in leadership that is reflected in the book can be identified with events in the decades before 70 C.E.,[30] and the concern with leadership is paralleled in 2 Baruch (see below, p. 282). Those who prefer a pre-70 date argue that the book seems to take the existence of the Jerusalem cult for granted and makes no explicit reference to the destruction of Jerusalem and its temple—an event that is central to the narratives in 2 Baruch and 4 Ezra.[31] Others have found an allusion to this event in L.A.B. 19:7, which dates the destruction of the First Temple to the 17th of Tammuz, the date in 70 C.E. on which the continual burnt offering (*tamid*) ceased in the Second Temple.[32] Support for a post-70 date also appears in 22:1-6, where Joshua berates the Israelites for building a sacrificial altar rather than teaching their sons the Torah. This addition to the biblical text parallels the situation after 70 when the study of the Torah replaced the sacrificial system.[33] In any case, whether one dates the work before, during, or after the Jewish War and the destruction of Jerusalem, its message is clear: in a time of deep distress and doubt as to whether the covenantal promises are still viable, God's actions in the past provide hope for the nation.

The Antiquities was composed in Hebrew and then translated into Greek, and from Greek into Latin, in which language alone it is extant.[34] Palestine is almost certainly its place of composition.[35] Its author is unknown, but the work came to be attributed to Philo of Alexandria, perhaps because it was transmitted with genuine works of Philo.[36]

Among the writings of the Jewish Pseudepigrapha the Antiquities of Pseudo-Philo has received relatively little treatment. Yet the work is valuable for what it reveals about several aspects of Jewish and Christian religion contemporary to it. It provides a significant witness to the theory and practice of first-century Jewish biblical interpretation.[37] As its treatment of the stories of Deborah (L.A.B. 30–33) and Jephthah's daughter (L.A.B. 39) indicates, it reflects an unusually positive attitude toward women.[38] A comparison with contemporary Jewish apocalypses demonstrates how a work that is not formally an apocalypse may employ motifs and structures of thought that are at home in apocalypses (see above). As a piece of narrative writing that interprets the Hebrew Bible, the Antiquities also sheds light on aspects of the literary and exegetical techniques and the theology of the New Testament Gospels and especially Luke–Acts.[39] Finally, Pseudo-Philo's expressed doubts about the question of the viability of the covenant suggest that Paul's wrestling with the same problem (esp. in Rom 9–11) is not a novelty with the apostle, but reflects similar contemporary Jewish speculation about the problem of theodicy.[40]

THREE APOCALYPTIC RESPONSES TO THE FALL OF JERUSALEM

The problems created by the destruction of Jerusalem are addressed in three apocalypses: 4 Ezra, 2 Baruch, and the Apocalypse of Abraham. While all three works stem from a common tradition, the relationship between 4 Ezra and 2 Baruch is especially close.

"Why?" and "Whither?" are the questions raised by these writers as they ponder the events of 70 C.E. The first question refers to the problem of theodicy: Why has a just God allowed the sinful Gentiles to defeat the covenant people and devastate their land and God's temple? The second question relates to reconstruction: What will take the place of the temple as the people attempt to pick up the broken pieces of their life and their religion? The two apocalypses differ in their answers to the first question, but they agree that the immediate remedy for the plight of Judaism lies in the Torah. In this respect they are in accord with developments in rabbinic circles.

Both 4 Ezra and 2 Baruch use the fall of Jerusalem in 587 B.C.E. as their fictional setting. Their alleged authors are two famous scribes: Ezra, the scribe who brought the Torah to Jerusalem in the fifth century, and Baruch, the secretary of Jeremiah. The literary structure of the two works depicts the brokenhearted and troubled scribes challenging God's justice and disputing with God or God's angels, receiving apocalyptic visions, and eventually becoming the agents of God's consolation of God's people.

4 Ezra

Second Esdras in the Apocrypha is in its present form a Christian writing that contains within it (in chaps. 3–14) a Jewish apocalypse commonly known as 4 Ezra.[41] This apocalypse has its fictional setting in the thirtieth year after the Babylonian destruction of Jerusalem, that is, in 557 B.C.E. It is ascribed to a certain Salathiel (Shealtiel), whom the Bible names as the father of Zerubbabel, the builder of the Second Temple.[42] In 4 Ezra, however, Salathiel is identified with Ezra the scribe, who in reality lived during the following century.[43] Evidence that we shall consider below indicates that the book should be dated at the end of the first century C.E., that is, approximately thirty years after the *Roman* destruction of Jerusalem.

Fourth Ezra is an apocalypse, a collection of revelatory visions held together by a narrative framework.[44] The "plot" of the narrative recounts Ezra's transformation from one who mourns over the destruction of Jerusalem and criticizes what he perceives to be God's injustice to one who understands God's ways in the world and transmits God's comforting and life-giving revelation.[45] The transformation takes place as a result of the revelations that are mediated by the angel Uriel and by God, "the Most High."[46] By scholarly consensus, the book divides cleanly into seven sections, each centering on a revelation.[47]

The first three sections recount dreams that contain disputative dialogs about theodicy, sometimes reminiscent of the book of Job (3:1—5:20; 5:21—6:35; 6:36—9:26).[48] Each begins with a prayer in which Ezra takes up the theme of divine justice. An angel appears and responds to Ezra. The two engage in a disputation. The section ends as Ezra fasts in preparation for another revelation.[49] The sequence—prayer and angelophany—is traditional (cf., e.g., 1 Enoch 12:3; Dan 9).

The first section (4 Ezra 3:1—5:20) begins with a disturbed Ezra mourning the destruction of Jerusalem. Ezra's prayer in 3:4-36 is less a petition than a complaint. Through his recital of history from Adam to the present he attributes Israel's present plight to the state of the human heart. Since the transgression of the first father, humanity has been burdened with "an evil heart." The problem is more acute with Israel. Although God had chosen them as the covenant people (vv 12-17) and given them the Torah, God did not remove the evil heart and thus allow the Torah to bear fruit (vv 20-22).[50] Moreover, the nation is now in ruins because God has punished the people for the sins their evil hearts led them to commit (vv 25-27). Carrying his complaint a step further, Ezra observes that the deeds of the Babylonians are no better than those of the Jews. He concludes by challenging God to compare Israel's deeds with those of the Gentiles (vv 28-36). Thus the problem of theodicy is clearly outlined. Since Adam, humanity has had a propensity to sin. The Creator has not removed this tendency even from the chosen people. Nonetheless, God holds them responsible for their deeds and punishes them at the hands of Gentiles, whose deeds are worse than those of the Jews. Ezra fails to understand "the way of the Most High," that is, God's way of conducting the world and God's injustice toward humanity.[51]

In response to Ezra's prayer, the angel Uriel appears and challenges Ezra to answer a series of riddles or questions about certain phenomena in this world (4:1-12).[52] When the seer is unable to do so, the angel asks how he expects to understand the way of the Most High. Such comprehension lies beyond human capacity (4:13-21). Ezra objects that he is not interested in fathoming *heavenly* things. Israel's suffering under the Gentiles is a matter of the *here and now*. Why does God permit it, and what will God do about it to vindicate "his name by which we are called"? (4:22-25).

This last question shifts the discussion in the direction of eschatology, which provides Ezra with the only solution that he will receive in his confrontation with the Almighty. From this point on, the tone of the dialog changes. Ezra is no longer the primary interlocutor, and his questions are less argumentative and more attempts to elicit information from the angel.[53] Presumed in Uriel's answers is a teaching of two ages. The present age is marked by sadness and infirmities (4:27), which are caused by the evil seed that was sown in Adam's heart from the beginning (4:30-32). Deliverance from this situation lies in the *eschaton* and the beginning of the age to come, and so Ezra asks the perennial apocalyptic question, "How long?" (4:33). Uriel responds that the time has been predetermined by God and cannot be rushed (4:34-37).

The questions and answers continue. Since the time is fixed, when it has arrived not even human sinfulness can hold it back (4:38-43). More time in the history of the world has passed than is yet to come (4:44-50). Certain events that will take place are the signs of the end (4:51—5:13). Ezra wakes up, and after Uriel has left, Ezra speaks with one of the Jewish leaders who is concerned that Ezra has abandoned his people (5:14-19). The section concludes as Ezra, following Uriel's command, fasts for seven days in preparation for the next revelation (5:20).

Ezra's second vision (5:21—6:35) parallels the first one. It begins as the grieving Ezra disputes with the angel and seeks to understand God's ways (5:21-40) and then turns to a series of questions that seek eschatological information (5:41-43). Different from the first section, however, the focus here is not on the anthropological problem of the human heart but on the dilemma of Israel's subjugation to the Gentiles. In his prayer Ezra stresses at length Israel's unique status as God's chosen people and asks why God has delivered the one to the many (God's unique people to the nations) rather than punishing Israel directly (5:23-30). This issue is not simply Israel's punishment, but their punishment *by the Gentiles*.[54] Uriel's responses again take the form of a challenge. Do you love Israel more than its Maker? (5:33). When Ezra protests that he wishes to understand God's ways and judgment, Uriel responds that it is not possible to understand God's judgment or the goal (*finis*) of God's love for the chosen people (5:34-40). His rejection of Ezra's quest for understanding is firmer than it was in the first dialog (cf. the firm rejections in 5:35, 40 with the rhetorical questions in 4:2, 11). As in the first discourse the focus shifts to eschatology and the question of who will be present at the end (*finis*, 5:41). Ezra wants to know whether God could not have arranged things so that the end would come sooner, and the angel again emphasizes through a set of analogies that God's own time is appropriate to the nature of things (5:43-49). After further discussion of the nearness of the end and the signs of its coming (5:50—6:28), Uriel, with words of encouragement not found in 5:13-15, commands Ezra to fast for another seven days before the next revelation (6:29-34).[55] The section closes with Ezra's fast (6:35).

The third discourse is by far the longest of the three (6:36—9:26).[56] In it the question of theodicy is pressed to its unanswerable limits. Ezra's prayer deals again with Israel's plight. After a long description of the six days of creation (6:38-54), the seer asks: if the world has been created for Israel, why is Israel dominated by the nations rather than in possession of its inheritance, and how long will this continue? (6:55-59). As in the first discourse, the angel expounds the teaching of the two ages. The sorrow and toil of this age, caused by Adam's transgression, will be overcome in the age to come, and it is to this that Ezra should direct his attention (7:1-16).

Ezra introduces a new motif and a new challenge to God's justice. The hope for an age to come is fine for the righteous, but what about the wicked, who can anticipate only punishment? (7:17-18). The angel asserts human responsibility. God gave the covenant and the Torah, and the wicked will be judged according to their deeds because they are responsible for these deeds (7:19-25). Then follows a description of the last days—a four-hundred-year reign of the Messiah,[57] the expunging of all life and a week when the earth returns to its primordial silence, the resurrection, and the great judgment over which God will preside (7:26-44). Judgment will be on the basis of deeds, and even the Gentiles will be punished for not having served the Most High and obeyed the commandments.[58]

Ezra now pursues a question that will occupy him through much of this discourse: who has not sinned? Thanks to the evil heart, the delights of paradise will be enjoyed by few, while many will be tormented (7:45-48). The angel dismisses the question. Things that are rare (here "the few" to be saved) are more precious than those in great quantity. God will rejoice over the few who are saved and will not grieve over the multitude that perish (7:49-61). Ezra laments the fate of humans, who are equipped with a mind to understand their future torment (7:62-69). Again the angel asserts human responsibility for sins knowingly committed (7:70-74). There now follows a long excursus on the "intermediate state," the situation of souls between death and the judgment (7:75-101). It is the most detailed discussion of the subject in our literature.[59]

Returning to the subject of the righteous and the wicked, Ezra inquires whether the wicked might be saved at the judgment through the intercession of the righteous (7:102-3). The angel's negative answer (7:104-5) leads to another lament over the human plight caused by Adam (7:116-26; cf. 7:62-69). According to the angel, Adam is not to blame. Life is a contest in which people must make the choice that Moses put to them (7:127-31). Ezra pleads the compassion of God, revealed to Moses (7:132-40; cf. Exod 34:6-7), which would pardon more than just a few; but the angel asserts that only a few will be saved (4 Ezra 8:1-3). The seer now addresses God, pleading for mercy (8:4-19, 20-36). The disputation continues but reaches an impasse. God assures Ezra, who doubts his own salvation, that he is among the righteous (8:48-54) but cuts short any more questions about the many who will perish (8:55). Ezra cannot love the creation more than the Creator does (8:47).

The angel states that the judgment is near. Ezra asks when it will come. Signs are again enumerated (8:61—9:6) and the judgment again predicted. The angel, like God, forbids any more questions about the punishment of the wicked (9:7-22) and commands Ezra to spend seven days preparing for the next revelation. This time he is not to fast, but he is to leave his house and to go to an uninhabited field, "where no house has been built" (9:24), and sustain himself on a diet of flowers (9:23-26).

The fourth and middle section (9:27—10:60) partakes of the characteristics of the first and second halves of the book and serves as a transition between them.[60] Like the previous sections, it begins by setting the scene and recounting Ezra's prayer (9:27-37) and continues with the appearance of what in retrospect is a supernatural figure with whom Ezra engages in a dialog (9:38—10:24). As its second half makes clear, the section also parallels the next two sections (chaps. 11–12 and 13) with their symbolic visions and angelic interpretations. The woman is transformed into a splendid vision of the heavenly Zion come to earth (10:25-27), and upon Ezra's cry Uriel appears and interprets the double vision of the woman and the city (10:29-59).[61] In his prayer Ezra laments Israel's inability to bring forth the fruit of the Torah that has been sown within them (9:29-37). It is an expansion on a subject that to this point has been an occasional but not a major topic of discussion.[62] His complaint is met by the appearance of a lamenting woman, who complains about the death of her son (9:38—10:27). Ezra consoles her with the promise of the resurrection and by comparing her loss to "the troubles of Zion" and "the sorrow of Jerusalem" (10:5-24). At this point the woman's face is gloriously transfigured, and then as the earth quakes she disappears and Ezra is confronted by the splendor of the heavenly Jerusalem (10:25-27). Uriel interprets the vision: the woman was Zion, mourning the loss of the earthly city (10:29-54). Uriel invites Ezra to enter the Holy City, to view its infinite splendor, and to "hear as much as your ears can hear" (10:55-57). The author does not make explicit whether the heavenly Jerusalem that Ezra visits and which will be revealed in the end time (cf. 7:26) will be a restored and glorified earthly Jerusalem or the heavenly place to which the resurrected righteous will ascend.[63] The section ends as Uriel promises new revelations in the form of dream visions (10:58-59).[64]

When we compare the vision and Ezra's response to it with the angelic interpretation, we can see how this section functions in the seer's own progress from complaint to consolation.[65]

Vision and Response	Interpretation	Ezra's Progress
The woman grieves	The woman is Zion	Ezra grieves over Zion
Ezra consoles her with promise of resurrection		Ezra's consolation can be applied to himself
The woman is transformed into a glorious city	The new Zion	because of the revealed promise of the new Zion

Thus the episode of Ezra and the woman parallels Ezra's previous interaction with the angel. Zion, like Ezra, grieves over the destruction of Jerusalem; and Ezra, like Uriel, speaks words of consolation. Ezra has undergone a profound religious reorientation.[66] Having given up his previous stance of antagonism, or at least puzzlement regarding the ways of the Most High, he assumes the role of the angelic interpreter and the consoler of the grieving one. A hint of the pivotal function of this section is given in Ezra's repeated statement that he dismissed the thoughts with which he had been engaged (9:39; 10:5). In spite of his own grief he begins to console the woman. Although Ezra continues to speak of the desolation of Zion (10:6-13, 20-23), for the first time in the book he utters words of hope. Similarly, the angel finally acknowledges the genuine character of Ezra's distress (10:39, 50) and speaks words of encouragement to him. In the glory of the heavenly Zion and in its promise, he will find consolation for the grief with which the book began. Now he is ready to receive visions of what God will do in the last days (10:58). The linkage between inquiring complaint and eschatological answer, which is internal to the first three sections, is repeated here as God answers Ezra's complaint with a vision of the glorious Jerusalem. The same connection will be made externally between the dialogical visions as a group (sections 1–4) and the symbolic visions as a group (sections 5–6).

Chapters 11–13 (sections 5 and 6) contain two dream visions of the end time together with their interpretations. The visions are traditional, based in part on Daniel 7. The interpretations also include traditional material, though in their present form they reflect the thought of the author of 4 Ezra.[67]

Chapters 11–12 (section 5) are an exposition of the four-kingdom vision in Daniel 7.[68] Like 2 Baruch 36–40 and Revelation 13 they understand the last kingdom to be the Roman Empire. The three heads of the eagle represent the three Flavian emperors (Vespasian, Titus, and Domitian) and thus indicate a date around the end of the reign of Domitian (± 96 C.E.).[69] The last kingdom is confronted by the Messiah, here depicted as the Lion from the tribe of Judah. Although he comes from the family of David, the Messiah is thought to be preexistent (12:32). He functions as accuser and judge of Rome (11:38-46; 12:32-33), bringing that empire and its oppression to an end. Conversely, he is the helper and deliverer of Israel. In these functions he differs from the one like a son of man in Daniel 7 but parallels the Chosen One in the Parables of Enoch (see above, pp. 250–53). After receiving this vision and its interpretation, Ezra gathers the people and speaks words of comfort to them (12:40-50). This consolation is again in marked contrast to Ezra's grief in the first half of the book.

The vision of the man from the sea and its interpretation are the subject matter of section 6 (chap. 13). The central figure is called "man" in the vision and "(my) son *or* servant" (*filius*) in the interpretation. Although he is called "Messiah," his characteristics and functions parallel those attributed to the Messiah in chapters 7 and 11–12. He is preexistent (6:26), protector of the righteous remnant (vv 23-29), judge (vv 37-38), and warrior (vv 9-11, 49).[70] The section ends with the seer's doxology (v 57), a feature typical of some apocalyptic visionary material (e.g., 1 Enoch 21–36) but again in notable contrast to Ezra's earlier complaints.

In the seventh and final section of 4 Ezra the seer is depicted as a prophet, indeed, the second Moses, while at the same time his scribal functions are stressed. At God's behest, Ezra admonishes the people to be obedient, promising them mercy and eternal life if they do so (vv 34-35). The section is remarkable in view of Ezra's previous complaints that only a few are able to be righteous. For this reason some scholars take it to be a later addition to the book.[71] As it stands, however, it resolves Ezra's previous skepticism. After this admonition, Ezra receives special divine inspiration, which enables him to dictate for future preservation twenty-four books—the writings of Moses and the rest of the Hebrew Scriptures, which had evidently been lost in the destruction of Jerusalem (14:21)—as well as seventy esoteric books received by Moses, which are to be read only by the wise (vv 5-7, 23-26, 44-48). Thus the portrait of the seer is brought into line with the historical Ezra, who, we are told, brought the Torah to Jerusalem (Neh 8:1-8). With this emphasis on Ezra's admonition that the people obey the Torah and his transmission of that Torah for future generations, the apocalypse concludes (4 Ezra 14:37-48). His receipt and transmission of revelation completed, Ezra will now be taken to heaven, "where you shall live with my Son [i.e., the Messiah] and with those who are like you, until the times are ended" (14:9).

The author of 4 Ezra has been badly scarred by the events of the year 70. The fall of Jerusalem, he asserts, was the result of Israel's sin. Indeed, so massive was the disaster that it must be that the number of the sinners vastly exceeds that of the righteous. The nature of the predicament is even deeper. Israel's sinfulness stands side by side with the nation's election and the gift of the Torah, which are unable to overcome the evil heart that has been with the human race since Adam.[72] Given these circumstances, Israel's punishment at the hands of sinful Gentiles is the more incomprehensible. Taken together, these observations and speculations verge on an indictment of the God who is creator and initiator of the covenant.

The writer of this apocalypse finds two answers to this line of questioning. The first, which is not totally different from the book of Job, is no answer at all. God simply pulls rank, maintaining that no human can hope to understand God's ways, asserting divine love for the creation, and finally forbidding any further questions by the seer. God's second answer takes up a traditional apocalyptic response. There is no explanation as to *why* God tolerates sin; instead the seer's attention is directed to God's *solution* of the problem: the coming judgment and the beginning of a new age that is free from the troubles that came into the present age with Adam's sin. The function of the visions in chapters 9–13 is to assure the seer that this age is coming and that it will come soon. At the same time, material in the dialogs reminds the reader that the time until the *eschaton* cannot be shortened.

Ezra's questions are well put and reflect intellectual and religious honesty. The answers he receives fall short of the rigors of systematic theological inquiry, but they appear to have been religiously satisfying to the author.[73] Perhaps this is an indication that "the odyssey of Ezra's soul," as it is recounted in the narrative, mirrors the religious experience of the author as he moved from sorrow and doubt to faith and hope in God's future.[74]

For all his agonized probing of the questions of theodicy, the author indicates by the structure of his book that the present grief is to be overcome by consolation—just as Ezra was so moved. God's answer is not an explanation, but it is a promise. Moreover, since the Judge holds people responsible for their deeds, obedience to the Torah is a possibility, though not an easy one, and to this end, when all is said and done, Ezra publishes the Scriptures.[75] As the age moves toward its end and the Roman eagle is on the verge of faltering in its final flight, God's people are called to faith and obedience while they await the glory of Zion.

The social context of 4 Ezra is uncertain. The book shows no certain connection with any known Jewish group.[76] Perhaps the author was associated in some way with the rabbis in Yavneh,[77] but we should not exclude that theological activity in response to the events of 70 C.E. took place in places other than Yavneh, and it is noteworthy that 4 Ezra appears to have made no impression on the rabbinic traditions. What we do know is that this author did not write in a social vacuum, since a comparison of 4 Ezra and 2 Baruch indicates that these two authors were in theological dialogue with one another (see below, pp. 283–85). There seems to be some evidence in 4 Ezra 14:44-47 that this author wrote his apocalypse not for general consumption, but with a learned audience in mind.[78] Nonetheless, 14:27-35 and Ezra's command to promulgate the twenty-four books of the Hebrew Scriptures to the public indicates the author's concern for more than a learned circle of the wise. Perhaps the wise were to serve as teachers and ministers to the public.[79] This is a function that is explicit in 2 Baruch (see below, p. 282).

Fourth Ezra was most likely composed in Hebrew and then translated into Greek and from Greek into a variety of languages.[80] Perhaps as early as the second century, a Christian editor prefaced the Greek apocalypse with two chapters (5 Ezra), which radically alter its tone.[81] The basic shift is evident in the repeated assertion that God has forsaken Israel and given the divine name to other nations (4 Ezra 1:24-26, 33-37; 2:10-11). Mother Zion must take leave of her children permanently (2:1-7). In her place is Mother Church, who awaits her sons in the resurrection (2:15-17, 30-32).[82] Ezra's admonition to the people failed (cf. 2:33 with chap. 14). His publication of the Scriptures was ineffectual. God will give his prophets to his new people, the church (1:38-40; 2:18). It is they and "the Son of God" who will inherit Mount Zion (2:42-47). In the late third century or early fourth century C.E. another Christian author composed an appendix to the book (2 Esdras 15–16 = 6 Ezra), which spoke to Christians during a time of persecution.[83]

2 Baruch

Like 4 Ezra, 2 Baruch is an apocalypse or collection of apocalypses.[84] Its revelatory components are held together by a running narrative that describes Baruch's transformation from one who bitterly laments the fall of Jerusalem to the consoler of his people, and that recounts how Baruch prepares his people for the transition from his leadership to that of the teachers who will succeed him when he departs this life. There is general consensus among scholars that, like 4 Ezra, 2 Baruch divides into seven major sections, although the extent of the units is less clear, and there is some disagreement as to where some of the sections begin and end and whether Baruch's epistle (chaps. 78–87) was part of the original composition.[85]

Chapters 1–9 describe the fall of Jerusalem, thus providing a setting for the rest of the apocalypse.[86] (There is no counterpart to this narrative in 4 Ezra.) The section interweaves narrative, possibly drawn from an earlier source,[87] with the kind of dialogue that will recur throughout the work. Baruch is depicted as a prophet (1:1) who is surprisingly the superior of Jeremiah (2:1; 5:5; 9:1; 10:2).[88] God announces that the city will be destroyed because of the sins of the people and commands Baruch and Jeremiah to depart because their good deeds and prayers are protecting the city from the destruction that must come (2:2). The distraught Baruch responds with a flurry of questions that reduce to three: the future of Israel and hence the honor of God (3:4-6); the future of the world and of the human race (3:7-8); the validity of God's promises to Moses (3:9).

God's initial response is brief (4:1). The destruction of the city and the captivity of the people are temporary. God has not canceled the covenantal promises or stripped Israel and the city of their status. The captivity is, moreover, chastisement rather than final punishment. The present crisis is not a sign of the coming annihilation of world and humanity. As for the present city, it is a mere shadow of the heavenly Jerusalem, which God revealed to the patriarchs and which God holds in reserve for the future (4:2-7). This motif of two worlds—the heavenly and the earthly—will return in the author's exposition.[89]

When Baruch worries that the enemy's victory will threaten God's name, he learns that it is God who will destroy the city (chap. 5). The ensuing narrative describes this destruction (chaps. 6–8). As in Ezekiel 8–11, God abandons the temple before it is captured. Both the opening of the city and the voice from the temple are mentioned in Josephus's account (*J.W.* 6.293–300 [§6.5.3]).[90] As for the temple furnishings and vessels, an angel commits them to the earth, where they are to be hidden until the latter times, when they and Jerusalem will be restored (6:5-10).[91] The section concludes as Baruch, along with Jeremiah, engages in the first of several seven-day fasts, which are preludes to revelation.[92] The motif of lamentation, repeated throughout this section (5:6; 6:2; 9:2), is typical of 2 Baruch and may be related to the biblical Jeremiah tradition (i.e., the book of Lamentations).

The second major section of the book begins a set of disputations between Baruch and God that corresponds to the disputations in sections 1–3 in 4 Ezra. Here, as in 4 Ezra 3, the section begins with a lament by the seer and depicts him in dialog with God (2 Bar 10–20). After Jeremiah has left for Babylon, Baruch goes to the temple to lament over Zion and to await a revelation about what will happen "at the end of days" (10:1-5), a subject about which he had earlier expressed concern (cf. 3:7-8). Baruch's lament begins with a beatitude for those who have not been born or who died before the destruction of Jerusalem (10:6-7; cf. 11:6-7). He then appeals to nature and humanity to join his lament. Under the circumstances, business as usual is inappropriate (10:8-19). Chapters 11–12 deal mainly with the paradox that Babylon prospers while Israel suffers (cf. 4 Ezra 3:28-36), and Baruch warns the Gentile nation of God's coming wrath. Another seven-day fast anticipates the revelation that follows (2 Bar 12:5).

Chapters 13–20 are a long, complex dialogue between God and Baruch on the subject of theodicy. The seer misperceives the present contrasting circumstances of Israel and the Gentiles (chap. 13). Because the Gentiles fail to appreciate their prosperity as God's blessing, they will fall victim to God's future wrath.[93] Israel's present misfortune, however, is divine chastisement that will later turn to mercy (cf. also 1:4; 4:1).[94] Baruch responds with a series of objections (chap. 14). Few of the nations that now prosper will still exist at the time of God's wrath (vv 1-3). The righteous, by contrast, have been carried off; God has not forgiven Zion for their sake but has punished her for the evil deeds of the wicked (vv 4-7). Obviously God's judgments cannot be known by mere mortals (vv 8-11; cf. 4 Ezra 5:35-40). Although the righteous who die await eternal life (2 Bar 14:12-13), those who remain suffer (vv 14-15). God's promise to Israel goes begging.

The world remains, but Israel—on whose account the world was made—passes away (vv 16-19; cf. 4 Ezra 6:59). Although God's response in chapter 15 alludes to Baruch's objections, it does not answer all of them. Verses 1-6 assert human responsibility on the basis of an assumed knowledge of the Torah; hence divine judgment is to be expected. Verses 7-8 contrast this world and the world to come. In the place of the present world, which is characterized by labor and misery, God has prepared for the righteous another world and a glorious crown.[95]

Significant in the dialog in chapters 17–20 is the mention of Moses (17:4) and the covenant and Torah. God again asserts human responsibility under the Torah (19:1-4) and then turns to a consideration of the end. What is important is not present distress but future glory. The time is near, and the destruction of Zion is God's way of hastening the end (19:4—20:2). God promises new revelation, and he commands Baruch to fast for seven days in preparation for it (20:3-6).

In the third section, this revelation again takes place in the context of a dialogue between Baruch and God, and it provides details about "the consummation of the times" (chaps. 21–30).[96] Chapter 21 is one of several lengthy prayers in the book. The extended doxology (vv 4-12) touches on the qualities of God that are the ground for Baruch's expectation that his petition will be heard (vv 8, 12). Baruch's complaint about the misery and instability of "this life" (vv 13-17) leads to a twofold petition that dwells on the problem of mortality. First is the question, "How long will the corruptible and the mortal continue?" (v 19). More important is Baruch's repeated and impassioned plea that God hasten the time of the end (vv 20-26). God answers the double petition in reverse order (cf. 4 Ezra 4:33-50). Employing a set of parabolic illustrations (2 Bar 22), God states that the time of the end has already been decreed and cannot hasten. Mortality must continue until the foreordained number of humans have been born (23:1-5). Nonetheless, in answer to Baruch's first query God promises that divine redemption has "drawn near" and is "not distant as before," and the judgment will take place (23:6—24:2).

In the dialogue that follows, God discusses how near the time is and the nature and extent of the woes that will come on the world (24:3—29:2). After the woes the Messiah will appear and the earth will blossom like paradise (29:3—30:1).[97] Then when the reign of the Messiah is complete and he has returned to heaven, the event awaited by Baruch will occur.[98] The dead will rise and mortality will come to an end (30:2-5; cf. 21:22-26).

The fourth section begins a second cycle in 2 Baruch's narrative. In it the elders' lament over the departure of their "father" (32:9) parallels Baruch's previous lament over his "mother" (3:1), and Baruch begins to play the role of instructor and comforter rather than the one in need of comfort.[99] In the narrative introduction, Baruch tells the people to assemble their elders for instruction (31:1-2). This instruction (31:3—34:1) is based in part on the previous revelation. The times are bad and will get worse. The (second) temple will be rebuilt and destroyed "until the time." Then when God renews the creation, it will be renewed and perfected forever (32:3-6), but the people are to prepare their hearts by faithful adherence to the Torah (32:1-2). When Baruch announces that he must leave the people for the present, they lament his absence (32:7—33:3; cf. 4 Ezra

5:16-19). He assures them that his departure is only temporary for the purpose of receiving new revelation (2 Bar 34). The scene as a whole foreshadows chapters 45–46 and 77, raising in a preliminary way the problem of a leadership vacuum.

Chapters 35–47 parallel chapters 10–34. Baruch returns to the temple and laments over Zion (chap. 35; cf. chaps. 10–12). God responds, this time with a vision and its interpretation (chaps. 36–40). Like the revelation in chapters 29–30, the vision, or at least its interpretation,[100] emphasizes the role of the Messiah (39:7—40:4). Like 4 Ezra 11:1—12:3, it may represent older tradition. Its imagery parallels Daniel 2, 4, 7, and 4 Ezra 4:13-18. In common with the Danielic visions it predicts the destruction of a great power. Second Baruch 39 interprets the vision in terms of the four kingdoms of Daniel 7, with the last kingdom being Rome (cf. 4 Ezra 11–12). Like 4 Ezra 12:10-19 and different from Daniel 7, the central figure (here and in 4 Ezra, the Messiah) is the executor of divine judgment against Israel's enemies. As in 2 Baruch 29–30 (and chap. 72) the time of the Messiah precedes the end of the corruptible world (40:3). After another exchange about the final fate of apostates and proselytes (chaps. 41–42), God informs Baruch that he must soon leave this world and commands the seer to gather the people for some testamentary instruction (chap. 43).

In the fifth section Baruch assembles the people, informs them of his imminent departure from this world, fasts for seven days, and receives a new revelation from God (chaps. 44–52). The scene in chapters 44–47 parallels chapters 31–34, except that now Baruch tells the people he is leaving them permanently (cf. 4 Ezra 12:40-50). His speech is a reprise of themes familiar to the reader. Adherence to the Torah will bring the consolation of Zion (2 Bar 44:3-7). This will mean the end of corruption and mortality and the beginning of a new world that will not pass away (vv 8-15). The people again object, protesting that there will be no one to teach them the Torah and to lead them on the paths of life (46:1-3). Baruch assures them that there will be no lack of leadership. The wise will be there, and the people should prepare to submit to their wisdom and to obey the Torah (46:4-5). Then the good things he announced will come to pass (46:6).

Now Baruch sets out for Hebron, where he fasts seven days in preparation for a final revelation (chap. 47). Chapters 48–52 consist of a prayer and ensuing dialog. The extended doxology focuses on God as Creator and Lord of the times (48:1-10; cf. 21:4-12). The complaint in vv 11-17 parallels 21:13-17 somewhat. The petition in 48:18-24 suits Baruch's situation admirably. It is a departing leader's intercessory prayer in behalf of his people (cf. Jesus' prayer in John 17). They are God's people, God's "little ones," in need of God's compassionate help. They will find this in the divine Wisdom that is resident in the Torah. As in 2 Baruch 25–27 God responds with reference to the coming woes and the judgment (48:25-41). Verses 38-47 focus on the fate of the wicked, and vv 48-50 treat the hope of the righteous, who will be relieved of the labors of this world.

This motif leads to a discussion of the resurrection and the resurrection body (chaps. 49–52), expanding on 30:2-5. Baruch's question in chapter 49 follows naturally from the context, and indeed from much of the previous discussion. In the resurrection will the righteous be rid of those bodies that have partaken of the weakness and evil of this world (chap. 49)? God states that after recognition has taken place (chap. 50),[101] the righteous and the wicked will be separated (51:1-6). Those who have been faithful to the Torah and have trusted in its wisdom will ascend into the heights of heaven, be transformed into the likeness of the stars and the angels (cf. Dan 12:3; 1 Enoch 104:2), and enjoy the blessings of paradise and the world—now invisible—that does not die (2 Bar 51:1-13). Thus the problem of mortality and corruptibility, as it related the nature of human beings, is resolved by means of his two-worlds scheme.[102] After some further observations on the unhappy fate that awaits those who have turned from Torah and denied their future (51:14—52:3), the author returns to the future reward of the righteous, which allows them to rejoice in their present sufferings (52:3-7).

The sixth section of 2 Baruch contains a vision about the dark and bright waters in a cloud (chap. 53), Baruch's prayer requesting an interpretation (chap. 54), an appearance by the angel Ramiel, who interprets the vision at great length (chaps. 55–74), Baruch's response (chap. 75), and Ramiel's command that Baruch set his house in order (chap. 76). As in chapters 36–40 Baruch responds to his vision with a prayer. The doxology acknowledges God as omniscient and the revealer (54:1-5). It is on these grounds that Baruch asks for an interpretation (vv 6, 20). The major part of the prayer is, however, a hymn of praise. As such it stands in striking contrast to the laments that have pervaded previous chapters (contrast esp. v 10 with 10:6).

Turning to the subject of theodicy, Baruch affirms what God has asserted on a number of occasions, namely, human responsibility. Though it was Adam who first sinned and brought misery and death into the world (23:4-5; 56:5-6), each descendant of Adam is his own Adam (54:14-19; contrast 54:15 with 48:42-43).[103] Ramiel's interpretation of the vision divides the history of Israel into alternating periods of righteousness and wickedness. The sin of Adam was foundational and brought to the world all the evils that Baruch is experiencing in his own time (56:5-6). The alternating periods of good and evil focus on covenant, Torah, and Zion; judgment, eternal reward, and eternal punishment—topics central to Baruch's exposition throughout the book. The interpretation of the last black waters describes again the woes to come (chap. 70). According to chapter 72, as in 39:7—40:4, the Messiah will function as judge over the Gentiles. The detailing of the criterion for salvation or destruction of the Gentiles is unique to this literature, and the references to "those who have trodden down Israel" (72:4) speaks to Israel's defeat by Rome. After the Messiah has subdued all things, the consummation will take place and the evils that Adam brought will be reversed (73:1—74:1; cf. 56:5-6). It will be a physical world, with women giving birth, bodies not subject to disease, reapers bringing in the harvest, wild animals and children playing together, and people not suffering an untimely death. It will be the end of what is corruptible, and the beginning of what is not corruptible (74:2).

Baruch responds with a doxology of God's unsearchable goodness, compassion, and wisdom (75:1-6). In two parallel verses (vv 7-8) he lays out the two alternatives before Israel: to obey the God of the exodus (and the Torah) and thus to remember the divine chastisement and rejoice; or to reject God (and the Torah) and thus to revert to previous wickedness and the grief that characterizes Israel's present existence.

Baruch is now ready for his farewell (chap. 76). In keeping with the heavy stress on the Torah and the previous references to the exodus, the section is reminiscent of the last chapters of Deuteronomy and their depiction of Moses' last days (cf. 4 Ezra 14).[104] Baruch is to instruct the people so that they can survive the last times. Then after forty days he will receive a vision of the whole earth and depart—not to die—but be preserved by God until the consummation (2 Bar 76).[105] Baruch's farewell is reminiscent of chapters 31–34 and 44–47. The motif of sin and punishment is repeated. The issue of leadership is discussed, and Baruch assures the people that the Torah will spawn its interpreters in spite of the evident darkness of the present situation. At the request of the people he writes two epistles to the exiled tribes and sends them via eagle.[106]

Chapters 78–87 purport to be the epistle that Baruch sent to the tribes exiled in Assyria. In their content, themes, and wording they have much in common with chapters 1–77, and in a way they summarize the issues discussed in the apocalypse.[107] Chapters 78–80 recapitulate the narrative in chapters 1–9. Chapters 81–82 offer consolation, largely with reference to the coming judgment of the Gentiles. Chapters 83–84 contain admonitions to prepare for the imminent judgment by obeying the Torah. Chapter 85 stresses the nearness of the end and the finality of the judgment (cf. 23:6—24:2). A majority of scholars think the epistle is part of the original composition, but there are some dissenters.[108] For the placement of an author's epistle at the end of an apocalyptic collection, one may compare 1 Enoch 92–105 (see above, pp. 110–14). For the content of a "text" being placed *after* a narrative that describes it, one may compare 1 Enoch 14–16 and 1 Enoch 84.

Second Baruch focuses on two issues: temple and Torah. The Romans' destruction of Jerusalem and its temple has raised the question of God's justice, and the author presents some answers. God was chastising Israel but will surely punish the Gentiles responsible for Israel's desolation.[109] The present tribulations notwithstanding, covenantal promises are intact. The Zion destroyed by the Roman armies will be restored. The judgment and access to the age and world of incorruption are near. However, between destruction and the hope of a new age lie the lamentable facts of life in the present. It is not by accident that this author speaks so often of "sorrow, grief, and lamentation" and that his book contains a number of laments. Reality as the author perceives it is a world marked by trouble, grief, and death—an understandable point of view in the wake of the Jewish War. Although the root of the situation was Adam's sin, his transgression has constantly repeated, and sinners are wholly responsible for their deeds. The accumulation of such sin had to be judged, and this happened in the destruction of Jerusalem. But the God who chastens the people will have mercy: the age and world of sorrow will give way to the age and world that does not die; mortality will surrender to incorruptibility; death will be overcome by life—all this in God's good time. The author encourages his people to obey the Torah (which the nation has forsaken) in the meantime. Such obedience is possible for those who heed the teaching of the leaders whom God will provide,[110] and it will fill the vacuum left by the desolation of Zion and prepare the souls of God's people for the joys of the world to come.

Precisely how the future reversal will take place is unclear. Although the author contrasts this present corrupt world with the incorruptible realm of heaven (4:2-6; 51:7-14), and although he describes the resurrected righteous soaring in the heights of heaven, he also envisions the renewal of creation (29:2-8; 73:1—74:1) and the restoration of Zion (6:5-10; 32:3-6). Most probably we are dealing with different traditions that stand in tension with one another. Yet they must have made sense to the author. Perhaps he expects that the righteous now dead will ascend to heaven after their resurrection, that the renewed creation will endure, and that those who have lived a long and full life will ascend to heaven.[111] Such a scenario has precedents in early Jewish texts, notably in 1 Enoch and perhaps Daniel 12:1-3.[112]

The precise dating of the apocalypse is uncertain. Arguments based on its relationship to 4 Ezra are tenuous[113] because that relationship is uncertain. I simply suggest that it was written toward the end of the first century C.E.[114] The author is still deeply grieved by the events of the year 70. Unlike the author of 4 Ezra, however, he has not produced studied speculations on theodicy. His interest is primarily "pastoral" and practical. His own grief has given way to consolation. His admonitions to "prepare your souls" are part of that consolation and, together with his exhortations to heed God's sages and teachers, they focus on the practical task of reconstruction.

Second Baruch in its entirety is extant in one Syriac manuscript and one Arabic manuscript representing a translation from Syriac.[115] The Syriac version was translated from Greek, which itself may have been a translation of a Semitic original.[116]

The Relationship between 4 Ezra and 2 Baruch

This discussion has shown that there is an especially close relationship between 4 Ezra and 2 Baruch. Both apocalypses are pseudonymously attributed to scribes in antiquity and employ the first destruction of Jerusalem in 587 B.C.E. as a fictional setting for a treatment of the second destruction in 70 C.E. The apocalypses have a similar narrative line. The scribe, in a state of grief and emotional turmoil, disputes with God or God's angel about the lack of divine justice that has permitted the Gentiles to overrun the city and sanctuary of the covenant people. As the story progresses, the divine appeal to an eschatological resolution transforms the seer into the role of consoler. The revelations that catalyze this transformation occur both in dialogs that involve dispute, along with queries for eschatological information, and in symbolic dreams that are interpreted by God or God's angel. The apocalypses end with the seer playing the role of a second Moses, providing hope for the people and providing for the ongoing instruction in the Torah.

In addition to this parallel in structure, the two apocalypses have many formal, thematic, and verbal parallels.[117] A few of these include a concern about the viability of the covenant; the appeal to a doctrine of the two ages/worlds as an answer to present misery; a focus on the place of Adam as the cause or originator of human sin and death; dream visions that depict the coming of a transcendent Messiah at the conclusion of a four-kingdom period in history.

Taken together these structural, formal, thematic, and verbal parallels almost certainly indicate a literary relationship between the two apocalypses.[118] This need not mean that one of the authors necessarily had the other's work in front of him, but could indicate that one of them had at some time read the other's apocalypse (or heard it read) and had digested its contents. Among scholars who accept this hypothesis there are four points of view: 4 Ezra was dependent on 2 Baruch;[119] 2 Baruch was dependent on 4 Ezra;[120] both were dependent on a common source;[121] we cannot determine the direction of the dependence.[122]

While the last of these options is the most cautious, five factors may constitute some cumulative evidence that tips the balance in favor of the priority of 4 Ezra. First, in 4 Ezra 14 the seer's role as a second Moses parallels the role of the biblical Ezra, who brought the Torah to Jerusalem according to Nehemiah 8:1-8. In 2 Baruch, however, none of the Mosaic characteristics ascribed to Baruch is paralleled in biblical or earlier postbiblical traditions about Baruch. Second, the narrative of the seer who undergoes a development from mourner to consoler is part of an organic narrative and formal development in 4 Ezra, while in 2 Baruch the seer seems much less in need of consolation.[123] Third, the sevenfold division in 4 Ezra is clean-cut and obvious, while in 2 Baruch the outline is messier, and the boundaries of the sections are more difficult to determine. Fourth, as has often been observed, it seems more likely that 2 Baruch has tried to tame 4 Ezra's speculations about Adam and the cause of sin, than that 4 Ezra has pushed 2 Baruch's rather tame observations into more dangerous theological territory.[124] Finally, the four-kingdom eschatology can be traced more easily to its Danielic source in 4 Ezra 11–12 than in 2 Baruch 36–40. To test these observations, it would be useful to compare parallel sections in 4 Ezra and 2 Baruch to see whether the shorter forms (in Baruch usually) are compressions of the longer forms, or the longer forms are expansions of the shorter forms.

If 2 Baruch is dependent on 4 Ezra, one can see a number of factors at work. First, in 2 Baruch the disputations are prefaced by a (traditional?) narrative about the destruction of Jerusalem that sets the stage for the material that follows, much as narrative in 1 Enoch 6–11 prepares one for the Enochic traditions in chapters 12–36 (see above, pp. 46–52). Second, "Baruch" portrays the seer in colors that derive from the Jeremianic tradition (notably the laments). Third, the narrative depicts extensive interaction between the seer and the people, including repeated concern about filling the leadership vacuum when Baruch leaves permanently. Fourth, in this respect the narrative takes on some of the characteristics of the testamentary form, including some elements drawn from biblical and postbiblical Mosaic tradition.[125] Fifth, in keeping with the democratizing of the seer's interaction with the people, Baruch's final transmission is not a corpus of esoteric wisdom for the few (4 Ezra 14:45-47), but a letter sent to the tribes in captivity (2 Bar 78–87). Finally, as noted, Baruch's theological speculations are tamer than some of Ezra's daring questions and formulations.

Doubtless, some of the aforementioned points can be argued in the opposite direction, and one may wish to accept a position of uncertainty. However that may be, a careful comparison of the two texts can be historically fruitful. In any case we have two authors in the post-destruction period in dialog with one another as they wrestle with the existential and theological questions that have arisen from the catastrophe of the year 70, and as they reshape tradition to fit what they perceive to be their situation and to fit the persona of the ancient figure with whom they identify their revelation.[126] There is perhaps some analogy for this in the composition of the early Christian Gospels.

The Apocalypse of Abraham

Like the book of Daniel, this seldom-read apocalypse divides into two major sections. The narrative section describes Abraham's conversion from idolatry, and the apocalyptic section depicts his ascent to heaven, where he is granted a vision of the enthroned Deity and revelations of the cosmos and of the future.

Chapters 1–8 recount Abraham's progress from his search for the true identity of the Mighty God to God's self-revelation to Abraham. A series of three incidents demonstrates the helplessness of idols (chaps. 1–5). The story focuses on Abraham's cogitations on these episodes, which begin with perplexity and end with inner laughter over the folly of idolatry. This folly is exemplified by Abraham's father, Terah the idol maker. In the climax of the story Abraham chides his father for foolishly resisting the obvious lesson of their experience, and he calls on the Creator for a theophany (chaps. 6–7). God answers the prayer of the seeker and commands him to depart from his father's house (cf. Gen 12:1), which is immediately reduced to ashes (Apoc. Abr. 8). This story draws on older traditions about Abraham's conversion from idolatry (cf. Jub. 11:16—12:31) and his escape from Ur (Heb. *'ûr* means "fire") of the Chaldeans (cf. Jub. 12:12-14; L.A.B. 6). The author expounds Genesis 12:1 and casts into narrative form traditional polemics that stress the helplessness of idols and the folly of idolatry.[127]

The theophany and sacrifice in Genesis 15 provide the occasion for Abraham's visions in the Apocalypse. Chapters 9–13 describe this occasion. Abraham hears the voice of God, who is revealed as Creator and who promises visions because Abraham has searched for God and has been named as God's "friend" (chap. 9; cf. Isa 41:8). Appropriately, Abraham's helper and guide to the heavenly regions is the archangel Yahoel, who bears the name of God (YHWH)[128] and is most closely associated with the divine throne (Apoc. Abr. 17–18). He appears to Abraham, strengthens him after his confrontation with God, and instructs him about the sacrifice (chaps. 10–12). The devil, here called Azazel (cf. 1 Enoch 6–16),[129] appears as a bird of prey (cf. Gen 15:11; Jub. 11:11), and deceitfully attempts to dissuade Abraham from offering the sacrifice (Apoc. Abr. 13–14). His intention is blocked by Yahoel (Iaoel), who commands him to leave and gives Abraham the necessary words of exorcism. The scene is reminiscent of other stories in which the angel of the Lord confronts Satan, who is attempting to frustrate God's purposes by disqualifying or annihilating God's agent.[130] Especially noteworthy is the parallel with

Zechariah 3, where the satan (the accusing angel) attempts to disqualify Joshua as high priest.[131] At stake here is Abraham's future as patriarch, for it is only in chapter 20 that he receives the promise of progeny.

Chapters 15–18 describe Abraham's ascent to heaven and his vision of God. The sacrificial birds, which Abraham has not slaughtered (chaps. 12, 15; cf. Gen 15:10), transport Abraham and Yahoel to heaven. The fire of the divine presence (Gen 15:17) increases and defines itself as the angelic entourage and finally the divine Glory itself (Apoc. Abr. 16–17). The hymn of praise that Yahoel has taught Abraham is the song of the angelic attendants of the throne (chap. 17; cf. chap. 10). Its repetitious recitation of divine names and attributes is paralleled in the angelic songs of later ascent texts of Jewish mysticism.[132] To the extended doxology is appended a brief petition that God accept the prayer and sacrifice of him who "sought" God and that God grant Abraham the revelation that was promised him. The description of God's throne in chapter 18 is drawn from Ezekiel 1.

God now grants Abraham a series of visions, which God interprets. From the highest heaven Abraham looks down on the seventh, sixth, and fifth heavens, which are inhabited by various classes of angels (Apoc. Abr. 19). Abraham's vision of the "powers of the stars" in the fifth heaven leads to God's command that he count them and to the promise that Abraham's innumerable descendants will be God's chosen people (chap. 20; cf. Gen 15:5). God's reference to Azazel's presence in the world causes the patriarch to inquire about the problem of evil.

Abraham's question leads to a second vision, which is divided into a number of segments. Structuring the whole are the format of vision, question, and answer and the device of a divine–human discourse about the problem of evil (cf. 4 Ezra and 2 Baruch passim). Abraham looks through the heavens to the earth beneath them and to the underworld and the place of torment (Apoc. Abr. 21; cf. 1 Enoch 17–32). Within the frame of this cosmic view Abraham sees like a great picture the events of history played out as a series of vignettes.[133] The picture is divided into a left side and a right side, which are inhabited by the Gentiles and by Israel, respectively, whom God has set apart as God's people (Apoc. Abr. 22). In effect the author has built the distinction between Jews and Gentiles into the cosmic structure.

The first vignette depicts the fall (chaps. 23–24). Abraham asks why God has permitted Azazel to rule over the wicked. God explains that God has delivered those who *will* to do evil into the power of the devil, who prods them to do evil. Abraham presses the question further: why does God permit sin to be willed? The answer at the beginning of chapter 24 is obscure, perhaps due to textual corruption; however, it refers to the Gentiles' ill-treatment of Israel—one of the author's special concerns.[134]

Abraham witnesses the murder of Abel. Then he sees human actions representing impurity, theft, passion, and desire, as well as their punishment (chap. 24; cf. T. Abr. 10).

The last segments of Abraham's vision center on the temple and its cult. In the first of these segments (Apoc. Abr. 25) he sees an idealized vision of the temple and its altar, which correspond to their heavenly counterparts beneath the throne of God.[135] This vision is marred, however, by the presence of cultic abominations: an idol like those that Terah made, which provokes God's jealousy or wrath (cf. Ezek 8:3, 5); and a man who "incites" child sacrifice (cf. 2 Kgs 21:4-7; 2 Chr 33:4-6, of Manasseh). Abraham asks why God permits this to happen and then condemns it (Apoc. Abr. 26). God cites the examples of Terah and Abraham, who freely chose, respectively, to continue in idolatry and to abandon it. God's will, however, is reserved for the coming days.

Chapters 27–29 are the main eschatological section of the Apocalypse of Abraham. Abraham sees the Gentiles destroy Jerusalem and burn the temple (chap. 27). God has permitted this as punishment for cultic abominations that Abraham had earlier witnessed. Abraham asks, "How, long?" (chap. 28). God responds in terms of Genesis 15:16. The precise chronology of this section is obscure. The division of the present age into twelve parts is, however, reminiscent of a similar division in 4 Ezra 14:12 and 2 Baruch 27; 53:6. In Apocalypse of Abraham 29, vv 3-13 have usually been identified as a Christian interpolation, describing Jesus and Jewish and Gentile responses to him. However, the vision (vv 3-6) is better read as a description of the anti-God figure who attracts Gentiles to him and leads some of the Jews astray; we need read only v 9b in the interpretation as a gloss possibly by a Christian interpolator.[136] The last part of chapter 29 describes the end time. Abraham's descendants will judge the lawless Gentiles. God will bring ten plagues on the world. The righteous among Abraham's descendants, whose number is predestined, will come to the temple, where they will offer righteous sacrifices and gifts in the new age. Their enemies will be destroyed. With this promise God concludes Abraham's vision and dismisses him.

Although Abraham has returned to earth, he continues to communicate with God, who presents something of an eschatological scenario (chaps. 30–31). The ten plagues are enumerated. They will be followed by the appearance of "my Chosen One," who will bear God's authority and will gather the dispersed Israel from the nations that have despised them.[137] These Gentiles and those who have mocked God will be delivered to eternal punishment. The Apocalypse ends with a prediction of Israel's slavery and the exodus (chap. 32), thus making a final contact with Genesis 15:13-14.

The purpose of the author of the Apocalypse of Abraham may be discerned in two themes that run through the book and unify it. The first of these is the tension between Israel's status as God's covenant people and its fate at the hands of the Gentiles. The ascription of the book to Abraham is related to his status as patriarch and as one with whom God made the covenant.[138] Israel is repeatedly identified as Abraham's descendants, a conception that is at the heart of Genesis 15. The distinction between Israel and the Gentiles is fundamental to the book, as is evident from the graphic division of the picture of the world into a left side and a right side. Also stressed on several occasions are the Gentiles' defeat, mistreatment, and ridicule of Israel. The apocalyptist asks why God has permitted this state of affairs, and, like the authors of 4 Ezra and 2 Baruch, he traces the roots of the problem to the fall.

The author explains the dilemma of Israel's suffering by means of a second theme that runs through the book: the practicing or the rejection of idolatry. The narrative section of the Apocalypse climaxes in God's initial appearance to Abraham. God chooses Abraham and commands him to leave Chaldea because he has searched after God and has rejected the idolatry of his father Terah. He is given the promise of descendants after he has parried the satanic temptation to cease from the sacrifice commanded by God. In connecting Israel's latter-day idolatry with that of Terah, the author indicts the people for reversing the decision of Abraham that led to his election, and the reference to "devilish idolatry" (chap. 26) suggests capitulation to Azazel. This leads quite naturally to Israel's punishment, ironically at the hands of the Gentiles. Like "Ezra" and "Baruch," this author finds his solution in the future: in appropriate judgments, a restored temple and sacrificial system, and eschatological joy for Israel.

Among the apocalypses we have studied in this chapter, the Apocalypse of Abraham is unique in its explicit indictment of the cult. With respect to this theme, what is the relationship between the author's narrative world and his real world? Is the author simply following biblical tradition, that the fall of Jerusalem in 587 B.C.E. was punishment for Manasseh's sin (2 Kgs 21:10-15)? Arguing against such a conclusion is the centrality of right and wrong cult in this work. It provides content for the crucial elements in the plot. It is the cause for Abraham's election, the means of his ascent, the reason for the destruction of Jerusalem, and a key element in the author's hope for the future. Thus it is likely that the author believes that the events of 70 C.E. were caused by wrong cultic activity, which he construes as idolatry.

The Apocalypse of Abraham parallels 4 Ezra and 2 Baruch at many points, indicating that it shares with these works a common apocalyptic tradition that was crystallized after 70 C.E. in response to that crisis.[139] These similarities notwithstanding, the Apocalypse has its own peculiarities and emphases. The common concern for the disparity between Israel's election and its present circumstances is here tied very naturally to the figure of the patriarch. The emphasis on cult is missing from 4 Ezra and for the most part from 2 Baruch (cf., however, 2 Bar 1–8; 64–66). Abraham's ascent and throne vision stand in a tradition that stretches from 1 Enoch 12–16 to the medieval mystical texts. The tradition is only alluded to in 2 Baruch 4:4 and 4 Ezra 3:13-14. On the other hand emphases in 4 Ezra and 2 Baruch are played down in the Apocalypse of Abraham. The extended discussions of theodicy have only brief counterparts in the Apocalypse. Totally lacking in the Apocalypse is a concern for Torah and teachers as indispensable constituents for reconstruction. In the place of a Davidic Messiah, this author awaits God's Chosen One.

The Apocalypse of Abraham is extant in Church Slavonic,[140] which translates a Greek text, most likely made from a Hebrew original.[141]

FLAVIUS JOSEPHUS

The first-century Jewish priest, "politician," soldier, apologist, and historian Flavius Josephus is important for our subject for several reasons. He was the author of the largest corpus of Jewish writings that has survived from the Greco-Roman period. These writings are a major source for our information about the history of the Jews (esp. in Palestine) in the Persian, Hellenistic, and early Roman periods. His *Jewish Antiquities* provides a window into first-century Jewish exegesis that interprets Scripture by recasting its narratives. He is the Jewish author from these times about whose life and activities we have the most information.

Josephus's Life and Career

This information comes primarily from his *Life*, an autobiographical appendix attached to the Antiquities, and from his *History of the Jewish War*. While we must read these sources with great care, looking for Josephus's biases, self-serving statements, and defensive and polemical intentions, we can garner from them a fair amount of data about his life and activities.[142]

Yosef ben Mattityahu was born in Jerusalem in 37/38 C.E. into a priestly family that traced its lineage back to Jonathan, the first of the Hasmonean high priests.[143] His father was a respected member of the Jerusalem community. After being educated by his parents, at the age of "about sixteen" he set out to gain some experience of the teachings of the Pharisees, the Sadducees, and the Essenes. Not satisfied with that experience, he placed himself under the tutelage of a desert ascetic named Bannus and became "his devoted disciple" (*zēlōtēs*). Returning to Jerusalem in his nineteenth year, he "entered public life, following the school of the Pharisees."[144] At the age of twenty-seven he traveled to Rome on a mission to free several Jewish priests whom Felix the procurator of Judea had sent to Rome on charges that were to be adjudicated by the emperor Nero. Having made the acquaintance of a Jewish actor named Aliturus, who was a favorite of Nero, he gained entrance to the imperial palace and was introduced to Poppaea, Nero's wife. Thus he was able to secure the release of the priests, and he returned home with some "large gifts" from the empress.[145]

The year was 64 C.E. and revolt against Rome was brewing. Precisely what position Josephus took on the issue is uncertain; his own accounts conflict with one another.[146] In any case, in the year 66/67, Josephus found himself in Galilee in command of a Jewish army that was in revolt against the Romans. Besieged in the city of Jotapata in central Galilee, he surrendered to Vespasian.[147] Thereafter he was kept under guard, for some of the time in Caesarea. Later, he was freed from his chains and accompanied the Roman army to Jerusalem, where he served as an adviser and interpreter for Titus during the siege that resulted in the destruction of the temple and the city. Thus he was an eyewitness of and a participant in many of the events in the Jewish War.

At the end of the war, Josephus accompanied Titus back to Rome. There Vespasian gave him an apartment in his former residence, honored him with the privilege of Roman citizenship, and granted him a pension and a large tract of land in Judea. After the death of Vespasian, Josephus remained in favor with Vespasian's two sons, Titus and Domitian, who succeeded him as the next two emperors (*Life* 426–30 [§76]). Thus honored and well looked after by the Romans, Josephus had the leisure to produce his substantial corpus of writings. It was when he became a Roman citizen under the patronage of the Flavian emperors Vespasian and Titus that Josephus received the name "Flavius" (and probably "Titus").[148]

Josephus's time in Rome was by no means without problems, however. His activities during the Jewish War and his history of the war came under strong criticism from some of his countrymen, including a certain Justus of Tiberias, who wrote his own account of the war. These criticisms and his loyalty to the imperial family notwithstanding, Josephus remained a staunch defender and a passionate interpreter of his people and their religion. He died late in the last decade of the first century or early in the second century C.E.[149]

Josephus's Writings

The corpus of Josephus's extant writings runs to almost 473,900 words in Greek, making it roughly 8 percent longer than Philo's preserved oeuvre and somewhat less than Philo's original output.[150] Like Philo's writings, the works of Josephus were preserved not by Jews but by Christians, perhaps because they provided external testimony to the figures of John the Baptist, Jesus of Nazareth, and his brother James the Just. Because of the size of his corpus, we can treat the works of Josephus only in brief summary, noting their presumed dates and some of the characteristics and major content of each writing. The bibliography lists more extensive treatments of Josephus's career and literary oeuvre.

The History of the Jewish War

The earliest of Josephus's known works was an Aramaic (or Hebrew) account of the Jewish War, written for the benefit of the "barbarians in the upper country" (Parthia and Babylon) in the months or years after the destruction of Jerusalem (*J. W.* 1.1–6 [Prol. 1–2]). Of its precise purpose, scope, and historical theses, we know nothing for certain.[151]

The first edition of the Greek version of the *War* (books 1–6) was completed before the death of Vespasian (79 C.E.).[152] According to Josephus (*J. W.* 1.1–3 [Prol. 1]), it was a complete revision of the Semitic version, but we do not know how thorough that revision was.[153] Josephus's stated purpose was to correct the accounts of other historians, who, he says, either wrote on the basis of hearsay or composed their works with the intention of flattering the Romans or slandering the Jews (*J. W.* 1.1–2 [Prol. 1]). Josephus, for his part, was an eyewitness of many of the events that he describes, and for the rest he consulted the diaries of Vespasian and Titus (*Life* 342, 358 [§65]; cf. *Ag. Ap.* 1.47–56 [§1.9–10]).

The *War* begins with a prologue that explains the purpose of the work and summarizes its contents (1.1–30 [Prol. 1–12]). Book 1 recounts the history of the Jews from the time of Antiochus IV Epiphanes to the death of Herod the Great (175–4 B.C.E.). Book 2 moves quickly into the events leading up to the revolt, while books 3–6 detail the course of the war from the appointment of Vespasian to the destruction of Jerusalem (67–70

C.E.). Book 7, which may have been composed during the reign of Domitian (81–96 C.E.),[154] recounts the last events of the war, principally the sieges of the Herodian fortresses, Herodium, Machaerus, and Masada, and the triumphal reception that Vespasian and Titus received in Rome (70–73 C.E.).

Since no other extensive accounts of the war have survived,[155] Josephus's vivid and detailed descriptions provide a valuable resource for understanding the causes of the revolt and for reconstructing the political, religious, social, and emotional context of the Jewish texts that we have discussed in this chapter. For these reasons the *War* is required reading for any serious interpreter of the texts discussed earlier in this chapter, as well as the four Gospels and the book of Acts.[156]

Its value as a source of historical information notwithstanding, the *War* is an interpretive piece of literature that presents an approach and a point of view quite different from that of Pseudo-Philo and the authors of 4 Ezra, 2 Baruch, and the Apocalypse of Abraham. The work is not pseudonymous and thus deals with named places and persons. It is less interested in theological explanations of historical causation—though they are present also—and more concerned with the nitty-gritty of political intrigue and social tension. And not least, the *War* reminds us that the empire had its own point of view about the events between 60 and 70 C.E.

In these respects, Josephus walks a tightrope.[157] He is a client of the Roman emperor, writing a history that would later be adopted as the empire's authorized version of the events he describes (*Life* 363). He does not hesitate to emphasize Titus's goodwill toward the Jews, for example, his attempt to avoid the destruction of the temple. At the same time, Josephus writes as a Jew, who both criticizes those of his own people whom he sees as the cause of the revolt and praises the virtues of his religion and the power of his God, who in the final analysis allowed Jerusalem to be destroyed on account of the sins that took place, notably in the temple. Josephus does speak in a voice that will please his Roman patrons because it justifies their severe measures against the Jews. Nonetheless, in blaming the destruction of Jerusalem and the temple on the Jews, he is expressing a point of view that is present also in 4 Ezra, 2 Baruch, and the Apocalypse of Abraham (see above, pp. 271, 277–79, 286–87). What is missing from Josephus is the grief of "Baruch," the puzzlement and intellectual agony of "Ezra," and the anger that both of these writers direct against the Romans as they assert that the instrument of God's judgment will be subject to that same judgment for its arrogant excesses. A conversation (or shouting match) between Josephus and the author of the last two visions of 4 Ezra would have made for interesting hearing.[158]

The Jewish Antiquities

The *Jewish Antiquities*, Josephus's second work, was completed in 93/94 C.E., the thirteenth year of the reign of Domitian (*Ant.* 20.267 [§12.1]). Its contents, which complement and in part overlap with the *Jewish War*, trace the history of his people from Adam to the inception of the Jewish War. At the time that he was writing the *War*, he considered a single history that would comprise the contents of both the *War* and the *Antiquities*, but the projected length of such a work led him to recount the history of the revolt in a separate volume. The effort required to construct an extended history of his people in a language that was not his first (Greek) led to his hesitation and to a considerable delay in the completion of the work (*Ant.* 1.Prol. 5–9 [§2]).

The Antiquities is a lengthy celebration and elaboration of the Jewish nation's history, constitution, culture, and virtues.[159] The model for his twenty-book "Ancient History" (Gk. *archaiologia*, *Ant.* 1.Prol. 5 [§2]; *Ag. Ap.* 1.1) appears to have been the twenty-book *Roman Antiquities* (*Romaïkē Archaiologia*) of Dionysius of Halicarnassus (7 B.C.E.).[160] For his part, Josephus begins his Antiquities not with the creation of the nation (Abraham or the exodus), but with the creation of the world (Gen 1:1). This narrative, drawn from the first book of Moses, is prefaced by a summary of the work that extols "the wisdom of our lawgiver, Moses," whose work has all the earmarks of natural philosophy (Gk. *physiologia*; *Ant.* 1.Prol. 18 [§4]). Other Jewish philosophers included Abraham and Solomon, and his portrayal of Judaism in philosophical terms is epitomized in his descriptions of the Pharisees, Sadducees, and Essenes (*Ant.* 18.11–25 [§1.2–6]; cf. *J.W.* 2.119–66 [§8.2–14]).[161] As in the *War*, his account of the Essenes is especially laudatory. Josephus explicates as the lesson of his history:

> men who conform to the will of God, and do not venture to transgress laws that have been excellently laid down, prosper in all things beyond belief, and for their reward are offered by God felicity; whereas, in proportion as they depart from the strict observance of these laws, things (else) practicable become impracticable, and whatever imaginary good thing they strive to do ends in irretrievable disaster.[162]

It is a world in which divine providence is always at work.[163] In keeping with his didactic prose, he often explicates the virtues or vices of his characters[164] in a way that is reminiscent of the biblical paraphrases of Philo of Alexandria (see above, pp. 215–16).

Books 1–10 of the Antiquities recount Israel's history through the Babylonian exile, and book 11, which concludes with a brief account of Alexander the Great, takes the history to the end of the period covered by the Bible. For these eleven books, Josephus employed the Bible as his principal source. Although he states that his account in translated from the records of the Hebrews (*Ant.* 1.Prol. 5 [§2]), he also employed its Greek translation.[165] This is suggested by his extensive use of Pseudo-Aristeas's account of the translation of the Torah (*Ant.* 12.11–118 [§2.1–15]) and his reference to it in his discussion of his sources (*Ant.* 1.Prol. 10–12 [§3]).[166] It is also indicated by his use of the Greek expanded version of the book of Esther (see above pp. 202–5) and probably his use of 1 Esdras with its story of Darius's bodyguards (see above, pp. 27–29). His text of the material from 1–2 Samuel is also drawn from the Greek translation.[167]

As is indicated by his use of the expanded versions of the Esther and Ezra materials, Josephus's presentation of the biblical materials reveals a Bible in the process of substantial interpretation,[168] and his elaborations of other parts of the biblical narratives indicate the use of current haggadic exegesis in written and oral sources, which is occasionally attested in parallel material in the contemporary Antiquities of Pseudo-Philo.[169] While Josephus employs the form of "rewritten Bible" attested in works like Jubilees and Pseudo-Philo, he differs from these examples of the genre in an important respect: he is consciously writing history as contemporary historians wrote their histories.[170]

Books 12 to 20 of the *Antiquities* are especially valuable because, alongside archeological and epigraphic evidence and some contextual material from historians of the Macedonian and Roman empires, Josephus is here our principal source for the events that he recounts. Apart from the Maccabean period, for which he employs 1 Maccabees as a major source (and for which we also have 2 Maccabees), Josephus provides some access to sources that have long been lost, for example, legends about the Tobiad family, the history of Nicolaus of Damascus, a wide variety of letters and imperial decrees, as well as material from Jewish and pagan historians.[171] Josephus's descriptions of the Herodian fortresses and palaces have been an important supplement and interpretive key to archeological remains in Judea, Samaria, and Galilee, and Transjordan.

Alongside Josephus's account of *events* in Jewish history, his descriptions of the four Jewish "philosophies" (Pharisees, Sadducees, Essenes, and the Fourth Philosophy) constitute evidence that complements and sometimes seems to contradict other sources such as the Qumran Scrolls and the New Testament.[172] In the case of the Essenes, Josephus's descriptions have been a crucial factor in identifying the group that was resident at Qumran, although there are some important differences to be accounted for—not least Josephus's complete silence on the major tenets of the apocalyptic and priestly theology evident in the Dead Sea Scrolls.[173] As for the Pharisees, Josephus provides the only contemporary evidence about the Pharisees apart from the highly polemical accounts in the New Testament.[174] Finally, Josephus's brief references to John the Baptist, Jesus of Nazareth, and James the brother of Jesus provide the only contemporary attestations to these persons outside the New Testament.[175]

The Life

Josephus's next work was an account of his life that was appended to Antiquities at 20.268.[176] It is generally believed that Josephus's purpose in writing the *Life* is to defend himself and his account of the Jewish War against the criticisms and attacks of his opponents, especially Justus of Tiberius, whom he addresses directly in *Life* 336–67 (§65).[177] An alternative explanation, based on careful literary analysis of the work, posits that Josephus intended the work to present him as a person whose deeds during his public life exemplified the virtues of the ideal aristocrat.[178] Thus this *Life* recommended him as "an unusually impressive spokesman for his nation"[179] and validated the contents of the Antiquities to which it was appended. The *Life* begins with Josephus's genealogy and a summary of the events of his life up to his return from Rome (1–16 [§1–3]). Its major part recounts his involvement in the Jewish War, principally explaining and defending his actions and criticizing the history written by Justus (17–425 [§4–76]). It concludes with a reference to his domestic life (he was married four times and had four children, two of whom died)[180] and a few comments about his life in Rome (427–30 [§78]).

Against Apion

In this apologetic and polemical work, Josephus celebrates the virtues of the Jewish people and their religion and way of life, while he relentlessly attacks the ignorance of its learned and ill-willed detractors (2.145 [§14]).[181] Thus the purpose and tendency sometimes implicit in his earlier works are made explicit here in his final surviving literary text.[182] In his opening paragraph (1.1–3 [§1]) he states his intention to respond to the scurrilous attacks against his claims about the antiquity of the Jews in the Antiquities. In order to allow time for his previous work to circulate, for his detractors to make their criticisms, and for him to compose his response, we should date *Against Apion* to some time between 96 and 100 C.E.[183] The title of the work seems to have been tagged on in the course of its transmission, since Apion is the object of his criticism only in the first half of book 2 (1–150 [§1–15]).[184] The rest of the work he directs against a host of named and unnamed opponents.

Josephus devotes the largest part of book 1 to a refutation of those who dispute the ancient origins of the Jews (1.1–218 [§1–23]). Hence the subtitle "Concerning the Antiquity of the Jews," which may reflect the work's original title.[185] His opening ploy is to criticize the inaccuracies of Greek historiography (1.6–46 [§2–9])—this in contrast to the care with which the Egyptians, Babylonians, and Chaldeans attended to their chronicles (1.29 [§6]). Similarly, the Jews in their priestly genealogies and in the twenty-two books of their Scriptures made accuracy their goal (1.30–46 [§7–8]). Moreover, as an eyewitness and participant of the Jewish War, and with reference to the diaries of the commanders, Josephus wrote an accurate account of the war, and in his Antiquities, as a trained priest, he properly "translated our sacred scriptures"—the accusations of his critics notwithstanding (1.47–56 [§9–10]).

Josephus now provides a table of contents (1.57–59 [§11]). (1) He argues that the lack of reference to the Jews in the Greek historians is due to the fact that the Jews were not engaged in maritime trade and hence had little opportunity for contact with the Greeks (1.60–68 [§12]). (2) Then, at great length, he quotes the historians of antiquity and anonymous sources that do, in fact, refer to the Jews (1.69–218 [§13–23]). His sources come from Egypt (1.69–105 [§13–16]), Phoenicia (1.106–27 [§17–18]), and Chaldea (1.128–60 [§19–21]), and, to beat his opponents at their own game, Greece (1.160–218 [§22–23]). The list of names is stunning, and the material quoted from sources now lost is of great value to the historian[186] and indicates that Josephus had access to a library of considerable size.[187] (3) Josephus spends the remainder of book 1 (219–320 [§24–25]) demonstrating the utter absurdity of those who slander the Jewish people (1.59 [§11]). Here he quotes at length a set of bizarre stories about Israelite origins in Egypt, and then takes the time to pick them apart piece by piece. The stories demonstrate the kind of anti-Semitism that marked the pogrom in Alexandria earlier in the century (see above, p. 214) and that would break out again in Egypt and Cyrene in 115–117 C.E.[188]

Josephus's narrative ends abruptly at 1.320 (§35) with the observation that he had come to the end of his scroll.[189] Thus, although he begins book 2 with a new dedication to his patron Epaphroditus (2.1; cf. 1.1; cf. also Luke 1:1-4 and Acts 1:1),[190] he notes that he will continue his refutation of "the rest of the writers who throw charges at us." Thus, finally, he launches his attack against Apion (2.2–144 [§1–13]). Apion, for the record, was an Alexandrian rhetorician who had moved to Rome in the 30s of the first century and who had opposed the Alexandrian Jews' request that Gaius Caligula grant them citizenship.[191] His attacks against the Jews were evidently contained in a five-volume *History of Egypt* (*Ag. Ap.* 2.10 [§2]). Josephus's attack on Apion, for its part, is riddled with sarcasm and filled with charges of lying, ignorance of the facts, stupidity, the inability to think clearly, and downright viciousness.[192] Perhaps most famous of Apion's calumnies was a story that he claims to have heard from a certain Apollonius Molon: the Jews worshiped an ass's head in the temple and kidnapped, ritually killed, and cannibalized a Greek each year (2.79–111 [§7–8]).[193] He ends his ad hominem invectives against Apion by describing his "just and appropriate death" (2.137–44 [§13]). Apion had ridiculed the rite of circumcision and other Jewish rituals. However, when he developed an ulcer on his genitals and had to be circumcised, he developed gangrene and died in terrible agony.

With Apion now disposed of on this cheery note, Josephus refers briefly to some attacks against Moses (2.145 [§14]). This provides a transition to his final topic—an encomium or disquisition in praise of the Jewish law, the Mosaic constitution (2.145–219 [§14–30]).

> Moses, the most ancient lawgiver, established a "theocracy" (2:164), which surpasses the constitutions of the Greeks because it makes piety the central virtue (2:170), and inculcates other virtues through both theory and practice. (2:169, 171–3)[194]

After contrasting Jewish religion and culture with Greek political, philosophical, and religious traditions (2.220–86 [§31–39]), Josephus summarizes the content of his book and concludes with a final encomium on the Jewish laws, a curse on the Apions and Molons of this world and the rest of the *liars*, and a word of dedication to Epaphroditus, who, in contrast to them, is "*the lover of truth*" (2.287–96 [§40–41]).

Against Apion is not an easy read. One is taken on a roller-coaster ride through strong emotions, claims of high religion, and the exercise of bitter invectives, on both sides. For Josephus it is a matter of religious and factual truth versus falsehood. His opponents, in the name of high culture, indulged in smear and prejudice. Through it all one gets a glimpse of that dark side of our humanity that is too often still with us.

The works of Josephus, for all of their impassioned pleas in behalf of the Jewish people and their religion and culture, and despite their polemics against the enemies and the critics and despisers of the Jews, had a short afterlife among Jews. Perhaps the reasons were complex. Josephus was himself an ambiguous character, given his role in the Jewish War, his "collaboration" with the Romans, and the resulting comforts that he enjoyed in Rome. As the rabbis transformed Judaism into a religion of the Torah that excluded the necessity of a temple, the story of the destruction of the temple became less relevant—as did the late-first-century apocalypses that fell out of use among Jews. "As the leaders of post-70 Judaism became less concerned with [the] enterprise [of making Jewish traditions understandable and respected in the Greek world], and more intent on reconstruction of Judaism in defiance of the harsh realities of history, historiography in general lost its appeal and relevance."[195] With the developing authority of the Hebrew canon, Israelite history was to be found in the narratives of Scripture, though these could be elaborated in the haggadah of the rabbinic commentaries. Apart from the medieval Hebrew elaboration of Josephus (so-called *Josippon*), the story of God's people recounted in Greek would be left for Christians to preserve and transmit, translating it also into Arabic, Ethiopic, Latin, and Slavonic.[196]

BIBLIOGRAPHY

History

The Jewish War and Its Aftermath

Schürer, *History*, 1:455–528. Martin **Goodman**, *The Ruling Class of Judaea: The Origins of the Jewish Revolt against Rome* (Cambridge: Cambridge Univ. Press, 1987); Richard A. **Horsley** and John S. **Hanson**, *Bandits, Prophets, and Messiahs* (New York: Harper & Row, 1985); James S. **McLaren**, *Power and Politics in Palestine: The Jews and the Governing of Their Land 100 BC–AD 70* (JSNTSup 63; Sheffield: JSOT Press, 1991); Jacob **Neusner**, "The Formation of Rabbinic Judaism: Yavneh (Jamnia) from A.D. 70–100," *ANRW* 2.19 (1979) 3–42. David M. **Rhoads**, *Israel in Revolution, 5–74 C.E. A Political History Based on the Writings of Josephus* (Philadelphia: Fortress Press, 1976) 68–181. E. Mary **Smallwood**, *The Jews under Roman Rule* (SJLA 20; Leiden: Brill, 1976) 256–355.

The Second Revolt

Schürer, *History*, 1:529–57. Glen W. **Bowersock**, "A Roman Perspective on the Bar Kochba War," in William S. **Green**, ed., *Approaches to Ancient Judaism* 2 (BJS 9; Missoula, Mont.: Scholars Press, 1980) 131–41. Werner **Eck**, "The Bar Kokhba Revolt: The Roman Point of View," *JRS* 89 (1999) 76–89. Joseph A. **Fitzmyer**, "The Bar Cochba Period," in idem, *Essays on the Semitic Background of the New Testament* (SBLSBS 5; Missoula, Mont.: Scholars Press, 1974) 305–54. Benjamin **Isaac** and Aharon **Oppenheimer**, "The Revolt of Bar Kokhba: Ideology and Modern Scholarship," *JJS* 35 (1985) 33–60. Leo **Mildenberg**, *The Coinage of the Bar Kokhba War* (Aarau: Sauerländer, 1984). Aharon **Oppenheimer**, "Bar Kokhba Revolt," *EDSS* 1:80–83. Peter **Schäfer**, *Der Bar Kokhba-Aufstand: Studien zum zweiten jüdischen Krieg gegen Rom* (TSAJ 1; Tübingen: Mohr Siebeck, 1981), discussion of the relevant primary sources and related matters. Peter **Schäfer**, *The Bar Kokhba War Reconsidered: New Perspectives on the Second Jewish Revolt against Rome* (TSAJ 100; Tübingen: Mohr Siebeck, 2003), conference papers on the state of the discussion. E. Mary **Smallwood**, *The Jews under Roman Rule* (SJLA 20; Leiden: Brill, 1976) 389–466. Yigael **Yadin**, *The Finds from the Bar Kokhba Period in the Cave of Letters* (Jerusalem: Israel Exploration Society, 1963). Yigael **Yadin**, *Bar Kochba: The Rediscovery of the Legendary Hero of the Second Jewish Revolt against Rome* (New York: Random House, 1971), popular treatment with a splendid set of photographs. Yigael **Yadin**, et al., *The Documents from the Bar Kokhba Period in the Cave of Letters* (2 vols.; Jerusalem: Israel Exploration Society, 1989, 2001).

The Book of Biblical Antiquities (Pseudo-Philo)

Translation: Daniel J. **Harrington**, *OTP* 2:297–377.

Texts, Other Translations, and Commentaries: M. R. **James**, *The Biblical Antiquities of Philo* (London: SPCK, 1917), extensive introduction, translation, reprinted in 1971 with a lengthy prolegomenon by Louis H. **Feldman**. Daniel J. **Harrington**, Jacques **Cazeaux**, Charles **Perrot**, and Pierre-Maurice **Bogaert**, *Pseudo-Philon: Les Antiquités Bibliques* (2 vols. SC 229–30; Paris: Cerf, 1976), introduction, critical text of the Latin with a facing French translation, commentary, extensive bibliography. Howard A. **Jacobson**, *A Commentary on Pseudo-Philo's Liber Antiquitatum Biblicarum with Latin Text and English Translation* (AGAJU 31; 2 vols.; Leiden: Brill, 1996).

Literature Survey: Daniel J. **Harrington**, "A Decade of Research on Pseudo-Philo's *Liber Antiquitatum Biblicarum*," *JSP* 2 (1988) 3–12.

Literature: Cheryl A. **Brown**, *No Longer Be Silent: First Century Jewish Portraits of Biblical Women* (Louisville: Westminster/John Knox, 1992). Bruce N. **Fisk**, *Scripture, Story and Exegesis in the Rewritten Bible of Pseudo-Philo* (JSPSup 37; Sheffield: Sheffield Academic Press, 2001). Frederick J. **Murphy**, *Pseudo-Philo: Rewriting the Bible* (New York: Oxford Univ. Press, 1993). Eckhart **Reinmuth**, *Pseudo-Philo und Lukas: Studien zum Liber Antiquitatum Biblicarum und seiner Bedeutung für die Interpretation des lukanischen Doppelwerks* (WUNT 74; Tübingen: Mohr Siebeck, 1994).

4 Ezra

Translations: The Apocrypha. Bruce M. **Metzger**, *OTP* 2:517–59. Michael E. **Stone**, *Fourth Ezra: A Commentary on the Book of Fourth Ezra* (Hermeneia; Minneapolis: Fortress Press, 1990).

Texts: Klaus **Berger**, *Synopse des Vierten Buches Ezra und der syrischen Baruch-Apokalypse* (TANZ 8; Tübingen: Franke, 1992), German translations of 4 Ezra and 2 Baruch in parallel columns in two forms that employ 4 Ezra and 2 Baruch, respectively, as the base text. Bruno **Violet**, *Die Ezra-Apokalypse, I: Die Überlieferungen* (GCS 18; Leipzig: Hinrichs, 1910), critical edition of the Latin; German and Latin translations of the other versions. Robertus **Weber**, ed., *Biblia Sacra Iuxta Vulgatam Versionem* (Stuttgart: Würtembergische Bibelanstalt, 1969) 2:1931–74, critical edition of the Latin based on Violet.

Commentaries: Jacob M. **Myers**, *I and II Esdras* (AB 42; Garden City, N.Y.: Doubleday, 1974) 107–354. **Stone**, *Fourth Ezra*. Michael A. **Knibb**, "The Second Book of Esdras," in R. J. **Coggins** and M. A. **Knibb**, *The First and Second Books of Esdras* (CBC; Cambridge: Cambridge Univ. Press, 1979), comments on the New English Bible translation. Bruno **Violet**, *Die Apokalypsen des Esra und des Baruch in deutscher Gestalt* (GCS 32; Leipzig: Hinrichs, 1924), extensive introduction, German translation, commentary.

Literature: G. H. **Box**, *APOT* 2:542–624, translation with text-critical and exegetical notes. Wolfgang **Harnisch**, *Verhängnis und Verheissung der Geschichte* (FRLANT 97; Göttingen: Vandenhoeck & Ruprecht, 1969), a study of the interpretation of time and history in 4 Ezra and

2 Baruch. Bruce W. **Longenecker**, *2 Esdras* (GAP; Sheffield: Sheffield Academic Press, 1995), an introduction to the book. Bruce W. **Longenecker**, *Eschatology and the Covenant: A Comparison of 4 Ezra and Romans 1–11* (JSNTSup 57; Sheffield: JSOT Press, 1991). Michael E. **Stone**, *Features of the Eschatology of IV Ezra* (HSS 35; Atlanta: Scholars Press, 1989). Alden L. **Thompson**, *Responsibility for Evil in the Theodicy of IV Ezra* (SBLDS 29; Missoula, Mont.: Scholars Press, 1977). Tom W. **Willett**, *Eschatology in the Theodicies of 2 Baruch and 4 Ezra* (JSPSup 4; Sheffield: Sheffield Academic Press, 1989).

2 Baruch

Translation: A. F. J. **Klijn**, *OTP* 2:615–52. R. H. **Charles**, rev. L. H. **Brockington**, *AOT*, 835–95.

Texts and Other Translations: Klaus **Berger**, *Synopse des Vierten Buches Ezra und der syrischen Baruch-Apokalypse* (TANZ 8; Tübingen: Franke, 1992), German translations of 4 Ezra and 2 Baruch in parallel columns in two forms that employ 4 Ezra and 2 Baruch, respectively, as the base text. Antonius M. **Ceriani**, "Apocalypsis Baruch Syriace," in *Monumenta Sacra et Profana* (Mediolani: Bibliotheca Ambrosiana, 1871) 5:113–80, *editio princeps* of the Syriac text of chaps. 1–87. S. **Dedering**, "Apocalypse of Baruch," *The Old Testament in Syriac* 4/3 (Leiden: Brill, 1973) 1–50, the Syriac text of chaps. 1–77. R. H. **Charles**, *The Apocalypse of Baruch* (London: Black, 1896), introduction, annotated translation, the Syriac text of chaps. 78–86. R. H. **Charles**, *APOT* 2:470–526.

Commentary: Pierre-Maurice **Bogaert**, *Apocalypse de Baruch* (2 vols.; SC 144–45: Paris: Cerf, 1969), introduction, French translation, commentary.

Literature: Frederick J. **Murphy**, *The Structure and Meaning of Second Baruch* (SBLDS 78; Atlanta: Scholars Press, 1985. Rivka **Nir**, *The Destruction of Jerusalem and the Idea of Redemption in the Syriac Apocalypse of Baruch* (SBLEJL 20; Leiden: Brill, 2003). Wolfgang **Harnisch**, *Verhängnis und Verheissung der Geschichte* (FRLANT 97; Göttingen: Vandenhoeck & Ruprecht, 1969), a study of the interpretation of time and history in 4 Ezra and 2 Baruch. Gwendolyn B. **Sayler**, *Have the Promises Failed? A Literary Analysis of 2 Baruch* (SBLDS 72; Atlanta: Scholars Press, 1984). Mark S. **Whitters**, *The Epistle of Second Baruch: A Study in Form and Message* (JSPSup 42; Sheffield: Sheffield Academic Press, 2003). Tom W. **Willett**, *Eschatology in the Theodicies of 2 Baruch and 4 Ezra* (JSPSup 4; Sheffield: Sheffield Academic Press, 1989).

The Apocalypse of Abraham

Translations: Richard **Rubinkiewicz**, *OTP* 1:681–705. A. **Pennington**, *AOT*, 363–91. G. H. **Box**, *The Apocalypse of Abraham* (London: SPCK, 1919), introduction, translation, textual and exegetical notes.

Flavius Josephus

Texts and Translation: Steve **Mason**, et al., *Flavius Josephus: Translation and Commentary* (11 vols.; Leiden: Brill, 2000–), literal translation with copious commentary, excursuses, appendices, essays, and indices. Benedictus **Niese**, *Flavii Iosephi Opera* (7 vols.; Berlin: Weidmann, 1885–95), definitive edition of Greek text. Étienne **Nodet**, *Flavius Josèphe: Les Antiquités Juives* (6 vols.; Paris: Cerf, 1992–), critical Greek text with apparatus and facing French translation. Folk **Siegert**, Heinz **Schreckenberg**, and Manuel **Vogel**, *Flavius Josephus: Aus meinem Leben (Vita)* (Tübingen: Mohr Siebeck, 2001), introduction, critical text, translation, and brief commentary on the *Life*. St. J. **Thackeray**, Ralph **Marcus**, Allen **Wikgren**, and Louis H. **Feldman**, *Josephus* (LCL 9 vols.; Cambridge: Harvard Univ. Press, 1926–1965), critical Greek text with facing English translation.

Concordances and Lexicon: Karl H. **Rengstorf**, et al., *A Complete Concordance to Flavius Josephus* (4 vols.; Leiden: Brill, 1973–83; Sup 1 with proper names by Abraham Schalit, 1968). Heinz **Schreckenberg**, "A Concordance to the Latin Text of *Contra Apionem*, in **Feldman** and **Levison**, eds., *Josephus' Contra Apionem*, 453–517. Henry St. J. **Thackeray** and Ralph **Marcus**, *A Lexicon to Josephus* (4 fascicles; Paris: Geuthner, 1930).

Bibliographies: Louis H. **Feldman**, *Josephus and Modern Scholarship (1937–1980)* (Berlin: de Gruyter, 1984). Louis H. **Feldman**, *Josephus: A Supplementary Bibliography* (New York: Garland, 1996). Heinz **Schreckenberg**, *Bibliographie zu Flavius Josephus* (ALGHJ 1; Leiden: Brill, 1968; supplementary volume, 1979).

Literature: Harold W. **Attridge**, *The Interpretation of Biblical History in the Antiquitates Judaicae of Flavius Josephus* (HDR 7; Missoula, Mont.: Scholars Press, 1976). Harold W. **Attridge**, "Josephus and His Works," in Michael E. **Stone**, ed., *Jewish Writings of the Second Temple Period* (CRINT 2/2; Assen: Van Gorcum; Philadelphia: Fortress Press, 1984) 185–232. Per **Bilde**, *Flavius Josephus between Jerusalem and Rome: His Life, His Works, and Their Importance* (JSPSup 2; Sheffield: JSOT Press, 1988), introduction to Josephus's life and writings with a survey of modern scholarship. Shaye J. D. **Cohen**, *Josephus in Galilee and Rome: His Vita and Development as a Historian* (Leiden: Brill, 1979). Gaalya **Cornfield**, ed., *Josephus: The Jewish War: Newly Translated with Extensive Commentary and Archeological Background Illustrations* (Grand Rapids: Zondervan, 1982), especially useful for the photographs and illustrations, but see the comment by Louis H. Feldman, "Josephus," 997. Louis H. **Feldman**, "Josephus," *ABD* 3:781–98. Louis H. **Feldman**, "Josephus Flavius," *EDSS* 1:427–31, Josephus especially in relation to the Essenes and the Qumran Scrolls. Louis H. **Feldman**, *Josephus's Interpretation of the Bible* (Berkeley: Univ. of California Press, 1998). Louis H. **Feldman**, *Studies in Josephus' Rewritten Bible* (JSJSup 58; Leiden: Brill, 1998). Louis H. **Feldman** and John R. **Levison**, eds., *Josephus' Contra Apionem: Studies in Its Character and Context with a Latin Concordance to the Portion Missing in Greek* (AGJU 34; Leiden: Brill, 1996), collection of articles related to *Against Apion*. Steve **Mason**, *Josephus and the New Testament* (2d ed.; Peabody, Mass.; Hendrickson, 2003), Josephus's life and career, detailed literary analysis of his works, as well as his relevance for New Testament studies. Steve **Mason**, *Flavius Josephus on the Pharisees: A Composition-Critical Study* (SPB 39; Leiden: Brill, 1991). Steve **Mason**, ed., *Understanding Josephus: Seven Perspectives* (JSPSup 32; Sheffield: Sheffield Academic Press, 1998). James S. **McLaren**, *Turbulent Times? Josephus and Scholarship on Judaea in the First Century C.E.* (JSPSup 29; Sheffield: Sheffield Academic Press, 1998). Tessa **Rajak**, *Josephus: The Historian and His Society* (London: Duckworth, 1983), Josephus, his life, his context, and his interpretation of the Jewish War.

The Testaments of the Twelve Patriarchs. T. Simeon 4:4—9.2 and T. Levi 1:1—2.7 in Armenian translation, Jerusalem Armenian Patriarchate manuscript J 1927 folio 30b, copied in Constantinople in 1649. Photograph is courtesy of the Armenian Patriarchate.

9

Texts of Disputed Provenance

THE PROBLEM

We come, finally, to an assortment of texts of uncertain origin. We do not know when they were written or where, and scholars dispute whether they were written by Jews or by Christians who had access to Jewish traditions and used them with some facility. All of the texts claim to recount events in the lives of biblical figures, and several of them allege to have been written by these persons. Since all of them are freely written narratives, they distinguish themselves from texts like Jubilees and Pseudo-Philo, which are guided, more or less, by the flow of the biblical narrative.

All of these texts, moreover, have been preserved only in manuscripts that are the products of Christian scribes. Despite this exclusive Christian manuscript attestation, earlier scholarship for the most part tended to assume or assert that these texts were Jewish compositions. More recently this axiom has been challenged. One must begin with what is given, namely, the Christian provenance of the manuscripts. This should be "the default position," and the burden of proof lies on the person who claims that they are texts of non-Christian Jewish origin that were copied by Christian scribes and sometimes interpolated with Christian elements.[1] Even apart from these explicit Christian elements, it is argued that there is no reason why a Christian, whose Bible included the "Old Testament," could not write a text about a biblical figure without making reference to Jesus. Whether this position works as a generalization may be debated in this respect: Are there points in a given text where one would expect an explicit reference to Jesus or Christian teaching rather than what one finds in the text? It is a point to which we shall return from time to time.

The question of Jewish or Christian provenance is of considerable importance for two reasons. Material from these texts is often cited uncritically as Jewish and hence as valid context for the New Testament. Conversely, the texts and their content are rarely integrated into the histories of Christianity, even at the minimalistic level that there were Christian scribes who thought it appropriate to copy the texts, and presumably there were others who read them for their edification.

Our survey begins with the Testaments of the Twelve Patriarchs, which are explicitly Christian in the form in which we have received them. As we move through the other five texts that follow, the issues become fuzzier, and the conclusions more difficult to draw with certainty.

The Testaments of the Twelve Patriarchs

The testamentary form is found already in the Bible. Genesis 49 depicts Jacob's deathbed scene. The patriarch gathers his twelve sons around him and makes a series of predictions about them and their descendants. The passage ends with Jacob's death and burial. In the last chapters of Deuteronomy, Moses announces his death and commissions Joshua as his successor (chap. 31). He then predicts the course of Israel's future in his "Song" (chap. 32) and pronounces his final blessing on the nation in the form of a series of predictions about eleven of the twelve tribes (chap. 33; Simeon is not mentioned). Then he dies and God buries him (chap. 34).

We have seen the expansion of these testamentary models in the Testament of Moses, which details the events that Moses foretold (see above, pp. 74–77); in the testaments of Abraham in Jubilees 20, 21, and 22, which are more concerned with ethical instruction than prediction and thus parallel the broader framework of Deuteronomy. A good part of 1 Enoch subsumes a variety of material under the category of Enoch's farewell instructions to his sons and descendants (see above, pp. 114–15, 221–22).

The Testaments of the Twelve Patriarchs is a collection of twelve self-contained units.[2] Each of these describes one of Jacob's sons on his deathbed (or just before his death), gathering his sons and making his testament in their presence. Following the biblical model, each Testament contains a prediction about the future of the tribe and sometimes of Israel in general. Similar to the testaments in Jubilees 20, 21, and 22, the contents of the Testaments of the Twelve Patriarchs (with the partial exception of the Testament of Levi) are controlled by ethical considerations. This emphasis is provided by the insertion of two interrelated elements into the biblical model. First, the patriarch narrates an event or events from his life that illustrate a particular virtue or vice, which is repeatedly mentioned. Then the patriarch addresses his sons, exhorting them to emulate his virtuous conduct or to avoid the example of his wickedness.

A common outline for most of the Testaments is as follows:[3]

A. Introduction, setting the scene
B. Narrative from the patriarch's life
C. Ethical exhortation
D. Prediction of the future
E. A brief second exhortation
F. Patriarch's death
G. His burial

Each Testament is prefaced by a title that states its theme. Although the introductions to the respective Testaments may or may not state that the patriarch is on his deathbed (Levi and Asher are in good health), in each case, after the aged patriarch transmitted his testament to the sons he has gathered around him, he dies. Narrative and exhortative sections are sometimes interwoven, and in two cases (Judah and Joseph) there are double narratives. Where the Bible provides details about an individual patriarch, the respective Testament employs and elaborates on them. Other Testaments draw on elements in the biblical story of Joseph. Occasionally a detail in the Blessing of Jacob or the Blessing of Moses has been elaborated into narrative. Only the Testament of Asher has no narrative (see below). Some of the narrative sections draw on traditional material, while others appear to have been created ad hoc. The exhortatory sections often employ themes, language, and forms typical of wisdom literature. The predictive sections are often designated as revelation. In some cases they employ the sin-punishment-repentance-salvation scheme that we have met in earlier apocalypses, usually specified as sin-exile-repentance-return.[4] These sections of the Testaments are perhaps the most stereotyped and contain many parallels to one another. They can be very short, and their content can be very general. More than any other section they give the impression of being ad hoc creations, inserted because the element is expected in the genre.

Our discussion of this document will sample seven Testaments that exemplify the formal characteristics of these writings, as well as their narrative technique and their ethical and eschatological contents.

The Testament of Reuben concerning Thoughts

The major part of this Testament consists of alternating narrative and related exhortation, with the exhortation sometimes introducing the narrative and indicating its function. The narrative sections elaborate three biblical stories: Reuben's unlawful intercourse with Bilhah, his father's concubine (Gen 35:22); Joseph's resistance to such conduct with his master's wife (Gen 39:1-18); and the story of the watchers and the women (Gen 6:1-4) as it is interpreted in 1 Enoch 6–11 (see above, pp. 47–50). After an introduction that sets the scene for the Testament (1:2-5a), Reuben addresses his brothers and sons, and recounts the consequences of the Bilhah incident; God struck Reuben with a disease in his "loins," the place of his sin, and Reuben repented (1:5b-10). Once more addressing his children, he states that he will instruct them about seven spirits of error appointed by Beliar to afflict human beings (2:1-2). In fact, the text describes two sets of seven spirits (2:3—3:2; 3:3-8). The first group of seven, to which an eighth is added (2:3—3:2), relates to bodily functions given at creation. The list may be an interpolation, since it is the second group of seven plus one that describes spirits that cause sin.[5] The Testament's second narrative section (3:9-15) again begins with an exhortation that explicates the moral of the story (3:9-10) and then recounts and elaborates on the circumstances of Reuben's sin (3:11-15). Next, a parallel section elaborates on the previous exhortation (4:1||3:10) as well as the consequences of Reuben's sin (4:2-4). Once again addressing his children and warning them against fornication (4:6-7), Reuben presents a positive example, briefly recounting the actions of his brother Joseph (4:8-11). Reuben introduces his final narrative section with the warning that "women are evil" and prone to lust (5:1-

5) and then cites the story of the watchers and the women who, according to this version, seduced the watchers (5:6-7; see above, p. 49). After a final warning against fornication and the jealousy that derives from it (6:1-4), Reuben moves into what appears to be his predictive section about the future negative interaction between his own descendants and those of Levi and Judah (6:5-6). In fact, reversing the previous pattern, this narrative in the future tense provides an introduction to a final exhortation that his sons grant Levi and Judah the honor they deserve (6:7-12). The Testament concludes with a description of Reuben's death and burial (7:1-2).

The Testament's narrative about Reuben and Bilhah is essentially exegetical and resolves several possible difficulties in the biblical story.[6] First, it absolves Bilhah of any blame in the incident: she had been bathing in a sheltered place when Reuben first saw her; she was asleep (albeit from overdrinking) and was unaware of the incident. Second, Reuben is severely punished for his sin and undertakes appropriate rituals of repentance. Third, Jacob does not sleep with Bilhah after the incident. In part these narrative elements are paralleled in Jubilees 33:2-8: Reuben spied Bilhah bathing, and although she awoke and found Reuben, she repulsed him; Jacob no longer slept with her. This suggests that the author of the Testament either knew the Jubilees account or shared a common tradition with it.[7]

These parallels notwithstanding, the author of the Testament takes the story in directions that suit his own interests and emphases and that find parallels elsewhere in the Testaments. The motif of drunkenness leading to sexual misconduct appears again in the Testament of Judah 11–16, where it is severely criticized. "Fornication" (*porneia*) is a major catchword in the Testament's narrative and exhortation (1:6; 3:3; 4:6, 7, 8, 11; 5:3, 5; 6:1, 4); it is a vice that the spirits of Beliar work in humans (3:3; 5:3). In spite of the narrative exculpation of Bilhah drawn from tradition, the exhortations emphasize that the basic problem is with women themselves, who are particularly prone to fornication and lust and who use their wiles and beauty to seduce men. To prove his case the author had cited Joseph and Potiphar's wife as positive and negative foils to Reuben and Bilhah (T. Reub. 4:8-11), and now he employs an element in the Enochic watcher tradition that implicitly blames the women (T. Reub. 5:6-7; cf. 1 Enoch 8:1-2). Bilhah's drunkenness is also consonant with this viewpoint. This author's low estimate of women is paralleled but probably unequaled in the Jewish literature of the Greco-Roman period. Joseph's positive example links this Testament to that of Joseph (see below). The reference to jealousy as a second vice (6:4-5) connects this Testament with the Testament of Simeon, which immediately follows it. The assertion of the primacy of the tribes of Levi (especially) and Judah expresses a motif that runs like a thread through the Testaments, and the prediction that Reuben's sons will rebel against Levi parallels Testament of Simeon 5:4 (cf. T. Dan 5:5-6).

Although the narrative and exhortative sections of the Testament focus on the vice of "fornication," its title identifies its theme as human thoughts (*ennoia*, 1:1). These thoughts and the mind (*dianoia*) in which they reside generate the decisions that result in sin and righteous conduct (3:12; 4:6, 8, 11; 5:3, 6, 7; 6:1, 2).[8] This emphasis on the internal origins of sin is paralleled in the second catalog of the "spirits of error" (3:3-7), which lists a range of sinful dispositions. Since all the other Testaments except Asher focus on specific vices and virtues, this emphasis on "thoughts" and "the mind," encapsulated in the title, suggests that along with its focus on a single vice, this first of the Testaments also functions to lay out the anthropological presupposition of the entire work.

The Testament of Simeon concerning Envy

The catchwords in this Testament are "envy" (*phthonos*) and "jealousy" (*zēlos*), which are virtually synonymous in this context.[9] In the first and largest part of the Testament, explicit moralizing narratives lead to exhortations that explicate the narratives and apply them to his children (2:1—5:3). Addressing his children in the first narrative, Simeon associates his strength and valor in battle (in the Shechem incident)[10] with the hard heart that would trigger his uncompassionate action against Joseph (2:1-5). This motif leads naturally to a discussion of his jealousy toward Joseph, which the Bible attributes to his brothers in general (Gen 37:11) but the Testament identifies as a characteristic of Simeon in particular (2:6-11). The cause of this envy is the influence of "the prince of deceit" and his "spirit of envy" (2:7; 3:1). Simeon's specific complicity in the plot against Joseph is probably deduced from the fact that Joseph later held Simeon hostage (Gen 42:24; cf. T. Sim. 4:2-3).[11] As in the Testament of Reuben, God punished the patriarch, and he repented of his sin (2:12-14). The exhortation that follows punctuates the narrative, employing the noun and verb "envy" five times (3:1-3).

The second narrative picks up the theme of Simeon's humiliation (3:4—4:3) and ends with reference to those qualities of Joseph that contrast with Simeon's envy and lack of compassion (cf. 4:4 with 2:4). The exhortation that follows both warns against jealousy and envy (like Simeon's) and encourages sincerity that derives from a "good" heart (like Joseph's) (4:5). A narrative verse that expands on Joseph's good qualities (4:6) leads to a related exhortation and an explication of how good and evil qualities work within humans (4:7-9). This use of explication in connection with narrative or exhortation occurs elsewhere in the Testaments (cf. 3:4-6). Mention of Joseph's love links this Testament to the second Joseph story in the Testament of Joseph (see below).

In the final section of narrative and exhortation, Simeon cites Joseph's lack of wickedness (lust) and exhorts his sons to avoid its opposite (fornication) (5:1-3). The use of Joseph's virtue as a foil to Simeon's vice and the mention of fornication parallels Testament of Reuben 4:8-10. The predictive section of the Testament begins by picking up the motif of fornication (T. Sim. 5:4ab) and continues with reference to the tribe's futile war against the sons of Levi (5:4c-6; cf. T. Reub. 6:5-6). Here and elsewhere in the Testaments, an appeal to the "writing [or words] of Enoch" supports a prediction of future sins with the authority of the venerable sage, but does not draw on any Enochic text that has survived.[12]

The predictive narrative continues in poetic form (6:1-7). Eschatological blessing to

Simeon's tribe will appear when his sons put away the envy of which he has spoken at length (6:2). Final salvation means the destruction of the "spirits of deceit," which are the cause of the wickedness that infected Simeon's life and would continue to plague his sons (6:6). The poem in which Simeon predicts the future parallels part of Ben Sira's hymn in honor of Wisdom (Sir 24:13-17) and, perhaps more significantly, his hymn in praise of the high priest Simon (Sir 50).[13] The parallels between the two poetic pieces in honor of the two men with the same name may reflect common tradition. Particularly interesting is the derogatory reference to the Samaritans in Sirach 50:26. Simeon's action against the Shechemites is hinted at in Testament of Simeon 5:6 (cf. Gen 49:6-7).[14] The concluding part of the eschatological section predicts Simeon's resurrection (T. Sim. 6:7; cf. 6:2) and looks forward to the incarnation of God, who will "save" Adam and humanity (6:5, 7). It is the first of several explicit christological passages in the Testaments. The closing exhortation asserts the dual sovereignty of Levi and Judah (7:1) and foresees a descendant of the two patriarchs who will be both "God and human," and who will "save all the Gentiles and the race of Israel" (7:2).

The Testament of Levi concerning Priesthood and Arrogance

The divine origin of the priesthood and God's resolution of the institution's abuses are the primary considerations in this Testament, a fact that is reflected in its title. Although the word "arrogance" (*hyperēphania*) never occurs in the body of the Testament, its presence here to summarize priestly misconduct reflects the Testament's use of abstract vices and virtues to typify human conduct. Although it is placed early in the collection, Levi's testament provides a thematic climax to the collection, in that it focuses on the patriarch whose descendants—especially the final one—are the mediators of salvation to Israel and the Gentiles. Levi's superiority over Judah, clear throughout the Testaments, is emphasized here by the almost complete absence of Judah (he appears only in 2:11; 8:14; 9:1) and by the traditional Davidic attributes assigned to Levi's descendants. Although my exposition will focus on this Greek Christian document, I shall note at the appropriate places where the text draws on a Jewish source—the Aramaic Levi Document (see above, pp. 159–65). The Testament can be outlined as follows:

A. Introduction	chap. 1
B. Levi's first commissioning vision and its consequences	2–7
C. Levi's second commissioning vision	8
D. Jacob's vision and Isaac's instruction of Levi	9
E. Exhortation and prediction	10
F. Biographical narrative	11–12
G. Exhortation	13
H. Apocalypse (a revealed review of history)	14–18
I. Conclusion	19

In Levi's first vision, an angel escorts him up through the seven heavens to the divine throne room, where God commissions him to be his priest until the *eschaton* (2:10). The angel, who later identifies himself as Israel's intercessory angel, returns Levi to earth and gives him a second commission—to destroy Shechem in retaliation for the rape of Dinah (5:3-7). The remainder of this section describes Levi's and Simeon's sack of Shechem, Jacob's reaction, and Levi's justification of the deed, which includes some polemics against the Samaritans that are paralleled in Ben Sira's hymn in honor of the high priest Simon (Sir 50).[15] The connection between Levi's commissioning as high priest and his action against Shechem is paralleled in Jubilees 30:18, where the priestly office is bestowed on him as a consequence of his destruction of the Shechemites.[16]

Among the striking features of this vision are its traditional form as a commissioning story (cf. 1 Enoch 12–16, on which see above, p. 50); its description of the angels in the sixth heaven as priests (T. Levi 3:5-6); and its christological references to Levi and Judah as the means through whom God will appear to "save the whole human race" (2:11), and to the son of God, who will visit all the nations and suffer at the hands of Levi's sons (4:4).[17] Surviving fragments of the Aramaic Levi Document 3 indicate that the author of the Testament has here drawn on a Jewish source, although a long interpolation in one Greek manuscript of the Testaments suggests that the author knew the source in a Greek rather than Aramaic form.[18] The vision, moreover, seems to be related to the account of Enoch's vision in 1 Enoch 14–16.[19]

In his second vision (chap. 8) seven angels invest Levi with the robes and paraphernalia of the high priestly office and make some predictions about his priestly descendants. This section parallels Jubilees 32:1 and the fragment of the Aramaic Levi Document 4–5 on which it is based (see above, p. 161).[20] In Testament of Levi 9 Levi's priestly status is confirmed by Jacob's vision and by the priestly instruction that Isaac transmits to Levi. The section is paralleled in fragments of the much longer section in the Aramaic Levi Document 5–10 (see above, p. 161). In Testament of Levi 10 an exhortation to observe Levi's commands has as its rationale a description of the sins that Levi's descendants will, in fact, commit at the "consummation of the ages." They include leading Israel astray (which will be the focus of the apocalypse in chaps. 14–18) and sinning against "the savior of the world." As a result the temple veil will be torn (cf. T. Benj. 9:4 and Mark 15:38; Matt 27:51)[21] and the people will be scattered as captives among the Gentiles. "The book of Enoch" is cited as authority for Levi's prediction. The passage as it stands is clearly Christian and appears to have no counterpart in the Aramaic Levi Document.

The biographical material in Testament of Levi 11–12, however, closely parallels a corresponding part in the Aramaic Levi Document 11–12 (see above, p. 161). Noteworthy in the section is that the genealogy concludes with the generation of Amram and does not mention his son Aaron, the high priestly patriarch.[22] Levi's exhortation to his sons in chapter 13 makes no reference to the cult, but employs the language of wisdom instruction, albeit without mention of the vices and virtues typical of the exhortative sections of the other Testaments. It emphasizes the teaching responsibilities of the priesthood, and the passage as a whole looks like a compressed paraphrase of the Aramaic Levi Document 13 (see above, p. 162).

Testament of Levi 14–18 is a historical apocalypse that traces the wicked history of the priesthood, twice citing "the writing/book of Enoch" as the source of its content and authority (14:1; 16:1). It can be divided into three parts. The first part (chaps. 14–15) traces the history of the priesthood, cataloging the sins of the priests (including their violence against "the savior of the world") and concluding with the appropriate punishment: the desolation of the temple and the scattering of the priests as captives among all the Gentiles (15:1; cf. 10:4). The second part (chaps. 16–17) provides a chronology of "seventy weeks" for the disintegration of the priesthood, again cataloging the priests' sins. Part 3 (chap. 18) presents the resolution of the situation—the appearance of "a new priest" and the inception of the *eschaton*. The new priest is the chief eschatological functionary. Some of the wording of the passages draws on Isaiah 11:1-9 and indicates that this figure has assumed traits of the expected Davidic king (cf. T. Levi 18:2, 5, 7; cf. also 4:5). His principal duties are to enact "true judgment," to reveal the knowledge of God, to bring sin and evil to an end and thus open the gates of paradise, to provide access to the tree of life, and to bind Beliar and his evil spirits. Chapter 18 is perhaps unmatched for its attribution of superlatives to a human figure.[23] The Christian character of this passage is evident in vv 6-7, 10-12, which read like an allusion to the account of Jesus' baptism and temptation in Mark 1:9-13.[24] Preserved fragments of the Aramaic Levi Document contain no counterpart to this apocalypse.[25]

With this passage the Testament of Levi moves to its logical conclusion: from the initial commissioning and ordination of Levi to the appearance and "investiture" of the last priest, who functions as the one who expunges the sin that has plagued the priesthood and humanity and brings the earth back to its primordial state. This glorification of the eschatological high priest must be read as the background for the rest of the statements in the Testaments regarding the latter-day descendant of Levi.

As it stands the Testament of Levi is a Christian document, with christological references woven into its accounts of the future priests' sins and its description of the eschatological priest. A comparison of the text with the fragments of the Aramaic Levi Document indicates that the author of the Testament has shaped a Jewish text of uncertain genre into a testament of christological import, compressing and omitting some of its sections and creating/adding others that fit his purpose.[26]

The Testament of Judah concerning Courage, the Love of Money, and Fornication

Given Judah's importance in the Testaments, it is not surprising that this is the longest of the Testaments.[27] Its title nicely summarizes the content of its narratives and exhortations.[28] The Testament contains all the elements typical of the Testaments, though sometimes in an order that suggests either displacement or a later accretion.

Central to this Testament is Judah's status as the patriarch of the tribe from which the royal dynasty will arise and whose latter-day heir will be the messianic king. Judah's strength, speed, and courage are vividly depicted in the first section (chaps. 2–7), which recounts engagement with a variety of wild animals. The long narrative about Judah's victorious military exploits against kings and armies shows that Judah himself acted as a king (chaps. 3–7). This narrative appears to have originally ended in chapter 7, and the reference to Judah's age (7:10) parallels the similar reference at the end of the next narrative (12:12). Chapter 9, which describes Judah's exploits against the sons of Esau, breaks the continuity between 8:3 and 10:1 and may be a secondary interpolation from Jubilees 37–38 or its source. The first narrative (T. Jud. 3–7, 9) provides a good example of the Testaments' use of traditional Jewish haggadah.[29]

The second narrative develops the story of Judah, his marriage to Bath Shua, and its consequences (Gen 38). The motif of Judah's drunkenness may be drawn from Genesis 49:11-12, but it fits well with Testament of Reuben 3:13 and its combination of drunkenness and fornication. Moreover, the narrative's depiction of both Bath Shua and Tamar as seductive, dangerous women is consonant with the appraisal of women in the Testament of Reuben.[30] Two exhortatory sections are based on this narrative (T. Jud. 13:1—17:1; 18:2—19:4). In form they weave together first-person narrative and second-person exhortation. Although the author places some implicit blame on Bath Shua, the emphasis differs considerably from that in the Testament of Reuben. Here Judah gets drunk and is thus carried away to fornication—on two occasions (11:1-2; 12:3). The Testament advocates not teetotalism but only a proper limit to one's drinking (14:3-8), a motif typical of the wisdom literature. A secondary but important motif in the narrative and exhortation is the evil that arises from the love of money. The motif of Judah's kingship appears in these sections in 12:4 and 15:5-6. The prediction in 17:2—18:1 looks like a secondary interpolation breaking apart two narrative-exhortatory sections that warn against fornication and the love of money.

Chapter 20 internalizes the eschatological battle between the two spirits and is reminiscent of column 4 of the Rule of the Community from Qumran (see above, pp. 139–40). The spirit of truth, who prods the righteous to good deeds, will also function as eschatological witness—interceding for the righteous and accusing the wicked. Of the two spirits we will hear more in the Testament of Asher (below). In chapter 21 the authority of Levi is superior to that of Judah. The final section, an eschatological prediction, follows the typical pattern of sin-punishment-repentance-salvation. Chapter 21, which may be modeled partly on Testament of Levi 18 (or an earlier form of it), describes the kingly Messiah, accreting to him many biblical titles. Here the kingly nature of Judah and his descendants reaches its climax in this Testament. The appearance of the Messiah will be followed by the resurrection and the *eschaton* (chap. 25).

The Testament of Issachar concerning Simplicity

This Testament is especially noteworthy for its thoroughgoing stress on ethics, even in its brief, pro forma eschatological section.[31] Simplicity (*haplotēs*) is an all-encompassing virtue that is especially consonant with hard labor and the agricultural life and contrasted with such vices as envy, slander, being a busybody, and lust.[32] The topic appears in popular Cynic and Stoic philosophical thought.[33]

After the typical introduction (1:1) there follow a pair of narrative sections. The first of these (1:2—2:5) elaborates the biblical story about Rachel, Leah, and the mandrakes (Gen 30:14-18). Rachel is cited as an example of sexual "continence" who eschews the love of sexual pleasure (T. Iss. 2). In this respect she will be followed by her sons, Issachar (3:5) and Joseph (Testament of Joseph, below), and she stands in contrast to Reuben and Judah, whose fornication is featured in their accounts of their lives.[34] In the second section (T. Iss. 3) Issachar speaks of his own life, effectively providing the reader with a catalog of virtues. That he was a farmer has been deduced from the blessing of Jacob (Gen 49:14-15).[35] Testament of Issachar 3:7-8 emphasizes that God blesses such upright conduct.

Chapters 4–5 are mainly exhortation, built on themes set forth in chapter 3. Issachar's sons are to emulate him and his virtues, and for this they are promised the rewards that he (and Judah and Levi) received. Typical of the late wisdom tradition are the initial address (4:1a; cf. Sir 6:23), the command "to walk" in the right way, the stress on Torah, and the promise of blessing for righteous conduct. The catalog-like form of the description of the righteous person in Testament of Issachar 4:2-6 is reminiscent of the description of love in 1 Corinthians 13:4-7. The explication of the "two great commandments"—to love God and one's neighbor—finds echoes elsewhere in the Testaments and is central to the book's piety (T. Iss. 5:1-2; cf. T. Zeb. 5:1; 8:1; T. Dan 5:1-3; T. Benj. 10:2-5).[36] In Testament of Issachar 4, as well as in chapters 6–7, the spirits of Beliar are the cause of sin and straying and are to be avoided.

Chapter 6 is the typical predictive section, presented as a revelation of the last times. Verses 1-2b are a reversal of the catalog in chapters 4–5. Issachar's sons will disobey his exhortation and will "forsake" all the virtues he has recommended and "cling" to all the vices he has denounced. For these sins they will be punished until they repent and are returned to their land (vv 2c-4).

Chapter 7 recapitulates briefly the form of the first part of the Testament: a description of some of Issachar's virtues, with "simplicity" notably missing (vv 1-6); a one-line exhortation to follow his example (v 7a); and the promise of God's blessing (v 7b-f), which provides a reversal of the prediction in chapter 6. After a final reference to "simplicity of heart" (v 7f) the Testament concludes typically with a description of the patriarch's death and burial (vv 8-9).

The Testament of Asher concerning the Two Faces of Vice and Virtue

Asher's Testament is unique among the Twelve Testaments in that the usual narrative about the patriarch's life is replaced by an exposition of the two ways of human conduct.[37] That is, instead of a story about the vices or the virtues of a particular son of Jacob, we learn about the ethical conduct of both good and evil people. The Testament's focus on the inner workings of human beings parallels somewhat the Testament of Reuben and its interest in the human mind and its thoughts.

A. Introduction		1:1-2
B. Exposition of the two ways and exhortation		1:3—6:3
1. Introduction	1:3-9	
2. The evil, two-faced person	2:1-10	
3. Exhortation to avoid this conduct	3:1-2	
4. The good, single-faced person	4:1-5	
5. Exhortation to emulate this	5:1—6:3	
C. Eschatological section		6:4—7:7
1. The ends of life for these two kinds of people	6:4-6	
2. The end times	7:1-7	
D. Conclusion: Asher's death and burial		8:1-2

The author begins by defining his approach to ethics. There are two ways of life that spring from two inclinations within the human, that issue to two kinds of actions and modes of living, and that lead to two ends (1:3-5). He then distinguishes between two kinds of people. In the one, the soul takes pleasure in the good, and its deeds are righteous; if it sins, it repents and overcomes the evil within (1:6-7). In the other, the inclination turns to evil and its deeds are wicked, being ruled by Beliar; even if it happens to do good, it perverts it to wickedness (1:8-9). These two alternatives are then explicated and nuanced. In a variety of ways, the wicked soul (or person) may have two faces—doing some good, but "on the whole" being evil (*kakos* = "vice" in the title [2:1-8]). Like certain animals, they are half-clean, but really unclean (Lev 11:5; Deut 14:7-8).[38] Asher exhorts his children not to be two-faced like these people (T. Ash. 3:1-2). He then lays out the alternative: people who may appear to be doing evil but who are really doing good. That is, "the whole is good" (4:1-4). Like other animals, they appear to be unclean, but are altogether clean (4:5). As with the previous exposition, this leads to an exhortation (5:1—6:3). One should see the twofold nature of all things (5:1-3). In the only autobiographical sentence in the Testament, Asher asserts that he had "tested all things," he "did not wander from the truth" (a two-ways allusion), and he searched out the commandments of the Most High" (cf. Jub. 23:26; 1 Enoch 99:10).[39] To act in this way—in spite of the double-faced character of one's deeds (T. Ash. 4:3, 4)—is to be single-faced (4:1; 5:4), a characteristic that is related to Issachar's "simplicity."[40]

Having completed his exposition of the two ways, Asher turns to the eschatological section of his Testament. Its first subsection describes the "ends" of the two ways, the judgment that comes to evil and good persons (6:4-6). From the look on a dying person's face one can determine that person's fate. A grimace indicates that the evil spirit that prodded one's actions (cf. Beliar in 1:8; 3:2) is dragging the soul to perdition. A calm appearance indicates that the angel of peace is leading the soul to eternal life. This portrayal of the moment of death (which has some parallels in Platonic speculation)[41] indicates that the Testament's two-ways ethic is combined with a two-spirits scheme, as is the case with the Rule of the Community from Qumran (see above, pp. 139–40).[42] The second part of the eschatological section looks toward a consummation in the end time (7:1-7), when "the Most High will visit the earth" (cf. 1 Enoch 25:3; Sir 16:18-19), albeit in the form of a human being (T. Ash. 7:2-3). Some of the terminology in chapters 6–7 suggests that the author of this Testament was interpreting Psalm 73, a text that employs "way" imagery (vv 2, 18, 24), together with Psalm 74.[43]

The Testament of Joseph concerning Self-Control

The biblical story of Joseph is a tale of the persecuted and exalted courtier,[44] an early example of the type of story we have seen in Daniel 3 and 6 (see above, pp. 20–22). In keeping with these later developments of this genre, the Testament of Joseph depicts the patriarch as a *righteous* man, persecuted but delivered, rewarded, and exalted. To make this point the author recounts two stories, the one greatly elaborating the incident of Joseph and Potiphar's wife and the other expounding the theme of Joseph's self-effacing love. Joseph's exemplary conduct in these two stories is a point of reference in a number of the other Testaments.

In the present text, the typical testamentary introduction (1:1) is followed by a poetic summary of Joseph's life (1:2—2:7), which contrasts the patriarch's troubles with God's deliverance. The style is reminiscent of biblical psalms of individual thanksgiving.[45] The repetition prepares us for the reference in 2:7 to Joseph's patience and endurance "in ten temptations," as well as for the episodic nature of the narrative that follows.

This first of the two stories (as also indicated in the title) describes Joseph's self-control (*sōphrosynē*) or more specifically "chastity" in the face of the seductive wiles of "the Egyptian woman" (chaps. 3–9). The author does not tell a plotted story but relates a series of episodes, which may have originated as a homiletical elaboration of Genesis 39:10, "and she spoke to Joseph day after day."[46] Several of these incidents suggest the influence of Hellenistic literature and tradition and of the Phaedra story in particular.[47] Depicted in this series of episodes is the struggle between two able, wily, and resourceful opponents (cf. T. Jos. 2:2)—the one driven by incessant lust, the other contending for chastity. The summary that follows (10:1-4, here not in the form of the usual direct, second-person imperative) stresses Joseph's patience and endurance (cf. 2:7). These virtues also characterize Abraham in the Book of Jubilees (see above, pp. 70–71) and Job in the Testament of Job (see below). The endurance of the spiritual athlete contending for virtue is a typical feature of Hellenistic moral philosophy and of Jewish martyr traditions,[48] and this virtue is important also in some apocalyptic literature.[49] Under this canon the worlds of the persecuted martyr and the virtuous hero are seen in a similar light.

After a brief exhortation based on this story (T. Jos. 10:1-4), the author turns to his second narrative (10:5—16:6), which relates events that chronologically precede those in the first narrative. Also episodic in nature, it describes how on a number of occasions Joseph's self-effacing love led him to keep his silence lest he put others (esp. his brothers) to shame. The motif is particularly striking in view of Genesis 40:14-15, where Joseph *reveals* how he had been kidnapped. Testament of Joseph 17 combines exhortation with narrative and underscores the theme of brotherly love, which vv 5-8 tie to Genesis 50:15-21. Such love leads one not to exalt oneself (T. Jos. 17:8; cf. 10:5). This characteristic of Joseph led to God's exaltation of the patriarch (cf. 10:3-5; 17:8—18:1), which is an essential part of the biblical story. Chapter 18 interweaves exhortation and narrative, presenting the idea that God does reward righteousness.

Joseph's revelation about the future comes in the form of a dream that is clearly Christian (chap. 19). From the twelve tribes of Israel, nine in the north, now dispersed, and three from the south, some of them dispersed, comes the virgin Mary, who gives birth to the Lamb of God, who is also the lion of Judah, who triumphs over those who assault him.[50] The conclusion of the Testament (chap. 20), which develops motifs in Genesis 50:24-26, is atypically long.

Summary

Certain concerns, themes, and theological conceptions pervade the Testaments as a whole. We have noted the centrality of the author's ethical concern, which runs through the narratives and exhortations. Concrete actions are the issue, as one would expect in a narrative genre based on biblical stories. The actions, however, are symptomatic of abstract vices and virtues, which are named throughout the narratives and exhortations and are highlighted in the titles of the individual Testaments: lust (which results in fornication), envy, jealousy, arrogance, courage, the love of money, simplicity, compassion and mercy, anger and deceit, natural goodness, hatred, self-control, a pure mind. These inward dispositions are, in turn, catalyzed or influenced by the activity of the two spirits, who stand in opposition to one another,[51] and who can also function judicially as accuser and advocate (T. Jud. 20) and punishing and rewarding angels (T. Ash. 6:4-6). Finally, we should note, the Testaments' teaching about right and wrong conduct reflects the influence of Hellenistic philosophy, employs language typical of Jewish wisdom teaching, and expresses concerns about issues in Jewish ritual law.[52]

Predictive sections describe the *eschaton* as the time when Beliar and his spirits will be bound. Another central theme is the priority of the tribes of Levi and Judah and of their eschatological leader(s).[53] This pairing is reminiscent of Zechariah 3–4 and is related to the Qumranic hopes regarding the Anointed One(s) of Aaron and Israel. The figure of Joseph is also prominent throughout the Testaments as an example of virtue and the avoidance of vice.[54] Common eschatological hopes include the appearance of an anointed priest and king, the binding of Beliar, the return from dispersion, the salvation of Israel and the Gentiles,[55] and the resurrection from the dead and life in paradise.[56]

Christian Provenance

The numerous clear references to Jesus the Messiah attest beyond a doubt that the present form of the collection of twelve Testaments is a Christian product. Moreover, all the manuscripts of the Testaments, whether in Greek or in a daughter version translated into Armenian or Slavonic, come from the hands of Christian scribes.[57] How these Testaments came into this form has been a hotly debated issue among scholars for the many centuries that they have been known in the Christian West since their publication in 1242 C.E.[58] Were they a fresh Christian composition? Were they an interpolated Jewish collection? Were they an expanded collection from a shorter Jewish set of testaments? To what extent did their author simply make use of Jewish traditions?

The last of these possibilities is as certain as the present Christian character of the collections. Since the beginning of the twentieth century scholars have known of two medieval texts, discovered in the Cairo synagogue genizah (storeroom), that contain large blocks of material from an Aramaic Levi Document and a Hebrew testament of Naphtali.[59] Fragments of the Aramaic Levi Document and of a Hebrew Naphtali text have also been uncovered among the Qumran Scrolls.[60] Various parallels between these texts and the Greek Testaments make clear that the author of the Testaments has made use of these ancient Jewish texts, either in their Semitic form or in a Greek translation. Parallels between the Greek Testaments and other ancient Jewish traditions are also evident and indicate an even broader use of Jewish material.[61] In the case of the Aramaic Levi Document, it is clear that the author of the Greek Testaments has compressed his source and added new material (see above, pp. 159–60). In addition to this source material, passages about the eschatological descendants of Levi and Judah parallel some of the messianic speculation in some of the Qumran Scrolls (see above, p. 151), as do some aspects of the two-spirits material in the Testaments.

The aforementioned sources and parallels, however, do not prove that the Greek Testaments are an expanded or interpolated form of an ancient Jewish collection of twelve patriarchal testaments. Moreover, various literary-critical attempts to extrapolate from the Greek Christian collection a Jewish collection of twelve or fewer testaments have gained no scholarly consensus.[62] What the Qumran finds appear to attest is a triad of testaments allegedly authored by Levi, Kohath, and Amram, which would have functioned to authenticate the priestly line. Of an ethically oriented corpus of twelve (or fewer) patriarchal testaments, there is no evidence. What we are left with in the Testaments of the Twelve Patriarchs is a Christian text whose author has dipped deeply into biblical and postbiblical Jewish tradition in a way that we can now only partly reconstruct.[63] What might we imply about that author and his context?

The Christian author of the Testaments of the Twelve Patriarchs stood with his feet in two worlds. In the first instance, he placed himself within the historical (if not ethnic) tradition of Israel. In that context, he drew not only on the biblical stories about the patriarchs, but on haggadic material that he knew either from tradition handed down to him in his Christian context or from non-Christian Jewish contemporaries with whom he had actual contact. The postbiblical character of his sources did not prevent him from treating them as authentic biblical exposition. He also understood the Torah as a basis for his ethical exposition, and he had knowledge of and drew on Jewish two-spirits anthropology and Jewish messianic speculation tied to the tribes of Levi and Judah. For him, however, there would not be two messianic figures, but one—Jesus Christ, descended from both Levi and Judah.[64] In the second instance, this Israelite context notwithstanding, he expressed his ethical instruction in categories that were at home in Hellenistic philosophy. This blending of Israelite tradition and Hellenistic forms and conceptions, however, is not surprising. We have seen it already in the Wisdom of Solomon and 4 Maccabees, and it characterized the ethical teaching of the apostle Paul.[65] It will reappear in the Testament of Job.

A cutoff date of the composition of the Testaments around 200 C.E. is provided by Origen's quotations from the corpus,[66] and other patristic material from the second century provides a viable context for some of the issues that are paramount to the corpus.[67] Their language of composition would have been Greek.[68]

Our conclusions about the Christian character of the Testaments have two implications. First, material from the Testaments should not be used uncritically to illustrate the forms of Judaism from which Christianity developed. Second, the Testaments should be integrated into histories of second-century Christianity to help portray the diversity of its religious expression.

The Testament of Job

The testamentary genre described in the previous section provides the outline and external form within which the biblical story of Job is here retold.

Central to the book as a whole is the contrast between heavenly realities and this world, which is the arena of Satan's activities. Job gains insight into this distinction and is contrasted with other characters who lack the insight. The unfolding plot depicts Job's insight in various stages and describes how certain other characters move from ignorance to knowledge, from unfaith to salvation, with Job always playing the mediating role.[69] At a number of key points, the author has reshaped the characters in the biblical book to deal with potential problems in its narrative.[70]

The book begins with the typical testamentary setting (A): the dying father gathers his children around him to recount the events of his life and to exhort the children on the basis of his example. Different from the Testaments of the Twelve Patriarchs, the narrative sections of the Testament of Job (B–D) predominate almost to the exclusion of other sections.

Job's Combat with Satan

The first narrative section (B) depicts a contest or battle between Satan and Job, who is here the king of Egypt (cf. Job 29:25; 31:36).[71] "Patience" (*makrothymia*) and "endurance" or "perseverance" (*hypomonē*) are the key words.[72] The initial episode in this section describes Job's conversion from paganism, his commission to raze the idolatrous temple, and his execution of this task (1:6—5:3). The episode has many of the features typical of angelophanic commissioning scenes. Job's pondering over "who this God is"— the functional equivalent of a prayer—is answered by the appearance of an angel who reveals the truth to Job and at his request (3:5b) authorizes him to destroy the temple. The episode is, however, much more than a commissioning scene. The angel is primarily a revealer. He exposes Satan as a deceiver who puts himself forward as God. By means of this revelation, Job is set apart from the rest of humankind, which remains subject to Satan's deceptions (3:4b, 5b). Job responds to this revelation by requesting permission to destroy the temple and thus to end Satan's cult and his deceptive spell over Job's compatriots and subjects. The angel warns Job that he is entering a struggle with Satan in which no holds are barred, but he assures Job that if he endures he will, like a true athlete, receive his reward and win his crown. God will equip him for the struggle. Job solemnly responds that he will endure until death, and he challenges Satan by demolishing his temple. This first section gives the biblical story a new twist. There Job is unaware of the bargain that Satan has struck with God. Here he provokes Satan into a dual and God more or less stands on the sidelines.[73] Thus the nature of Job's heroism is very different in the two texts.

In the next episode Satan appears in the first of several disguises (chaps. 6–8). As a beggar he should be welcome at Job's door (see chaps. 9–10). The servant girl is deceived, but Job, with his newfound wisdom, penetrates the disguise. The burnt loaf that Job offers Satan is symbolic of Job's refusal henceforth to participate in the cult, of which the offering of bread seems to have been a part, and it may also imply Job's burning of the temple (see above, p. 70, regarding the closely related story in Jub 12). Satan turns the imagery back on Job: the bread symbolizes Job's body, soon to be destroyed like the loaf. Job reasserts his readiness for the contest. At this point the narrative links up with the biblical story. Satan receives authority to attack Job (cf. T. Job 8:1 and Job 1:6-12).

We now move to the heart of the contest, ultimately derived from Job 1:13-21 and 2:7-10, but here greatly elaborated and divided into four distinct episodes. The first episode (T. Job 9–16) begins with a long description of Job's deeds of charity. In both form and literary function this section is the counterpart of the narrative sections of certain of the Testaments of the Twelve Patriarchs (e.g., Issachar and Zebulun). It defines pious conduct: looking after the poor, giving alms, not withholding wages, and the like. Satan directs his fury at the livestock of Job that were set aside for charitable purposes. Job loses the rest of his livestock. He responds to this first onslaught of Satan by praising God and refusing to blaspheme. He has won the first round.

In the next episode (T. Job 17–19) Satan assumes another disguise and deceives Job's countrymen. By distorting reality he enlists them against Job. Satan destroys Job's children, and his erstwhile subjects drive him away and plunder his house. Although Job is greatly distressed, he contemplates the goal of this contest. The heavenly city is of far greater worth than all that Job has given up by his voluntary entrance into battle with Satan. In spite of his deep distress over his children's death, Job blesses the name of the Lord. Satan has lost round two.

Now Satan turns his attacks on Job's person (chap. 20). In short order Job, who had been sitting on his throne, finds himself sitting on a dung heap, his body infested with worms. He responds not with complaint but by making certain that he suffers this affliction to the full (20:10). Again Satan has been bested, and we are now ready for the final round (chaps. 21–27).

Satan attempts to get at Job through Job's wife, Sitidos. He dons yet another disguise and deceives Sitidos. Roles are reversed from the first scene. The wife is a beggar, and Satan is the seller of bread. Whereas Job had freely given bread to the poor, his wife must now have herself sheared in public in order to pay for the bread. The lament in chapter 25 underscores the reversal of situations. His wife's public degradation completes Job's humiliation. She comes to him with the tale of woe, mocks his hopes for salvation, and urges him "to speak some word against the Lord and die." All this is of course a cleverly contrived plan of Satan, who is using Sitidos as his unwitting accomplice (23:13). Job responds to his wife with a word of encouragement. Then he unmasks Satan, who is comically depicted hiding behind Sitidos. Job challenges him to come out into the open and do battle. But the deceiver cannot fight in the open, and so with tears the spirit must concede defeat to Job, the human being, who has shown himself superior and victorious in the contest (27:3-8). The narrative, which began with the dialogue in chapter 4, is now resolved. Satan must withdraw, defeated—at least for the time being. The section concludes with the typical testamentary admonition that the children emulate the father's virtue, here his patience (27:10). This is the last we hear of this virtue.

Job's Debate with the Kings

This second narrative section of the book corresponds to the poetic section of the biblical book and describes Job's debate with his friends, here depicted as four kings. Once again Job's superior insight is pitted against others' lack of perception. The primary opposition is between Job and Elious, who is "filled with Satan" (41:7) and is his representative in this debate (cf. 27:9).

The brief narrative at the end of the prose section of the biblical book (2:11-13) is developed into an extended scene that depicts the kings' reaction to Job's situation (T. Job 28–30): astonishment, disbelief, and doubt as to his identity. This leads to Elious's lengthy lament (chap. 32), which contrasts Job's former glorious state with his present degradation. "Are you the one who. . . ? Where now is the splendor of your throne?" Some of the verses contrast Job's former charity and generosity to others with his present deprivation (vv 2a, 3a, 4a, 8a). To the repeated rhetorical question "Where now is your throne?" (chap. 33), Job responds, "My throne is in heaven." In this exchange Job's superior insight is again evident. Elious and his colleagues, as we shall see, misperceive reality. Job's present suffering does not prove that he has lost his kingdom, for this world is essentially transitory and changing, and prosperity may fade. But Job understands that he will be exalted in heaven, the place of unchanging, permanent realities, and the present existence of his throne there guarantees that exaltation. Eliphaz rejects this assertion out of hand, mocks his claim, and suggests that the kings leave. Baldas adopts a mediating position: Job may be "mentally disturbed." The next interchange tests this hypothesis (chaps. 35–38). Again Job contrasts heavenly and earthly things. The earth and its inhabitants are unstable—witness his present predicament. His heart is fixed on heavenly things. He will not disavow God, who has permitted his present situation. Baldas, with his human mind-set, is incapable of understanding heavenly things (38:8). He does not perceive Job's throne in heaven, nor can he see God's hand in Job's affliction. Sophar reasserts Job's mental derangement and offers the help of his physicians, which Job refuses because his "healing and treatment are from the Lord," who is superior to the physicians whom the Lord created (38:13; cf. Sir 38:1).

At this point the narrative is broken by the reappearance of Job's wife (T. Job 39–40). Because the debate picks up again in chapter 41, it is likely that chapters 39–40 have been interpolated into the present context, albeit for a specific purpose. When Sitidos appears, the kings fail to recognize her, and she identifies herself in the mode of the lament that had been raised for her in the marketplace (39:2-3; cf. chap. 25). The interchange between Job and his wife again contrasts his superior insight with the lack of perception on the part of others. Previously his wife had failed to perceive Satan's true identity. Here her lack of perception parallels that of the kings (one reason for its placement here). For Sitidos the death of her children is reality, and she asks that they have a memorial in the form of a proper burial. The kings agree. Job disputes their ignorance of reality—which is in heaven. The "tomb" (the house that fell on them) is empty. The children have been taken to heaven by the Creator, their king (cf. 2 Macc 7:11, 22-23, 27-29). Sitidos and the kings think Job is mad. Now Job *proves* the reality of his assertion. His wife and the kings are granted a vision of the heavenly realities: the enthroned Deity and the children enthroned by God's side. Sitidos is convinced. She has the memorial she has sought—in heaven—and she returns to the city, where she dies (T. Job 40:6-14). The story about Sitidos has two functions in its present context. Having likened Sitidos's lack of perception to that of the kings, the author uses the vision to bring her from ignorance to knowledge, from disbelief to faith. The kings have also had the vision and thus are responsible for their knowledge. Elious will be culpable for his action in what follows.

Elious denies what he knows to be true. He takes up the conversation that had been broken off, specifically Job's assertion of a throne in heaven. With words that are not recorded in the text here,[74] he exposes Job's "nonexistent portion." He does so as a spokesman of Satan, employing the satanic device of deception, confusing and contradicting reality.

Now God intervenes to resolve the plot (chap. 43). Eliphaz, Baldas, and Sophar have sinned by speaking falsely against Job, but they will be forgiven through Job's sacrificial intercession. With Elious it is a different matter. The heavenly reality he has denied is now refused him. His kingdom has passed away and his throne has decayed. His misconstrual of Job's situation becomes the reality of his own case. Job's relationship to his compatriots is restored, as is his fortune (chap. 44).

With the major elements in the story resolved we have arrived at the end of the biblical story. Job must now die (Job 42:17). To tell this story the author returns to the testamentary framework. The final ethical exhortation is brief and pro forma (T. Job 45:1-4). Job does not exhort his children to the endurance and patience of which we heard so much in the first narrative section. Rather, he paraphrases the double commandment in terms consonant with the content of the book: Job had not forgotten *God*, and his life had been a model of charity to *the poor and helpless*. The stricture against marrying foreign wives is frequent in the literature of this time.

Job Distributes His Possessions

This section (F) brings to a climax and resolution a number of elements in the book as a whole. Job apportions his earthly possessions among his sons, as was the custom, but he bequeaths a better inheritance to his daughters. The magical bands with which he invests them will lead them to a better world. Moreover, the bands transform the daughters' minds. They are no longer concerned with or troubled by earthly things but are enabled here and now to participate in the heavenly level and to join in the praise of the heavenly chorus. Thus Job transfers his special powers to his daughters.

This transfer is remarkable in light of the rest of the book. On three different occasions Job's insight has been contrasted with misperceptions by women (chaps. 7, 22–27, 39–40). Now Job's daughters become the knowledgeable ones, the true heirs of their father. This episode resolves clearly and definitively the inferior role of women in the book. Against the background of his earlier distinction between the earthly and the heavenly, Job distributes his earthly possessions to his sons and his heavenly gifts to his daughters. This action ascribes a higher religious status to these women than to their male contemporaries.[75] This development in the plot and the contrast between the outcomes for the male and female children of Job is remarkable. It is uncertain, however, whether the elevation of Job's daughters is an expression of the author's high regard for the status and roles of women in general or, perhaps more likely, whether it corresponds to the important social and religious role of certain women in the author's community.[76]

This section adds a twist to the testamentary genre. Job's highest "virtue," his insight, is not recommended in a typical exhortatory section but is bequeathed by means of a certain magical apparatus, which also acts as an amulet against the power of the enemy (47:11). The section is also the counterpart of the eschatological section of the testamentary genre, providing entree to heaven and eternal life and knowledge of "things present and future" (47: 11).

Message and Origin

The Testament of Job is in the first place an exhortation to patience and endurance in a troubled and unstable world. Permanence and stability are to be found only in heaven (33:2-9; 36:4-6). The world, by contrast, is in a state of flux. More than that, it is the arena in which Satan perpetrates his deceptions and illusions as he engages in combat with the believer. Salvation involves a revealed perception of these facts and of the present existence of one's reward in heaven. At the same time, this perception enables one to endure in the combat and thus obtain the reward (18:5-7). Endurance for Job is almost tantamount to faith or faithfulness. When Job was rich, charity and generosity were appropriate as piety. When he is cast into dire straits true religion is the endurance that resists the satanic temptation to fall into despair and thus curse God and accept the present miserable situation as ultimate reality. The lonely spiritual athlete, locked in mortal combat with Satan, is persistent and victorious. At the same time, he is the true "martyr," testifying—to friend, onlooker, and antagonist—to the spiritual realities that he knows to exist in spite of his predicament. Through this testimony he wins others to his side.

The provenance and date of the Testament of Job cannot be fixed with certainty. The description of Job as a king of Egypt and several other features in the text suggest that country as a place of origin.[77] But in what context and when? The personal mysticism depicted and the tendency toward ecstasy on the part of women in the last section may support an origin among the Jewish group known as the Therapeutae,[78] or to a similar group.[79] It seems better to reserve judgment, since we know relatively little about the sociology of Egyptian Judaism.[80] A probable allusion to the work in Tertullian (*Pat.* 14) indicates 200 C.E. as a terminus ad quem.[81] The book's Greek vocabulary suggests a date no earlier than the first half of the second century C.E.[82] The book's heavy dependence on the Greek translation of Job is an indication that it was composed in Greek.[83]

Although there is virtual consensus among scholars that the Testament of Job is a Jewish composition,[84] our only evidence for the text derives from Christian sources. These include the manuscripts of the Greek text and the Coptic and Slavonic versions (see n. 77), a possible allusion to the text in James 5:11 ("You have heard of Job's endurance [*hypomonē*]"),[85] and Tertullian's reference to the narrative detail in Testament of Job 20:9-10. This Christian evidence allows two explanations: Christians preserved and transmitted a Jewish work;[86] a Christian in close touch with Hellenistic Jewish traditions created a didactic text about a biblical saint.[87] This latter, "default" position cannot be disproved with total certainty. However, although the Testament is thoroughly concerned with "soteriology," Job's appeals to the heavenly world, and indeed his vision of the "glory of the heavenly one," totally miss the opportunity to describe the enthroned Christian Savior's presence there. It is Job's children and not the Christ who are crowned by the side of God. Two possible Christian allusions are of uncertain value. In 7:12 Satan likens the burnt loaf of bread to Job's destroyed body. Job's claim that his children's bodies have been taken to heaven from the building that collapsed on them recalls the New Testament story of Jesus' empty tomb. In neither instance, however, is a Christian interpretation necessary, nor is its function clear. We are left with a text that is thoroughly Jewish in its content, that evinces no demonstrable Christian elements,[88] but that is known only from Christian sources. In either case, the work is testimony to Christian interest in promoting "patience" and "endurance" in difficult circumstances by citing the example of Job. This is noteworthy in view of texts like 1 Peter and the Epistle to the Hebrews (see below), whose authors cite the suffering and exalted Christ as the example to be emulated.

Related Literature

Although the Testament of Job is one of the less familiar Pseudepigrapha, its traditions and its theology are related to a wide variety of Jewish and Christian literature. The first episode closely parallels traditions about Abraham in Jubilees. Abraham comes to a knowledge of the true God and recognizes the folly of idols. He defeats Satan's attempt to destroy the crops, and he burns down the local idolatrous temple (Jub. 11:15—12:15; cf. Apocalypse of Abraham, above, p. 285). The story of the sacrifice of Isaac in Jubilees 17:15—18:19 is set in the framework of a heavenly conflict between the prince of *mastēmā* and the angel of the Presence that is reminiscent of the prologue of the biblical book of Job. This story depicts Abraham as a model of patience and endurance, a characteristic attached to him through ten different trials (19:8). The Testament of Joseph speaks of *Joseph's* patience and endurance through ten trials. Common to these works is the idea of life as a struggle to be endured and the use of patriarchal examples to make the point. The Testament of Job is unique among these in its emphasis on Job's knowledge of heavenly realities. Other Hellenistic Jewish texts and non-Jewish texts also depict the struggle of the spiritual athlete.[89]

The second narrative in the Testament of Job (chaps. 28–43) has affinities with the Wisdom of Solomon, which sets the story of the suffering and exalted hero in the midst of a debate over the existence of heavenly reality, specifically immortality. As in the case of Elious, the antagonists lose the immortality they have denied.[90]

Jewish apocalyptic literature and the Qumran corpus provide other parallels. The appeal to a revealed knowledge of heavenly realities as a dynamic for endurance under stress is essential to the message of 1 Enoch 92–105 (see above, pp. 110, 112, 113). The motif appears also in the Parables of Enoch and in 2 Baruch 4:2-4 (see above, pp. 249 and 278). Salvation both as knowledge and as a present reality is typical of the Qumran Hymns.[91] The ecstatic angelic liturgy of Job's daughters has parallels in the Qumran literature (see above, pp. 151–54).

On the Christian side the closest parallel is perhaps the Epistle to the Hebrews, particularly chapters 10–12. Life is a struggle to be endured, and the victor's crown is promised as reward. The author encourages his readers by citing the example of past heroes of faith, the last of these being Jesus. The ground of one's hope is in the realities of the heavenly world. Revealed knowledge brought down from heaven as salvation from a world under the spell of Satan is essential to the theology of the Fourth Gospel.[92]

The Testament of Abraham

This didactic but entertaining story about the last day of Abraham's life is preserved in two recensions (text forms).[93] Although the relationship between the two recensions is complex in a number of respects, the longer of the two is by far the more interesting and preserves a more original form of the story's plot and of many of its narrative elements.[94] The time for Abraham's death has arrived. Out of special consideration for God's "friend," God dispatches Michael to announce his death and to command the patriarch to put his affairs in order, that is, to make his testament. At first Abraham refuses to follow Michael, but then he agrees when God promises that he can take a tour of the whole universe. During this chariot ride Abraham calls down divine punishment on sinners whom he sees in the act of transgression. Fearing that sinless Abraham will annihilate the whole human race, God orders the patriarch up to heaven to see the judgment process and learn mercy. When Abraham successfully intercedes for a soul whose righteous deeds and sins are equally balanced in the judgment scale, he decides that he should also intercede for the sinners whom he had previously condemned. They are brought back to life, and he has learned about the compassion of a long-suffering God. Michael escorts him back to earth and again orders him to make his testament. Once more he refuses, and then God sends Death, who relentlessly presses the patriarch despite his protests and finally takes his soul by a subterfuge. Abraham never does make his testament.

The book is neatly divided into two parallel and symmetrical parts. Each begins as God summons the messenger of death and ends with Abraham in the typical testamentary situation, on his bed surrounded by the members of his household.[95]

Part I		Part II	
Chapter		Chapter	
1	God summons Michael: Go, tell Abraham he will die, so that he can make his testament.	16	God summons Death: Go, bring Abraham to me.
2	Michael leaves, goes to Abraham, who sits at Mamre.		Death leaves, goes to Abraham, who sits at Mamre.
	Abraham sees him, rises to meet him.		Abraham sees him, rises to meet him.
	Michael greets honored father, righteous soul, friend of God.		Death greets honored Abraham, righteous soul, friend of God.
	Abraham returns the greeting, notes Michael's glory and beauty.		Abraham returns the greeting, notes Death's glory.
	Whence are you?		Who are you, and whence?
	Michael replies elusively.		I tell you truth: I am Death.
	————		Abraham contradicts him, then refuses to follow.
2–3	They go to his house, conversing.	17	They go in the house: Death is silent.
	The talking tree: a hint.		————
	Isaac, Abraham wash his feet.		(Abraham's sullen inhospitality)
4	They prepare the room.		
	Michael returns to heaven.		Death stays.
5	They eat, go to bed.		Abraham goes to bed, orders Death away.

5–7	Isaac's dream, interpretation; Michael reveals identity, mission		Are you Death? Discuss how Death comes to different people.
7	Abraham refuses to go.		———
8–9	Michael's ascent, return: Make your testament!		Death stays.
9	Abraham asks to see all the world.		Show me all your rottenness.
10	Abraham sees, calls down various kinds of death.		Death unmasks, shows Abraham various kinds of death; servants die.
11–13	Sees judgment; Michael explains.		———
14	They pray for the dead; revived.	18	They pray for dead; revived.
	———	19	Further delays, refusal; Death explains vision.
15	Michael returns Abraham to Sarah, Isaac, servants, who rejoice.	20	Isaac, Sarah, servants mourn.
	Make your testament! No! Michael returns to heaven.		Abraham is suddenly taken. Michael takes soul to heaven.

Binding these two parts together is a double narrative thread: God's command that Abraham prepare for death and Abraham's refusal to do so. The plot moves through the two parts from God's initial command to its fulfillment with Abraham's death. Each of the two parts has its own pace and tone, corresponding to its relative place in the development of the plot. Part I is lengthy and rambling, and it has more than its share of humorous touches: the double entendre in Michael's identification of himself (chap. 2); the picture of the disturbed patriarch afraid to admit that he hears trees talking and sees teardrops turning to pearls (chap. 3); Michael unable to cope with Abraham's repeated refusals and making repeated trips to the divine throne room for new orders (chaps. 4, 8, 9, 15), once with the excuse that he needed to stop by the restroom.[96]

When Michael fails in his mission, we move to part II, where a totally different pace and tone pervade. The divine messenger is "merciless, rotten Death." His identification of himself is quick and to the point. Abraham's continued refusals are met not by repeated trips to the throne room but by Death's pursuit of Abraham into the inner rooms of his house, right to his bed. This time Abraham's request for a revelation results in a fierce vision that strikes terror in the patriarch's heart, and he falls into "the faint of death." Again Abraham's family gathers around his bed, not to rejoice over his return but to mourn his imminent death. Now there is no command to make his testament, only the sudden, unexpected death about which he had inquired moments before. God's command is finally fulfilled. The plot is resolved.

Whereas the testaments we have previously discussed use the deathbed situation as a setting for ethical and eschatological instruction that is often not essentially connected with this setting, the Testament of Abraham focuses on the problem of death itself and right and wrong attitudes about its relationship to God's judgment. By means of his plot-line the author underscores the inevitability of death while at the same time dealing sympathetically with the universal human fear of death and aversion to it. He employs the figure of Abraham to both ends. Abraham's righteousness could not save him from death:

> Even upon [pious, all-holy, righteous, hospitable Abraham] there came the common, memorable, bitter cup of death and the uncertain end of life. (Chap. 1; Stone, adapted)

Although the author ascribes to the patriarch some of the virtues traditionally attributed to him (righteousness, hospitality), he has glaringly omitted the most celebrated of these: Abraham's obedient faith. Indeed, he has created a satirical portrait of the biblical and traditional Abraham.[97] He fears God's summons to "go forth" (cf. T. Abr. 1 and Gen 12:1),[98] and his haggling with God (contrast Gen 18:22-32) takes on the character of disobedience.[99] Through this satire the author transforms the exceptional patriarch into a character whose fear of death places him in solidarity with the rest of humanity and with whom his readers can empathize.[100]

Not only has our author reversed the traditional theme of Abraham's obedient faith, but he has also employed the motif of Abraham's righteousness to counter wrong (and self-righteous) ideas about the relationship between death and divine judgment.[101] Because he has not sinned, Abraham has no sympathy for sinners, and he invokes divine judgment on them in the form of sudden death (chap. 10). The Bible itself describes the prophets doing this, and contemporary Jewish literature is replete with wishes, prayers, and statements about God's judgment of sinners. God responds to this traditional attitude by reference to Scripture, namely, Ezekiel 18. The righteous one not only fails to understand sinners, he also fails to comprehend the long-suffering mercy of the Creator, who does not desire the death of his creatures but grants them time to repent. When Abraham has learned his lesson by viewing the judgment process and has repented and prayed (here for the restoration of those whose death he had invoked), God makes yet another point. Persons who suffer an untimely death are not punished after death.[102] Thus to call down sudden death on sinners in the hope of catching them in their sins before they have a chance to repent is not only contrary to God's merciful intent but also counterproductive. The act itself prevents its intended result.

In the corresponding section of part II, our author treats the problem of death in a more programmatic fashion. At Abraham's request Death unmasks himself, and this causes the untimely demise of seven thousand (!) of Abraham's servants (chap. 17). In the discussion that follows, Death reveals himself as the universal devastator of humanity. What Abraham did in an ad hoc manner is Death's full-time occupation. Moreover, these deaths are untimely at the rate of seventy-one to one (chap. 20). This very fact, however, mitigates Death's effectiveness and validity, for, as we learned from chapter 14, such deaths deliver one from postmortem judgment.

Abraham must die, as must all human beings. Nonetheless, Death's self-description, when read in the light of God's previous revelation, neutralizes Death's sting. Premature death saves one from postmortem judgment and eternal destruction. When such judgment takes place God's mercy is operative. On the basis of these consoling principles our author sweetens "the bitter cup" and tempers the first part of his message, which asserted the inevitability of death.

In his trip to heaven Abraham receives a double vision of the judgment process: the separation of the souls into the two gates leading to life and destruction (chap. 11) and the judgment before Abel, the son of Adam (chaps. 13–14). Both scenes imply that the soul goes to its eternal destiny shortly after death. A bodily resurrection is not envisioned, and the references to the second and third judgments look like interpolations into the text.[103] The main judgment scene is probably a piece of tradition. Its description of the two angelic scribes and the book is paralleled in a number of other Jewish writings.[104] The stated rationale for Abel's position as judge is that he is the son of Adam, and therefore he judges all of Adam's subsequent progeny. The ascription to him of judicial powers may derive from his status as protomartyr,[105] or the title "son of Adam" might conceivably reflect the title "son of man" in 1 Enoch 37–71, where this figure is enthroned as judge.[106] The balancing of righteous deeds versus sins may reflect Egyptian ideas attested in the *Book of the Dead*.[107]

Although the Testament of Abraham does not recast biblical narrative as other Jewish texts do (e.g., Jubilees, the Genesis Apocryphon, Pseudo-Philo), it does draw significantly on biblical texts and on exegetical traditions attested elsewhere.[108] Specially noteworthy among these traditions is the Jewish haggadah about the death of Moses and his attempts to delay it.[109] Moreover, similar to the Book of Jubilees and the Testament of Job, we find the movement of traditions between the figures of Job and Abraham.[110] Yet another parallel is the comic narrative about the failure of the righteous man to understand the presence of an angel, as this is recounted in the book of Tobit (see above, pp. 30–31, 33). In addition to the use of Jewish tradition, this "well-read" author has drawn on Egyptian tradition, as we have seen, and also on motifs from Homer's *Odyssey,* among others.[111]

The long recension of the Testament of Abraham has been preserved in twenty-three Greek manuscripts dating from the fourteenth to the eighteenth centuries, and the short recension, in eight manuscripts from the eleventh to the fifteenth centuries.[112] Daughter versions were translated into Coptic, Ethiopic, Arabic, as well as Church Slavonic and Romanian.[113] Although the Greek of both recensions (the short more than the long) has many Semitic characteristics, there is no sure evidence that the work was composed in Hebrew or Aramaic.[114]

In its present form the Testament of Abraham is a Christian text, transmitted in a wide range of Christian circles. Moreover, the Greek of the long recension has been influenced by the New Testament.[115] Nonetheless, one major element in the story almost certainly points to its non-Christian origin. In the judgment scene, which is central to the story, the judge of all humanity is the glorified, enthroned Abel, who is flanked by several named angels. The presence of these figures and the absence of the exalted Christ in such a scene seem unimaginable in a text that was composed by a person who was by any definition a Christian.[116]

The date of the Testament is difficult to fix. Its earliest attestation is a fragmentary fifth-century Sahidic Coptic papyrus whose text is closest to the short recension. This places the long recension somewhat earlier, although its Greek vocabulary dates from a later period. If the work is of Jewish rather than Christian origin, as seems to be the case, it may have been composed as early as the first century C.E.,[117] most likely in Egypt.[118]

The Life of Adam and Eve

The Genesis story of Adam and Eve inspired a large volume of Jewish and early Christian literature.[119] Two recensions or text forms of one such work—one preserved in Greek and the other in Latin—have traditionally have been called the Apocalypse of Moses and the Vita Adae et Evae. We shall refer to them as the Greek Life (of Adam and Eve) and the Vita (Adae et Evae), respectively. It should be emphasized, however, that these are only two examples from a complex tradition in which manuscripts or groups of manuscripts often play out their own variations, sometimes creating new themes and sometimes drawing on (oral) tradition.[120]

The Greek Life of Adam and Eve

This shorter and simpler of the two recensions is primarily an account of Adam's death, its cause and its cure. Chapters 1–4 retell Genesis 4:1-25: the birth of Cain and Abel, the murder of Abel, and the birth of Seth.[121] The main function of the section is to introduce Seth, who will be the recipient of important traditions and in other ways a central figure in the action that follows. Once Seth has appeared, the author turns quickly to Adam's terminal illness (5:1-2) and devotes the remainder of the book to the events surrounding Adam's death. Most of the elements of the testamentary genre (see above, p. 302) occur in these chapters, but they are incorporated into a broader plot that embodies the author's message.

When Adam sees that he is going to die, he summons his children (5:2). Because they do not understand what death is (5:4—6:3), Adam recites briefly the story of the temptation, the fall, and the expulsion from the garden (chaps. 7–8). Unlike the typical testamentary narrative, this recital does not present Adam's conduct as an example but explains the reason for his present plight. He has sinned and therefore must die. As we shall see, the necessity of Adam's death is an essential part of the author's message.

The author now interrupts the testamentary form with a narrative sequence that dramatizes his message (9:3—13:6). Seeking to put off the time of his death, Adam dispatches Eve and Seth to the garden in search of the oil of mercy, which will bring him relief (9:3). Along the way Seth is attacked by a beast (chaps. 10—12). God's curse in Genesis 3:15 is in effect. When Seth and Eve pray for the oil of mercy, the angel Michael responds,

> [The oil of mercy] *will be yours not now but at the end of the times.* Then all flesh from Adam to that great day will arise. . . . Then the joy of the garden will be given to them. (Life 13:2-4)

This twofold assertion—not now but at the end—is central to the message of the book and will be repeated later.

Having eliminated the possibility that Adam can escape death, the author returns us to the testamentary form he had temporarily abandoned in chapter 5. Knowing that he is going to die, Adam asks Eve to gather the children and to recount to them the story of the temptation, the fall, and the expulsion from the garden (chap. 14). Like its briefer counterpart in chapters 7–8, this lengthy and artful elaboration of the events in Genesis 3 explains to Adam's children the reason for his death (Life 15–34). The detailed account of the expulsion from the garden repeats the earlier sequence of Adam's petition and God's response (cf. chaps. 27–29 and 9–13). Adam seeks mercy (27:4; cf. 9:3; 13:1 and the request for the oil of mercy). God commands the angels to continue with the expulsion (27:4—28:1). When Adam pleads for access to the tree of life (28:2) God repeats the twofold assertion of chapter 13:

> You shall *not* take from it *now.* . . . If you keep yourself from all evil as one willing to die, when again the resurrection comes to pass *I shall raise you up.* And then [fruit] from the tree of life *will be given to you.* (28:3-4)

Now Adam pleads for fragrant herbs from the garden to offer incense. God allows him to take these, as well as seeds with which to grow food, and then Adam and Eve are expelled from the garden (chap. 29). The section concludes with the stereotyped testamentary exhortation that the children not follow their parents' example (chap. 30; contrast 5:4—6:3).

The author's narration of the deathbed events continues to focus on Adam's fate, namely, his death and burial (chaps. 31–42).[122] After giving instructions about the disposal of his body, Adam asks Eve to pray because he is not yet certain of God's mercy (31:3-4). Her repetitious confession of sin is typical of the book's emphasis on Eve's primary responsibility for the fall (32:1-2).[123] Through this confession she is presumably lessening Adam's fault in the hope that God will have mercy on him. In answer to her prayer she is given a vision of the heavenly throne room and of Adam's salvation (chaps. 33–37). God then summons the heavenly entourage and gives instructions for the burial of Adam and Abel (38:1—41:2). God's last word repeats the now familiar double formula:

> Adam, Adam, . . . I told you that you are earth and *to earth you shall return* [cf. Gen 3:19]. Again I promise you the resurrection; *I shall raise you up on the last day* in the resurrection with every nation of humanity that is from your progeny. (*Life* 41)

Adam's burial completes those events relating to his death and shaped by the testamentary genre.

Chapters 42–43 describe Eve's death and burial. Seth receives special instructions for her burial, together with the command "Lay out in this manner every person that dies until the day of the resurrection, . . . and do not mourn beyond six days" (43:2-3). Eve's death and burial close the narrative.

Speculation about the salvation of Adam and Eve is central to this book. Will God have mercy on the people responsible for the presence of sin and death in this world? The answer is twofold. Death is an inevitable consequence of Adam's (and Eve's) sin. No amount of bargaining and praying can alter this fact (cf. the Testament of Abraham, above, pp. 322–25). Adam has been cut off from the tree of life, and the most he can take from the garden are seeds to grow food to eat and incense to accompany his prayer. The prayer provides a bridge from condemnation to ultimate salvation, which is the author's second point. In spite of Adam's death, God responds to the prayers that have been offered by Adam, Eve, Seth, and the angels and has mercy on the first father. God receives his spirit and promises the resurrection of his body. Thereafter he will have access to the joy and the eternal sustenance he left behind in the garden.

The author's interest, however, is broader. Adam and Eve will participate in a general resurrection. The specifications for burial in chapters 38–43 apply to "every person who dies." If the death and trouble Adam and Eve brought into the world are a universal malady, the resurrection provides a remedy for all "the holy people" who descend from him. Proper burial is performed in the hope of the resurrection and as a sign of it. Because of this hope, mourning must give way to joy. It must not extend beyond six days, because the seventh day is symbolic of the eternal rest.[124]

In summary, our author admits the inevitability of death for everyone but expresses his faith in the resurrection. As Adam was God's creature and image, so it is with all humanity; and the Creator will redeem the creature in the resurrection.[125]

The Latin Life of Adam and Eve

Latin, Armenian, and Georgian-language versions of the Life of Adam and Eve preserve a somewhat different form of the story, which overlaps with approximately one-half of the Greek Life.[126] Here we shall treat the Vita Adae et Evae.[127]

	Vita	Greek Life
1. Penitence, devil's narrative, Cain's birth	1:1—22:2	———
2. Birth of (Cain) Abel, Seth, et al.	22:3—24:2	1:1—5:1a
3. Adam's revelations to Seth	25–29	———
4. Adam's sickness, journey to the garden, testamentary situation	30–44	5:1b—14:3
5. Eve's narrative, exhortation	———	15–30
6. Adam's death, Eve's vision, Adam's burial	45—48	31:1—42:2
7. Eve's testament	49:1—50:2	———
8. Eve's death, burial	50:3—51:3	42:3—43:4

The material found in the Vita but not in the Greek Life occurs in three blocks (1, 3, 7).

The narrative thread that binds together chapters 1–22 of the Vita is Adam and Eve's quest for food, although other episodes and themes are interspersed. When Adam and Eve are driven from the garden they find the earth devoid of food (1:1—4:2). They hope that acts of penitence will obtain divine favor and bring them the gift of food (4:3—6:2). While Eve is standing in the waters of the Tigris, Satan appears in the guise of an angel (cf. Greek Life 17) and again deceives Eve (7:1—10:3). When she asks him why he has tricked them he tells the story of his expulsion from heaven (chaps. 11–17).[128] The story of Cain's birth is narrated as a separate incident (chaps. 18–21). After Cain's birth God sends Adam seeds to grow the food for which he has been searching (22:2). Seen as a whole this narrative sequence is an elaborate version of Adam's request and receipt of herbs and seeds at the end of Eve's narrative in Greek Life 29:3-6.

In chapters 25–29 of the Vita, Adam transmits secret knowledge to Seth. In the first part of this instruction (25:1—29:1) he relates his ascent to the heavenly garden and his vision of God after his expulsion from the garden. Its theme (God's threat of death, Adam's petition, God's promise) parallels the last part of Eve's narrative in Greek Life 27–29, and it appears that a major part of Eve's narrative in the Greek Life has been transformed into a heavenly throne vision. The second part of Adam's instruction to Seth is a historical apocalypse that transmits eschatological secrets that Adam learned after eating of the tree of knowledge (29:2-10). The content of this part has no parallel in the Greek Life.

In Greek Life 14 Adam asks Eve to recount the story of the fall, and Eve's narrative follows. In the corresponding place in the Vita (chap. 44), Adam tells Eve to recount the story *after his death*, and so Eve's long narrative is dropped at this point. After Adam's death and immediately before her own, Eve gathers her children. Instead of telling the story of the fall, however, she repeats Michael's instructions that the children should write the story of their parents' lives on stone and clay tablets so that it survives two judgments by water and fire (chaps. 49–50). This section is also unparalleled in the Greek Life.

The precise relationships between the Greek Life and the Vita, and indeed among all the versions of the Life of Adam and Eve, is a complex literary problem that can be solved only by a full text-critical and literary-critical analysis of all the recensions of this work.[129] With some caution, however, we may make a few suggestions as to the relationships between the Greek and the Latin versions of the Life of Adam and Eve.[130]

Section 1 (Vita 1–22) is largely an expansion of the end of Eve's narrative in Greek Life 29. It is told as third-person narrative before the time of Adam's final days rather than retrospectively in the first person as a piece of testamentary biography. The penitence of Adam and Eve doubtless has a theological rationale, and their bathing in the Jordan and Tigris rivers may allude to rituals practiced by the Jewish and/or Christian groups that generated and transmitted this literature.[131] The role played by the devil in this section (chaps. 9–10) dramatizes the continuing problem of temptation after the fall. The devil's narrative about his fall reflects theological speculation (chaps. 11–17), and Greek Life 39:1-3 may indicate knowledge of this tradition.[132] The story of the birth of Cain (chaps. 18–21) is more ambiguous. It may be an elaboration of Greek Life 25:3, although the latter could be a fleeting allusion to the longer story. In section 2 the account of Adam's ascent to the heavenly garden (Life 25:1—29:1) transforms the heart of Eve's narrative into a heavenly throne vision perhaps because a theology of a transcendent God preferred to depict a theophany in the heavenly garden rather than God's descent to earth à la Genesis 3.[133] Adam's second revelation to Seth about the future of the world (Vita 29:2-10) and Eve's testament (section 3, Vita 49–50) present the kind of apocalyptic material that is at home in testamentary literature.[134] These sections may have been drawn from an Adamic testament also alluded to by Josephus (*Ant.* 1.70–71 [§2.3]).[135] In short, the Greek version is the more original form of the Life of Adam and Eve. The Vita is an expansion of the earlier work, although it may contain some original elements that have dropped out of the Greek Life[136] and some original wording now revised in the Greek Life.

Introductory questions about these Adamic texts are not easily answered. The date of composition of the various recensions cannot be determined with any certainty. The extant manuscripts of the various recensions all date from the medieval period or later.[137] A comparison of the Vita with some Christian texts that make use of it places the date of the Latin version in the third or fourth century,[138] which indicates an earlier date for the form of the Greek Life, perhaps the second to fourth centuries.[139] All of the versions appear to go back to various forms of a text in Greek, which may have been the language of the work's composition.[140]

The major introductory problem is the book's provenance. Was it composed as a non-Christian Jewish text, or as a Christian text that drew deeply from Jewish narrative exegetical traditions? That the authors of the Greek Life and the Vita knew such traditions is clear. In the mid-first century the apostle Paul assumes that his Corinthian audience knows a tradition about Eve and Satan similar to that in Greek Life 17 (2 Cor 11:3, 14). The author of the Vita knows a first-century tradition related to that in Josephus, Ant. 1.70–71 (§2.3). Romans 5, as well as 4 Ezra and 2 Baruch, attest first-century Jewish speculation about Adam's sin and its consequences (see above, pp. 271, 281, 283). The earliest form of the Life has been shaped by the testament form familiar to us from Jewish parallels. Thus Jewish literary and theological elements are in place in the first century that could support postulating a first- to second-century Jewish origin for these texts. In addition, the earliest form(s) of the text contains no explicitly Christian elements.[141] Especially noteworthy is the total absence of Christian soteriology with reference to the future salvation of Adam and of humanity in the resurrection of the dead. This absence stands out the more because such elements enter the later manuscript tradition.[142] Taken together, these factors could indicate non-Christian Jewish authorship for the Greek Life and the Vita.

This evidence is not decisive, however, and other considerations suggest Christian authorship. Negatively, first-century attestations of traditions similar to those found in the Life of Adam and Eve do not prove that these first-century authors knew these traditions *in the context of a Life of Adam and Eve*.[143] Positively, all manuscripts of the Life of Adam and Eve are the products of Christian scribes. Moreover, some Christians of the second century were well versed in Jewish haggadic tradition, as the Testaments of the Twelve Patriarchs attest (see above, pp. 314–15), and thus the Jewish content of the versions of Life by no means excludes Christian authorship. Finally, second- and early-third-century Christian writings that treat the sin and the fate of the first parents sometimes do so without reference to Christ, while employing some striking parallels with these Adam and Eve texts.[144] This interest is noteworthy because it marks an increasing attention to the first parents at a time when the Enochic story of the Watchers and the women still provides an important explanation for the presence of evil in the world.[145] A comparative study of these partly competing traditions and their theological functions is a desideratum for historians for early Christian thought.

In light of the above-mentioned considerations and in the present state of the discussion, the provenance of the versions of the Life of Adam and Eve is uncertain, but seems to tip in favor of Christian authorship of the Life of Adam and Eve in the versions in which it is now extant. One would hope that scholars of Jewish and early Christian literature working cooperatively may eventually reach some consensus on the matter. In the meantime the versions should not be used uncritically as attestations of first-century Jewish religious thought or as certain testimonies to an as yet undefined sector of the second- or third-century church. Nonetheless, the Christian translations of these texts, from Rome or Africa to areas of eastern Europe and perhaps Egypt,[146] and the prolific copying of the manuscripts over fifteen centuries, should be more closely studied and the data incorporated into the history of the Christian church.

Joseph and Aseneth

The patriarch Joseph is a prominent figure in some of the literature that we have studied. A significant part of Genesis is devoted to his story, which becomes a prototype of later Jewish stories about the persecution and exaltation of the righteous person (see above, p. 312). Various of the Testaments of the Twelve Patriarchs present him as a paragon of virtue, especially chastity. Against this background, one element in the biblical stories stands out. Contrary to the patriarchal admonitions of Genesis,[147] Joseph married a non-Israelite woman, who was, moreover, the daughter of an Egyptian priest! (Gen 41:45). The story that has come to be known as Joseph and Aseneth deals with this problem constructively, describing Aseneth's conversion from idolatry and attributing to her the status of prototypical proselyte.[148] Its traditional title notwithstanding, it is primarily a story about Aseneth.[149] The work has been preserved in a long and a short text form. For our purposes, we recount mainly narrative elements that are present in both forms.[150] Where the versification differs between the two text forms, the versification of the short form follows that of the long form.

Aseneth is introduced as the daughter of Pentepheres, the priest of Heliopolis, a virgin of peerless beauty whose hand in marriage is sought by suitors from far and near, among them Pharaoh's son (chap. 1). She scorns them all and lives in virginal isolation in a great tower (chap. 2). When Joseph announces his intention to dine with Pentepheres, the priest informs Aseneth that he wishes her to marry Joseph, who is a pious and wise man (chaps. 3–4). Aseneth scornfully refuses to have anything to do with this "alien and fugitive . . . this son of the shepherd from the land of Canaan . . . who slept with" the wife of his master and whom "his master threw in prison" (4:9-11 [11-14]).

When Joseph arrives, Aseneth retreats to her tower (chap. 5). As she peeks through her window, however, she is shocked at his resplendent appearance and repents of her rash words because the shepherd's son from Canaan is, in fact, "the son of God" (chap. 6).

Joseph, who has caught Aseneth peeking at him from her window, refuses to have anything to do with her, supposing her to be another one of those Egyptian women who are trying to bed him. When Pentepheres assures Joseph that Aseneth "is a virgin who detests men," Joseph agrees to see her and to accept her as his "sister" (chap. 7). But when Aseneth arrives and attempts to give him a sisterly kiss, he restrains her and refuses. It is improper for a man who with his mouth blesses the living God and partakes of sacred food to kiss a strange woman who with her mouth blesses dead and deaf idols and partakes of the polluted food of their cult (8:5). Aseneth is deeply chagrined at her rejection, but Joseph prays for her conversion, employing language about the conversion that will recur later. He promises to return in a week (chaps. 8–9).

Aseneth retreats to her tower, where she mourns, fasts, and repents for seven days. She exchanges her royal robes for sackcloth and destroys her idols, throwing them out the window, together with her rich foods (chaps. 9–10). Aseneth is alone, forsaken by her parents and hated by all because of her repudiation of her idols. (Chapter 11 of the long text recounts how she gradually comes to the decision to seek "refuge" with the God of Joseph, who, she has heard, is merciful, filled with pity, long-suffering, not reckoning the sin of the humble.) In her lengthy prayer (chaps. 12–13) she confesses her sin of idolatry and asks to be delivered from "the Lion" (the devil), the "father of the gods of the Egyptians," who pursues her like a lion. She points to her acts of penitence and repudiation as signs of her true repentance and asks forgiveness for her idolatry and her blasphemy against God's son.

In answer to her prayer the morning star arises in the eastern sky, and with a blaze of light an angel appears in her room and commands Aseneth to replace her mourning garments with bridal array. God has accepted her confession. Her name has been written in the book of life, and from this day she will be renewed, re-created, and given new life, and she will eat the bread of life and drink the cup of immortality. This wording indicates that Joseph's prayer is fulfilled. God will give her to Joseph as a bride, and her name will be changed to "City of Refuge," symbolizing her status as the prototypical proselyte (chap. 15).

The angel then commands Aseneth to bring a honeycomb that mysteriously appears in her storehouse. He places his hand on her head, thereby transmitting to her "the ineffable mysteries of God," and he tells her eat of the honeycomb, made by the bees of paradise from the roses of life. Because she has participated in these rites, the angel tells her, she will never die. An obscure passage follows, which describes the appearance of the honeycomb and the bees that exit from it (16:1—17:5 [6]). When Aseneth turns her back momentarily, the angel vanishes and then Aseneth sees a fiery chariot ascending toward the eastern sky (17:6 [7]).

In a manner that parallels the narrative technique in the Testament of Abraham (see above, pp. 323–24), the author repeats the plot-line of chapters 3–8, albeit with significant changes (chaps. 18–20) that resolve the complication that had arisen in the first narrative cycle.[151] The servant announces that Joseph will come to dine. Aseneth orders the meal to be prepared. She adorns herself with special bridal array and her face is gloriously transfigured. Joseph arrives once again. Aseneth goes out to meet him. This time they embrace—for a long time—and their spirits are revived. (In the long text they kiss three times, and Aseneth receives "the spirit of life," "the spirit of wisdom," and "the spirit of truth.") Aseneth is fit to be Joseph's bride. Her parents return and rejoice at her beauty (in the long text they are astonished at her beauty). Amid glorious ceremonies and feasting Pharaoh joins Joseph and Aseneth in marriage (chap. 21). Thus the plot begun in chapter 1 comes to its conclusion.

Chapter 22 describes Aseneth's meeting with Joseph's father, Jacob. Simeon and Levi are introduced as Aseneth's friends and protectors. This provides a transition to the second part of the story (chaps. 23–29). Pharaoh's son reappears as Joseph's rival, madly in love with Aseneth (cf. 1:7-9 [11-14]). He vainly seeks the help of Simeon and Levi in murdering Joseph. Finally he enlists the help of the sons of Bilhah and Zilpah. Their attempted kidnapping of Aseneth and murder of Joseph are stymied by the efforts of Simeon, Levi, and Benjamin, who strikes the prince with a mortal blow. Later, when Pharaoh dies, Joseph becomes sole ruler of Egypt. The story about Pharaoh's son, which began in chapter 1, is employed mainly as a short second act that draws motifs from the main story[152] and serves the didactic purposes of the author. It demonstrates how God protects the new convert, and in the actions of Simeon, Levi, and Benjamin it exemplifies the conduct that "is proper for a man who worships God."[153]

This second part of the story is, in effect, a replay of the biblical account of Dinah and Shechem (Gen 34). The role of Shechem is played by Pharaoh's son, with Levi and Simeon assuming their biblical roles as the young woman's protectors. This is noteworthy because later rabbinic legends identify Aseneth as the daughter of Dinah and Shechem and thus solve the problem of Joseph's marriage to an Egyptian woman by maintaining that she was in reality an Israelite.[154] If such a tradition does lie behind this part of Joseph and Aseneth, the author has incorporated it into a story that solves the problem of Genesis 41:45 in a different way. Aseneth is an Egyptian who married Joseph after she is converted to the religion of Israel. It is this story that governs the present form of Joseph and Aseneth and dominates the reader's attention.

Aseneth's conversion is twofold. First, chapters 4–6 depict her change in attitude toward Joseph. At first she spurned "the son of the shepherd from the land of Canaan," saying she would marry the king's firstborn son. When she sees Joseph, however, she acknowledges him to be "the son of God" and likens his advent to a solar epiphany.[155] Second, by describing Joseph in language appropriate for the pharaoh's son,[156] she is not only making a marital choice but is also adumbrating her conversion from the gods of Egypt to the God of Joseph. This conversion and its implications are the main subject of chapters 2–23.

Aseneth's status as an idolatress constitutes a twofold problem for her. First, because she worships "dead and deaf idols," she is cut off from "the living God."[157] She exists in the realm of death and corruption, deprived of eternal life and incorruptibility (8:5-7). Moreover, her idolatry has defiled her. For seven days she does not dare to open her polluted mouth to address the living God (10:17[20]—11:3; 12:6).[158] Second, her state of defilement imperils her relationship to Joseph. A man who has blessed the living God and has partaken of the food and drink of immortality may not kiss the polluted mouth of an idolatress (8:5). The marriage of Joseph and Aseneth is forbidden.

Through her conversion Aseneth passes from death to life (8:9 [10]).[159] After she has destroyed her gods and their sacrificial food and drink (10:12-13 [13-14]), she engages in a mourning ritual, evidently lamenting her sojourn in the realm of death (10:14-17 [15-20]).[160] When the angel announces that God has accepted her acts of repentance and that her name is now written in the book of life (15:2-4 [2-3]), he enacts rituals that dramatize this fact and confer on her a new status that reverses her former deprivation. She receives the mysteries of God (16:13-14 [7-8]) in the place of the ignorance of her idolatry (12:4-5 [4-6]). She partakes of the food and drink of immortality (16:13-16 [7-9]). Her investiture in bridal array transfigures her appearance and beauty beyond recognition, testifying to the eternal life that is now hers (chaps. 18–19). Joseph may now kiss her, thus conferring on her the spirit of life, wisdom, and truth (19:11 [3]).[161] Their marriage resolves the plot of chapters 2–23.

Aseneth's is no ordinary conversion, for she does not marry an ordinary man. Joseph is the prototype of the persecuted and exalted righteous man (see above, p. 312). Imbued with a special measure of God's spirit, he is mighty, wise, and clairvoyant (4:7-8 [9]; 6:1-7). Glorious in appearance and resembling the angel,[162] he is called by the angelic title "son of God" and is set apart from mere mortals (6:5-7 [1-3]).[163] For such a one a special bride is required. Aseneth becomes a very special person. The angelophany has its typical commissioning function. The angel announces Aseneth's change of

name. As in parallel biblical epiphanies, the name change denotes a change from individual to collective and matriarchal or foundational status.[164] Aseneth, who sought
refuge, will be a city of refuge (15:7 [6]; cf. 13:12). The first proselyte is the prototype of
future proselytes. She is both woman and city, proselyte and congregation of proselytes.
The immortality she has gained is promised to all who follow her example and thereby
become citizens of her city.

Although the plot of Joseph and Aseneth and its theme seem clear enough, its
nuances, message, and function as these relate to the text's setting in a religious context
and in time and place are the subject of considerable dispute.[165] This is to no small
degree due to the obscurity of a number of passages. Here are a few examples. Why is
Joseph described as if he were an angel, and what do we make of Aseneth's physical
transformation? Is there a hidden meaning behind the detailed descriptions of Aseneth's
tower and of the honeycomb and the bees? Do the rituals over which the angel presides
have any counterparts in the author's religious world? Here we can only summarize and
briefly comment on some of the options for interpreting this rich, colorful, multifaceted,
and, finally, elusive text.

A majority of scholars find a distinct connection between the story's characters and
plot-line and the author's world. This is a story written by a Jew about Gentiles and Jews,
and especially about a woman who converts from the worship of idols to faith in the God
of Israel. As such the story relates to a world where Jews and Gentiles live in a common
environment and interact with one another.[166] It is a milieu in which "Jews lived in
dynamic tension with Gentiles and struggled to maintain a distinctive Jewish identity;
one in which table fellowship and intermarriage with Gentiles, including even marriage
between a convert to Judaism and a born Jew, were live issues."[167] The angelic rituals,
however, seem to be part of the book's fiction rather than actual mystery initiation rites in
the author's religious community.[168] That the author chose to write a story in which a
Jewish–Gentile marriage is at the center of the plot and in which erotic elements play a
significant role suggests further that intermarriage and not just conversion to Judaism is
of importance to that author.[169]

While it is possible that the author may have had in mind an audience that included
potential Gentile converts, it seems more likely that the book was intended for a Jewish
audience,[170] albeit one that may well have included proselytes, who would have found
assurance in the book's promise that God protected those who "fled to him for refuge."[171]

Two stimulating and controversial studies have drawn very different conclusions
about the origins and setting of Joseph and Aseneth, focusing in both cases on the
epiphany scene. According to the first of these, the text is an allegory that justifies the
existence of the temple that Onias IV built in Heliopolis.[172] This ingenious interpretation builds on a detailed analysis of the honeycomb ritual in chapter 16. While it
accounts for many otherwise obscure details in the text as a whole and it presents a
coherent interpretation of the work, it leaves unanswered a major question: Why would
an author wishing to justify the exodus of Jewish priests from Jerusalem to Heliopolis
seek to make this case by creating a story about the conversion of an Egyptian woman

and her marriage to an Israelite? The text at hand seems much closer to the real world of Jews and Gentile converts.[173]

According to the second interpretation, Aseneth is a Christian text probably of the third century that draws on Neoplatonic and Jewish mystical sources. Aseneth's prayer is an angelic adjuration paralleled by other texts that prescribe or describe how "humans have the means to initiate, indeed to compel [mystical] encounters, whether the descent of the divine or the ascent of the human."[174] Its "drama of the bees is . . . the drama of the fate of souls."[175] The book is not about "conversion" from idol worship, but transformation from a human being to an angel.[176] The literary material from late antiquity that is adduced to support this interpretation is impressive and provides a new history-of-religions context within which to read this text. However, whether the ritual sequence adds up to an adjuration is unclear. Aseneth's prayer is not an appeal for an epiphany but an extensive confession of sin and a petition for protection from demonic forces and for the pardoning of her sin, and it ends with the request that God protect Joseph and allow her to be his servant. And when the angel does appear, Aseneth is surprised.[177]

When one reads these interpretations of the text alongside more traditional readings, one has the feeling that one is herding cats or participating in a greased pig contest. The story's many obscure and elusive elements defy simple solution, and the notion of an "obvious" meaning is quickly dispelled. For the present author, it is most satisfying to read the text as a religious myth that explains the origins of proselytism: Aseneth is the city of refuge and the mother of proselytes. The myth's kerygmatic content is straightforward: eternal life and immortality are to be found only in the God of Israel, whose worship excludes idolatry. This God is a "merciful and compassionate God, long-suffering, full of mercy and gentle, and not reckoning the sin of a humble person" (11:10; cf. Exod 34:6). This God accepts the repentant idolater. Aseneth's marriage to a son of God reflects biblical imagery about the marriage of YHWH and Israel and may be parabolic of the covenantal relationship between the proselyte and God.[178] In accepting proselytes God promises deliverance from the fury of the devil, who is piqued by the conversion (12:9-11 [10]). The second part of the story underscores this by demonstrating that God "is with" the new convert, protecting her in mortal danger (26:2; 27:10-11). But this is one person's opinion about a complex issue.

There are other unsettled issues as well. Scholars debate whether the long or the short text is more original.[179] Not unrelated to this is an issue raised by feminist critics: What attitude about women is reflected in the two text forms, and might one or the other of them have been written by a woman?[180] The place of writing is generally thought to have been Egypt because of the book's fictional setting; however, Syria has also been suggested.[181] If it was written in Egypt, its message would have a special bite. Pharaoh and an Egyptian priest acknowledged the God of Israel. Aseneth deserted her Egyptian gods and rejected Pharaoh's son in order to embrace the religion of Israel and marry an Israelite. What better precedents? The book can be ascribed to no known group.[182] The time of its composition is disputed.[183] There is some consensus that it was composed in Greek.[184]

Joseph and Aseneth was popular among Christians and was translated into Syriac,

Armenian, Latin, Slavonic, and Ethiopic.[185] It is preserved only in manuscripts that are the products of Christian scribes. It is not difficult to understand this popularity among Christians. The rituals performed by the angel could be understood as foreshadowing the Christian Eucharist.[186] Moreover, the attention paid to Aseneth's rejection of Joseph and her subsequent acknowledgment of him as "son of God"[187] may also have been understood in terms of one's rejection and acceptance of Jesus as "son of God."[188] For this reason, it should be studied in light of Christian allegorical interpretations of the Bible.

The Prayer of Manasseh

The Prayer of Manasseh claims to be the penitential prayer that moved God to forgive the wicked king of Judah and restore him from his captivity in Babylon to his throne in Jerusalem (2 Chr 33:12-13).[189] The text is preserved only in Christian sources, which are of two kinds. The first is the Odes, a collection of hymns and prayers that forms an appendix to the book of Psalms in three Greek biblical manuscripts from the fifth, sixth, and tenth centuries and in some daughter translations.[190] Two church manuals provide the second set of sources: the third-century *Didascalia Apostolorum* (*Teaching of the Apostles*) and the fourth-century *Apostolic Constitutions*, which preserves parts of the *Didascalia*. Both manuals set the prayer in a narrative context that conflates and expands the accounts of Manasseh's reign in 2 Kings 21 and 2 Chronicles 33. Although the Greek text of the Prayer has a strong Semitic flavor, its use of phrases paralleled in the Greek Bible and some of its linguistic constructions suggest that it was composed in Greek.[191]

The Prayer is composed in the first-person singular but has relatively few counterparts among the individual laments of the canonical Psalter. Its closest parallel is Psalm 51, whose language it appears to echo.[192] Despite its prevalent concern with the covenant, it differs significantly from such penitential prayers as Ezra 9, Nehemiah 9, Daniel 9, Baruch 1:15—3:8, the Prayer of Azariah, the Qumran Words of the Heavenly Luminaries, and Tobit 3:2-6.[193] Its focus is consistently personal rather than national, and it lacks the language of the Deuteronomic tradition that permeates these prayers.[194] Instead it is laced with wording that alludes to the biblical Manasseh narratives in 2 Kings 21 and 2 Chronicles 33 and, in one place, to the prayer's narrative context in the church manuals.

In the opening verse of his prayer Manasseh addresses God with a pair of epithets that anticipate the two themes of the prayer's invocation (vv 1-7). God is the "Almighty," whose power is active in creation (vv 2-5a). "The God of our Fathers, of Abraham and Isaac and Jacob and their righteous descendants," is the one whose wrath and mercy are operative in the covenant (vv 5b-7). Manasseh's invocation of God as the "Almighty" expresses his repentance from his polytheistic worship of rival gods, as does his acknowledgment that this God has "made the heaven and the earth with all their order" (v 2).[195] The reference to God's shackling the sea and sealing the abyss, an allusion to the myth about the Creator bringing order from chaos by taming the great sea monster (cf., e.g.,

Job 28:8-11), may be a confession that Manasseh's own imprisonment is an act of God. Manasseh's reference to the covenant emphasizes God's compassion for those who repent (vv 5b-7).

This motif prepares us for Manasseh's confession of his sin (vv 8-10). Its introduction recalls the theme of the covenantal God in v 1 and sets up the traditional distinction between the righteous (the patriarchs) and the sinner (Manasseh), who is in need of repentance in order to become righteous (v 13).[196] Manasseh's confession emphasizes the quality and quantity of his sins. While v 9c recalls Ezra's confession (Ezra 9:6), the combined language of v 9a, 9c with reference to the multitude of Manasseh's sins may be an inverted allusion to the covenantal promises about the multitude of Abraham's descendants (Gen 22:17; 15:5). The verb "they are multiplied" corresponds to the same verb in 2 Kings 21:6 and 2 Chronicles 33:6, and the doubling of the verb "I have sinned" (v 12) emphasizes the point. The vivid reference to the physical conditions of Manasseh's imprisonment ("I am unworthy to look up . . . I am weighted down," lit. "bent down," v 10) complements v 9c. The mention of his iron chains (v 10), which has no basis in 2 Kings 21 or 2 Chronicles 33, does have a counterpart in the prayer's narrative context, which may indicate that the narrative and the prayer were composed together. Manasseh's lack of "relief" from his torment also suggests an allusion to the specific conditions of his imprisonment. This particular complaint and its repetition in v 13b recalls a similar repetition in the confession of the "mighty kings" in 1 Enoch 63:1, 5, 6, 8. The language of the second half of v 10 refers to details in 2 Kings 21:2 and 2 Chronicles 32:2, 6.

The words "and now," which are traditional in Jewish prayers,[197] introduce Manasseh's petition for relief and forgiveness (vv 11-15). The image in v 11 suggests a parallel between Manasseh's physical and spiritual condition. As the king kneels, he also submits his will ("heart") to God. The appeal for God's goodness is a request for the covenantal blessing (Deut 30:15) that God promises to those who repent (Deut 30:1-10). Verse 12 recapitulates his prior confession, and v 12b is one of several resonances of Psalm 51 (cf. Ps 51:3). Manasseh's petition proper occupies only one verse. First he asks twice that God grant him relief (Pr Man 13b).[198] This is followed by a triad of negative imperatives that God not act as judge ("Do not destroy me . . . do not be angry with me . . . do not condemn me"). The pairing of "evil things" (v 13e) and God's "goodness" (v 14a) employs traditional terms for the curses and the blessings of the covenant. The rationale for mercy is God's status as "the God of those who repent" (v 13f), reprising v 7. The king's acknowledgment of his unworthiness and his need for much mercy (v 14) echo v 9cd ("I am unworthy . . . because of the multitude of my iniquities"). The wording of v 14b recalls Psalm 51:1. Manasseh's prayer concludes with the promise to praise God (Pr Man 15). Parallel to this promise is the statement that "all the host of heaven sing your praises." Coming from one who had instituted the worship of the host of heaven (cf. v 2), it is a fitting reinforcement of his repentance from polytheism and a suitable reprise of the prayer's opening invocation of the "Lord Almighty."

Central to the Prayer of Manasseh is the belief that repentance is a divine gift that allows the worst of sinners to be accepted back into the covenant and have its curses turned to blessing. Even Manasseh, whose apostasy caused the destruction of the temple and the Holy City, could be forgiven and, according to the narrative context, reckoned to be righteous as Abraham was (*Ap. Con.* 2.22.16; cf. Gen 15:6). This moralizing focus on the vices and virtues of a biblical figure is typical of Jewish and Christian literature of the Greco-Roman period (cf. Jubilees, Testament of Job, Testaments of the Twelve Patriarchs).

As we have seen, verbal allusions to details in the 2 Kings and 2 Chronicles narratives indicate that the prayer was composed in the voice of Manasseh. A question rarely discussed or even mentioned is whether the prayer was composed as an integral part of the narrative context in which it stands in the *Didascalia* and the *Apostolic Constitutions*, or whether it is an independent composition that was later placed in that narrative context. Two factors may support the former alternative. All the other compositions in the Odes are drawn from biblical narrative contexts.[199] The prayer and the narrative share at least one detail (Pr Man 10) that is missing from both 2 Kings 21 and 2 Chronicles 33. Claiming to recount a story in "the fourth book of Kings"[200] and "the second book of Chronicles," the narrative begins with a compressed revision of 2 Kings 21 with a few details from 2 Chronicles 33. Turning to 2 Chronicles, it mentions Manasseh's exile, elaborates the Chronicler's account by detailing the terrible conditions of Manasseh's imprisonment, picks up the report of his prayer and recounts the prayer, describes how a fire miraculously melted his chains, returns to the Chronicler's account of Manasseh's return to Jerusalem, adds that he worshiped God wholeheartedly and "was reckoned righteous," and concludes with a summary of the Chronicler's report of Manasseh's restoration of the Jerusalem cult. As a whole, the rewritten narrative, including the prayer, emphasizes the severity of God's judgment, the sincerity of Manasseh's repentance, God's direct intervention and restoration of the covenantal relationship, and Manasseh's transformation from sinner to righteous, attested by his deeds. Thus the simplest explanation may be that the prayer was created as an integral part of the narrative.

Whether the text was composed by a Jew or a Christian is debated. The lack of any clear Christian elements and the supposed presence of postbiblical Jewish elements have led most commentators to ascribe the work to a Jewish author sometime in the centuries around the turn of the era.[201] While such a Jewish origin can by no means be excluded, and is perhaps probable, it should be noted that the text as we have it in the church manuals—narrative and prayer—fits well in a context that deals with the issue of repentance to which the manuals admonish the bishops to address themselves. In that respect it is a rare instance in which we can know for certain the Christian context of a text that is generally included in collections of Jewish texts—in this case, the Apocrypha. That the prayer also had a liturgical function in some circles of the church is indicated by its presence in the collection of Odes and by other data.[202] Its inclusion in modern editions of the Apocrypha or deuterocanonical books notwithstanding, the Prayer is considered canonical only by the Eastern Orthodox churches. This doubtless reflects its preservation in church manuals of Syrian provenance.

SUMMARY

We have reached a variety of conclusions in this chapter. The Testaments of the Twelve Patriarchs is a Christian text that draws on a wealth of Jewish tradition. The Life of Adam and Eve is quite probably a Christian composition, which also draws on Jewish tradition. The Testament of Abraham, the Testament of Job, and Joseph and Aseneth seem to be of Jewish origin, but this is not absolutely certain. The Prayer of Manasseh is a toss-up.

These findings lead to some further conclusions. The material in these texts can be used as witnesses to the ongoing life of Jewish religious thought and practice, and as context for early Christianity, only with great care, and the rules for such use need to be worked out methodically. Given their Christian transmission, the texts should be seen as a part of the Christian story, alongside the more theological and philosophical writings of the fathers, apologists, and exegetes of the early and medieval church and in conjunction with the so-called New Testament Apocrypha. In doing so, we will create a picture of the church that is more variegated than the one that focuses exclusively on the writings of the patristic tradition. To this corpus must also be added texts of indubitable Jewish origin, such as 1 Enoch, 4 Ezra, and 2 Baruch, which were translated into a wide variety of languages. If we sort these texts by language, we can contribute to profiles of Christianity in the various regions: Ethiopia, Coptic Egypt, Armenia, the various Slavic areas, Greece, and Rome and North Africa. Further, if we think about things in this way, we will begin to see in new ways how the churches were more Jewish than we might have thought and how the churches placed their ancient scriptures in a context that was broader than the canon. Finally, we shall broaden our knowledge of the working theology and the religious practice of the churches.

BIBLIOGRAPHY

The Testaments of the Twelve Patriarchs

Translations: Marinus de Jonge, *AOT*, 506–600 (for a revised version, see Harm W. **Hollander** and Marinus **de Jonge**, *The Testaments of the Twelve Patriarchs: A Commentary* [SVTP 8; Leiden: Brill, 1985]). Howard C. **Kee**, *OTP* 1:775–828.

Text: Marinus **de Jonge**, et al., eds., *The Testaments of the Twelve Patriarchs* (PVTG 1:2; Leiden: Brill, 1978), critical edition of the Greek text.

Commentary: **Hollander** and **de Jonge**, *Testaments*, introduction, translation, and commentary.

Literature: Jürgen **Becker**, *Untersuchungen zur Entstehungsgeschichte der Testamente der Zwölf Patriarchen* (AGAJU 8; Leiden: Brill, 1970). Harm W. **Hollander**, *Joseph as an Ethical Model in the Testaments of the Twelve Patriarchs* (SVTP 6; Leiden: Brill, 1981). Marinus **de Jonge**, ed.,

Studies on the Testaments of the Twelve Patriarchs (SVTP 3; Leiden: Brill, 1975), articles on textual criticism, exegesis, and the history of research. Marinus **de Jonge**, "The Testaments of the Twelve Patriarchs: Central Problems and Essential Viewpoints," *ANRW* 2.20.1 (1987) 359–420. Marinus **de Jonge**, *Jewish Eschatology, Early Christian Christology and the Testaments of the Twelve Patriarchs: Collected Essays* (Leiden: Brill, 1991) 147–326, collection of de Jonge's papers with a full bibliography of his publications. Robert **Kugler**, *Testaments of the Twelve Patriarchs* (GAP; Sheffield: Sheffield Academic Press, 2001). George W. E. **Nickelsburg**, ed., *Studies on the Testament of Joseph* (SBLSCS 5; Missoula, Mont.: Scholars Press, 1975), collection of working papers. Eckhard **von Nordheim**, *Die Lehre der Alten*, vol. 1: *Das Testament als Literaturgattung im Judentum der hellenistisch-römischen Zeit* (ALGHJ 13; Leiden: Brill, 1980) 1–114.

The Testament of Job

Translations: Russell P. **Spittler**, *OTP* 1:829–68. R. **Thornhill**, *AOT*, 617–48.

Texts and Other Translations: S. P. **Brock**, *Testamentum Iobi* (PVTG 2; Leiden: Brill, 1967) 1–59, critical edition of the Greek text. Robert A. **Kraft**, *The Testament of Job* (SBLTTPS 5/4; Missoula, Mont.: Scholars Press, 1974), Greek text with apparatus, translation, and annotated bibliography by Russell Spittler.

Literature Survey: Russell P. **Spittler**, "The Testament of Job: A History of Research and Interpretation," in Michael A. **Knibb** and Pieter W. **van der Horst**, *Studies on the Testament of Job* (SNTSMS 66; Cambridge: Cambridge Univ. Press, 1989) 7–32.

Literature: **Knibb** and **van der Horst**, *Studies*.

The Testament of Abraham

Translations: E. P. **Sanders**, *OTP* 1:871–902 (some of the best readings for Recension B [ms. E] are in the footnotes). N. **Turner**, *AOT*, 393–421 (translation of Recension A with four interpolations from Recension B).

Texts and Other Translations: Francis **Schmidt**, *Le Testament grec d'Abraham* (TSAJ 2; Tübingen: Mohr Siebeck, 1986), introduction, critical edition of the Greek texts of the two recensions, French translation. M. R. **James**, *The Testament of Abraham* (TextsS 2/2; Cambridge: Cambridge Univ. Press, 1892), introduction, critical edition of the Greek texts of the two recensions, summary of the Arabic version, translation of the related Coptic Testament of Isaac and Testament of Jacob. Nicolae **Roddy**, *The Romanian Version of the Testament of Abraham: Text, Translation, and Cultural Context* (SBLEJL 19; Atlanta: Society of Biblical Literature, 2001). Michael E. **Stone**, *The Testament of Abraham* (SBLTTPS 2/2; Missoula, Mont.: Scholars Press, 1972), reprint of James's Greek texts with a facing translation.

Literature: Dale C. **Allison Jr.**, *Testament of Abraham* (CEJL; Berlin: de Gruyter, 2003), introduction, translation of the two recensions in parallel columns, commentary. Mathias **Delcor**, *Le Testament d'Abraham* (SVTP 2; Leiden: Brill, 1973), introduction, translation and commentary on Recension A, translation of the Greek and the versions of Recension B, translation of the Testament of Isaac and Testament of Jacob. Jared W. **Ludlow**, *Abraham Meets Death: Narrative Humor in the Testament of Abraham* (JSPSup 41; Sheffield: Sheffield Academic Press, 2002).

Phillip B. **Munoa** III, *Four Powers in Heaven: The Interpretation of Daniel 7 in the Testament of Abraham* (JSPSup 28; Sheffield: Sheffield Academic Press, 1998). George W. E. **Nickelsburg**, ed., *Studies on the Testament of Abraham* (SBLSCS 6; Missoula, Mont.: Scholars Press, 1976), articles mainly on the recensional problem and parallel traditions, annotated bibliography, translation of the Coptic version of Recension B, translation with apparatus of the Slavonic version of Recension B. Francis **Schmidt**, "Le Testament d'Abraham" (2 vols.; diss., Strasbourg, 1971), extensive introduction, edition of the Greek of the short recension, translation of both recensions now superceded by his *Testament* (above).

The Books of Adam and Eve

Translations: M. D. **Johnson**, *OTP* 2:249–95. Gary A. **Anderson** and Michael E. **Stone**, eds., *A Synopsis of the Books of Adam and Eve* (2d ed.; SBLEJL 17; Atlanta: Scholars Press, 1999).

Texts: Konstantin von **Tischendorf**, *Apocalypses Apocryphae* (1866; repr. Hildesheim: Olms, 1966) 1–22, critical edition of the Greek text of *Apocalypse of Moses*. Wilhelm **Meyer**, "Vita Adae et Evae," in *Abhandlungen der königlichen Bayerischen Akademie der Wissenschaften: Philosophisch-philologische Klasse* 14/3 (1878) 187–250; and J. H. **Mozley**, "Documents: The 'Vita Adae,'" *JTS* 30 (1929) 121–49, Latin text of the *Life*.

Literature: Marinus **de Jonge**, *Pseudepigrapha of the Old Testament as Part of Christian Literature: The Case of the Testaments of the Twelve Patriarchs and the Greek Life of Adam and Eve* (SVTP 18; Leiden: Brill, 2003) 181–240. Marinus **de Jonge** and Johannes **Tromp**, *The Life of Adam and Eve and Related Literature* (GAP; Sheffield: Sheffield Academic Press, 1997). John R. **Levison**, *Portraits of Adam in Early Judaism: From Sirach to 2 Baruch* (JSPSup 1; Sheffield: Sheffield Academic Press, 1988) 163–90. Michael E. **Stone**, *A History of the Literature of Adam and Eve* (SBLEJL 3; Atlanta: Scholars Press, 1992). George W. E. **Nickelsburg**, "Some Related Traditions in the Apocalypse of Adam, the Books of Adam and Eve, and 1 Enoch," in Bentley **Layton**, ed., *The Rediscovery of Gnosticism*, vol. 2: *Sethian Gnosticism* (SHR 41; Leiden: Brill, 1980) 515–39.

Joseph and Aseneth

Translations: Christoph **Burchard**, *OTP* 2:177–247, translation of the long text. D. **Cook**, *AOT*, 465–503, translation of the short text.

Texts: Christoph **Burchard** with Carsten **Burfeind** and Uta Barbara **Fink**, *Joseph und Aseneth* (PVTG 5; Leiden: Brill, 2003), introduction with bibliography, the long text with full apparatus of the Greek and the versions. Marc **Philonenko**, *Joseph et Aséneth* (SPB 13; Leiden: Brill, 1968), introduction, short Greek text, annotated French translation.

Literature: Gideon **Bohak**, *Joseph and Aseneth and the Jewish Temple in Heliopolis* (SBLEJL 10; Atlanta: Scholars Press, 1996). Christoph **Burchard**, *Untersuchungen zu Joseph und Aseneth* (WUNT 8; Tübingen: Mohr, 1965). Christoph **Burchard**, *Der Dreizehnte Zeuge* (FRLANT 103; Göttingen: Vandenhoeck & Ruprecht, 1970) 59–88. Randall D. **Chesnutt**, *From Death to Life: Conversion in Joseph and Aseneth* (JSPSup 16; Sheffield: Sheffield Academic Press, 1995). Edith M. **Humphrey**, *Joseph and Aseneth* (GAP; Sheffield: Sheffield Academic Press, 2000), introduction to the major issues, rhetorical-literary reading. Ross Shepard **Kraemer,** *When Joseph Met Aseneth: A Late Antique Tale of the Biblical Patriarch and His Egyptian Wife, Reconsidered* (New York: Oxford Univ. Press, 1998). Dieter **Sänger,** *Antikes Judentum und die Mysterien: Religionsgeschichtliche Untersuchungen zu Joseph und Aseneth* (WUNT 2/5; Tübingen: Mohr Siebeck, 1980). Angela **Standhartinger,** *Das Frauenbild im Judentum der Hellenistischen Zeit: Ein Beitrag anhand von 'Joseph und Aseneth'* (AGAJU 26; Leiden: Brill, 1995).

The Prayer of Manasseh

Translations: The Apocrypha. James H. **Charlesworth,** *OTP* 2:625–37. Herbert E. **Ryle,** *APOT* 1:612–26. R. Hugh **Connolly,** *Didascalia Apostolorum: The Syriac Version Translated and Accompanied by the Verona Latin Fragments, with an Introduction and Notes* (1929; repr. Oxford: Clarendon, 1969) 68–76. See also A. C. **Coxe,** "Constitutions of the Holy Apostles," *ANF* 7:406–7.

Texts: Alfred **Rahlfs,** *Psalmi cum Odis* (SVTG 10; Göttingen: Vandenhoeck & Ruprecht, 1967) 361–63. Fransiscus Xaverius **Funk,** *Didascalia et Constitutiones Apostolorum* (2 vols.; Paderborn: Schoeningh, 1905) 1:80–91, Greek text of the Constitutions and Latin text of the *Didascalia* on facing pages. Marcel **Metzger,** *Les Constitutions Apostoliques* (3 vols.; SC 320, 329, 336; Paris: Cerf, 1985–86) 1:210–23.

Commentaries: Daniel J. **Harrington,** "Prayer of Manasseh," in James L. **Mays,** ed., *The HarperCollins Bible Commentary* (San Francisco: HarperSanFrancisco, 2000) 872–74. George W. E. **Nickelsburg,** "Prayer of Manasseh," in John **Barton** and John **Muddiman,** eds., *The Oxford Bible Commentary* (Oxford: Oxford Univ. Press, 2001) 770–73. Eva **Osswald,** *Das Gebet Manasses* (JSHRZ 4/1; Gütersloh: Mohn, 1974).

Notes

Prologue: Exile—Return—Dispersion

1. See below, chapters 3 and 9.

2. John Bright, *A History of Israel* (2d ed.; Philadelphia: Westminster, 1971) 346. For a discussion of the Jews' life in exile, see Albertz, *Israel in Exile*, 98–111.

3. For a summary of three not mutually exclusive options for explaining the origins of the synagogue, see George W. E. Nickelsburg, *Ancient Judaism and Christian Origins: Diversity, Continuity, and Transformation* (Minneapolis: Fortress Press, 2003) 155, where I draw on the discussions by Lee Levine, *The Ancient Synagogue: The First Thousand Years* (New Haven: Yale Univ. Press, 2000) 22–23; and Gruen, *Diaspora*, 119–23.

4. Klaus Baltzer (*Deutero-Isaiah: A Commentary on Isaiah 40–55* [Hermeneia; Minneapolis: Fortress Press, 2001] 25–26) suggests multiple authorship. Albertz (*Israel in Exile*, 376–433) refers to the "Deutero-Isaiah group" and sees chaps. 40–55 as the product of two editions.

5. The date for the collection is almost universally placed at the end of the sixth century. Baltzer (*Deutero-Isaiah*, 30–32) opts for a date between 450 and 400.

6. Ibid., 18–22.

7. "Anointed" translates the Hebrew *mashiah*, a term that the preexilic texts apply to the reigning monarch of Israel or Judah. Later it became a designation for a future ruler. Its Greek translation is *christos* (= Christ). See Nickelsburg, *Ancient Judaism*, 91–95.

8. Sheshbazzar has often been identified with Shenazzar, the son of King Jehoiachin, but the identification is unlikely; see Albertz, *Israel in Exile*, 120–23.

9. On the events from 520 to 515, see ibid., 124–32.

10. For one reconstruction of the events of the end of the sixth century, see Paul D. Hanson, *The Dawn of Apocalyptic* (Philadelphia: Fortress Press, 1985). For two critiques of his position, see Grabbe, *Judaism*, 1:107–11; and Berquist, *Judaism*, 182–84.

11. Hanson, *Dawn*, 32–208.

12. Third Isaiah lacks the angelology and the hope of resurrection and eternal life that characterize 1 Enoch and Daniel, as well as the visionary forms that develop in the apocalyptic literature (see below, pp. 52, 82, 112–13), for which reason I refrain from calling Third Isaiah's eschatology "apocalyptic."

13. For three different assessments of the evidence and the arguments, see Grabbe, *Judaism*, 1:136–38; Robert North, "Ezra," *ABD* 2:726–28; Berquist, *Judaism*, 110–19.

14. On the difference between Ezra's and Nehemiah's reforms, see Berquist, *Judaism*, 117–19.

15. On the problems of dating 1–2 Chronicles see Ralph W. Klein, "Chronicles, Books of 1–2," *ABD* 1:994–95.

16. See ibid., 999–1000. In correspondence dated October 2004, Klein expressed his doubt that the Chronicler espoused a restorationist theology.

17. See Bezalel Porten, "Elephantine Papyri," *ABD* 2:445–55.

1. TALES OF THE DISPERSION

1. See below, p. 83.

2. Bickerman, *Four Strange Books*, 92; Collins, *Daniel*, 24–38.

3. The doxologies may be an editorial element that unifies stories of diverse origin and genre or subgenre; see Collins, *Daniel*, 36; also Matthias Henze, "The Ideology of Rule in the Narrative Frame of Daniel (Dan 1–6)," *SBLSP* 38 (1999) 537. The difference between stories of contest and stories of conflict was noted by W. Lee Humphreys, "A Life-style for Diaspora: A Study of the Tales of Esther and Daniel," *JBL* 92 (1973) 211–23. Drawing on both the Hebrew/Aramaic and the Greek texts of Daniel, Wills (*Jew*) provides a detailed and sophisticated discussion of the complex tradition history behind the collection and the genre and respective settings of the stories. See also Collins, *Daniel*, 38–52. For some issues relating to the question of genre and the classification of the stories, see the discussion between Wills and Nickelsburg in *GNP* 2:504–19.

4. On the ancient legendary figure of Daniel see S. B. Frost, "Daniel," *IDB* 1:761.

5. For a detailed comparison see Collins, *Daniel*, 38–40; and below, n. 15.

6. There are historical problems with this sequence. Babylon fell not to the Medes under Darius but to Cyrus, the king of the Medo-Persian Empire. Darius was a later Persian king; see below, n. 14.

7. In addition to foreshadowing motives in subsequent chapters, the story is shorter and more sketchy than chaps. 2–6. Wills (*Jew*, 79–81) is uncertain whether the story was composed by the editor of the collection or adapted from an earlier source.

8. For details see Collins, *Daniel*, 162–70. On the origins of the imagery of four metals representing successive ages, as attested in Hesiod, a Greek author of the eighth century B.C.E. (*Works and Days* 1.109–201), and the Persian *BahmanYasht*, see Collins, *Daniel*, 164.

9. John J. Collins, *The Apocalyptic Vision of the Book of Daniel* (HSM 16; Missoula, Mont.: Scholars Press, 1977) 43–44.

10. Collins, *Daniel*, 174.

11. The events described fit the reign of Nabonidus rather than that of Nebuchadnezzar. Among the Dead Sea Scrolls is the *Prayer of Nabonidus*, a version of the present story with Nabonidus as the central figure. It is doubtless descended from a form of the story earlier than that preserved in Dan 4. For a translation see Vermes, *Scrolls*, 329; idem, *Complete Scrolls*, 573; García Martínez, *Scrolls*, 289; Wise, Abegg, and Cook, *Scrolls*, §46. For a detailed comparative discussion of Dan 4 in its Aramaic and Greek forms and the Qumran text, see Wills, *Jew*, 86–121. On Dan 4, the Qumran text, and other sources on Nabonidus, see Collins, *Daniel*, 216–21; idem, DJD 22:83–93.

12. For another connection with chap. 4, cf. 5:4 with the *Prayer of Nabonidus*. Just as Dan 4

has changed Nabonidus to Nebuchadnezzar, so chap. 5 has changed Belshazzar's father from Nabonidus to Nebuchadnezzar—a common practice of associating a story about a less-familiar figure with a better-known figure.

13. For a vivid musical interpretation of the dramatic potential of this story, cf. William Walton's *Belshazzar's Feast*.

14. This is evidently Darius I, king of Persia, who reigned after Cyrus (522–486 B.C.E.). See H. H. Rowley, *Darius the Mede* (Cardiff: Univ. of Wales Press, 1935).

15. For the story of Ahiqar see J. Rendel Harris, Agnes Smith Lewis, and F. C. Conybeare, *APOT* 2:715–84; and J. M. Lindenberger, *OTP* 2:479–507. For the formal similarities in these stories see Nickelsburg, *Resurrection*, 48–58; idem, "The Genre and Function of the Markan Passion Narrative," *HTR* 73 (1980) 153–63, repr. with responses in *GNP* 2:473–519. See also Humphreys, "Lifestyle"; Wills, *Jew*, 44–49.

16. The nature of their wisdom varies. Joseph predicts the future by interpreting dreams. Ahiqar is a composer of proverbs, and his quick thinking spares his own life and saves his nation. Mordecai is notable for his cleverness in the midst of palace intrigues.

17. See esp. Wills, *Jew*, 74–152.

18. Collins, *Daniel*, 47–48.

19. On the problems of equating or not equating the position of the characters in the story with that of the stories' authors, see ibid., 48. See the discussion of Henze, "Ideology," 534–39.

20. Collins, *Daniel*, 51–52, following Humphreys, "Life-style."

21. Collins, *Daniel*, 66–67; see also Wills, *Jew*, 150–51. But note the demur of Henze, "Ideology," 534–36.

22. On the two translations see Collins, *Daniel*, 3–11. For a date of ca. 100 B.C.E. for the Old Greek see ibid., 8–9.

23. Gruen (*Diaspora*, 170–74) offers a different interpretation that plays down the similarities to the other Danielic stories. The author directs humorous "barbs at the foibles and failings of Jews who run their own affairs in the diaspora: at hypocrisy, false religiosity, inverted values, the ethical indifference of the elite, and the unprincipled vacillation of the rank and file." Some of his exegetical observations seem to me more to the point than others. That Susanna expects not to be rescued is no more indicative of a vacillation in her faith than the statement of the three young men in Dan 3:17. That a few elements in the story call into question her innocence seems to fly in the face of the story's genre. At other points, Gruen is on the mark, and his reading should be consulted.

24. Daniel's name, which denotes God as judge, is also appropriate to the young man's function in the story.

25. Cf. v 12||Gen 39:10; v 23||39:9; v 26||39:14-15; v 39||39:18.

26. The history of the interpretation of Susanna documents many attempts to focus on one or the other of these elements as the central point of the story; see Moore, *Additions*, 84–91. For a provocative feminist reading, see Levine, "Hemmed in on Every Side," who also notes (p. 187) the parallel between Susanna's vulnerability as a woman and Israel's status in the text as an exiled people.

27. Moore, *Additions*, 91; Collins, *Daniel*, 438.

28. Verses 54-55 and 59-60 contain a wordplay in Greek that involves the respective words for the trees and for cutting. Bruce Metzger reproduces the effect in English with this paraphrase: "under a *clove* tree . . . the angel will *cleave* you"; "under a *yew* tree . . . the angel will *hew* you asunder" (*Oxford Annotated Apocrypha, Expanded Edition* [New York: Oxford Univ. Press, 1977] ad

loc.). For arguments supporting a Semitic original see Moore, *Additions*, 81–84; as Metzger's note indicates and Collins observes (*Daniel*, 427–28), wordplays in one language can be re-created in a translation.

29. Collins, *Daniel*, 426.

30. Most modern translations entitle the story "Bel and the Dragon." Here I follow the judgment of Moore (*Additions*, 141–42) and Collins (*Daniel*, 414) that the story refers to a living snake that was a cult object in the temple.

31. Moore (*Additions*, 121–25) argues that the two parts of the story may originally have been separate.

32. The term "living God" (Bel, vv 5, 6, 24, 25) occurs several times in Dan 4–6, as do certain cultic terms. However, only chap. 3 and 5:4 make specific reference to idolatry.

33. Cf. Isa 44:9–20; Wis 13–14; Epistle of Jeremiah; Apoc. Abr. 1–8.

34. A number of legendary expansions in Bel and the Serpent heighten the miracle as it is described in Dan 6; see Nickelsburg, "Stories," 40.

35. For the former possibility see Wills, *Jew*, 134–38. For possible indications of independent development see Collins, *Daniel*, 411–12.

36. For details see Collins, *Daniel*, 410–11.

37. The versification used here follows that of standard translations of the Apocrypha. Editions of the Greek Daniel begin versification with v 24 (i.e., English v 1 becomes v 24, etc.).

38. For these prayers in general see Rodney A. Werline, *Penitential Prayer in Second Temple Judaism: The Development of a Religious Institution* (SBLEJL 13; Atlanta: Scholars Press, 1998). For a detailed exposition of the Prayer of Azariah see 168–79.

39. Cf. Dan 9:7; Bar 1:15; 2:6. Cf. also, e.g., Pss. Sol. 2:16–18 and 8:30–40 for the same idea in the context of covenant theology.

40. Cf. Bar 2:29 for an explicit citation of Deut 28:62.

41. Cf. 1 Macc 4:30–34; 2 Macc 3:15–24; 3 Macc 2; and Esth 14–15, an addition to the Greek translation of Esther, placed after 4:17 in the canonical book with the same effect.

42. Reference to the lack of a prophet could have been made at *any* time that the author believed there was no prophet.

43. Verse 25 has been taken over from v 22 in the original, which has dropped out of some mss. of the Greek. Perhaps the author of the addition displaced it for the above-mentioned reason.

44. The original story does not actually describe the deliverance but only the king's discovery of the miracle. In order to insert the prayer before that discovery the author of the addition must mention the deliverance here.

45. Pfeiffer, *History*, 448; Gerhard von Rad, "Job 38 and Ancient Egyptian Wisdom," in idem, *The Problem of the Hexateuch and Other Essays* (trans. E. W. Trueman Dicken; New York: McGraw-Hill, 1955) 285–86.

46. Moore, *Additions*, 44–49; Collins, *Daniel*, 198–205.

47. We know little about the reasons for the inclusion or insertion of hymnic material in biblical narratives or the functions of this material. For other examples see Exod 15; 1 Sam 2; Luke 1:46–55, 68–79.

48. The discussion here is a somewhat condensed form of my treatment of the story in "Bible Rewritten," 131–35.

49. For further details see Crenshaw, "Contest," 80.

50. Ibid., 81.

51. The Gk. *alētheia* reflects the Aramaic *qushṭaʾ* (Talshir, *Commentary*, 154), which has this range of meanings; see Nickelsburg, "Bible Rewritten," 132 n. 247.

52. See Frank Zimmermann, "The Story of the Three Guardsmen," *JQR* 54 (1963/64) 181–82.

53. See the discussion and references in Nickelsburg, "Bible Rewritten," 133 nn. 250, 251.

54. For parallels with both Daniel and Esther see Torrey, "Story," 187–88.

55. See Crenshaw, "Contest," 77–79. Especially noteworthy is the similarity between 1 Esd 4:6–9 and the series in Eccl 3:1–9, cited in ibid., 85–86.

56. See Pohlmann, *Studien*, 44.

57. See Torrey, "Story," 185–86; Zimmermann, "Story," 185, 197–98; Pfeiffer, *History*, 251–57; Pohlmann, *Studien*, 40–47; Hilhorst, "Speech," 141–48.

58. See Paul Humbert, "'Magna est veritas et praevalet' (3 Esra 4:35)," *OLZ* 31 (1928) 148–50; Hilhorst, "Speech," 145–46.

59. See Torrey, "Story," 197; Pohlmann, *Studien*, 38. The identification occurs very late in the story and breaks into the context.

60. See Wills, *Jew*, 194–96.

61. See Pfeiffer, *History*, 252–54; Crenshaw, "Contest," 74–76.

62. On the language see C. C. Torrey, "The Nature and Origin of '1 Esdras,'" *AJSL* 23 (1906) 128–30; Zimmermann, "Story," 183–94; Pohlmann, *Studien*, 48–49; Talshir, *Origin*, 81–102. On the time and place see Nickelsburg, "Bible Rewritten," 134–35.

63. On this very difficult problem see Torrey, "Nature and Origin," 116–41; Pfeiffer, *History*, 233–50; Pohlmann, *Studien*, 32–73. On the relationship between Ezra-Nehemiah and 1 Esdras, see Tamara Cohn Eskenazi, *In an Age of Prose: A Literary Approach to Ezra-Nehemiah* (SBLMS 36; Atlanta: Scholars Press, 1988) 155–74; Talshir, *Origin*.

64. In this discussion I have retained the Greek name *Tobit*, which is found in all modern translations of this book. It translates the Semitic name *Tobi* (lit. "my good"), attested in the Qumran Aramaic Tobit mss., a hypocoristicon (shortened pet name) for either *Tobiah* ("YHWH is my good") or *Tobiel* ("God is my good"); see Moore, *Tobit*, 99–100; Fitzmyer, *Tobit*, 92–93. Otherwise, I have adopted the Semitic forms of the characters' names, all of which are attested in the Qumran mss.: Tobiah, which modern translations render by the Greek "Tobias"; and Hannah, which they render as "Anna."

65. The sequence of events is reminiscent of the court tales discussed in the previous section.

66. On the tragic (or are they comical) aspects of this situation, see Moore (*Tobit*, 131) and the literature he cites.

67. There is a wordplay in the names of Tobit's relatives: Azariah = "YHWH has helped"; Ananiah = "YHWH has had mercy"; Shemaiah = "YHWH has heard." All hint at the salvation yet to be revealed through Raphael.

68. See, however, Moore (*Tobit*, 220), who thinks that Raguel may be simply encouraging his guest to "relax," "enjoy yourself," "feel good."

69. The element of the demonic is evident in the figure of Asmodeus, but may also be present in the cause of Tobit's blindness. For birds as the agents of Satan, see Jub. 11:11 and Mark 4:4, 15. This reading would enhance the symmetry between the stories of Tobit and Sarah.

70. For Gruen (*Diaspora*, 151), Tobit's comparison of his pious deeds with the sins of his compatriots evinces "more than a touch of arrogance" and "perhaps also excessive swagger." The story of the Pharisees and the tax collector (Luke 18:9–14) comes to mind. However, Tobit

recounts these events after he has, by his own admission, been "scourged," and in context the narration sets the reader up for the cognitive dissonance of unexpected consequences. If Gruen rightly intuits that this attitude existed prior to Tobit's suffering, however, we have a reason for Tobit's scourging.

71. Both are tales from a wisdom tradition that focus on the problem of theodicy. The wealthy hero in each case is a righteous and pious man who loses his wealth and health, engages in a bitter dispute with his wife, wishes he were dead, and eventually has everything restored to him. For further details see Devorah Dimant, "Use and Interpretation of Mikra in the Apocrypha and Pseudepigrapha," in M. J. Mulder, ed., *Mikra* (CRINT 2/1; Philadelphia: Fortress Press; Assen: Van Gorcum, 1988) 417–19; George W. E. Nickelsburg, "Tobit and Enoch: Distant Cousins with a Recognizable Resemblance," *SBLSP* 27 (1988) 54–55, repr. with response by Robert Doran in *GNP* 1:217–39, 254–63 (see 217–18).

72. Zimmermann (*Tobit*, 24–27) argues that chaps. 13 and 14 date after 70 C.E. However, both chapters are found in several of the pre-Christian Aramaic and Hebrew mss. of Tobit among the Dead Sea Scrolls.

73. Ps. 89:32–34; Pss. Sol. 7:8–10; 10:1–4; 18:4–7; Wis 12:22.

74. The material relating to Raphael is structured after the typical biblical form describing an angelic appearance. Not infrequently these biblical passages construe the angel as God's presence. That Tobit is, in a sense, an extended angelophany was pointed out to me by Norman R. Petersen. Other elements in my discussion also reflect his insights, now gathered in Petersen, "Tobit."

75. See 3:11; 4:19; 11:1, 14, 16–17; 12:6.

76. On this issue see esp. Levine, "Diaspora as Metaphor," 107–9.

77. See Beverly Bow and George W. E. Nickelsburg, "Patriarchy with a Twist: Men and Women in Tobit," in Amy-Jill Levine, ed., *"Women like This": New Perspectives on Jewish Women in the Greco-Roman World* (SBLEJL 1; Atlanta: Scholars Press, 1991) 127–43; Levine, "Diaspora as Metaphor."

78. See George W. E. Nickelsburg, "The Search for Tobit's Mixed Ancestry: A Historical and Hermeneutical Odyssey," *RevQ* 17, nos. 65–68 (1996) (= F. García Martínez and Émile Puech, eds., *Hommage à Józef T. Milik* [Paris: Gabalda, 1996]) 349–59, repr. in *GNP* 1:241–53; Dennis R. MacDonald, "Tobit and the *Odyssey*," in idem, ed., *Mimesis and Intertextuality in Antiquity and Christianity* (Harrisburg: Trinity International, 2001) 11–40; Nickelsburg, "Tobit, Genesis, and the *Odyssey*: The Complex Web of Intertextuality," in MacDonald, ed., *Intertextuality*, 41–55.

79. Nickelsburg, "Tobit, Genesis and the *Odyssey*," 48–51.

80. Parallels between Tobit and the *Odyssey* were first noted by Carl Fries, "Das Buch Tobit und die Telemachie," *ZWT* 53 (1911) 54–87, an article that has been all but neglected in the literature. For a compelling case for a connection between Tobit and the *Odyssey*, see MacDonald, "Tobit and the *Odyssey*," as well as my critique in "Tobit, Genesis, and the *Odyssey*."

81. See Pfeiffer, *History*, 269–71; Will Soll, "Misfortune and Exile in Tobit: The Juncture of a Fairy Tale Source and Deuteronomic Theology," *CBQ* 51 (1989) 209–31; Wills, *Jewish Novel*, 73–76.

82. Soll, "Misfortune"; Nickelsburg, "Tobit and Enoch."

83. For the term "didactic novel" see Wills (*Jewish Novel*, 88–92), who develops a detailed analysis for how the whole comes together.

84. Nickelsburg, "Tobit and Enoch." I remain intrigued by the fact that at least in part the suffering and deliverance in this book are attributed to an angelic duel that is paralleled in 1 Enoch 6–11.

85. See Petersen, "Tobit"; Wills, *Jewish Novel*, 77–78; Gruen, *Diaspora*, 148–58; David McCracken, "Narration and Comedy in the Book of Tobit," *JBL* 114 (1995) 401–18; Moore, *Tobit*, index, *sub* "comedy," "humor," and "irony"; Anathea Porter-Young, "Alleviation of Suffering in the Book of Tobit: Comedy, Community, and Happy Endings," *CBQ* 63 (2001) 35–54; J. R. C. Cousland, "Tobit: A Comedy in Error?" *CBQ* (2003) 535–53.

86. See Zimmermann, *Tobit*, 15–21; Moore, *Tobit*, 42–43; Fitzmyer, *Tobit*, 52–54. Places suggested include the eastern dispersion, Egypt, Antioch in Syria, and Palestine. J. T. Milik ("La Patrie de Tobie," *RB* 73 [1966] 523–30) suggests that Tobit is a Samaritan writing touched up to make it orthodox in Judean circles.

87. On this issue see Levine, "Diaspora as Metaphor."

88. J. Lebram ("Die Weltreiche in der jüdischen Apokalyptik," *ZAW* 76 [1964] 328–31) suggests a date soon after Alexander's conquest of the Persian Empire and argues that the scheme of events in 14:4–7 has been altered by a later editor. See, however, Moore, *Tobit*, 42.

89. An analysis of the Aramaic of the Qumran fragments of Tobit leads Joseph A. Fitzmyer ("The Aramaic and Hebrew Fragments of Tobit from Cave 4," *CBQ* 57 [1995] 665–67) to situate the composition of Tobit between the end of the second century B.C.E. (the time of the composition of Daniel) and the beginning of the second century C.E. See also idem, *Tobit*, 52, where he tends to agree with the commonly held dating for Tobit.

90. That Tobit was composed in Aramaic rather than Hebrew is argued by Fitzmyer, "Fragments," 665–72; idem, *Tobit*, 18–27; Moore, *Tobit*, 33–39; Matthew Morgenstern, "Language and Literature in the Second Temple Period," *JJS* 48 (1997) 139–40. For the most sustained argument against authorship in Hebrew (rather than Aramaic), see Fitzmyer, *Tobit*, 21–25. In conversation Hanan Eshel has noted that it would be strange for a book composed in Aramaic, a widely known language, to be translated into the less accessible Hebrew. See the comments of David Noel Freedman, quoted by Moore, *Tobit*, 34.

91. See W. M. W. Roth, "For Life, He Appeals to Death (Wis 13:18)," *CBQ* 37 (1975) 21–47, who discusses Isa 40:18—41:7; 44:9–20; 46:5–8; Jer 10:3–8; Hab 2:18–19; Pss 115:4–8; 135:15–18; Wis 13:10–19; 15:7–13; Epistle of Jeremiah; Bel and the Serpent; Jub. 12:2–5; 20:8–9.

92. Cf. vv 67–70 with Jer 10:2–5. For details see Moore (*Additions*, 357–58), who also notes the influence of Isa 44 and 46; Pss 115 and 135; Deut 4:27–28 (ibid., 319–23). For yet another pseudepigraphic Jeremianic letter, cf. the Paraleipomena of Jeremiah.

93. I interpret vv 6–7 to be referring to a common topic. For the idea cf. Wis 1:6–10. The Greek verb *ekzētein* frequently has connotations of judgment and refers to searching out for the purpose of requiting. Cf. 1 Enoch 104:7–8, and see Werline, *Penitential Prayer*, 111–12.

94. The formulas occur in vv 16, 23, 29, 40, 44, 49, 52, 56, 64, 65, 69, 72.

95. Greek *hothen*, in vv 14, 22, 63; "from these things," v 28; cf. v 71; "(how), therefore," vv 39, 44, 49, 51, 56, 64, 68.

96. Cf. Deut 32:17.

97. This motif is drawn from Jer 10:5.

98. For similar negative formulations in an anti-idol polemic, cf. Isa 44:9–10, 18–20.

99. See Jonathan A. Goldstein, *1 Maccabees* (AB 41; Garden City, N.Y.: Doubleday, 1976) 36.

100. Subtracting seven generations of forty years from 597 B.C.E., the year of the first deportation; see Moore, *Additions*, 334–35.

101. On the details see Naumann, *Untersuchungen über den apokryphen Jeremiasbrief*, 3–31. Cf. 1 Enoch 99:7 and 104:9, where idolatry presents a threat in a Palestinian document.

102. For a possible Qumran fragment of the Greek, see Maurice Baillet, DJD 3:143 and pl. 30.2. Hanan Eshel has suggested in conversation that the identification of the fragment is uncertain, however. Its five partially preserved lines contain only twenty-two letters or letter fragments and only two fully preserved words ("therefore" and "them"). For Hebrew as the original language see Moore, *Additions*, 326–27.

2. PALESTINE IN THE WAKE OF ALEXANDER THE GREAT

1. For details on the event and the archeological finds relating to it, see Paul W. Lapp and Nancy L. Lapp, eds., *Discoveries in the Wâdî ed-Dâliyeh* (AASOR 41; Cambridge: American School of Oriental Research, 1974); Mary Joan Winn Leith, DJD 24 (1997); Douglas M. Gropp, DJD 28 (2001) 3–116.

2. See Pierre Grelot, "La légende d'Hénoch dans les apocryphes et dans le Bible," *RevScRel* 46 (1958) 5–26; VanderKam, *Enoch and Growth*, 23–109.

3. See Milik, *Books of Enoch*, 6; Nickelsburg, *1 Enoch 1*, 9–10. On the ten Qumran mss. of "the Book of Giants," a related Enochic composition not included in 1 Enoch, see Nickelsburg, *1 Enoch 1*, 10–11. For the content of that text see briefly Nickelsburg, *1 Enoch 1*, 172–73. For these texts see Loren T. Stuckenbruck, DJD 36:1–94; Émile Puech, DJD 31:9–115; Stuckenbruck, *The Book of the Giants from Qumran* (TSAJ 63; Tübingen: Mohr Siebeck, 1997). For commentary see Stuckenbruck, *Book of the Giants;* John C. Reeves, *Jewish Lore in Manichaean Cosmology* (HUCM 14; Cincinnati: Hebrew Union College Press, 1992).

4. In this chapter I shall discuss chaps. 72–82 and 1–36. For chaps. 83–90 see chapter 3 below. For chaps. 91–105 see chapter 4 below, where the collection as a whole is also discussed. For chaps. 37–71 see chapter 7 below.

5. For these texts see Milik, *Books of Enoch*, 274–97 (mss. b, c, d); Florentino García Martínez and Eibert J. C. Tigchelaar, DJD 36:95–171 (mss. a and b); Nickelsburg and VanderKam, *1 Enoch*, 100–116. Manuscript a contains only parts of the synchronistic calendar; ms. b, parts of this calendar and fragments of 1 Enoch 76–82; ms. c, fragments of chaps. 76–78; ms. d, three fragments from the end of the book, now missing in the Ethiopic version. For a tabulation see García Martínez and Tigchelaar, DJD 36:96. For discussions of the Book of the Luminaries, on which I am here dependent, see VanderKam, *Calendars*, 17–27; briefly Nickelsburg and VanderKam, *1 Enoch*, 6–8.

6. VanderKam, in Nickelsburg and VanderKam, *1 Enoch*, 6.

7. Translation by VanderKam, ibid., 96. For another example of a title in the middle of a narrative, cf. 1 Enoch 14:1.

8. For the correspondence or noncorrespondence of the Enochic calculations to empirical reality, I am dependent on comments by my former student Jay Cassel and my colleague Robert Mutel.

9. See Milik, *Books of Enoch*, 275.

10. Ibid., 296–97.

11. Michael E. Stone, "The Book of Enoch and Judaism in the Third Century B.C.E.," 489–90.

12. For the texts see García Martínez, *Scrolls*, 451–55; Vermes, *Complete Scrolls*, 335–56; Wise, Abegg, and Cook, *Scrolls*, §§72–73, 75–76. See also J. T. Milik, *Ten Years of Discovery in the Wilderness of Judaea* (SBT 1/26; London: SCM, 1959) 107–18; idem, *Books of Enoch*, 274–84, 93–95.

13. For a summary discussion, see James C. VanderKam, "Calendrical Texts and the Origins of the Dead Sea Scroll Community," in Michael O. Wise, Norman Golb, John J. Collins, and Dennis G. Pardee, eds., *Methods and Investigation of the Dead Sea Scrolls and the Khirbet Qumran Site: Present Realities and Future Prospects* (Annals of the New York Academy of Science 722; New York: New York Academy of Science, 1994) 371–88. For a summary see VanderKam, *Calendars*, 113–16.

14. Ancient Hebrew and Aramaic documents can be dated quite closely on the basis of the handwriting. For a brief summary see Frank Moore Cross, *The Ancient Library of Qumran* (3d ed.; Minneapolis: Fortress Press, 1995), 92–95. For a detailed analysis see idem, "The Development of the Jewish Scripts," in G. Ernest Wright, ed., *The Bible and the Ancient Near East*, FS W. F. Albright (Garden City, N.Y.: Doubleday, 1961) 133–20. See also Brian Webster, "Chronological Index of the Texts from the Judaean Desert," DJD 39:351–77. On the dating of chaps. 1–11 see Milik, *Books of Enoch*, 6.

15. See below, pp. 83–86.

16. The author of chaps. 20–36 has reused the traditions in chaps. 17–19, with eschatological additions that have parallels in chaps. 1–5. See in particular 25:3–6 and 27:2. For other parallels and for a detailed analysis of the content and function of chaps. 1–5 as a whole, see Hartman, *Asking for a Meaning*; and the summary in Nickelsburg, *1 Enoch 1*, 132.

17. On the relationship of 1:1–2 to the Blessing of Moses and the Balaam oracles see Nickelsburg, *1 Enoch*, 137–41. On the form of the oracle in 1 Enoch 1–5 see Paul D. Hanson, *The Dawn of Apocalyptic* (Philadelphia: Fortress Press, 1975) index, p. 425, *sub* "Salvation-judgment oracle."

18. Cf. Sir 16:26–28; 43:1–12; Pss. Sol. 18:11–14; T. Naph. 3. See Argall, *1 Enoch and Sirach*, 101–7, 159–61.

19. For the details of this analysis see Nickelsburg, *1 Enoch 1*, 165–68.

20. Ibid., 166.

21. See John J. Collins, "Methodological Issues in the Study of 1 Enoch: Reflections on the Articles of P. D. Hanson and G. W. Nickelsburg," *SBLSP* 13 (1978) 320–21; George W. E. Nickelsburg, "Reflections upon Reflections: A Response to John Collins' 'Methodological Issues in the Study of 1 Enoch,'" *SBLSP* 13 (1978) 313–14.

22. Nickelsburg, *1 Enoch 1*, 170–71.

23. For the alternative possibilities see Paul D. Hanson, "Rebellion in Heaven, Azazel, and Euhemeristic Heroes in *1 Enoch* 6–11," *JBL* 96 (1977) 220–27; Nickelsburg, *1 Enoch 1*, 171–72; Devorah Dimant, "1 Enoch 6–11: A Methodological Perspective," *SBLSP* 13 (1978) 323–39; Carol A. Newsom, "The Development of *1 Enoch* 6–19: Cosmology and Judgment," *CBQ* 42 (1980) 310–29.

24. In 6:8 he is the tenth of Shemihazah's lieutenants, while in 10:8 he is the angel most responsible for the rebellion, as is hinted by his prominence in 8:1–3. See Dimant, "1 Enoch 6–11," 323–24.

25. For the alternatives see Nickelsburg, *1 Enoch 1,* 191–93; Hanson, "Rebellion," 227–31.

26. For some of the complexities of tracing the development of this tradition in 1 Enoch see Hanson, "Rebellion," 220–26; Nickelsburg, "Apocalyptic and Myth in 1 Enoch 6–11," *JBL* 96 (1977) 401–4.

27. For the Qumran prognosticative documents see 4Q318, 4Q186, and 4Q561 in García Martínez, *Scrolls,* 451–52, 456–57; Vermes, *Scrolls,* 367–71; idem, *Complete Scrolls,* 357–62; Wise, Abegg, and Cook, *Scrolls,* §§34, 70, 146.

28. This section is based on my commentary *1 Enoch 1,* 229–75.

29. Cf. Pss. Sol. 8:13; CD 5:6–7.

30. Cf. Ezra 9. Ezra the scribe and priest comes to Jerusalem, where he finds that some of the Jews, including priests, have married foreign women and thus defiled the holy race and, of course, the priesthood. He prays in their behalf (cf. Ezra 9:6 with 1 Enoch 13:5) and orders the marriages dissolved. In 1 Enoch 16 the damage is irreparable and the angelic priests are under irrevocable judgment.

31. For details see the excursus "Sacred Geography in 1 Enoch 6–16," in Nickelsburg, *1 Enoch 1,* 238–47; see also David W. Suter, "Why Galilee? Galilean Regionalism in the Interpretation of *1 Enoch* 6–16," *Hen* 25 (2003) 167–211.

32. E.g., Homer, *Od.* 11 (see esp. 11.576–600); Plato, *Rep.* 10.614–21; *Phaedo* 113D–114C; Plutarch, *Mor.* 563–68.

33. Influence from Babylonian geography is argued by P. Grelot, "La géographie mythique d'Hénoch et ses sources orientales," *RB* 65 (1969) 33–69. Much of Grelot's argument is built on a comparison with the Babylonian epic about Gilgamesh's search for immortality. For further connections between Babylonian mythology and the Enoch traditions, see VanderKam, *Enoch and the Growth of an Apocalyptic Tradition.* These parallels notwithstanding, one should note the close analogy between this text and the Greek *nekyia.* Similarly the fiery river, Pyriphlegethon (cf. 17:5), is known in Greek but not in Babylonian sources. See also Glasson, *Greek Influence,* 8–11.

34. The original order of these verses appears to have been 18:6–11, 19:1–2, 18:12–16, and 19:3. The text as it now stands has two visions in a row (18:10–11 and 12–13), the first having no interpretation, the second having two (18:14–16 and 19:1–2). See Nickelsburg, *1 Enoch 1,* 287.

35. See Nickelsburg, *1 Enoch 1,* 37–42.

36. See ibid., 57–62.

37. See Argall, *1 Enoch and Sirach,* for a detailed comparison of these two works.

38. The form of his name differs in the Greek and Hebrew texts of 50:27. See Skehan and Di Lella, *Ben Sira,* 3–4, 557, 579–80.

39. On the translation see Benjamin G. Wright III, *No Small Difference.*

40. Ben Sira was not the only author in the Hellenistic period composing sapiential material reminiscent of the book of Proverbs. See the text entitled 4QInstruction found in at least eight fragmentary Qumran mss. and discussed below, pp. 169–72.

41. Jan Liesen, "Strategic Self-References in Ben Sira," in N. Calduch-Benages and J. Vermeylen, eds., *Treasures of Wisdom: Studies in Ben Sira and the Book of Wisdom,* FS M. Gilbert (BETL 143; Leuven: Leuven Univ. Press and Peeters, 1999) 63–74. On Ben Sira as a scribe see Stadelmann, *Ben Sira*; Mack, *Wisdom and Hebrew Epic,* 89–107; John G. Gammie, "The Sage in Sirach," in John G. Gammie and Leo G. Perdue, eds., *The Sage in Israel and the Ancient Near East* (Winona Lake, Ind.: Eisenbrauns, 1990) 355–72; Wolfgang Roth, "On the Gnomic-Discursive Wisdom of Jesus Ben Sirach," *Semeia* 17 (1980) 59–79.

42. See esp. Sanders, *Ben Sira and Demotic Wisdom.*

43. See Mack (*Wisdom and Hebrew Epic*, 96), who finds no precedents for this in Jewish wisdom literature.

44. On 51:23 and the question of whether Ben Sira had a "house of instruction" or a group of students, see Collins, *Jewish Wisdom*, 36–39. For a different opinion see Skehan and Di Lella, *Ben Sira*, 420–23.

45. Contra Tcherikover (*Hellenistic Civilization*, 146–47), who cites 8:1–2 and 13:2, 7, 15–23. These passages contrast rich and poor and warn against association with the mighty but do not explicitly address the poor. On banquets and banqueting see Hans Volker Kieweler, "Beinehmen bei Tisch," in Egger-Wenzel and Krammer, eds., *Einzelne*, 191–215; Collins, *Jewish Wisdom*, 32–33; Benjamin G. Wright III and Claudia V. Camp, "Who Has Been Tested by Gold and Found Perfect," *Hen* 23 (2001) 165.

46. This claim is argued at length by Stadelmann (*Ben Sira*, 40–176), who is followed by Saul M. Olyan, "Ben Sira's Relationship to the Priesthood," *HTR* 80 (1987) 261–86, esp. 263–67. Mack (*Wisdom and Hebrew Epic*, 104–7) speaks of the priestly scholar-sage, who stands in the image of Moses. Collins (*Jewish Wisdom*, 37–38) believes that Stadelmann's evidence is not probative, but he does not engage Stadelmann and Olyan at length. Gammie ("Sage in Sirach," 364–65) and Coggins (*Sirach*, 49) take a mediating position: Ben Sira could have belonged to a priestly family, without (regularly) officiating in the temple. For a description of the scribes as "retainers" of the priestly and governing class, see Anthony J. Saldarini, *Pharisees, Scribes, and Sadducees* (Wilmington, Del.: Glazier, 1988) 243–76, esp. 254–57, who does not exclude that scribes "may have been drawn from the priests and Levites" (p. 273). He is followed by Richard Horsley and Patrick Tiller, "Ben Sira and the Sociology of the Second Temple," in Philip R. Davies and John M. Halligan, eds., *Temple Studies III: Studies in Politics, Class and Material Culture* (JSOT-Sup 340; Sheffield: Sheffield Academic Press, 2002) 74–107; Benjamin G. Wright III, "'Fear the Lord and Honor the Priest': Ben Sira as Defender of the Jerusalem Priesthood," in Beentjes, ed., *Ben Sira in Modern Research*, 189–222.

47. For the structure see the overview by Johannes Marböck, "Structure and Redaction History in the Book of Ben Sira: Review and Prospects," in Beentjes, ed., *Ben Sira in Modern Research*, 61–79. For its composition see ibid., 76–79. See also Maurice Gilbert, "The Book of Ben Sira: Implications for Jewish and Christian Traditions," in Shemaryahu Talmon, ed., *Jewish Civilization in the Hellenistic-Roman Period* (JSPSup 10; Sheffield: Sheffield Academic Press, 1991) 81–91.

48. See Thomas R. Lee, *Studies in the Form of Sirach 44–50* (SBLDS 75; Atlanta: Scholars Press, 1986); Mack, *Wisdom and Hebrew Epic*; Jean Louis Ska, "L'éloge des Pères dans le Siracide (Si 44–50) et le canon de l'Ancien Testament," in Calduch-Benages and Vermeylen, eds., *Treasures of Wisdom*, 181–93.

49. Cf. Dan 12:12; Rev 22:7.

50. James A. Sanders (DJD 4:79–85) has published an earlier form of the Hebrew version of the poem, which was included in a ms. of the canonical Psalter explicitly ascribed to David, and he argues that Ben Sira has adopted a traditional poem (pp. 84–85). This is disputed by Skehan and Di Lella, *Ben Sira*, 74, 576–77; and by Marböck, "Structure," 76. See also Collins, *Jewish Wisdom*, 53.

51. Cf. 6:23–31.

52. Collins, *Jewish Wisdom*, 37.

53. See Alexander A. Di Lella, "Fear of the Lord as Wisdom: Ben Sira 1:11–30," in Beentjes, ed., *Ben Sira and Modern Research*, 113–33. For a broader study that argues that the fear of Lord is

the central theme in Sirach, see Josef Haspecker, *Gottestfurcht bei Jesus Sirach: Ihre religiöse Struktur und ihre literarische und doktrinäre Bedeutung* (AnBib 30; Rome: Biblical Institute Press, 1967).

54. For the contrast between the personified Wisdom and the wicked woman, cf. Prov 1:20—2:19. Cf. also 4Q184 (John M. Allegro, DJD 5:82–84; and the review by John Strugnell in *RevQ* 7 [1970] 263–68; García Martínez, *Scrolls*, 379–80; Vermes, *Scrolls*, 273–74; idem, *Complete Scrolls*, 395–96; Wise, Abegg, and Cook, *Scrolls*, §132); cf. also the two women in Rev 12 and 17–18.

55. On the scope of Ben Sira's wisdom see Alexander A. Di Lella, "The Meaning of Wisdom in Ben Sira," in Leo G. Perdue, Bernard Brandon Scott, and William Johnston Wiseman, eds., *In Search of Wisdom: Essays in Memory of John G. Gammie* (Louisville: Westminster/John Knox, 1993) 133–48; Collins, *Jewish Wisdom*, 42–79.

56. On wisdom and Torah in Sirach see Eckhard J. Schnabel, *Law and Wisdom from Ben Sira to Paul: A Tradition Historical Enquiry into the Relation of Law, Wisdom, and Ethics* (WUNT 16; Tübingen: Mohr Siebeck, 1985) 8–92; more briefly, Collins, *Jewish Wisdom*, 54–61.

57. For earlier texts that seem to presume the identification, cf. Deut 4:6; Ezra 7:14, 25; see Collins, *Jewish Wisdom*, 54. For a somewhat later text, cf. Bar 3:9—4:4, on which see below, pp. 95–96.

58. See Johannes Marböck, *Weisheit im Wandel: Untersuchungen zur Weisheitstheologie bei Ben Sira* (BBB 37; Bonn: Peter Hanstein, 1971; repr. as BZAW 272; Berlin: de Gruyter, 1999) 17–97; Maurice Gilbert, "L'éloge de la Sagesse (Siracide 24)," *RTL* 5 (1974) 326–48; Skehan and Di Lella, *Ben Sira*, 326–38; more briefly, Mack, *Wisdom and Hebrew Epic*, 162–64, 235–36 n. 11; Collins, *Jewish Wisdom*, 49–53.

59. Hans Conzelmann, "Die Mutter der Weisheit," in Erich Dinkler, ed., *Zeit und Geschichte*, FS R. Bultmann (Tübingen: Mohr Siebeck, 1964) 225–34; Hengel, *Judaism*, 1:157–59; Collins, *Jewish Wisdom*, 49–50.

60. Skehan and Di Lella, *Ben Sira*, 327–28, 331, following Skehan, "Structures in Poems on Wisdom: Proverbs 8 and Sirach 24," *CBQ* 41 (1979) 365–79.

61. Sirach here conflates two traditional ideas: the tree of wisdom and the tree of life. See Howard N. Wallace, "Tree of Knowledge and Tree of Wisdom," *ABD* 6:656–60. On the tree of wisdom cf. 1 Enoch 28–32; 82:2–3; Argall, *1 Enoch and Sirach*, 32–35; Nickelsburg, *1 Enoch 1*, 343.

62. On prophecy and the scribal office see Stadelmann, *Ben Sira*, 177–207. See also Mack, *Wisdom and Hebrew Epic*, 98–99, 126–27. On the problem of the relationship between prophecy and office of the scribes, see George W. E. Nickelsburg, "Wisdom and Apocalypticism in Early Judaism: Some Points for Discussion," *SBLSP* 33 (1994) 727–28, repr. in *GNP* 1:283–85.

63. See Walter Baumgartner, "Die literarischen Gattungen in der Weisheit des Jesus Sirach," *ZAW* 34 (1914) 161–98; Hengel, *Judaism*, 1:134–35.

64. See George W. E. Nickelsburg, *Ancient Judaism and Christian Origins: Diversity, Continuity, and Transformation* (Minneapolis: Fortress Press, 2003) 52–53.

65. On the ambiguities of the relationship between Ben Sira and the Deuteronomic tradition, see Mack, *Wisdom and Hebrew Epic*, 113, 120. However, on Ben Sira's use of a two-ways theology that is related to Deuteronomy (Sir 15:17||Deut 30:15), see Nickelsburg, *Resurrection*, 164 n. 21. The vitalistic language in 24:12–22 and its connection with the Mosaic Torah (v 23) fits well with the notion of covenantal blessing as life.

66. Cf. 17:12; 24:23; 28:7; 39:8; 41:19; 42:2; 44:18, 20, 22; 45:5. In 45:7, 15, 17, 24 he speaks of the priestly covenant, and in 45:25 and 47:11 of the Davidic covenant. For a discussion of Ben

Sira's theology as an expression of "covenantal nomism," see E. P. Sanders, *Paul and Palestinian Judaism* (Philadelphia: Fortress Press, 1977) 329–46. Mack (*Wisdom and Hebrew Epic*, see index, p. 252) works in a more restricted way with actual occurrences of the term and in a broader way with a plurality of covenants.

67. For similar catalogs cf. 1 Macc 2:49–64 and Heb 11:1—12:13. For a superb treatment of the hymn, its sources, and its function in Sirach, see Mack, *Wisdom and Hebrew Epic*.

68. On these poems see Marböck, *Weisheit im Wandel*; Otto Rickenbacher, *Weisheits Perikopen bei ben Sira* (OBO 1; Fribourg: Universitätsverlag; Göttingen: Vandenhoeck & Ruprecht, 1973); more briefly, Skehan and Di Lella, *Ben Sira*, ad loc.; Collins, *Jewish Wisdom*, 46–54.

69. Nuria Calduch-Benages, "Trial Motive in the Book of Ben Sira with Special Reference to Sir 2, 1–6," in Beentjes, ed., *Ben Sira and Modern Research*, 135–51.

70. The materials in chaps. 2, 4, and 6 have a similar structure: one seeks Wisdom, who provides blessings after and through difficulty.

71. See above, pp. 32–33.

72. See below, pp. 95–96. For Ben Sira's reference to Deuteronomy see above, n. 65.

73. Cf. John 1:1–18; Phil 2:5–11; Col 1:15–20; Heb 1:1–3.

74. See the nicely crafted discussion by Collins, *Jewish Wisdom*, 62–74.

75. On this topic see Reinhold Bohlen, *Die Ehrung der Eltern bei Ben Sira: Studien zur Motivation und Interpretation eines familienethischen Grundwortes in frühhellenistischer Zeit* (TThSt 51; Trier: Paulinus, 1991).

76. Collins, *Jewish Wisdom*, 64–74.

77. His sections on women include 7:19–26; 9:1–9; 22:3–5; 25:16—26:18; 42:12–14. Especially problematic are passages like 22:3; 25:19, 24; 42:14. For a detailed discussion and extremely negative assessment that attributes to Ben Sira a personal bias against women, see Warren C. Trenchard, *Ben Sira's View of Women: A Literary Analysis* (BJS 38; Chico, Calif.: Scholars Press, 1982). This assessment is shared by Coggins, *Ben Sira*, 85–90; and to some degree by Collins, *Jewish Wisdom*, 72.

78. Skehan and Di Lella (*Ben Sira*, 90–92) argue that Ben Sira's attitude toward women is paralleled and even exceeded in contemporary documents. See also Claudia V. Camp, "Understanding a Patriarchy: Women in Second-Century Jerusalem through the Eyes of Ben Sira," in Amy-Jill Levine, ed., *"Women like This": New Perspectives on Jewish Women in the Greco-Roman World* (SBLEJL 1; Atlanta: Scholars Press, 1991) 1–39. On the culture of honor and shame, see ibid.; idem, "Honor and Shame in Ben Sira: Anthropological and Theological Reflections," in Beentjes, ed., *Ben Sira and Modern Research*, 171–87; David A. deSilva, "The Wisdom of Ben Sira: Honor, Shame, and the Maintenance of the Values of a Minority Culture," *CBQ* 58 (1996) 433–65, who cites neither of Camp's articles.

79. See the collection edited by Egger-Wenzel and Krammer, *Einzelne*.

80. Cf. 6:5–17; 9:10–16; 11:29—12:18; 13:15–23; 19:13–17; 22:19–26; 27:16–21; 37:1–6. See the papers in Frederich V. Reiterer, ed., *Freundschaft bei Ben Sira: Beiträge des Symposiums zu Ben Sira Salzburg, 1995* (BZAW 244; Berlin: de Gruyter, 1966); Jeremy Corley, "Friendship according to Ben Sira," in Egger-Wenzel and Krammer, eds., *Einzelne*, 65–72; Corley, *Ben Sira's Teaching on Friendship* (BJS 316; Providence: Brown Univ. Program in Judaic Studies, 2002).

81. Thus Corley, "Friendship"; idem, *Ben Sira's Teaching*.

82. See Roland E. Murphy, "Sin, Repentance, and Forgiveness in Sirach," in Egger-Wenzel and Krammer, eds., *Einzelne*, 261–70.

83. Victor Morla Asensio, "Poverty and Wealth: Ben Sira's View of Possessions," in Egger-Wenzel and Krammer, eds., *Einzelne*, 152–78.

84. Wright and Camp, "Tested by Gold," 153–73, quotation from 154 n. 2.

85. Mack, *Wisdom and Hebrew Epic*, 112–17; Olyan, "Priesthood," 267–72.

86. Mack, *Wisdom and Hebrew Epic*, citations in index, p. 257; Collins, *Jewish Wisdom*, 106–8; Johannes Marböck, "Der Hohepriester Simon in Sir 50: Ein Beitrag zur Bedeutung von Priestertum und Kult im Sirachbuch," in Calduch-Benages and Vermeylen, eds., *Treasures of Wisdom*, 215–29.

87. Schnabel, *Law and Wisdom*, 39–42.

88. Nickelsburg, *Ancient Judaism*, 39–41.

89. See Jack T. Sanders, "When Sacred Canopies Collide: The Reception of the Torah of Moses in the Wisdom Literature of the Second Temple Period," *JSJ* 32 (2001) 121–36.

90. See Nickelsburg, *1 Enoch 1*, 58–59.

91. Cf. Pss. Sol. 3, on which see below, p. 244.

92. James L. Crenshaw, "The Problem of Theodicy in Sirach: On Human Bondage," *JBL* 94 (1975) 48–55.

93. For this section as an attack on Epicureanism see Hengel, *Judaism*, 1:141, tentatively; and Gerhard Maier, *Mensch und freier Wille* (WUNT 12; Tübingen: Mohr, 1971) 88–90.

94. See Nickelsburg, *Resurrection*, 164 n. 121, for a comparison of the Qumran Rule of the Community (1QS 3:13—4:26) with Sir 15:11ff. The latter might be considered a critique of something like the former. For an extensive discussion of this passage, see Ursel Wicke-Reuter, *Göttliche Providenz und menschliche Verantwortung bei Ben Sira und in der Frühen Stoa* (BZAW 298; Berlin: de Gruyter, 2000) 106–87.

95. On free will in Sirach see Jean Hadot, *Penchant mauvais et volonté libre dans la Sagesse de Ben Sira (L'Ecclésiastique)* (Brussels: Presses Universitaires de Bruxelles, 1970); Maier, *Mensch und freier Wille*, 60–115.

96. Argall, *1 Enoch and Ben Sira*, 136–54.

97. See Collins, *Jewish Wisdom*, 84–89. On the topic as a whole see Gian Luigi Prato, *Il problema della teodicea in Ben Sira* (AnBib 65; Rome: Biblical Institute Press, 1975).

98. See Collins, *Jewish Wisdom*, 92–94; for a different opinion see Émile Puech, "Ben Sira 48:11 et la Résurrection," in Harold W. Attridge, John J. Collins, and Thomas H. Tobit, eds., *Of Scribes and Scrolls: Studies on the Hebrew Bible, Intertestamental Judaism, and Christian Origins Presented to John Strugnell on the Occasion of his Sixtieth Birthday* (College Society Resources in Religion 5; Lanham, Md.: Univ. Press of America, 1990) 81–90.

99. On this text see Ralph Hildesheim, *Bis dass ein Prophet aufstand wie Feuer: Untersuchungen zum Prophetenverständnis des Ben Sira in Sir 48, 1—49, 16* (TThSt 58; Trier: Paulinus, 1996) 119–24, 238.

100. Doubting Ben Sira's hope in a future Davidic king are Collins, *Jewish Wisdom*, 103; and Martha Himmelfarb, "The Wisdom of the Scribe, the Wisdom of the Priest, and the Wisdom of the King according to Ben Sira," in Randal A. Argall, Beverly A. Bow, and Rodney A. Werline, eds., *For a Later Generation: The Transformation of Tradition in Israel, Early Judaism, and Early Christianity*, FS G. W. E. Nickelsburg (Harrisburg: Trinity International, 2000) 98. Olyan ("Priesthood," 281–84) argues for Ben Sira's belief in a future Davidic king.

101. Collins (*Jewish Wisdom*, 109–11) disputes the authenticity of the passage and sees it as a later interpolation that spoke of conditions during the Maccabean period. For arguments supporting the authenticity of the text, however, see Skehan and Di Lella, *Ben Sira*, 420–23;

Johannes Marböck, "Das Gebet um die Rettung Zions Sir 36,1–22 (G:33,1–13a; 36,16b–22) im Zusammenhang der Geschichtsschau ben Sira," in J. B. Bauer and Johannes Marböck, eds., *Memoria Jerusalem: Freundesgabe Franz Sauer* (Graz: Akademisches Drück- u. Verlaganstalt, 1977) 93–115; Benjamin G. Wright III, "'Put the Nations in Fear of You': Ben Sira and the Problem of Foreign Rule," *SBLSP* 38 (1999) 77–93, esp. 83–85, 91–93.

102. Skehan and Di Lella, *Ben Sira*, 8–10. Although most scholars agree that this Simon is Simon II, James C. VanderKam (*From Joshua to Caiaphas* [Minneapolis: Fortress Press, 2004] 141–57) argues that Ben Sira is referring to Simon I, who was high priest roughly a century earlier. Even if that is the case, we can set Ben Sira's approximate dates on the basis of the reference to his grandson in the prologue; see Skehan and Di Lella, *Ben Sira*, 8–9.

103. See Tcherikover, *Hellenistic Civilization*, 143–45; Hengel, *Judaism*, 1:131–53.

104. E.g., on 15:11—18:14 see above, pp. 60–61; on 41:8–9 see below, n. 105. Similarly, 3:21–24 might be a warning against apocalyptic speculation (contra Hengel, *Judaism*, 1:139). On the possibility of Ben Sira's polemics against Enochic apocalypticism, see Argall, *1 Enoch and Sirach*, 250.

105. We might find one such reference in 41:8–9; so Tcherikover, *Hellenistic Civilization*, 145; Hengel, *Judaism*, 1:151. However, the expression "forsake the covenant/law" refers in Dan 11:30; Jub. 23:16; 1 Macc 1:15; and 2:21 to the radical apostasy of the Hellenistic reform of 175 and after, a time considered too late by both Tcherikover (*Hellenistic Civilization*, 143) and Hengel (*Judaism*, 1:131).

106. A number of scholars have argued that Ben Sira reflects Stoic influence, directly or indirectly; see, e.g., Hengel, *Judaism*, 1:146–50; Marböck, *Weisheit im Wandel*, 170–71; David Winston, "Theodicy in Ben Sira and Stoic Philosophy," in Ruth Link-Salinger, ed., *Of Scholars, Savants, and Their Texts: Studies in Philosophy and Religious Thought*, FS Arthur Hyman (New York: Peter Lang, 1989) 239–49; Collins, *Jewish Wisdom*, 84–89; Wicke-Reuter, *Göttliche Providenz*. For an argument against Stoic influence, see Sharon Lea Mattila, "Ben Sira and the Stoics: A Reexamination of the Evidence," *JBL* 119 (2000) 473–501. More radical Hellenistic influence on Ben Sira is proposed by Th. Middendorp, *Die Stellung Jesus ben Siras zwischen Judentum und Hellenismus* (Leiden: Brill, 1973) 7–34. This position, however, has not generally been accepted; see, e.g., Volker Kieweler, *Ben Sira zwischen Judaism und Hellenismus: Eine Auseinandersetzung mit Th. Middendorp* (BEATAJ 30; Frankfurt: Peter Lang, 1992). For a thorough discussion of Ben Sira's relationship to Jewish, Greek, and Egyptian wisdom traditions, see Sanders, *Ben Sira and Demotic Wisdom*.

107. Mack, *Wisdom and Hebrew Epic*, 91–92, 95, 114, 120–37.

108. Sanders, *Ben Sira and Demotic Wisdom*, 58.

109. Ben Sira's constructive use and transformation of Hellenistic philosophical thought and ethical instruction is argued by Marböck, *Weisheit im Wandel*; and Wicke-Reuter, *Providenz*; and Bohlen, *Ehrung*, who finds it in Ben Sira's interpretation of the commandment to honor one's parents.

110. Mack (*Wisdom and Hebrew Epic*, citations in index, p. 257) sees the glorifying of Simon at the end of his hymn to the heroes as essential to Ben Sira's purpose. On the variety of attitudes about the priesthood, see Olyan, "Priesthood."

111. See Argall, *1 Enoch and Sirach*, 8–11; Benjamin G. Wright III, "Putting the Puzzle Together: Some Suggestions concerning the Social Location of the Wisdom of Ben Sira," *SBLSP* 35 (1996) 133–49; idem, "Fear the Lord," 218–22.

112. Mack, *Wisdom and Hebrew Epic*, 150–56.

113. Camp, "Understanding a Patriarchy," 38.

114. On the prologue see Skehan and Di Lella, *Ben Sira*, 132–35. On the translation see Wright, *No Small Difference*.

115. For the Qumran fragments see Maurice Baillet, DJD 3:75–77; for a Hebrew form of the poem in Sir 51:13–22, see James A. Sanders, DJD 4:79–85. For the Masada ms. see Yigael Yadin, *The Ben Sira Scroll from Masada* (Jerusalem: Israel Exploration Society, 1965); John Strugnell, "Notes and Queries on 'The Ben Sira Scroll from Masada,'" *Eretz Israel* 9 (1969) 109–19. See also Corrado Martone, "Ben Sira Manuscripts from Qumran and Masada," in Beentjes, ed., *Ben Sira and Modern Research*, 81–94.

116. On the history of the Hebrew text see Di Lella, *Hebrew Text of Sirach*; Yadin, *Scroll*, 5–11; Strugnell, "Notes," 119. For the work that has been done on the text of Sirach, see Harrington, "Sirach Research," 164–70; Reiterer, "Recent Research," 26–34.

117. On the references to Ben Sira in rabbinic literature see G. H. Box and W. O. E. Oesterley, "Sirach," in *APOT* 1:297–98; Jonas C. Greenfield, "Ben Sira 42.9–10," in Philip R. Davies and Richard T. White, eds., *A Tribute to Geza Vermes: Essays on Jewish and Christian Literature* (JSOTSup 100; Sheffield: Sheffield Academic Press, 1990) 167–73; Benjamin G. Wright III, "B. Sanhedrin 100b and Rabbinic Knowledge of Ben Sira," in Calduch-Benages and Vermeylen, eds., *Treasures of Wisdom*, 41–50.

118. See Box and Oesterley, "Sirach," 270–71; on its use in the early church, ibid., 298–303.

3. REFORM—REPRESSION—REVOLT

1. I use the term "pious" to refer to those Jews who opposed their compatriots' hellenizing ways. They are usually called *Hasidim* in the scholarly literature. This Hebrew term, which may be roughly translated "loyalists" (i.e., those loyal to the Torah), is used of a "group of mighty warriors" who made common cause with Mattathias (1 Macc 2:42). On the difficulties of using this term broadly and indiscriminately, however, see John J. Collins, *The Apocalyptic Vision of the Book of Daniel* (HSM 16; Missoula, Mont.: Scholars Press, 1977) 201–5; Philip Davies, "Hasidim in the Maccabean Period," *JJS* 28 (1977) 127–40; George W. E. Nickelsburg, "Social Aspects of Palestinian Jewish Apocalypticism," in David Hellholm, ed., *Apocalypticism in the Mediterranean World and the Near East* (Tübingen: Mohr Siebeck, 1983) 641–54; Nickelsburg, *Ancient Judaism*, 176–78. See also below, p. 91.

2. See Gruen, *Heritage and Hellenism*, 9–12.

3. See 1:27, 29; 2:1; cf. also 18:9–11; 30:17–21; chap. 48. On Jubilees as an extension of Mosaic discourse that authorizes itself through the device of angelic dictation, and a comparison with the Qumran Temple Scroll, see Hindy Najman, *Seconding Sinai: The Development of Mosaic Discourse in Second Temple Judaism* (JSJSup 77; Leiden: Brill, 2003) 43–69.

4. For a detailed study of this author's techniques for rewriting of the biblical text, see Endres, *Biblical Interpretation*, 196–225; and van Ruiten, *Primaeval History Interpreted*.

5. For a reading of Jubilees that focuses especially on the book's chronology and calendar, see VanderKam, *Book of Jubilees*, 23–84; see also idem, "Studies on the Prologue and *Jubilees 1*," in Randal A. Argall, Beverly A. Bow, and Rodney A. Werline, eds., *For a Later Generation: The Transformation of Tradition in Israel, Early Judaism, and Early Christianity*, FS G. W. E. Nickelsburg (Valley Forge, Pa.: Trinity International, 2000) 273–79. On the calendar and chronology in

Jubilees see Matthias Albani, "Zur Rekonstruktion eines verdrängten Konzepts: Der 364-Tage Kalendar in der gegenwärtigen Forschung," in Albani, Frey, and Lange, eds., *Studies*, 79–125; Uwe Glessmer, "Explizite Aussagen über kalendarische Konflikte im Jubiläenbuch: Jub 6,22–32.33–38," in Albani, Frey, and Lange, eds., *Studies*, 127–64; Werner Eiss, "Das Wochenfest im Jubiläenbuch und im antiken Judentum," in Albani, Frey, and Lange, eds., *Studies*, 165–78; Ben Zion Wacholder, "The Date of the Eschaton in the Book of Jubilees: A Commentary on Jub. 49:22–50:5, CD 1:1–10, and 16:2–3," *HUCA* 56 (1985) 87–101.

6. Wacholder, "Date," 87–101.

7. On the Sabbath laws in Jubilees see Lutz Doering, "The Concept of the Sabbath in the Book of Jubilees," in Albani, Frey, and Lange, eds., *Studies*, 179–205.

8. On these tablets and their function see Florentino García Martínez, "The Heavenly Tablets in the Book of Jubilees," in Albani, Frey, and Lange, eds., *Studies*, 243–60; Martha Himmelfarb, "Torah, Testimony, and Heavenly Tablets: The Claim to Authority of the *Book of Jubilees*," in Benjamin G. Wright, ed., *A Multiform Heritage: Studies on Early Judaism and Christianity in Honor of Robert A Kraft* (Scholars Press Homage Series 24; Atlanta: Scholars Press, 1999) 25–28.

9. On the angel of the Presence as the one who dictates the book to Moses, see James C. VanderKam, "The Putative Author of the Book of Jubilees," *JSS* 26 (1981) 209–17.

10. See Hindy Najman, "Interpretation as Primordial Writing: Jubilees and Its Authority Conferring Strategies," *JSJ* 30 (1999) 379–410.

11. On Jubilees' dependence on the traditions in 1 Enoch 6–16, see Nickelsburg, *1 Enoch 1*, 72–75; James C. VanderKam, "The Angel Story in the Book of Jubilees," in Esther G. Chazon and Michael Stone, eds., *Biblical Perspectives: Early Use and Interpretation of the Bible in Light of the Dead Sea Scrolls: Proceedings of the First International Symposium of the Orion Center for the Study of the Dead Sea Scrolls and Associated Literature, 12–14 May 1996* (STDJ 28; Leiden: Brill, 1998) 151–70. For its dependence on the Aramaic Levi Document see Pierre Grelot, "Le livre des Jubilés et le Testament de Levi," in P. Casetti, O. Keel, and A. Schenker, eds., *Mélanges Dominique Barthélemy: Études bibliques offertes à l'occasion de son 60ᵉ anniversaire* (OBO 38; Fribourg: Éditions Universitaires; Göttingen: Vandenhoeck & Ruprecht, 1981) 111–20; Robert A. Kugler, *From Patriarch to Priest: The Levi-Priestly Tradition from Aramaic Levi to Testament of Levi* (SBLEJL 9; Atlanta: Scholars Press, 1996) 139–69. On the tradition about Abraham's ten trials see below, p. 71.

12. For similar stories see T. Job. 1–5 and Apoc. Abr. 1–2. On these books see below, pp. 315–22, 285–88. On the stories of Abraham's conversion from idolatry, see George W. E. Nickelsburg, "Abraham the Convert," in Michael E. Stone and Theodore A. Bergren, eds., *Biblical Figures outside the Bible* (Harrisburg: Trinity International, 1998) 151–67. For the ongoing history of this tradition in Christian chronography, see William Adler, "Abraham and the Burning of the Temple of Idols: Jubilees Traditions in Christian Chronography," *JQR* 77 (1986–87) 95–117.

13. On this passage see James C. VanderKam, "The *Aqedah*, *Jubilees*, and PseudoJubilees," in Craig Evans and Shemaryahu Talmon, eds., *The Quest for Context and Meaning: Studies in Intertextuality in Honor of James A. Sanders* (BIS; Leiden: Brill, 1997) 241–61; Leroy-Andrew Huizenga, "The Battle for Isaac: Exploring the Composition and Function of the Aqedah in the Book of Jubilees," *JSP* 13 (2002) 33–59.

14. For a later rabbinic reference to the traditions, see *m. ʾAbot* 5:4. On the possibility of other source material behind Jubilees, see James Kugel, "Reuben's Sin with Bilhah in the *Testament of*

Reuben," in David P. Wright, David Noel Freedman, and Avi Hurvitz, eds., *Pomegranates and Golden Bells: Studies in Biblical, Jewish, and Near Eastern Ritual, Law, and Literature in Honor of Jacob Milgrom* (Winona Lake, Ind.: Eisenbrauns, 1995) 550–54.

15. The motif of Abraham's faithfulness in connection with the sacrifice becomes traditional. Cf. Sir 44:20 (which is older than Jubilees); 1 Macc 2:52; Jdt 8:24–27; Heb 11:17; Jas 2:21–23.

16. On this issue see Betsy Halpern-Amaru, *The Empowerment of Women in the Book of Jubilees* (JSJSup 60; Leiden: Brill, 1999). See also Christine Hayes, "Intermarriage and Impurity in Ancient Jewish Sources," *HTR* 92 (1999) 15–25, who writes independently of Halpern-Amaru.

17. Cf., e.g., chaps. 10; 11; 17:16; 48:2–19. On Jubilees' use of the traditions in 1 Enoch 6–16 see above, n. 11.

18. On this passage and its relationship to Ps 90 see James Kugel, "The Jubilees Apocalypse," *DSD* 1 (1994) 322–37.

19. Nickelsburg, *Resurrection*, 46–47; Jonathan A. Goldstein, "The Date of the Book of Jubilees," *PAAJR* 50 (1983) 63–86. Robert Doran ("The Non-Dating of Jubilees: Jub 34–38; 23:14–32 in Narrative Context," *JSJ* 20 [1989] 8–9) is skeptical of Goldstein's dating. Michael A. Knibb ("Jubilees and the Origins of the Qumran Community: An Inaugural Lecture in the Department of Biblical Studies delivered on Tuesday 17 January 1989" [London: King's College, 1989] 20 n. 52), citing the first edition of the present book, which in turn reflected my discussion in *Resurrection*, 46–47, favors a date before 167 B.C.E., but doubts that one can be so precise in identifying the events on which I base the dating.

20. On this passage see Nickelsburg, *Resurrection*, 31–33.

21. On the children chiding the parents see Doran, "Non-Dating," 9–10. For a parallel cf. 1 Enoch 90:6. On this section of 1 Enoch see below, pp. 83–86.

22. For a more detailed discussion of the dating see VanderKam, *Textual and Historical Studies*, 207–85 (for a summary see idem, *Book of Jubilees*, 17–21); Nickelsburg, "Bible Rewritten," 101–3.

23. Cf. 1 Macc 1:15; 2 Macc 4:12–14; Josephus, *Ant.* 12.241 (§5.1).

24. Knibb ("Jubilees," 14–15") opts for this high dating. Doran ("Non-Dating of Jubilees," 11) declines to date the book, but thinks the book's insistence on group solidarity is more appropriate before 167 than afterward.

25. See the detailed discussion by VanderKam, *Textual and Historical Studies*, 207–85.

26. See my review of VanderKam in *JAOS* 100 (1980) 84; Goldstein, "Date," 74–83.

27. Gruen (*Heritage and Hellenism*, 28–40), who is not concerned with Jubilees, documents considerable hellenization during the Hasmonean period. However, the issues he discusses are not of concern to the author of Jubilees. The lack of allusion both to the hellenizing practices of the Hasmonean rulers and to the figure of Antiochus IV argues against a date in the Hasmonean period. One could harmonize the two dates by positing two stages of composition, as does Davenport (*Eschatology*, 10–18); however, see Nickelsburg, "Bible Rewritten," 102 n. 62.

28. For two options as to its relationship to Genesis–Exodus, see Ben Zion Wacholder, "Jubilees as the Super Canon: Torah-Admonition versus Torah-Commandment," in Moshe Bernstein, Florentino García Martínez, and John Kampen, eds., *Legal Texts and Legal Issues: Proceedings of the Second Meeting of the International Organization for Qumran Studies Cambridge 1995, Published in Honour of Joseph M. Baumgarten* (STDJ 23; Leiden: Brill, 1977) 195–211; Himmelfarb, "Torah, Testimony and Heavenly Tablets." For Jubilees' concept of revelation in comparison with contemporary Jewish texts, see George W. E. Nickelsburg, "The Nature and Function

of Revelation in 1 Enoch, Jubilees, and Some Qumranic Documents," in Esther G. Chazon and Michael E. Stone, eds., *Pseudepigraphical Perspectives: The Apocrypha and Pseudepigrapha in Light of the Dead Sea Scrolls: Proceedings of the International Symposium of the Orion Center for the Study of the Dead Sea Scrolls and Associated Literature, 12–14 January 1997* (STDJ 31; Leiden: Brill, 1999) 91–119.

29. Knibb, "Jubilees."

30. For a variety of explanations of the issues see, e.g., Endres, *Biblical Interpretation*, 233–36; VanderKam, "The Origin and Purposes of Jubilees," in Albani, Frey, and Lange, eds., *Studies*, 19; idem, "Jubilees' Exegetical Creation of Levi the Priest," *RevQ* 17 (1996) 359–73; Halpern-Amaru, *Empowerment of Women*, 148–55; Hayes, "Intermarriage"; Liora Ravid, "Purity and Impurity in the Book of Jubilees," *JSP* 13 (2002) 61–86.

31. On these texts and versions, as well as on the Latin version, of which a sizable part has been preserved, see VanderKam, *Textual and Historical Studies*, 1–18.

32. See Wacholder, "Super Canon."

33. On the identification of this work see Charles, *Assumption*, xlv–1, who gathers information about two ancient texts, one called "Testament of Moses," the other, "Assumption of Moses." Johannes Tromp, the most recent commentator on the present work (*Assumption*, 115–16), agrees that the work's genre is that of a testament (a farewell discourse), but argues that its ancient name was the "Assumption of Moses" and that the "Testament of Moses" mentioned in ancient documents was, in reality, the Book of Jubilees (see above, pp. 69–74). The problem is complex; neither the incipit of Jubilees nor the reference to Jubilees in the Qumran Damascus Document (CD 16:3–4) calls it "Testament of Moses," nor is Jubilees generically a testament. The confusion may be due to later, inconsistent application of names to earlier works. Here I use the generic title that has come into common usage in the past two decades.

34. See the papers of John Collins, George Nickelsburg, and Jonathan Goldstein in Nickelsburg, ed., *Studies on the Testament of Moses*, 15–52. This conclusion is contested by Tromp (*Assumption*, 109–11, 120–23), who maintains the literary integrity of the work and dates its composition ca. 1–25 C.E. He states that "in the 1980's . . . Nickelsburg's point of view [that the text has been interpolated] has met with increasing doubt" but cites no literature to support the claim. Priest (*OTP* 1:920–21) states that my proposal "has been widely accepted," though he himself supports the later date. See also the spate of literature from the 1980s and 1990s cited by Hofmann, *Assumptio Mosis*, 25 n. 103, which does, in fact, accept my position. Hofmann (*Assumptio Mosis*, 297) finally opts for a date in the first century C.E., but in my view a comparison between the Testament of Moses and the literature of the second century B.C.E. to the first century C.E. can be levered in either direction.

35. Tromp (*Assumption*, 121) doubts that the historical pattern in this text has its roots in the latter part of Deuteronomy. He correctly notes that the pattern occurs elsewhere in the Hebrew Bible but misses the obvious: this text is framed by events uniquely narrated in Deut 31–34 (Moses' preparation for his death and his last words) and contains many verbal echoes of Deut 31–33. See Hofmann, *Assumptio Mosis*, esp. 81–189.

36. The one extant ms. of the Testament of Moses is missing its last page or pages, but a summary of its ending may well have been preserved elsewhere; see below, p. 419 n. 109. It is curious that the announcement of Moses' death in chap. 1 must wait nine chapters for Joshua's response (11:1). Perhaps an old narrative expansion of Deut 30–34 has been reworked with the material about the history of Israel; cf. Günther Reese, "Die Geschichte Israels in der Auffassung des frühen Judentums" (diss., Heidelberg, 1967) 89–93.

37. For an ingenious attempt to see behind chap. 6 an earlier description of the attacks of Antiochus and Apollonius, see Jonathan A. Goldstein, "The Testament of Moses: Its Content, Its Origin, and Its Attestation in Josephus," in Nickelsburg, ed., *Studies on the Testament of Moses*, 44–47.

38. It is uncertain who the "messenger" is that serves as the agent of divine vengeance (10:2). He is usually identified as the angel Michael (see Nickelsburg, *Resurrection*, 29), but Tromp ("Taxo the Messenger of the Lord," *JSJ* 21 [1990] 200–209) identifies him with the martyred and exalted Taxo.

39. See the discussion in Tromp, *Assumption*, 270–85. The passage could, in fact, parallel the juxtaposition of Satan and "the messenger" in 10:1–2. See Nickelsburg, *Resurrection*, 29–31.

40. Collins, *The Apocalyptic Vision of the Book of Daniel* (HSM 10; Missoula, Mont: Scholars Press, 1977) 198–201.

41. Cf. the discussion of 1 Enoch 12–16 above, p. 51; and the discussion of 1 Enoch 85–90 below, p. 86.

42. Charles, *Assumption*, xxxv–xlv; David H. Wallace, "The Semitic Origin of the Assumption of Moses," *TZ* 11 (1955) 321–28.

43. For an important discussion of myth and symbol in Dan 7–12 see Collins, *Apocalyptic Vision*, 95–152. On this issue and in other specific matters I am indebted to this work. For a detailed commentary on the individual visions see idem, *Daniel*.

44. Collins, *Daniel*, 280–94.

45. For a more elaborate use of this pattern of vision and interpretation see the discussion of 1 Enoch 20–36 above, pp. 51–52.

46. The Aramaic of 7:17 reads "four kings." By changing one easily confused letter we get "four kingdoms," which is the reading of the Greek and Latin translations. This is supported by the Aramaic and the versions of 7:23, which explain the fourth beast as a "fourth kingdom."

47. Collins, *Daniel*, 313–19.

48. For Israel as *the people* of the holy ones see ibid., 317, 322.

49. For an image of the god Pan as a goat running with his feet of the ground, see Philippe Borgeaud, *The Cult of Pan in Ancient Greece* (Chicago: Univ. of Chicago Press, 1988) pl. 4.

50. Collins, *Daniel*, 334–35. On the background of this idea in Isa 14 see Nickelsburg, *Resurrection*, 14–15, 69–70.

51. R. H. Charles, *A Critical and Exegetical Commentary on the Book of Daniel* (Oxford: Clarendon, 1929) 242–52.

52. Rodney A. Werline, *Penitential Prayer in Second Temple Judaism: The Development of a Religious Institution* (SBLEJL13; Atlanta: Scholars Press, 1998) 65–108. Cf. also the Qumran prayer called *The Words of the Heavenly Lights*, in García Martínez, *Scrolls*, 414–18; Vermes, *Scrolls*, 250–53; idem, *Complete Scrolls*, 364–67; Wise, Abegg, and Cook, *Scrolls*, §127.

53. Cf., e.g., 1 Enoch 12–16; 3 Bar. 1; Tob 3; Luke 3:21–22; 9:29; cf. above, p. 26, and the unquestionable instance of an interpolated prayer.

54. See Collins, *Daniel*, 347–48.

55. See Benjamin J. Hubbard, *The Matthean Redaction of a Primitive Apostolic Commissioning* (SBLDS 19; Missoula, Mont.: Scholars Press, 1974) 25–67. The revelations in the NT book of Revelation are framed by the same structure in chaps. 1 and 22:6–19.

56. For points of contact with Jewish and Near Eastern revelatory literary forms, see Collins, *Daniel*, 402.

57. This portrayal of two corresponding levels of reality here and in chaps. 7–8 has precursors in ancient Israelite literature; cf. Judg 5:19–20.

58. Collins, *Daniel*, 378–90.

59. Ibid., 402–3.

60. Richard Clifford, "History and Myth in Daniel 10–12," *BA* 220–21 (1975–76) 25.

61. Ibid.

62. On this and other matters relating to the interpretation of 12:1–3, see Nickelsburg, *Resurrection*, 11–27; Collins, *Daniel*, 390–94.

63. This verse may presume and allude to 1 Enoch 24–27; see Nickelsburg, *1 Enoch 1*, 315–16.

64. See below, pp. 207–8.

65. Nickelsburg, *Resurrection*, 11–15.

66. See the discussion in Nickelsburg, *1 Enoch 1*, 541–42.

67. For a much more detailed discussion of this vision see Tiller, *Commentary;* Nickelsburg, *1 Enoch 1*, 364–408.

68. Noah and Moses, first represented by animals, are transformed into human beings, which suggests in the imagery of the allegory that they have become angels (Tiller, *Commentary*, 259, 295–96). It is also possible that their transformation is depicted so that they can carry out tasks inappropriate to animals, namely, building the ark and tabernacle (note the use of the passive in 89:50 with respect to the temple); see Nickelsburg, *1 Enoch 1*, 375. Cf. also 86:3, where the stars become bulls in order to mate with heifers.

69. Cf. Dan 8:15 and 7:13, where one like a "son of man" is perhaps contrasted with the beasts.

70. For reference to three kinds of giants cf. Syncellus's text of 1 Enoch 7:2–3, which is supported by Jub. 7:22; see Nickelsburg, *1 Enoch 1*, 185.

71. On this tendency in 1 Enoch see Milik, *Books of Enoch*, 43; Nickelsburg, *1 Enoch 1*, 172.

72. 1 Enoch 20 mentions these three angels in addition to the other four. In chaps. 21–36 the seven escort the seer through the universe, and in 81:5 either the seven or the three (the texts differ) return him to earth.

73. Cf., e.g., Pss 74:1; 79:13; 95:7; Isa 53:6; Jer 50:6; Ezek 34; Zech 13:7.

74. On blindness cf. Isa 56:10; 59:9–10; on straying cf. Ps 119:176; Isa 53:6; Jer 50:6.

75. See esp. Ezek 34 and its juxtaposition of scattered sheep, wild beasts, and derelict shepherds.

76. See Nickelsburg, *1 Enoch 1*, 391–93.

77. R. H. Charles, *APOT* 2:255; Hengel, *Judaism,* 1:187–88; Nickelsburg, *1 Enoch 1*, 391.

78. Deut 32:8; Sir 17:17; Jub. 15:31; Dan 10:13, 20.

79. Isa 56:11; Ezek 34; Zech 13:7.

80. Isa 56:11; Ezek 34; Zech 13:7.

81. Jer 25:11–12; 29:10, as interpreted in Dan 9:2, 24–27; see Tiller, *Commentary*, 51–60; Nickelsburg, *1 Enoch 1*, 391–92.

82. See the detailed discussion by Tiller, *Commentary*, 63–78; Nickelsburg, *1 Enoch 1*, 397–98.

83. Milik, *Books of Enoch*, 44; Tiller, *Commentary*, 74–79.

84. Cf. also 1 Enoch 1 and T. Mos. 10:3–7.

85. The idea is also implied in Dan 12:2; Nickelsburg, *Resurrection*, 19–23.

86. See Tiller, *Commentary*, 380; Nickelsburg, *1 Enoch 1*, 405–6. The term "destroyed" (Aram. ʿ*ebad*?) is ambiguous, but in the vision it does refer to the activity of the disobedient shepherds.

87. Charles, *APOT* 2:260; see, however, Nickelsburg, *1 Enoch 1*, 406–7.

88. This author's notion of salvation is most closely paralleled in the apostle Paul's notion of the second Adam. See Tiller, *Commentary*, 19–20, 384; Nickelsburg, *1 Enoch 1*, 407.

89. For a (very sketchy) apocalypse with almost the same scope, cf. the Apocalypse of Weeks, 1 Enoch 93:1–10 + 91:11–17, on which see below, pp. 110–11, and in more detail, Nickelsburg, *1 Enoch 1*, 398–99.

90. See Tiller, *Commentary*, 61–79.

91. See ibid., which opts for composition in the Maccabean period. I have argued for an earlier date, before the appearance of the Hasmoneans, Nickelsburg, *1 Enoch 1*, 360–61, 396–98.

92. See above, n. 68. By analogy with 89:1, 9, 36, 38 the construction of the desolating sacrilege would require that the birds representing the Seleucids be transformed into men.

93. See Goldstein, "Testament of Moses," 48–50.

94. On the text's provenance see Tiller, *Commentary*, 101–26; Nickelsburg, *1 Enoch 1*, 361–63, 398–400.

95. Collins, *Apocalyptic Vision*, 194–210.

96. In Jubilees Moses is the recipient of angelic revelation. For each of the visions in Dan 7–12 there is an angelic mediator or interpreter. In 1 Enoch 85–90 Enoch has a dream vision that is not interpreted. The Testament of Moses indicates no source for the prophet's message.

97. See Collins, *Apocalyptic Vision*, 80, 87–88. Connected to this determinism is a sense of order implied in the periodizing of history, for example, in the Animal Vision.

98. For an entree into the problems of defining revelatory literature, see John J. Collins, "Apocalypse: Toward the Morphology of a Genre," *Semeia* 14 (1979) 1–20.

99. See above, n. 1.

4. The Hasmoneans and Their Opponents

1. Our major Jewish primary sources for this period are 2 Macc 8–15 (Judas); 1 Macc 5–16 (Judas, Jonathan, and Simon); Josephus, *J.W.* 1.54–119 (§§2.3—5.4); *Ant.* 12.327—13.432 (§§12.8.1—13.16.6) (Hyrcanus through Alexandra).

2. See Grabbe, *Judaism*, 1:304.

3. For the other works see below, pp. 277–83, as well as 3 Baruch and the Paraleipomena of Jeremiah. On the figure of Baruch, cf. Jer 32, 36, 43, and 45.

4. For this meaning of "to read in one's hearing" see H. Orlinsky, "The Septuagint as Holy Writ and the Philosophy of the Translators," *HUCA* 46 (1975) 94–96.

5. Moore (*Additions*, 291) suggests that 2:5—3:8 may originally have been three independent prayers; his divisions are unconvincing, however. "And now . . ." (2:11) would hardly begin a prayer, and 2:31–35 and 3:6–8 are logically related (see above) and represent similar clusters of motifs that are hardly coincidental.

6. See, e.g., Rodney A. Werline, *Penitential Prayer in Second Temple Judaism: The Development of a Religious Institution* (SBLEJL 13; Atlanta: Scholars Press, 1998) 92–103; and standard versions of the Apocrypha.

7. See Carey A. Moore, "Toward the Dating of the Book of Baruch," *CBQ* 36 (1974) 312–17; idem, *Additions*, 291–93. For a close comparative analysis of the two prayers see Werline, *Penitential Prayer*, 66–108.

8. See 1:15 and 2:1–2 and note the contrast between "we" in Jerusalem and "they" in dispersion in 2:3–5.

9. Noted by Jonathan Goldstein, "The Apocryphal Book of Baruch," *PAAJR* 46–47 (1979–80) 196 n. 48.

10. Cf. 1:12 and Jer 27:12.

11. Cf. Deut 30:1–5 but also 1 Kgs 8:47; cf. also Tob 13:7.

12. The passage may be redactional; the reference to the dead refers to 3:4 However, the direct address to Israel and the appellative "God" (rather than "Lord") are at home in the poem.

13. Cf. Ezek 37 for the exposition of this idea.

14. On the giants see above, pp. 47–79. The verbiage is drawn from Gen 6:4, but the reference to their making war and to their destruction reflects 1 Enoch 6–11, and their lack of knowledge ironically alludes to their fathers' having brought secrets to earth; see Walter Harrelson, "Wisdom Hidden and Revealed according to Baruch (Baruch 3:9–44)," in Eugene Ulrich, et al. eds., *Priests, Prophets and Scribes: Essays on the Formation and Heritage of Second Temple Judaism in Honour of Joseph Blenkensopp* (JSOTSup 149; Sheffield: Sheffield Academic Press, 1992) 164–65.

15. Cf. esp. 3:37—4:2 with Sir 24:8–11, 24.

16. Cf. 4:7–8 with Deut 32:17–18 and 4:25 with Deut 33:29 (LXX).

17. Cf. Deut 30:7, and for the image of the enemy personified as a woman with children, cf. Isa 47:1–9.

18. Cf. Isa 49:14–23; 54:1–13; 60:4–9.

19. Cf. Isa 52:1–2.

20. On the relationship of chap. 5 to Pss. Sol. 11 see Moore, *Additions*, 314–16.

21. This is the thesis of Mukenge, *L'unité littéraire*.

22. See Pfeiffer, *History*, 415–16.

23. On the relationship between Bar 1:15—3:8 and Dan 9 see above, n. 7. On chap. 5 and Pss. Sol. 11 see Moore, *Additions*, 314–16; Steck, *Das apokryphe Baruchbuch*, 240–42; Mukenge, *L'unité littéraire*, 330–56. According to all three, either Pss. Sol. 11 is dependent on Bar 5, or both are dependent on a common source.

24. Tov, *Septuagint Translation*, 111–33, 165. On the Hebrew original of Bar 3:3—5:9 see Burke, *Poetry of Baruch*.

25. This dating, first argued by Goldstein ("Apocryphal Book of Baruch"), has found support from Steck (*Baruchbuch*, 294–303) and Mukenge (*L'unité littéraire*, 412–26).

26. If one plays down the importance of the fictional setting and emphasizes the discrepancies between the narrative and the circumstances of 164, then a date higher in the second century, or perhaps earlier, may seem more plausible. Moore (*Additions*, 260) suggests the early part of the second century B.C.E.; however, his arguments are at least partly met by Goldstein, "Apocryphal Book of Baruch."

27. See also Philip S. Esler, "'By the Hand of a Woman': Culture, Story and Theology in the Book of Judith," in John J. Pilch, ed., *Social Scientific Models for Interpreting the Bible: Essays by the Context Group in Honor of Bruce J. Malina* (BIS 53; Leiden: Brill, 2001) 99–100. He sees in Judith "a profound message concerning how the God of the ancient Israelites dealt with his people," viz., that this God "exalts the lowly and crushes the arrogant who oppress them" (ibid., 99). Wills (*Jewish Novel*, 156) thinks it "simplistic to try to reduce any literary work to one 'main' theme," but notes that "the motive force behind the *Book of Judith* is the reversal of weak and strong, male and female."

28. On this strange character see Adolfo D. Roitman, "The Mystery of Arphaxad (Jdt 1); A New Proposal," *Hen* 16 (1995) 301–10.

29. Cf., e.g., Jdt 6:2 and Isa 45:5. This tension governs the outline of the book as it is laid out by Zenger, *Historische und legendarische Erzhälungen*, 449–85. In this he is followed by Otzen, *Tobit and Judith*, 71–73, 129–30.

30. Esler ("By the Hand of a Woman," 92–96) counts thirteen lies (10:12–13; 11:7; 11:11–19; 13:3) in addition to ambiguous statements. On irony in Judith see Alonso-Schöckel, "Narrative Structures," 8–11; Moore, *Judith*, 78–85; Esler, "By the Hand of a Woman," 96–98.

31. The wordplay is that of Paul Winter ("Judith, Book of," 1024) and is worthy of our author's irony.

32. Craven, *Artistry and Faith*; Wills, *Jewish Novel*, 132–57.

33. See Moore, *Judith*, 56.

34. For this scheme, much too complex and intricate to be explicated here, see Craven, *Artistry and Faith*, 47–112, and the summary by Moore, *Judith*, 57–59.

35. Adolfo D. Roitman, "Achior in the Book of Judith: His Role and Significance," in VanderKam, ed., *No One*, 31–45.

36. See, in detail, the perceptive analysis of Gruen, *Diaspora*, 162–70.

37. See F. Zimmermann, "Aids for the Recovery of the Hebrew Original of Judith," *JBL* 57 (1938) 67–74; Grintz, *Sefer Yehudith*, 56–63; Moore, *Judith*, 67. On the Greek and Latin versions of Judith see Otzen, *Tobit and Judith*, 140–41. On the Syriac version see J. P. M. van der Ploeg, *The Book of Judith (Daughter of Merari): Syriac Text with Translation and Footnotes* (Kottayam, Kerala: St. Ephrem Ecumenical Research Institute, 1991); idem, "Some Remarks on a Newly Found Syriac Text of the Book of Judith," in F. García Martínez, A. Hilhorst, and C. J. Labuschagne, eds., *The Scriptures and the Scrolls: Studies in Honour of A. S. van der Woude on the Occasion of his 65th Birthday* (VTSup 49; Leiden: Brill, 1992) 124–34.

38. For two summaries see Otzen, *Tobit and Judith*, 114–18; Craven, "The Book of Judith in the Context of Twentieth-Century Studies of the Apocryphal/Deuterocanonical Books," *CurBS* 1 (2003) 202–9. For some notable contributions to the discussion see Amy-Jill Levine, "Sacrifice and Salvation: Otherness and Domestication in the Book of Judith," in VanderKam, ed., *No One*, 17–30; Pamela J. Milne, "What Shall We Do with Judith? A Feminist Reassessment of A Biblical 'Heroine,'" *Semeia* 63 (1993) 37–58; Wills, *Jewish Novel*, 142–52; Levine, "Sacrifice and Salvation," repr. in Athalya Brenner, ed., *A Feminist Companion to Esther, Judith and Susanna* (Feminist Companion to the Bible 7; Sheffield: Sheffield Academic Press, 1995) 208–23; Jan Willem van Henten, "Judith as Alternative Leader: A Rereading of Judith 7–13," in ibid., 224–52; Mieke Bal, "Head-Hunting: 'Judith' on the Cutting Edge of Knowledge," in ibid., 253–85; Alexander A. Di Lella, "Women in the Wisdom of Ben Sira and the Book of Judith: A Study in Contrasts and Reversals," in J. A. Emerton, ed., *Congress Volume: Paris, 1992* (VTSup 61; Leiden: Brill, 1995) 39–52; Stocker, *Judith, Sexual Warrior*.

39. Van Henten, "Judith as Alternative Leader," 247–52. See also Di Lella ("Women," 52), who argues that the "author [of Judith] . . . intended to challenge . . . many of Ben Sira's sexist biases against women."

40. On the use of deceit in the culture in which Judith was written see Esler, "By the Hand of a Woman," 91–98.

41. From the concluding sentence of Milne's crackling criticism ("What Shall We Do," 55) of those who would make Judith a feminist statement in any meaningful sense.

42. Amy-Jill Levine, "Sacrifice and Salvation: Otherness and Domestication in the Book of Judith," in VanderKam, ed., *No One*, 17–30. See, however, Wills (*Jewish Novel*, 144–45), who notes that this element is part of a typical paradigm according to which the heroes are never able to integrate into the society that they have rescued from danger.

43. Pfeiffer, *History*, 292–95; Craven, *Artistry and Faith*, 65–74; Wills, *Jewish Novel*, 134–35; Otzen, *Tobit and Judith*, 81–90. Gruen (*Diaspora*, 162–64) attributes the inaccuracies to the author's humor. For Craven (*Artistry and Faith*), they are explained by the author's art; see in brief Moore, *Judith*, 58 n. 33.

44. A.-M. Dubarle, *Judith*, 1:137–56; Otzen, *Tobit and Judith*, 74–79.

45. See Sidnie Ann White, "In the Steps of Jael and Deborah: Judith as Heroine," in VanderKam, ed., *No One*, 5–16; Wills, *Jewish Novel*, 146–48.

46. Esler, "By the Hand of a Woman," 78–91.

47. Levine ("Sacrifice and Salvation," 18) notes in addition to the explicit reference to Genesis "the resonance between the name of the town and the Hebrew for 'virgin'" (*bĕtûlāh*).

48. The term "parabolic" is drawn from Haag (*Studien zum Buch Judith*), who sees the book as a freely composed parabolic presentation of the forces inherent in and behind the empirical history of Israel. See also Otzen, *Tobit and Judith*, 91–92; Judith H. Newman, "The Past as Blueprint for Present: Salvation by Typology in Judith 9," in idem, *Praying by the Book: The Scripturalization of Prayer in Second Temple Judaism* (SBLEJL 14; Atlanta: Scholars Press, 1999) 117–54.

49. So Otzen (*Tobit and Judith*, 92–93), who warns against the use of the term "apocalypticism" in the context. But see below, p. 203, on the first addition to the book of Esther.

50. See 8:4–6; 9:1; 10:5; 11:13; 12:2, 5–9; 13:4–7; 16:18, 24. For a summary see Otzen, *Tobit and Judith*, 104–5. For more particulars see Grintz, *Sefer Yeudith*, 47–51.

51. See Moore, *Judith*, 235–36.

52. For my somewhat more detailed discussion of the date of Judith, see Nickelsburg, "Stories," 50–51.

53. Dubarle, *Judith*, 1:131–32.

54. Pfeiffer, *History*, 294.

55. Grintz, *Sefer Yehudith*, 15–55.

56. Pfeiffer, *History*, 294–95; Enslin and Zeitlin, *Judith*, 26–31.

57. In Dan 3 the final redactor of Daniel certainly intends Nebuchadnezzar to be a figure for Antiochus.

58. See Enslin and Zeitlin, *Judith*, 28–30.

59. See H. L. Ginsberg, "The Oldest Interpretation of the Suffering Servant," *VT* 3 (1953) 400–401.

60. On the location of a Simeonite settlement in this area, see Grintz, *Sefer Yehudith*, 132–35.

61. Moore, *Judith*, 67–70. Otzen (*Tobit and Judith*, 132–34) also settled for a Hasmonean date.

62. Cf. also 2 Macc 7 (below, p. 109), where the mother of the seven brothers speaks in the idiom of Second Isaiah's Zion figure.

63. Like Tobit, Judith may also draw on non-Israelite material. In a paper presented in the 2003 Annual Meeting of the Society of Biblical Literature, Deborah Gera argued for parallels in Herodotus. Mark S. Caponigro ("Judith, Holding the Tale of Herodotus," in VanderKam, ed., *No One*, 47–69) also suggests Herodotus as a model for Judith, but cites none of Gera's parallels.

64. See the notes by the editor and B. Bayer, "Judith, Book of," in *EncJud* 10:460–61. For a comprehensive study from a feminist point of view, see Stocker, *Judith*. On the visual arts see Nira Stone, "Judith and Holofernes: Some Observations on the Development of the Scene in Art," in VanderKam, ed., *No One*, 73–93.

65. Williams, *Structure of 1 Maccabees*, 72–107; for this summary see pp. 131–37. For a similar analysis of Judith, see above, n. 34.

66. On this opposition see Tcherikover, *Hellenistic Civilization*, 188–92; Goldstein, *1 Maccabees*, 212–13.

67. Verses 43, 52–53 allude to this opposition.

68. For other examples of religious zeal that wins priestly credentials, cf. Exod 32:25–29 and Jub. 30:17–19.

69. For the propriety of these examples see Goldstein, *1 Maccabees*, 6–7, 240–41. For similar catalogs see above, chapter 2, n. 67.

70. Nickelsburg, *Resurrection*, 97–102. For different conclusions about the relationships among these stories, see Norbert J. Hofmann, *Die Assumptio Mosis: Studien zur Rezepzion massgültige Überlieferung* (JSJSup 67; Leiden: Brill, 2000) 245–57.

71. The form of this epilogue is typically biblical; cf., e.g., 1 Kgs 22:39; and below, on 1 Macc 16:23–24. However, the negative "have not been recorded" is best paralleled in John 20:30; 21:25.

72. Note the preparations in 3:47–49; the dismissal of those not fit (3:56); and the practice of slaughtering all males, taking spoils, and total annihilation of the city in 5:28, 35, 51; cf. Lawrence E. Toombs, "War, Ideas of," *IDB* 4:797–98.

73. Goldstein, *1 Maccabees*, 395.

74. On the date of composition see ibid., 63. In his literary analysis of the book, Williams (*Structure*, 108–27) suggests that 14:16—16:24 *may have been* written as an appendix to the book, which would have been completed during Simon's reign. This is by no means certain.

75. Ibid., 14–16.

76. Only chaps. 14–15, set in the reign of Demetrius I, seem to move beyond the scope of 2:19–22, which mentions Antiochus IV and Antiochus V.

77. See Goldstein, *1 Maccabees*, 34, and the references listed in ibid., n. 70.

78. For the same idea cf. above, pp. 32–33 (Tobit), and below, pp. 107 (2 Maccabees), 238, 244–46 (Psalms of Solomon), and 278 (2 Baruch).

79. Nickelsburg, *Resurrection*, 97–102. See above, n. 70.

80. Ibid., 102–9.

81. For other instances of the author's view of strictly appropriate retribution, cf. 4:26, 38, 42; 5:10.

82. For another resurrection passage cf. 12:39–45.

83. Daniel R. Schwartz, "The Other in 1 and 2 Maccabees," in Graham N. Stanton and Guy G. Stroumsa, eds., *Tolerance and Intolerance in Early Judaism and Christianity* (Cambridge: Cambridge Univ. Press, 1998) 30–37.

84. Doran, *Temple Propaganda*, 109.

85. For a summary of the problem see Gruen, *Diaspora*, 75–76. For some possibilities see Goldstein, *2 Maccabees*, 34; Doran, *Temple Propaganda*, 77–109; Wills, *Jewish Novel*, 193–201.

86. Nickelsburg, *Resurrection*, 177–80.

87. See Gerbern S. Oegema, "Portrayals of Women in 1 and 2 Maccabees," in Ingrid Rosa Kitzberger, ed., *Transformative Encounters: Jesus and Women Re-viewed* (BIS 43; Leiden: Brill, 2000) 244–64.

88. On the parallel between Judas and Nehemiah in 2 Macc 1:10—2:18, see Theodore A. Bergren, "Nehemiah in 2 Maccabees 1:10—2:18," *JSJ* 28 (1997) 270.

89. For other instances of evident anti-Hasmonean sentiment see Goldstein, *1 Maccabees*, 78–80.

90. This is suggested by Goldstein (ibid., 85–89) and by myself in the previous version of this book and in greater detail in "1 and 2 Maccabees—Same Story, Different Meaning," *CTM* 42 (1971) 515–26, repr. in *GNP* 2:659–74.

91. Doran, *Temple Propaganda*, 114.

92. Goldstein, *1 Maccabees*, 84–85.

93. Ibid., 34–36. On the second letter see Bergren, "Nehemiah," 249–70.

94. This section is a summary of my detailed commentary on these chapters, Nickelsburg, *1 Enoch 1*, 430–535.

95. For the word *epistolē* see 100:6 and the editor's superscript in the Chester Beatty papyrus. On this word and the genre of these chapters, see Milik, *Books of Enoch*, 47, 51–52; Nickelsburg, *1 Enoch 1*, 420, 430–31.

96. One section of the Apocalypse (91:11–17) has been misplaced in the Ethiopic version. The original order, attested by the Aramaic, is 91:1–10, 18–19; 92; 93:1–10; 91:11–17; 93:11–14; 94; see Milik, *Books of Enoch*, 260–70; Nickelsburg, *1 Enoch 1*, 414–15.

97. The Aramaic text in question is 4QEn^g. References can be found in Milik, *Books of Enoch*, 260–70, ad loc.

98. Nickelsburg, *1 Enoch 1*, 420, 461, 471, 484, 497, 506, 516–17.

99. Ibid., 416–18.

100. Ibid., 486–88.

101. See George W. E. Nickelsburg, "Riches, the Rich, and God's Judgment in 1 Enoch 92–105 and the Gospel according to Luke," *NTS* 25 (1979) 324–44; idem, "Revisiting the Rich and the Poor in 1 Enoch 92–105 and the Gospel according to Luke," *SBLSP* 37 (1998) 2:579–605, repr. with a response by John S. Kloppenborg in *GNP* 2:527–88.

102. See Nickelsburg, *1 Enoch 1*, 419–20.

103. Nickelsburg, *Resurrection*, 119.

104. Cf. also 1QS 8:4–7.

105. See, e.g., Charles, *Enoch*, 222; Tcherikover, *Hellenistic Civilization*, 258–59, 492; Nickelsburg, *Resurrection*, 113.

106. Tcherikover, *Hellenistic Civilization*, 258–59, 492.

107. See above, pp. 73–74.

108. For some other parallels between the redactional framework and the Epistle, cf. 81:1||103:2; 81:4||102:4–5; 103:3; 104:5, 7; 82:4||99:10; 91:3–4, 18–19||94:1–5. For a detailed discussion of the problem see Nickelsburg, *1 Enoch 1*, 334–38.

109. For details see ibid., 109–11.

110. For details see ibid., 335–37.

111. For detailed arguments supporting and adding nuances to this hypothesis, see ibid., 25–26, 334–38. For critiques of this argument by Patrick A. Tiller, James C. VanderKam, and John J. Collins and my response to them, see *GNP*, 365–86, 414–17.

112. VanderKam, "The Birth of Noah," in Zdzislaw J. Kapera, ed., *Intertestamental Essays in Honour of Jósef Tadeusz Milik* (Kraków: Enigma, 1992) 213–31; Nickelsburg, *1 Enoch 1*, 540, 543–44.

5. The People at Qumran and Their Predecessors

1. For an early published account, see G. Lankester Harding in DJD 1:5–6. For a fascinating account of the events relating to the discovery and purchase of the scrolls by one of the major players, see John C. Trever, *The Dead Sea Scrolls: A Personal Account* (rev. ed.; Upland, Calif.: Upland Commercial Printers, 1988). For an excellent overview see James C. VanderKam, *The Dead Sea Scrolls Today* (Grand Rapids: Eerdmans, 1994) 1–16.

2. In DJD 39:29–89 the unnumbered mss. and the numbered mss. including those with superscript letters add up to about 930. So also Emanuel Tov in private correspondence, February 2005. Cf. VanderKam, *Scrolls*, 29.

3. On the controversies that swirled around scrolls and the delays in their publication, see VanderKam, *Scrolls*, 187–200.

4. Volumes 8 and 9 were submitted to Oxford Univ. Press in 1987 and 1988, private communication from Eugene Ulrich, May 2004.

5. The series also includes several volumes on the manuscript finds and other discoveries elsewhere in the Judean Desert and in the Wadi ed-Daliyeh in the central hill country fifteen miles north of Jericho. For the history of the series see Emanuel Tov in DJD 39:1–25.

6. For this tally see Schiffman, *Reclaiming the Dead Sea Scrolls*, 34.

7. For a summary count of the mss. of biblical books see VanderKam, *Scrolls*, 30–32. For a detailed accounting of all the scroll material, see the various lists in DJD 39:27–322.

8. For a summary see VanderKam, *Scrolls*, 16–20. For a detailed discussion see Brian Webster in DJD 39:351–446. For a more skeptical view see Joseph Atwill and Steve Braumheim (with the participation of Robert Eisenman), "Redating the Radiocarbon Dating of the Dead Sea Scrolls," *DSD* 11 (2004) 143–57.

9. See Hartmut Stegemann, "How to Connect Dead Sea Scroll Fragments," in Shanks, ed., *Understanding the Dead Sea Scrolls*, 245–55.

10. On the technologies employed to read and interpret the scrolls, see the summary by Magen Broshi, "The Dead Sea Scrolls, the Sciences and New Technologies," *DSD* 11 (2004) 133–42.

11. On the archeology of Qumran see the excellent volume by Magness, *Archaeology of Qumran*. On the chronology and the two phases of occupation between 100 B.C.E. and 68 C.E., see ibid., 47–69. For the paleographical dating of the scrolls see DJD 39:378–446. The dating of the individual texts discussed below is indicated in the notes.

12. For a summary discussion see Charlotte Hempel, "Qumran Community," *EDSS* 2:746–51.

13. See the postscript by Yaʿakov Sussmann in DJD 10:220; and the discussion by Joseph A. Fitzmyer, "The Qumran Community: Essene or Sadducean?" *HeyJ* 36 (1995) 467–76.

14. On the proliferation of Jewish sects and groups in the Greco-Roman period, see the discussion and bibliography in Nickelsburg, *Ancient Judaism*, 160–81, 233–43. On the use of the term "Essene," see Albert Baumgarten, "Who Cares and What Does It Matter? Qumran and the Essenes," *DSD* 11 (2004) 174–90. For recent discussions and hypotheses on Qumran origins, see F. García Martínez and J. Trebolle Barrera, *The People of the Dead Sea Scrolls* (Leiden: Brill, 1995); Philip R. Davies, *Sects and Scrolls: Essays on Qumran and Related Topics* (South Florida Studies in the History of Judaism 134; Atlanta: Scholars Press, 1996); Gabriele Boccaccini, *Beyond the Essene Hypothesis: The Parting of the Ways between Qumran and Enochic Judaism* (Grand

Rapids: Eerdmans, 1998). For a discussion of Boccaccini see Wido van Peursen, "Qumran Origins: Some Remarks on the Enochic/Essene Hypothesis," *RevQ* 20, no. 78 (2001) 243–53. See also Charlotte Hempel, "The Community and Its Rivals according to the Community Rule from Caves 1 and 4," *RevQ* 21 (2003) 47–81.

15. Nickelsburg, *Ancient Judaism*, passim.

16. Ibid., passim.

17. On the discoveries in the Cairo Genizah in the late nineteenth century, see Stefan C. Reif, "Cairo Genizah," *EDSS* 1:105–8. The Cairo Damascus Documents were acquired by Solomon Schechter in 1896 (ibid., 105) and published by him in 1910 as *Documents of Jewish Sectaries*. The volume was reprinted with a prolegomenon by Joseph A. Fitzmyer (New York: KTAV, 1970). For an early translation and commentary see R. H. Charles, "The Zadokite Fragments," *APOT* 2:785–834.

18. For a history of the pre-Qumran scholarship, see Davies, *Damascus Covenant*, 5–14.

19. Credit for this identification belongs to Eleazar Sukenik of the Hebrew University in Jerusalem, who purchased several of the early scrolls. However, an Essene identification of the first scrolls (Isaiah Scroll, the Habakkuk Commentary, and the Rule of the Community, known then as the "Manual of Discipline") was put forth in the first press release on the discovery in 1948. See the interesting comment by Trever, *Dead Sea Scrolls*, 25; see also 76.

20. For a tabulation of the fragments see Joseph M. Baumgarten, DJD 18:3–4. For summary descriptions of the mss. see Hempel, *Damascus Texts*, 21–24. The fragments are published in full by Baumgarten, DJD 18.

21. On the ambiguity of this division, however, see below, p. 125.

22. For the comparative tabulation of the Cairo mss. and the Qumran fragments, see Baumgarten, DJD 18:3–4.

23. The aforementioned tabulation suggests that in 4Q266 the Admonition and the Laws contained roughly nine and eighteen columns, respectively. On the reconstruction of the scrolls see Hartmut Stegemann, "Toward Physical Reconstructions of the Qumran Damascus Document Scrolls," in Baumgarten, Chazon, and Pinnick, eds., *Damascus Document*, 177–200.

24. Joseph M. Baumgarten, "The Damascus Document," *EDSS* 1:167; cf. Hempel, *Damascus Texts*, 71–73, who notes the scholarly neglect of the Laws in pre- and early post-Qumran studies of the document.

25. Baumgarten, DJD 18:11–12; Hempel, *Laws of the Damascus Document*, 30–34.

26. On the community or communities behind the document see Hempel, "Community Origins in the Damascus Document in the Light of Recent Scholarship," in Donald W. Parry and Eugene Ulrich, eds., *The Provo International Conference on the Dead Sea Scrolls: Technological Innovations, New Texts, and Reformulated Ideas* (STDJ 30; Leiden: Brill, 1999) 316–29, esp. 328–29; Hempel, *Damascus Texts*, 54–65; see also her conclusion, 87–88. On the problems of extracting history from the Damascus Document see Grossman, *Reading for History*.

27. Hempel, *Laws of the Damascus Document*, 187–92; idem, *Damascus Texts*, 44–54.

28. Stegemann, "Reconstructions," 200 n. 80. For paleographic details see Baumgarten, DJD 18:26–30, 96, 116–18, 124, 138–40, 170–72, 185–87, 193–94.

29. For the many attempts to outline the Admonition and reconstruct the history of its literary growth, see Hempel, *Damascus Texts*, 44–49. My segmentation of the text follows mainly that of Hempel, ibid., 26–33.

30. George W. E. Nickelsburg, "*1 Enoch* and Qumran Origins: The State of the Question

and Some Prospects for Answers," in Kent H. Richards, ed., *SBLSP* 25 (1986) 341–60. Cf. Hempel, "Community Origins," 328–29.

31. Davies, *Damascus Covenant*, 161–62; Hempel, *Damascus Texts*, 31–32.

32. On the legislation for the organization of the camps see Hempel, *Laws of the Damascus Document*, 105–40. On the question of women at Qumran see Magness, *Archaeology*, 163–87; Eileen Schuller, "Women in the Dead Sea Scrolls," in Flint and VanderKam, eds., *Dead Sea Scrolls after Fifty Years*, 2:117–44; and the articles by Rob Kugler and Esther Chazon, Moshe J. Bernstein, Maxine Grossman, and Benjamin G. Wright III in *DSD* 11 (2004) 167–73, 191–261.

33. Hempel, *Damascus Texts*, 77–79.

34. See Baumgarten, DJD 18:4–5.

35. In his edition Baumgarten (DJD 18:3) places the fragment in the Admonition. In his later article ("Damascus Document," 167) he places it in the Laws. For the problem of the placement see Baumgarten, DJD 18:143; Stegemann, "Reconstructions," 189; Charlotte Hempel, "The Laws of the Damascus Document and 4QMMT," in Baumgarten, Chazon, and Pinnick, eds., *Damascus Document*, 80–81.

36. Does this subscript refer to the source of the book's laws, or does it preserve the title of the book, which would also have stood at its no longer preserved incipit? See Baumgarten, DJD 18:78 and also 32, who cites Hartmut Stegemann, *The Library of Qumran*, 116–17.

37. See, e.g., Baumgarten, DJD 18:11–22, and his articles cited on p. 6; Lawrence H. Schiffman, *The Halakhah at Qumran* (SJLA 16; Leiden: Brill, 1975), citations in the index, pp. 152–53; Hempel, *Laws of the Damascus Document*.

38. For other halakic texts in the Qumran corpus see Elisha Qimron and John Strugnell, DJD 10 (on which see below, pp. 147–49); Joseph Baumgarten, et al., eds., DJD 35. For translations of some of these texts see García Martínez, *Scrolls*, 77–92; Vermes, *Complete Scrolls*, 220–34; Wise, Abegg, and Cook, *Scrolls*, §§54–61.

39. Hempel, *Laws of the Damascus Document*; and in summary, idem, *Damascus Texts*, 49–53.

40. For an argument in favor of the Sadducean character of Qumran halakah, see Lawrence H. Schiffman, "The Sadducean Origins of the Dead Sea Scroll Sect," in Shanks, ed., *Understanding the Dead Sea Scrolls*, 35–49; Schiffman, *Reclaiming the Dead Sea Scrolls*, 83–112, 154–57. For a response to Schiffman's article see James C. VanderKam, "The People of the Dead Sea Scrolls: Essenes or Sadducees," in Shanks, ed., *Understanding the Dead Sea Scrolls*, 50–62. See also the detailed discussion of the halakah in 4QMMT by Yaʿakov Sussmann in DJD 10:179–200 and its carefully phrased conclusion on p. 200. On references to the Sadducees in the Mishnah see Fitzmyer, "Qumran Community," 467–76, who sees these as references to Zadokite, i.e., Qumranic, halakah.

41. On the Qumran laws in relation to Pharisaic and rabbinic law see Baumgarten, DJD 18:18–22; Lawrence H. Schiffman, "The Pharisees and Their Legal Traditions according to the Dead Sea Scrolls," *DSD* 8 (2001) 262–77.

42. Schiffman, "Pharisees and Their Legal Traditions," 265–70; Baumgarten, DJD 18:21; Albert I. Baumgarten, "Seekers after Smooth Things," *EDSS* 2:856–59.

43. Baumgarten, DJD 18:15–16.

44. On these two attitudes toward the temple see Hempel, *Laws of the Damascus Document*, 31. On this subject as it relates also to the Essenes see Joseph M. Baumgarten, *Studies in Qumran Law* (SJLA 24; Leiden: Brill, 1977) 39–97.

45. See Nickelsburg, *Ancient Judaism*, 56.

46. On the complexities of the text and the histories that it preserves, see, e.g., Hempel, *Laws*

of the Damascus Document; idem, *Damascus Texts,* 54–70; idem, "The Earthly Essene Nucleus of 1QSa," *DSD* 3 (1996) 252–69, which relates the early history of the Damascus community to an early stratum in 1QSa (on which see below, pp. 150–51). See also Sarianna Metso, "The Relationship between the Damascus Document and the Community Rule," in Baumgarten, Chazon, and Pinnick, eds., *Damascus Document,* 85–93.

47. See Baumgarten, DJD 18:9–10; Hempel, *Damascus Texts,* 58–60.

48. For an introduction see Lim, *Pesharim.* For a more detailed study, with texts and translations, see Horgan, *Pesharim.*

49. On the problem of extracting history from the *pesharim* see Lim, *Pesharim,* 67–69.

50. For a list of the mss. see ibid., 1–2.

51. For the paleographic data see ibid., 21–22.

52. On the Kittim see ibid., 65–67.

53. For the date of the ms. see ibid., 21; Horgan, *Pesharim,* 11.

54. The term has its roots in Third Isaiah (see above, p. 12), where it denotes righteous as opposed to unrighteous Israel. It is a favorite term in the Scrolls, and we meet it elsewhere, notably in 1 Enoch; see above, pp. 47, 110, etc.

55. Some passages refer only to "the Priest who (does something wrong)." The qualifying relative clause is an explication of the concept "wicked," which term is then usually not used.

56. See Lim, *Pesharim,* 67–72.

57. Adam S. van der Woude, "Wicked Priest or Wicked Priests? Reflections on the Identification of the Wicked Priest in the Habakkuk Commentary," *JJS* 33 (1982) (= Geza Vermes and Jacob Neusner, eds., *Essays in Honour of Yigael Yadin*) 349–59.

58. Lim, *Pesharim,* 72–74.

59. See Gert Jeremias, *Der Lehrer der Gerechtigkeit* (SUNT 2; Göttingen: Vandenhoeck & Ruprecht, 1963) 36–126. Although 1QpHab 10:6–13 stands next to the references to the Wicked Priest's building projects, the juxtaposition of literal and metaphorical uses of building language occur elsewhere in the literature; cf. 1 Enoch 99:12–14.

60. See Grabbe, *Judaism,* 1:304.

61. The Facile Interpreters are not mentioned by name in the commentary on 3:4, but a comparison with the other passages indicates that they are meant.

62. On the Epistle of Enoch see above, pp. 111.

63. See Yigael Yadin, "Pesher Nahum Reconsidered," *IEJ* 21 (1971) 1 n. 2.

64. See Lim, *Pesharim,* 31–33.

65. Ibid., 27–29. For translations see García Martínez, *Scrolls,* 185–91; Vermes, *Scrolls,* 320–23; idem, *Complete Scrolls,* 466–69; Wise, Abegg, and Cook, *Scrolls,* §20; for texts and translations see García Martínez and Tigchelaar, *Scrolls,* 312–29.

66. Cf. CD 1:18, which quotes this section of Isaiah, substituting the word *dārash* in the quotation of 30:10.

67. For these texts and the problems of defining them see Lim, *Pesharim,* 44–53.

68. For a discussion of this text with bibliography see George J. Brooke, "Florilegium," *EDSS* 1:297–98.

69. For a discussion of this text with bibliography see Annette Steudel, "Melchizedek," *EDSS* 1:535–37.

70. For a discussion of this text see Annette Steudel, "Testimonia," *EDSS* 2:936–38.

71. See Emanuel Tov, "Joshua, Book of," *EDSS* 1:431–34.

72. Émile Puech, "Hodayot," *EDSS* 2:365.

73. For 1QH^b see Jozef T. Milik, DJD 1:136–38. For the 4QH fragments (4Q427–31) see Eileen Schuller, DJD 29:69–232. For the parallels between these fragments and 1QH^a, see Schuller, DJD 29:72–73.

74. See Puech, "Hodayot," 365, 368.

75. Ibid., 368.

76. Ibid., 366. On the dating of 4QH^b see Schuller, DJD 29:129–30.

77. Advances in the methods used to reconstruct scrolls on the basis of destruction patterns resulted in the reordering of some of the columns from the editio princeps. Texts are cited according to the new numbers (see e.g., García Martínez and Tigchelaar, *Scrolls*, 146–203), with the old numbering given in parentheses.

78. On these hymns and their authorship see Jeremias, *Lehrer der Gerechtigkeit*, 168–267. For the Teacher's authorship of hymns in both groups see also briefly Puech, "Hodayot," 366–67.

79. On these hymns see Kuhn, *Enderwartung*. For the broader context of the kind of realized eschatology spelled out here, see Nickelsburg, *Resurrection*, 144–69.

80. For an opinion different from my own, cited in the previous note, see Émile Puech, *La croyance des Esséniens en la vie future: Immortalité, résurrection, vie éternelle?* (EBib n.s. 21–22; Paris: Gabalda, 1993) 335–419.

81. See Kuhn, *Enderwartung*, 29–33.

82. For an introduction to the Rule see Metso, *Serek Texts*. In my revision of this section I was greatly helped by the draft manuscript of this book, which Prof. Metso kindly sent me.

83. On the dating of 1QS see Cross, "Jewish Scripts," 158. For the dating of the Cave 4 fragments see Philip S. Alexander and Geza Vermes, DJD 26:7–9, 29–30, 45, 68–69, 89–90, 133–34, 157, 172, 190, 197–98, 202.

84. On these hypotheses see Metso, *Textual Development*, 6–11.

85. For the full publication of the Cave 4 fragments see Alexander and Vermes, DJD 26. For tabulations of the parallels between 1QS and the Cave 4 fragments, see ibid., 1–3. For a short account see Michael A. Knibb, "Rule of the Community," *EDSS* 2:794–95; Metso, *Serek Texts*. For more detail see idem, *Textual Development*, 13–68.

86. For a detailed discussion of the topic of wealth and possessions in the Rule of the Community see Catherine M. Murphy, *Wealth in the Dead Sea Scrolls and in the Qumran Community* (STDJ 40; Leiden: Brill, 2002) 103–62.

87. On the Qumran community and its opponents see Hempel, "Community and Its Rivals."

88. Klaus Baltzer, *The Covenant Formulary* (trans. John Bowden; Philadelphia: Fortress Press, 1971) 167–69.

89. For a similar expansion of the benediction in oracular form cf. 1 Enoch 1:8, on which see Lars Hartman, *Asking for a Meaning: A Study of 1 Enoch 1–5* (ConBNT 12; Lund: Gleerup, 1979) 5, 32–38, 44–48, 132–36; and in summary, Nickelsburg, *1 Enoch 1*, 147.

90. On the curses and 1 Enoch see Rodney A. Werline, "The Curses of the Covenant Renewal Ceremony in 1QS 1.16—2.19 and the Prayers of the Condemned," in Randal A. Argall, Beverly A. Bow, and Rodney A. Werline, eds., *For a Later Generation: The Transformation of Tradition in Israel, Early Judaism, and Early Christianity*, FS G. W. E. Nickelsburg (Harrisburg: Trinity International, 2000), 280–88.

91. On the use of the imagery of the two ways to shape ethical instruction see Nickelsburg, *Resurrection*, 157–64, and the literature cited in the notes; idem, "Seeking the Origins of the Two Ways Tradition in Jewish and Christian Texts," in Benjamin G. Wright, ed., *A Multiform Heritage: Studies on Early Judaism and Christianity in Honor of Robert A. Kraft* (Scholars Press

Homage Series 24; Atlanta: Scholars Press, 1999) 95–108; Robert A. Kraft, "Early Developments of the 'Two-Ways Tradition(s),' in Retrospect," in Argall, Bow, and Werline, eds., *For a Later Generation*, 136–43; Nickelsburg, *1 Enoch 1*, 454–56.

92. On the covenantal form here see Baltzer, *Formulary*, 98–112. For other occurrences of the maskil see CD 12:21; 13:22; 1QS 9:12, 21; 1QH^a 22:11. Cf. also Dan 12:3, where it applies to the wise teachers during the Antiochan persecution, on which see above, p. 82.

93. See Nickelsburg, *Resurrection*, 165–66.

94. On the arguments as to whether the section on the two spirits was composed at once or reflects one or several redactions, see Metso, *Textual Development*, 113 and n. 19.

95. Metso, *Serek Texts*.

96. For a summary see ibid.

97. Ibid.

98. For a summary of the discussion see Metso, *Textual Development*, 9–11.

99. Ibid., 124–28; idem, *Serek Texts*.

100. Metso, *Serek Texts*.

101. For a comparison of the Qumran Scrolls and Josephus see Todd S. Beall, *Josephus' Description of the Essenes Illustrated by the Dead Sea Scrolls* (SNTSMS 58; Cambridge: Cambridge Univ. Press, 1998). For some additional issues see Nickelsburg, *Ancient Judaism*, 167–75.

102. For a summary see Sarianna Metso, "The Relationship between the Damascus Document and the Community Rule," in Baumgarten, Chazon, and Pinnick, eds., *Damascus Document*, 84–93.

103. For a summary see Knibb, "Rule of the Community," 794–96; Metso, *Serek Texts*. For a detailed discussion see Metso, *Textual Development*, 69–149.

104. Alexander and Vermes, DJD 26:9–12.

105. Metso, *Textual Development*, 68–149.

106. Sukenik, *Dead Sea Scrolls of the Hebrew University*, 35.

107. For a physical description of the scroll and photographs, see ibid., pp. 35–36, figs. 11–13, 26–27, and pls. 16–34.

108. For a transcription and translation of 1QM and the Cave 4 fragments, see Duhaime, "War Scroll," in *DSSHAGT*; García Martínez and Tigchelaar, *Scrolls*, 1:112–45; 2:970–91.

109. See, e.g., Duhaime, "War Scroll," in *DSSHAGT*, 80; Davies, "War," 966.

110. For the influence of Ezek 38–39 (the prophecy about God of Magog) and Dan 11–12 on the War Scroll, see Davies, *1QM*, 85, 100, 116; idem, "War," 967.

111. For an explication of these seven periods see John J. Collins, "The Mythology of Holy Warfare in Daniel and the Qumran War Scroll: A Point of Transition in Jewish Apocalyptic," *VT* 25 (1975) 605–7.

112. Davies, *1QM*, 26–28.

113. Yadin, *Scroll of the War*, 278; Davies, "War," 967.

114. On these towers see Yadin, *Scroll of the War*, 187–90.

115. On the seven periods see Collins, "Mythology," 605–7.

116. Duhaime, "War Scroll," in *DSSHAGT*, 87.

117. Davies, "War," 966.

118. Duhaime, "War Scroll," in *DSSHAGT*, 83–84; Davies, "War," 966–67. For a comparison of 1QM with Roman military manuals see Jean Duhaime, "The *War Scroll* from Qumran and the Greco-Roman Tactical Treatises," *RevQ* 13 (1988) 133–51. See also the detailed discussion in Yadin, *Scroll of the War*, 141–83.

119. On the reference to the Seleucids see Hanan Eshel, "The Kittim in the *War Scroll* and in the Pesharim," in David Goodblatt, Avital Pinnick, and Daniel R. Schwartz, eds., *Historical Perspectives: From the Hasmoneans to Bar Kochba in Light of the Dead Sea Scrolls: Proceedings of the Fourth International Symposium of the Orion Center for the Study of the Dead Sea Scrolls and Associated Literature, 27–31 January 1999* (STDJ 37; Leiden: Brill, 2001) 32–37.

120. See the summary and conclusions in Duhaime, "War," in *DSSHAGT,* 83–84.

121. Davies, *1QM.*

122. Collins, "Mythology." For the view that the dualism in 1QM (and 1QS and CD) involves a late reworking of the texts, see Jean Duhaime, "Dualistic Reworking in the Scrolls from Qumran," *CBQ* 49 (1987) 32–56.

123. *Israel:* 1:9–10 (God of Israel); 2:7 (all the tribes of Israel); 2:9; 3:13; 5:1; 6:6 (God of Israel); 10:8 (God of Israel); 10:9 (your nation Israel); 12:16; 13:1–2 (God of Israel); 13:13 (God of Israel); 14:4 (God of Israel); 15:1, 13 (God of Israel); 16:1 (God of Israel); 17:7 (covenant of Israel); 17:8; 18:3 (God of Israel); 18:6 (God of Israel); 19:8. *Nation:* 1:5, 12; 3:13; 6:6 (the holy ones of his nation, perhaps an exception); 10:9 (your nation Israel), 10 (a nation of holy ones of the covenant); 12:1, 8 (the nation of his holy ones); 12:15; 13:7, 9; 14:12; 18:7; 19:7. *Covenant:* 1:2; 10:10; 12:3; 13:7; 14:8, 10; 17:7, 8; 18:7, 8.

124. See Collins, *Apocalypticism,* 108. The two texts are also tied together by a common interest in the eschatological war.

125. See Collins, "Mythology." On the scroll's use of Daniel (and the Hebrew Bible in general), see Duhaime, "War Scroll," in *DSSHAGT,* 87–88. See also the index in Yadin, *Scroll of the War,* 362–63.

126. Nickelsburg, *1 Enoch 1,* 362, 464.

127. Davies, "War," 967–68.

128. For transcriptions of the six mss., a composite text, a translation, and detailed discussion, see Qimron and Strugnell, DJD 10.

129. Originally, the editors presented the text as a letter, possibly from the Teacher of Righteousness; see Elisha Qimron and John Strugnell, "An Unpublished Halakhic Letter from Qumran," in [J. Amitai, ed.], *Biblical Archaeology Today: Proceedings of the International Congress on Biblical Archaeology Jerusalem, April 1984* (Jerusalem: Israel Exploration Society, 1985) 400–407. Most discussions continue to consider it to be a letter. In its formal publication Strugnell (DJD 10:113–14) discusses its literary genre and hesitantly concludes that it is a public treatise. In his "second thoughts" on the document, he shies away from the term "epistle," emphasizing that the preserved text lacks the introductory and concluding formulas typical of epistles; see John Strugnell, "MMT: Second Thoughts on a Forthcoming Edition," in Eugene Ulrich and James VanderKam, eds., *The Community of the Renewed Covenant* (Notre Dame: Univ. of Notre Dame Press, 1994) 57–73, esp. 67, a somewhat different form of his appendix in DJD 10:203–6. However one describes its genre, the "we/you" language and the formal appeals to action in part C identify it as a piece of two-party communication.

130. For the terminology see Strugnell and Qimron, DJD 10:1, 46, 63, 139. For a translation of *maʿăśeh* and *děbārim* (B 1) as "deeds" or "practices" rather than "precepts" and "rulings," see Florentino García Martínez, "4QMMT in a Qumran Context," in Kampen and Bernstein, eds., *Reading 4QMMT,* 15–27.

131. Strugnell, DJD 10:203. If it was not original to the document, it was perhaps added when the document lost its setting as a piece of communication and served rather as an epitome of laws and practices that differentiated the Qumranites from the temple establishment. Such a change in function might also explain how an introduction and a conclusion typical of a letter might have dropped from the document.

132. Qimron and Strugnell, DJD 10:44. For 4Q325 (*Mishmarot* D), as one example, see Vermes, *Complete Scrolls*, 349–50; Wise, Abegg, and Cook, *Scrolls*, §75. On the calendar at Qumran see James C. VanderKam, *Calendars in the Dead Sea Scrolls: Measuring Time* (London and New York: Routledge, 1998).

133. Lawrence H. Schiffman ("Miqtsat Maʿasei ha-Torah," 558–59) lists the following topics: Gentile wheat may not be brought into the temple; the cooking of offerings; Gentile sacrifices; the purity of those preparing the red cow; the purity of hides; the place of slaughtering and offering sacrifices; prohibition of the slaughter of pregnant animals; forbidden sexual unions; the exclusion of the blind and deaf from the "purity of the temple"; impurity of liquid streams from one vessel to another; dogs may not enter Jerusalem; the fruit of the fourth year is to be given to the priests; the cattle tithe is to be given to the priests; purification rituals of the leper; impurity of human bones; marriages between priests and Israelites are forbidden. In several cases the introductory "And concerning x" appears as a subtopic under Schiffman's topics. It is uncertain how many other topics may have been lost in the gap between the last preserved material in part B and the first preserved material in part C.

134. See Moshe J. Bernstein, "The Employment and Interpretation of Scripture in 4QMMT: Preliminary Observations," in Kampen and Bernstein, eds., *Reading 4QMMT*, 29–51.

135. Qimron and Strugnell, DJD 10:57 n. 3.

136. For this expression with the verb *dārash* rather than *biqqēsh* (as here), cf. CD 6:7; 7:18; Jub. 1:12; 23:26.

137. For "good" and "evil" as shorthand for the covenantal blessings and curses, see Deut 30:15; Jer 32:42. See Nickelsburg, *1 Enoch 1*, 484.

138. On this dating see Ada Yardeni, DJD 10:3–6, 14, 16–18, 21–25, 28–34, 38–39.

139. See above, pp. 124, 127, 129, and below, p. 153.

140. Strugnell, DJD 10:109–21; Strugnell, "Second Thoughts," 70–73; Schiffman, "Miqtsat Maʿasei ha-Torah," 559.

141. Strugnell, DJD 10:114–21.

142. Ibid., 120; idem, "Second Thoughts," 72; Hanan Eshel, "4QMMT and the History of the Hasmonean Period," in Kampen and Bernstein, eds., *Reading 4QMMT*, 53–65.

143. For the four instances see Lawrence H. Schiffman, "The Temple Scroll and the Systems of Jewish Law of the Second Temple Period," in Brooke, ed., *Temple Scroll Studies*, 251. VanderKam ("People of the Dead Sea Scrolls," 58–59) reduces the number to three.

144. For a detailed commentary on the halakah in MMT see Elisha Qimron, DJD 10:123–77. For a discussion that places MMT's laws in their historical context, not least in cautious comparison to Sadducean law, see Yaʿakov Sussmann, DJD 10:179–200. See also Yaʿakov Elman, "Some Remarks on 4QMMT and the Rabbinic Tradition, or, When Is a Parallel Not a Parallel," in Kampen and Bernstein, eds., *Reading 4QMMT*, 99–128. For an emphasis on the parallels with Sadducean law see briefly Schiffman, "Miqtsat Maʿasei ha-Torah," 559. For a more hesitant appraisal see Joseph M. Baumgarten, "Sadducean Elements in Qumran Law," in Ulrich and Vanderkam, eds., *Community of the Renewed Covenant*, 30–36.

145. The fragments of its two columns were left behind by the Bedouin and recovered in the subsequent archeological excavation of the cave. For a photograph see DJD 1, pl. 24. Stephen J. Pfann has edited a group of papyrus fragments from Cave 4, written in a cryptic script, which he ingenioiusly argues are the remains of eight or nine mss. of this Rule. For his transcription and discussion of the fragments see DJD 36:515–74. The identification is considered by some to be problematic because of the size of the fragments; see DJD 36, pls. 35–38.

146. It is unclear to me that the gathering of the congregation will take place in the *aftermath* of the war, as is suggested by Schiffman, "Rule of the Congregation," 797.

147. Ibid., 798.

148. For these alternative translations see Knibb, *Qumran Community*, 153; García Martínez and Tigchelaar, *Scrolls*, 103.

149. For bibliography and a brief discussion see Dennis E. Smith, "Meals," *EDSS* 1:530–32.

150. Annette Steudel, "*ʾḥryt hymym* in the Texts from Qumran," *RevQ* 16 (1993) 230–31.

151. See, e.g., Frank Moore Cross, *The Ancient Library of Qumran and Modern Biblical Studies* (3d ed.; Minneapolis: Fortress Press, 1995) 77; Knibb, *Qumran Community*, 155; Schiffman, *Reclaiming the Dead Sea Scrolls*, 333–34.

152. Schiffman, "Rule of the Congregation," 797.

153. This is suggested by Hartmut Stegemann (*The Library of Qumran* [Grand Rapids: Eerdmans, 1998] 122), who refers to it as the Essenes' "oldest congregational rule." See further Steudel, "Texts from Qumran," 230–31 n. 33.

154. On the parallel to the Damascus Document see Charlotte Hempel, "The Earthly Essene Nucleus of 1QSa," *DSD* 3 (1996) 262–66.

155. See John J. Collins, *The Scepter and the Star: The Messiahs of the Dead Sea Scrolls and Other Ancient Literature* (New York: Doubleday, 1995) 74–101.

156. For these texts see ibid., 56–67, 154–75.

157. See Nickelsburg, *Ancient Judaism*, 109–10.

158. For the texts, translations, and photographs of all the mss., see Carol A. Newsom, DJD 11:173–401, pls. 16–31. For the most complete English translations see García Martínez, *Scrolls*, 419–31; Wise, Abegg, and Cook, *Scrolls*, §101. For a composite text and translation that allow one to navigate through the fragmentary mss. and see what is preserved of each song, see Newsom, et al., "Angelic Liturgy."

159. Newsom, et al., "Angelic Liturgy," 3; Newsom, "Songs of the Sabbath Sacrifice," *EDSS* 2:887. The exposition that follows is heavily indebted to Newsom, *EDSS* 2:887–88; Newsom, et al., "Angelic Liturgy," 3. For a fuller discussion, see idem, "'He Has Established for Himself Priests': Human and Angelic Priesthood in the Qumran Sabbath *Shirot*," in Lawrence H. Schiffman, ed., *Archaeology and History in the Dead Sea Scrolls: The New York University Conference in Memory of Yigael Yadin* (JSPSup 8; JSOT/ASOR Monograph Series 2; Sheffield: Sheffield Academic Press, 1990) 101–20.

160. Cf., e.g., Exod 32:25–29; Num 25:1–13 (cf. 1 Kgs 18, where Elijah functions as a priest); Jub. 30:18–20; 1 Macc 2:23–26.

161. For the text and translation of these songs, which must be reconstructed from a number of mss., one is best referred to the composite text by Brent Strawn in Newsom, et al., "Angelic Liturgy," 175–89.

162. Newsom, et al., "Angelic Liturgy," 8–9. For a detailed exegesis see idem, "Merkabah Exegesis in the Qumran Sabbath Shirot," *JJS* 38 (1987) 11–30.

163. On 1 Enoch 14–16 and Ezek 1–2 see Nickelsburg, *1 Enoch 1*, 254–66.

164. On the liturgical or nonliturgical function of the songs as this relates especially to the additional Sabbath sacrifice in the Jerusalem temple, see Newsom, et al., "Angelic Liturgy," 3–4; idem, *EDSS* 2:888. One problem with attributing to them a liturgical function is that the thirteen songs are appropriate only the first quarter of the year. Did one repeat the collection of thirteen for each quarter of the year? This is suggested by Johann Maier, "*Shirê ʿÔlat hash-Shabbat:* Some Observations on Their Calendric Implications and on Their Style," in Julio Trebolle Barrera and

Luis Vegas Montaner, eds., *The Madrid Qumran Congress: Proceedings of the International Congress on the Dead Sea Scrolls, Madrid 18–21 March, 1991* (STDJ 11/2; Leiden: Brill, 1992) 543–53. Newsom ("Angelic Liturgy," 3–4; *EDSS* 2:888) is less certain. However, the same question pertains if they were used for what was not technically a liturgical purpose.

165. Newsom, *EDSS* 2:888.

166. Newsom, et al., "Angelic Liturgy," 4. In more detail see the exposition by Nitzan, *Qumran Prayer*, 282–318.

167. Newsom, *EDSS* 2:888–89; idem, "He Has Established," 115.

168. The possible relationship between a defunct Jerusalem cult and the Angelic Liturgy was made in the first publication on this text by John Strugnell, "The Angelic Liturgy at Qumrân—4Q Serek Šîrôt ʿÔlat Haššabāt," in *Congress Volume: Oxford 1959* (VTSup 7; Leiden: Brill, 1960) 35. See also Newsom, et al., "Angelic Liturgy," 4; Newsom, *EDSS* 2:889; idem, "He Has Established," 115. For the notion that glorifying God is like offering sacrifices, cf. 11QPs[a] 18:7–10. For the emphasis on God as king, and its concern with the kingship of God, see Anna Maria Schwemer, "Gott als Königsherrschaft in den Sabbatliedern aus Qumran," in Martin Hengel and Anna Maria Schwemer, eds., *Königsherrschaft Gottes und himmlischer Kult im Judentum, Urchristentum und in der hellenistischen Welt* (Tübingen: Mohr Siebeck, 1991) 45–118.

169. See Newsom, *EDSS* 2:887.

170. Newsom, et al., "Angelic Liturgy," 4–5; idem, *EDSS* 2:887. On the paleographical dating of the mss. see DJD 11:173–74, 197–98, 221–22, 239–40, 253–54, 293–94, 308.

171. Newsom ("Angelic Liturgy," 5; *EDSS* 2:887) leans toward an early, extra-Qumranic provenance. Fletcher-Lewis (*All the Glory of Adam*, 394) thinks the text is sectarian.

172. Newsom, "Merkabah Exegesis."

173. For details on the acquisition of the scroll and its unrolling see Yadin, *Temple Scroll*, 1:1–8.

174. The scroll is roughly 1.5 meters longer than the great Isaiah Scroll (1QIsa[a]). For details regarding the physical characteristics of the Temple Scroll and the state of its preservation, see ibid., 1:9–17.

175. For photographs of the scroll, see the plates in ibid., 3:1–82.

176. In my discussion, I have been greatly helped by the introduction by Crawford, *Temple Scroll*, and by the summary article by García Martínez, "Temple Scroll." For the distinction between issues on which there is consensus and those on which scholars disagree, see García Martínez, "Temple Scroll," 930.

177. My outline reflects mainly that of Crawford, *Temple Scroll*, 29. On alternative proposals regarding the sources see the summaries in ibid., 22–24; García Martínez, "Temple Scroll," 929–30.

178. Yadin (*Temple Scroll*, 1:46, 2:1) sees Exod 34 as the base text, while Crawford (*Temple Scroll*, 33–34) emphasizes the importance of Exod 24.

179. On the covenantal context see the outline in Crawford, *Temple Scroll*, 29.

180. Yadin, *Temple Scroll*, 2:2–3. On the author's use of Scripture, see Swanson, *Temple Scroll*.

181. Yadin, *Temple Scroll*, 2:46; Crawford, *Temple Scroll*, 33–34.

182. Yadin, *Temple Scroll*, 2:50–57; Crawford, *Temple Scroll*, 50.

183. See Crawford, *Temple Scroll*, 49; García Martínez, "Temple Scroll," 929.

184. For a helpful road map through this section see Crawford, *Temple Scroll*, 49–57.

185. The preserved text, following Lev 23:23 and Num 29:1–6, mentions only the "Day of

Memorial," so also Yadin, *Temple Scroll*, 2:111–12. Crawford (*Temple Scroll*, 55) refers to this as the Fall New Year, a designation that appears in the later rabbinic calendar; see Maier, *Temple Scroll*, 85.

186. Crawford, *Temple Scroll*, 50–51, 54.

187. Yadin, *Temple Scroll*, 1:99; Baruch Levine, "The Temple Scroll: Aspects of Its Historical Provenance and Literary Character," *BASOR* 232 (1978) 7–11; James C. VanderKam, "The Temple Scroll and the Book of Jubilees," in Brooke, ed., *Temple Scroll Studies*, 214–18.

188. On this section see Crawford, *Temple Scroll*, 36–42; and in great detail, Yadin, *Temple Scroll*, 1:200–276.

189. Yadin, *Temple Scroll*, 2:203.

190. Crawford, *Temple Scroll*, 39.

191. Ibid.

192. Magen Broshi, "The Gigantic Dimensions of the Visionary Temple in the Temple Scroll," in Shanks, ed., *Understanding the Dead Sea Scrolls*, 113–15.

193. Yadin, *Temple Scroll*, 1:274–75.

194. Crawford, *Temple Scroll*, 42.

195. On the purity regulations in general see ibid., 42–49. On the problem of the terminology about the relationship of the city to the temple, see ibid., 48–49; see also the discussion by Lawrence H. Schiffman, "The Theology of the Temple Scroll," *JQR* 85 (1994) 118–21; and the response by Jacob Milgrom, "The City of the Temple," *JQR* 85 (1994) 125–28.

196. On this section as a whole see Crawford, *Temple Scroll*, 57–62.

197. Yadin, *Temple Scroll*, 2:246.

198. On the Law of the King see ibid., 1:344–62.

199. On these laws about the king's wife see ibid., 353–57; Crawford, *Temple Scroll*, 59–60.

200. Crawford, *Temple Scroll*, 62.

201. On the alternatives for understanding the relationship of the Temple Scroll to scriptural law, see García Martínez, "Temple Scroll," 930.

202. Schiffman, "Theology," 123.

203. For the alternatives see García Martínez, "Temple Scroll," 931–21; Crawford, *Temple Scroll*, 24–26.

204. Swanson, *Temple Scroll*, 237–39; Crawford, *Temple Scroll*, 25. For a much earlier date, around the mid-fifth century, see Hartmut Stegemann, "The Origins of the Temple Scroll," *Congress Volume: Jerusalem 1986* (VTSup 40; Leiden: Brill, 1988) 234–56.

205. García Martínez, "Temple Scroll," 932. On the details of this law see Lawrence H. Schiffman, "*Miqtsat Maʿaśeh ha-Torah* and the *Temple Scroll*," *RevQ* 14 (1990) 442–48.

206. On the dating of the mss. see García Martínez, "Temple Scroll," 927–28; Crawford, *Temple Scroll*, 12–16.

207. Crawford, *Temple Scroll*, 24.

208. Ibid., 13–14; García Martínez, "Temple Scroll," 928.

209. On the two scribes see Yadin, *Temple Scroll*, 1:9–12; and in summary, Crawford, *Temple Scroll*, 12.

210. Schiffman, "*Temple Scroll*," 435–57.

211. Yadin, *Temple Scroll*, 1:398–99.

212. Levine, "Temple Scroll," 7.

213. Schiffman, "*Temple Scroll*," 456–47; Crawford, *Temple Scroll*, 28–29; García Martínez, "Temple Scroll," 930–32.

214. VanderKam, "Temple Scroll," 210–36. On Jubilees at Qumran see above, p. 74.

215. VanderKam, "Temple Scroll," 231.

216. For an argument that Jubilees and the Temple Scroll are two parts of one work, see Ben Zion Wacholder, *The Dawn of Qumran: The Sectarian Torah and the Teacher of Righteousness* (HUCM 8; Cincinnati: Hebrew Union College Press, 1983) 61–62; see, however, the critique of VanderKam, "Temple Scroll," 232; and in much more detail, Hindy Najman, *Seconding Sinai: The Development of Mosaic Discourse in Second Temple Judaism* (JSJSup 77; Leiden: Brill, 2003), 43–69.

217. For these texts see above, pp. 124, 149, 153.

218. On the Cairo Genizah see above, p. 373 n. 17. Of the six pages, two are preserved almost in their entirety with only one lacuna in the ms., two are missing about a quarter of the text, and only about 20 percent of the other two remains. Thus about 30 percent of the text on the six pages has been preserved. The total length of the original document is uncertain. See Stone, "Levi, Aramaic," 487. For photographs of the ms. see Drawnel, *Aramaic Wisdom Text*, pl. VI–IX; Greenfield, Stone, and Eshel, *Aramaic Levi Document*, 52–55.

219. For the text see M. de Jonge, et al., eds., *The Testaments of the Twelve Patriarchs: A Critical Edition of the Greek Text* (PVTG 1/2: Leiden: Brill, 1978) 25, 46–48; and for a text and translation see Drawnel, *Aramaic Wisdom Text*, 98–101; Greenfield, Stone, and Eshel, *Aramaic Levi Document*, 60–109.

220. For the formal editions with Aramaic texts, notes, and translations, see J. T. Milik, DJD 1:87–91 (Cave 1); Jonas C. Greenfield and Michael E. Stone, DJD 22:1–63 (Cave 4).

221. It is the overlaps between the Genizah and Mt. Athos fragments that establish the sequence of the fragments. Overlaps between the Qumran fragments and the Mt. Athos and Genizah fragments help to establish the Aramaic text, but not the sequence. For details and discussion of the overlaps and the sequencing of the fragments, see Kugler, *From Patriarch to Priest*, 52–59; Drawnel, *Aramaic Wisdom Text*, 32–55; Greenfield, Stone, and Eshel, *Aramaic Levi Document*, 11–19, as well as the reconstruction on the page before page 1.

222. Because Levi's prayer almost certainly presupposes the Dinah story (see below), I follow the order of Kugler (*Patriarch to Priest*, 34–59) and Greenfield, Stone, and Eshel (*Aramaic Levi Document*, 18–19) rather than that of Drawnel (*Aramaic Wisdom Text*, 54), who places Levi's prayer before the Dinah story. Given the various textual witnesses, citation of the passages within the context of the whole reconstructed document is problematic. Since I follow the order of Greenfield, Stone, and Eshel, I employ their chapter and verse enumeration.

223. See Drawnel, *Aramaic Wisdom Text*, pl. VI; Greenfield, Stone, and Eshel, *Aramaic Levi Document*, 52.

224. See Drawnel, *Aramaic Wisdom Text*, pl. VII; Greenfield, Stone, and Eshel, *Aramaic Levi Document*, 53. For the calculation see Greenfield, Stone, and Eshel, *Aramaic Levi Document*, 2.

225. For these wars see Greenfield, Stone, and Eshel, *Aramaic Levi Document*, 12, 119. Drawnel (*Aramaic Wisdom Text*, 230–33), relying on a reconstruction by Puech ("Testament de Lévi," 518–22), relates this incident to the selling of Joseph, but the parallels to Gen 37 are not that close. See the critique of Puech's reconstruction in Greenfield, Stone, and Eshel, *Aramaic Levi Document*, 117–18.

226. Kugler, *Patriarch to Priest*, 57–58; Greenfield, Stone, and Eshel, *Aramaic Levi Document*, 12–13.

227. For the two options see Kugler, *Patriarch to Priest*, 57–58; Greenfield, Stone, and Eshel, *Aramaic Levi Document*, 12–13.

228. Given the dependence of this part of Jubilees on the Aramaic Levi Document (Kugler, *Patriarch to Priest*, 139–69) and the lack of any other exegetical trigger in the Genesis story, the connection is warranted (ibid., 67, 161–62). For other connections between violent zeal and priestly appointment, cf. Exod 32:25–29; Num 25:6–13; 1 Macc 2:23–26. See Greenfield, Stone, and Eshel, *Aramaic Levi Document*, 142, 145.

229. Greenfield, Stone, and Eshel, *Aramaic Levi Document*, 126–27, which cites David Flusser, "Qumran and Jewish Apotropaic Prayers," *IEJ* 16 (1966) 200.

230. On this element see Nickelsburg, *1 Enoch 1*, 206.

231. For details see Greenfield, Stone, and Eshel, *Aramaic Levi Document*, 33–34. See also Drawnel, *Aramaic Wisdom Text*, 213.

232. On this term see Drawnel, *Aramaic Wisdom Text*, 216–17; Greenfield, Stone, and Eshel, *Aramaic Levi Document*, 129–30.

233. Greenfield, Stone, and Eshel, *Aramaic Levi Document*, 125–26.

234. See ibid., 20–21, 184–86.

235. For this motif cf. 1 Enoch 10:16, 20, 22.

236. In 1 Enoch 20–36 Enoch is also accompanied by seven angels; cf. also 81:5 and see Nickelsburg, *1 Enoch 1*, 207.

237. Greenfield, Stone, and Eshel, *Aramaic Levi Document*, 39–41, 147–54.

238. Although Drawnel (*Aramaic Wisdom Text*, 255) acknowledges that this instruction deals mainly with "legal injunctions," he characterizes it as "wisdom instruction," perhaps a confusing use of the terminology. It is uncertain exactly why Isaac rather than Jacob instructs Levi, since it was Jacob who invested him. See ibid., 40–41. However, cf. Testament of Isaac 4, a much later Christian text, which may or may not know this text.

239. Drawnel, *Aramaic Wisdom Text*, 254.

240. Following the division in Greenfield, Stone, and Eshel, *Aramaic Levi Document*, 75–93. For a different division see Drawnel, *Aramaic Wisdom Text*, 257–58.

241. For an analogy with the inspection of sacrificial animals, see Drawnel, *Aramaic Wisdom Text*, 272–73.

242. On the list see Greenfield, Stone, and Eshel, *Aramaic Levi Document*, 165–67.

243. On the metrology in this text see ibid., 41–44; Drawnel, *Aramaic Wisdom Text*, 280–93.

244. On this section as a later addition to the text see Greenfield, Stone, and Eshel, *Aramaic Levi Document*, 44.

245. Ibid., 189–90.

246. Ibid., 184–88.

247. See ibid., 198.

248. On the poem's poetic structure see Greenfield and Stone, DJD 22:12–13.

249. Greenfield, Stone, and Eshel (*Aramaic Levi Document*, 216–19) do not attempt to place the fragment. Drawnel (*Aramaic Wisdom Text*, 37) states that it cannot be connected with any possible context in the Aramaic document, but in his translation (373) he juxtaposes it to the end of the wisdom poem. For another Aramaic text dubbed a Levi Apocryphon by its editor (4Q540–41), see Émile Puech, DJD 31:213–56. It has some similarities to T. Levi 18, but there is no certain evidence that it was a part of the present text; see Greenfield, Stone, and Eshel, *Aramaic Levi Document*, 31–32.

250. After a long discussion, Drawnel (*Aramaic Wisdom Text*, 96) comes to no certain conclusion.

251. On 1 Enoch see Nickelsburg, *1 Enoch 1*, 28–35. On Tobit see above, p. 34.

252. On the Testaments of the Twelve Patriarchs and the form of the testament, see below, pp. 302–14. On the problems of identifying this as a testament, see Greenfield, Stone, and Eshel, *Aramaic Levi Document*, 25–28; Drawnel, *Aramaic Wisdom Text*, 85–87.

253. On this see above, p. 114, and Nickelsburg, *1 Enoch 1*, 410–15.

254. On the didactic character of the text see Drawnel, *Aramaic Wisdom Text*, 78–85.

255. Greenfield, Stone, and Eshel, *Aramaic Levi Document*, 34–35.

256. Drawnel, *Aramaic Wisdom Text*, 269–93.

257. See VanderKam, *From Joshua to Caiaphas*, 122–95.

258. See above, n. 228.

259. George W. E. Nickelsburg, "Aaron," in *RAC* Sup 1:2–5.

260. On Noah's priesthood see Andrei A. Orlov, *The Enoch-Metatron Tradition* (TSAJ 107; Tübingen: Mohr Siebeck, 2005) 204–33.

261. On the calendar see Greenfield, Stone, and Eshel, *Aramaic Levi Document*, 20.

262. Kugler, *Patriarch to Priest*, 139–69.

263. Ibid., 29–31.

264. Nickelsburg, "Aaron," 4.

265. H. W. Hollander and M. de Jonge, *The Testaments of the Twelve Patriarchs: A Commentary* (SVTP 8; Leiden: Brill, 1985) 82–85.

266. See William F. Stinespring, "Testament of Isaac," in *OTP* 1:903–11.

267. See Greenfield, Stone, and Eshel, *Aramaic Levi Document*, 19–20.

268. For the dating of the Cave 4 mss. see Greenfield and Stone, DJD 22:3, 27, 37, 44, 54, 62.

269. Greenfield, Stone, and Eshel, *Aramaic Levi Document*, 19.

270. Greenfield, Stone, and Eshel (*Aramaic Levi Document*, 19–20) suggest this range of dates. Drawnel (*Aramaic Wisdom Text*, 63–75) argues for a date in the early Hellenistic period, perhaps ca. 300 B.C.E.

271. On the Aramaic of the Levi Document see Greenfield, Stone, and Eshel, *Aramaic Levi Document*, 22–25; Drawnel, *Aramaic Wisdom Text*, 55–61.

272. Greenfield, Stone, and Eshel, *Aramaic Levi Document*, 20–22.

273. For the text and photographs of the scroll see James A. Sanders, DJD 4. For a second edition that includes discussion of a three-column fragment published later and a foldout photograph of the whole scroll, see idem, *Dead Sea Psalms Scroll*.

274. For a table of contents of the scroll and an index that lists the psalms in their canonical sequence, see Sanders, DJD 4:5–6. On the organization of the scroll see Flint, *Dead Sea Psalms Scrolls*, 73–98.

275. For texts, translations, and discussion of these noncanonical pieces see Sanders, DJD 4:53–93; idem, *Dead Sea Psalms Scroll*, 93–137.

276. Flint, *Dead Sea Psalms Scrolls*, 40–41.

277. This was argued first by Sanders, *Dead Sea Psalms Scroll*, 10–14. For a detailed examination and confirmation of this hypothesis see Flint, *Dead Sea Psalms Scrolls*, 203–27.

278. Flint, *Dead Sea Psalms Scrolls*, 198–200.

279. On the date of the scroll see Sanders, DJD 4:6–9.

280. Flint, *Dead Sea Psalms Scrolls*, 189–94. He also notes the dispersal of Davidic psalms throughout the collection and suggests that the collection included fifty-two Davidic psalms, one for each week of the solar calendar, ibid., 189–93.

281. On the relationship between the Hebrew and Greek compositions see Sanders, DJD 4:54–64. For further discussion of this Hebrew psalm see idem, "The Qumran Psalms Scroll (11QPs^a) Reviewed," in Matthew Black and William A. Smalley, eds., *On Language, Culture, and Religion: In Honor of Eugene A. Nida* (The Hague: Mouton, 1974) 84–88; idem, "A Multivalent Text: Psalm 151:3–4 Revisited," in Reuben Ahroni, ed., *Biblical and Other Studies in Honor of Sheldon H. Blank* (HAR 8; Columbus: Ohio State Univ. Press, 1984) 167–84.

282. Sanders, DJD 4:61–63.

283. On the relationship between these *two* Hebrew pieces and Greek Psalm 151, see ibid., 60–61.

284. Ibid., 53.

285. My exposition draws on ibid., 67–90.

286. For the notion that pious deeds can serve in lieu of sacrifices, see above, pp. 60, 142, and below, p. 244.

287. Sanders, DJD 4:69–70.

288. Robert Polzin, "Notes on the Dating of the Non-Massoretic Psalms of 11QPs^a," *HTR* 60 (1967) 468–76.

289. See Dieter Lührmann, "Ein Weisheitpsalm aus Qumran (11QPs^a XVIII)," *ZAW* 80 (1968) 87–98.

290. On the problem of the Hasidim see Nickelsburg, *Ancient Judaism*, 176–78.

291. On synagogues in early Judaism see the discussion in ibid., 154–59.

292. For the six Cave 4 mss. and the one Cave 1 ms. see John Strugnell and Daniel J. Harrington, DJD 24:1. For another possible ms. see ibid., 501–3. For the fragmentary condition of the mss. see ibid., pls. 1–31.

293. See Charlotte Hempel, "The Qumran Sapiential Texts and the Rule Books," in Charlotte Hempel, Armin Lange, and Hermann Lichtenberger, eds., *The Wisdom Texts from Qumran and the Development of Sapiential Thought* (BETL 159; Leuven: Peeters, 2002) 281–83.

294. For these estimates see Strugnell and Harrington, DJD 24: 18–19.

295. See the list in Tigchelaar, *To Increase Learning*, 148–50.

296. Ibid., 155–57.

297. See, e.g., ibid., 191–200.

298. Collins, *Jewish Wisdom*, 118; Harrington, "Sapiential Work," 825.

299. For the translation of this word see Strugnell and Harrington, DJD 34:3; and Eibert J. C. Tigchelaar, "The Addressees of 4Q Instruction," in Daniel K. Falk, Florentino García Martínez, and Eileen M. Schuller, eds., *Sapiential, Liturgical, and Poetical Texts from Qumran: Proceedings of the Third Meeting of the International Organization for Qumran Studies Oslo 1998: Published in Memory of Maurice Baillet* (STDJ 35; Leiden: Brill, 2000) 65–69.

300. For photographs of the ms. see DJD 34, pls. 4–6. For the text, a translation, and notes, see ibid., 88–131. For a translation and brief notes see Daniel J. Harrington, *Wisdom Texts from Qumran* (London: Routledge, 1996) 42–49.

301. See Murphy, *Wealth*, 163–209.

302. See Harrington, *Wisdom Texts from Qumran*, 47.

303. Translation here and below, in ibid., 44.

304. For an address in the second-person singular, probably to the wife of the student, cf. 4Q415 2 2:1–9, ibid., 57.

305. On this column see Strugnell and Harrington, DJD 34:81–88; Tigchelaar, *To Increase Learning*, 175–93.

306. On eschatology in 4QInstruction see Goff, *Wisdom*, 168–215.

307. Ibid., 192–93.

308. The expression occurs in 4Q415 6 4; 24 1; 4Q416 2 1:5; 2 3:9; 2:3:14, 18, 21; 17 3; 4Q417 1 1:8, 18, 21; 1 2:3; 4Q418 10a-b 1; 43–45 1:4, 14, 16; 77 2; 77 4; 123 2:4; 172 1; 184:2. On the verbs see Torleif Elgvin, "The Mystery to Come: Early Essene Theology of Revelation," in Frederick H. Cryer and Thomas L. Thompson, eds., *Qumran between the Old and New Testaments* (JSOTSup 290; Sheffield: Sheffield Academic Press, 1998) 133.

309. On the meaning of the expression see Elgvin, "Mystery to Come," 131–39; Strugnell and Harrington, DJD 34:32; Collins, *Jewish Wisdom*, 121–25; Goff, *Wisdom*, 51–79.

310. Goff, *Wisdom*, 169.

311. Torleif Elgvin, "Wisdom and Apocalypticism in the Early Second Century BCE—The Evidence of 4QInstruction," in Lawrence H. Schiffman, Emanuel Tov, and James C. VanderKam, eds., *The Dead Sea Scrolls Fifty Years after Their Discovery* (Jerusalem: Israel Exploration Society, 2000) 235–36.

312. Goff, *Wisdom*, 73–79.

313. Werline, *Penitential Prayer*, 111–13.

314. Elgvin, "Mystery to Come," 131, without reference to this verb.

315. For a comparison and contrast between 4QInstruction and the Wisdom of Ben Sira, see Daniel J. Harrington, "Two Early Jewish Approaches to Wisdom: Sirach and Qumran Sapiential Work A," in Hempel, Lange, and Lichtenberger, eds., *Wisdom Texts*, 263–75.

316. For different opinions on whether the intended readers were actually poor, see Collins, *Jewish Wisdom*, 118–19; Tigchelaar, "Addressees," 69–71. In much more detail see Goff, *Wisdom*, 127–67.

317. Strugnell and Harrington, DJD 34:27.

318. 4Q417 1 1:9; 4Q418 126 2:5. See Strugnell and Harrington (DJD 34:29): "especially to be noted [is] the *absence from 4Q415ff. of any trace of hypostatized Wisdom.*"

319. See Goff, *Wisdom*, 197–214.

320. Nickelsburg, *1 Enoch 1*, 58–59.

321. Ibid., 478–79.

322. Cf. 1 Enoch 1–5. See Tigchelaar, *To Increase Learning*, 182–84.

323. On the parallels between 4QInstruction and 1 Enoch and for different opinions on the relationship between the two works, see Elgvin, "The Reconstruction of Sapiential Work A," *RevQ* 16 (1993–95) 561; idem, "Mystery to Come," 146–47; Strugnell and Harrington, DJD 34:35; Loren T. Stuckenbruck, "4QInstruction and the Possible Influence of Early Enochic Traditions: An Evaluation," in Hempel, Lange, and Lichtenberger, eds., *Wisdom Texts*, 245–61; Tigchelaar, *To Increase Learning*, 212–17; Goff, *Wisdom*, 185–89.

324. See the discussion in Nickelsburg, *1 Enoch 1*, 58–61.

325. For a linguistic comparison of 4QInstruction with the larger Qumran corpus, see Strugnell and Harrington, DJD 34:22–31.

326. Tigchelaar, *To Increase Learning*, 194–203.

327. Strugnell and Harrington, DJD 34:21–22, 36.

328. See Tigchelaar, "Addressees," 62–75.

329. On the dating of the mss. see Strugnell and Harrington, DJD 34:42, 74–76, 144–47, 214–17, 476, 506–7, 535.

330. For a description of the scroll and an account of its unrolling, see Avigad and Yadin, *Genesis Apocryphon*, 12–26. For photographs of the scroll see Emanuel Tov, ed., *The Dead Sea*

Scrolls on Microfiche: A Comprehensive Facsimile Edition of the Texts from the Judean Desert (Leiden: Brill, 1993) microfiche 126. For the recoverable contents of the scroll before its renewed study see Joseph A. Fitzmyer, *The Genesis Apocryphon of Qumran Cave 1: A Commentary* (2d ed.; Rome: Biblical Institute Press, 1971) 48–75.

331. For a description of the rephotographing of the scroll and text and translation of the contents, see Morgenstern, Qimron, and Sivan, "Hitherto Unpublished Columns." My comments on these columns are based on this publication.

332. My analysis here summarizes my article "Patriarchs Who Worry about Their Wives: A Haggadic Tendency in the Genesis Apocryphon," in Michael E. Stone and Esther G. Chazon, eds., *Biblical Perspectives: Early Use and Interpretation of the Bible in Light of the Dead Sea Scrolls. Proceedings of the First International Symposium of the Orion Center for the Study of the Dead Sea Scrolls and Associated Literature, 12–14 May 1996* (STDJ 28; Leiden: Brill, 1998) 138–58, repr. in *GNP* 1:177–99. I also make use of the perceptive comments and criticisms by Eileen Schuller in *GNP* 1:200–212.

333. Nickelsburg, "Patriarchs," 138–41," repr. in *GNP* 1:178–82.

334. See the comments by Schuller in *GNP* 1:204–5.

335. Ibid., 205.

336. Nickelsburg, "Patriarchs," 141–44, repr. in *GNP* 1:181–84.

337. James C. VanderKam, "The Birth of Noah," in Zdzislaw J. Kapera, ed., *Intertestamental Essays in Honour of Jozef Tadeusz Milik* (Kraków: Enigma Press, 1992) 215–26; Nickelsburg, *1 Enoch 1*, 540, 543–44.

338. For this conclusion see Nickelsburg, "Patriarchs," 157–58, repr. in *GNP* 1:198–99, where I dispute the hypothesis that both 1 Enoch and the Apocryphon draw their material from a "Book of Noah."

339. See Richard C. Steiner, "The Heading of the *Book of the Words of Noah* on a Fragment of the Genesis Apocryphon: New Light on a 'Lost' Work," *DJD* 2 (1995) 66–71.

340. For a later but perhaps similar vision and its interpretation see 2 Bar. 36–40. In the Apocryphon see 19:14–17, where Abram is symbolized by a cedar tree. Perhaps it is not coincidental that in 1 Enoch, both Noah and Abraham are associated with the plant of righteousness; see Nickelsburg, *1 Enoch 1*, 220, 444–45.

341. Morgenstern, et al., "Columns," 32. Where the Book of Noah ended is uncertain. The order of Ham, Shem, Japheth in Jub. 9:1–13 suggests that Ham's division of his portion was recounted somewhere between 1QapGen 16:20 and 17:7. Thus the Book of Noah could have ended in the bottom half of col. 17. In Jubilees the narrative between the apportionment of the land and Abram's arrival at Bethel (when 1QapGen 19 picks up) covers ninety-four verses (10:1—13:4) and contains material about Noah, the tower of Babel, and Abram.

342. On "the problem of the length of the original 1QapGen scroll," see Schuller in *GNP* 1:209–11, esp. 210 n. 27.

343. Nickelsburg, "Patriarchs," 147, repr. in *GNP* 1:187.

344. On this text as an example of the genre *wasf* see Moshe H. Goshen-Gottstein, "Philologische Miszellen zu den Qumrantexten," *RevQ* 2 (1959–60) 46–48. On the poetry of the passage see James C. VanderKam, "The Poetry of 1Q Ap Gen, XX, 2–8a," *RevQ* 10 (1979) 57–66.

345. Nickelsburg, "Patriarchs," 147–49, repr. in *GNP* 1:167–90.

346. The expression "I, Abram," occurs in 20:11; 21:15. The first person runs from 19:7 to 21:21, where it is followed by eleven lines of biblical paraphrase. Only at l. 34 does Abram reenter as a character, and from there to the end of col. 22 he is mentioned in the third person. On the

change from first person to third person, also in the book of Tobit, see James E. Miller, "The Redaction of Tobit and the Genesis Apocryphon," *JSP* 8 (1991) 53–61.

347. On this dream, see B. Dehandschutter, "Le rêve dans l'Apocryphe de la Genèse," in W. C. van Unnik, ed., *La littérature juive entre Tenach et Mischna* (RechBib 9; Leiden: Brill, 1974) 48–55; Marianne Luijken Gevirtz, "Abram's Dream in the Genesis Apocryphon: Its Motifs and Their Function," *Maarav* 8 (1992) 229–43. For a parallel to the dream cf. T. Abr. 7; and see above, n. 340.

348. In the Prayer of Nabonidus, Daniel appears as an exorcist. In Dan 2 and 5 he is victorious in a contest with Chaldeans, sages, and magicians.

349. See Joseph A. Fitzmyer, *The Genesis Apocryphon of Qumran Cave 1 (1Q20): A Commentary* (3d ed.; BO 18B; Rome: Biblical Institute Press, 2004) 191.

350. See Nickelsburg, "Patriarchs," 150–52, repr. in *GNP* 1:190–92.

351. On the problem of the social setting of this element in the text see Nickelsburg, "Patriarchs," 151–53, repr. in *GNP* 1:192–93.

352. On the Apocryphon's possible dependence on Jubilees see Fitzmyer, *Genesis Apocryphon*, 20–21.

353. Moshe Bernstein, "Pseudepigraphy in the Qumran Scrolls: Categories and Functions," in Esther G. Chazon and Michael E. Stone, eds., *Pseudepigraphical Perspectives: The Apocrypha and Pseudepigrapha in Light of the Dead Sea Scrolls: Proceedings of the International Symposium of the Orion Center for the Study of the Dead Sea Scrolls and Associated Literature, 12–14 January 1997* (STDJ 31; Leiden: Brill, 1999) 15–17.

354. In the Enochic corpus, where the story of the watchers and the women predominates, there is scarcely any allusion to Gen 1–3.

355. See Nickelsburg, "Patriarchs," 152–54, repr. in *GNP* 1:192–95. See also the comments by Schuller, *GNP* 1:207, as well as her reference to James C. VanderKam, "The Granddaughters and Grandsons of Noah," *RevQ* 16 (1994) 457–61. On the arguments for and against Essene authorship, see Fitzmyer, *Genesis Apocryphon*, 22–25.

356. See Fitzmyer, *Genesis Apocryphon*, 29–37. See the discussion and opinions on date in ibid., 26–28.

357. For texts and translations of the various mss. see the bibliography. For a detailed discussion of the texts architectural descriptions, see Chyutin, *New Jerusalem Scroll*.

358. On the size of the city see Magen Broshi, "Visionary Architecture and Town Planning in the Dead Sea Scrolls," in Devorah Dimant and Lawrence H. Schiffman, eds., *Time to Prepare the Way in the Wilderness: Papers on the Qumran Scrolls* (STDJ 16; Leiden: Brill, 1995) 12.

359. For this summary in greater detail see Crawford, *Temple Scroll*, 69–73.

360. Ibid., 71.

361. García Martínez, "New Jerusalem," 609–10.

362. Crawford, *Temple Scroll*, 73.

363. Ibid.; García Martínez, "New Jerusalem," 608–9. For some uncertainty as to its genre see Collins, *Apocalypticism*, 59.

364. Crawford, *Temple Scroll*, 74–75; García Martínez, "New Jerusalem," 610.

365. García Martínez, "New Jerusalem," 606–7.

366. Ibid., 610; Crawford, *Temple Scroll*, 74.

367. García Martínez, "New Jerusalem," 610. Crawford (*Temple Scroll*, 75) suggests 200–100 B.C.E.

368. García Martínez, "New Jerusalem," 609–10.

6. ISRAEL IN EGYPT

1. On Elephantine and the papyri see Bezalel Porten, "Elephantine Papyri," *ABD* 2:445–55. On the story of Ahiqar see above, p. 347 n. 15.

2. Tcherikover and Fuks, *Corpus Papyrorum Judaicarum*.

3. For two summaries of the discussion see Tov, "Jewish-Greek Scriptures"; Peters, "Septuagint." For a more detailed treatment see Ulrich, *Dead Sea Scrolls and Origins*, 202–23. For a comprehensive introduction to the topic see Jobes and Silva, *Invitation*.

4. Jobes and Silva, *Invitation*, 29–37.

5. Ibid., 34.

6. Robert A. Kraft, "Greek Jewish Scriptures," in Jacob Neusner and Alan Avery-Peck, eds., *Dictionary of Religious Writings in Late Antiquity: Pagan, Judaic, Christian* (Leiden: Brill, forthcoming).

7. Tov, "Jewish-Greek Scriptures," 230–31; Peters, "Septuagint," 1097–1100; Jobes and Silva, *Invitation*, 37–42.

8. Ulrich, *Dead Sea Scrolls and Origins*, 34–50, 79–120.

9. Jobes and Silva, *Invitation*, 119–66.

10. Ibid., 86–102.

11. Ibid., 183–205.

12. Collins, *ABD* 6:2–6.

13. For a discussion of the time and place of origin of the books see Collins, "Development." On the date of the collection see ibid., 454; idem, *OTP* 1:467.

14. Collins, *Sibylline Oracles*, 24–25.

15. Collins, *OTP* 2:362.

16. Collins, *Sibylline Oracles*, 64–70.

17. See, however, Gruen, *Heritage and Hellenism*, 279–81, who is doubtful.

18. Collins, *Sibylline Oracles*, 80–87.

19. Ibid., 25–27.

20. Ibid., 57–62.

21. Collins, *OTP* 1:371 nn. u2, v2.

22. Collins, *Sibylline Oracles*, 27–28.

23. Ibid., 28.

24. On the similarities between this passage and Wis 5 see Nickelsburg, *Resurrection*, 92 n. 168. Note, however, the contrasting earthly and heavenly settings. On Wis 5 see below, pp. 207–8. On the temple in Sib. Or. 3 see Collins, *Sibylline Oracles*, 44–53; Andrew Chester, "The Sibyl and the Temple," in William Horbury, ed., *Templum Amicitiae: Essays on the Second Temple Presented to Ernst Bammel* (JSNTSup 48; Sheffield: Sheffield Academic Press, 1991) 39–47.

25. Collins, *Sibylline Oracles*, 37–44; idem, *Apocalyptic Imagination*, 95–98. This dating is disputed by Nikiprowetzky (*La Troisième Sibylle*), who argues for a unitary authorship for the book; by Gruen (*Heritage and Hellenism*, 271–83), who thinks the book is a conglomeration of material of diverse origins; and by Buitenwerf (*Book III of the Sibylline Oracles*). Here I have followed the response to these critiques by Collins, "Third Sibyl."

26. See Collins, *Sibylline Oracles*, 53–55; idem, "The Sibyl and the Potter: Political Propa-

ganda in Ptolemaic Egypt," in Lukas Bormann, Kelly del Tredici, and Angela Standhartinger, eds., *Religious Propaganda and Missionary Competition in the New Testament World: Essays Honoring Dieter Georgi* (Leiden: Brill, 1994) 57–69; Gruen, *Heritage and Hellenism*, 288–90; Collins, "Third Sibyl," 18–19.

27. For the historical problems relating to Demetrius see Hadas, *Aristeas*, 7–8.

28. Ibid., 28–32.

29. Ibid., 47–48.

30. Ibid., 121.

31. Ibid., 48–50.

32. Ibid., 42. Cf. also 1 Esdr 3:1—4:41.

33. Hadas, *Aristeas*, 40–43. On the place of God and the imitation of God in such treatises see Erwin R. Goodenough, "The Political Philosophy of Hellenistic Kingship," *YCS* 1 (1928) 65–72.

34. Hadas, *Aristeas*, 5–9.

35. See Elias Bickerman, "Zur Datierung des Pseudo-Aristeas," in idem, *Studies in Jewish and Christian History* (AGAJU 9; 3 vols.; Leiden: Brill, 1976) 1:123–36; Hadas, *Aristeas*, 54; Goldstein, "Message," 8–18.

36. M. A. L. Beavis ("Anti-Egyptian Polemic in the Letter of Aristeas 130–165 [The High Priest's Discourse]," *JSJ* 18 [1987] 145–51) argues that the author distinguishes between educated Egyptian Greeks and animal-worshiping Egyptians.

37. Hadas, *Aristeas*, 54–59.

38. See ibid., 59–66; Goldstein, "Message," 18. Tcherikover ("Ideology") stresses the book's duality. Jews are to remain Jews, but they are to seek to participate in Greek culture. See also Carl R. Holladay, "Jewish Responses to Hellenistic Culture in Early Ptolemaic Egypt," in Per Bilde, et al., eds., *Ethnicity in Hellenistic Egypt* (Studies in Hellenistic Civilization 3; Aarhus: Aarhus Univ. Press, 1991) 148–49.

39. Hadas, *Aristeas*, 66–84.

40. In addition to its abrupt beginning see 2:25, which presumes a part of the text now missing; see Hadas, *Maccabees*, 4–5.

41. Tcherikover ("Maccabees," 2–3) suggests dependence on a Ptolemaic historian.

42. On the parallels see Tromp, "Formation," 311–28.

43. On the background of this detail see ibid., 3–5.

44. On the historical problems relating to this legend see Hadas, *Maccabees*, 10–11; Tcherikover, "Maccabees," 6–8; Tromp, "Formation."

45. Nickelsburg, *Resurrection*, 90–92.

46. Tcherikover, "Maccabees," 1–2.

47. See the detailed analysis by Cousland, "Reversal," 39–51.

48. For the comic elements in 3 Maccabees and esp. its description of Ptolemy, see Wills, *Jewish Novel*, 204; Gruen, *Heritage and Hellenism*, 232–34.

49. Tcherikover, "Maccabees," 25–26.

50. Gruen, *Heritage and Hellenism*, 222–36.

51. For some alternatives see Cousland, "Reversal," 40–42.

52. See also the conclusion of Cousland, ibid., 51.

53. See the detailed argument of Tcherikover, "Maccabees," 11–18. See also Parente, "Maccabees," 177.

54. Collins, *Between Athens and Jerusalem*, 106–11. For a critique see Parente, "Maccabees," 175–77.

55. Bacchisio Motzo, "Il Rifacimento Greco di Ester e il III Mac.," in idem, *Saggi di Storia e Letteratura Giudeo-Ellenistica* (CScA 5; Florence: Le Monier, 1924) 272–90. See also Carey A. Moore, "On the Origins of the LXX Additions to the Book of Esther," *JBL* 92 (1973) 384–85, evidently independently of Motzo. Winston (*Wisdom*, 24 n. 34) thinks that Motzo's arguments for the direction of dependence were based on his dating of 3 Maccabees. The arguments, however, seem to be literary. Parente ("Maccabees," 156–57, 168, esp. n. 79) is dismissive of Motzo and Moore, and offers little evidence to support his claim. For a couple of points to support the dependence of Greek Esther on 3 Maccabees, see below, pp. 203–5.

56. Hadas, *Maccabees*, 8–10.

57. See ibid., 11–12.

58. For these parallels and similarities see Nickelsburg, *Resurrection*, 90–91, esp. nn. 157–66.

59. On the secondary character of these passages see Moore, *Additions*, 153–54. On the religious dimension see ibid., 153; Crawford, "Additions," 945–50.

60. See the literature cited in Crawford, "Additions," 155.

61. E. J. Bickerman, "The Colophon of the Greek Book of Esther,'" *JBL* 63 (1944) 339–62; but see Moore (*Additions*, 250) for a dating in the reign of Ptolemy IX, ca. 114 B.C.E.

62. Crawford, "Additions," 948. On Mordecai in the tradition of Joseph and Daniel see Nickelsburg, *Resurrection*, 50–51.

63. Crawford, "Additions," 948–49.

64. Ibid., 969; and see the discussion of the Thanksgiving Hymns and the War Scroll above, pp. 136, 145.

65. For other details of the relationship of this chapter to the Hebrew see Crawford, "Additions," 950–51.

66. For a similar use of documents see above, p. 196, regarding Aristeas; and see Moore, *Additions*, 191; Crawford, "Additions," 953.

67. Comparisons with 3 Maccabees are based on Motzo, "Rifacimento," 275–80.

68. Crawford, "Additions," 956. On this and other elements in similar prayers see Nickelsburg, *1 Enoch 1*, 205–6.

69. See the brief but excellent exposition by Crawford, "Additions," 959.

70. Nickelsburg, *1 Enoch 1*, 256.

71. For the difference between the two Esthers in the Hebrew and Greek texts, see Crawford, "Additions," 962. The calm and courageous queen becomes "a delicate Victorian."

72. Nickelsburg, *Resurrection*, 50–51.

73. Motzo, "Rifacimento," 287–90.

74. See Richard J. Clifford, "Proverbs as a Source for Wisdom of Solomon," in Calduch-Benages and Vermeylen, *Treasures of Wisdom*; Larcher, *Études*, 179–261; John J. Collins, "Cosmos and Salvation: Jewish Wisdom and Apocalyptic in the Hellenistic Age," *HR* 17 (1977) 128–34; Shannon Burkes, "Wisdom and Apocalyptic in the Wisdom of Solomon," *HTR* 95 (2002) 21–44; Dieter Georgi, "Das Wesen der Weisheit nach der 'Weisheit Salomos,'" in Jacob Taubes, ed., *Gnosis und Politik* (Munich: W. Fink, 1984) 66–91.

75. James M. Reese, "Plan and Structure in the Book of Wisdom," *CBQ* 27 (1965) 391–99; Addison G. Wright, "The Structure of Wisdom 11–19," *CBQ* 27 (1965) 28–34; idem, "Numerical Patterns in the Book of Wisdom," *CBQ* 29 (1967) 524–38; idem, "The Structure of the Book of Wisdom," *Bib* 48 (1967) 165–84; Maurice Gilbert, "La structure de la prière de Salomon (Sg 9)," *Bib* 51 (1970) 301–31; idem, *Critique;* idem, "Wisdom Literature," 301–6. Scholars debate

the precise genre of the text, however. On the problem see Collins, *Jewish Wisdom*, 181–82. For Reese, especially (*Influence*, 117–21), Wisdom is a protreptic, a treatise that made "an appeal to follow a meaningful philosophy as a way of life." So also Winston, *Wisdom*, 18–20. For Gilbert ("Wisdom Literature," 306–9) it is an encomium, a text that demonstrates and praises the glories of Wisdom, rather than appealing to one to seek and follow it.

76. On the unity of the three parts of the Wisdom of Solomon see Gilbert, "Wisdom Literature," 306–9; Devorah Dimant, "Pseudonymity in the Wisdom of Solomon," in Natalio Fernán-dez Marcos, ed., *La Septuaginta en la Investigacion Contemporanea* (V Congress of the IOSCS) (Madrid: Biblia Poliglota Matritense Instituto, 1985); Collins, *Jewish Wisdom*, 180–81.

77. See Frederic Raurell, "From *Dikaiōsynē* to *Athanasia* (Wis 1,1.15)," in Calduch-Benages and Vermeylen, eds., *Treasures of Wisdom*, 330–49.

78. See Kolarcik, *Ambiguity*; Karina Martin Hogan, "The Exegetical Background of the 'Ambiguity of Death' in the Wisdom of Solomon," *JSJ* 30 (1999) 1–24; A. P. Hayman, "The Survival of Mythology in the Wisdom of Solomon," *JSJ* 30 (1999) 125–39.

79. Nickelsburg, *Resurrection*, 58–62.

80. For a slightly different literary organization that sees 3:1—4:19 as a single unit at the center of chaps. 1–6, see Pancratius C. Beentjes, "Wisdom of Solomon 3,1–4,19 and the Book of Isaiah," in J. Van Ruiten and M. Vervenne, eds., *Studies in the Book of Isaiah*, FS Willem A. M. Beuken (BETL 132; Leuven: Leuven Univ. Press and Peeters, 1997) 413–20. See also Collins, *Jewish Wisdom*, 182; Gilbert, "Wisdom Literature," 302.

81. On death and immortality in the Wisdom of Solomon see John J. Collins, "The Root of Immortality: Death in the Context of Jewish Wisdom," *HTR* 71 (1978) 186–92; idem, *Jewish Wisdom*, 185–90.

82. Clifford, "Proverbs," 256–59.

83. See Robert J. Miller, "Immortality and Religious Identity in Wisdom 2–5," in Elizabeth A. Castelli and Hal Taussig, eds., *Reimagining Christian Origins: A Colloquium Honoring Burton L. Mack* (Valley Forge, Pa.: Trinity International, 1996) 199–213. For a discussion of this section of Wisdom in relation to Job and Qohelet, see Vittoria d'Alario, "La Réflexion sur le sens de la vie en SG 1–6: Une réponse aux questions de Job et de Qohélet," in Calduch-Benages and Vermeylen, eds., *Treasures of Wisdom*, 313–29. See also Michael Kolarcik, "Universalism and Justice in the Wisdom of Solomon," in Calduch-Benages and Vermeylen, eds., *Treasures of Wisdom*, 288–301.

84. See above, n. 74.

85. Nickelsburg, *Resurrection*, 128–29.

86. Ibid., 62–82; see also Lothar Ruppert, *Der Leidende Gerechte* (FB 5; Würzburg: Echter Verlag, 1972) 70–105.

87. Nickelsburg, *Resurrection*, 62; David Seeley, "Transumptive Narration and the Structure of Wisdom 1–5," *SBLSP* 27 (1988) 245–48.

88. Beentjes, "Wisdom of Solomon."

89. On Wisdom in the Wisdom of Solomon, with some comparison with Qumran, see David Winston, "Wisdom in the Wisdom of Solomon," in Leo G. Perdue, Bernard B. Scott, and William J. Wiseman, eds., *In Search of Wisdom: Essays in Memory of John G. Gammie* (Louisville: Westminster John Knox, 1993) 149–64.

90. On the persona of Solomon in this book see Dimant, "Pseudonymity." On the king and wisdom, as the motif may reflect the book of Proverbs, see Clifford, "Proverbs," 261–62. On the "mystical" quest for Wisdom (and its similarities to Philo's religion, see below, pp. 216–17), see

David Winston, "The Sage as Mystic in the Wisdom of Solomon," in John G. Gammie and Leo G. Perdue, eds., *The Sage in Israel and the Ancient Near East* (Winona Lake, Ind.: Eisenbrauns, 1990) 383–97.

91. Michael E. Stone, "List of Revealed Things in the Apocalyptic Literature," in Frank Moore Cross, et al., eds., *Magnalia Dei: The Mighty Acts of God,* FS G. Ernest Wright (Garden City, N.Y.: Doubleday, 1976) 436–37.

92. See Winston, *Wisdom,* 198–99; Collins, *Jewish Wisdom,* 185–86.

93. On the sophisticated structure of this prayer see Gilbert, "Structure."

94. See Winston, *Wisdom,* 31–32, 42.

95. See Reese, *Influence,* 46–49; Burton L. Mack, *Logos und Sophia* (SUNT 10; Göttingen: Vandenhoeck & Ruprecht, 1973) 90–95; and Luca Mazzinghi, "La Sapienzia, presente accanto a Dio e all' Uomo: Sap 9,9b, 10c e la Figura di Iside," in Calduch-Benages and Vermeylen, eds., *Treasures of Wisdom,* 357–67.

96. See Winston, *Wisdom,* 182; Collins, "Cosmos," 133.

97. See Collins, "Cosmos," 125–28.

98. See Reese, *Influence,* 98–102; Winston, *Wisdom,* 227.

99. On this motif in Wisdom and the book of Proverbs, see Clifford, "Proverbs," 259–61.

100. See Gilbert, *Critique,* esp. pp. 252–57.

101. On the exodus in Wisdom see Cheon, *Exodus Story.*

102. On Wisdom of Solomon and Philo see Winston, *Wisdom,* 59–63.

103. Ibid., 22–23.

104. For a survey of proposed dates between 220 B.C.E. and 50 C.E. see ibid., 20–25, which argues for the date in Caligula's reign. Collins (*Jewish Wisdom,* 178–79) suggests a date between 30 B.C.E. and 70 C.E.

105. Miller, "Immortality."

106. See Jack T. Sanders, "When Sacred Canopies Collide: The Reception of the Torah of Moses in the Wisdom Literature of the Second Temple Period," *JSJ* 32 (2001) 121–36. See above, pp. 53, 62.

107. See Larcher, *Études,* 11–84; William Horbury, "The Wisdom of Solomon in the Muratorian Fragment," *JTS* n.s. 45 (1994) 149–59; idem, "The Christian Use and the Jewish Origins of the Wisdom of Solomon," in John Day, Robert P. Gordon, and H. G. M. Williamson, eds., *Wisdom in Ancient Israel: Essays in Honour of J. A. Emerton* (Cambridge: Cambridge Univ. Press, 1995) 182–96.

108. This section is an abridged form of my paper "Philo among Greeks, Jews, and Christians," in Roland Deines and Karl-Wilhelm Niebuhr, eds., *Philo and the New Testament: Wechselseitige Wahrnehmungen: I. Internationales Symposium zum Corpus Judeo-Hellenisticum Novi Testamenti: 1.–4. Mai 2003, Eisenach/Jena* (WUNT 172; Tübingen: Mohr Siebeck, 2004), 53–72, used here with kind permission of Mohr Siebeck.

109. To these two one might add Joshua ben Sira (see above, pp. 53–54). We know a few other names like Aristobulus, Artapanus, Eupolemus, Ezekiel the tragedian, and Philo the epic poet, but possess only fragments of their writings. For a summary of what we know about Philo and his family see Jenny Morris, "The Jewish Philosopher Philo," in Schürer, *History,* 3/2:813–17.

110. For Alexander's decoration of the temple gates see Josephus, *J.W.* 5.205 (§5.3). Actually, Alexander refused the loan to Agrippa, but granted it to his wife, Cypros (Josephus, *Ant.* 18.159–60 [§6.3]).

111. On Tiberius Julius Alexander see Morris, "Philo," 815 n. 14.

112. The precise number in the database of the Philo Concordance Project is 437,433 words, cited by Kåre Fuglseth, in a private communication, June 2003. This does not include works preserved in Armenian, on which see Morris, "Philo," 820–21 n. 33.

113. For a list of Philo's lost works, see Morris, "Philo," 868.

114. The paraphrase includes *On the Creation of the World; On the Life of Abraham; On the Life of Joseph; On the Decalogue; On the Special Laws; On the Virtues; On Rewards and Punishments. On the Life of Moses* appears to have been a companion treatise to these.

115. *Questions and Answers on Genesis, Questions and Answers on Exodus,* on which see Morris, "Philo," 826–30.

116. This group consists of nineteen treatises named after episodes in the Genesis account. On these see ibid., 830–53.

117. For his citations of the prophets as oracles of God see *Cher.* 49; *Plant.* 38; *Conf.* 44; *Flight* 197; *Names* 139, 169; *Dreams* 2.172.

118. On these works see Morris, "Philo," 856, 858–59, 864–66.

119. Ibid., 856–58. For Philo's possible time with the Theraputae see Erwin W. Goodenough, *An Introduction to Philo Judaeus* (2d ed.; New York: Barnes & Noble, 1962) 31–32; cf. *Spec. Laws* 3.1–6.

120. On the problems relating to this work see Morris, "Philo," 866–68.

121. On the problems relating to these works see ibid., 859–64.

122. On the problems of historical reconstruction see ibid.; Goodenough, *Introduction,* 58–60.

123. On Philo's education and knowledge of Greek culture see M. Alexandre, "La culture profane chez Philon," in *Philon d'Alexandrie: Lyon 11–15 Septembre 1966: Colloques nationaux du Centre National de la Recherche Scientifique* (Paris: Éditions du Centre national de la recherche scientifique, 1967) 105–29.

124. Harry A. Wolfson, *Philo* (2 vols.; Cambridge: Harvard Univ. Press, 1962) 1:307.

125. Ibid., 1:111–13.

126. On the *Logos* in Philo see Goodenough, *Introduction,* 100–110.

127. Peder Borgen, "Philo of Alexandria," *ABD* 5:339–40.

128. Philo's mysticism was worked out first by Goodenough, *By Light, Light.* For a summary see idem, *Introduction,* 134–60.

129. Goodenough, *Introduction,* 7.

130. In this respect, he was in a real sense a spiritual forebear of Moses Mendelssohn, the Jewish sage who was also a respected man of letters and a philosopher of the Enlightenment. On Mendelssohn see Amos Elon, *The Pity of It All: A History of Jews in Germany 1743–1933* (New York: Holt, 2002) 33–55, 60–66.

131. See Elisabeth Kübler-Ross, *On Death and Dying* (London: Tavistock, 1970). For two other examples of Philo's psychological and political insights, see Nickelsburg, "Philo," 62. On Philo and politics see Goodenough, *Politics of Philo,* 1–128; and more briefly idem, *Introduction,* 52–74.

132. On Philo's generally negative view toward women, see Judith Romney Wegner, "The Image of Woman in Philo," *SBLSP* 21 (1982) 551–63; D. Sly, "The Plight of Woman: Philo's Blind Spot?" in Wendy E. Helleman, ed., *Hellenization Revisited: Shaping a Christian Response with the Greco-Roman World* (Lanham, Md.: Univ. Press of America, 1994) 174–88.

133. Borgen, "Philo of Alexandria," 335.

134. On rabbinical hermeneutics see H. L. Strack and Günther Stemberger, *Introduction to the Talmud and Midrash* (repr. Minneapolis: Fortress Press, 1996) 15–30.

135. Ibid., 233–359.

136. I. Heinemann, "Die Allegoristik der hellenistischen Juden ausser Philon," *Mnem* 5 (1952) 133–35; David Dawson, *Allegorical Readers and Cultural Revision in Ancient Alexandria* (Berkeley: Univ. of California Press, 1992) 74–82.

137. For two overviews see David T. Runia, *Philo in Early Christian Literature: A Survey* (CRINT 3/3; Assen: Van Gorcum; Minneapolis: Fortress Press, 1993) 63–86; Gregory E. Sterling, "Philo and the New Testament," in Deines and Niebuhr, eds., *Philo and the New Testament*, 21–52.

138. Runia, *Philo*, 66–74.

139. Ibid., 132–56.

140. Ibid., 157–83.

141. Ibid., 212–34.

142. Ibid., 13–15.

143. Ibid., 344–47.

144. See the summary by Francis I. Andersen (*OTP* 1:93–94), who notes that there is actually a third text form and that the textual relationships between the short and longer recensions are complex. See also Orlov, *Enoch–Metatron Tradition*, 225–26.

145. My authority for the short recension is the translation by Andersen, *OTP* 1:102–221.

146. Cf. 2 Enoch 1–2 with 1 Enoch 12:1–3.

147. The type of comment made by Enoch in 2 Enoch 8:8 and 10:4 (wonderment rather than question) corresponds to 1 Enoch 21:8; 22:2; and 24:5; and the double question in 2 Enoch 18:2 parallels 1 Enoch 21:4.

148. On Enoch's intercession for the angels (2 Enoch 7:4–5) cf. 1 Enoch 15:2.

149. On the parallels between these lists, see Ulrich Fischer, *Eschatologie und Jenseitserwartung in hellenistischen Diasporajudentum* (BZNW 44; Berlin: de Gruyter, 1978) 48–49.

150. The long recension makes perfunctory reference to an eighth and ninth heaven and places the throne room in the tenth heaven (21:6—22:1a).

151. Orlov, *Enoch–Metatron Tradition*, 155–56.

152. See ibid., 283–85, 289–91.

153. There seems to be some contradiction between 1 Enoch 14:21 and 22–24; see Nickelsburg, *1 Enoch 1*, 264. However, there is a major difference between "come here" in 1 Enoch 15:1 and the extensive description in 2 Enoch 22.

154. Orlov, *Enoch Metatron Tradition*, 203–7. Cf. 1 Enoch 14:1; 15:1.

155. Orlov, *Enoch–Metatron Tradition*, 188–200.

156. See Marc Philonenko, "La Cosmogonie du 'Livre des Secrets d'Hénoch,'" in *Religions en Égypte hellénistique et romaine* (Paris: Presses Universitaires de France, 1969) 113–16; Shlomo Pines, "Eschatology and the Concept of Time in the Slavonic Book of Enoch," in R. J. Z. Werblowsky and C. J. Bleeker, eds., *Types of Redemption* (NumenSup 18; Leiden: Brill, 1970) 75–82.

157. Orlov, *Enoch–Metatron Tradition*, 239–44.

158. See Vaillant, *Hénoch*, 37 nn. 17–19.

159. See esp. the Aramaic of 1 Enoch 93:2 (4QEn^g 1 3:22; J. T. Milik, *The Books of Enoch: Aramaic Fragments from Qumran* [Oxford: Clarendon, 1976] 264).

160. For this interpretation see Orlov, *Enoch–Metatron Tradition*, 59–61, 216–19.

161. Cf., e.g., 2 Enoch 50:4 with 1 Enoch 95:5; 2 Enoch 50:5 with 1 Enoch 94:8; 2 Enoch 53:1-3 with 1 Enoch 98:7-8; and 2 Enoch 53:4—54:1 with 1 Enoch 104:12—105:2.

162. See John J. Collins, "The Genre Apocalypse in Hellenistic Judaism," in David Hellholm,

ed., *Apocalypticism in the Mediterranean World and the Near East: Proceedings of the International Colloquium on Apocalypticism, Uppsala, August 12–17, 1979* (Tübingen: Mohr Siebeck, 1983) 536.

163. For details see Fischer, *Eschatologie*, 53–62; see also John J. Collins, *The Apocalyptic Imagination* (New York: Crossroad, 1984) 198.

164. Continuity is an issue of concern in some other testamentary works; cf. T. Mos. 11:9-19; 2 Bar. 31–33; 44–46; 77; 4 Ezra 12:40-50.

165. Orlov, *Enoch-Metatron Tradition*, 304–33.

166. Ibid., 313–17, 328–29.

167. Ibid., 254–303.

168. Ibid., 232–34, 248–52.

169. Ibid., 207–8. For a translation of 3 Enoch see Philip Alexander, "3 (Hebrew Apocalypse of) Enoch," in *OTP* 1:223–315.

170. See Charles, *APOT* 2:426; Philonenko, "Cosmogonie," 113–16; Fischer, *Eschatologie*, 40–41.

171. The date is asserted by Gershom Scholem (*Ursprung und Anfänge der Kabbala* [Studia Judaica 3; Berlin: de Gruyter, 1962] 64), who is followed by Jonas C. Greenfield ("Prolegomenon," in Hugh Odeberg, *3 Enoch* [repr. New York: KTAV, 1973] xviii) and by Fischer (*Eschatologie*, 40–41).

172. Orlov, *Enoch-Metatron Tradition*, 327. See also Pines, "Eschatology," 74–75.

173. See Vaillant, *Hénoch*, xi–xiii; Pines, "Eschatology," 73. Andersen (*OTP* 1:94) is cautious about the possibility that some Semitic written material may stand behind the Greek.

174. On the alleged Christian origin of 2 Enoch see Arie Rubinstein, "Observations on the Slavonic Book of Enoch," *JJS* 13 (1962) 3–4, 10–15. See also Milik, *Books of Enoch*, 107–12. For an argument in favor the Christian authorship of the Melchizedek story see Beverly A. Bow, "Melchizedek's Birth Narrative in 2 Enoch 68–73: Christian Correlations," in Randall A. Argall, Beverly A. Bow, and Rodney A. Werline, eds., *For a Later Generation: The Transformation of Tradition in Israel, Early Judaism, and Early Christianity*, FS G. W. E. Nickelsburg (Harrisburg: Trinity International, 2000) 33–41. For a refutation of Milik's arguments, see the review of Milik by Rainer Stichel in *Byzantinoslavica* 39 (1978) 65. In refutation of the proposal that 2 Enoch is "a specimen of Bogomil propaganda," composed in Slavonic between the twelfth and fifteenth centuries, see Orlov, *Enoch-Metatron Tradition*, 324. On the Bogomils, a medieval dualistic Christian sect, see below, p. 409 n. 140. On the Jewish authorship of 2 Enoch see Greenfield, "Prolegomena," xviii–xxi; Collins, *Apocalyptic Imagination*, 195.

7. THE ROMANS AND THE HOUSE OF HEROD

1. Josephus portrays Hyrcanus as weak and irresolute. For another side of his personality, see VanderKam, *From Joshua to Caiaphas*, 385.

2. Erich Gruen (private communication, May 2004) notes that "Judaea was not made a province, [there were] no troops, administrators, or direct rule. Yielding up the title of king may have been a concession to the third party of Jews who wanted no monarchy; it need not represent a Roman imposition."

3. Ibid.

4. Roller, *Building Program*, 85–238; Netzer, *Palaces*.

5. Roller, *Building Program*, 54–65.

6. According to Mark 6:17 Herodias was first married to Antipas's brother Philip, presumably the tetrarch. Josephus indicates, however, that Herodias's first husband was Herod, the son of Herod the Great, and that Philip the Tetrarch was married to Salome, the daughter of Herod and Herodias; see Schürer, *History*, 1:344.

7. On the difficulties of dating this census see ibid., 399–427.

8. My versification follows the editions of Wright and Brock. The alternate versification in parentheses and brackets denotes the edition of Gray.

9. Johannes Tromp ("The Sinners and the Lawless in Psalm of Solomon 17," *NovT* 35 [1993] 356) argues that the sinners in vv 5–6 (6–7) are the Romans, but this does not fit the claim that they set up a kingdom. See also Kenneth Atkinson, "Herod the Great, Sosius, and the Siege of Jerusalem (37 B.C.E.) in Psalm of Solomon 17," *NovT* 38 (1996) 315; idem, "On the Herodian Origin of Militant Davidic Messianism at Qumran: New Light from *Psalm of Solomon* 17," *JBL* 118 (1999) 440–41.

10. Atkinson, "Herod the Great" (see also the literature cited in ibid., 314 n. 3); idem, "Herodian Origin," 442–44.

11. On the translation of these tenses see Tromp, "Sinners," 347; Atkinson, "Herod the Great," 315–16.

12. It is a matter of dispute to what extent Herod's Idumean ancestry was an issue in his own time. See Richardson, *Herod*, 54–62; Atkinson, "Herodian Origin," 443 n. 22.

13. All mss. read "the anointed, the Lord." Robert R. Hann ("Christos Kyrios in PsSol 17:32: 'The Lord's Anointed' Reconsidered," *NTS* 31 [1985] 620–27) argues that this text is correct. However, for this reading as a mistranslation of the original Hebrew, "the Anointed of the Lord," see Marinus de Jonge, "The Expectation of the Future in the Psalms of Solomon," in idem, *Jewish Eschatology, Early Christian Christology and the Testaments of the Twelve Patriarchs: Collected Essays of Marinus de Jonge* (NovTSup 63: Leiden: Brill, 1991) 14–15.

14. This is the case here whether that figure be Pompey or Herod. Cf., e.g., Ps 2; the Parables of Enoch, on which see below, pp. 248–56, where the opponents of the Son of Man/Anointed One are "the kings and the mighty"; 4 Ezra 11–12.

15. Atkinson, "Herodian Origin," 444. In *I Cried to the Lord*, 139, he pushed the date back to before 40–37 B.C.E.

16. This notion is reminiscent of a saying of Jesus (Matt 6:25–33||Luke12:22–32), and the parallel between Pseudo-Solomon's reference to "kings and rulers" and Jesus' citation of Solomon is especially noteworthy.

17. P. N. Franklyn ("The Cultic and Pious Climax of Eschatology in the Psalms of Solomon," *JSJ* 18 [1987] 3 n. 7) places this psalm among the Psalms of the Nation, noting that it does not mention the polarization of the sinners against the pious (my criterion). However, its parallel to Ps 6, which he places among the Psalms of the Individual, is striking. Moreover, Ps 5, which he places among the Psalms of the Individual, has no polarizing reference to the sinners.

18. See the summary in Atkinson, *I Cried to the Lord*, 5–6.

19. Jerry O'Dell, "The Religious Background of the Psalms of Solomon," *RevQ* 3 (1961) 241–59; Robert B. Wright, "The Psalms of Solomon, the Pharisees, and the Essenes," in Robert A. Kraft, ed., *1972 Proceedings IOSCS Pseudepigrapha* (SBLSCS 2; Society of Biblical Literature, 1972) 136–54; Robert R. Hann, "The Community of the Pious: The Social Setting of the Psalms of Solomon," *SR* 17 (1988) 184–89; Ernest-Marie Laperrousaz, "Le milieu d'origine du 17e Psaulmes (apocryphes) de Salomon," *REJ* 150 (1991) 557–64.

20. Franklyn, "Cultic and Pious Climax," 17; Atkinson, *I Cried to the Lord*, 8, 220–22.

21. See also the frequent use of *hosios*, 2:36 (40); 3:8 (10); 4:6 (7), 8 (9); 8:23 (28), 34 (40); 9:3 (6); 10:6 (7); 12:4 (5), 6 (7); 13:10 (9), 12 (11); 14:3 (2), 10 (7); 15:3 (5), 7 (9).

22. For the problem of identifying these people with a group called the Hasidim, however, see Nickelsburg, *Ancient Judaism*, 176–78. For a detailed profile of the community, see Hann, "Community." On the setting of the Psalms in communal worship, see Atkinson, *I Cried to the Lord*, 211–18.

23. See Atkinson, *I Cried to the Lord*, 211, 218–20.

24. Multiple authorship is presumed in ibid., 1–2, 212–20. For an attempt to discover redactional levels in the psalms, see Schüpphaus, *Psalmen Salomos*. See, however, Atkinson, *I Cried to the Lord*, 138, on 17:11–20.

25. Some of the psalms of the righteous and pious could very well antedate the time of Pompey.

26. For some problems with the scheme presented by Franklyn ("Cultic and Pious Climax") see, e.g., above, n. 17.

27. Trafton (*Syriac Version*, 187–206) argues that both the Greek and the Syriac go back to a Hebrew original.

28. For an example of the historicizing of an apocalyptic tradition about Antiochus's judgment see Nickelsburg, *Resurrection*, 79–80.

29. It is possible that most of chap. 6 is a revision of materials that originally described Antiochus rather than a wholesale interpolation; see Jonathan A. Goldstein, "The Testament of Moses: Its Content, Its Origin, and Its Attestation in Josephus," in George W. E. Nickelsburg, ed., *Studies on the Testament of Moses* (SBLSCS 3; Cambridge: Society of Biblical Literature, 1973) 45–47.

30. For this expression see E.-M. Laperrousaz, "Le Testament de Moïse," *Sem* 19 (1970) 122.

31. On the Testament of Moses as an interpretation of Deuteronomy see above, p. 75.

32. Adela Yarbro Collins, "Composition and Redaction."

33. For a detailed discussion of the place of the revised Testament in the time after Varus's campaign see the articles by John J. Collins in Nickelsburg, ed., *Studies on the Testament of Moses*, 28–30, 38–39.

34. See R. H. Charles, *The Book of Enoch* (Oxford: Clarendon, 1912) 66, for some significant differences from the rest of 1 Enoch. For chaps. 37–71 as a late addition to an earlier collection see above, pp. 114–15.

35. Cf. Isa 14:4; Mic 2:4; Hab 2:6; Num 23:7, 18; 24:3, 15, 20, 21, 23. See above, p. 47, for the dependence of 1 Enoch 1:2–3 on the Balaam oracles.

36. The title "book of parables" occurs in 68:1, a later addition to the work.

37. E.g., 99:4–5; 100:1–6; 102:1–3.

38. The phrasing of the title may derive from Num 16:22; cf. also 2 Macc 3:24.

39. The unqualified term appears in 1 Enoch 62:7 and 69:27.

40. See Maurice Casey, "The Use of Term 'Son of Man' in the Similitudes of Enoch," *JSJ* 7 (1976) 11–29.

41. See Collins, "Heavenly Representative," 111–33.

42. Cf. the parallelism between chaps. 53 and 54 and cf. 55:4.

43. Some mss. read "righteousness" for "the Righteous One," but cf. 52:9.

44. According to Charles (*APOT* 2:210), 39:1–2 is an interpolation. The parallel with the

early chapters of 1 Enoch suggests rather that the last line of 39:2 is a displaced variant from the end of 38:6.

45. Nickelsburg, *Resurrection*, 74–75.

46. Cf. 7:6; 8:4; 9:1–11; 10:1–22; 89:69–71, 76–77; 90:14, 17; 97:5; 99:3; 104:1.

47. Nickelsburg, *Resurrection*, 74 n. 102; in greater detail, Theisohn, *Richter*, 119–21.

48. See above, pp. 57–59.

49. See Dieter Georgi, "Der vorpaulinische Hymnus Phil. 2:6–11," in Erich Dinkler, ed., *Zeit und Geschichte*, FS R. Bultmann (Tübingen: Mohr Siebeck, 1964) 277–78.

50. Theisohn, *Richter*, 55–59.

51. Suter (*Tradition and Composition*, 45–49) believes that 54:6; 54:7—55:2; 55:3—56:4 constitute an a-b-a' unit that is a midrash on Isa 24:17–18, 19–20, 21–23, in which he also detects an a-b-a' structure. The similarity is noteworthy, but his argument ignores the fact that 53:1–7 and 54:2 locate the punishment of the kings in the mighty in a different place from that of the hosts of Azazel. See also the critique by Walck, "Son of Man," 51–53.

52. Jonas C. Greenfield and Michael E. Stone, "The Enochic Pentateuch and the Date of the Similitudes," *HTR* 70 (1977) 58; Walck, "Son of Man," 33–36.

53. See below, p. 253, on 68:1.

54. For details see Nickelsburg, *Resurrection*, 70–74.

55. Ibid., 72.

56. In 64:1–2; 65:1—67:3; 67:4—68:1, as in 54:1—56:4, Suter (*Tradition*, 49–52) sees an a-b-a' midrash on Isa 24:17–23. The two-verse, eighteen-verse, eleven-verse components seem out of balance. See also Walck, "Son of Man," 53–54.

57. Josephus, *Ant.* 17.168–72 (§6.5). See Greenfield and Stone, "Pentateuch," 60; Walck, "Son of Man," 36–38. See, however, Suter, *Tradition*, 24.

58. On this passage see Michael A. Knibb, "The Translation of 1 Enoch 70:1: Some Methodological Issues," in Ada Rapoport-Albert and Gilliam Greenberg, eds., *Biblical Hebrews, Biblical Texts: Essays in Memory of Michael P. Weitzman* (JSOTSup 333; Sheffield: Sheffield Univ. Press, 2001) 340–54.

59. For a summary of the various interpretations of chap. 71 and its relationship to chaps. 37–70, see Walck, "Son of Man," 221–46.

60. John J. Collins, "The Jewish Apocalypses," *Semeia* 14 (1979) 39–40.

61. Collins, "Heavenly Representative," 124–25; Pieter G. R. de Villiers, "Revealing the Secrets: Wisdom and the World in the Similitudes of Enoch," *Neot* 17 (1983) 50–68.

62. Milik (*The Books of Enoch* [Oxford: Clarendon, 1976] 91–98) dates the work ca. 270 C.E. For a critique see Greenfield and Stone, "Enochic Pentateuch"; and the review of Milik by the present writer in *CBQ* 40 (1978) 417–18. Knibb ("Date of the Parables") disputes Milik at many points but finds the silence of Qumran significant and accepts a date near 100 C.E. For a summary of various proposals see Walck, "Son of Man," 20–39.

63. See above, n. 62.

64. See Suter, *Tradition*, 174 n. 57.

65. This section summarizes Nickelsburg, "Son of Man," 142–49.

66. David R. Catchpole, "The Poor on Earth and the Son of Man in Heaven: A Re-appraisal of Matthew xxv.31–46," *BJRL* 61 (1979) 378–83.

67. For Matthew's knowledge of the Enochic Son of Man traditions see Theisohn, *Richter*, 161–201. Walck ("Son of Man," 257–380) is a bit more hesitant.

68. Milik, *Books of Enoch*, 91–92. John Collins ("Heavenly Representative," 126) suggests that

the parables' identification of that son of man with Enoch may be a Jewish response to Christian belief.

69. Also espousing a date around this time are Mearns, "Dating the Similitudes"; Walck, "Son of Man," 38–39.

70. The reference to idols in 46:7 does not exclude the possibility that the author had some Jewish rulers in mind when he used the broad generic category, "the kings and the mighty."

71. Like the author of this document, some early Christians conflated the originally separate figures of the Servant, the one like a son of man, and the Messiah. See Nickelsburg, "Son of Man," 138–49.

72. See the discussion by M. Knibb, *The Ethiopic Book of Enoch* (2 vols.; Oxford: Clarendon, 1978) 2:38–42, and the bibliography cited by him (2:36 nn. 2–3). James C. VanderKam ("The Textual Base for the Ethiopic Translation of 1 Enoch," in D. M. Golomb, ed., *Working with No Data: Studies in Semitic and Egyptian Presented to Thomas O. Lambdin* [Winona Lake, Ind.: Eisenbrauns, 1987] 247–62) is dubious of a direct Aramaic-Ethiopic connection in 1 Enoch. Although no Greek translation of the Parables has survived, the existence of such may be attested in a couple of passages in Origen and the *Apocalypse of Peter*; see Nickelsburg, *1 Enoch 1*, 87, 91.

73. It is not impossible that this author used the history of Jason of Cyrene rather than its epitome, 2 Maccabees. See, however, Hadas, *Maccabees*, 92–95.

74. On 4 Maccabees as a thoroughly Hellenistic document, philosophically and rhetorically, see Redditt, "Concept of *Nomos*"; and deSilva, "Noble Contest."

75. For a discussion of this topic in Philo, 4 Maccabees, and early Christianity, see David C. Aune, "Mastery of the Passions: Philo, 4 Maccabees, and Early Christianity," in Wendy E. Helleman, ed., *Hellenization Revisited: Shaping a Christian Response with the Greco-Roman World* (Lanham, Md.: Univ. Press of America, 1994) 125–58.

76. For the passages see ibid., 149.

77. Redditt, "Concept of *Nomos*," 250–51.

78. Ibid., 251–54.

79. For an (unconvincing in my view) argument that 4 Maccabees espouses a belief in a resurrection of the body, see Ulrich Fischer, *Eschatologie und Jenseitserwartung im hellenistischen Diasporajudentum* (BZNW 44; Berlin: de Gruyter, 1978)101–5. See also Klauck, *4. Makkabäerbuch*, 672–74.

80. Sam K. Williams, *Jesus' Death as Saving Event* (HDR 2; Missoula, Mont.: Scholars Press, 1975) 137–61; David R. Seeley, *The Noble Death: Graeco-Roman Martyrology and Paul's Conception of Salvation* (JSOTSup 28; Sheffield: JSOT Press, 1990), esp. 87–99.

81. See above, pp. 70–71, and below, pp. 312–13, 320.

82. Elias J. Bickerman, "The Date of Fourth Maccabees," in *Louis Ginzberg Jubilee Volume* (New York: American Academy of Jewish Research, 1945) 105–12. Breitenstein (*Beobachtungen zu Sprache*) cites other linguistic rhetorical usage in the book as evidence for its composition between 100 and 135 C.E. John Collins (*Between Athens and Jerusalem*, 187) and Redditt ("Concept of *Nomos*," 266–68) favor the earlier date.

83. See Hadas, *Maccabees*, 109–13. See also John Collins, *Between Athens and Jerusalem*, 188; Redditt, "Concept of *Nomos*," 268–69.

84. DeSilva, "Noble Contest," 34–52.

85. Hadas, *Maccabees*, 103–9. So also Redditt, "Concept of *Nomos*," 264.

86. Hadas (*Maccabees*, 95–96) favors a date ca. 40 C.E. and suggests that it may have been written around that year in response to Caligula's attempt to have his statue erected in the

Jerusalem temple. While this event could be in the background, the more general purpose of dealing with Jewish life in the Diaspora seems more likely. See Redditt, "Concept of *Nomos*," 264–66; deSilva, "Noble Contest," 34–52.

87. Hadas, *Maccabees*, 127–35.

88. Townshend, *APOT* 2:658–62. With an eye toward the usage of Eastern Orthodoxy it is now included in editions of the RSV and NRSV.

8. Revolt—Destruction—Reconstruction

1. According to Josephus (*Ant.* 18.4 [§1.1]), the opponent of the census was "Judas a Gaulanite from a city called Gamala." In *Ant.* 20.102 this same person, the father of the aforementioned two sons, is called Judas the Galilean. On the problem of identifying him with the Judas who stirred up a revolt in Galilee in 4 B.C.E. (*Ant.* 17.271 [§10.5]), see E. Mary Smallwood, *The Jews under Roman Rule*, 153 n. 40.

2. According to Acts 21:38 this Egyptian was a contemporary of Paul.

3. On the Second Revolt in Palestine, led by Bar Kochba, see the bibliography below on pp. 296–97.

4. Opinions differ on the nature, the importance, and the centrality of the rabbinic activity in Yavneh (Jamnia). For the importance of Yohanan ben Zakkai's "academy" in Jamnia, see the summary discussion by Jacob Neusner, "The Formation of Rabbinic Judaism: Yavneh (Jamnia) from A.D. 70–100," 3–42, esp. 21–42. Contrary to what was a commonly accepted theory, the activity at Yavneh did not constitute a formal "council" that made definitive decisions, e.g., about the canon of Scripture; see Jack P. Lewis, "What Do We Mean by Jabneh?" *JBR* 32 (1964) 125–32; idem, "Jamnia (Jabneh), Council of," *ABD* 3: 634–37. For caution regarding the institutional nature of the activity at Yavneh, see Neusner's comment ("Formation," 41), "But the nature of the 'gathering' at Yavneh—whether it was some sort of 'academy,' or a nascent political institution, or merely an inchoate assembly of various sorts of sectarians, professions, pre-70 authorities, or whatever—is simply unilluminated." For a skeptical appraisal of the importance and centrality of Yavneh and an argument for much more proliferated rabbinic activity, see Catherine Hezser, *The Social Structure of the Rabbinic Movement in Roman Palestine* (TSAJ 66; Tübingen: Mohr Siebeck, 1997), esp. 171–80, 195–99, 407–8, 492–94.

5. The abrupt ending of the Antiquities had led M. R. James (*Biblical Antiquities*, 60–65) and John Strugnell ("Philo [Pseudo] or Liber Antiquitatum Biblicarum," *EncJud* 13:408) to suggest that the original ending of the text has been lost. Feldman (in James, *Biblical Antiquities*, lxxvii), Perrot (*Pseudo-Philon*, 2:21–22), and Jacobson (*Commentary*, 1:253–54) contest this hypothesis.

6. For discussions of Pseudo-Philo's literary and exegetical techniques see Murphy, *Pseudo-Philo*, 9–25; Jacobson, *Commentary*, 1:211–13, 224–41; Fisk, *Do You Not Remember?*; Christopher T. Begg, "The Golden Calf Episode according to Pseudo-Philo," in Marc Vervenne, ed., *Studies in the Book of Exodus: Redactions—Reception—Interpretation* (BETL 126; Leuven: Leuven Univ. Press, 1996) 577–94.

7. See also Josephus, *Ant.* 5.182 (§3.3), noted by James, *Biblical Antiquities*, 146.

8. George W. E. Nickelsburg, "Good and Bad Leaders in Pseudo-Philo's *Liber Antiquitatum Biblicarum*," in John J. Collins and George W. E. Nickelsburg, eds., *Ideal Figures in Ancient Judaism: Profiles and Paradigms* (SBLSCS 12; Missoula, Mont.: Scholars Press, 1980) 49–65. See

also Murphy (*Pseudo-Philo*, 233–41), who distinguishes between persons who are formally leaders (judges and the like) and those who do not hold such an office. See also idem, "The Martial Option in Pseudo-Philo," *CBQ* 57 (1995) 676–88.

9. For other references to postmortem judgment cf. 3:10; 16:3; 23:13; 25:7.

10. On covenant in Pseudo-Philo see Frederick J. Murphy, "The Eternal Covenant in Pseudo-Philo," *JSP* 3 (1988) 43–57; and in summary, idem, *Pseudo-Philo*, 244–46.

11. See 18:3–6; 23:4–9; 32:1–4; 40:2.

12. See 9:3–4, 7; 10:2; 11:1; 19:2; 22:7; 30:7.

13. For the term or the idea see 4:11; 7:4; 8:3; 11:2, 5; 30:7.

14. Jacobson, *Commentary*, 1:380.

15. See Murphy, *Pseudo-Philo*, 21.

16. On sin and punishment ("moral causality") in Pseudo-Philo, see ibid., 247–48.

17. On idolatry in Pseudo-Philo see ibid., 252–54.

18. On the Torah in Pseudo-Philo see Eckhart Reinmuth, "Beobachtungen zum Verständnis des Gesetzes im Liber Antiquitatum Biblicarum (Pseudo-Philo)," *JSJ* 20 (1989) 151–70.

19. See, e.g., 9:3; 12:8; 18:10–11; 19:9; 30:4; 35:3; 49:3. On the issue see Fisk, *Do You Not Remember?* 190–263.

20. See Perrot, *Pseudo-Philon*, 2:43–47.

21. See 18:5–6; 23; 32:1–10; and Fisk, *Do You Not Remember?* 264–313.

22. For God as the principal actor in the Antiquities see Murphy, *Pseudo-Philo*, 223–29; Jacobson, *Commentary* 1:242–45.

23. Perrot, *Pseudo-Philon*, 2:57–59; Murphy, *Pseudo-Philo*, 260–61.

24. Murphy, *Pseudo-Philo*, 260. For a broad picture see Nickelsburg, *Ancient Judaism*, 90–108.

25. Nickelsburg, *Ancient Judaism*, 92–93.

26. See 3:10; 16:3; 19:12–13; 23:13; 25:7; 36:4.

27. L. Cohn, "An Apocryphal Work Ascribed to Philo of Alexandria," *JQR* 10 (1898) 327; James, *Biblical Antiquities*, 30–33; perhaps Strugnell, "Philo," 408; Harrington ("Pseudo-Philo," 299) thinks "A date around the time of Jesus seems most likely," but cites no reasons for not dating it later in the first century. Bogaert (*Pseudo-Philon*, 2:66–74) allows for wider range of dates before 70 C.E.

28. Harrington, *Pseudo-Philon*, 2:77–78; Strugnell, "Pseudo-Philo," 408.

29. For the parallels to 4 Ezra and 2 Baruch see James, *Biblical Antiquities*, 46–58; Arthur J. Ferch, "The Two Eons and the Messiah in Pseudo-Philo, 4 Ezra, and 2 Baruch," *AUSS* 15 (1977) 135–52; but cf. Feldman, in James, *Biblical Antiquities*, liv–lv. For the writings of Josephus see ibid., lvii–lxiv. For some comparisons with passages in Josephus see Christopher T. Begg, "The Transjordanian Altar (Josh 22:10–34) according to Josephus (Ant 5.100–114) and Pseudo-Philo (L.A.B. 22:1–10)," *AUSS* 35 (1997) 5–19; idem, "The Massacre of the Priests of Nob in Josephus and Pseudo-Philo," *EstBib* 55 (1997) 171–98; idem, "The Retellings of the Story of Judges 19 by Pseudo-Philo and Josephus: A Comparison," *EstBib* 58 (2000) 33–49.

30. See the summary above, pp. 263–64; and, in detail, Rhoads, *Israel in Revolution*.

31. Harrington, "Pseudo-Philo," 299; Murphy, *Pseudo-Philo*, 6. See also Bogaert, *Pseudo-Philon*, 2:67–74.

32. For a compelling set of arguments in support of this passage as an allusion to the Second Temple, see Jacobson, *Commentary*, 199–206.

33. Ibid., 206–7.

34. James, *Biblical Antiquities*, 28–29; Strugnell, "Philo," 408; Harrington, *Pseudo-Philon*,

2:75–77; Jacobson, *Commentary*, 215–24. Fragments of the Hebrew original have been preserved in the medieval *Chronicles of Jerahmeel*. For a text and translation of these fragments see Daniel J. Harrington, *The Hebrew Fragments of Pseudo-Philo's Liber Antiquitatum Biblicarum Preserved in the Chronicles of Jerahmeel* (SBLTT 3; Missoula, Mont.: Society of Biblical Literature, 1974).

35. Harrington, "Pseudo-Philo," 300; Jacobson, *Commentary*, 210–11. See also Daniel J. Harrington, "The 'Holy Land' in Pseudo-Philo, 4 Ezra, and 2 Baruch," in Shalom M. Paul, et al., eds., *Emanuel: Studies in Hebrew Bible, Septuagint and Dead Sea Scroll in Honor of Emanuel Tov* (VTSup 94; Leiden: Brill, 2003) 661–64.

36. James, *Biblical Antiquities*, 26–27; Feldman, in ibid., xxii–xxiv.

37. Daniel J. Harrington, "Philo, Pseudo-," *ABD* 5:354. See above, n. 6.

38. Perrot, *Pseudo-Philon*, 2:52–53; Pieter W. Van der Horst, "Portraits of Biblical Women in Pseudo-Philo's *Liber Antiquitatum Biblicarum*," *JSP* 5 (1989) 29–46; Cynthia Baker, "Pseudo-Philo and the Transformation of Jephthah's Daughter," in Mieke Bal, ed., *Anti-Covenant: Counter-Reading Women's Lives in the Hebrew Bible* (Bible and Literature Series 22; Sheffield: Almond Press, 1989) 175–209; Betsy Halpern-Amaru, "Portraits of Women in Pseudo-Philo's *Biblical Antiquities*," in Amy-Jill Levine, ed., *"Women like This": New Perspectives on Jewish Women in the Greco-Roman World* (SBLEJL 1; Atlanta: Scholars Press, 1991) 83–106; Murphy, *Pseudo-Philo*, 258–59; Brown, *No Longer Be Silent*; Mary Therese DesCamp, "Why Are These Women Here? An Examination of the Sociological Setting of Pseudo-Philo through Comparative Reading," *JSP* 16 (1997) 53–80, who goes so far as to suggest that the author of the Antiquities was a woman. Jacobson (*Commentary*, 1:250–51) also notes the tendency but thinks that it has been overemphasized by those of the aforementioned authors whom he cites.

39. Richard Bauckham, "The Liber Antiquitatum Biblicarum of Pseudo-Philo and the Gospels as 'Midrash,'" in R. T. France and David Wenham, eds., *Studies in Midrash and Historiography* (Gospels Perspectives 3; Sheffield: JSOT Press, 1983) 33–76; Daniel J. Harrington, "Birth Narratives in Pseudo-Philo's *Biblical Antiquities* and the Gospels," in Maurya P. Horgan and Paul Kobelski, eds., *To Touch the Text*, FS Joseph A. Fitzmyer (New York: Crossroad, 1989) 316–24; Reinmuth, *Pseudo-Philo und Lukas*; idem, "Beobachtungen zur Rezeption der Genesis bei Pseudo-Philo (L.A.B.1–8) und Lukas (APG 7.2–17)," *NTS* 43 (1997) 552–69. See also William W. Reader, "The Twelve Jewels of Revelation 21:19–20: Tradition History and Modern Interpretations," *JBL* 100 (1981) 444–48.

40. Romans was written in the mid-50s. For a look at the issue in the broader context of Paul's writings see Eckart Reinmuth, "'Nicht Vergeblich' bei Paulus und Pseudo-Philo, Liber Antiquitatum Biblicarum," *NovT* 33 (1991) 97–123.

41. Esdras is the Greek form of the Hebrew name Ezra. Because Saint Jerome included 2 Esdras in his Latin translation of the Bible (the Vulgate) it has come to be included in the Apocrypha. The Latin mss. generally separate the Jewish core of this work from its Christian additions, giving each its own enumeration, which is often as follows:

The canonical Ezra-Nehemiah	= 1 Ezra
2 Esdras 1–2 of our Apocrypha	= 2 Ezra
1 Esdras of our Apocrypha	= 3 Ezra
2 Esdras 3–14 of our Apocrypha	= 4 Ezra
2 Esdras 15–16 of our Apocrypha	= 5 Ezra

42. Cf. Ezra 3:2; 5:2; Neh 12:1.

43. The identification is explicit in 4 Ezra 3:1, but this may be an explanatory gloss by a scribe. Ezra's name is mentioned in 6:10; 7:2, 25; 8:2, 20; 14:2, 38, as well as in the Christian additions in 1:1; 2:10, 33, 42.

44. On the genre "apocalypse" see above, pp. 86–87. The major part of my discussion here follows the first edition of this book, but it has been refined by articles and books published since 1981, esp. the commentary of Michael Stone (*Fourth Ezra*).

45. See the groundbreaking article by Earl Breech, "These Fragments I Have Shored against My Ruins: The Form and Function of 4 Ezra," *JBL* 92 (1973) 267–74. For a refinement of the hypothesis see Stone, *Fourth Ezra*, 28–33, 50–51, and in the commentary, ad loc.

46. On Ezra's progress as it is attested in the form of the visions see Frances Flannery-Dailey, *Dreamers, Scribes, and Priests: Jewish Dreams in the Hellenistic and Roman Eras* (JSJSup 90; Leiden: Brill, 2004) 212–20.

47. See, e.g., Stone, *Fourth Ezra*, 50–51.

48. For these episodes as dreams see Flannery-Dailey, *Dreamers*, 212–15.

49. Stone (*Fourth Ezra*, 118) differs slightly in his division, placing the fasts at the beginning of the respective units, citing "setting and time" as the beginning of the unit. In each case, however, the time of the vision is mentioned *after* the fast (5:21; 6:36; cf. 3:1; 9:27; 11:1; 13:1; 14:1).

50. For a thorough discussion of this problem see Harnisch, *Verhängnis*, passim.

51. On "the way of the Most High" in 4 Ezra see Stone, *Fourth Ezra*, 24–28.

52. The subject matter is drawn from "lists of revealed things" found in the sapiential and apocalyptic literature; see the important article by Michael E. Stone, "Lists of Revealed Things in the Apocalyptic Literature," in Frank M. Cross, Werner E. Lemke, and Patrick D. Miller, eds., *Magnalia Dei, the Mighty Acts of God: Essays on the Bible and Archaeology in Memory of G. Ernest Wright* (Garden City, N.Y.: Doubleday, 1976) 414–54.

53. Stone, *Fourth Ezra*, 24.

54. Ibid., 27.

55. Cf. also 6:29 with 5:14; it is the earth that quakes and not Ezra's body that shutters.

56. It is 2.3 and 3.5 times as long as sections 1 and 2, respectively.

57. On the Messiah in 4 Ezra see Stone, *Fourth Ezra*, 207–11.

58. On this passage see Nickelsburg, *Resurrection*, 138–40.

59. One brief treatment of the subject occurs in 1 Enoch 22, on which see Nickelsburg, *1 Enoch 1*, 300–309. The section here very likely reproduces a traditional discussion of the topic; see Stone, *Fourth Ezra*, 22.

60. For a critical analysis of the literature on this section see Edith McEwan Humphrey, *The Ladies and the Cities: Transformation and Apocalyptic Identity in Joseph and Aseneth, 4 Ezra, the Apocalypse and the Shepherd of Hermas* (JSPSup 17; Sheffield: Sheffield Academic Press, 1995) 57–81. For an analysis of this episode as a dream and its aftermath, see Flannery-Dailey, *Dreamers*, 194–97.

61. On this double structure of the section and its parallels in the first three sections, see Stone, *Fourth Ezra*, 29.

62. Ibid., 306.

63. For the ambiguity see ibid., 335; Humphrey, *Ladies*, 73–76.

64. Flannery-Dailey (*Dreamers*, 197) suggests that Ezra's status as a priest makes him eligible to enter the sacred precincts.

65. This interpretation was worked out by Breech, "Fragments."

66. For a detailed discussion of this issue and its implications see Stone, *Fourth Ezra*, 31–33.

67. On the messianic teaching of 4 Ezra see Stone, *Fourth Ezra*, 207–11.

68. For the author of 4 Ezra as an expositor of Scripture see Michael A. Knibb, "Apocalyptic and Wisdom in 4 Ezra," *JSJ* 13 (1992) 67–72.

69. On this interpretation see Stone, *Fourth Ezra*, 9–10, 367–68; Knibb, "2 Esdras," 104–5. According to Lorenzo DiTommaso ("Dating the Eagle Vision of 4 Ezra: A New Look at an Old Theory," *JSP* 20 [1999] 3–38), the vision dates from 218 C.E., although in view of Clement of Alexander's evident knowledge of the work (± 190), the text may be a later revision of an earlier text from the end of the first century.

70. A. Peter Hayman ("The 'Man from the Sea' in 4 Ezra 13," *JJS* 49 [1998] 1–16) argues that in the vision, which revives ancient mythic tradition, the "man" is actually YHWH. According to the interpretation, however, the figure is "my son" (vv 33, 52), "the one whom the Most High has been keeping for many ages" (v 26).

71. See, e.g., E. P. Sanders, *Paul and Palestinian Judaism* (Philadelphia: Fortress Press, 1977) 409–18, who stresses the difference between 4 Ezra's view of the few and the many and the covenantal theology that was typical of Palestinian Judaism.

72. On 4 Ezra's pessimism regarding Israel's ability to keep the Torah, see Michael Desjardins, "Law in 2 Baruch and 4 Ezra," *ScRel/StRel* 14 (1985) 31–36. John R. Levison (*Portraits of Adam in Early Judaism* [JSPSup 1; Sheffield: JSOT Press, 1988] 113–27) rightly finds some ambiguity in 4 Ezra's assessment of the consequences of Adam's sin.

73. Stone, *Fourth Ezra*, 36.

74. Ibid., 31–33.

75. Michael P. Knowles, "Moses, the Law, and the Unity of 4 Ezra," *NovT* 31 (1989) 273–74. For Desjardins ("Law"), who emphasizes Ezra's pessimism, the glass is, however, half empty. For an emphasis on this point see the reading of 4 Ezra by Longenecker, *Eschatology and the Covenant*, 149–57.

76. Stone, *Fourth Ezra*, 38. Longenecker (*2 Esdras*, 107) suggested that he is "a learned scribe with Pharisaic sympathies."

77. Bruce W. Longenecker, "Locating 4 Ezra: A Consideration of Its Social Setting and Functions," *JSJ* 28 (1997) 270–93.

78. See Knibb, "Apocalyptic and Wisdom"; Longenecker, "Locating 4 Ezra," 284–85; idem, *2 Esdras*, 100–108. Stone (*Fourth Ezra*, 431) is less certain.

79. See Longenecker, "Locating 4 Ezra," 285–93. Cf. also Philip S. Esler, "The Social Function of 4 Ezra," *JSNT* 53 (1994) 99–123, who employs social scientific methods to arrive at his conclusion that the author sought to manage or eliminate the cognitive dissonance between the Jews' belief in their covenantal status and the realities of 70 C.E.

80. See Stone, *Fourth Ezra*, 1–9. The daughter versions of the Greek include the Latin, Syriac, Slavonic, Ethiopic, Coptic, Arabic, Armenian, and Georgian.

81. On 5 Ezra see Graham N. Stanton, "5 Ezra and Matthean Christianity," *JTS* 28 (1977) 67–83; Theodore A. Bergren, "The People Coming from the East in 5 Ezra 1:28," *JBL* 108 (1989) 675–83; Longenecker, *2 Esdras*, 114–20. For a text and translation see Theodore A. Bergren, *Fifth Ezra: The Text, Origin and Early History* (SBLSCS 25; Atlanta: Scholars Press, 1990).

82. The author's imagery about the mother sending her children off and the mother receiving her children back draws on the Jewish traditions about Mother Zion, attested in Baruch and 2 Macc 7, on which see above, pp. 96, 108–9. The immediate contextual reference, however, is 4 Ezra 9–10.

83. See Longenecker, *2 Esdras*, 112–14. On a date between 262 and 313 C.E. see Theodore A. Bergren, *Sixth Ezra: The Text and Origin* (New York: Oxford Univ. Press, 1998) 116–32. On the religious affiliation of the author see idem., *Sixth Ezra*, 103–15. See also idem, "Prophetic Rhetoric in 6 Ezra," in Randall A. Argall, Beverly A. Bow, and Rodney A. Werline, eds., *For a Later Generation: The Transformation of Tradition in Israel, Early Judaism, and Early Christianity*, FS G. W. E. Nickelsburg (Valley Forge, Pa.: Trinity International, 2000) 25–32.

84. On the genre "apocalypse" see above, pp. 86–87.

85. The five recent scholars who have treated the matter agree that there are major breaks between chaps. 20 and 21 and between chaps. 52 and 53, but they disagree as to the divisions within chaps. 1–20, 21–52, and 53–77/87. See Bogaert, *Apocalypse de Baruch*, 1:64–76; Thompson, *Responsibility*, 122–24; Sayler, *Have the Promises Failed?* 14–39; Murphy, *Structure*, 11–29; and Willett, *Eschatology*, 80–95. See also Whitters, *Epistle*, 35–48. At all points of disagreement a decision is difficult, because the text indicates many points of transition. My division favors mainly that of Sayler. Different from these scholars, John F. Hobbins ("The Summing Up of History in 2 Baruch," *JQR* 89 [1998] 53–54) opts for a fourfold division.

86. For Sayler (*Have the Promises Failed?* 14–15), the first section ends with the end of the first day (5:7), which breaks up the author's narrative about the destruction of Jerusalem.

87. See George W. E. Nickelsburg, "Narrative Traditions in the Paraleipomena of Jeremiah and 2 Baruch," *CBQ* 35 (1973) 60–68.

88. In the parallel version of this narrative in the *Paraleipomena of Jeremiah* the roles are reversed, as they seem to be in 2 Bar. 33:1–2.

89. For the author's distinction between the earthly Zion and the heavenly Jerusalem see Murphy, *Structure*, 70–116.

90. In Par. Jer. 4:2 God does not destroy the walls but opens the gates.

91. On the legend about the restoration of the temple paraphernalia and on the restoration as a reference to the *eschaton* rather than to the Second Temple (from the text's fictive point of view), see Hobbins, "History," 56–57, esp. nn. 25–26.

92. Cf. 2 Bar. 12:5; 21:1; 43:3; 47:2.

93. See Krister Stendahl, "Hate, Non-Retaliation, and Love: 1QS x, 17–20 and Romans 12:19–21," *HTR* 55 (1962) 343–55.

94. For this formula see above, pp. 32–33, 59, 107, 210, 238, 244–46, 278. Cf. Pss. Sol. 3, which contrasts God's chastisement of the righteous and God's punishment of the sinner.

95. On this motif in 2 Baruch see Murphy, *Structure*, 31–67.

96. The end of the section is indicated by the fact that the activity outlined in 20:6 has been completed; see Sayler, *Have the Promises Failed?* 21.

97. Cf. 1 Enoch 10:16—11:2.

98. On this passage see Bogaert, *Apocalypse*, 2:265; A. F. J. Klijn, "The Sources and Redaction of the Syriac Apocalypse of Baruch," *JSJ* 1 (1970) 65–76.

99. Sayler, *Have the Promises Failed?* 25. For some detailed parallels between section 4 and section 2 that help to indicate the limits of this section, see Sayler, *Have the Promises Failed?* 25–27.

100. On the differences between this vision and its interpretation see Harnisch, *Verhängnis*, 257–59.

101. See Nickelsburg, *Resurrection*, 84–85.

102. On the relationship between the author's anthropology and his two-worlds concept see Murphy, *Structure*, 52–63.

103. For the figure of Adam in 2 Baruch and the book's emphasis on human responsibility in relation to Adam, see Levison, *Portraits,* 129–44. These sections on Adam (23:4–5; 48:42–43; 54:15; 56:5–6) have counterparts in 4 Ezra (3:4–11, 20–27; 4:30–32; 7:11–14; 7:116–31).

104. For the many parallels between 2 Baruch and Deuteronomy see Murphy, *Structure,* 120–32.

105. For this emendation of 76:2, which is based on 13:3; 25:1, see Charles, *APOT* 2:519.

106. Par. Jer. 7.

107. On the epistle see Whitters, *Epistle.*

108. For the most detailed argument against the originality of the epistle see Sayler, *Have the Promises Failed?* 98–101. For a thorough discussion of the pros and cons, see Whitters, *Epistle,* 23–33. If the epistle is original, it can still be construed as part of the last section of the seven-part outline I have proposed following primarily Sayler.

109. Frederick J. Murphy ("*2 Baruch* and the Romans," 104 [1985] 663–69) suggests that the author is presenting a pacifist alternative to the Jews' taking God's justice into their own hands. This interpretation fits with the ideas laid out in the article by Stendahl cited in n. 93 above.

110. On this author's belief that obedience to the Torah is possible, see Michel Desjardins, "Law in 2 Baruch and 4 Ezra," 26–31.

111. For two very different views on this issue, the one positing the eventual dissolution of this earthly world and the other emphasizing the notion of restoration and renewal, see Murphy, *Structure*; Hobbins, "History."

112. See George W. E. Nickelsburg, "Where Is the Place of Eschatological Blessing?" in Esther G. Chazon, David Satran, and Ruth A. Clements, eds., *Things Revealed: Studies in Early Jewish and Christian Literature in Honor of Michael E. Stone* (JSJSup 89; Leiden: Brill, 2004) 53–71.

113. See, e.g., G. H. Box, "IV Ezra," *APOT* 2:553–54.

114. Bogaert (*Apocalypse,* 1:294–95) suggests the year 96. Nicolae Roddy ("'Two Parts: Weeks of Seven Weeks': The End of the Age as *Teminus ad Quem* for *2 Baruch,*" *JSP* 14 [1996] 3–14) reads the evidence differently, but arrives at roughly the same date.

115. For details see Whitters, *Epistle,* 4–12. Part of 2 Bar. 12–14 in Greek has also been preserved in a fragmentary Oxyrhynchus papyrus; see Bogaert, *Apocalypse,* 1:40–43. The epistle as a separate document has been preserved in numerous Syriac mss.; see ibid., 1:43–56.

116. For arguments in favor of a Semitic original see Charles, *APOT* 2:472–74. Bogaert (*Apocalypse,* 1:378–80) favors Greek as the original language. See also Whitters, *Epistle,* 15–18. Nir's claim (*Destruction*) that 2 Baruch is a Christian composition is, in my view, unconvincing. It is based on an oversimplified view of Judaism in the Greco-Roman period and early Christianity. To achieve her reading she must bracket out such demonstrably Jewish works as 1 Enoch and Jubilees, and the Qumran corpus in general as not really (or actually?) Jewish but ideologically proximate to the world of Christianity. See her comments on pp. 6–13.

117. For details see Berger, *Synopse.* For a list of parallels see Charles, *Apocalypse of Baruch,* 170–71.

118. See Sayler, *Have the Promises Failed?* 130.

119. For a list of scholars see Bogaert, *Apocalypse,* 1:26.

120. See ibid., as well as Box, *APOT* 2:553; Metzger, *OTP* 2:522.

121. Klijn, *OTP* 1:620.

122. Charles, *APOT* 2:477; Stone, *Fourth Ezra,* 39. In the first edition of this book I favored this option (p. 287).

123. On 4 Ezra see Stone, *Fourth Ezra,* 24–28, 31–33; Flannery-Dailey, *Dreamers,* 212–20.

On 2 Baruch see Murphy, *Structure*, 141. There is some debate as to whether Ezra's interaction with the people is integral to the narrative as it is in 2 Baruch; see Sayler, *Have the Promises Failed?* 155; Longenecker, "Locating 4 Ezra," 292 n. 75.

124. See, e.g., Box, *APOT* 2:553; Metzger, *OTP* 2:522.

125. Cf., e.g., T. Mos. 11.

126. For more see Sayler, *Have the Promises Failed?* 130–34.

127. Cf. Isa 44:9–20, Bel and the Serpent, and the Epistle of Jeremiah.

128. Gershom Scholem, *Major Trends in Jewish Mysticism* (New York: Schocken, 1971) 68–69.

129. See Lester L. Grabbe, "The Scapegoat Tradition: A Study in Early Jewish Interpretation," *JSJ* 18 (1987) 153–58; Daniel Stökl, "Yom Kippur in the Apocalyptic *imaginaire* and the Roots of Jesus' High Priesthood: Yom Kippur in Zechariah 3, 1 Enoch 10, 11QMelkizedeq, Hebrews and the Apocalypse of Abraham 13," in Jan Assmann and Guy G. Stroumsa, eds., *Transformations of the Inner Self in Ancient Religions* (SHR 83; Leiden: Brill, 1999) 351–61.

130. Cf. Zech 3; Jub. 17:16—18:16; 48; Mark 1:12–13; 8:32–33.

131. See Stökl, "Yom Kippur," 358–61. See also, with reference to Matt 22:13, Ryszard Rubinkiewicz, *Die Eschatologie von Henoch 9–11 und das Neue Testament* (ÖBS; Lublin: Österreichisches Katholisches Bibelwerk, 1980) 97–113.

132. Scholem, *Major Trends*, 61. Steven Weitzmann ("The Song of Abraham," *HUCA* 65 [1994] 31–33) suggests that the song may reflect a traditional exegesis of Gen 14:22, attested already in Philo, *Drunkenness* 105–7.

133. Cf. 1 Enoch 85–90; see above, pp. 83–86.

134. On the problem in this passage see Arie Rubinstein, "A Problematic Passage in the Apocalypse of Abraham," *JJS* 8 (1957) 45–50.

135. On the heavenly temple and throne see above, pp. 50–51, 152–53, 250.

136. See Robert G. Hall, "The 'Christian Interpolation' in the *Apocalypse of Abraham*," *JBL* 107 (1988) 107–12, who suggests that the figure may represent the emperor Hadrian.

137. On the Chosen One see above, pp. 249–53.

138. For the centrality of the covenant in the *Apocalypse* see Ryszard Rubinkiewicz, "La Vision de l'histoire dans l'Apocalypse d'Abraham," *ANRW* 2, *Principat* 19.1:137–51.

139. Box (*Apocalypse of Abraham*) mentions many of these parallels in his notes.

140. On the recensions of the Slavonic text see Émile Turdeanu, "L'Apocalypse d'Abraham en Slave," *JSJ* 3 (1972) 153–80, repr. in idem, *Apocryphes Slaves et Roumains de l'Ancien Testament* (SVTP 5; Leiden: Brill, 1981) 172–200. On the Greek see Box, *Apocalypse*, xv. Rubinkiewicz (*OTP* 1:684) suggests that the Slavonic text of 20:5, 7; 22:5 may contain interpolations originating with the Bogomils (a medieval Balkan sect of Manichean origin). Even if this is the case, it does not affect our positing the Jewish origin of the text in the decades after 70 C.E. So also Rubinkiewicz, *OTP* 2:683. On the Bogomils see Malcolm Lambert, *Medieval Heresies: Popular Movements from Bogomil to Hus* (New York: Holmes & Meier, 1976) 12–23.

141. On the Hebrew see Arie Rubinstein, "Hebraisms in the Slavonic 'Apocalypse of Abraham,'" *JJS* 4 (1953) 108–15; idem, "Hebraisms in the Apocalypse of Abraham," *JJS* 5 (1954) 132–35.

142. See the discussions of Rajak, *Josephus*, 11–45; Feldman, "Josephus," 981–83; Mason, *Flavius Josephus on the Pharisees*, 311–71; idem, *Josephus and the New Testament*, 34–52. Feldman follows the account in the *Life* quite closely, rejecting, however, some of its obvious exaggerations. Rajak responds to some of the skeptics, who doubt the veracity of much of Josephus's auto-

biography. Mason is skeptical at many points. For a strongly critical analysis of Josephus as a historian see Cohen, *Josephus*.

143. This paragraph draws on Josephus, *Life* 1–12 (§§1–2). For two different readings of the problems connected with Josephus's genealogy, see Rajak, *Josephus*, 15–17; Mason, *Josephus and the New Testament*, 38–39.

144. Josephus's account here (*Life* 10–12 [§2]) is problematic; he enters his studies at around sixteen years old and completes them in his nineteenth year, having spent three years with Bannus. When did he subject himself to the rigors of study with the Pharisees, Sadducees, and Essenes? See Mason, *Josephus and the New Testament*, 39–41. Since the arithmetic does not add up, perhaps there is a corruption in the text. Alternatively, "around sixteen" and "in my nineteenth year" does allow for more than three years. Perhaps, also, Josephus's studies with the three groups were more cursory than he claims. On the interpretation of the wording of *Life* 10–12 (§2), I follow Mason, *Flavius Josephus*, 342–56.

145. For these events see *Life* 13–16 (§3). According to *Ant.* 20.195 (§8.11), Poppaea was a God-fearing women who took up the case of the Jews. Feldman ("Josephus," 982) suggests that the imperial gifts were Nero's attempt to encourage Josephus to use his influence to quiet the unrest in Israel.

146. Mason, *Josephus and the New Testament*, 44–46.

147. For Josephus's strange and suspicious account of this event, see *J.W.* 3.340–408 (§§8.1–9) and the discussion by Mason, *Josephus and the New Testament*, 43–45.

148. Josephus never uses the name Flavius in his writings; the name appears, however, in the writings of a number of the early church fathers, e.g., Minucius Felix, *Octavius* 33 (late second/early third century); Clement of Alexandria, *Stromata* 1.21 (147.2–3) (late second/early third century); Eusebius, *Ecclesiastical History* 1.5.3 (311 C.E.).

149. The terminus a quo for Josephus's death is usually set at 100 C.E., presumably the date of Agrippa II's death, which is presumed in *Life* 359 (§65). On the problem of that date see Rajak, *Josephus*, 237–38. In *Ant.* 20.267 (§12.1) he dates the completion of that work to the thirteenth year of Domitian's reign (93/94 C.E.). In *Life* 428 (§76) Josephus mentions no emperor after Domitian, whose reign ended in 96 C.E. A date very late in the century at least is indicated by the dating of *Against Apion*, on which see below, p. 294–96.

150. For the size of Josephus's corpus I am dependent on a communication from Steve Mason (8/19/04). The numbers are *Jewish War* (125,292 words); *Antiquities* (312,276); *Life* (15,289); *Against Apion* (20,520). The part of *Against Apion* preserved only in Latin (52–113 [§5–9]) adds somewhat to this count. For the word count of Philo's preserved works, see above, p. 213, and on his lost works, see p. 395 n. 113.

151. Mason, *Josephus and the New Testament*, 64–65.

152. According to Cohen (*Josephus*, 236) books 1–6 were completed during the reign of Titus (79–81 C.E.); see also Feldman, "Josephus," 983–84. Mason (*Josephus and the New Testament*, 64) indicates a date for the completion of most of it before the death of Vespasian. See *Ag. Ap.* 1.50–51, where Josephus states that he presented copies of the *War* to both Vespasian and Titus; cf. also *Life* 361.

153. Mason, *Josephus and the New Testament*, 65.

154. Cohen, *Josephus*, 237; Feldman, "Josephus," 983–84.

155. There are some brief references to it in the Roman historians, e.g., Dio Cassius 65.4–10; Suetonius, *Vespasian* 4–5.

156. See Mason, *Josephus and the New Testament*.

157. For this analysis in more detail, see ibid., 60–65.

158. Josephus believed that Daniel had predicted the Roman destruction of the temple (*Ant.* 10.276–81 [§11.7]; Per Bilde, "Josephus and Jewish Apocalypticism," in Steve Mason, ed., *Understanding Josephus*, 53), but he anticipates no judgment on the Romans.

159. Mason, *Josephus and the New Testament*, 100–120. Here he argues against the commonly accepted theory that the *Antiquities* is primarily an apologetic work, a position he espoused in his first edition (64–66).

160. Thackeray, *Josephus*, 4:ix; Attridge, "Josephus," 217; Feldman, *Josephus's Interpretation of the Bible*, 7–8. However, see Mason, *Josephus and the New Testament*, 99.

161. Mason, *Josephus and the New Testament*, 111–16.

162. *Ant.* 1.Prol. 14 (§3), trans. LCL. See Attridge, "Josephus," 217, 224.

163. Attridge, *Interpretation*, 71–107.

164. Ibid., 109–44.

165. On his biblical sources see ibid., 30–33. See, however, Aden Nodet (*Flavius Josèphe*, 1:xxv–xxvi), who believes that Josephus worked only from the Hebrew Bible.

166. Feldman, "Josephus," 986–87.

167. Eugene Ulrich, *The Dead Sea Scrolls and the Origins of the Bible* (Grand Rapids: Eerdmans, 1999) 184–201.

168. See Attridge, *Interpretation*.

169. Attridge, "Josephus," 211–12; Feldman, *Interpretation*, 51–56. On the parallels in Pseudo-Philo see the citations in Feldman, *Interpretation*, 753; idem, *Studies*, 603–4. For discussions of some specific examples see the articles by Christopher Begg cited above in n. 29.

170. On Josephus's rewriting of the Bible see Feldman, *Studies*; more briefly, idem, *Interpretation*, 14–73. On his "historiographical predecessors" see ibid., 3–13.

171. On these sources see Louis Feldman, "The Sources of Josephus' Antiquities Book 19," *Latomus* 21 (1962) 320–33; Attridge, "Josephus," 211–16; Timothy P. Wiseman, *Death of an Emperor: Flavius Josephus* (Exeter: Univ. of Exeter Press, 1991) xii–xiv.

172. See Nickelsburg, *Ancient Judaism*, 160–75.

173. Bilde ("Josephus and Jewish Apocalypticism," 43–45) notes Josephus's interest in Essene prophecy and interpretation of biblical prophecy but does not comment on his failure to deal with most of the tenets of their apocalyptic theology.

174. See Mason, *Flavius Josephus on the Pharisees*.

175. On the problems associated with these texts see Mason, *Josephus and the New Testament*, 213–50.

176. Attridge, "Josephus," 188; Feldman, "Josephus," 982; Steve Mason, *Josephus and the New Testament*, 121.

177. See Feldman, "Josephus," 982–83; Mason, *Josephus and the New Testament* (1st ed. 1992) 73–76.

178. Mason, *Josephus and the New Testament* (2d ed.), 121–31. (Citations of Mason, *Josephus and the New Testament,* are to the second edition unless otherwise indicated.)

179. Ibid., 121.

180. Ibid., 52. See *J.W.* 5.418 (§9.4); *Life* 414 (§75), 426–27 (§76).

181. For two different assessments of the quality of the work see Mason, *Josephus and the New Testament*, 77 ("he creates a model of religious apologetics that has seldom been matched"); John

M. G. Barclay, "Josephus v. Apion: Analysis of an Argument," in Mason, ed., *Understanding Josephus*, 221 ("the argumentative fire-power is often disappointing").

182. There is no evidence that Josephus wrote the historical and theological works that he projects in *Ant.* 20.267–69 (§22.1).

183. Attridge ("Josephus," 227–28) suggests the last years of Domitian or the reign of Nerva (96–98 C.E.); Mason (*Josephus and the New Testament* [1st ed.] 77) proposes 97–100 C.E.

184. Mason, *Josephus and the New Testament*, 132.

185. Ibid.

186. Attridge, "Josephus," 228.

187. See Thackeray, *Josephus* 4:11, who identifies Josephus's patron Epaphroditus as a Roman grammarian who amassed a library of thirty thousand books.

188. See Schürer, *History,* 1:529–33.

189. Mason, *Josephus and the New Testament*, 79.

190. On the parallel with Luke's books see Mason, *Josephus and the New Testament*, 190–92.

191. Attridge, "Josephus," 228.

192. Ibid., 228–29.

193. See Bezalel Bar-Kochva, "An Ass in the Jerusalem Temple—The Origins and Development of the Slander," in Feldman and Levison, eds., *Josephus's Contra Apionem*, 310–26.

194. Summary by Attridge, "Josephus," 229.

195. Ibid., 231.

196. Ibid., 231–32. On the use of Josephus in the early church fathers see Michael E. Hardwick, *Josephus as an Historical Source in Patristic Literature through Eusebius* (BJS 128; Atlanta: Scholars Press, 1989).

9. TEXTS OF DISPUTED PROVENANCE

1. The pioneer in this scholarly "movement" was Marinus de Jonge of the University of Leiden, whose prolific work on especially the Testaments of the Twelve Patriarchs is copiously cited below. On the methodological issues see Robert A. Kraft, "Setting the Stage and Framing Some Central Questions," *JSJ* 32 (2001) 371–95.

2. For three comprehensive introductions to the Testaments see Hollander and de Jonge, *Testaments*, 1–85; M. de Jonge, "The Testaments of the Twelve Patriarchs: Central Problems and Essential Viewpoints," *ANRW* 2.20.1 (1987) 359–420; Kugler, *Testaments*.

3. On the possible relationship between this outline and the biblical covenant forms see Klaus Baltzer, *The Covenant Formulary* (trans. John Bowden; Philadelphia: Fortress Press, 1972) 141–63. For a discussion of the form in the respective testaments see von Nordheim, *Lehre*, 1:1–107. For a summary see Hollander and de Jonge, *Testaments*, 27–41.

4. On this pattern see Hollander and de Jonge, *Testaments*, 53–56.

5. Thus de Jonge, "Testaments," 516 n. 3, though not Hollander and de Jonge, *Testaments*, 91–95.

6. For more details see the excellent analysis by James Kugel, "Reuben's Sin with Bilhah in the *Testament of Reuben*," in David P. Wright, David Noel Freedman, and Avi Hurvitz, eds., *Pomegranates and Golden Bells: Studies in Biblical, Jewish, and Near Eastern Ritual, Law, and Literature in Honor of Jacob Milgrom* (Winona Lake, Ind.; Eisenbrauns, 1995) 525–54.

7. For a detailed comparison see ibid., 550–54.

8. See Hollander and de Jonge, *Testaments*, 87.

9. Ibid., 109–10.

10. Ibid., 112.

11. Cf. also *Tg. Ps.–J.* Gen 42:24, which specifies Simeon as the one who plotted Joseph's death.

12. See Nickelsburg, *1 Enoch 1*, 96. Cf. T. Levi 10:5; 14:1; 16:1; T. Jud. 18:1; T. Zeb. 3:4; T. Dan 5:6; T. Naph. 4:1; T. Benj. 9:1.

13. See Hollander and de Jonge, *Testaments*, 123–24.

14. Ibid., 122.

15. On the exegetical moves that justify the deed see Bruce N. Fisk, "One Good Story Deserves Another: The Hermeneutics of Invoking Secondary Biblical Episodes in the Narratives of *Pseudo-Philo* and the *Testaments of the Twelve Patriarchs*," in Craig A. Evans, ed., *The Interpretation of Scripture in Early Judaism and Christianity: Studies in Language and Tradition* (JSPSup 33; Sheffield: Sheffield Academic Press, 2000) 233–36. For a possible historical setting for Sir 50:26 and T. Levi 7:2–3 see James D. Purvis, *The Samaritan Pentateuch and the Origins of the Samaritan Sect* (HSM 2; Cambridge: Harvard Univ. Press, 1955) 119–29.

16. On the relationship between priestly office and zealous action see above, p. 384 n. 228.

17. In the Gospels it is the priestly leaders who initiate the conspiracy against Jesus and carry out his first trial; see George W. E. Nickelsburg, "The Genre and Function of the Markan Passion Narrative," *HTR* 73 (1980) 153–83, repr. in *GNP* 2:473–503.

18. On this text see Greenfield, Stone, and Eshel, *Aramaic Levi Document*, 60–65.

19. See George W. E. Nickelsburg, "Enoch, Levi, and Peter: Recipients of Revelation in Upper Galilee," *JBL* 100 (1981) 375–400, repr. in *GNP* 2:427–57; and the critical comments by Hanan and Esther Eshel, "Separating Levi from Enoch," in *GNP* 2:458–68.

20. Aramaic Levi Document 4 contains the end of a vision in which seven angels have spoken with Levi. In chap. 5 Jacob invests Levi.

21. On this motif in the Testaments and in early Christian literature see de Jonge, "Two Interesting Interpretations."

22. See also the Qumran Testament of Kohat, which provides instructions for Amram's sons (plural).

23. Chapter 18 itself does not say that the new priest will be a descendant of Levi, but the implication can be drawn from the context of the other Testaments, which speak of a descendant or descendants from Levi and Judah. That this priest will receive revelation (18:2) indicates that he is not purely a divine figure.

24. It describes the opening of heaven, the voice like that of a father to a son, the spirit resting on him in the water, the defeat of Satan, mention of the angels (the holy ones) and, in Mark one reads of the paradisiacal coexistence of humanity and the beasts. For early Christian interpretations of Jesus' baptism as the commissioning of Jesus as the anointed priest, see Tertullian, *On Baptism* 7.1; Cyril of Jerusalem, *Catechetical Lectures* 10.1; 21.5–6; *De uno domine* 11; *De sacro chrism.* 5–6; Pseudo-Clement, *Recognitions* 1.44.6—48.6; Armenian *Penitence of Adam* 41–42; *Vita* 41–42.

25. See, however, the text cited above, chapter 5, n. 249.

26. For comparisons of the Testament and the Aramaic text see M. de Jonge, "The Testament of Levi and 'Aramaic Levi,'" *RevQ* 13, nos. 49–52 (1988) (= Florentino García Martínez and Émile Puech, eds., *Mémorial Jean Carmignac* [Paris: Gabalda, 1988]) 367–85; and, at the

appropriate places, the commentaries in Greenfield, Stone, and Eshel, *Aramaic Levi Document*; and Drawnel, *Aramaic Wisdom Text*. See also M. de Jonge, "Levi, the sons of Levi and the Law, in *Testament Levi* X, XIV–XV and XVI," in Maurice Carrez, Joseph Doré, and Pierre Grelot, eds., *De la Tôrah au Messie: Études d'exégèse et d'herméneutique bibliques offertes à Henri Cazelles* (Paris: Desclée, 1980) 513–23, repr. in de Jonge, *Jewish Eschatology*, 180–90.

27. Hollander and de Jonge, *Testaments*, 184.

28. The word "courageous one" occurs in the text only in 15:6, but the kind of exploits recounted in the first narrative surely imply courage as well as strength and military adeptness.

29. Hollander and de Jonge, *Testaments*, 185–86.

30. Cecila Wassén, "The Story of Judah and Tamar in the Eyes of the Earliest Interpreters," *LT* 8 (1994) 354–59.

31. On this Testament see M. de Jonge, "Testament Issachar als 'typisches Testament,'" in de Jonge, *Studies*, 291–316.

32. See J. Amstutz, *ΑΠΛΟΤΗΣ: Eine begriffsgeschichtliche Studie zum jüdisch-christlichen Griechisch* (Theophaneia 19; Bonn: Hanstein, 1968); and the summary by de Jonge in *Studies on the Testaments*, 302–5.

33. Hollander and de Jonge, *Testaments*, 234.

34. On the Testaments' positive and negative portrayals of continence and fornication, and their relationship to some Jewish and early Christians attitudes, see Marinus de Jonge, "Rachel's Virtuous Behavior in the *Testament of Issachar*," in David L. Balch, Everett Ferguson, and Wayne A. Meeks, eds., *Greeks, Romans, and Christians: Essays in Honor of Abraham J. Malherbe* (Minneapolis: Fortress Press, 1990) 340–52, repr. in de Jonge, *Jewish Eschatology*, 301–12.

35. See esp. Gen 49:15 LXX, where he is called *geōrgos*, as he is in T. Iss. 3:1.

36. For a discussion of these passages and others related to them see M. de Jonge, "The Two Great Commandments in the Testaments of the Twelve Patriarchs," *NovT* 44 (2002) 378–92; Matthias Konradt, "Menschen oder Bruderliebe? Beobachtungen zum Liebesgebot in den Testamenten der Zwölf Patriarchen," *ZNW* 97 (1988) 296–310.

37. For literature on the imagery of the two ways see above, chapter 5, n. 91. On the Testament of Asher see Nickelsburg, *Resurrection*, 161–62; see also Marinus de Jonge, "The Testaments of the Twelve Patriarchs and the 'Two Ways,'" in Esther G. Chazon, David Satran, and Ruth A. Clements, eds., *Things Revealed: Studies in Early Jewish and Christian Literature in Honor of Michael E. Stone* (JSJ 89; Leiden: Brill, 2004) 303–17.

38. Hollander and de Jonge, *Testaments*, 348.

39. On these texts see above, pp. 92–111; Nickelsburg, *1 Enoch 1*, 493–94.

40. Hollander and de Jonge, *Testaments*, 338–41.

41. Plato, *Phaedo* 107D–108C; *Rep.* 10.614–21.

42. Other texts that combine the imagery of two ways with the two spirits are *Barn.* 18–20 and the *Mandates* of the Shepherd of Hermas; on the latter see Nickelsburg, *Resurrection*, 160–61.

43. Note the following parallels: one's "end," 6:4||73:17; "terror," 6:5||73:19; God's angel or God guides one to eternal life/glory, 6:6||73:23–34; the holy place/meeting places will be destroyed, 7:2||74:8; God's breaking the dragon's head through water or on the water, 7:3||74:13.

44. See Nickelsburg, *Resurrection*, 49.

45. Harm W. Hollander, "The Ethical Character of the Patriarch Joseph," in Nickelsburg, ed., *Studies on the Testament of Joseph*, 17–18; Hollander and de Jonge, *Testaments*, 367–68.

46. Richard I. Pervo, "The Testament of Joseph and Greek Romance," in Nickelsburg, ed., *Studies on the Testament of Joseph*, 17–18.

47. Ibid., 15–28. He cites and provides a critique of Martin Braun, *History and Romance in Graeco-Oriental Literature* (Oxford: Blackwell, 1938). See also Hollander and de Jonge, *Testaments*, 372.

48. Hollander, "Ethical Character"; Hollander and de Jonge, *Testaments*, 370.

49. Cf., e.g., Rev 1:9; 2:2, 3, 19; 3:10; 13:10; 14:12.

50. For details see Hollander and de Jonge, *Testaments*, 408–9.

51. On this supposition see Nickelsburg, *Resurrection*, 36–37, 158–59. For the many passages in the Testaments that reflect this angelology see Hollander and de Jonge, *Testaments*, 47–50.

52. On the first two of these see the summary in Hollander, *Joseph*, 94–95. On the latter see Dixon Slingerland, "The Nature of *Nomos* (Law) within the *Testaments of the Twelve Patriarchs*," *JBL* 106 (1986) 39–48.

53. On the Levi and Judah passages see Hollander and de Jonge, *Testaments*, 56–61; M. de Jonge, "Two Messiahs in the Testaments of the Twelve Patriarchs?" in Jan W. van Henten, et al., eds., *Tradition and Re-interpretation in Jewish and Early Christian Literature: Essays in Honour of Jürgen C. Lebram* (SPB 36; Leiden: Brill: Leiden, 1986) 150–62, repr. in de Jonge, *Jewish Eschatology*, 191–203.

54. Hollander, *Joseph*.

55. Hollander and de Jonge, *Testaments*, 64–67; M. de Jonge, "The Future of Israel in the Testaments of the Twelve Patriarchs," *JSJ* 17 (1985) 196–211, repr. in idem, *Jewish Eschatology*, 164–79.

56. On resurrection in the Testaments see Nickelsburg, *Resurrection*, 34–37, 141–42; H. C. C. Cavallin, *Life after Death* (ConBNT 7/1; Lund: Gleerup, 1974) 53–57; Hollander and de Jonge, *Testaments*, 61–63.

57. On the ms. tradition see Hollander and de Jonge, *Testaments*, 10–16. For much more detail see the articles by H. J. de Jonge, H. W. Hollander, H. E. Gaylord, and Th. Korteweg in M. de Jonge, ed., *Studies*, 45–173. See also M. de Jonge, "The Transmission of the Testaments of the Twelve Patriarchs by Christians," *VC* 47 (1993) 1–28.

58. For a summary of the history of scholarship see Hollander and de Jonge, *Testaments*, 1–8, and the literature cited there. For a detailed history see H. Dixon Slingerland, *The Testaments of the Twelve Patriarchs: A Critical History of Research* (SBLMS 21; Missoula, Mont.; Scholars Press, 1977). On the first publication of the texts and early studies on it see M. de Jonge, "Robert Grosseteste and the Testaments of the Twelve Patriarchs," *JTS* n.s. 42 (1991) 115–25; H. J. de Jonge, "Die Patriarchentestamente von Roger Bacon bis Richard Simon," in de Jonge, *Studies*, 3–42. For a critical discussion of the possibilities see de Jonge, "Testaments."

59. See, e.g., R. H. Charles, *APOT* 2:361–67. On the genizah see Stefan C. Reif, "Cairo Genizah," *EDSS* 1:105–8.

60. On the Levi texts see above, pp. 159–65. On the Naphtali text see Michael E. Stone, DJD 22:73–82.

61. Hollander and de Jonge, *Testaments*, 17–27.

62. See the discussion in de Jonge, "Control Problems," 405–20.

63. See ibid., 85: "A fortiori, it is practically impossible to answer the question whether there ever existed Jewish Testaments in some form. If they existed, we shall never be able to reconstruct them with any degree of certainty."

64. De Jonge, "Two Messiahs."

65. See Marinus de Jonge, "Light on Paul from the *Testaments of the Twelve Patriarchs?*" in L. Michael White and O. Larry Yarbrough, eds., *The Social World of the First Christians: Essays in Honor of Wayne A. Meeks* (Minneapolis: Fortress Press, 1995) 100–115. He argues that parallels between Paul and the *Testament* "illustrate the continuity in content and diction between Hellenistic-Jewish and early Christian parenesis."

66. Hollander and de Jonge, *Testaments*, 15–16.

67. Ibid., 67–83. For more detail see M. de Jonge, "Hippolytus' 'Benedictions of Isaac, Jacob and Moses' and the Testaments of the Twelve Patriarchs," *Bijdr* 46 (1985) 245–60; idem, "Two Interesting Interpretations of the Rending of the Temple Veil in the Testaments of the Twelve Patriarchs," *Bijdr* 46 (1985) 350–62; idem, "The Pre-Mosaic Servants of God in the Testaments of the Twelve Patriarchs and in the Writings of Justin and Irenaeus," *VC* 39 (1985) 157–70; repr., respectively, in idem, *Jewish Eschatology*, 204–19, 220–32, 262–76.

68. Hollander and de Jonge, *Testaments*, 27–29.

69. My approach to this book is largely indebted to John J. Collins, "Structure and Meaning in the Testament of Job," *SBLSP* (1974) 1:35–52. See also his later discussion, "Testaments," in Stone, ed., *Jewish Writings*, 349–54.

70. Christopher T. Begg, "Comparing Characters: The Book of Job and the Testament of Job," in W. A. M. Beuken, ed., *The Book of Job* (BETL 114; Leuven: Leuven Univ. Press and Peeters, 1994) 433–45.

71. Ibid., 437.

72. For a detailed study of this terminology, its connotations, and its use in the *Testament* and in the Greco-Roman world, see Cees Haas, "Job's Perseverance in the *Testament of Job*," in Knibb and van der Horst, eds., *Studies*, 117–54.

73. Begg, "Comparing Characters," 436–40.

74. It is possible that 41:7 alludes to the lament now at 32:1–12; see Kraft, *Testament of Job*, 74, note on 41:7.

75. On the contrasting portrayals of women in the first and last parts of the book see Collins, "Structure," 48; idem, "Testaments," 352–53; Pieter van der Horst, "Images of Women in the Testament of Job," in Knibb and van der Horst, eds., *Studies*, 93–116; Randall D. Chesnutt, "Revelatory Experiences Attributed to Biblical Women in Early Jewish Literature," in Amy-Jill Levine, ed., *"Women like This": New Perspectives on Jewish Women in the Greco-Roman World* (SBLEJL 1; Atlanta: Scholars Press, 1991) 115–19; Susan Garrett, "The 'Weaker Sex' in the *Testament of Job*," *JBL* 112 (1993) 55–70.

76. See the skeptical commends by Garrett, "Weaker Sex." Begg ("Comparing Characters," 441) takes a less dim view of the Testament's characterization of Job's wife.

77. Spittler, "Testament of Job," 833–34. The fifth-century fragment of a Coptic translation of the Testament may also point in this direction; see Cornelia Römer and Heinz J. Thissen, "P. Köln Inv. Nr. 3221: Das Testament des Hiob in Koptischer Sprache, ein Vorbericht," in Knibb and van der Horst, eds., *Studies*, 33–45.

78. On this hypothesis see ibid., 833–34. See Collins, "Testaments," 353–54.

79. Van der Horst, "Images," 114–15.

80. See the reservations of Collins ("Testaments," 354), who modifies his previous opinion ("Structure," 50–51); Garrett, "Weaker Sex," 70; see also Schaller, *Testament Hiobs*, 309–11, for a more detailed discussion.

81. Tertullian refers to a narrative detail that we find in T. Job 20:9–10. The earliest ms. evidence is the fifth-century Coptic fragment (above, n. 77). The Greek mss. date from the eleventh, twelfth, and thirteenth centuries; see Brock, *Testamentum Iobi*, 3.

82. Schaller, *Testament Hiobs*, 311–12.

83. Ibid., 307–8. For details on this dependence see idem, "Das Testament Hiobs und die Septuaginta-Übersetzung des Buches Hiob," *Bib* 61 (1980) 277–406.

84. See Schaller, *Testament Hiobs*, 308; van der Horst, "Images," 106–16.

85. Christoph Burchard (*Der Jacobusbrief* [HNT 15/1; Tübingen: Mohr Siebeck, 2000] 202) thinks that an allusion to the Testament is not demonstrable; however, given the very different portrayal of Job in the biblical book, James's offhand comment presumes knowledge of some such haggadic tradition.

86. For a sustained argument to this effect see van der Horst, "Images," 106–16.

87. For a critique of the thesis that a Jewish work has been interpolated by a Christian Montanist, see ibid. For a detailed study of the book that concludes it is the composition of a single author, see Berndt Schaller, "Zur Komposition und Konzeption des Testaments Hiobs," in Knibb and van der Horst, eds., *Studies*, 46–92.

88. For a critical appraisal of other possible Christian elements see van der Horst, "Images," 109–11.

89. See Haas, "Job's Perseverance." See also the discussion of 4 Maccabees, above, pp. 256–58.

90. In Wisdom of Solomon the wise man knows the mysteries of God whereas his enemies do not (2:22). He is exalted to heaven in spite of his suffering. His life is described as *mania* (5:4; cf. T. Job 35:6; 49:1–3). The enemies propose to see whether he is the servant of God (Wis 2:17; cf. T. Job 36–37). Great emphasis is placed on the recognition (Wis 5:4; cf. T. Job 30), where the situation of Wisdom of Solomon is reversed, and one thinks of Isa 14, which stands behind Wisdom of Solomon; see above, p. 208.

91. On the presence of eternal life see above, pp. 136–37, 205. On salvation as knowledge, see Nickelsburg, *Ancient Judaism*, 73–75 and 215 n. 39.

92. On this and other NT texts, see ibid., 83–85

93. The best guide for a detailed study of the Testament of Abraham is the fine commentary by Allison, *Testament of Abraham*.

94. On the relationship of the two recensions see the articles by George W. E. Nickelsburg, Francis Schmidt, Raymond A. Martin, and Robert A. Kraft in Nickelsburg, ed., *Studies on the Testament of Abraham*, 23–137. For more recent and detailed discussions that assert the priority of the plot outline of the long recension, see Ludlow, *Abraham Meets Death*, 119–51; Allison, *Testament of Abraham*, 12–27.

95. I developed this outline in my article "Structure and Message in the Testament of Abraham," in my *Studies in the Testament of Abraham*, 85–86, and employed in the first edition of this book. Allison (*Testament of Abraham*, 43–47) has elaborated on the outline, indicating in particular how the first section consists of four parallel episodes (1:1—4:5; 4:5—7:12; 8:1—9:6; 9:7—15:10), which he lays out in tabular form (pp. 46–47). See also the detailed graphics in Ludlow, *Abraham Meets Death*, 119–43.

96. For a detailed and sophisticated study of humor in the Testament of Abraham, see Ludlow, *Abraham Meets Death*. See also Lawrence M. Wills, "The *Testament of Abraham* as a Satirical Novel," in *The Jewish Novel in the Ancient World* (Ithaca: Cornell Univ. Press, 1995) 245–56, as well as the commentary on all the relevant passages in Allision, *Testament of Abraham*.

97. See Wills, *Jewish Novel*, 249–56.

98. Ludlow (*Abraham Meets Death*, 13) thinks that my parallel with Genesis "seems to owe more to the cleverness of the interpreter, Nickelsburg, than to the intention of the author," but offers no explanation for this judgment.

99. There are seven refusals of one kind or another: chaps. 7, 9, 15, 16, 17, 19, 20.

100. See Allison, *Testament of Abraham*, 174.

101. On this aspect of the message of Testament of Abraham see A. B. Kolenkow, "The Genre Testament and the Testament of Abraham," in Nickelsburg, ed., *Studies on the Testament of Abraham*, 143–47.

102. The idea is not unique here; cf. 1 Enoch 22:12–13.

103. On these judgments see George W. E. Nickelsburg, "Eschatology in the Testament of Abraham: A Study of the Judgment Scenes in the Two Recensions," in idem, ed., *Studies in the Testament of Abraham*, 23–47; Allison, *Testament of Abraham*, 253–306.

104. Allison, *Testament of Abraham*, 37–39; cf. Nickelsburg, *Resurrection*, 39–40.

105. Cf. 1 Enoch 22:7, where he is the advocate of all the persecuted righteous; and *Tg. Neof.* Gen 4:8, which may presume an identification of Abel with the persecuted righteous man in Wis 2, 4–5, who judges his persecutors (see above, pp. 207–8).

106. Munoa (*Four Powers in Heaven*) argues that this part of the *Testament* interprets Dan 7 and reflects the "one like a son of man" in that chapter. I do not find his argument compelling, nor does Allison (*Testament of Abraham*, 245 n. 17, 281). For my own doubts about a connection with 1 Enoch 37–71, see Nickelsburg, "Eschatology," 36.

107. See Schmidt, "Le Testament d'Abraham," 1:71–78 (summarized by Nickelsburg in *Studies on the Testament of Abraham*, 32–34); Allison, *Testament of Abraham*, 256–67. For drawings of Egyptian scenes see Danielle Ellul, "Le Testament d'Abraham: Mémoire et source d'imaginaire, la pesée des âmes," *Foi et vie* 89 (1990) 73–82. A judgment scene like the present one may be presupposed in 1 Enoch 41:1–2, 9; 61:8; 2 Enoch 49:2 (B); 52:15–16. For the metaphor of God's weighing the human spirit and heart cf. Prov 16:2; 21:2; 24:12.

108. Allison, *Testament of Abraham*, 49–50.

109. See Samuel E. Loewenstamm, "The Testament of Moses" and "The Testament of Abraham and the Texts concerning Moses' Death," in Nickelsburg, ed., *Studies on the Testament of Abraham*, 185–225; Esther Glickler Chazon, "Moses' Struggle for His Soul: A Prototype for the Testament of Abraham, the Greek Apocalypse of Ezra, and the Apocalypse of Sedrach," *SecCent* 5 (1985–86) 151–64.

110. Allison, *Testament of Abraham*, 49–50, 69–70, 128–31, 308–10, 316–18, 327–29. On the fluctuation of Joban and Abrahamic traditions in Jubilees and the Testament of Job, see above, pp. 70, 361 n. 12.

111. Allison, *Testament of Abraham*, 168–69.

112. Schmidt, *Testament*, 1–32. For a summary see Allison, *Testament of Abraham*, 4–7.

113. Schmidt, *Testament*, 33–44; Allison, *Testament of Abraham*, 8–11.

114. See Allison, *Testament of Abraham*, 15–16.

115. See ibid., passim, esp. 28, 239–41, and the index as well.

116. See also the judgment of ibid., 28–31.

117. Ibid., 34–40.

118. See Schmidt, "Testament," 1:71–76, 101–10, 119; Delcor, *Testament d'Abraham*, 67–69; Allison, *Testament of Abraham*, 32–33.

119. See Stone, *History*.

120. Johannes Tromp, "The Story of Our Lives: The *qz*-Text of the *Life of Adam and Eve*, the Apostle Paul, and the Jewish-Christian Oral Tradition concerning Adam and Eve," *NTS* 50 (2004) 205–23.

121. Elements in Eve's dream (Greek Life 2:2–3 and esp. in the form in Vita 22:4) suggest an exegetical development from Gen 4:11.

122. Certain contradictions in this section (is it Adam's body or his spirit that are assumed to heaven?) suggest that these chapters conflate two traditions; see Johannes Tromp, "Literary and Exegetical Issues in the Story of Adam's Death and Burial (*GLAE* 31–42)," in Judith Frishman and Lucas van Rompay, eds., *The Book of Genesis in Jewish and Oriental Christian Interpretation: A Collection of Essays* (Traditio Exegetical Graeca 3; Louvain: Peeters, 1997) 25–41.

123. Cf. Greek Life 9:2; 10:1–2; 14:2; 21:6.

124. The idea is clearer in Vita 51:2.

125. See John L. Sharpe III, "The Second Adam," *CBQ* 35 (1973) 35–46. For the relationship of creation and redemption with reference to resurrection cf. 2 Macc 7:11, 22–23, 27–29.

126. For a synopsis of the texts see Anderson and Stone, eds., *Synopsis*. For a detailed tabulation of the parallels among the versions see de Jonge and Tromp, *Life*, 26–27. See also Johannes Tromp, "The Textual History of the *Life of Adam and Eve* in the Light of a Newly Discovered Latin Text-Form," *JSJ* 33 (2002) 28–41.

127. For a preliminary probe into the textual history of the Latin version see Tromp, "Textual History."

128. This section is based ultimately on Isa 14, which is an important source of Jewish demonic speculation. See Nickelsburg, *Resurrection*, 69–82, for examples.

129. I have not here dealt with the Slavonic version of the Life, which seems to occupy an intermediate stage in the development of the recensions; see briefly Nickelsburg, "Bible Rewritten," 114–15; and, in more detail, idem, "Some Related Traditions," 524–25. On the problem as a whole see de Jonge and Tromp, *Life*, 28–44.

130. Here I draw on my publications cited in the previous note. De Jonge and Tromp (*Life*, 28–44) also believe that the Greek version is prior to the Armenian, Georgian, and Latin.

131. Nickelsburg, "Some Related Traditions," 538. Cf. Vita 29:10; 42:2–5; Greek Life 37:3.

132. See de Jonge and Tromp, *Life*, 41–42.

133. See Nickelsburg, "Some Related Traditions," 526–28. Johannes Tromp ("On Human Disobedience to the Order of Creation [4Q521, fr. 2, and Latin *Life of Adam et Eve* 29c]," *RevQ* 21 [2003] 115) thinks there is no doubt that this section was composed in Latin by a medieval Christian author.

134. Nickelsburg, "Some Related Traditions," 529–32.

135. Ibid., 525.

136. On the question of omissions vs. additions in the textual tradition see Johannes Tromp, "The Role of Omissions in the History of the Literary Development of the Greek *Life of Adam and Eve*," *Apocrypha* 14 (2003) 257–75.

137. According to Stone (*History*), the earliest mss. are Greek, eleventh century (p. 9); Latin, ninth century (pp. 25–30); Slavonic, fourteenth century (pp. 31–33); Armenian, seventeenth century (p. 36); Georgian, fifteenth–sixteenth century (p. 38).

138. Stone, *History*, 22, 56–57.

139. See de Jonge and Tromp, *Life*, 75–77.

140. Ibid., 66–67; Stone and Gideon Bohak (in Stone, *History*, 46–53) leave open the possibility that the Greek was translated from a Semitic original.

141. Stone, *History*, 57–61.

142. De Jonge and Tromp, *Life*, 75.

143. See M. de Jonge, "The Greek Life of Adam and Eve and the Writings of the New Testament," in *Pseudepigrapha*, 228–40.

144. See de Jonge, "The Christian Origin of the Greek Life of Adam and Eve," in idem, *Pseudepigrapha*, 181–200; idem and L. Michael White, "The Washing of Adam in the Acherusian Lake (Greek Life of Adam and Eve 37:3) in the Context of Early Christian Notions of the Afterlife," in ibid., 200–227; de Jonge and Tromp, *Life*, 66–75.

145. See Nickelsburg, *1 Enoch 1*, 87–95.

146. On the Coptic fragments see de Jonge and Tromp, *Life*, 17.

147. See Gen 24:3–4, 37–38; 27:46—28:1 and the expansion of these admonitions in Jub. 20:4; 22:20; 30:7–16. See also Tob 4:12–13.

148. According to Johannes Tromp ("Response to Ross Kraemer: On the Jewish Origin of Joseph and Aseneth," in Athalya Brenner and Jan Willem van Henten, eds., *Recycling Biblical Figures* [Studies in Theology and Religion 1; Leiden: Deo, 1999] 267–68), the goal of this author was not exegetical, i.e., to deal with a difficulty in the biblical text, and he notes that other texts (Philo, Josephus, and Jubilees) appear to have had no such problem. The fact remains, however, that most of *Joseph and Aseneth* is devoted to the removal of the impediment to this marriage. See Kraemer, *When Aseneth Met Joseph*, 20, which was written after Tromp's aforementioned critique of her previous presentation of the material.

149. See Kraemer, *When Aseneth Met Joseph*, 3.

150. On these two text forms see below, p. 337.

151. Looking at the texts from a different point of view, Humphrey (*Joseph and Aseneth*, 105) finds a chiastic structure in chaps. 1–21.

152. Cf. 23:10, "son of God"; 27:10–11, Aseneth's appeal to her conversion.

153. See 22:13 (8); 23:9, 10, 12 (long text); 28:7 (4); 29:3; cf. 4:7 (9); 8:5–7.

154. For the parallel sources see Victor Aptowitzer, "Asenath, the Wife of Joseph," *HUCA* 1 (1924) 243–56; Philonenko, *Joseph*, 32–43. For a somewhat longer discussion of the parallels that I see between those traditions and the present text, see Nickelsburg, "Narrative Writings," 66–68. Kraemer (*When Aseneth Met Joseph*, 307–18) dismisses the traditions as late, but does not refer to my discussion. In a later treatment (Ross Kraemer, "When Aseneth Met Joseph: A Postscript," in Randall A. Argall, Beverly A. Bow, and Rodney A. Werline, eds., *For a Later Generation: The Transformation of Tradition in Israel, Early Judaism, and Early Christianity*, FS G. W. E. Nickelsburg [Harrisburg: Trinity International, 2000] 130–31) she finds the parallels to the Shechem story "intriguing," but sees no need to appeal to the later rabbinic material. The material seems relevant to me because the rabbinic tradition deals with Aseneth's parentage by reference to the Shechem story, while the present story about Aseneth's eligibility to marry Joseph is followed by a reprise of the Shechem story. This hardly seems coincidental.

155. He comes from the east (5:2). The solar language is explicit in 6:2 (5). See Kraemer, *When Aseneth Met Joseph*, 156–67. The contrast of Aseneth's former scorn of Joseph with her present acclamation of him as a "son of God" is reminiscent of the wicked's change of mind in Wis 2 and 5. On the relationship of Wis 2, 4–5 and Gen 37–45, see Nickelsburg, *Resurrection*, pp. 49–58.

156. For Egyptian texts describing the pharaoh as the son of Re, the sun god, see J. B. Pritchard, ed., *Ancient Near Eastern Texts* (3d ed.; Princeton: Princeton Univ. Press, 1969) 234, 254, 370–71.

157. For the contrast see 8:5; cf. also 11:8–10; 12:1, 5. The expression "living God" is traditional (see Bel and the Serpent, above, pp. 24–26).

158. Other references to Aseneth's mouth are 8:5 and 11:15; cf. 13:13 (9).

159. Cf. 15:4–5 (3–4); 16:16 (9). The language of realized eschatology in these formulations is most closely paralleled in the hymns of Qumran (1QH 3 [11]:19–23; 11 [19]:3–14 [see above, pp. 136–37]; cf. Jos. Asen. 15:12 [13]) and Philo's description of Therapeutic belief (*On the Contemplative Life* 13 [see Nickelsburg, *Resurrection*, 169]).

160. Suggested by Prof. Jonathan Z. Smith in correspondence (October 1976). It fits the author's death/life polarity.

161. On kissing in Joseph and Aseneth and the issue of Jewish identity see Christoph Burchard, "Küssen in *Joseph und Aseneth*," *JSJ* 36 (2005) 316–23.

162. Chapters 5–6 are an epiphany scene. On the resemblance of Joseph and the angel see 14:9 (8).

163. On Joseph's and Aseneth's supernatural beauty see O. Betz, "Geistliche Schönheit," in Otto Michel and Ulrich Mann, eds., *Die Leibhaftigkeit des Wortes: Theologische und seelsorgische Studien und Beiträge als Festgabe für Adolf Köberle zum sechsigsten Geburtstage* (Hamburg: Im Furche, 1958) 76–79.

164. See Burchard (*Untersuchungen*, 112–21), who cites such passages as Isa 62:4–5; Gen 17:5, 15; 32:28; Matt 16:17–19.

165. See the review of the literature and the disputed issues in Humphrey, *Joseph and Aseneth*. See also idem, "On Bees and Best Guesses: The Problem of *Sitz im Leben* from Internal Evidence as Illustrated by *Joseph and Aseneth*," *CurBS* 7 (1999) 223–36. See also Gideon Bohak, "From Fiction to History: Contextualizing *Joseph and Aseneth*," *SBLSP* 35 (1996) 273–84; Randall Chesnutt, "From Text to Context: The Social Matrix of *Joseph and Aseneth*," *SBLSP* 35 (1996) 285–302; Angela Standhartinger, "From Fictional Text to Socio-Historical Context: Some Considerations from a Textcritical Perspective on *Joseph and Aseneth*," *SBLSP* 35 (1996) 302–18.

166. Philonenko, *Joseph et Aséneth*; Burchard, *Untersuchungen*, 112–21; idem, "Joseph and Aseneth," 188–95; Nickelsburg, "Stories," 69–71; Sänger, *Antikes Judentum*; Chesnutt, *From Death to Life*; Standhartinger, *Frauenbild*; Humphrey, *Joseph and Aseneth*, 48–62; John J. Collins, "*Joseph and Aseneth*: Jewish or Christian?" *JSP* 14 (2005) 97–112.

167. Chesnutt, *From Death to Life*, 254.

168. Christoph Burchard, "Joseph et Aséneth: Questions actuelles," in Willem van Unnik, ed., *La littérature juive entre Tenach et Mischna: Quelques problèmes* (RechBib 9; Leiden: Brill, 1974) 96–100; Sänger, *Antikes Judentum*, 148–90; Chesnutt, *From Death to Life*, 216–53.

169. Nickelsburg, "Stories," 71. So also, apparently, Collins, "*Joseph and Aseneth*." See also Burchard, "Joseph and Aseneth," 188–89.

170. Burchard, "Joseph and Aseneth," 194–95. My reasons for suggesting a Gentile audience ("Stories," 69–70) have been addressed by Chesnutt, *From Death to Life*, 258–59, but see ibid., pp. 260–61.

171. Nickelsburg, "Stories," 70.

172. Bohak, *Joseph and Aseneth*.

173. For three reviews of Bohak see Albert Pietersma, *JNES* 59 (2000) 141–43 (mainly in agreement with the book); Harold W. Attridge, *CBQ* 60 (1998) 555–57 (the thesis is generally persuasive, but speculative at some points); C. T. R. Hayward, *JSS* 14 (1999) 133–35 (the thesis in general does not seem to be firmly grounded, and the author does not do justice to the work of other scholars and engage their theories in depth).

174. Kraemer, *When Aseneth Met Joseph*, 90.

175. Ibid., 295.

176. Kraemer, "When Aseneth Met Joseph Revisited," 131–32.

177. See George J. Brooke, "Men and Women as Angels," *JSP* 14 (2005) 159–77. For other reviews of Kraemer's study that are both appreciative of the new material that she has brought to the discussion and critical of her conclusions, see Humphrey, *Joseph and Aseneth*, 35–37, 55–57; Randall D. Chesnutt, *JBL* 119 (2000) 761–62; Angela Standhartinger, *JAOS* 120 (2000) 488–89. See also the discussion in Kraemer, "When Aseneth Met Joseph Revisited," 128–35.

178. See Isa 52:1–2; 54:1–13; 61:10–11; 62:1–2, where the imagery of remarriage and rein-vestiture is prominent and the imagery fluctuates between woman and city. Cf. also Eph 5:22–23; Rev 21:1–2.

179. Supporting the long text are Burchard, *Untersuchungen*, 4–90; idem, "The Text of *Joseph and Aseneth* Reconsidered," *JSP* 14 (2005) 83–96; idem, *Joseph und Aseneth;* Chesnutt, *From Death to Life*, 65–69; Humphrey, *Joseph and Aseneth*, 17–27. Favoring the short text are Philonenko, *Joseph et Aséneth*; Standhartinger, *Frauenbild*, 33–47 and passim; Kraemer, *When Aseneth Met Joseph*, 50–89.

180. See Humphrey, *Joseph and Aseneth*, 64–78.

181. Chesnutt, *From Death to Life*, 76–80; Humphrey, *Joseph and Aseneth*, 28–37; Burchard, *Untersuchungen*, 140–43.

182. Chesnutt, *From Death to Life*, 184–216.

183. Humphrey, *Joseph and Aseneth*, 28–38.

184. Burchard, *Untersuchungen*, 91–99.

185. Burchard, *Joseph und Aseneth*, 1–34.

186. On the possible light that the rituals may shed on the Pauline understanding of the Eucharist, see Christoph Burchard, "The Importance of Joseph and Aseneth for the Study of the New Testament: A General Survey and a Fresh Look at the Lord's Supper," *NTS* 33 (1987) 102–34.

187. Aseneth's concern about her blasphemy of Joseph is mentioned at length in both chaps. 6 and 13, and one has the impression that it is a sin of almost as great magnitude as her idolatry.

188. For the polarity of rejection and confession of Jesus as son of God, cf. Mark 14:61–64; 15:39; Matt 26:63–66; 27:40, 54. On the relationship of these passages to Wis 2 and 5 (see above, n. 155), see Nickelsburg, "The Genre and Function of the Markan Passion Narrative," *HTR* 73 (1980) 153–84, repr. in *GNP*, 2:473–503.

189. My discussion here is a compression of my commentary "Prayer of Manasseh," which should be consulted for additional details.

190. A few Syriac mss. also append the prayer to 2 Chronicles.

191. Herbert E. Ryle, "The Prayer of Manasses," *APOT* 1:614–15.

192. James H. Charlesworth, "The Prayer of Manasseh," *OTP* 2:630.

193. On these texts see above, pp. 80, 94–95, 26, 30.

194. See above, p. 366 n. 6.

195. In Deut 4:19; 17:3; Isa 24:21; 40:26, the Greek noun *kosmos* ("order") translates the Hebrew ṣābāʾ ("host"); it was "the host of heaven" whose idolatrous worship Manasseh had insti-tuted in Jerusalem. See Osswald, *Gebet*, 23, 26.

196. On the distinction between the righteous and the sinners, see Pss. Sol. 3, above, pp. 244.

197. Nickelsburg, *1 Enoch 1*, 206.

198. The verb "forgive" (RSV, NRSV) seems to be an overtranslation of Gk. *anes.*

199. Ode 14 is an expansion of Luke 2:14.

200. From the counting of the Greek Bible, which begins with 1 Samuel.

201. Ryle, "Prayer," 612; Charlesworth, "Prayer," 627–28. Harrington ("Prayer," 797) is more cautious. Osswald (*Gebet*, 20) cites vv 1 and 8 as proof of Jewish origin, but an appeal to the patriarchs in a Christian pseudepigraphon is quite appropriate.

202. See also Chanoine André Rose, "Le Prière d'Azarias (Dan 3,26–45) et le Cantique de Manasse dans la tradition chrétienne et dans la liturgie," in A. M. Triacca and A. Pistoia, eds., *Liturgie, conversion et vie monastique: Conférences Saint-Serge, XXXVe Semaine d'études liturgiques, Paris, 28 juin–1er juillet 1988* (Rome: C. L. J.–Edizioni liturgiche, 1989) 294–305.

Charts

MAJOR FIGURES IN THE SELEUCID DYNASTY

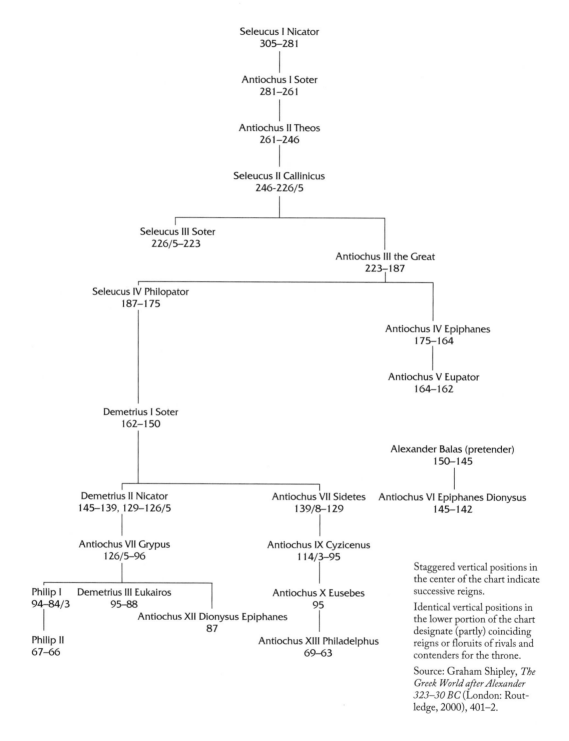

Seleucus I Nicator
305–281

Antiochus I Soter
281–261

Antiochus II Theos
261–246

Seleucus II Callinicus
246-226/5

Seleucus III Soter
226/5–223

Antiochus III the Great
223–187

Seleucus IV Philopator
187–175

Antiochus IV Epiphanes
175–164

Antiochus V Eupator
164–162

Demetrius I Soter
162–150

Alexander Balas (pretender)
150–145

Demetrius II Nicator
145–139, 129–126/5

Antiochus VII Sidetes
139/8–129

Antiochus VI Epiphanes Dionysus
145–142

Antiochus VII Grypus
126/5–96

Antiochus IX Cyzicenus
114/3–95

Philip I
94–84/3

Demetrius III Eukairos
95–88

Antiochus XII Dionysus Epiphanes
87

Antiochus X Eusebes
95

Philip II
67–66

Antiochus XIII Philadelphus
69–63

Staggered vertical positions in the center of the chart indicate successive reigns.

Identical vertical positions in the lower portion of the chart designate (partly) coinciding reigns or floruits of rivals and contenders for the throne.

Source: Graham Shipley, *The Greek World after Alexander 323–30 BC* (London: Routledge, 2000), 401–2.

THE HASMONEAN HOUSE

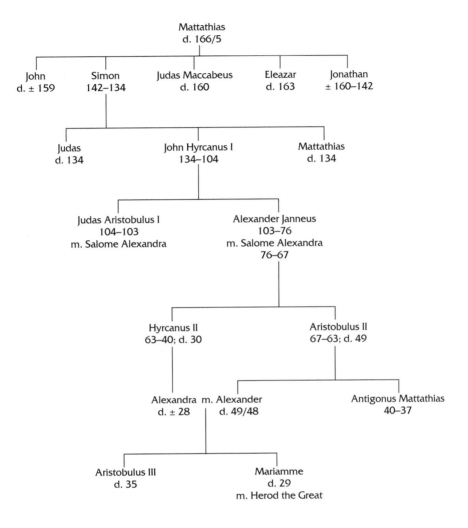

Mattathias
d. 166/5

John
d. ± 159

Simon
142–134

Judas Maccabeus
d. 160

Eleazar
d. 163

Jonathan
± 160–142

Judas
d. 134

John Hyrcanus I
134–104

Mattathias
d. 134

Judas Aristobulus I
104–103
m. Salome Alexandra

Alexander Janneus
103–76
m. Salome Alexandra
76–67

Hyrcanus II
63–40; d. 30

Aristobulus II
67–63; d. 49

Alexandra
d. ± 28

m. **Alexander**
d. 49/48

Antigonus Mattathias
40–37

Aristobulus III
d. 35

Mariamme
d. 29
m. Herod the Great

d. = died
m. = married

The House of Herod

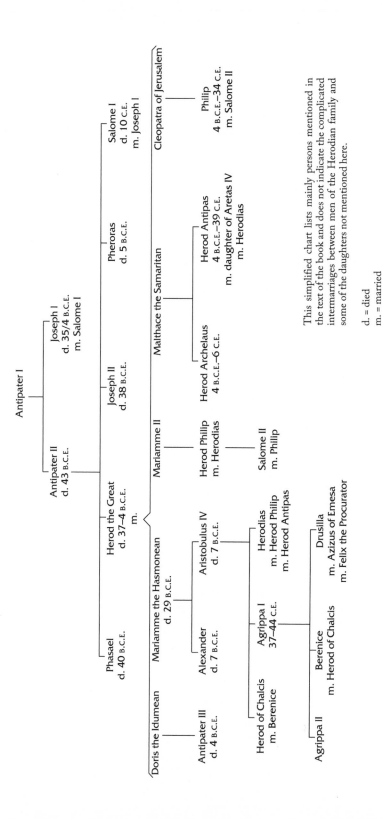

Index of Subjects

Boldface type indicates works treated in detail in this book and page numbers of the major discussions of these works. A few citations enclosed in parentheses ( ) indicate that the subject is mentioned not on the book page but in a text cited on that page.

Index of Modern Authors